T0022033

6 - 12

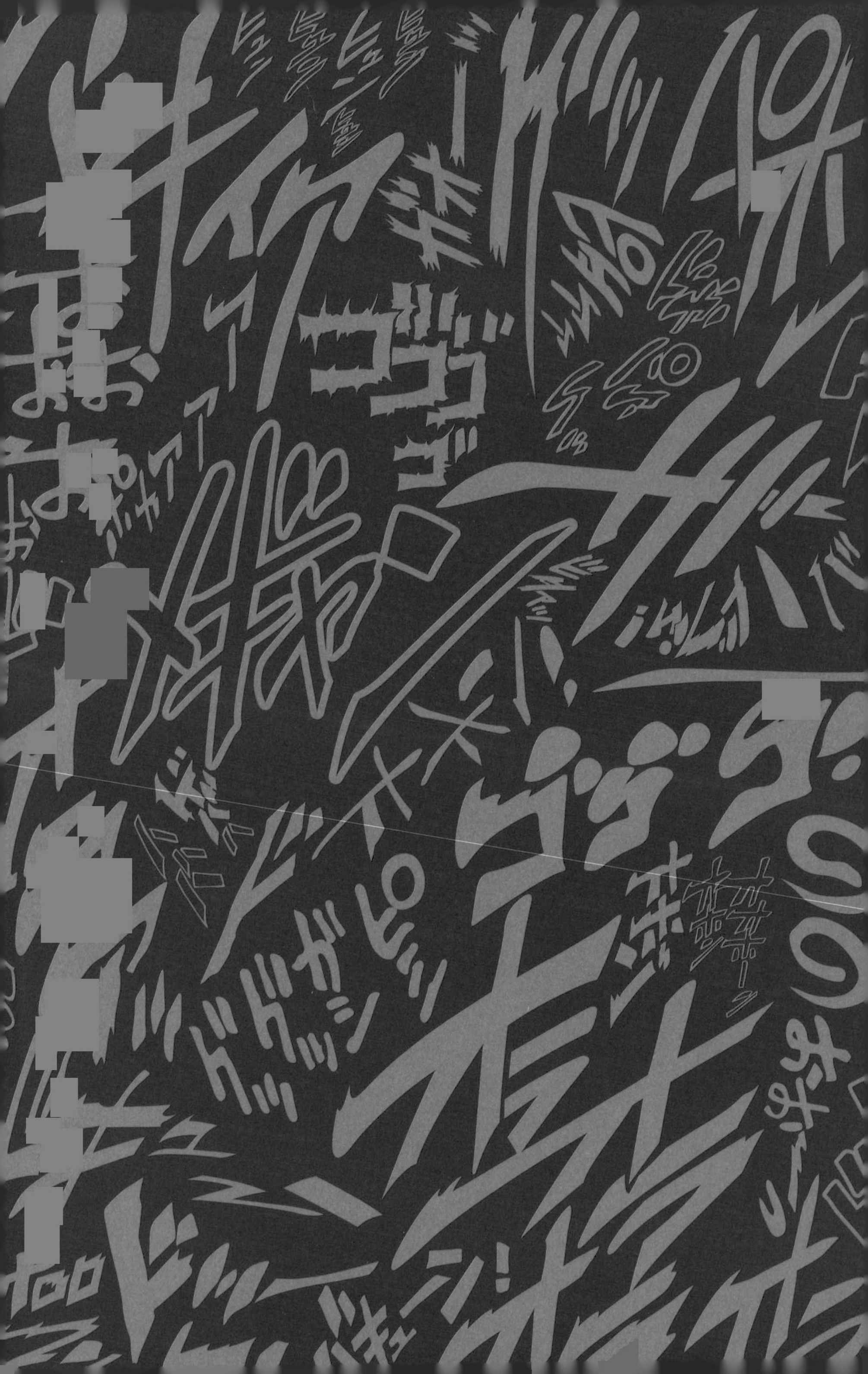

10

JoJo's BIZARRE ADVENTURE

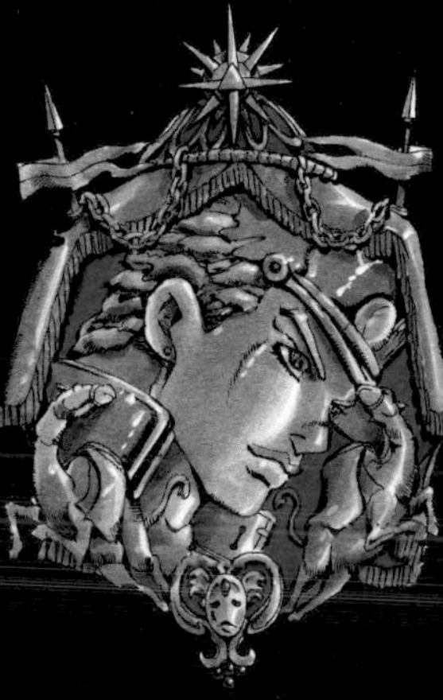

PART 3
STARDUST CRUSADERS

荒 木 飛 呂 彦

HIROHIKO ARAKI

JoJo's Bizarre Adventure
PART 3 STARDUST CRUSADERS

CONTENTS

CHAPTER 134: DIO's World PART 1

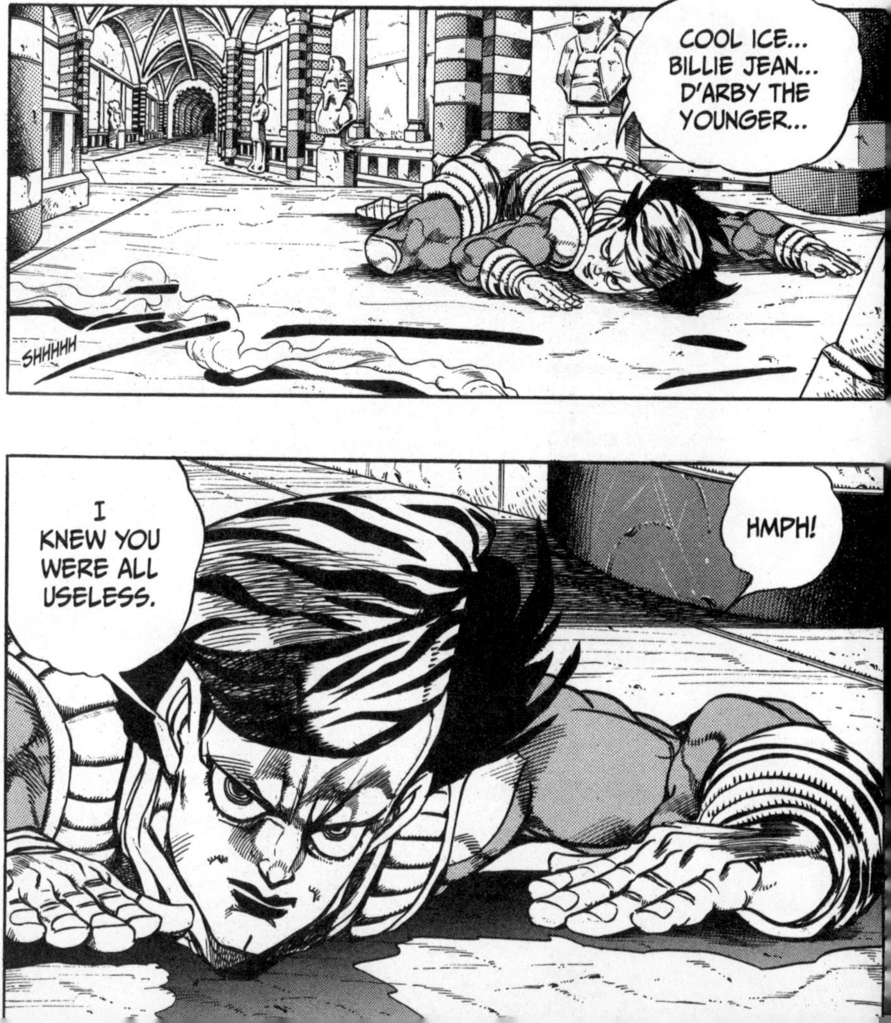
COOL ICE... BILLIE JEAN... D'ARBY THE YOUNGER...
SHHHHH
HMPH!
I KNEW YOU WERE ALL USELESS.

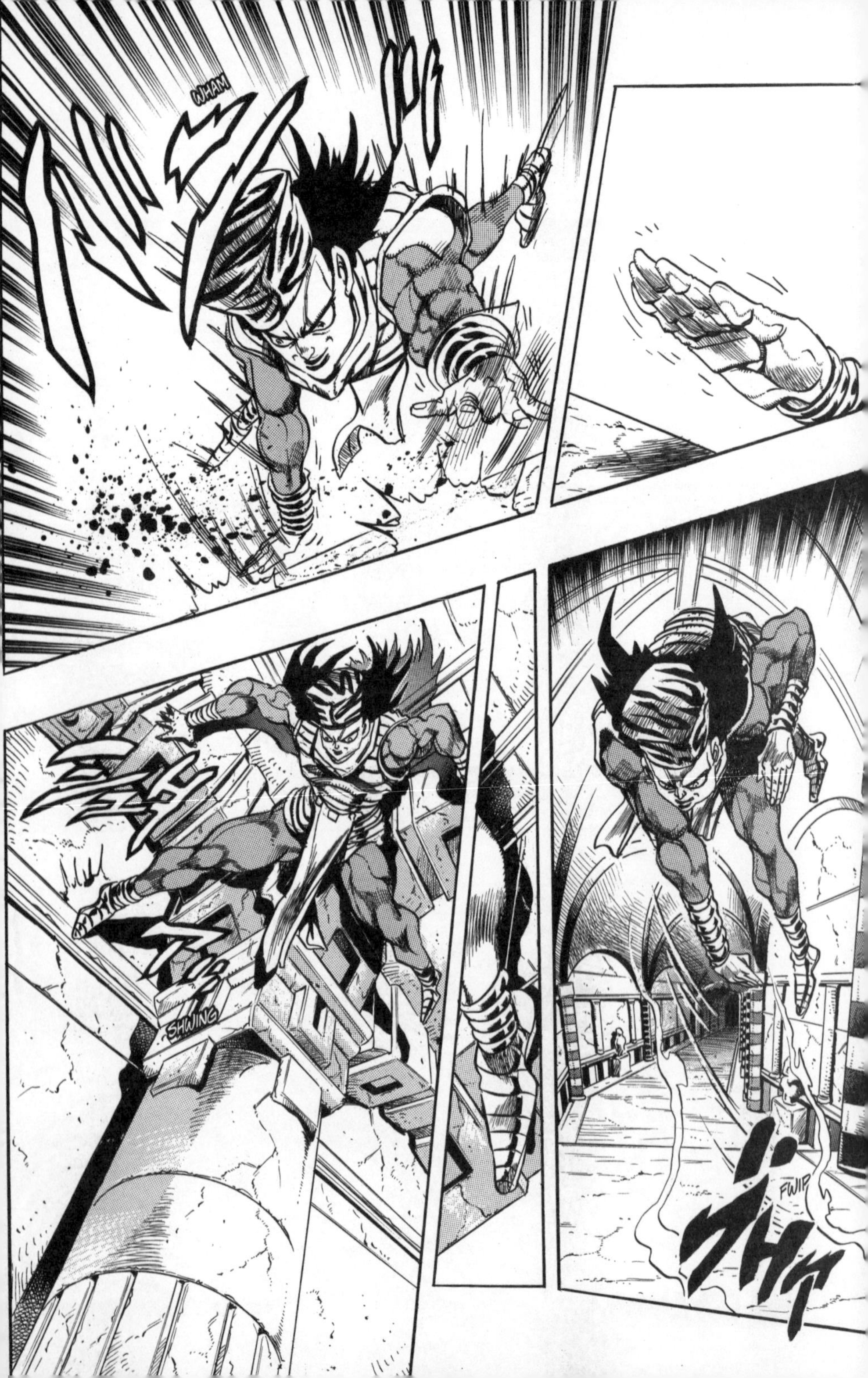
WHAM
FWIP
SHWING

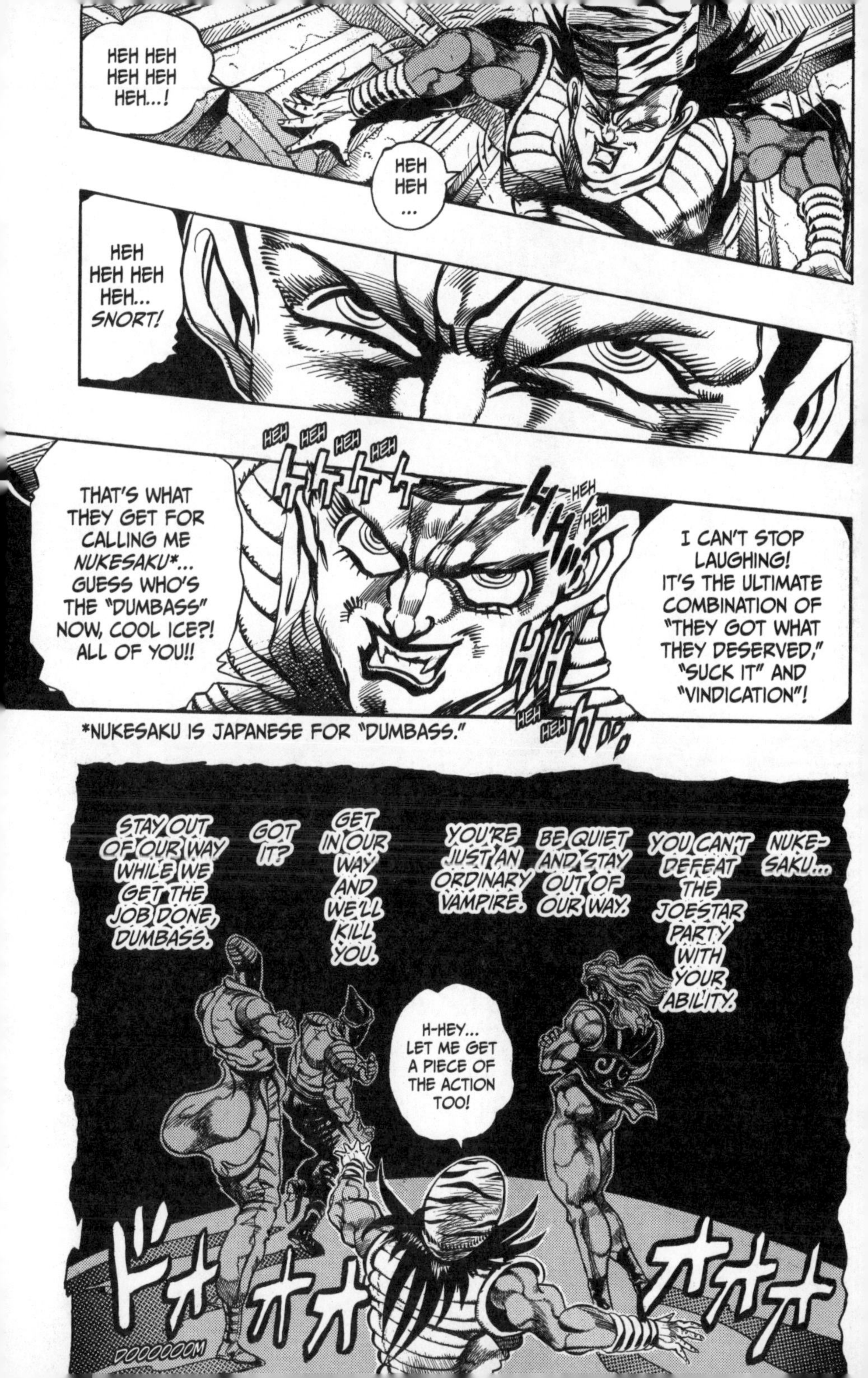
HEH HEH HEH HEH HEH...!
HEH HEH ...
HEH HEH HEH HEH... SNORT!
HEH HEH HEH HEH
I CAN'T STOP LAUGHING! IT'S THE ULTIMATE COMBINATION OF "THEY GOT WHAT THEY DESERVED," "SUCK IT" AND "VINDICATION"!
HEH HEH
THAT'S WHAT THEY GET FOR CALLING ME NUKESAKU*... GUESS WHO'S THE "DUMBASS" NOW, COOL ICE?! ALL OF YOU!!
HEH HEH
NUKE-SAKU...
YOU CAN'T DEFEAT THE JOESTAR PARTY WITH YOUR ABILITY.
BE QUIET AND STAY OUT OF OUR WAY.
YOU'RE JUST AN ORDINARY VAMPIRE.
GET IN OUR WAY AND WE'LL KILL YOU.
GOT IT?
STAY OUT OF OUR WAY WHILE WE GET THE JOB DONE, DUMBASS.
H-HEY... LET ME GET A PIECE OF THE ACTION TOO!
DOOOOOOM

*NUKESAKU IS JAPANESE FOR "DUMBASS."

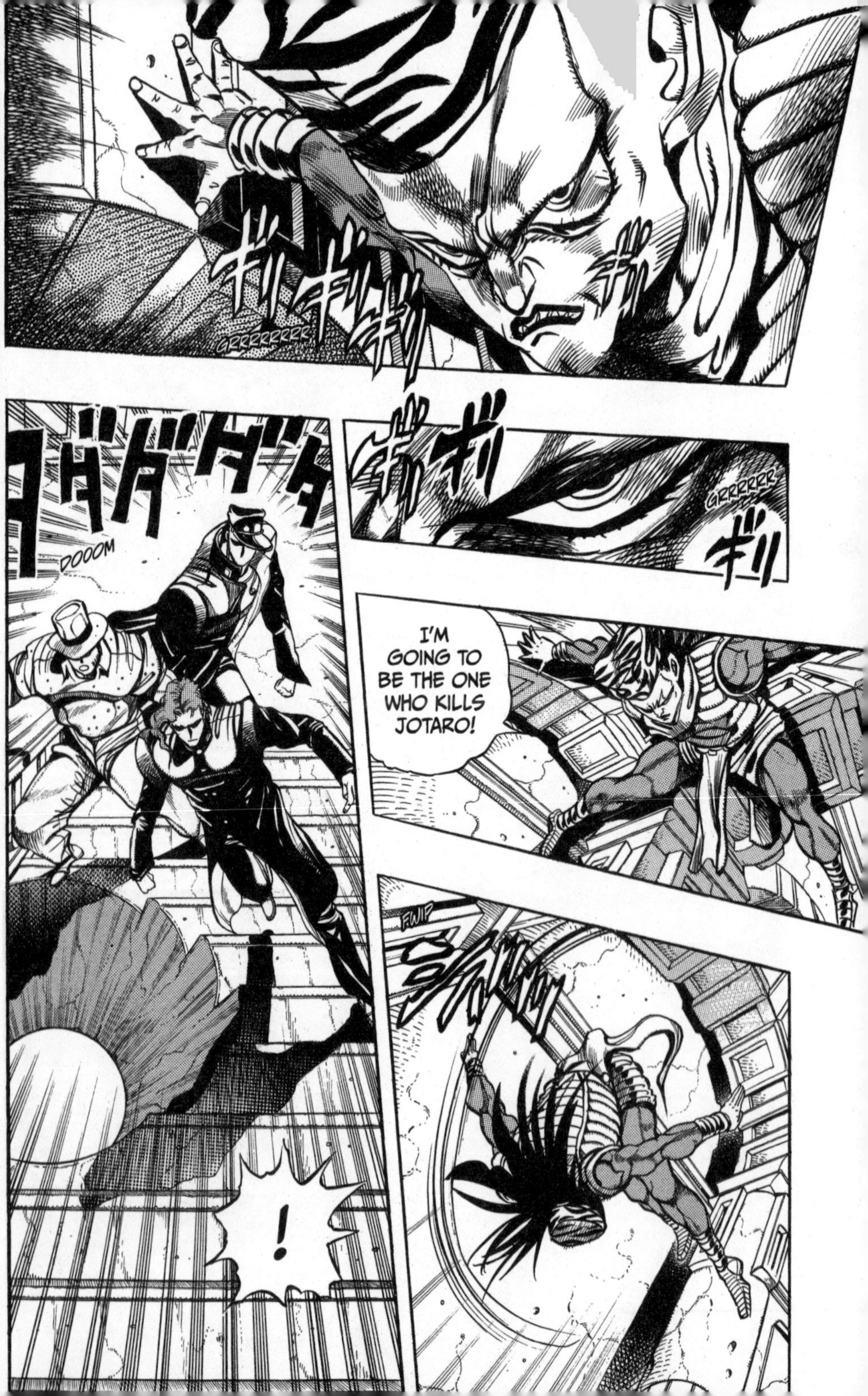
GRRRRRRRR
GRRRRRR
DOOOM
I'M GOING TO BE THE ONE WHO KILLS JOTARO!
FWIP
!

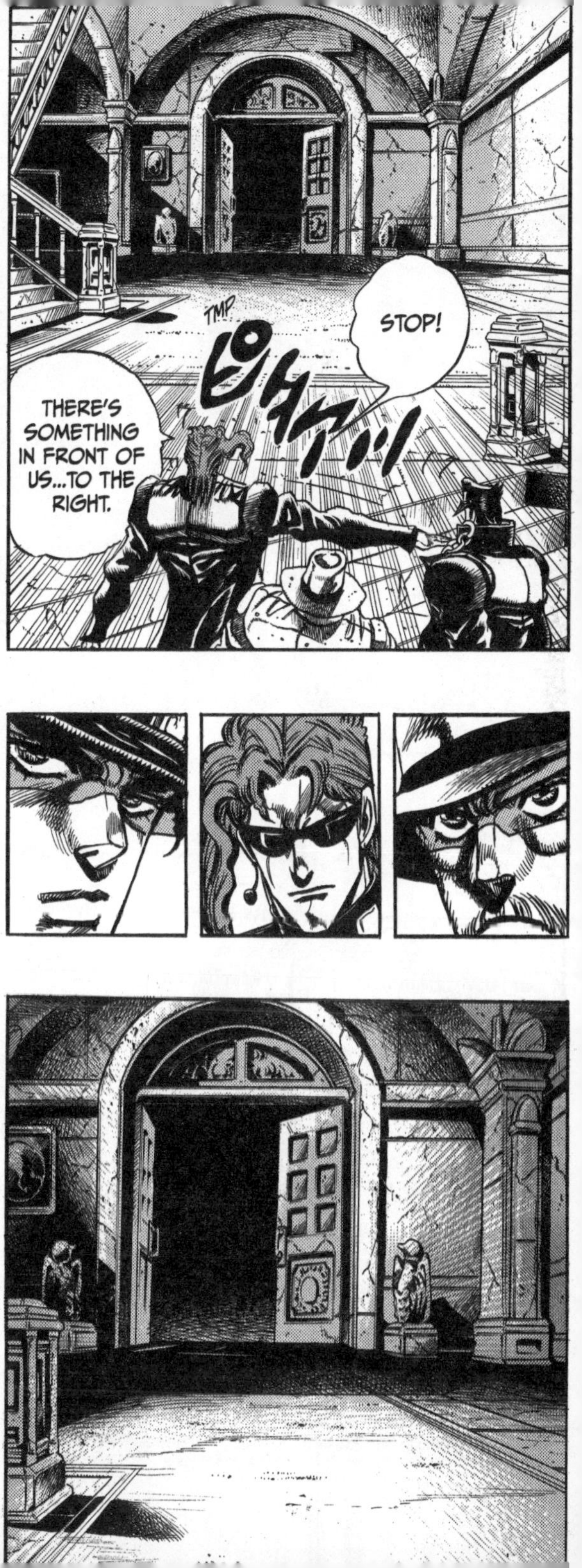
STOP!
TMP
THERE'S SOMETHING IN FRONT OF US...TO THE RIGHT.

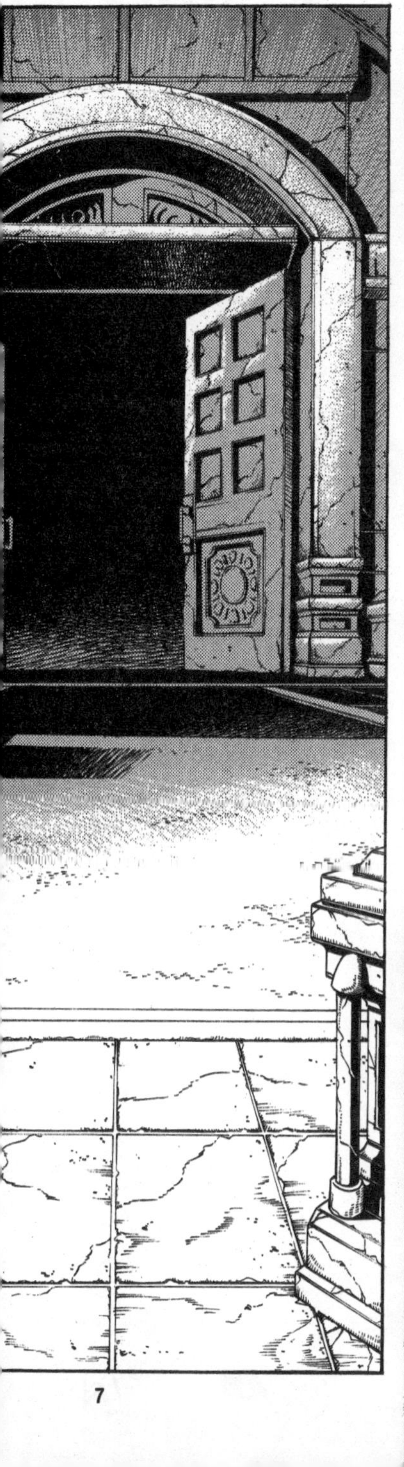

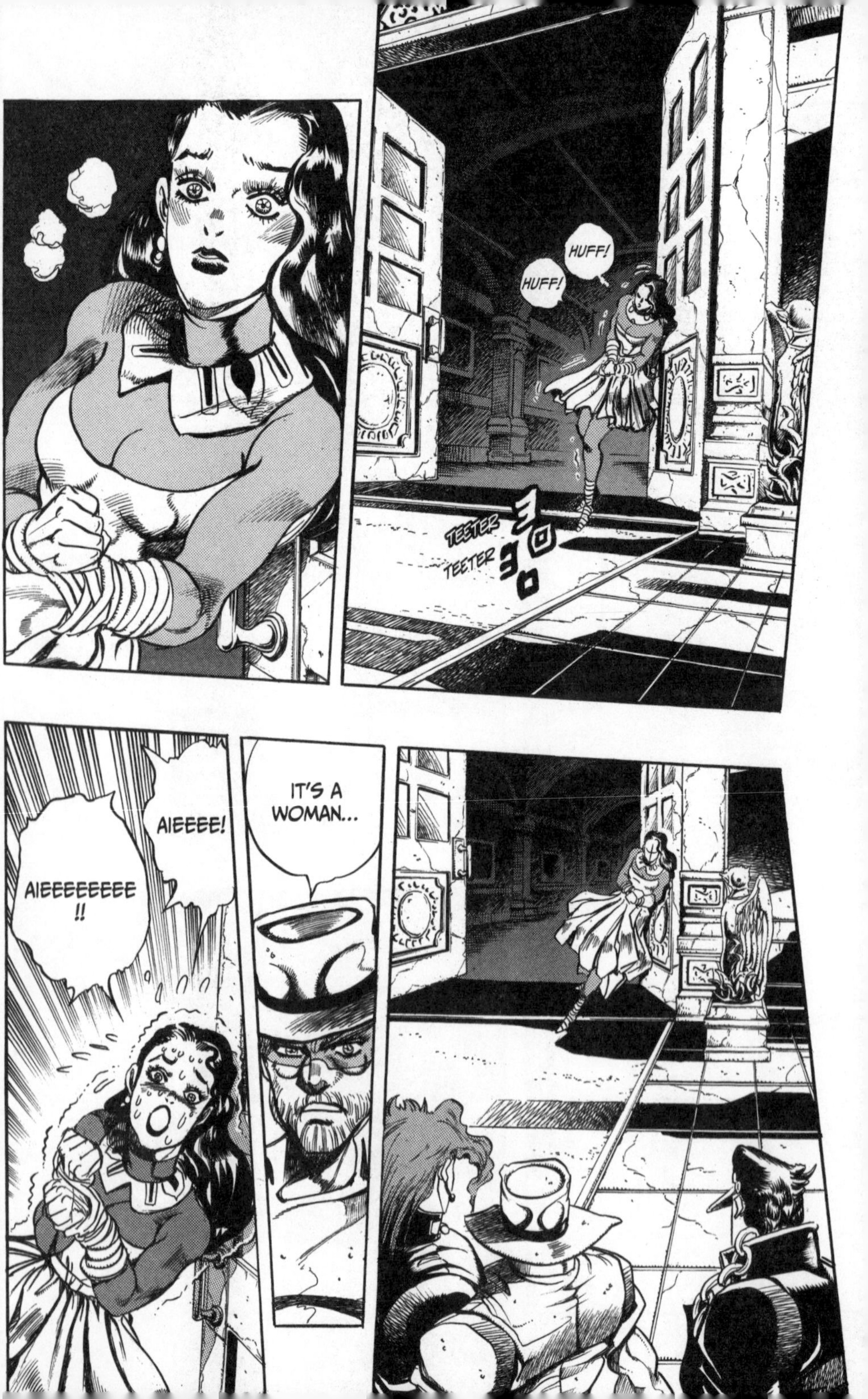
HUFF!
HUFF!
TEETER
TEETER
IT'S A WOMAN...
AIEEEE!
AIEEEEEEEE !!

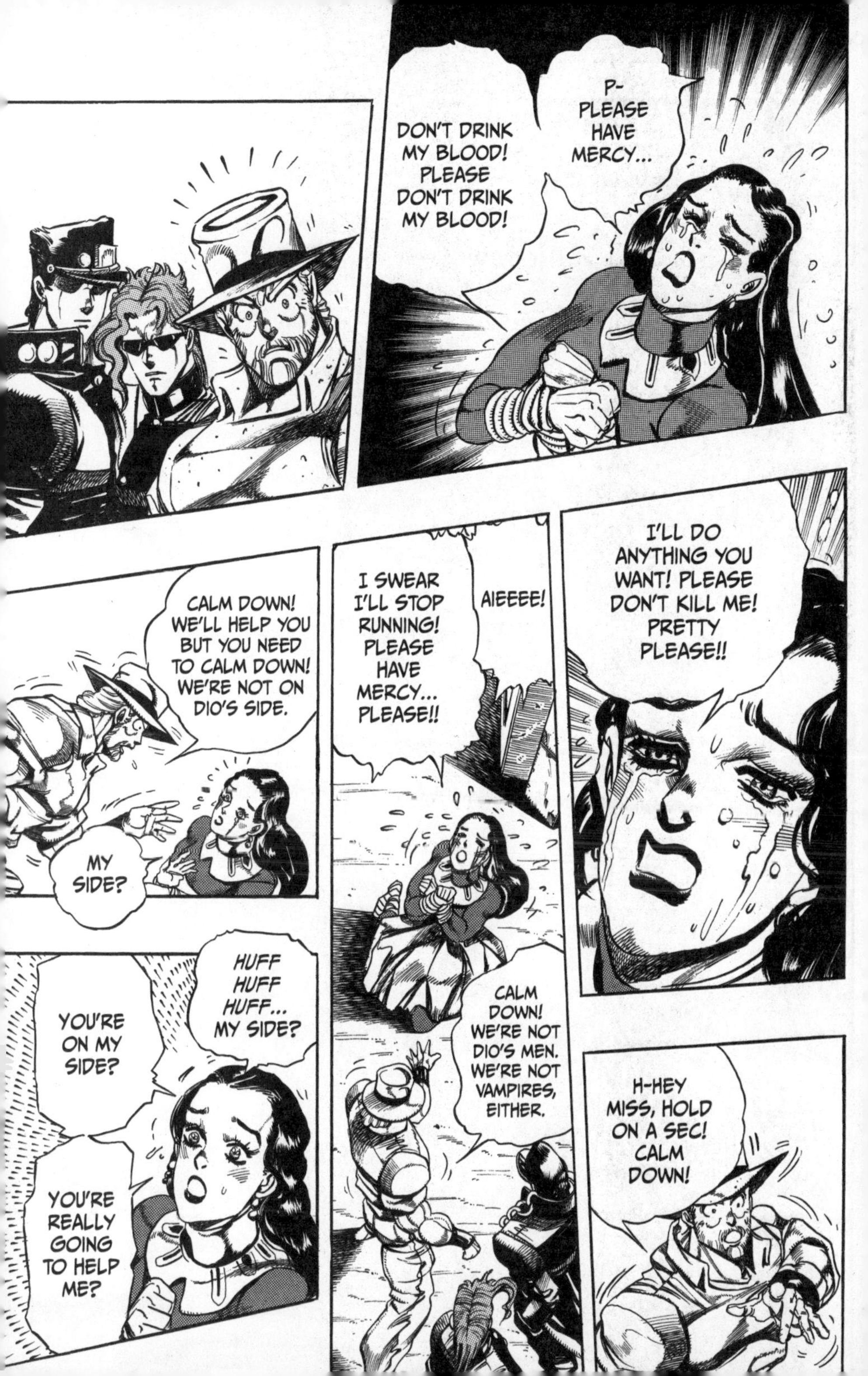
P- PLEASE HAVE MERCY...
DON'T DRINK MY BLOOD! PLEASE DON'T DRINK MY BLOOD!
I'LL DO ANYTHING YOU WANT! PLEASE DON'T KILL ME! PRETTY PLEASE!!
AIEEEE!
I SWEAR I'LL STOP RUNNING! PLEASE HAVE MERCY... PLEASE!!
CALM DOWN! WE'LL HELP YOU BUT YOU NEED TO CALM DOWN! WE'RE NOT ON DIO'S SIDE.
MY SIDE?
H-HEY MISS, HOLD ON A SEC! CALM DOWN!
CALM DOWN! WE'RE NOT DIO'S MEN. WE'RE NOT VAMPIRES, EITHER.
HUFF HUFF HUFF... MY SIDE?
YOU'RE ON MY SIDE?
YOU'RE REALLY GOING TO HELP ME?

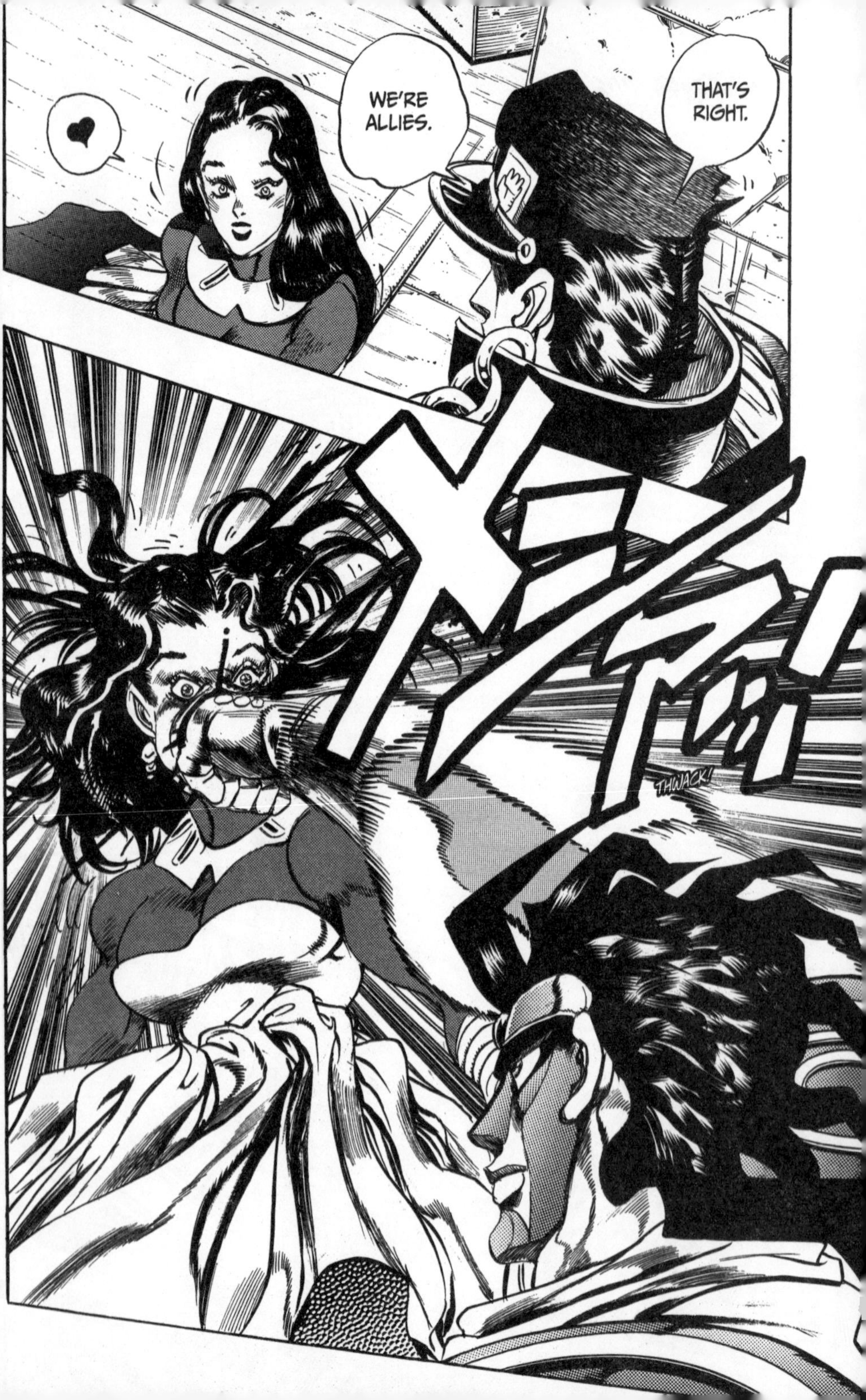
THAT'S RIGHT.
WE'RE ALLIES.
THWACK!

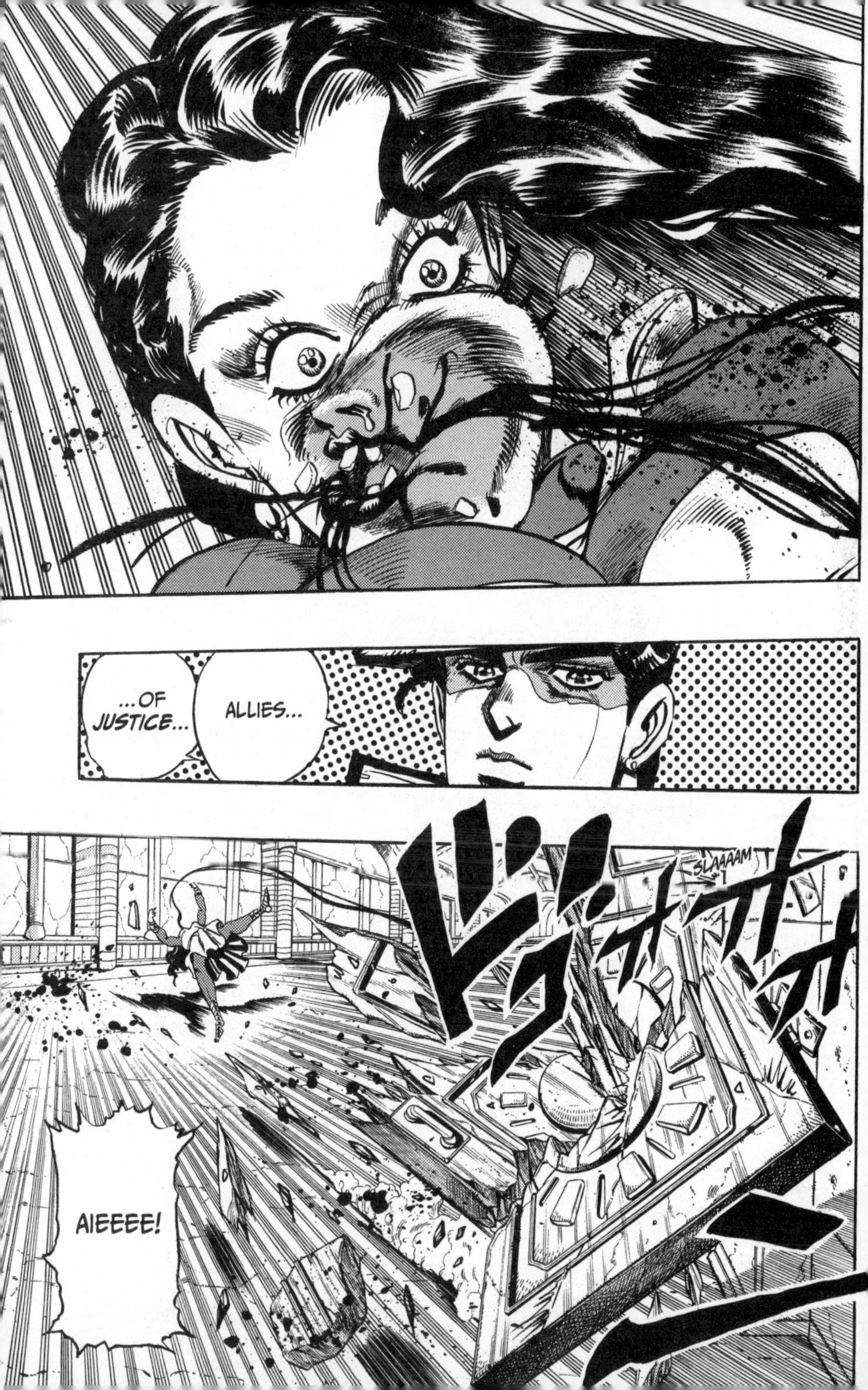
ALLIES...
...OF JUSTICE...
SLAAAAM
AIEEEE!

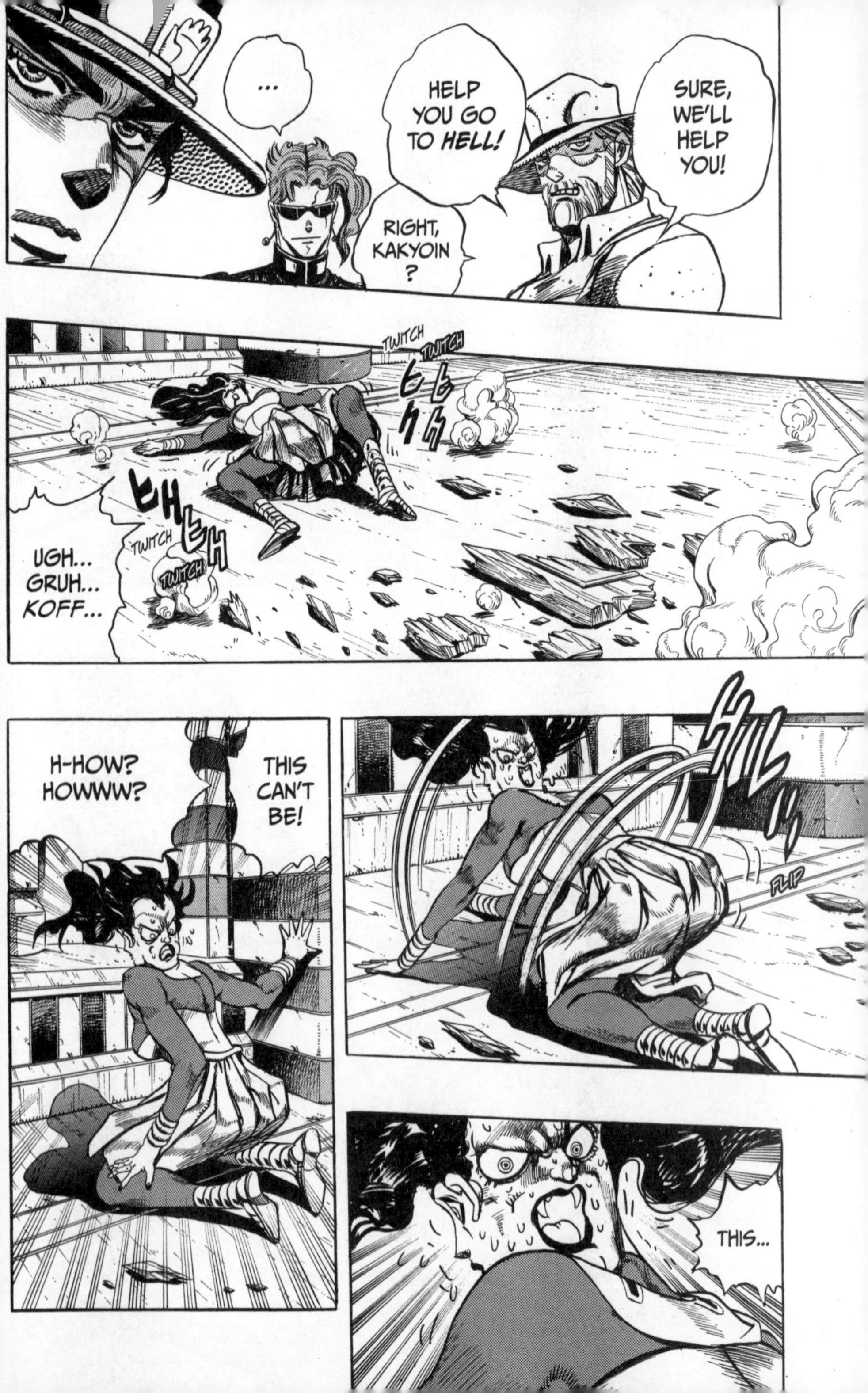
SURE, WE'LL HELP YOU!
HELP YOU GO TO HELL!
RIGHT, KAKYOIN?
...
TWITCH
TWITCH
ヒクヒク
UGH... GRUH... KOFF...
TWITCH
TWITCH
ヒクヒク
FLIP
THIS CAN'T BE!
H-HOW? HOWWW?
THIS...

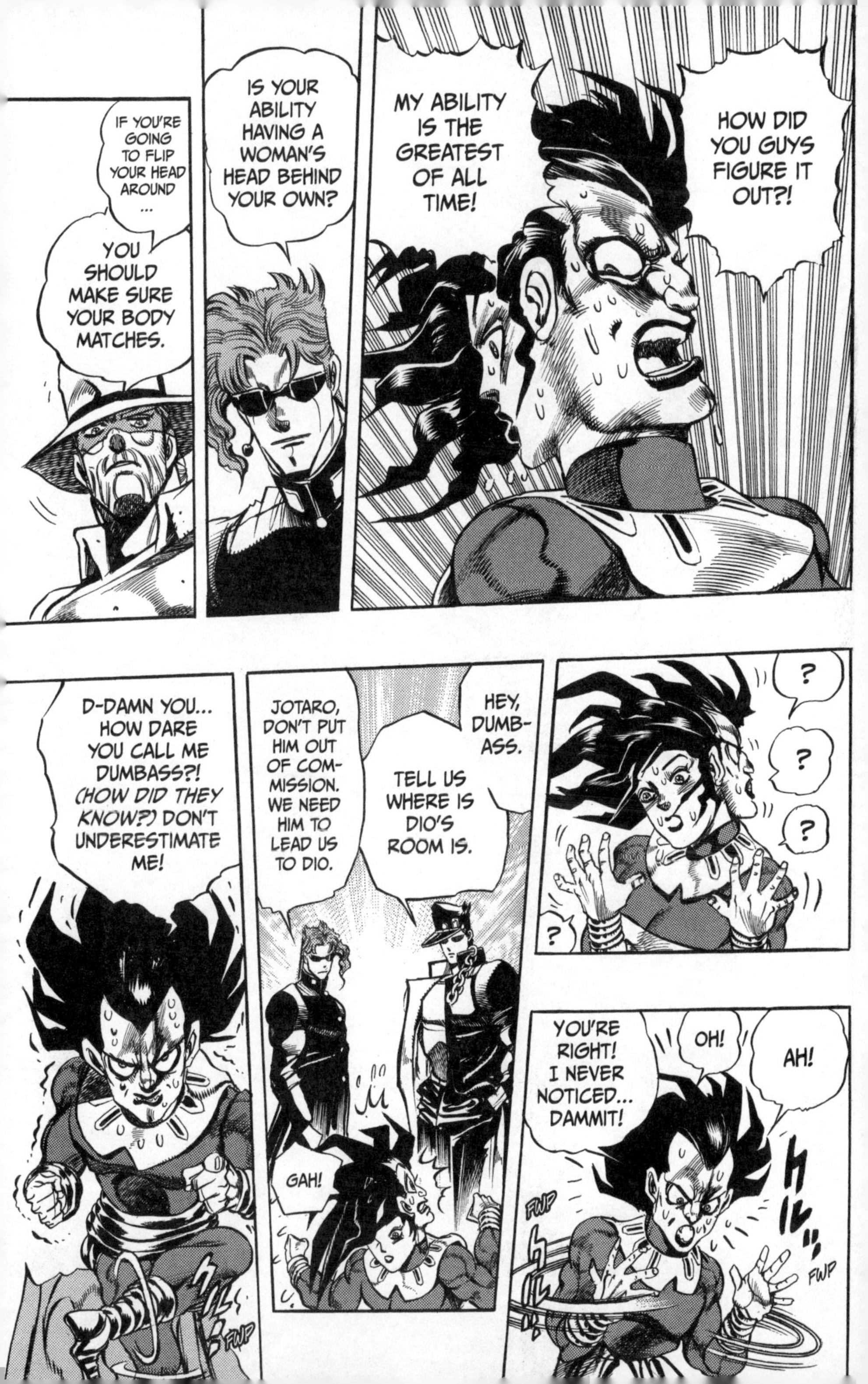
HOW DID YOU GUYS FIGURE IT OUT?!
MY ABILITY IS THE GREATEST OF ALL TIME!
IS YOUR ABILITY HAVING A WOMAN'S HEAD BEHIND YOUR OWN?
IF YOU'RE GOING TO FLIP YOUR HEAD AROUND ...
YOU SHOULD MAKE SURE YOUR BODY MATCHES.
?
?
?
?
AH!
OH!
YOU'RE RIGHT! I NEVER NOTICED... DAMMIT!
FWP
FWP
HEY, DUMBASS.
TELL US WHERE IS DIO'S ROOM IS.
JOTARO, DON'T PUT HIM OUT OF COMMISSION. WE NEED HIM TO LEAD US TO DIO.
GAH!
D-DAMN YOU... HOW DARE YOU CALL ME DUMBASS?! (HOW DID THEY KNOW?) DON'T UNDERESTIMATE ME!
FWP

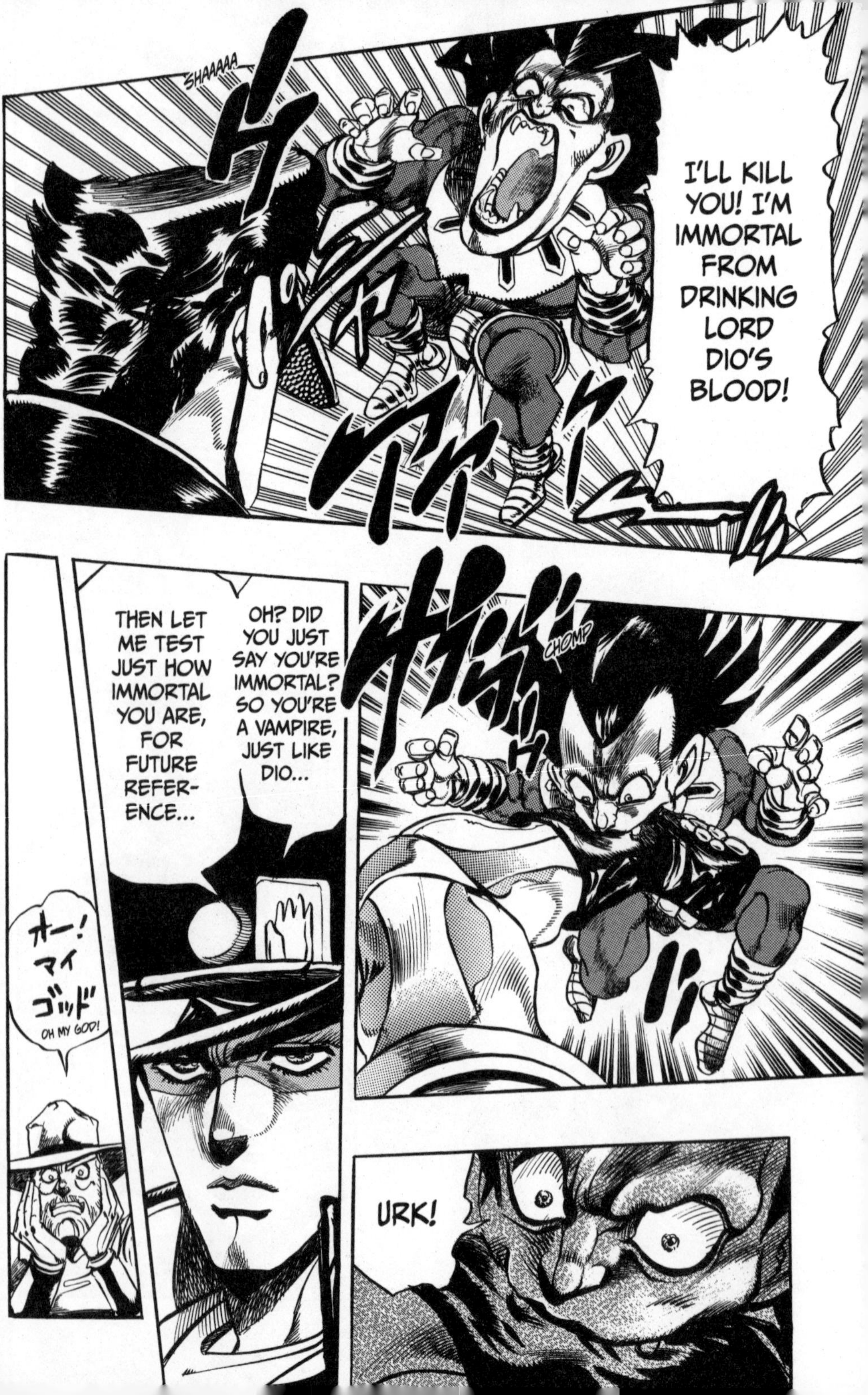
I'LL KILL YOU! I'M IMMORTAL FROM DRINKING LORD DIO'S BLOOD!
SHAAAAA
CHOMP
URK!
OH? DID YOU JUST SAY YOU'RE IMMORTAL? SO YOU'RE A VAMPIRE, JUST LIKE DIO...
THEN LET ME TEST JUST HOW IMMORTAL YOU ARE, FOR FUTURE REFERENCE...
オー!マイゴッド
OH MY GOD!

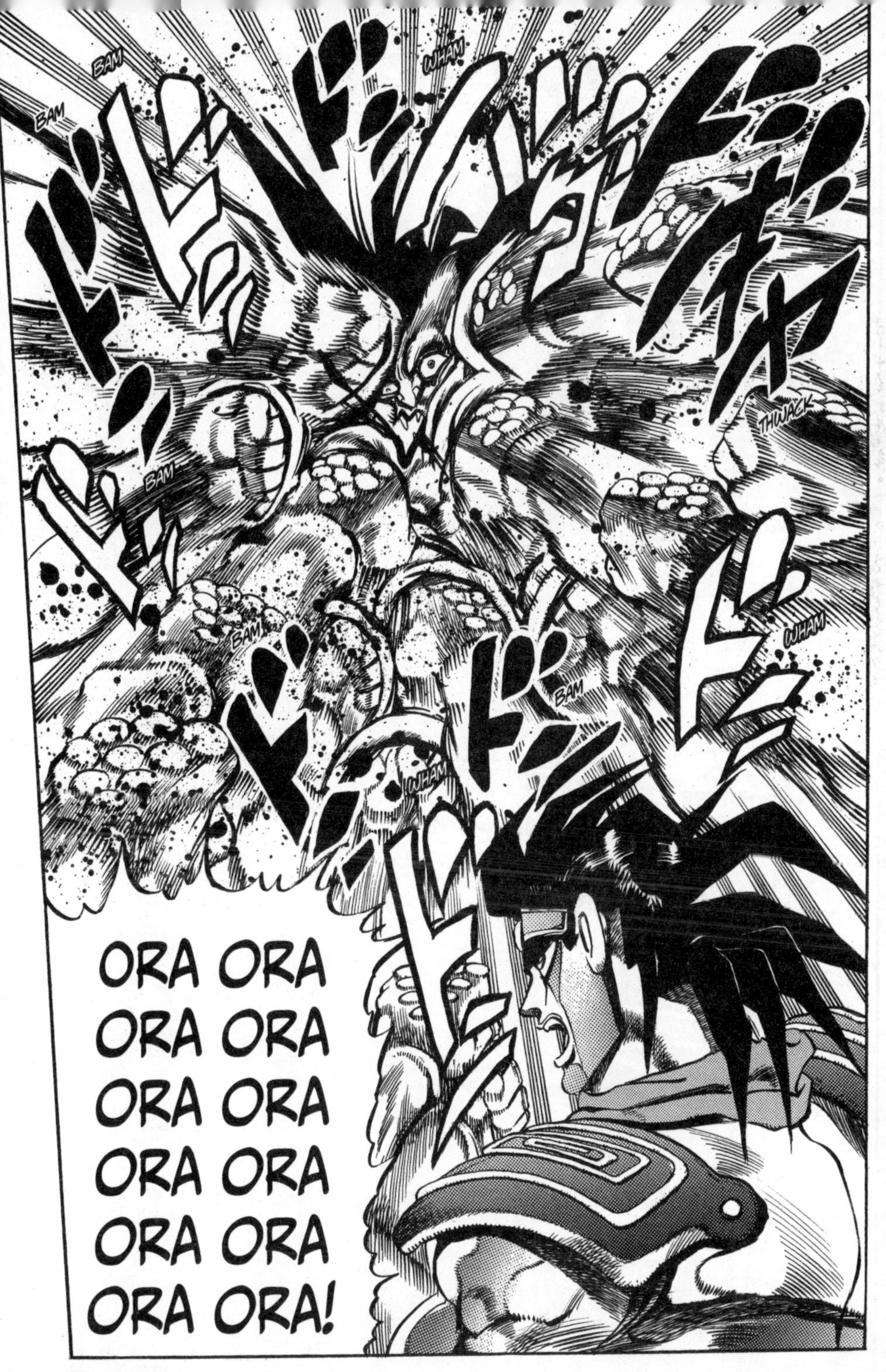
WHAM
BAM
BAM
THWACK
BAM
WHAM
BAM
BAM
WHAM
ORA ORA
ORA ORA
ORA ORA
ORA ORA
ORA ORA
ORA ORA!

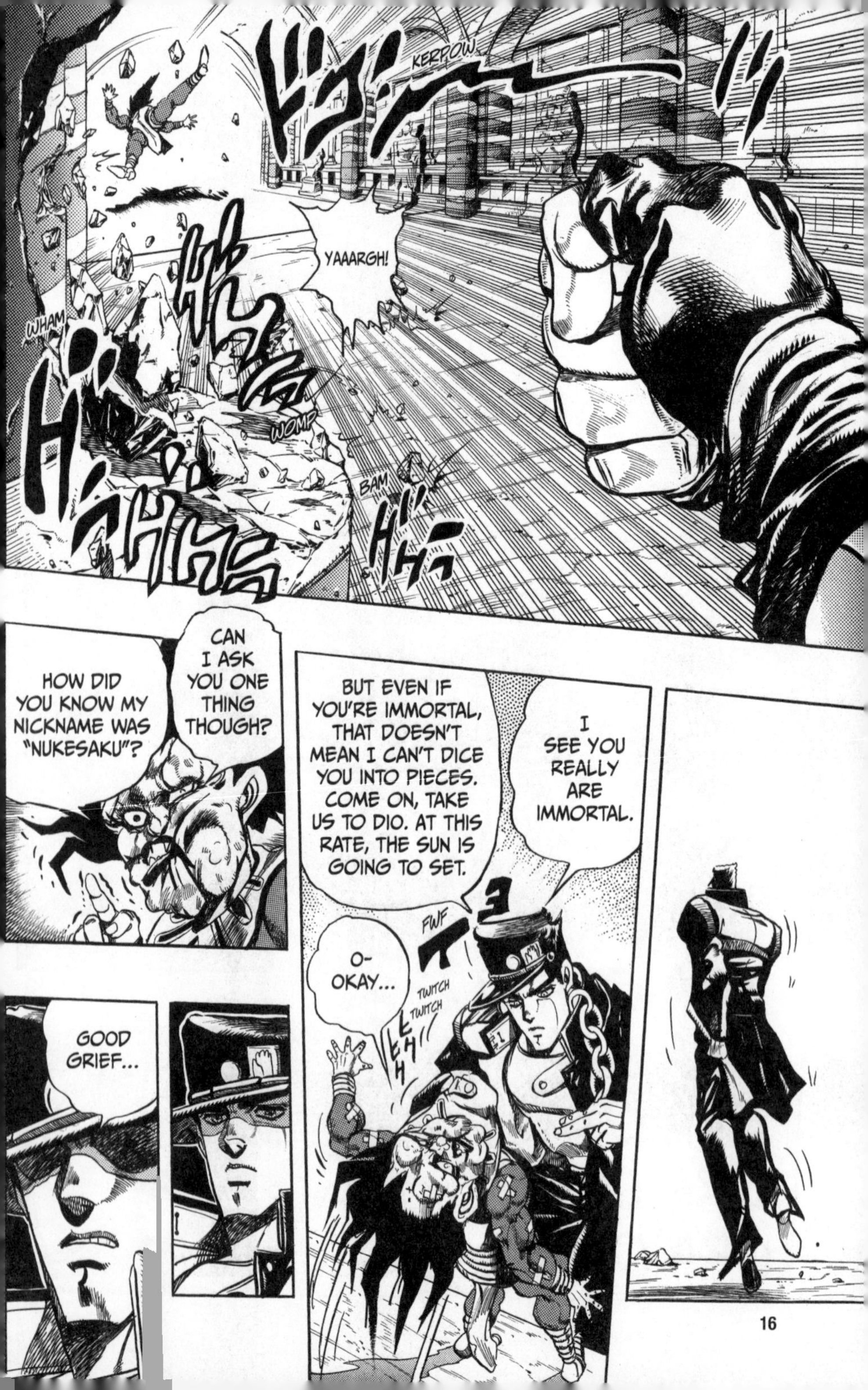
KERPOW
YAAARGH!
WOMP
BAM
WHAM
I SEE YOU REALLY ARE IMMORTAL.
BUT EVEN IF YOU'RE IMMORTAL, THAT DOESN'T MEAN I CAN'T DICE YOU INTO PIECES. COME ON, TAKE US TO DIO. AT THIS RATE, THE SUN IS GOING TO SET.
FWF
O-OKAY...
TWITCH TWITCH
CAN I ASK YOU ONE THING THOUGH?
HOW DID YOU KNOW MY NICKNAME WAS "NUKESAKU"?
GOOD GRIEF...

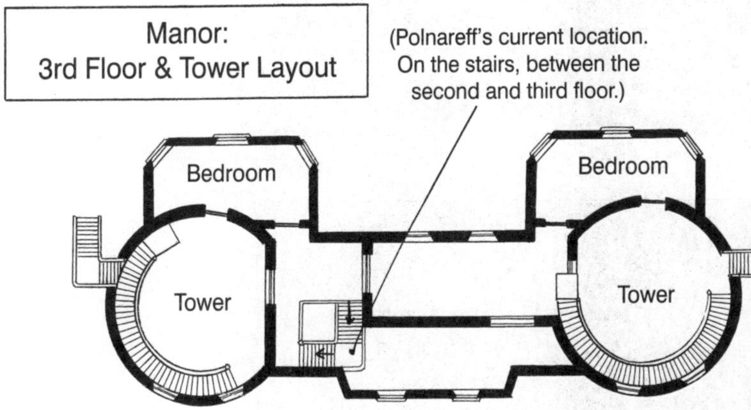
Manor:
3rd Floor & Tower Layout
(Polnareff's current location.
On the stairs, between the
second and third floor.)
Bedroom
Bedroom
Tower
Tower

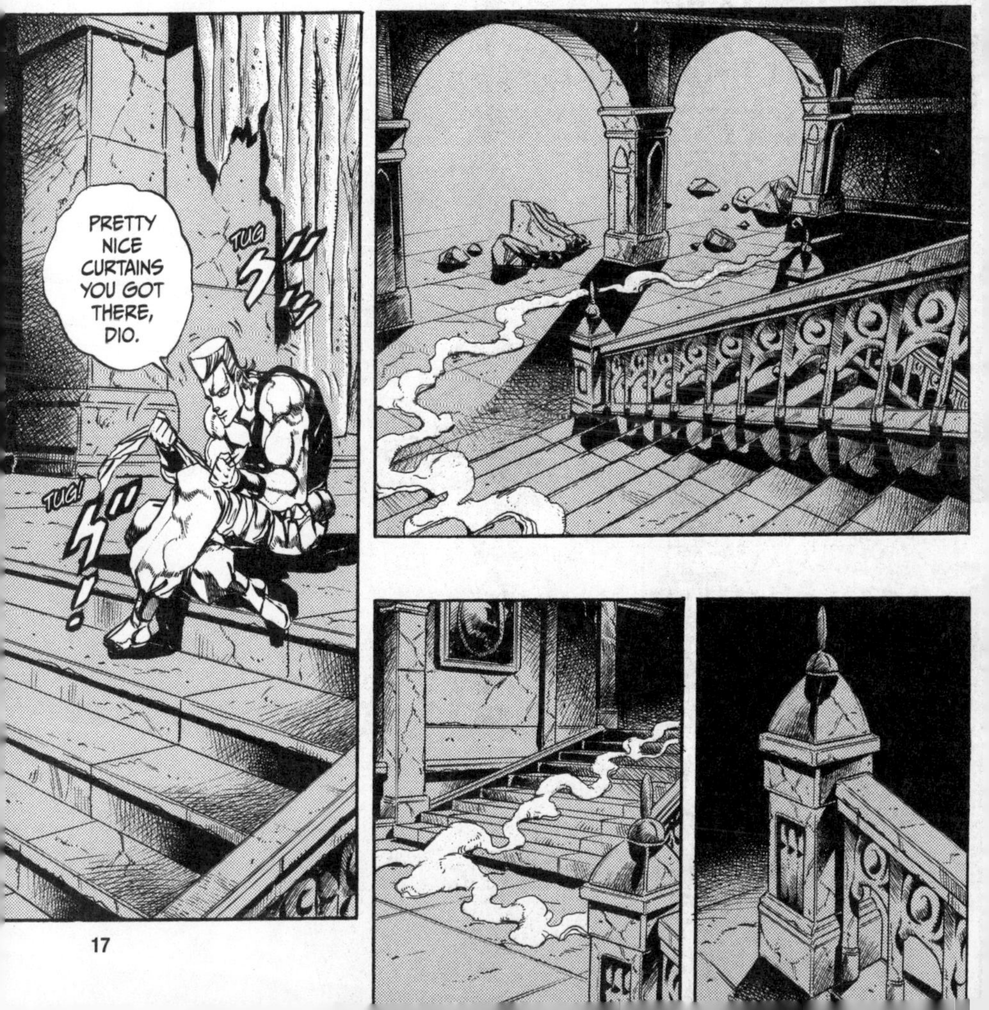
PRETTY NICE CURTAINS YOU GOT THERE, DIO.
TUG
TUG!

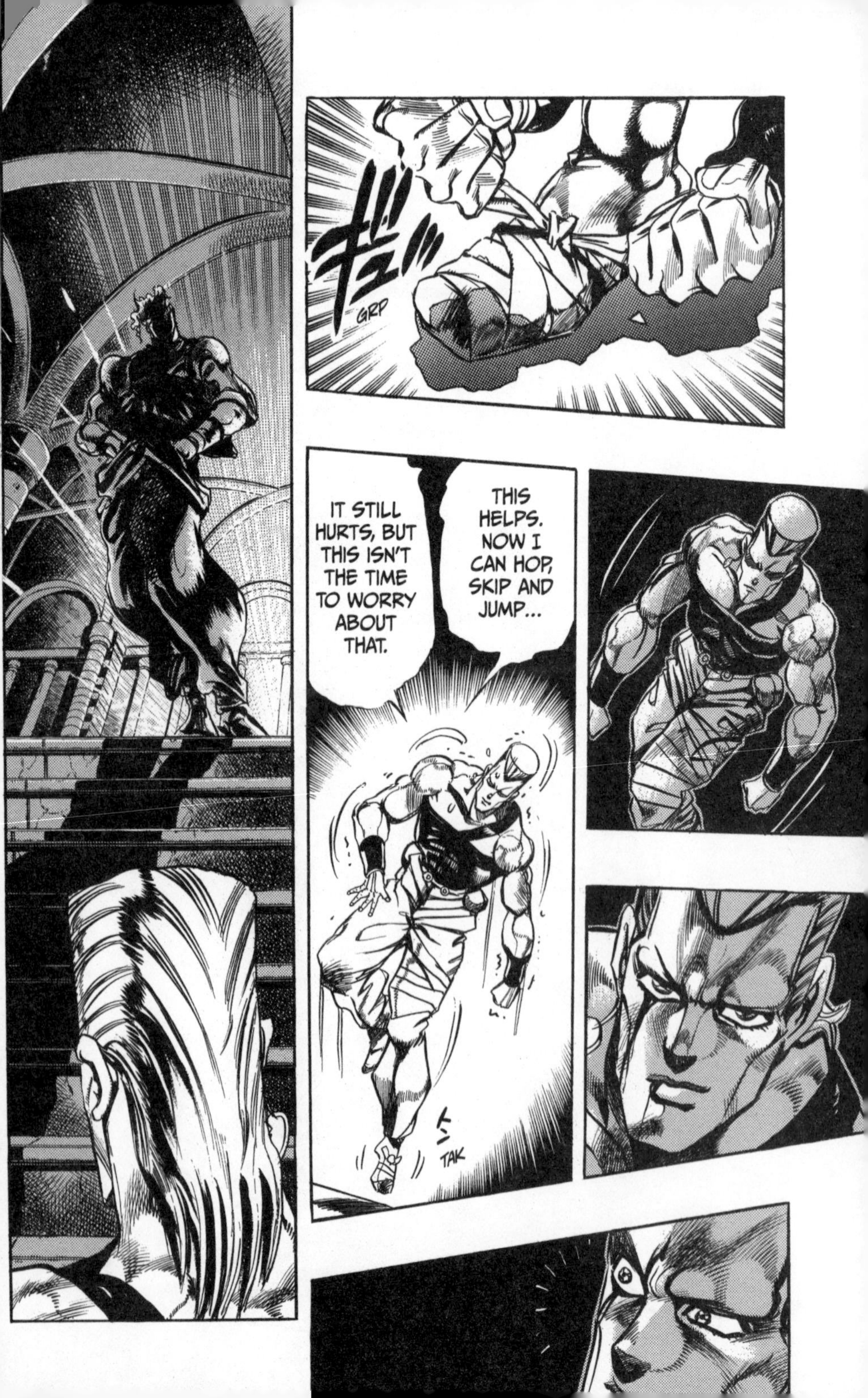
GRP
THIS HELPS. NOW I CAN HOP, SKIP AND JUMP...
IT STILL HURTS, BUT THIS ISN'T THE TIME TO WORRY ABOUT THAT.
TAK

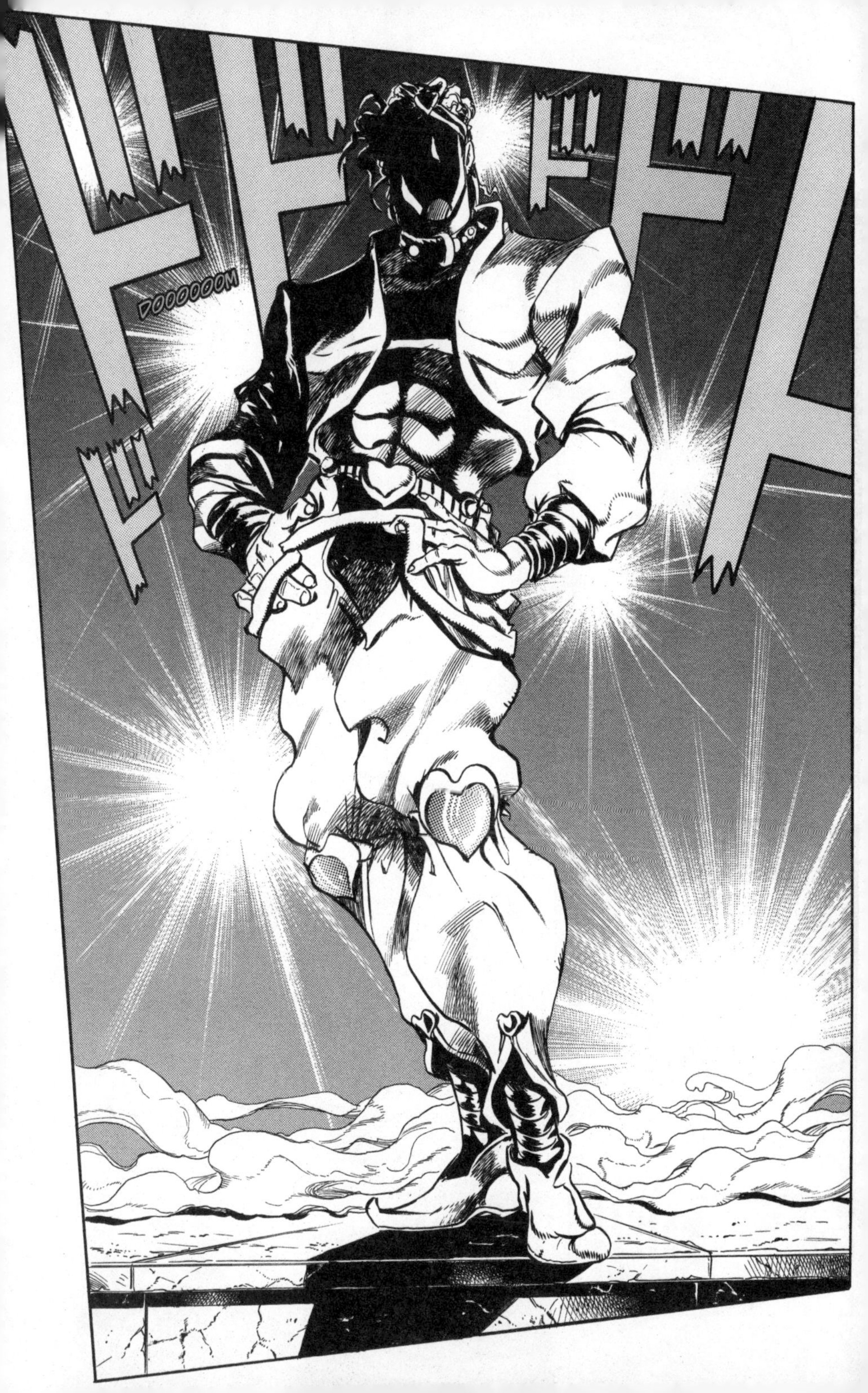
ドドドドドドド
DOOOOOOM

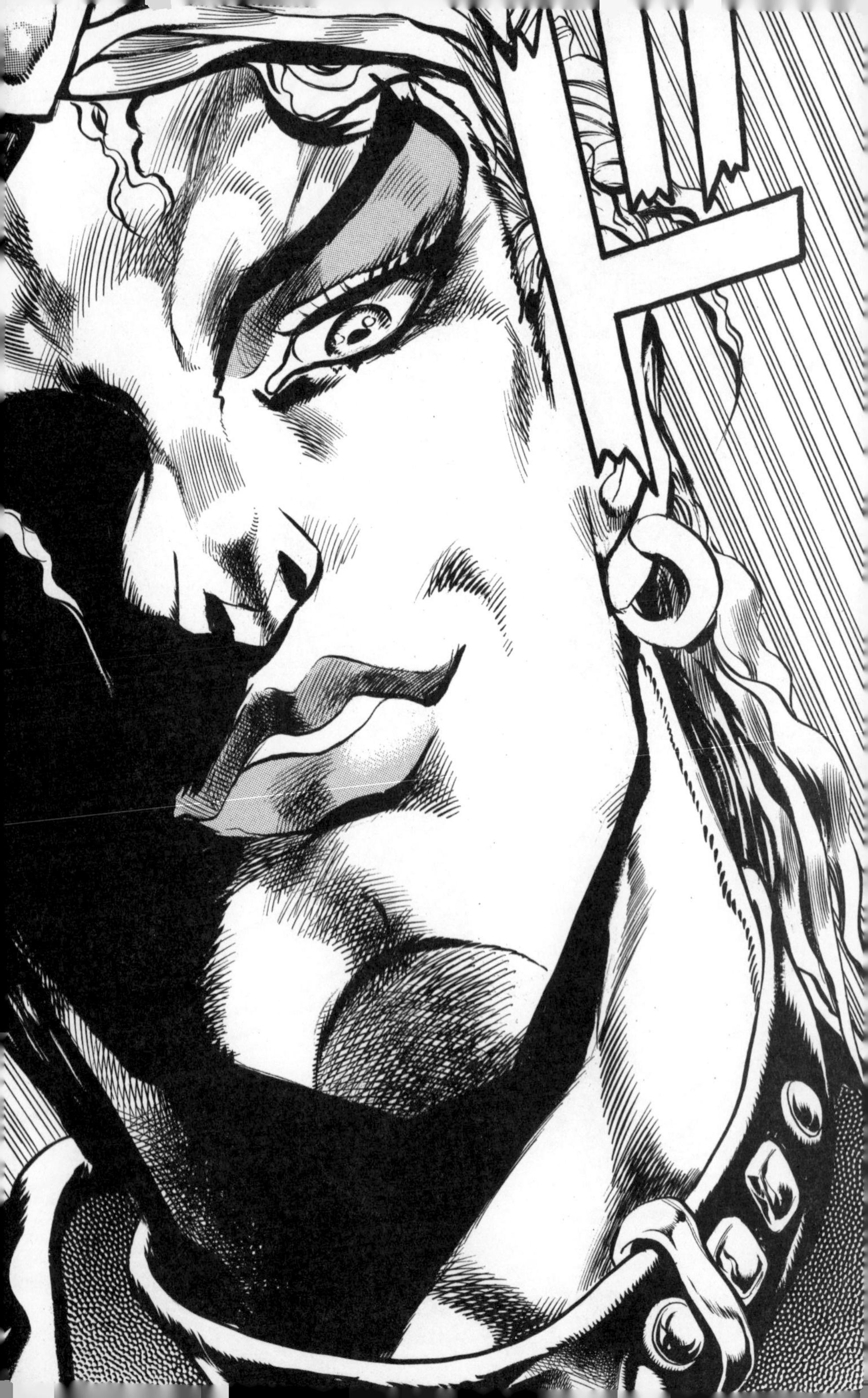

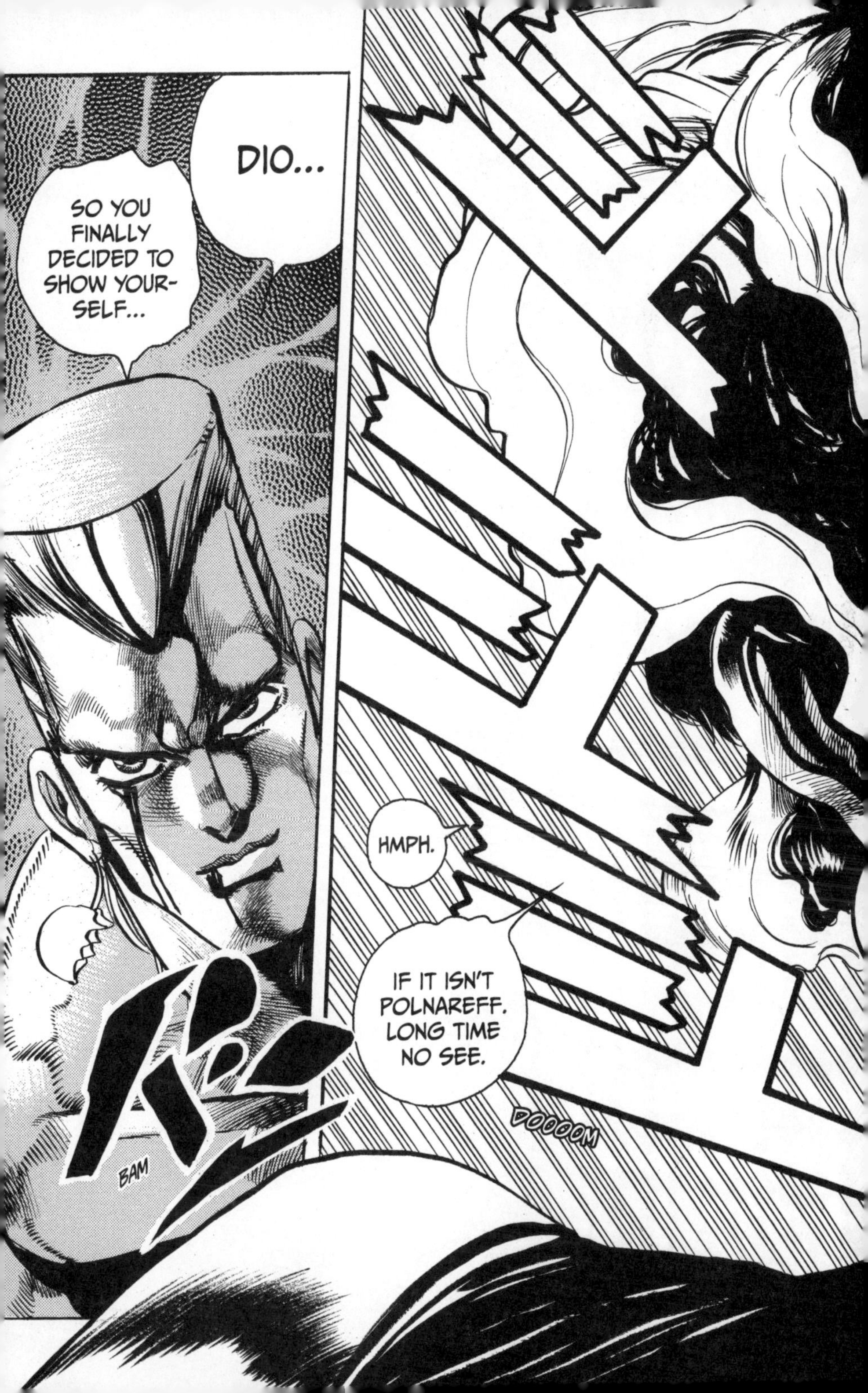
HMPH.
IF IT ISN'T POLNAREFF. LONG TIME NO SEE.
DOOOOM
DIO...
SO YOU FINALLY DECIDED TO SHOW YOUR-SELF...
BAM

THE WORLD 21

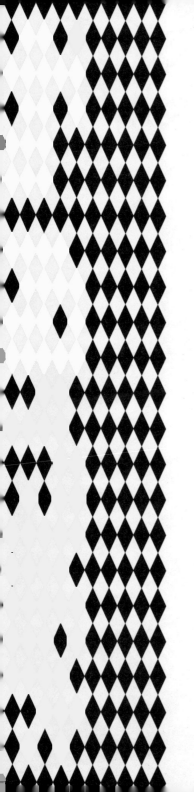

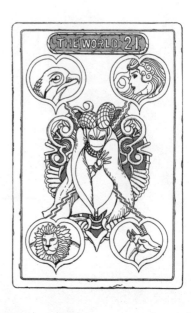

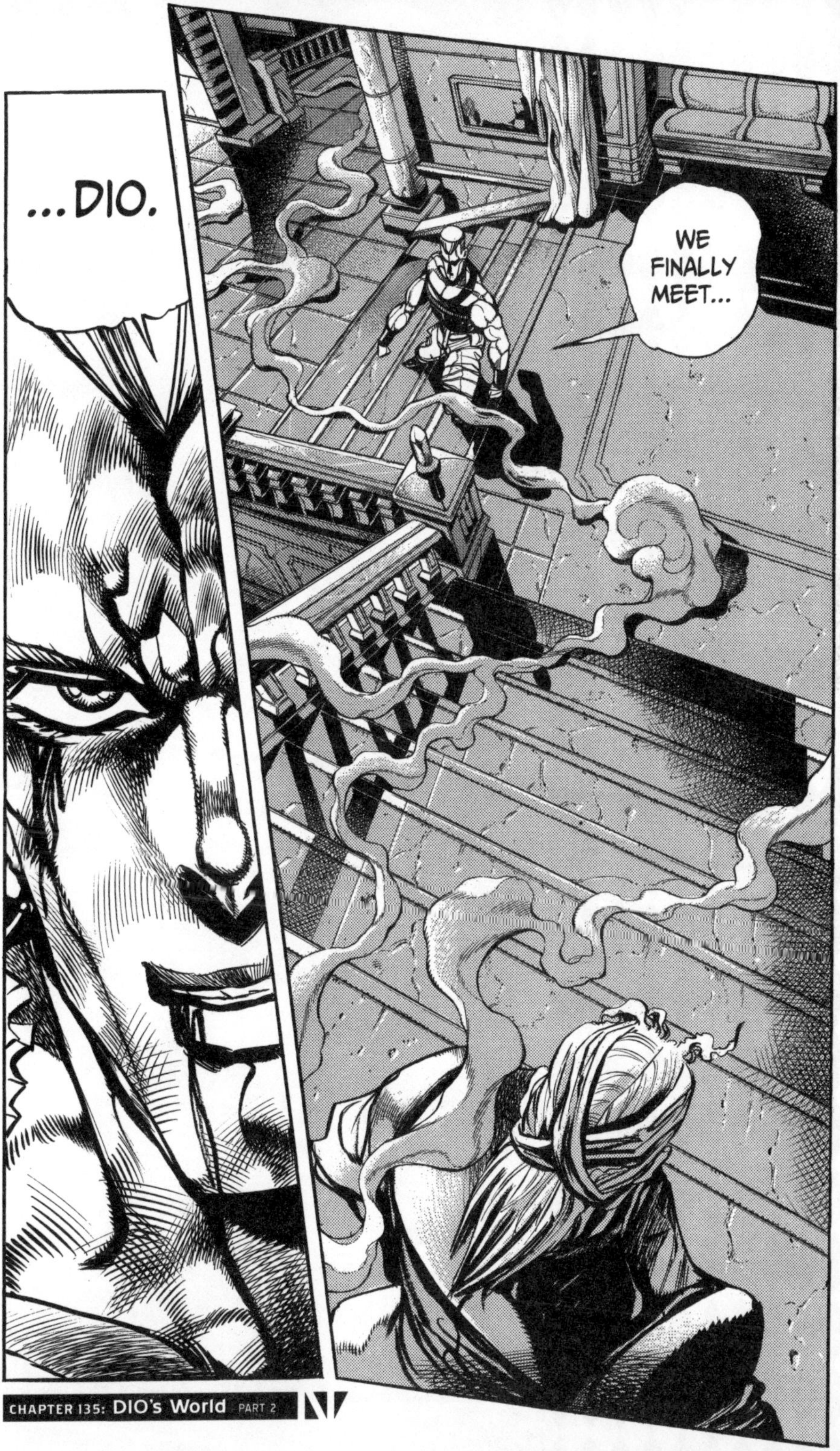
WE FINALLY MEET...
...DIO.

CHAPTER 135: DIO's World PART 2

CHAPTER 135: DIO's World PART 2

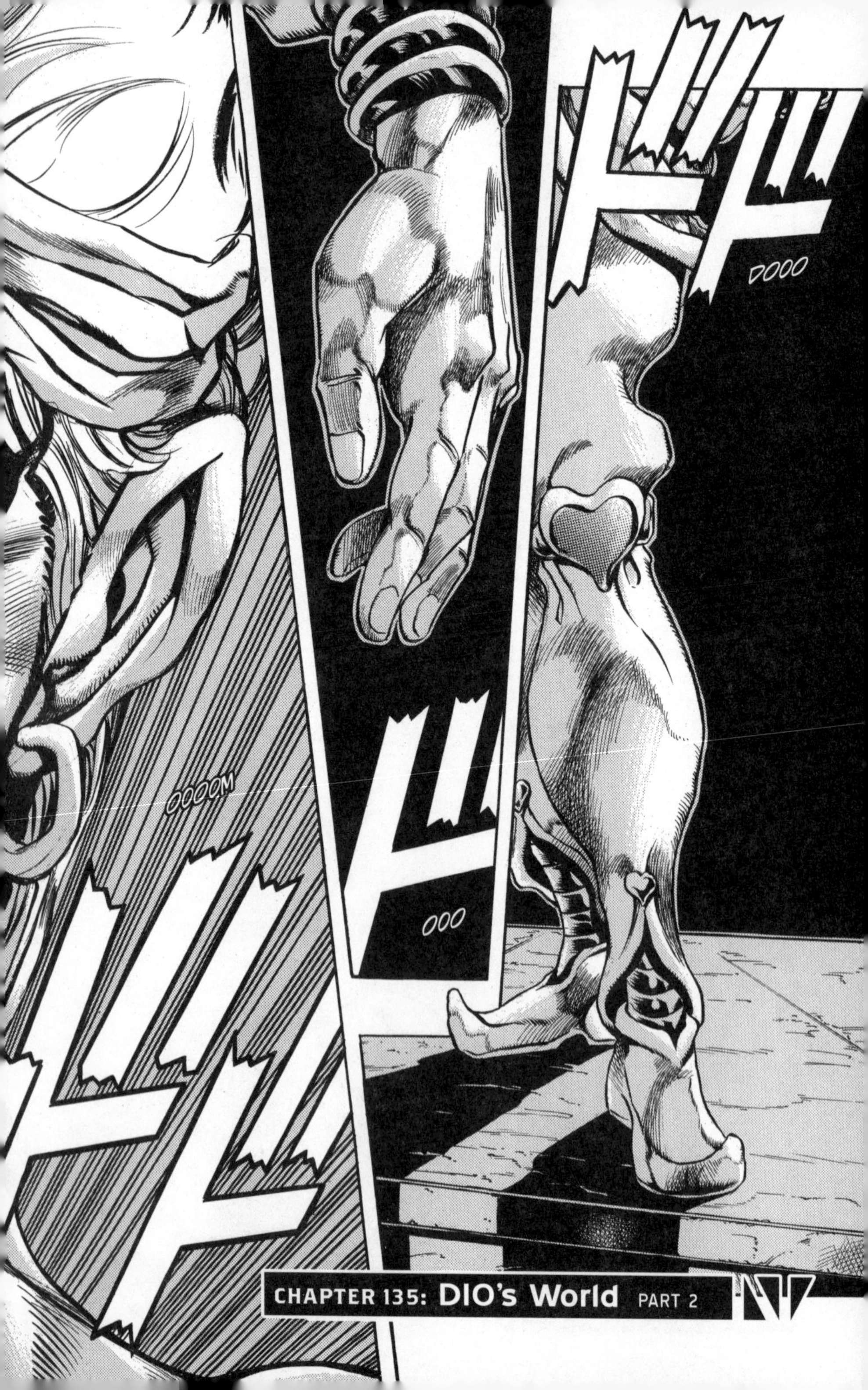
DOOO
OOO
OOOOM

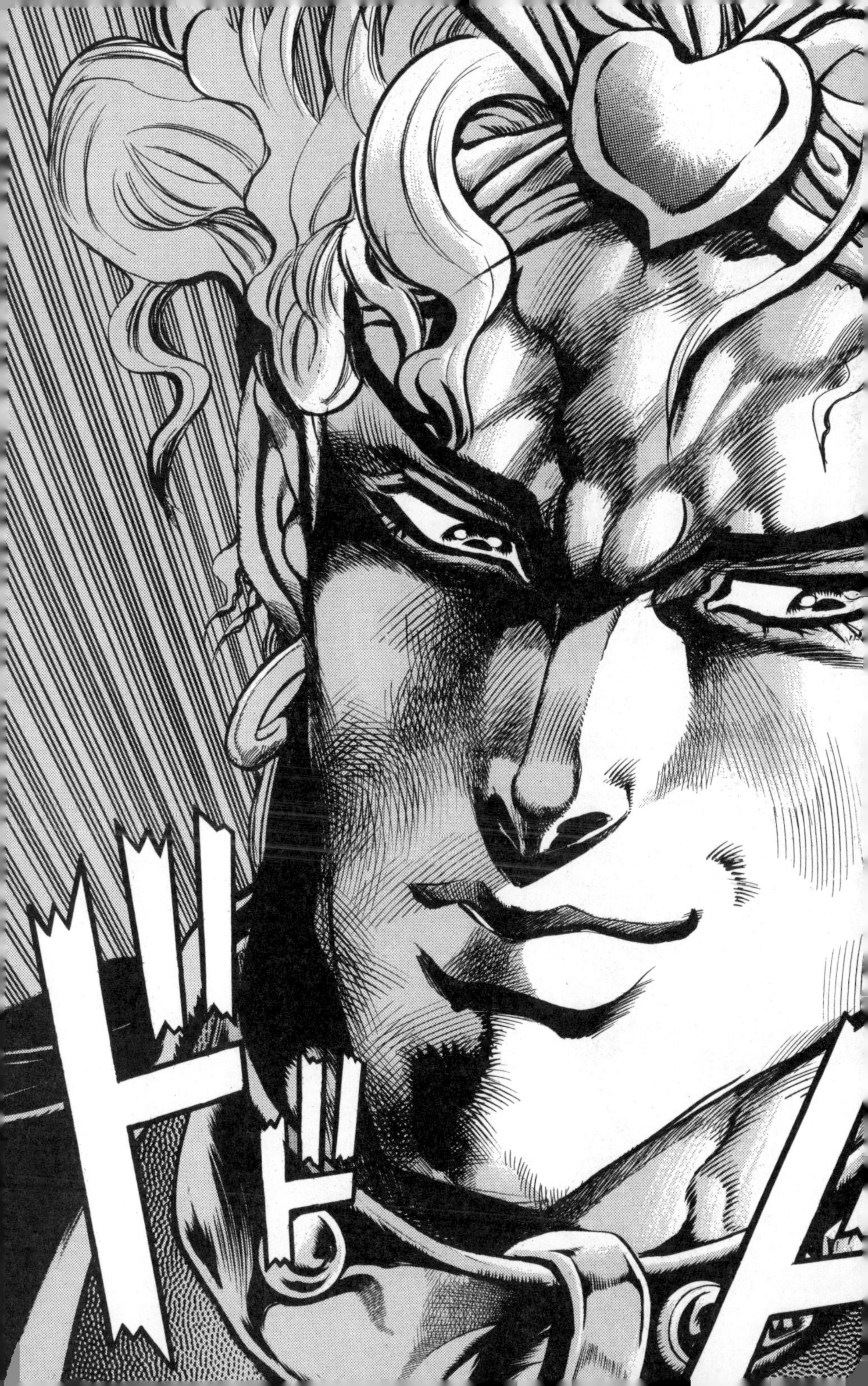
ド
ド

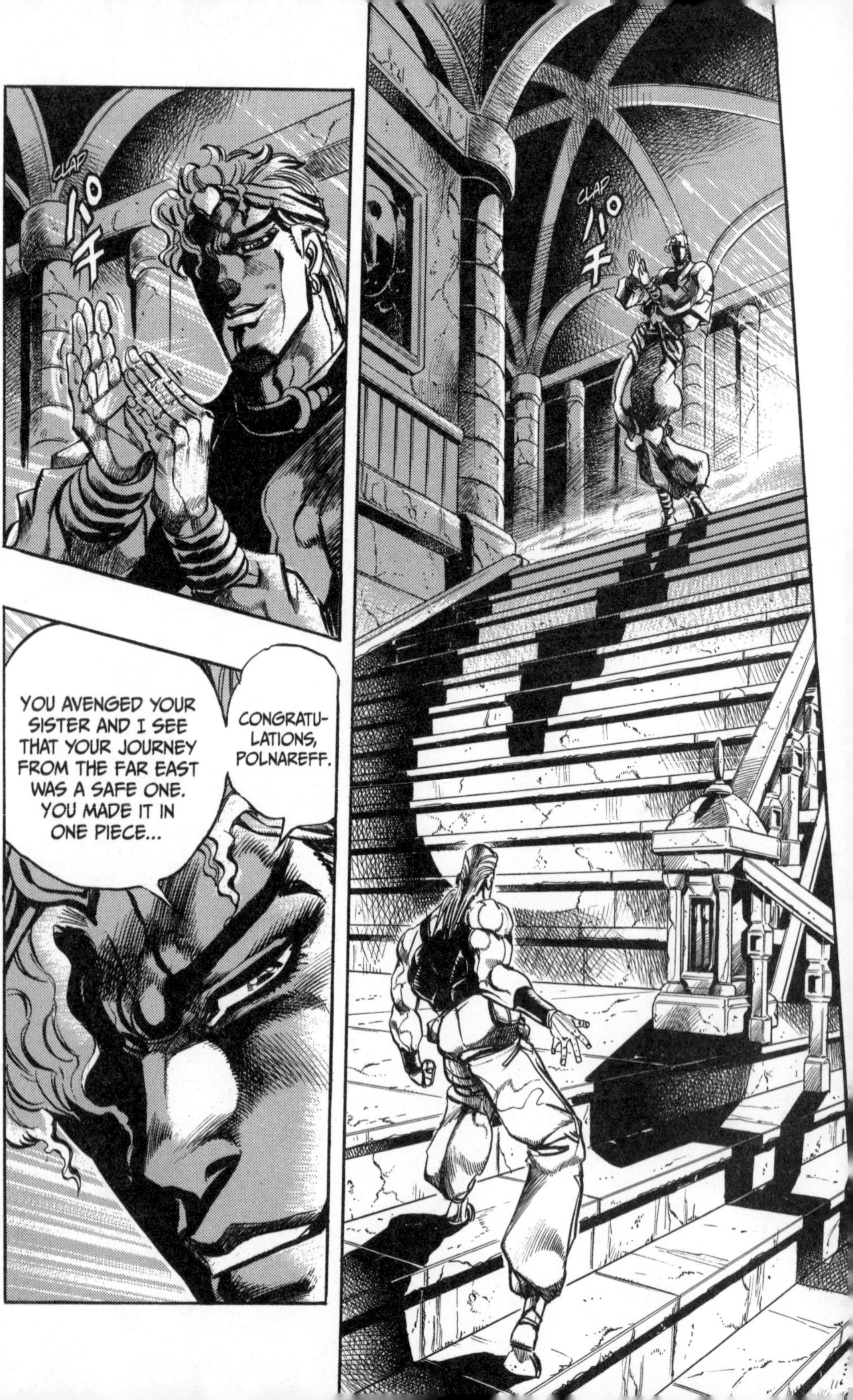
CLAP
パチ
CLAP
パチ
CONGRATULATIONS, POLNAREFF.
YOU AVENGED YOUR SISTER AND I SEE THAT YOUR JOURNEY FROM THE FAR EAST WAS A SAFE ONE. YOU MADE IT IN ONE PIECE...

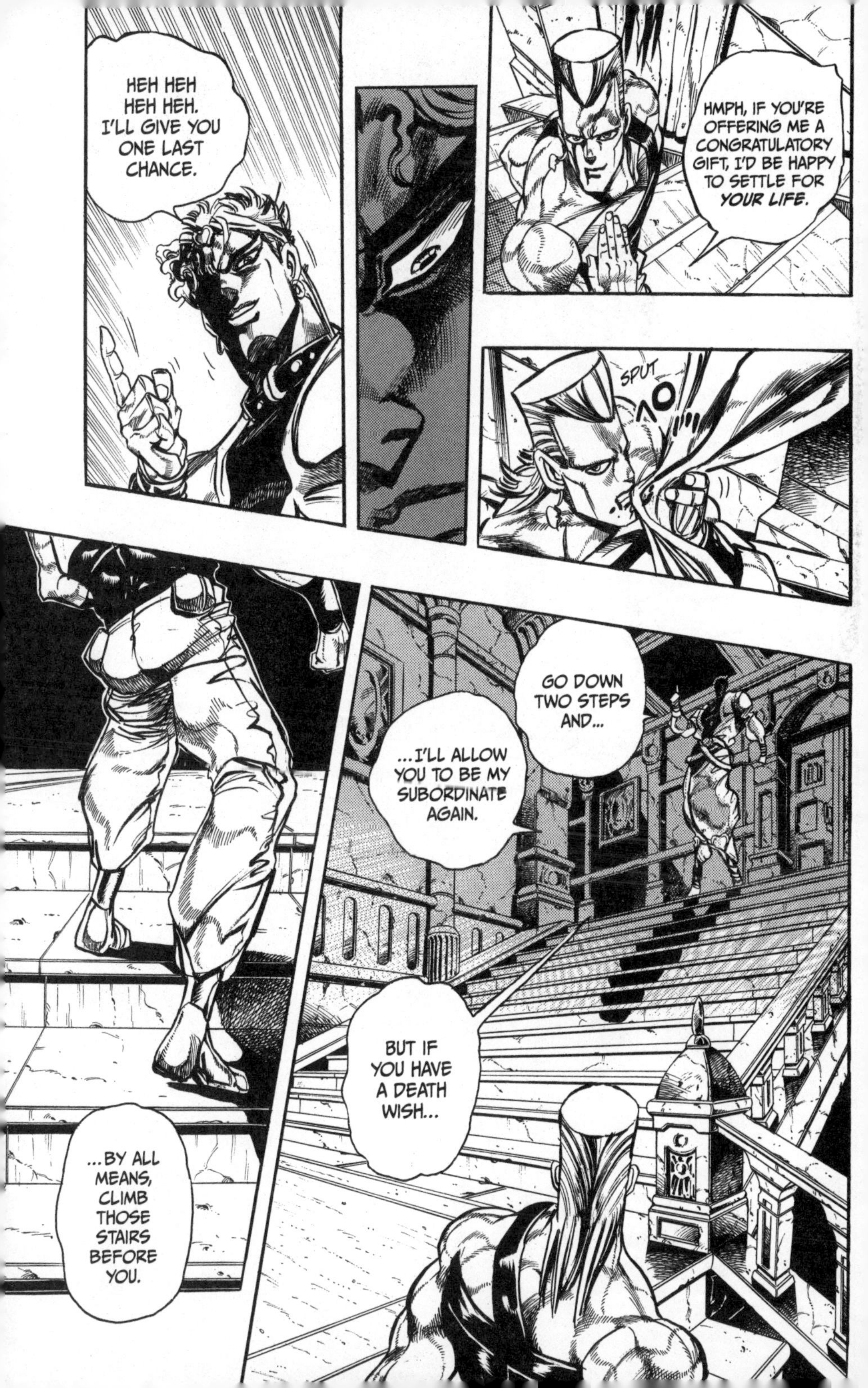
HMPH, IF YOU'RE OFFERING ME A CONGRATULATORY GIFT, I'D BE HAPPY TO SETTLE FOR *YOUR LIFE*.
SPUT
HEH HEH HEH HEH. I'LL GIVE YOU ONE LAST CHANCE.
GO DOWN TWO STEPS AND...
...I'LL ALLOW YOU TO BE MY SUBORDINATE AGAIN.
BUT IF YOU HAVE A DEATH WISH...
...BY ALL MEANS, CLIMB THOSE STAIRS BEFORE YOU.

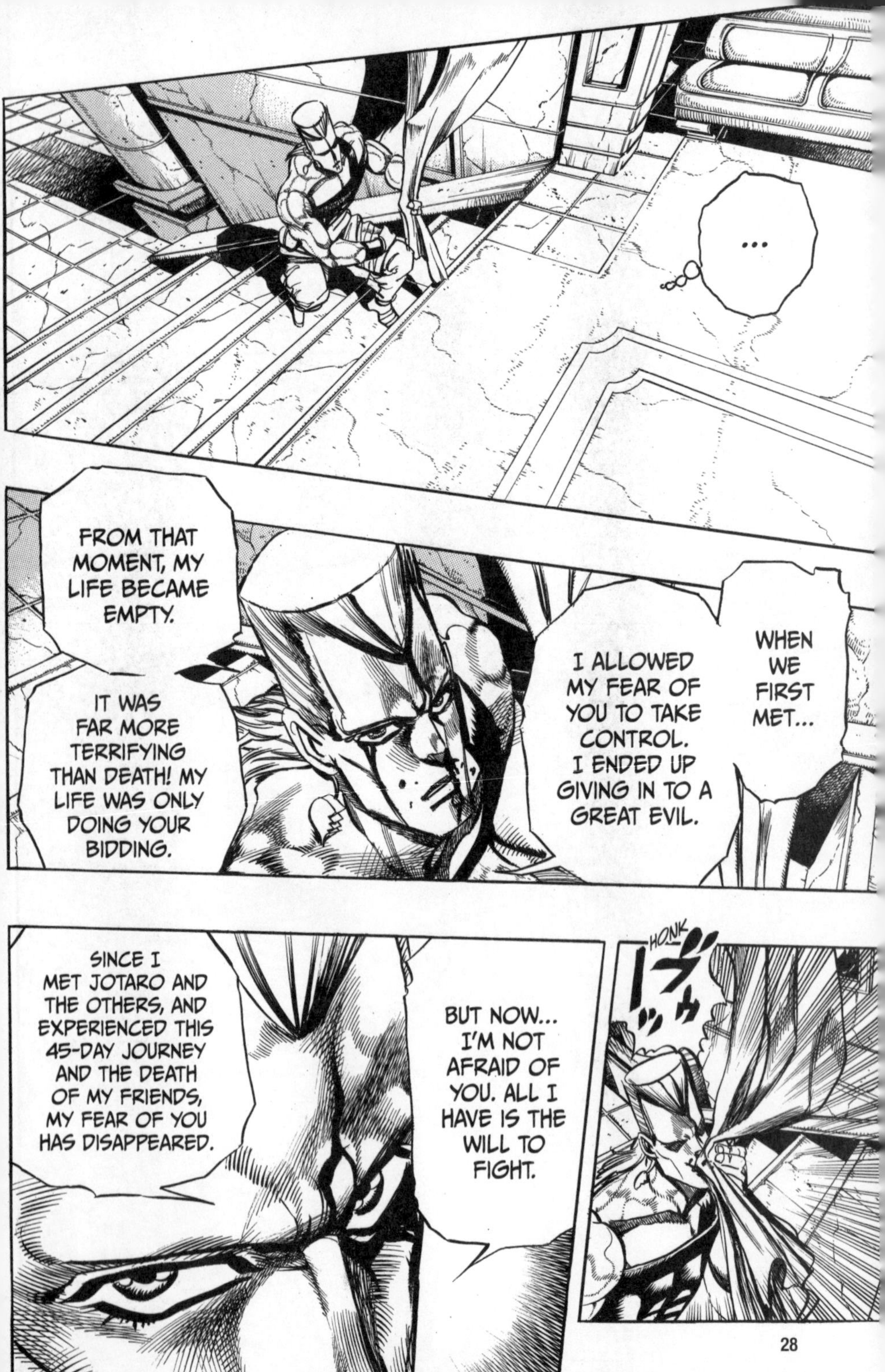
...
WHEN WE FIRST MET...
I ALLOWED MY FEAR OF YOU TO TAKE CONTROL. I ENDED UP GIVING IN TO A GREAT EVIL.
FROM THAT MOMENT, MY LIFE BECAME EMPTY.
IT WAS FAR MORE TERRIFYING THAN DEATH! MY LIFE WAS ONLY DOING YOUR BIDDING.
HONK
SINCE I MET JOTARO AND THE OTHERS, AND EXPERIENCED THIS 45-DAY JOURNEY AND THE DEATH OF MY FRIENDS, MY FEAR OF YOU HAS DISAPPEARED.
BUT NOW... I'M NOT AFRAID OF YOU. ALL I HAVE IS THE WILL TO FIGHT.

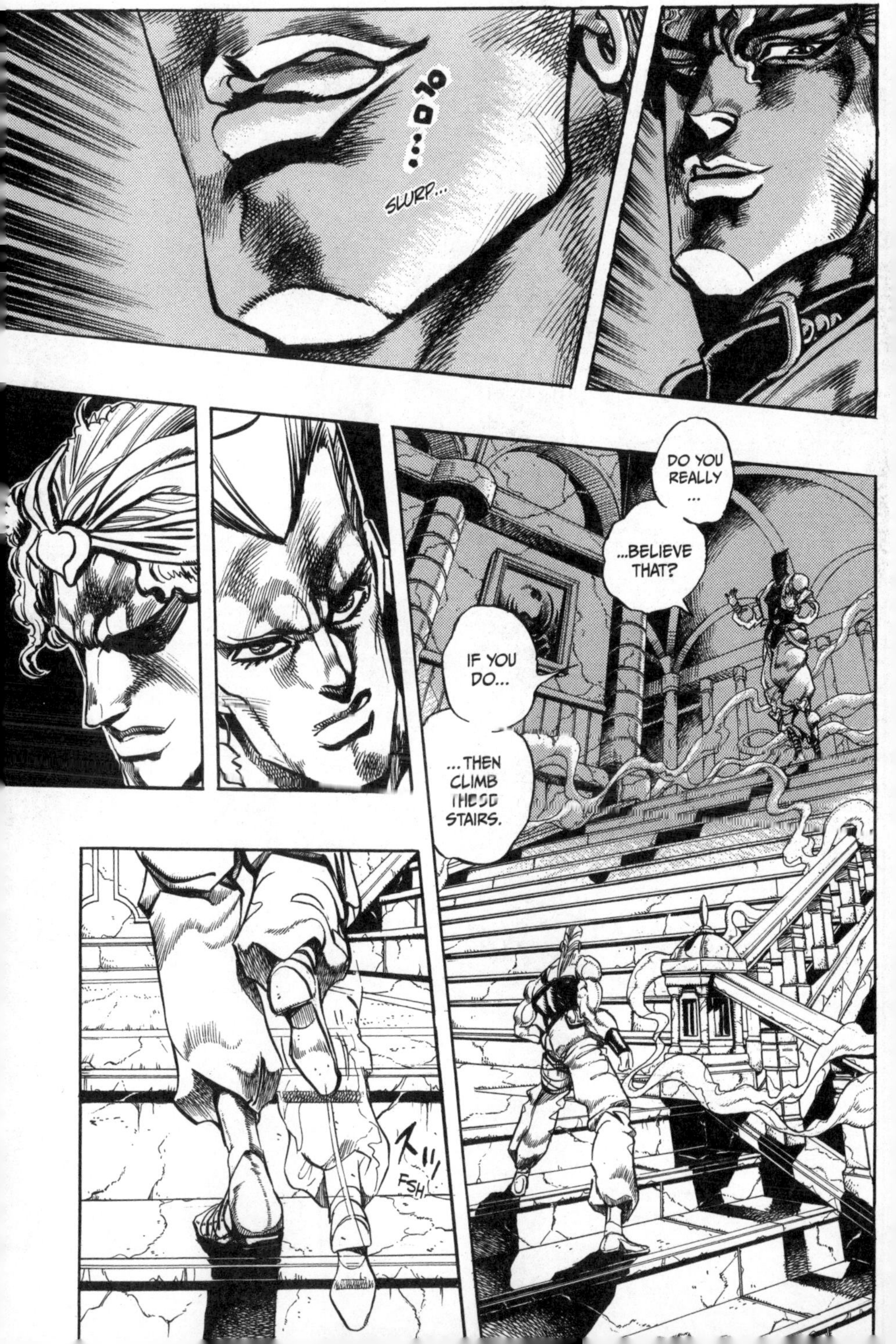
SLURP...
DO YOU REALLY ...
...BELIEVE THAT?
IF YOU DO...
...THEN CLIMB THESE STAIRS.
FSH

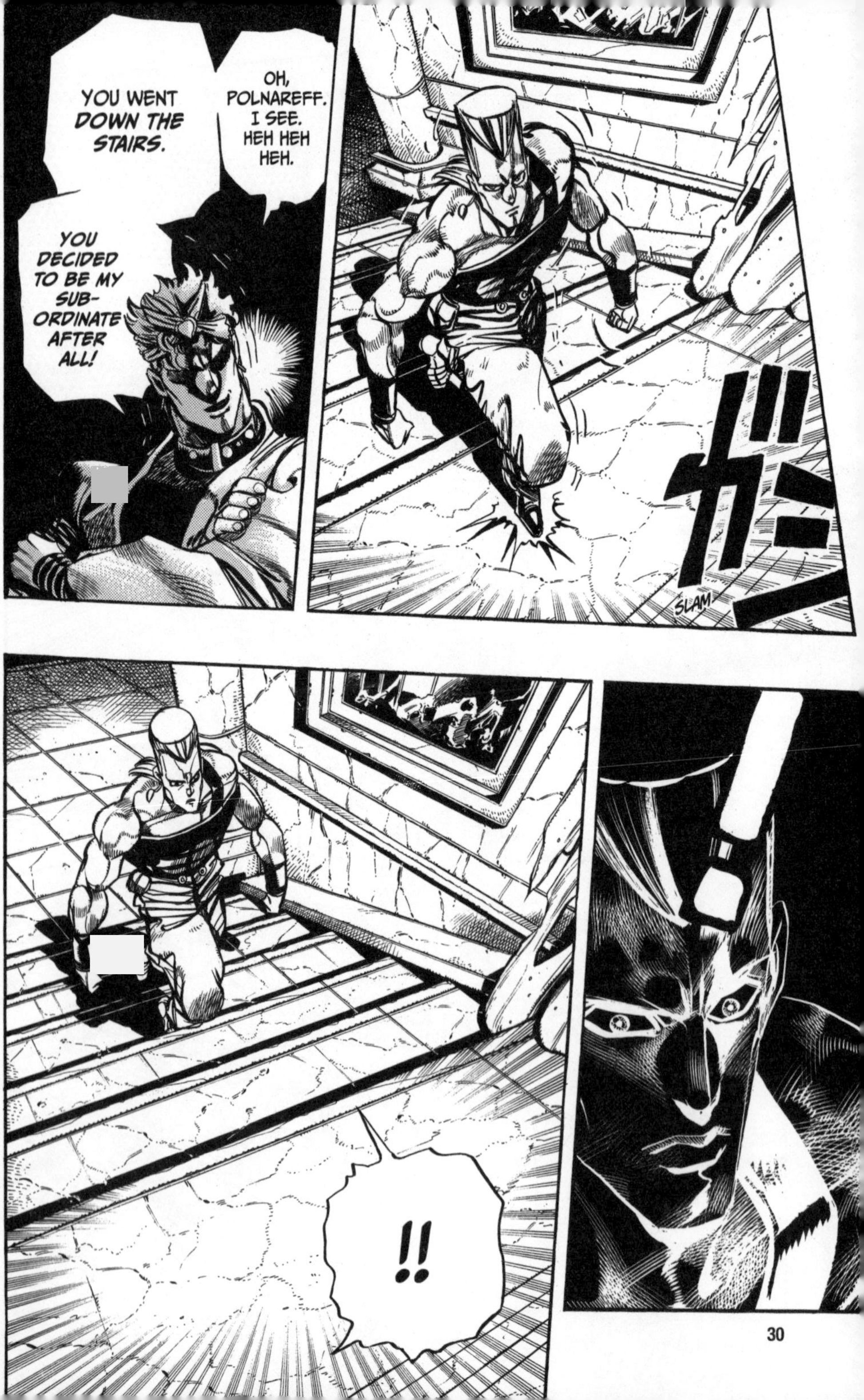
SLAM
OH, POLNAREFF. I SEE. HEH HEH HEH.
YOU WENT DOWN THE STAIRS.
YOU DECIDED TO BE MY SUB-ORDINATE AFTER ALL!
!!

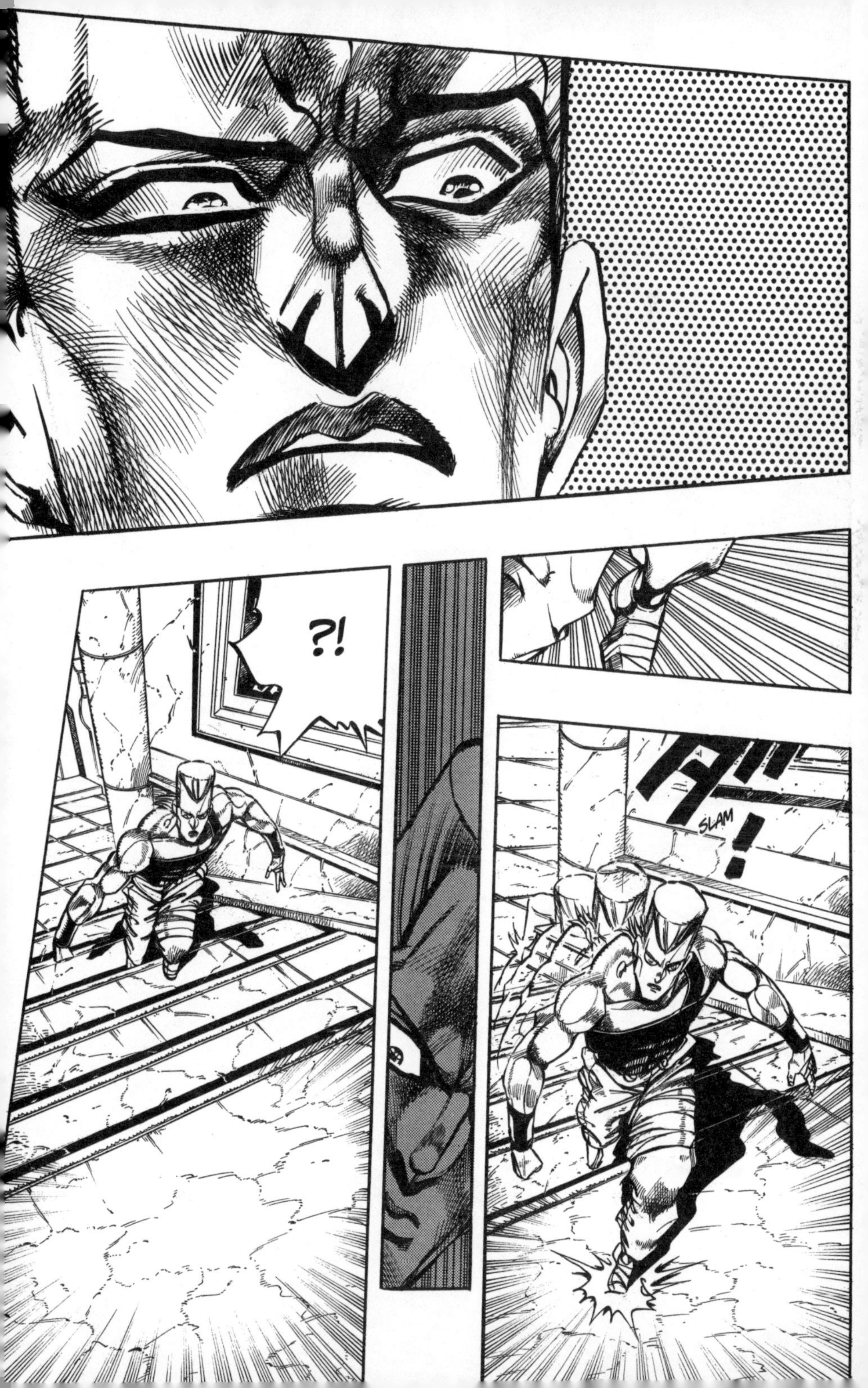
SLAM
?!

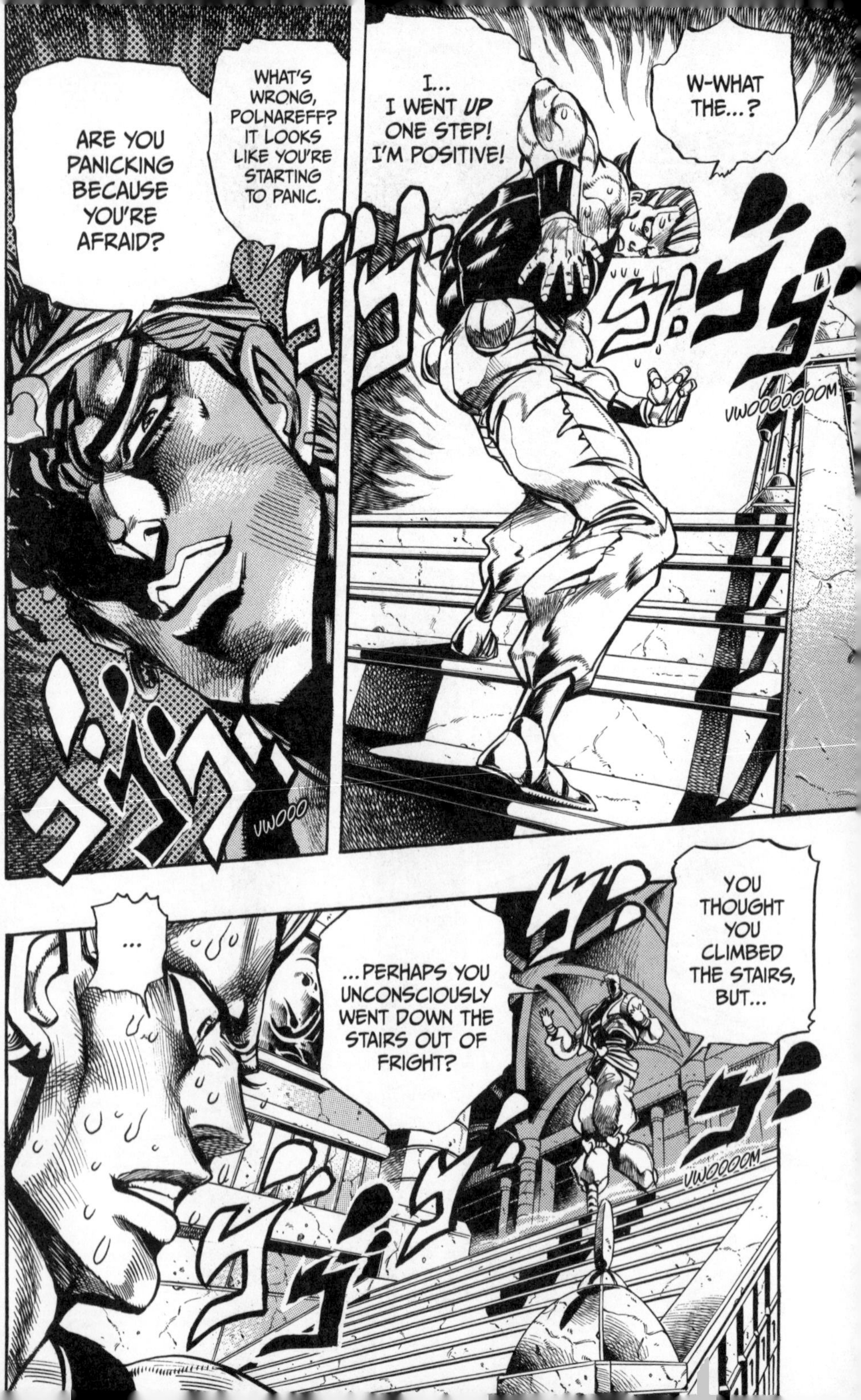
W-WHAT THE...?
I... I WENT *UP* ONE STEP! I'M POSITIVE!
VWOOOOOOOM
WHAT'S WRONG, POLNAREFF? IT LOOKS LIKE YOU'RE STARTING TO PANIC.
ARE YOU PANICKING BECAUSE YOU'RE AFRAID?
VWOOO
YOU THOUGHT YOU CLIMBED THE STAIRS, BUT...
VWOOOOM
...PERHAPS YOU UNCONSCIOUSLY WENT DOWN THE STAIRS OUT OF FRIGHT?
...

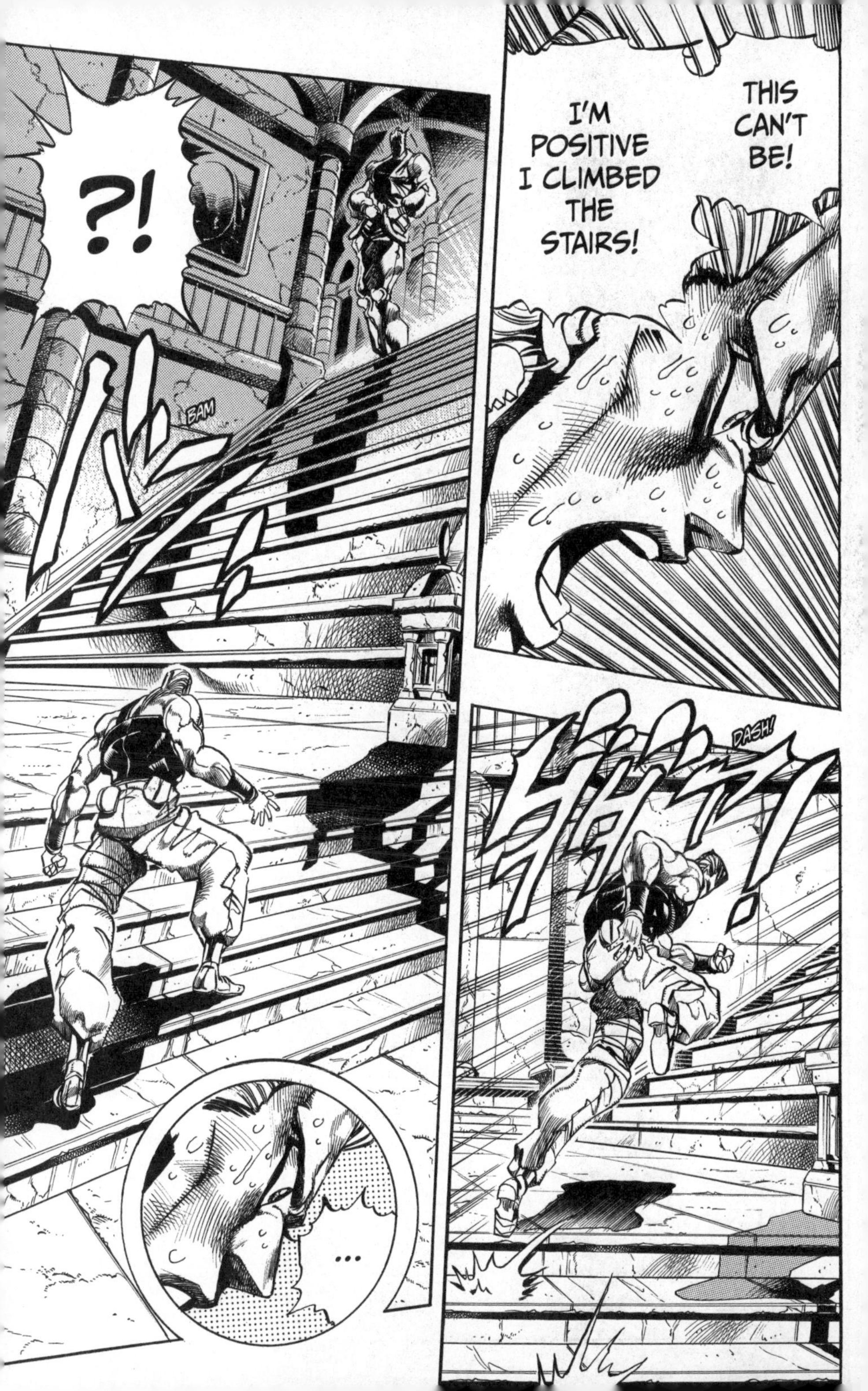
THIS CAN'T BE!
I'M POSITIVE I CLIMBED THE STAIRS!
DASH!
?!
BAM
...

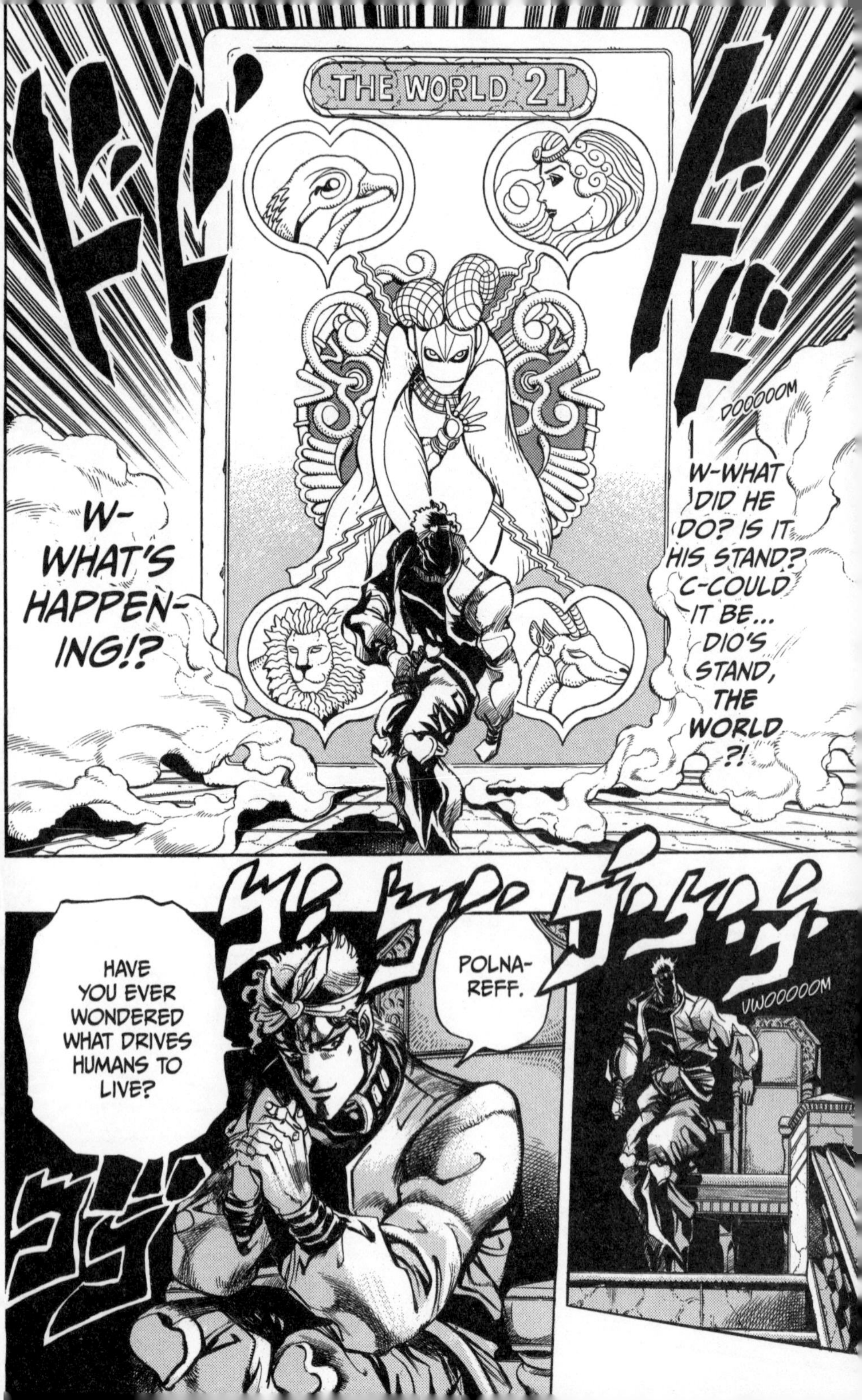
THE WORLD 21
DOOOOOM
W-WHAT DID HE DO? IS IT HIS STAND? C-COULD IT BE... DIO'S STAND, THE WORLD ?!
W-WHAT'S HAPPEN-ING!?
UWOOOOOM
POLNA-REFF.
HAVE YOU EVER WONDERED WHAT DRIVES HUMANS TO LIVE?

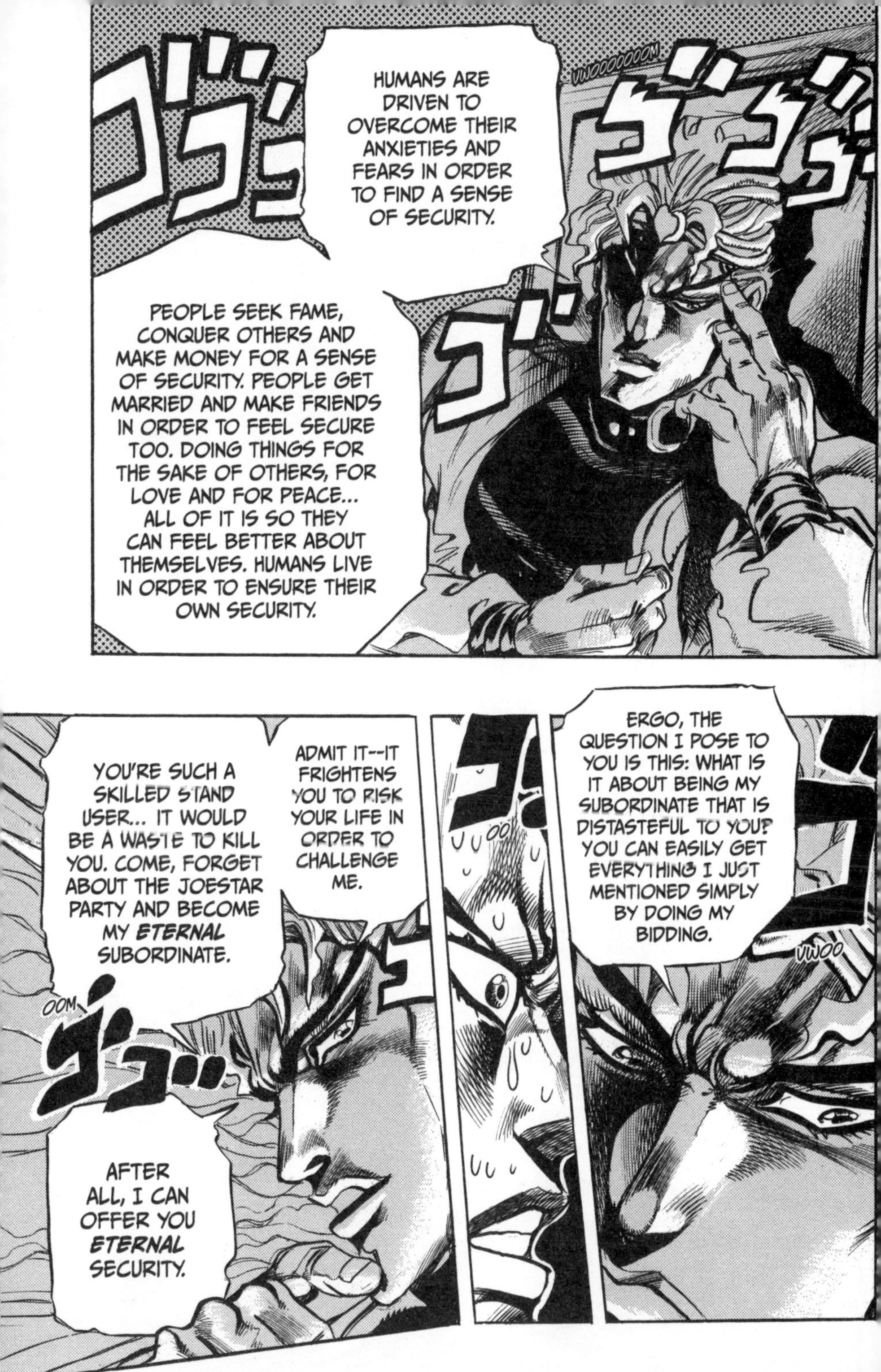
VWOOOOOOOOM
HUMANS ARE DRIVEN TO OVERCOME THEIR ANXIETIES AND FEARS IN ORDER TO FIND A SENSE OF SECURITY.
PEOPLE SEEK FAME, CONQUER OTHERS AND MAKE MONEY FOR A SENSE OF SECURITY. PEOPLE GET MARRIED AND MAKE FRIENDS IN ORDER TO FEEL SECURE TOO. DOING THINGS FOR THE SAKE OF OTHERS, FOR LOVE AND FOR PEACE... ALL OF IT IS SO THEY CAN FEEL BETTER ABOUT THEMSELVES. HUMANS LIVE IN ORDER TO ENSURE THEIR OWN SECURITY.
ERGO, THE QUESTION I POSE TO YOU IS THIS: WHAT IS IT ABOUT BEING MY SUBORDINATE THAT IS DISTASTEFUL TO YOU? YOU CAN EASILY GET EVERYTHING I JUST MENTIONED SIMPLY BY DOING MY BIDDING.
VWOO
ADMIT IT--IT FRIGHTENS YOU TO RISK YOUR LIFE IN ORDER TO CHALLENGE ME.
YOU'RE SUCH A SKILLED STAND USER... IT WOULD BE A WASTE TO KILL YOU. COME, FORGET ABOUT THE JOESTAR PARTY AND BECOME MY ETERNAL SUBORDINATE.
OOM
AFTER ALL, I CAN OFFER YOU ETERNAL SECURITY.

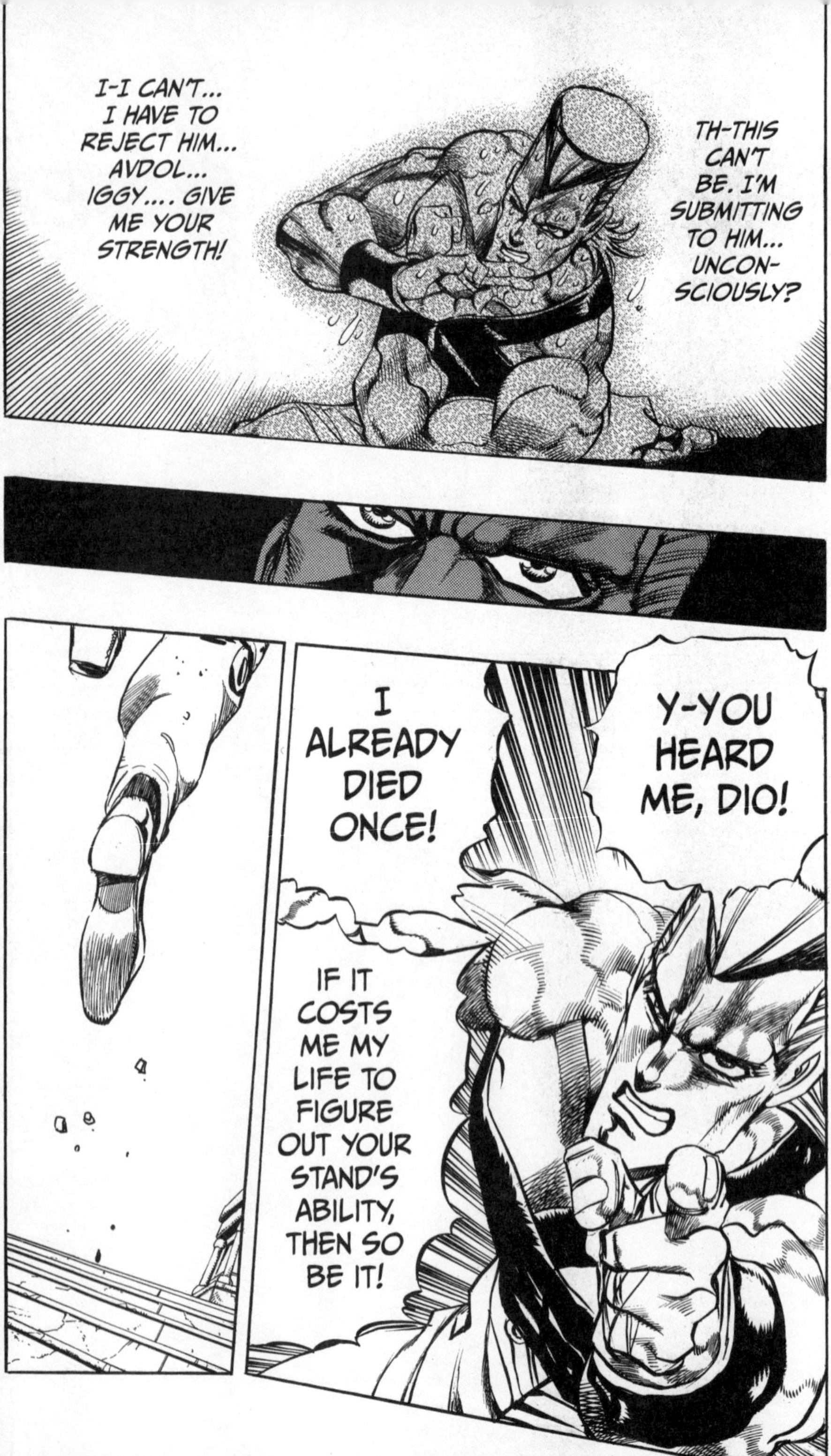
TH-THIS CAN'T BE. I'M SUBMITTING TO HIM... UNCON-SCIOUSLY?
I-I CAN'T... I HAVE TO REJECT HIM... AVDOL... IGGY.... GIVE ME YOUR STRENGTH!
Y-YOU HEARD ME, DIO!
I ALREADY DIED ONCE!
IF IT COSTS ME MY LIFE TO FIGURE OUT YOUR STAND'S ABILITY, THEN SO BE IT!

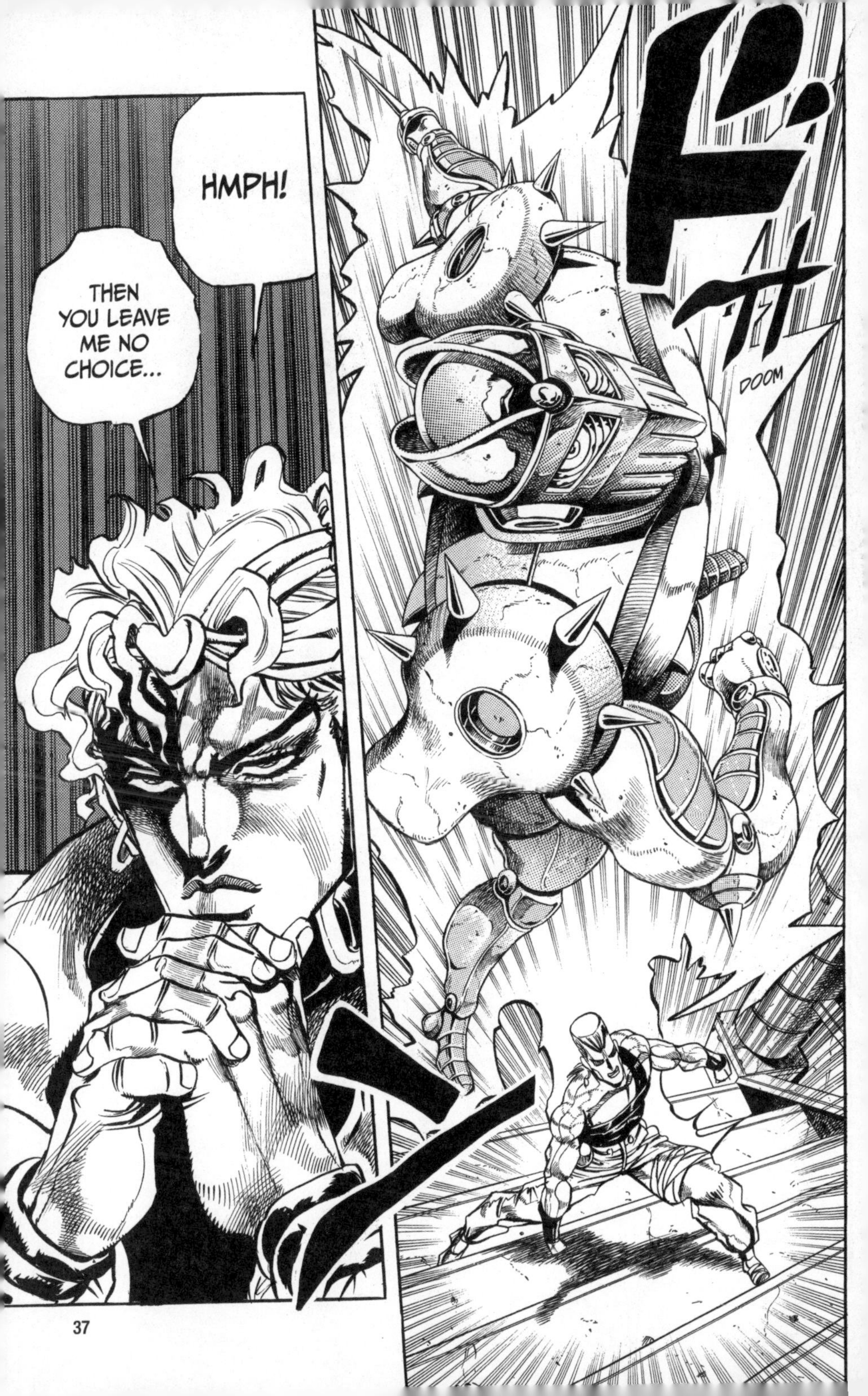
DOOM
HMPH!
THEN YOU LEAVE ME NO CHOICE...

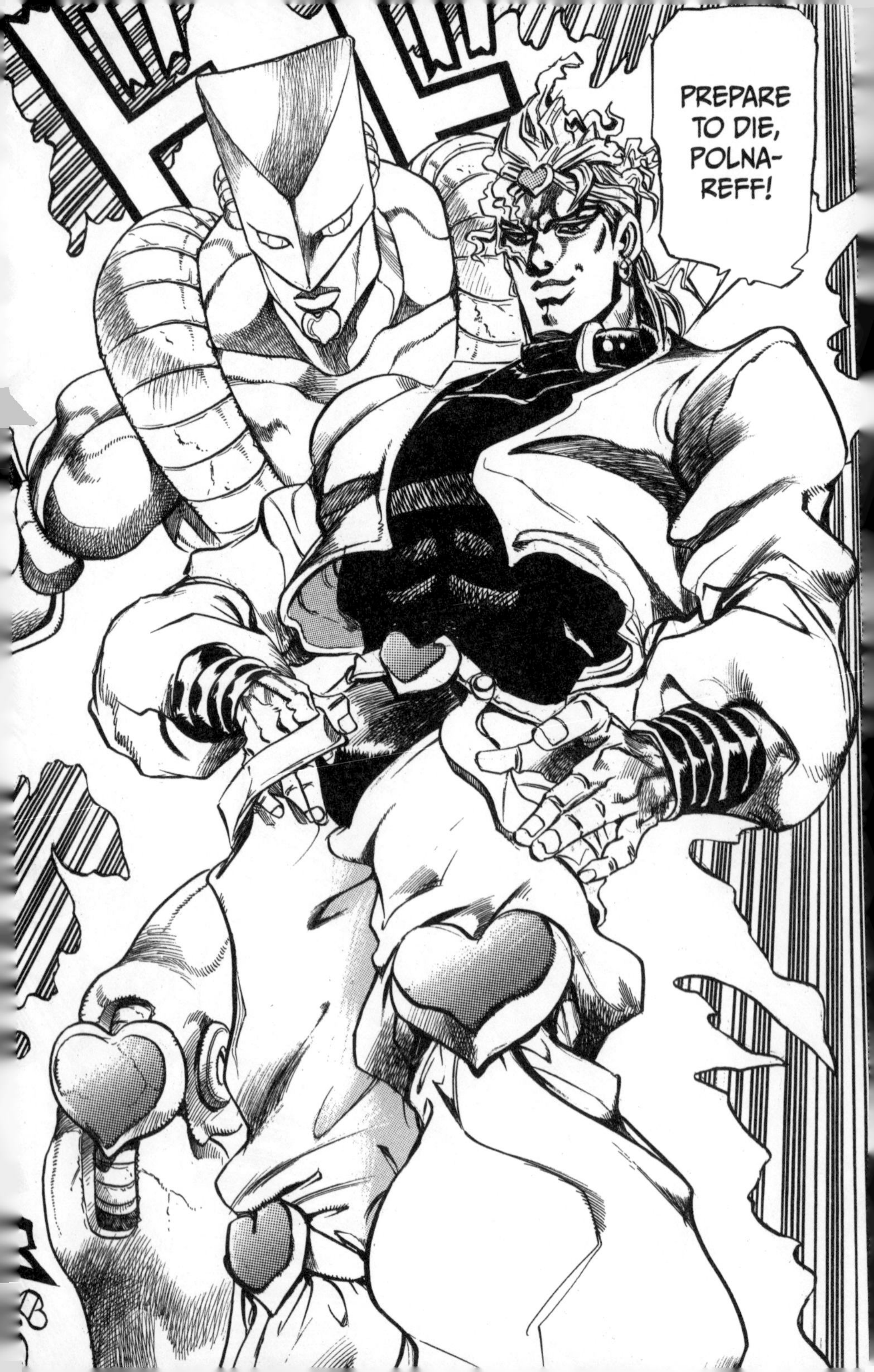
PREPARE TO DIE, POLNA-REFF!

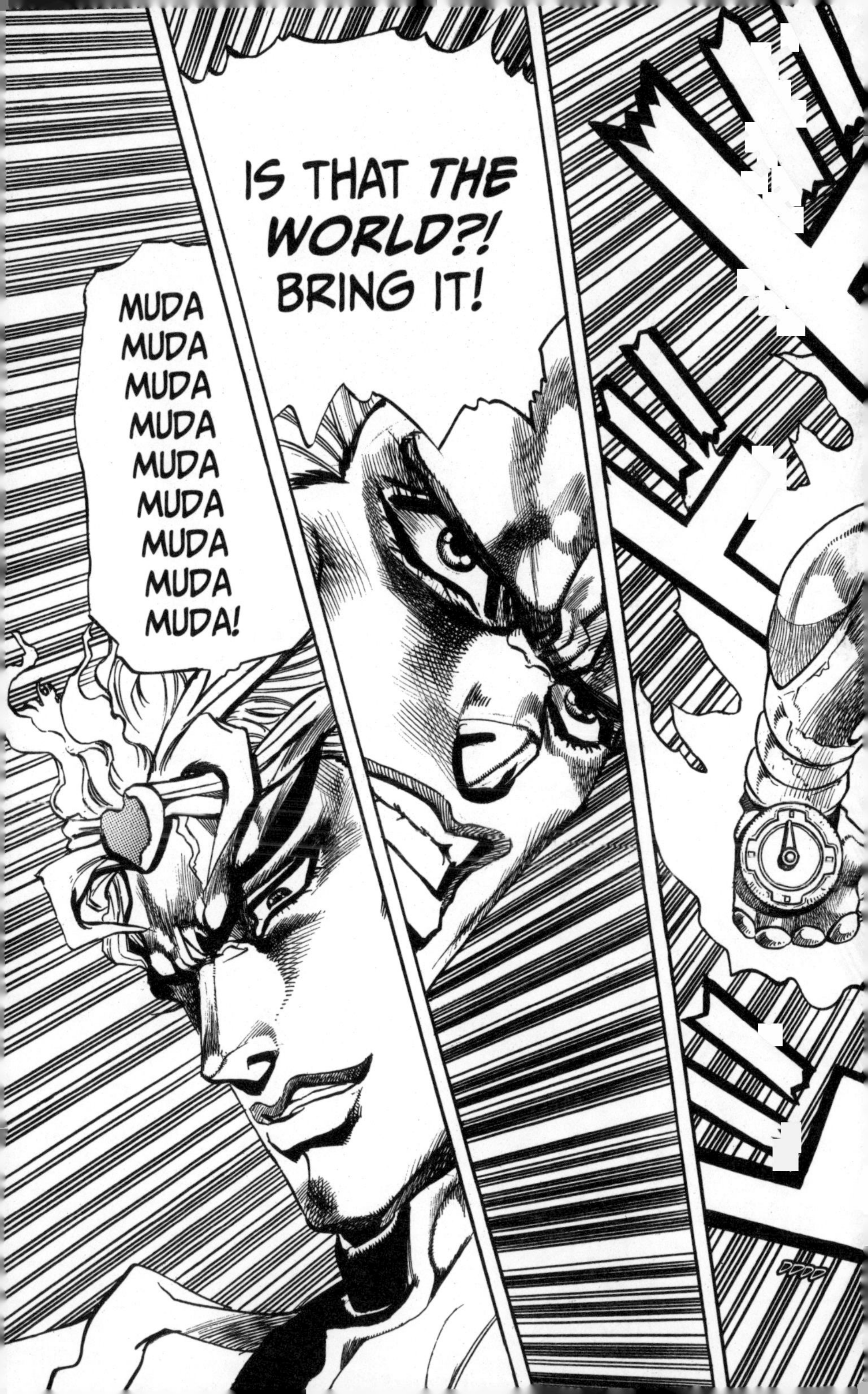
IS THAT *THE WORLD*?! BRING IT!
MUDA MUDA MUDA MUDA MUDA MUDA MUDA MUDA MUDA!

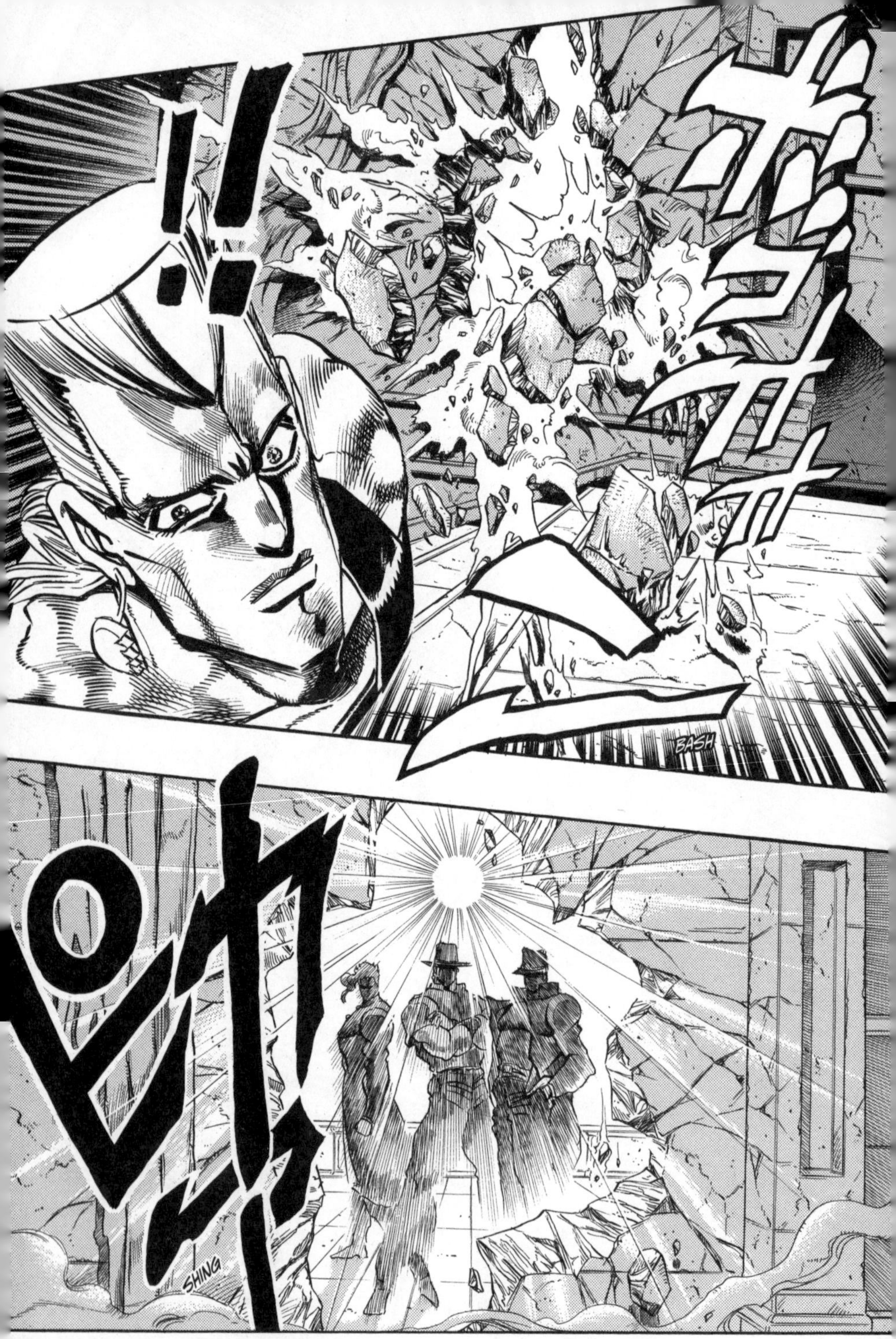
!!
BASH
SHING

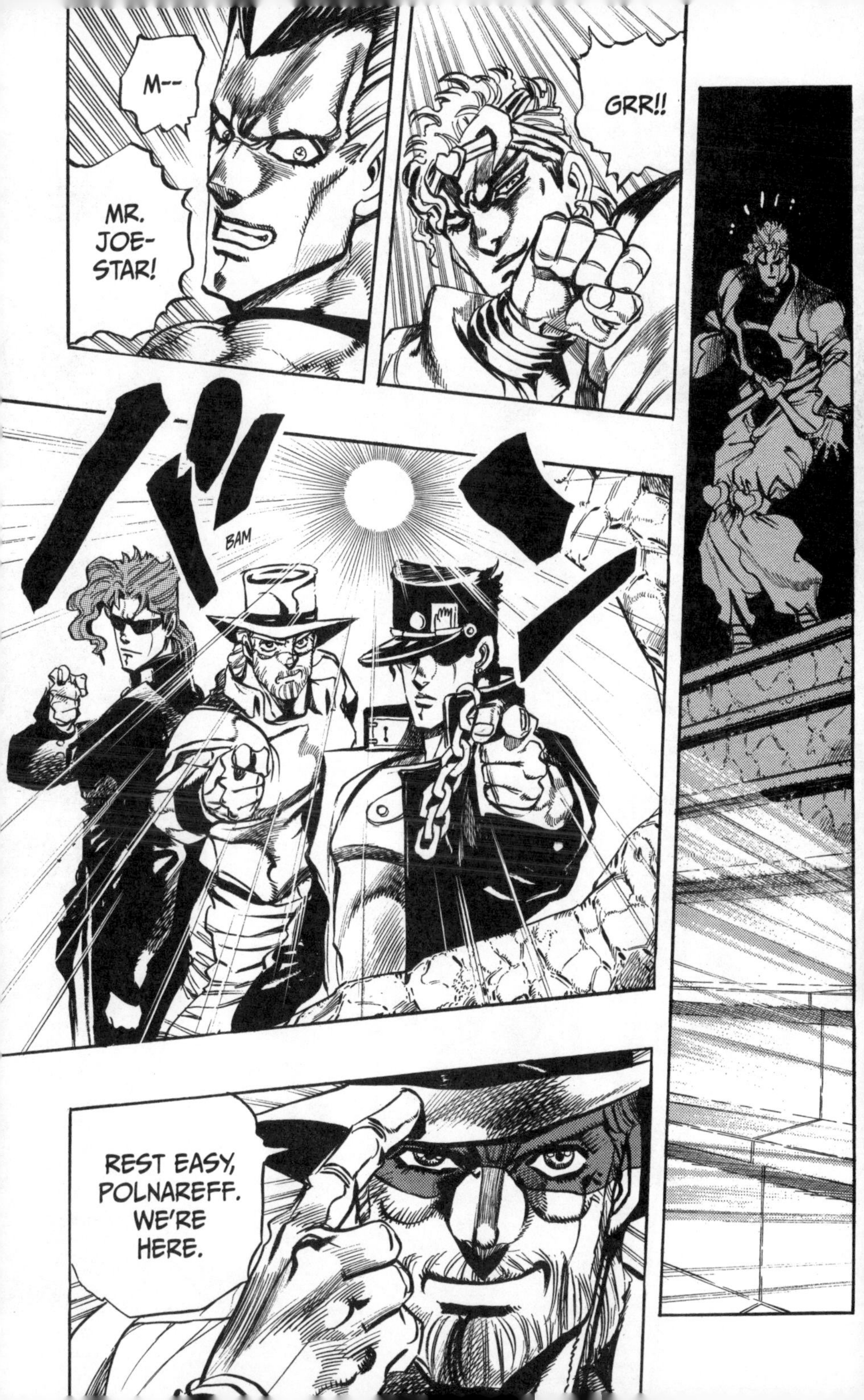
GRR!!
M--
MR. JOE-STAR!
BAM
REST EASY, POLNAREFF. WE'RE HERE.

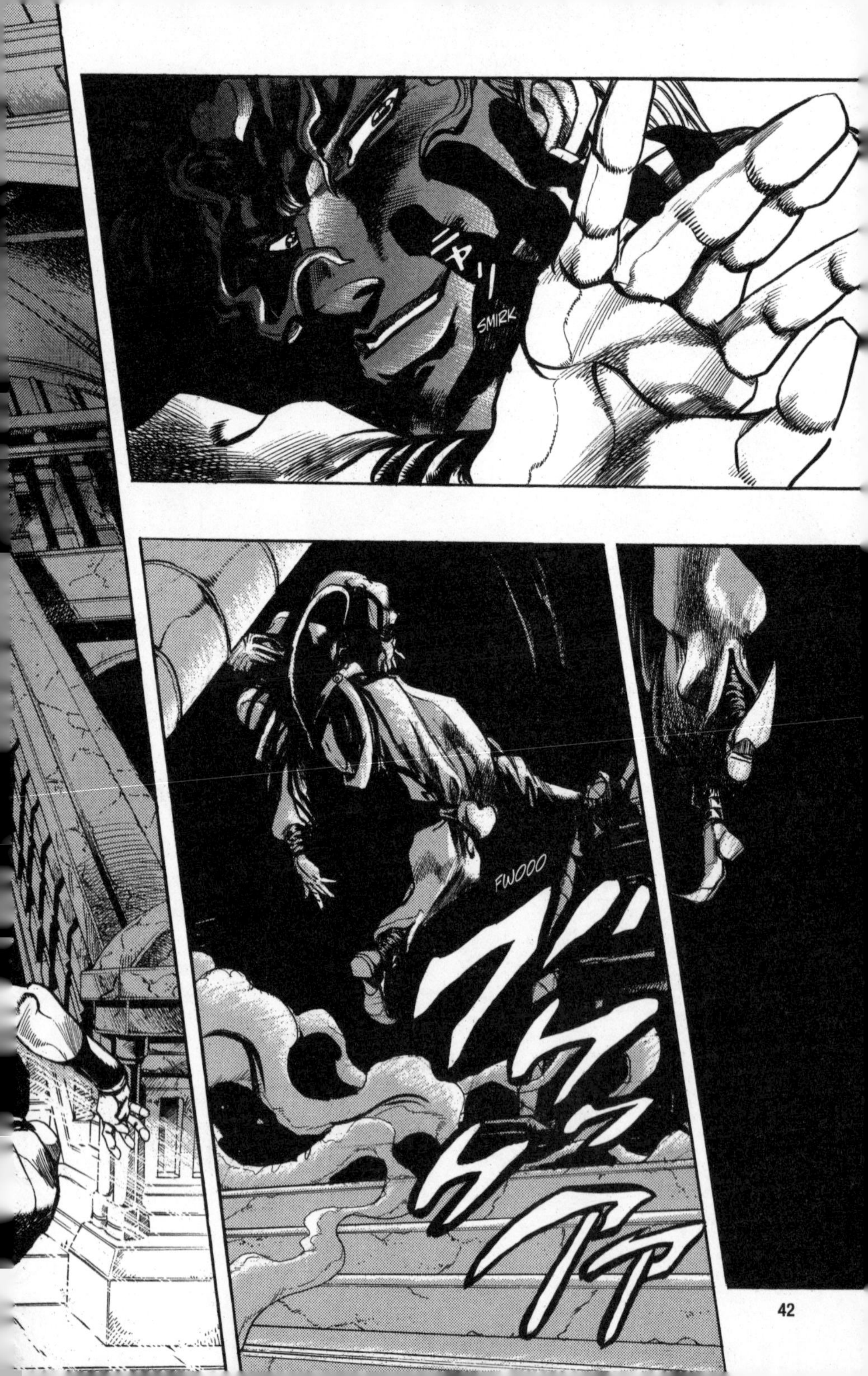
SMIRK
FWOOO

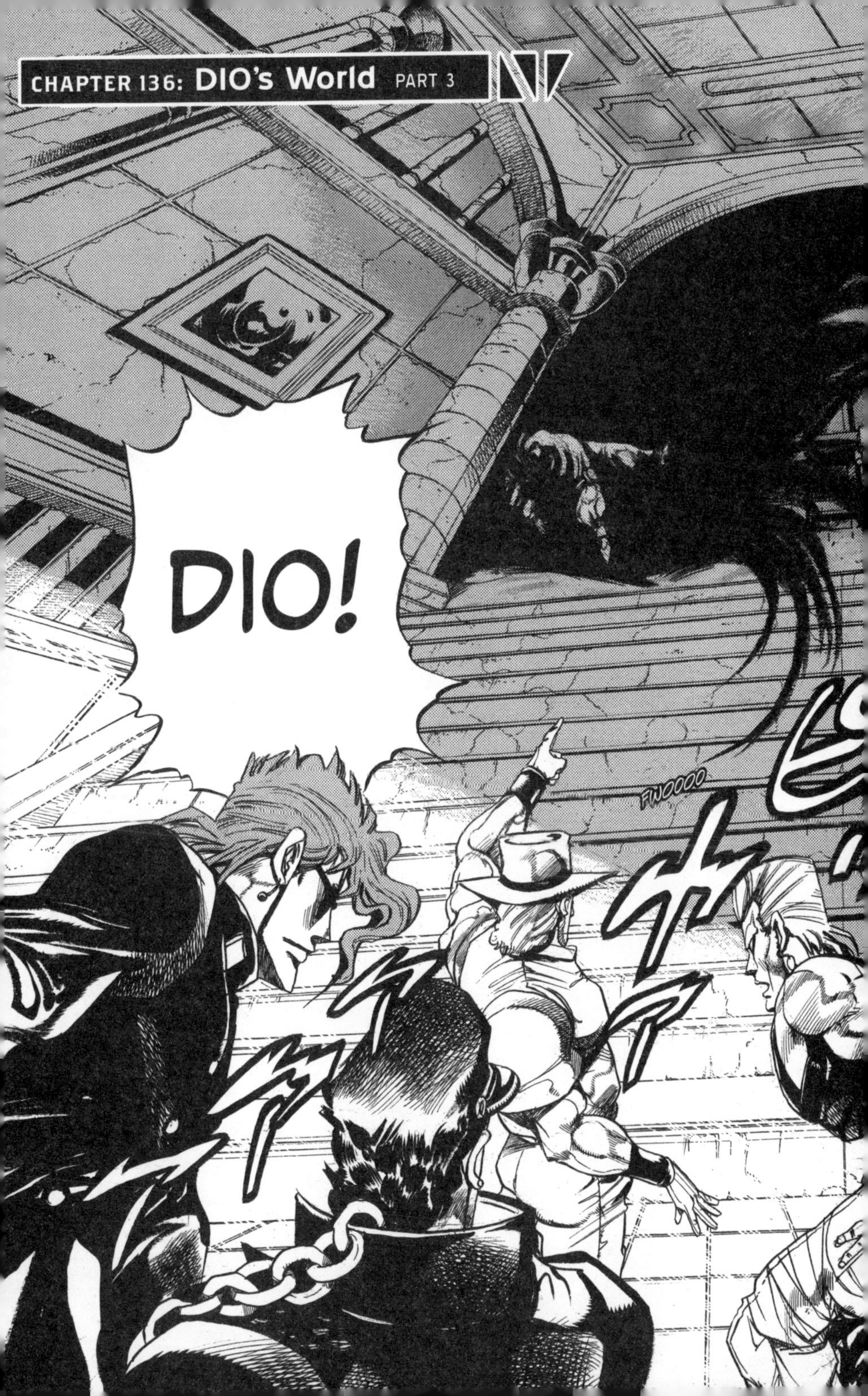
CHAPTER 136: DIO's World PART 3
DIO!
FWOOOO

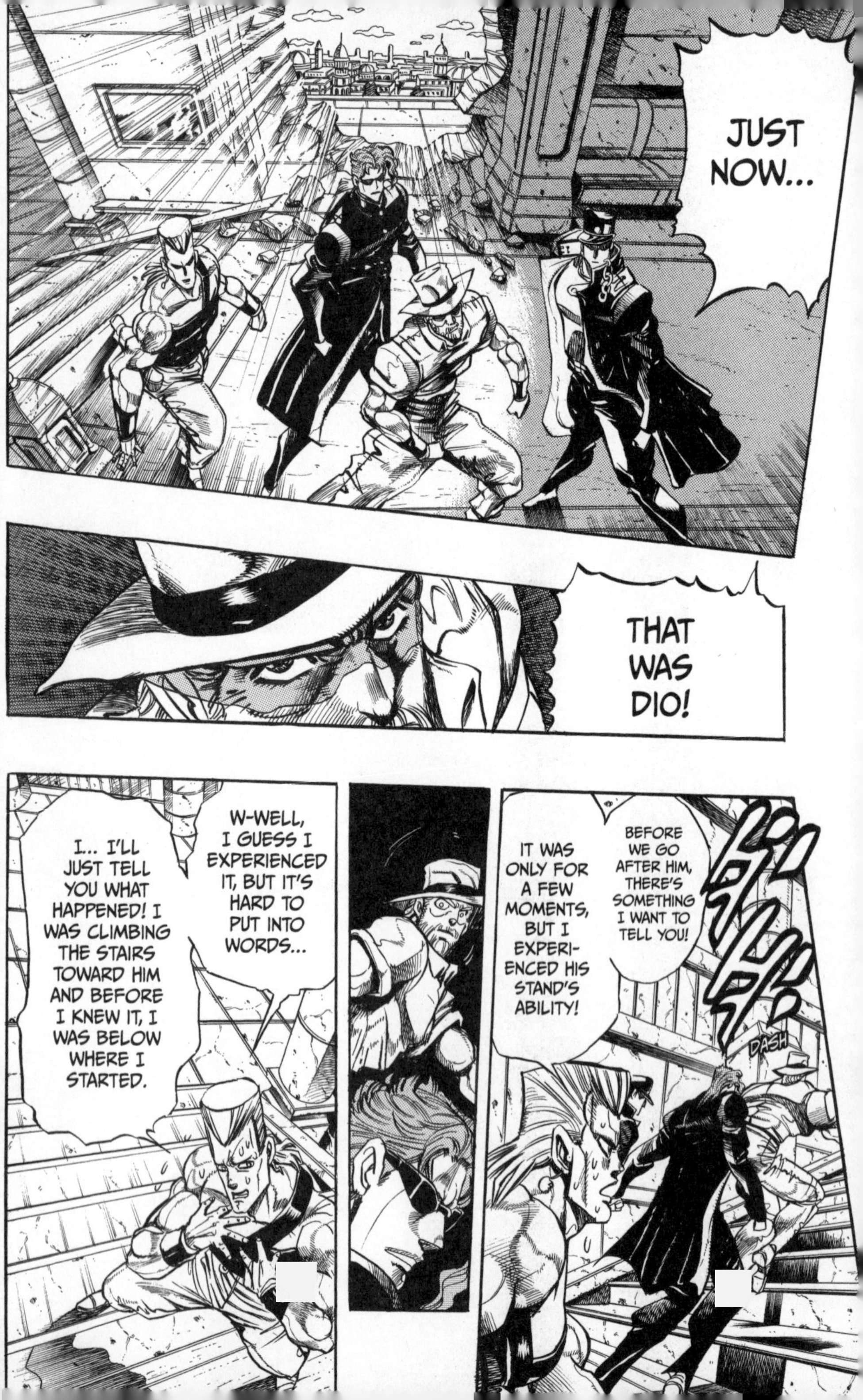
JUST NOW...
THAT WAS DIO!
BEFORE WE GO AFTER HIM, THERE'S SOMETHING I WANT TO TELL YOU!
IT WAS ONLY FOR A FEW MOMENTS, BUT I EXPERIENCED HIS STAND'S ABILITY!
DASH
W-WELL, I GUESS I EXPERIENCED IT, BUT IT'S HARD TO PUT INTO WORDS...
I... I'LL JUST TELL YOU WHAT HAPPENED! I WAS CLIMBING THE STAIRS TOWARD HIM AND BEFORE I KNEW IT, I WAS BELOW WHERE I STARTED.

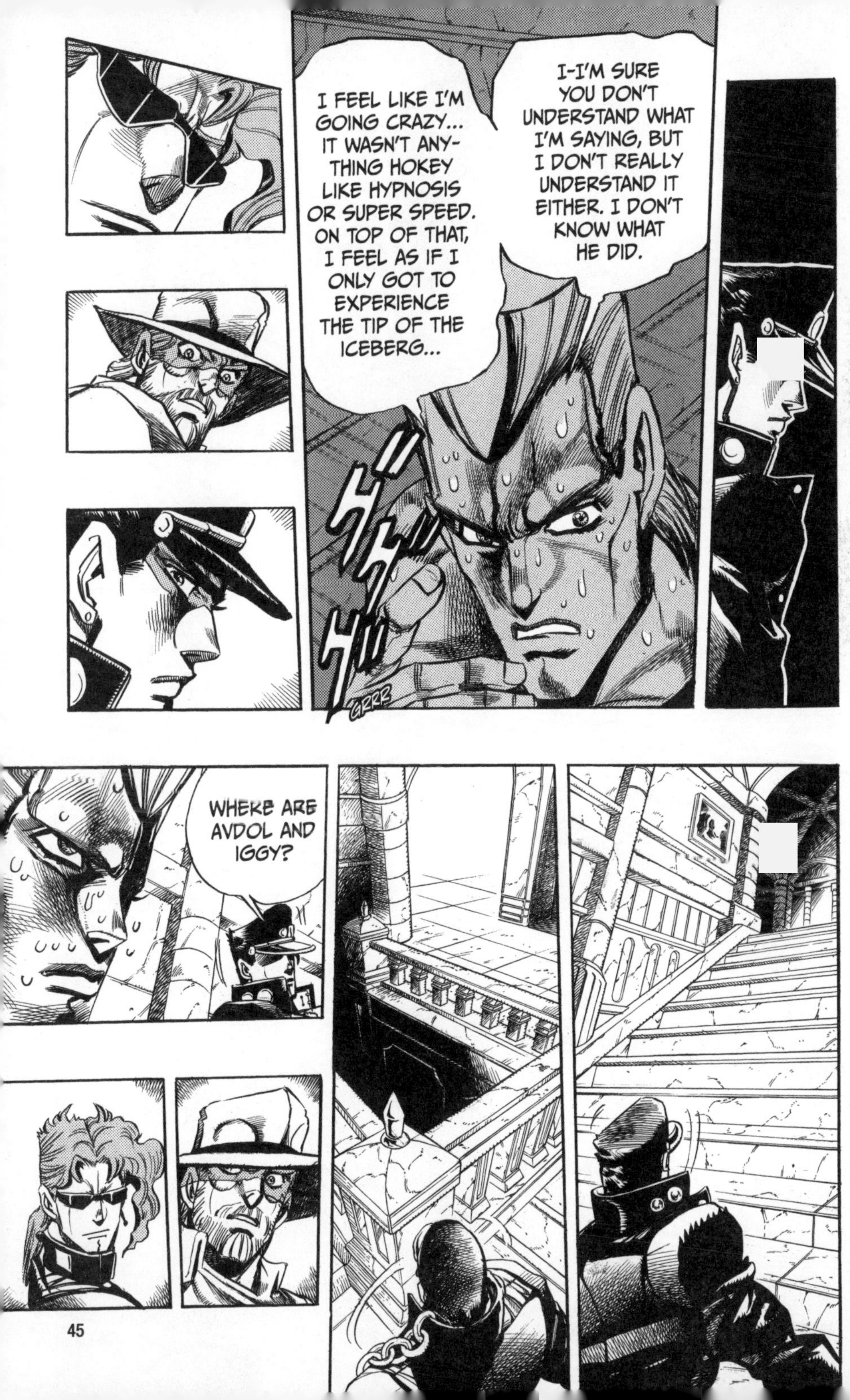
I-I'M SURE YOU DON'T UNDERSTAND WHAT I'M SAYING, BUT I DON'T REALLY UNDERSTAND IT EITHER. I DON'T KNOW WHAT HE DID.
I FEEL LIKE I'M GOING CRAZY... IT WASN'T ANYTHING HOKEY LIKE HYPNOSIS OR SUPER SPEED. ON TOP OF THAT, I FEEL AS IF I ONLY GOT TO EXPERIENCE THE TIP OF THE ICEBERG...
GRRR
WHERE ARE AVDOL AND IGGY?

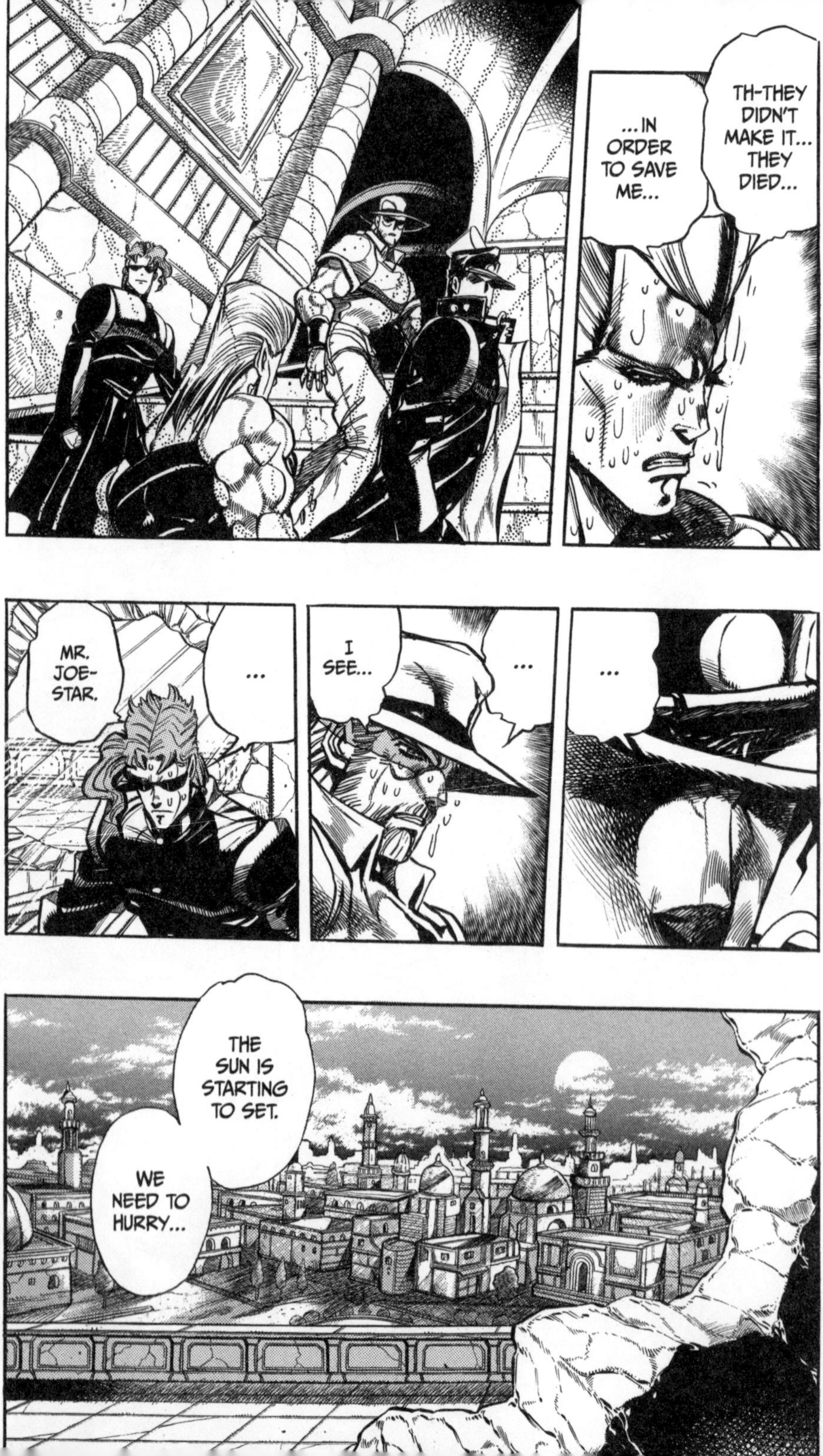
TH-THEY DIDN'T MAKE IT... THEY DIED...
...IN ORDER TO SAVE ME...
...
...
I SEE...
...
MR. JOE-STAR.
THE SUN IS STARTING TO SET.
WE NEED TO HURRY...

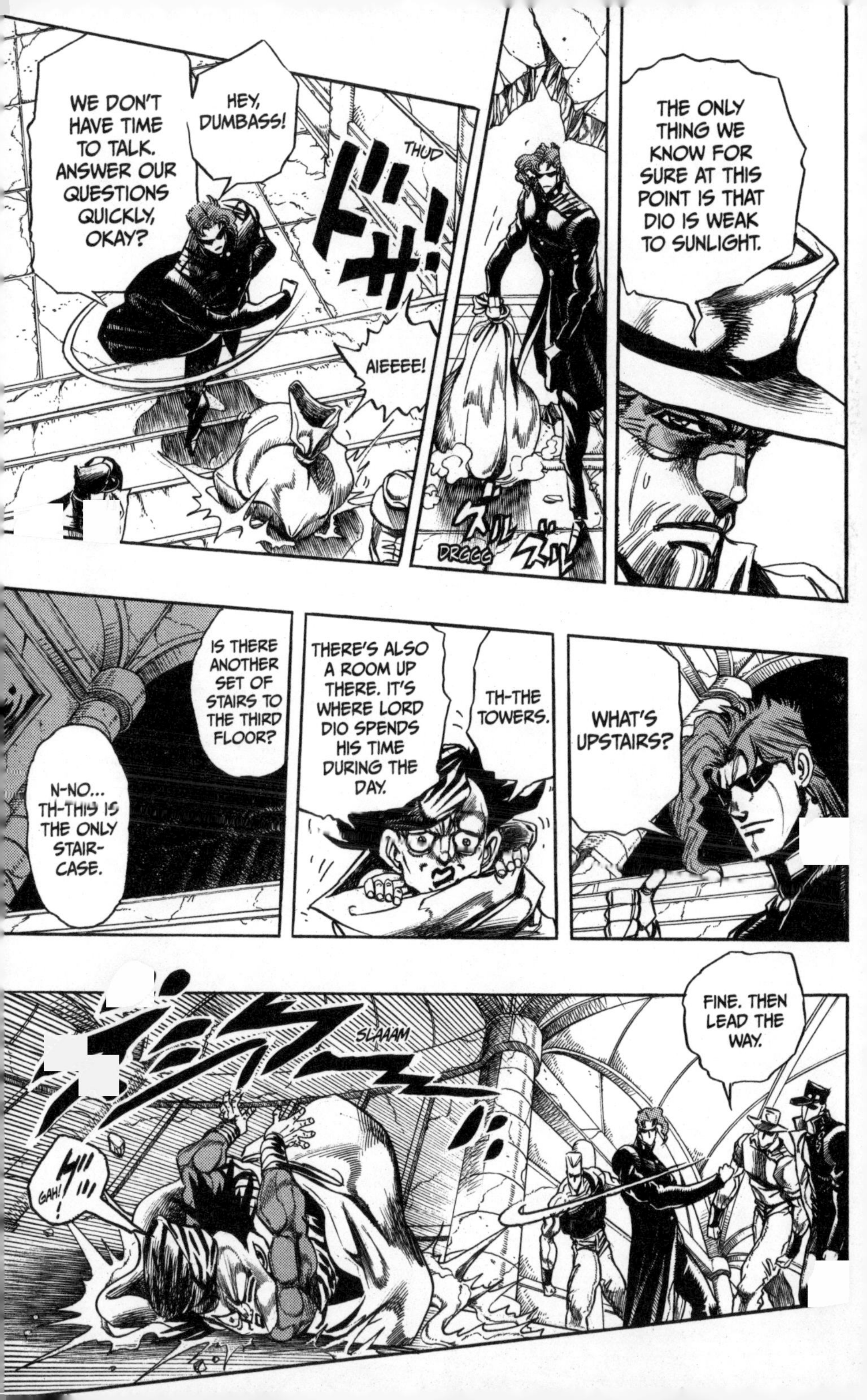
THE ONLY THING WE KNOW FOR SURE AT THIS POINT IS THAT DIO IS WEAK TO SUNLIGHT.
DRGGG
HEY, DUMBASS!
WE DON'T HAVE TIME TO TALK. ANSWER OUR QUESTIONS QUICKLY, OKAY?
THUD
AIEEEE!
WHAT'S UPSTAIRS?
TH-THE TOWERS.
THERE'S ALSO A ROOM UP THERE. IT'S WHERE LORD DIO SPENDS HIS TIME DURING THE DAY.
IS THERE ANOTHER SET OF STAIRS TO THE THIRD FLOOR?
N-NO... TH-THIS IS THE ONLY STAIR-CASE.
FINE. THEN LEAD THE WAY.
SLAAAM
GAH!

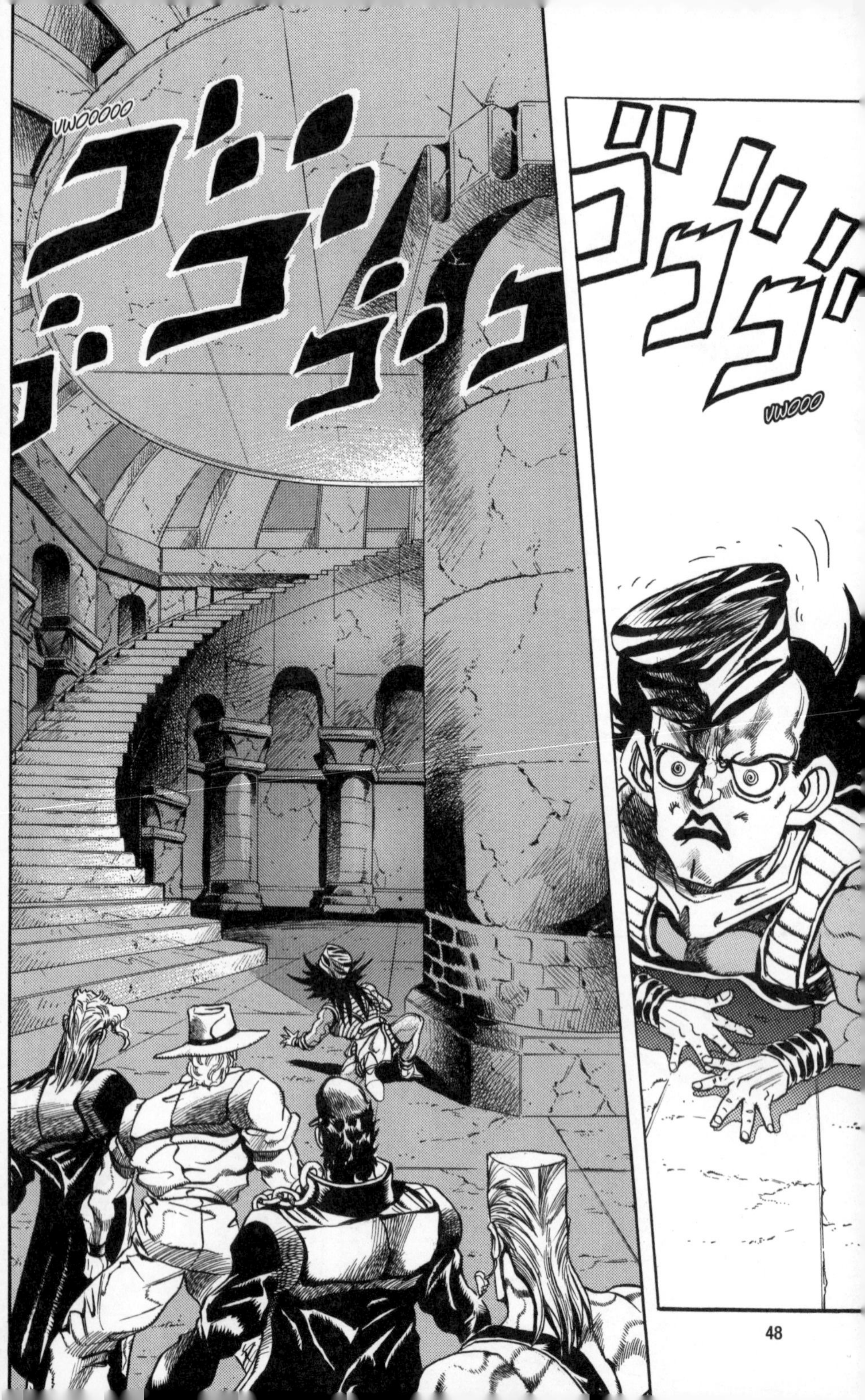
ゴゴゴゴ
VWOOO
ゴゴゴゴゴゴゴ
VWOOOOO

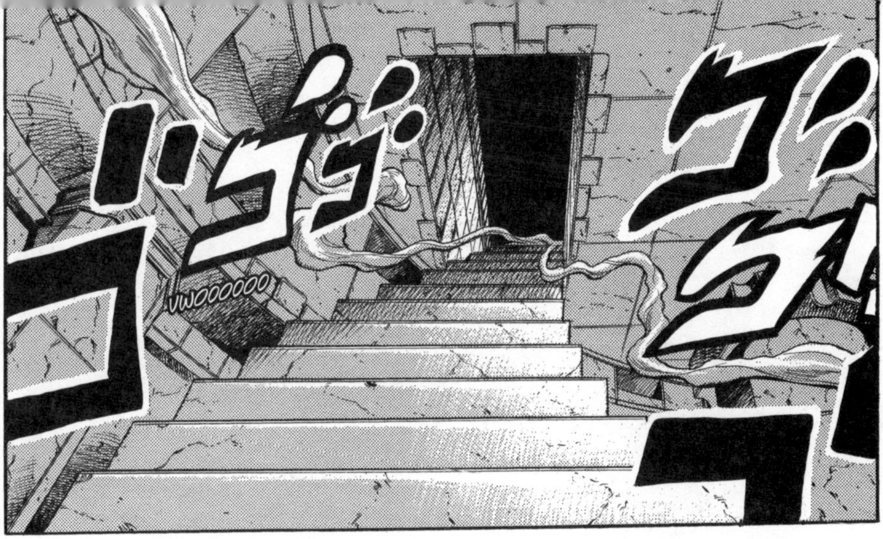
VWOOOOOO
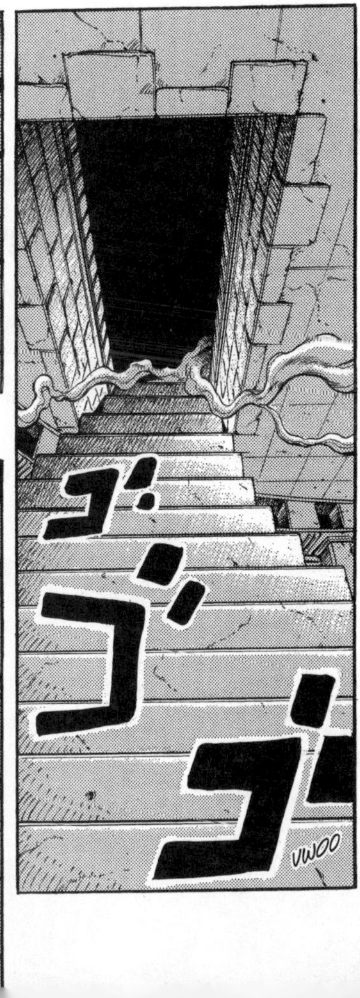
VWOO
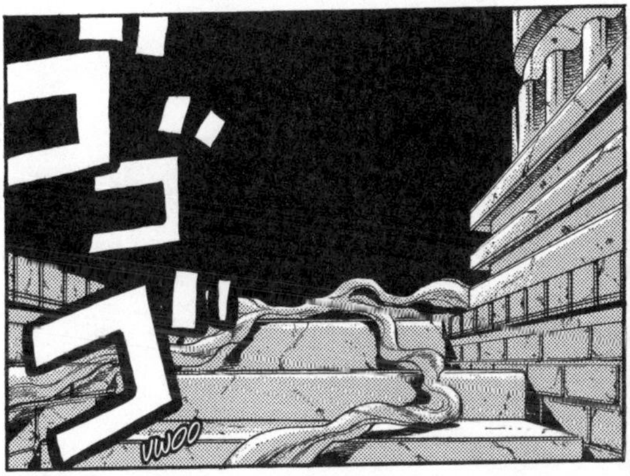
VWOO
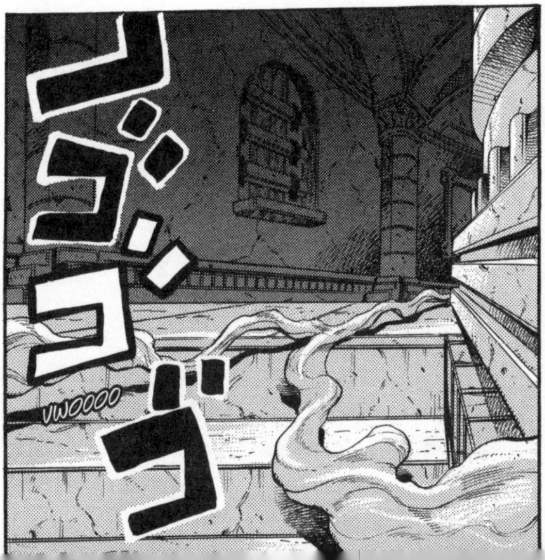
VWOOOO

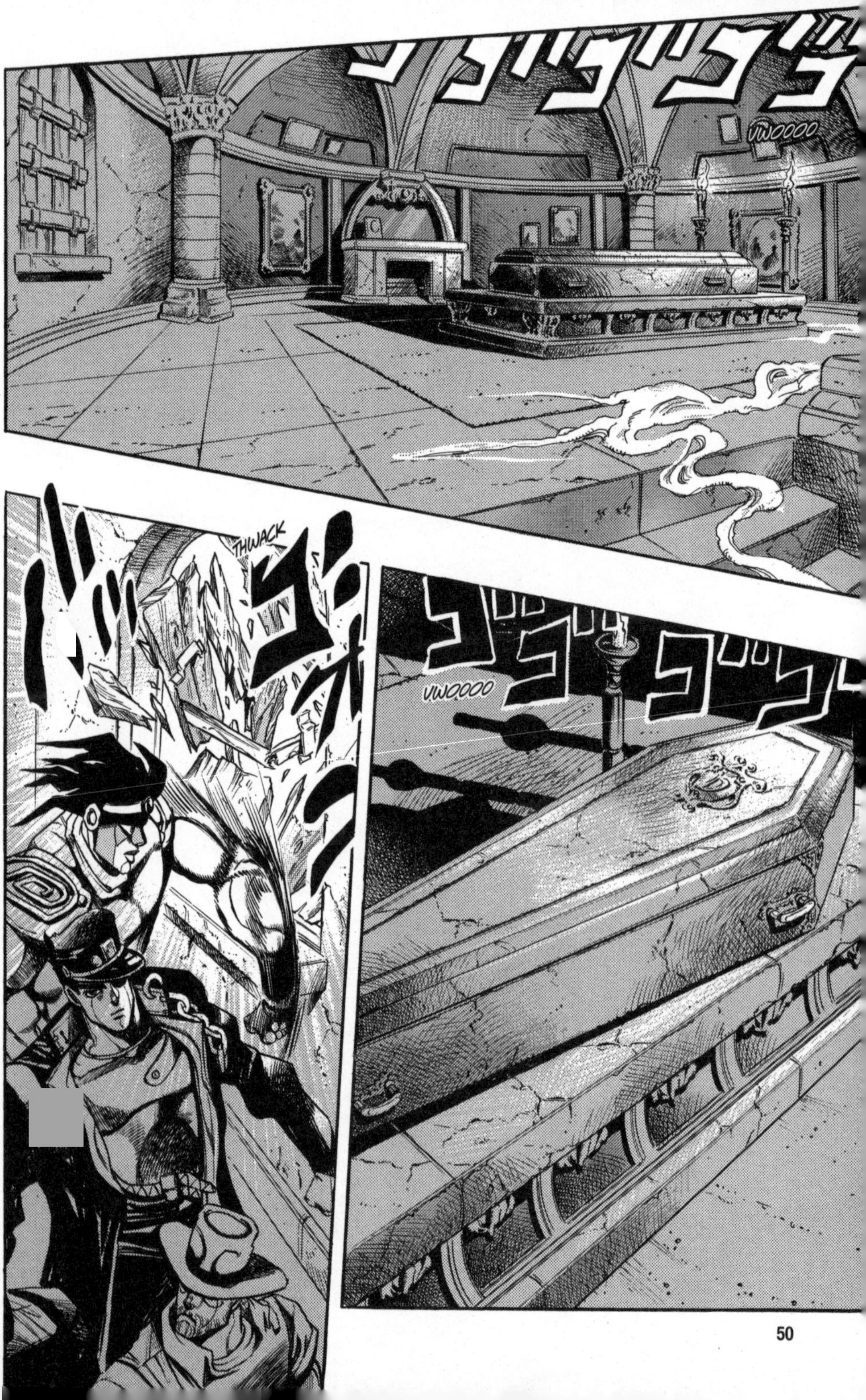
VWOOOO
VWOOOO
THWACK

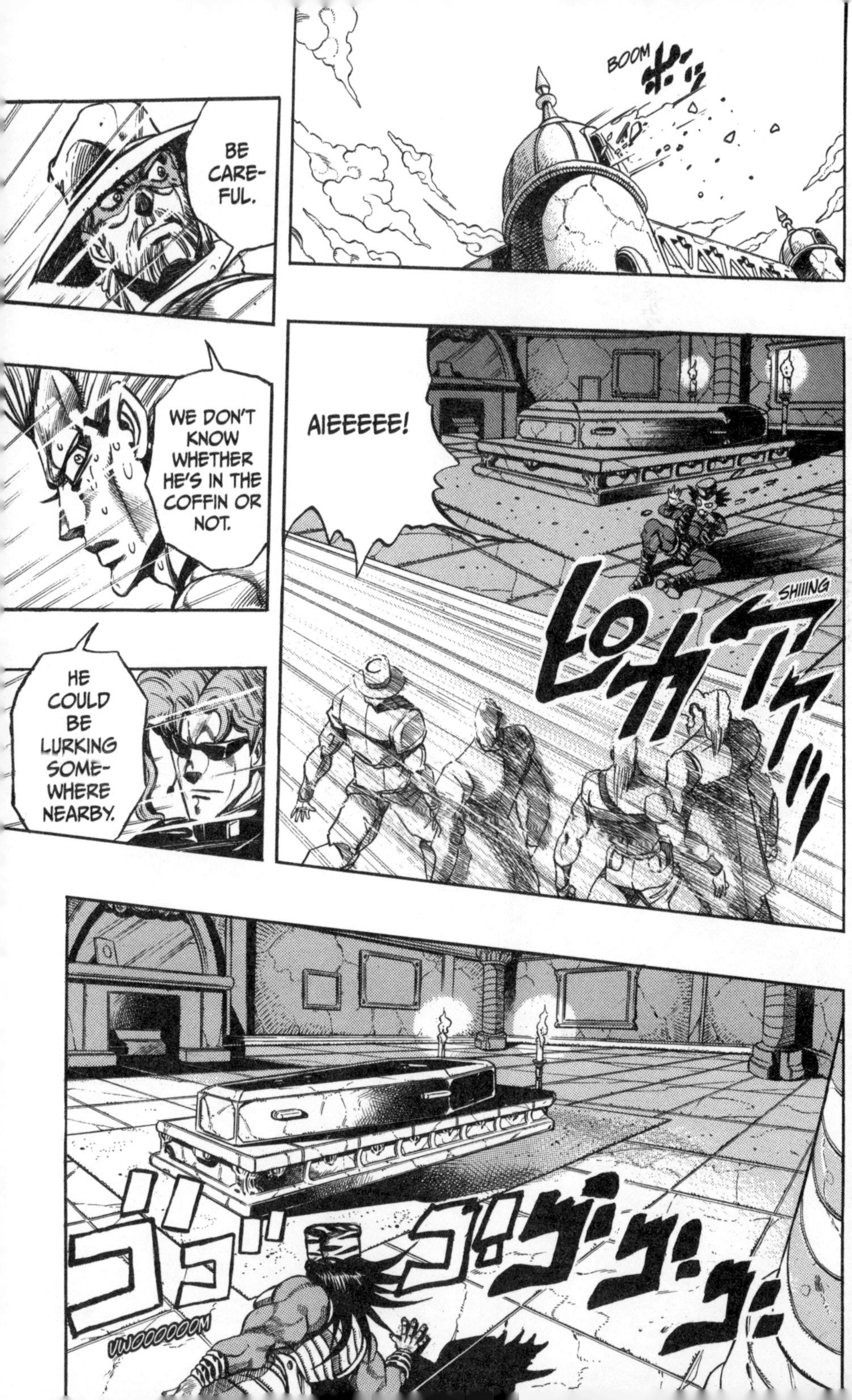
BOOM
BE CAREFUL.
AIEEEEE!
SHIIING
WE DON'T KNOW WHETHER HE'S IN THE COFFIN OR NOT.
HE COULD BE LURKING SOMEWHERE NEARBY.
UWOOOOOOM

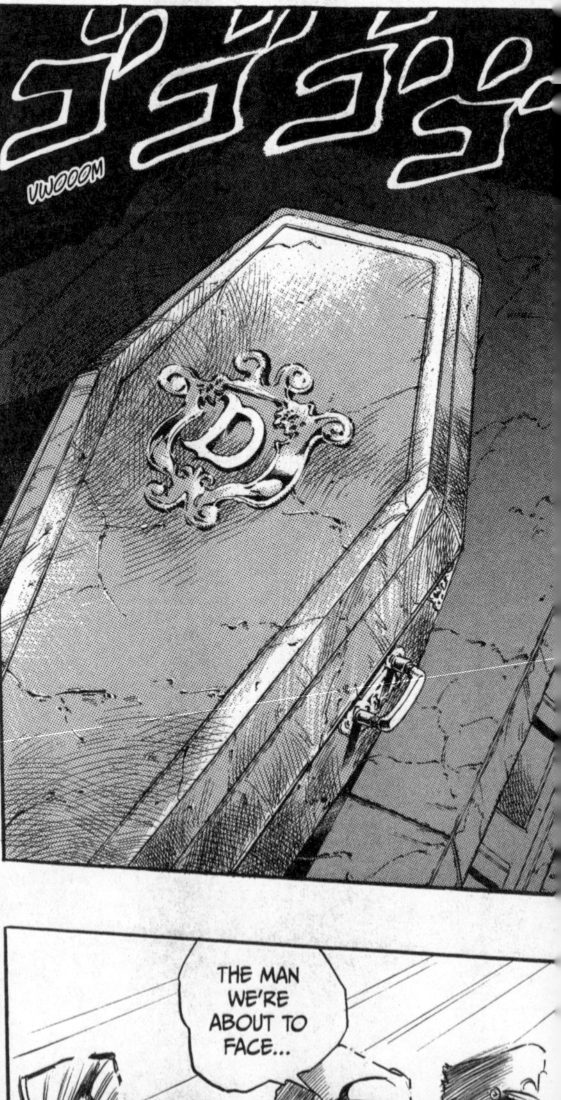
VWOOOM

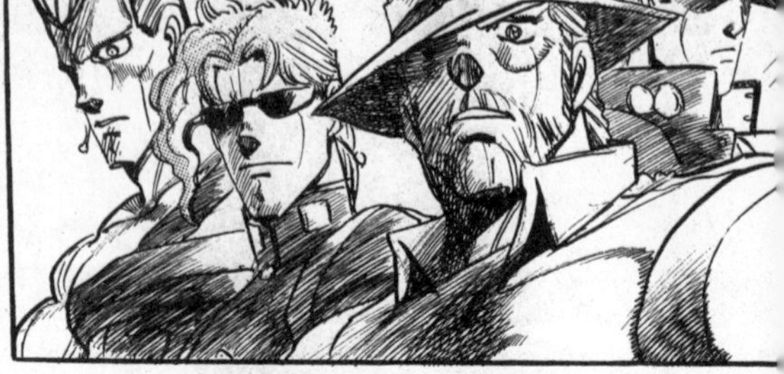
THE MAN WE'RE ABOUT TO FACE...

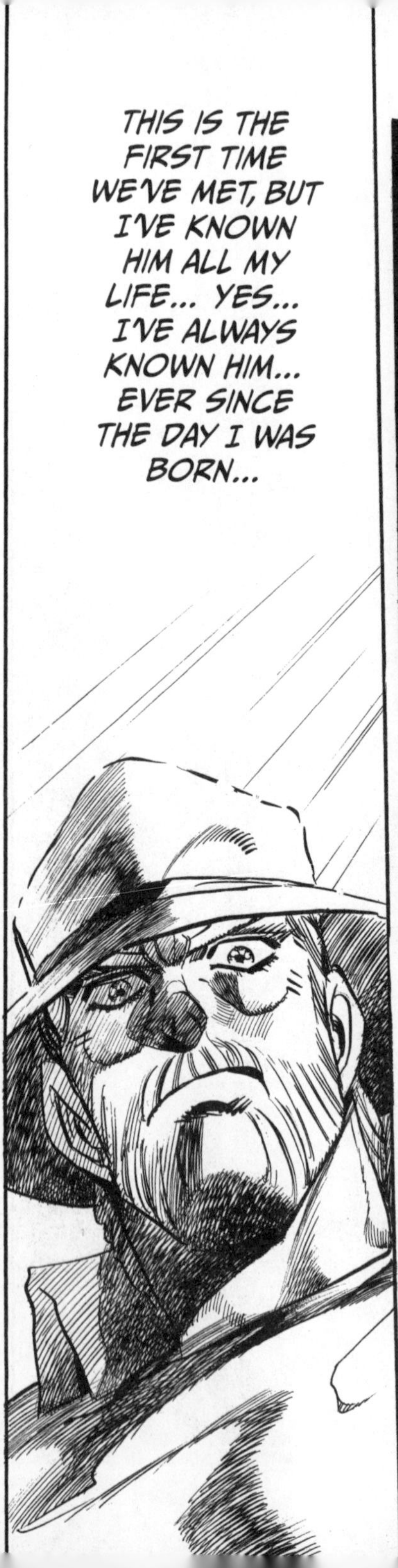
THIS IS THE FIRST TIME WE'VE MET, BUT I'VE KNOWN HIM ALL MY LIFE... YES... I'VE ALWAYS KNOWN HIM... EVER SINCE THE DAY I WAS BORN...

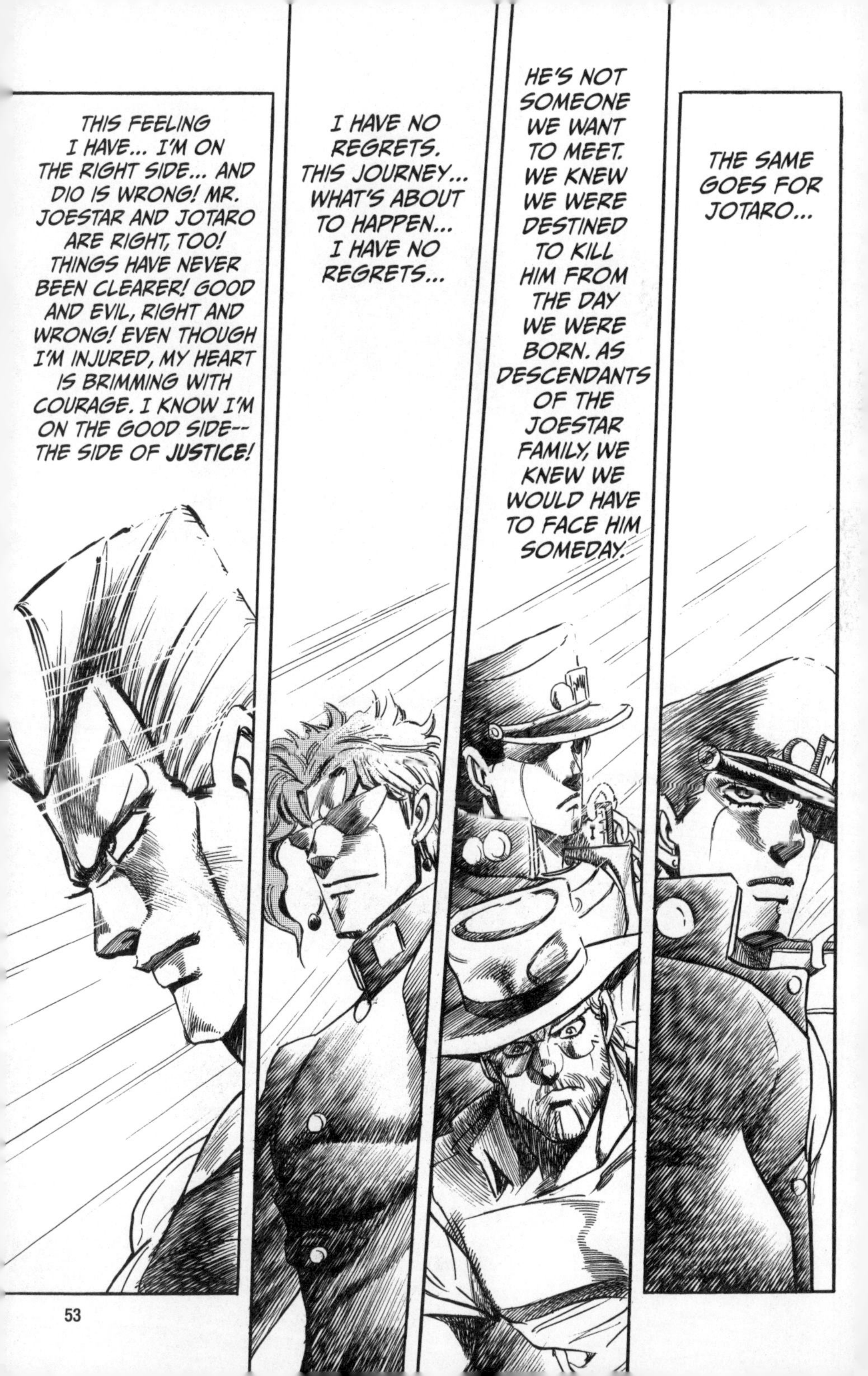
THIS FEELING I HAVE... I'M ON THE RIGHT SIDE... AND DIO IS WRONG! MR. JOESTAR AND JOTARO ARE RIGHT, TOO! THINGS HAVE NEVER BEEN CLEARER! GOOD AND EVIL, RIGHT AND WRONG! EVEN THOUGH I'M INJURED, MY HEART IS BRIMMING WITH COURAGE. I KNOW I'M ON THE GOOD SIDE-- THE SIDE OF **JUSTICE!**
I HAVE NO REGRETS. THIS JOURNEY... WHAT'S ABOUT TO HAPPEN... I HAVE NO REGRETS...
HE'S NOT SOMEONE WE WANT TO MEET. WE KNEW WE WERE DESTINED TO KILL HIM FROM THE DAY WE WERE BORN. AS DESCENDANTS OF THE JOESTAR FAMILY, WE KNEW WE WOULD HAVE TO FACE HIM SOMEDAY.
THE SAME GOES FOR JOTARO...

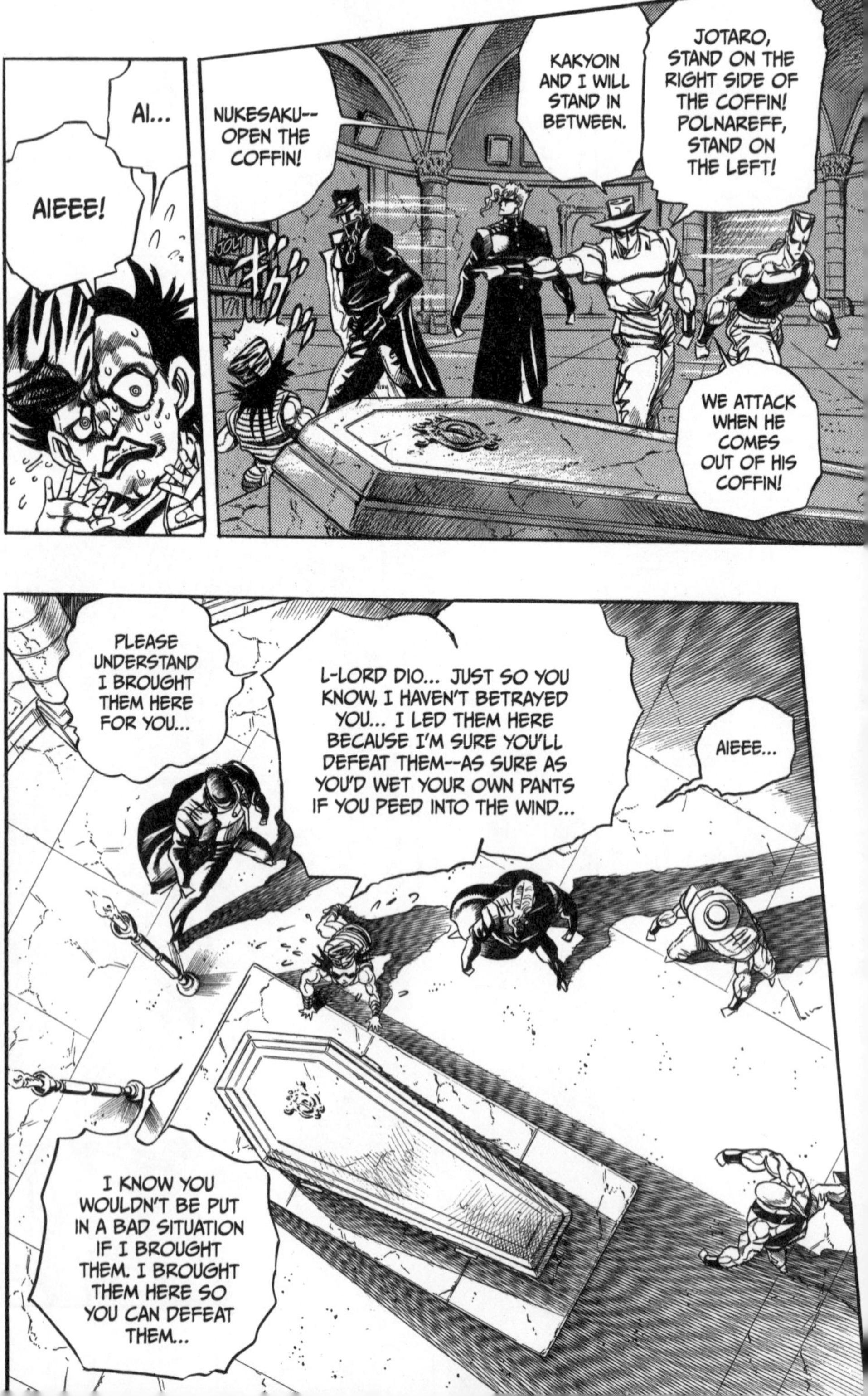
JOTARO, STAND ON THE RIGHT SIDE OF THE COFFIN! POLNAREFF, STAND ON THE LEFT!
KAKYOIN AND I WILL STAND IN BETWEEN.
WE ATTACK WHEN HE COMES OUT OF HIS COFFIN!
NUKESAKU-- OPEN THE COFFIN!
JOLT
AI...
AIEEE!
AIEEE...
L-LORD DIO... JUST SO YOU KNOW, I HAVEN'T BETRAYED YOU... I LED THEM HERE BECAUSE I'M SURE YOU'LL DEFEAT THEM--AS SURE AS YOU'D WET YOUR OWN PANTS IF YOU PEED INTO THE WIND...
PLEASE UNDERSTAND I BROUGHT THEM HERE FOR YOU...
I KNOW YOU WOULDN'T BE PUT IN A BAD SITUATION IF I BROUGHT THEM. I BROUGHT THEM HERE SO YOU CAN DEFEAT THEM...

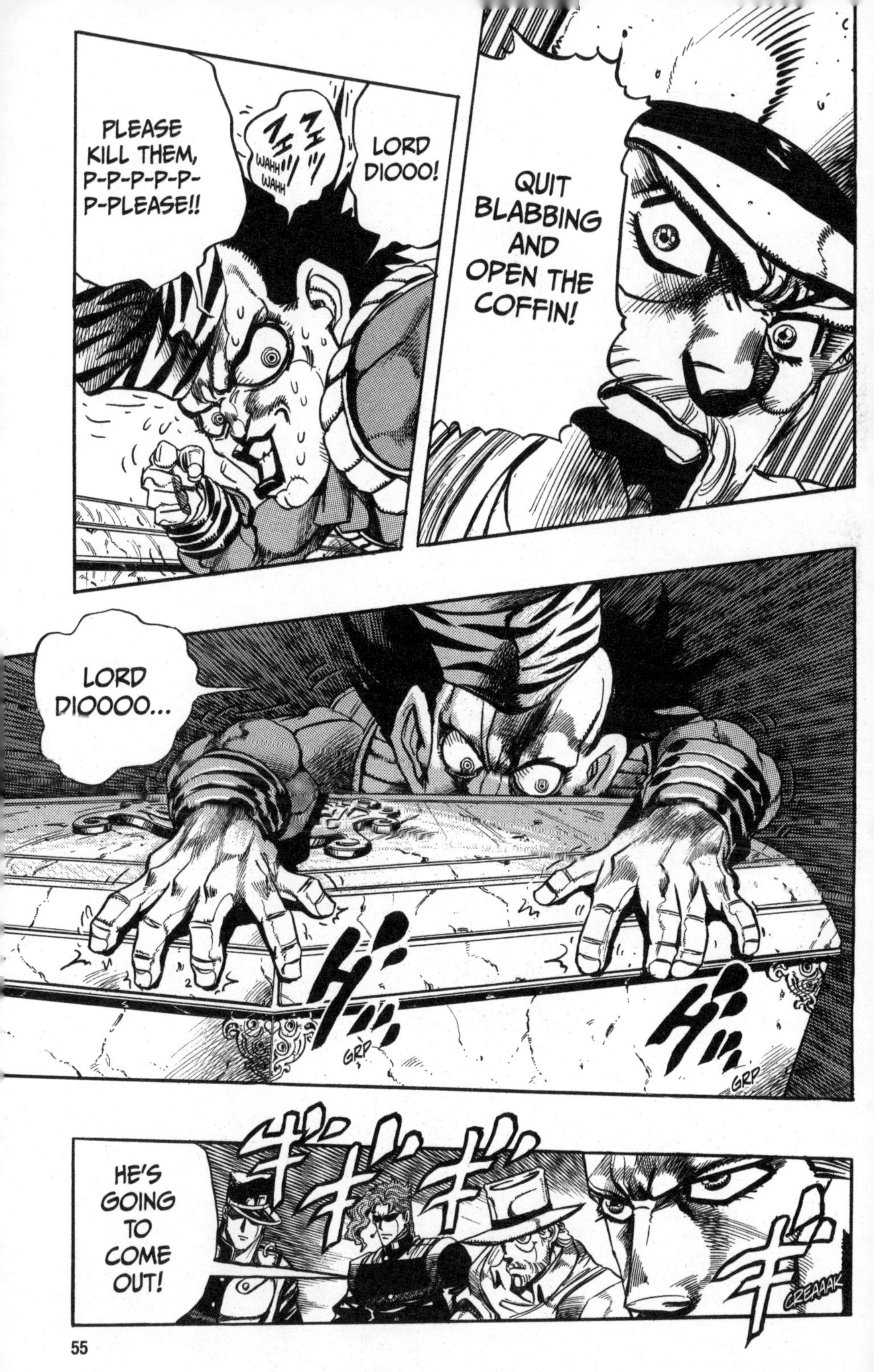
QUIT BLABBING AND OPEN THE COFFIN!
LORD DIOOO!
WAHH WAHH
PLEASE KILL THEM, P-P-P-P-P-P-PLEASE!!
LORD DIOOOO...
GRP
GRP
HE'S GOING TO COME OUT!
CREAAAK

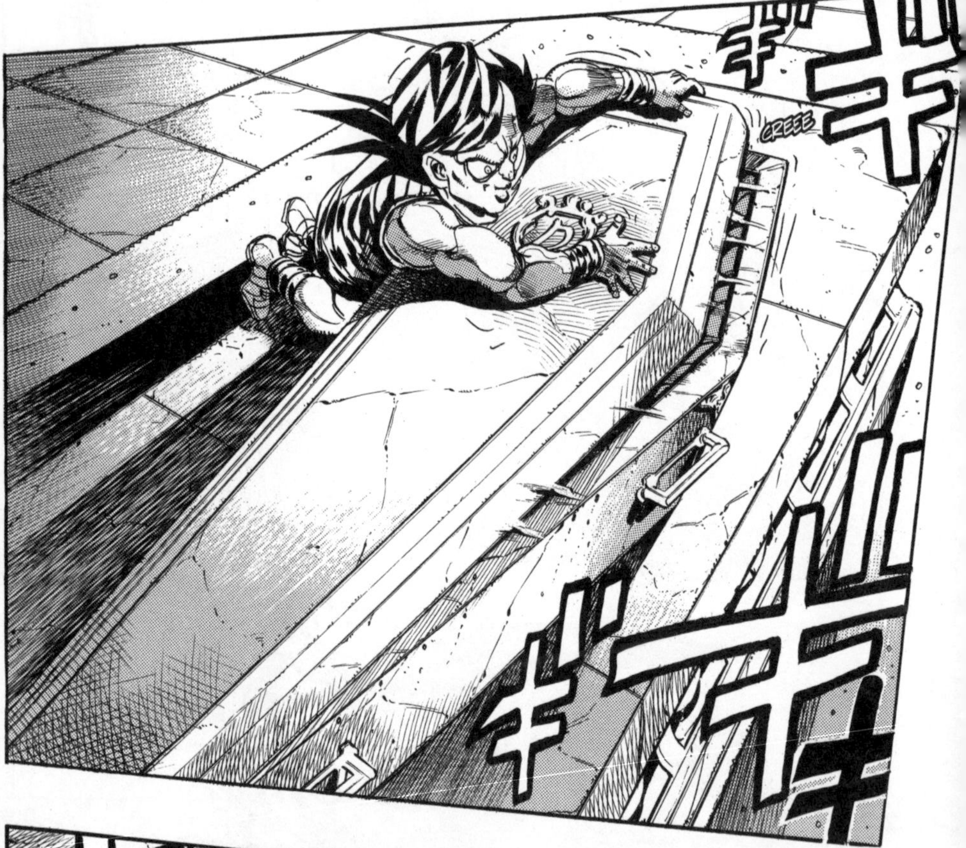
CREEE
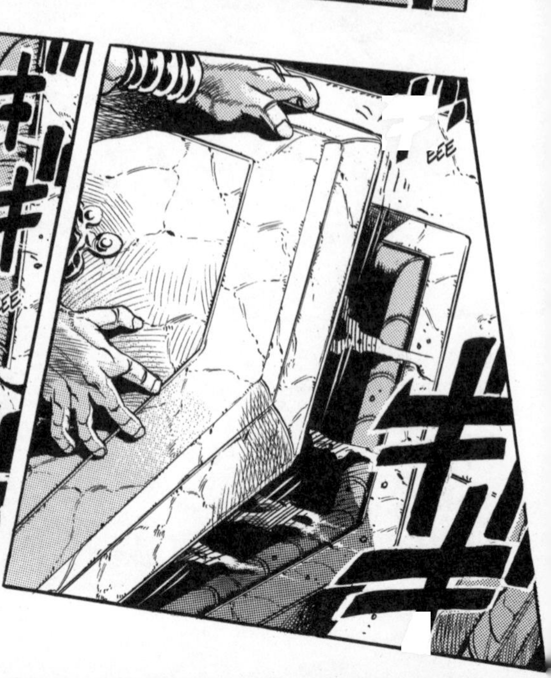
EEE
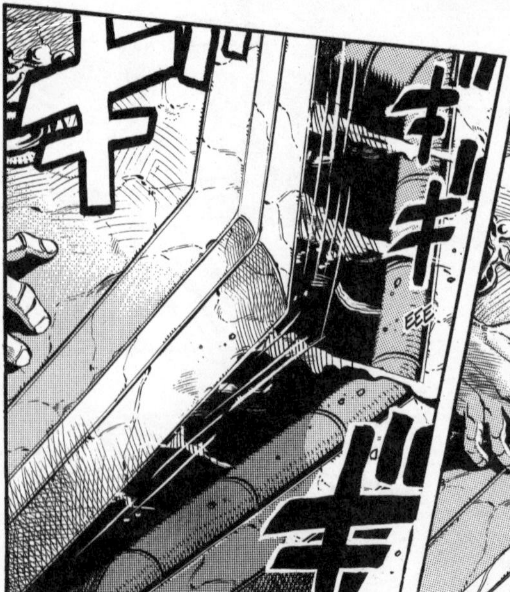
EEE

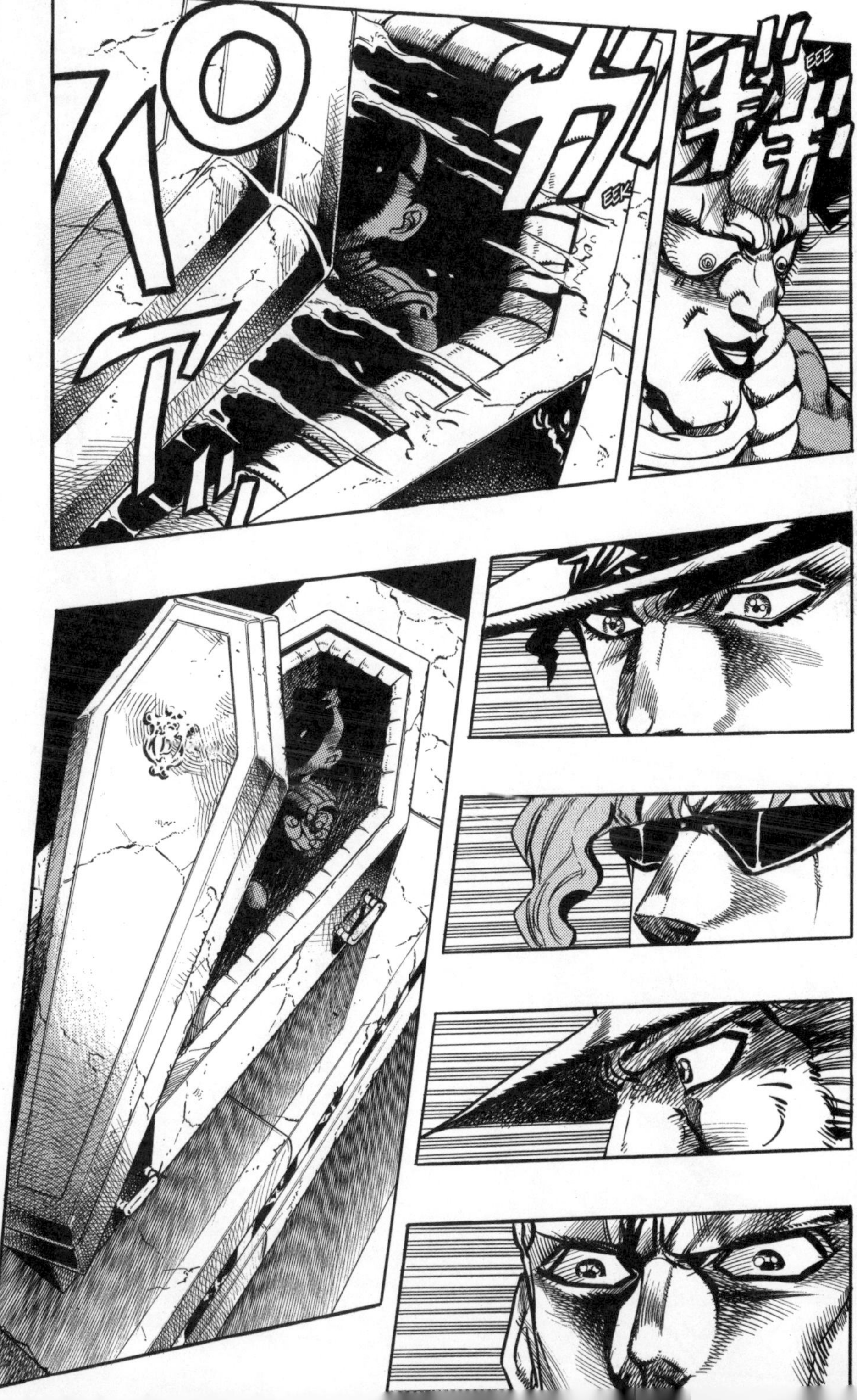
EEE
EEK

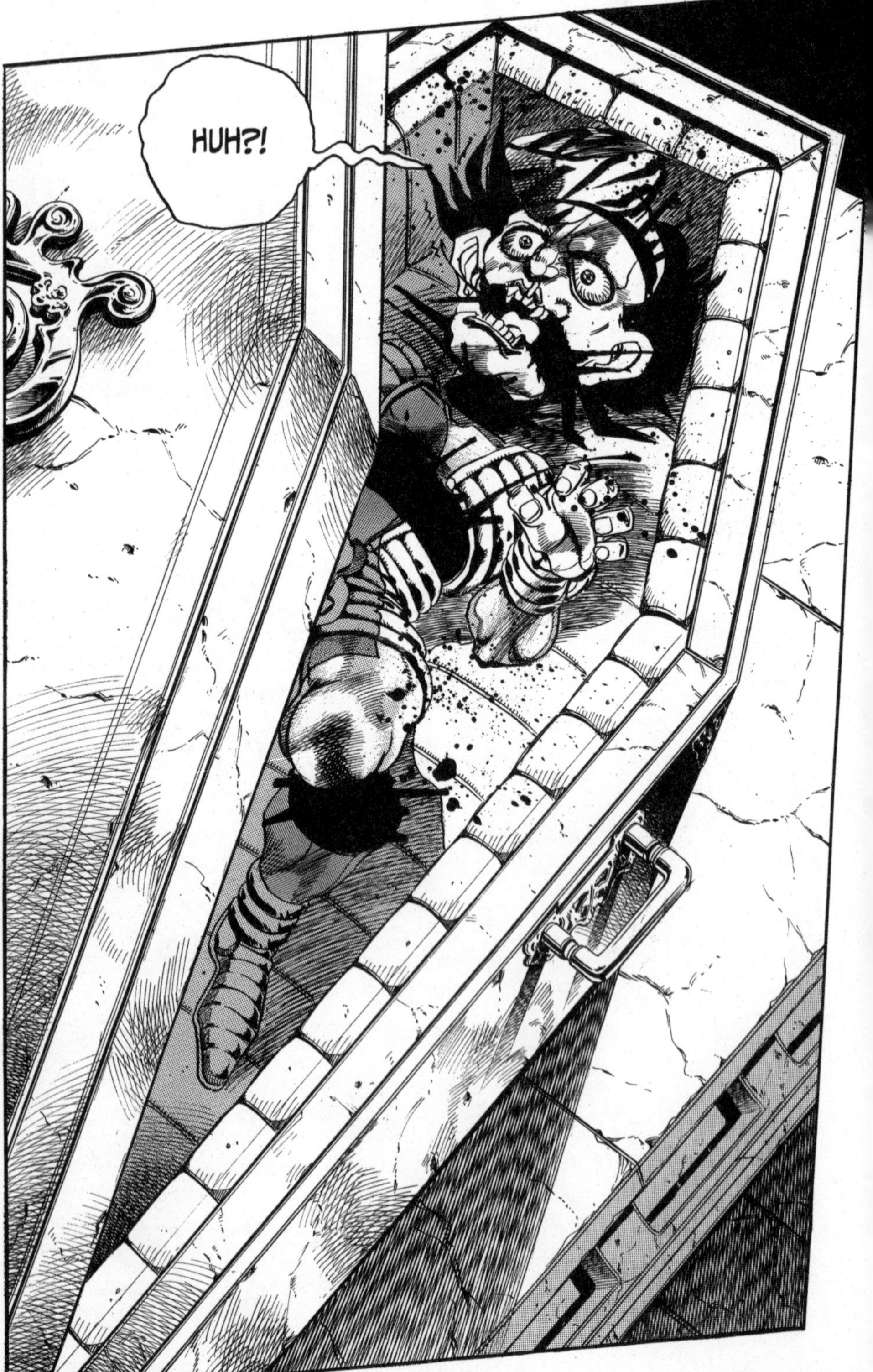
HUH?!

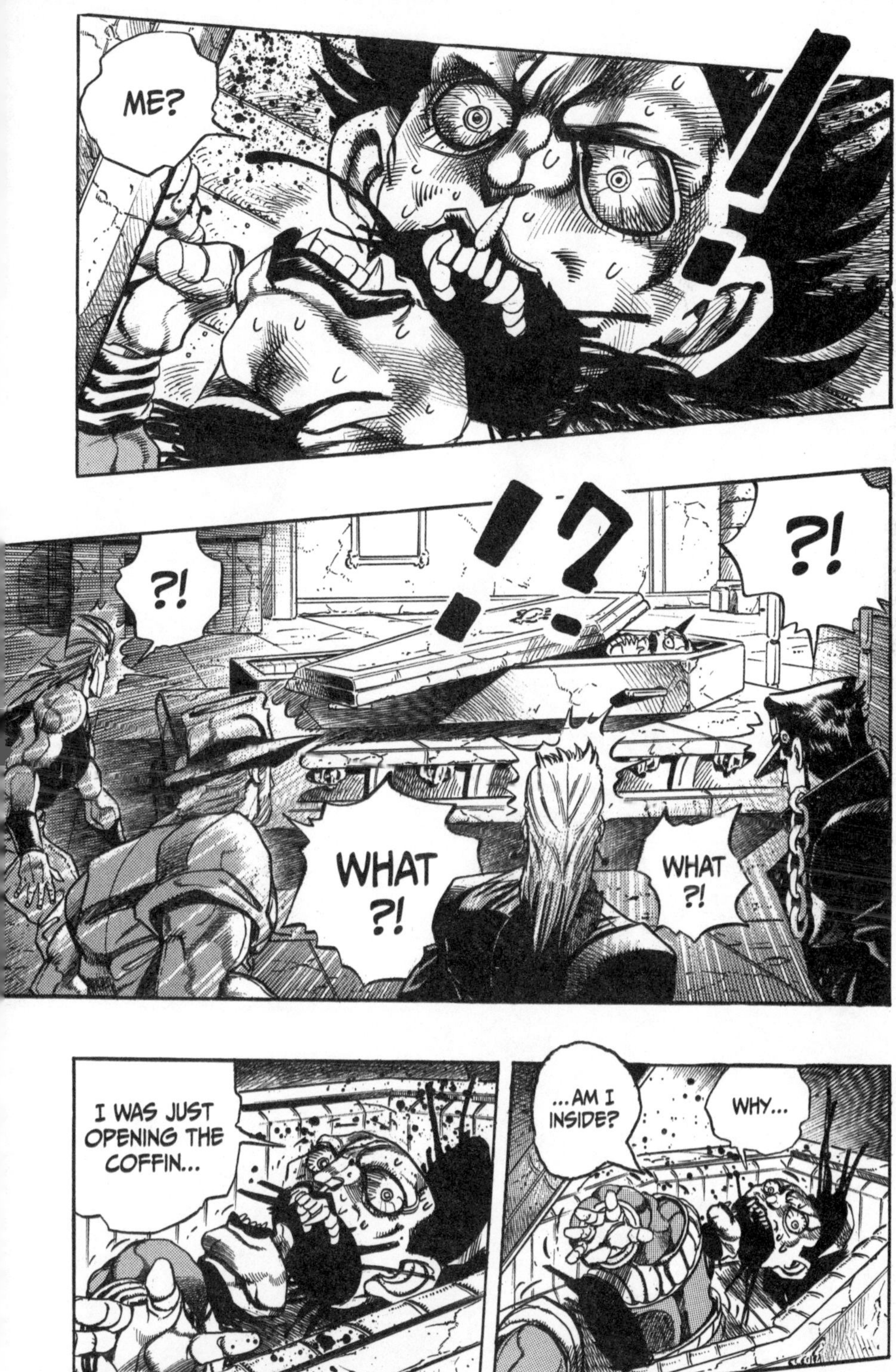
!
ME?
?!
!?
?!
WHAT ?!
WHAT ?!
WHY...
...AM I INSIDE?
I WAS JUST OPENING THE COFFIN...

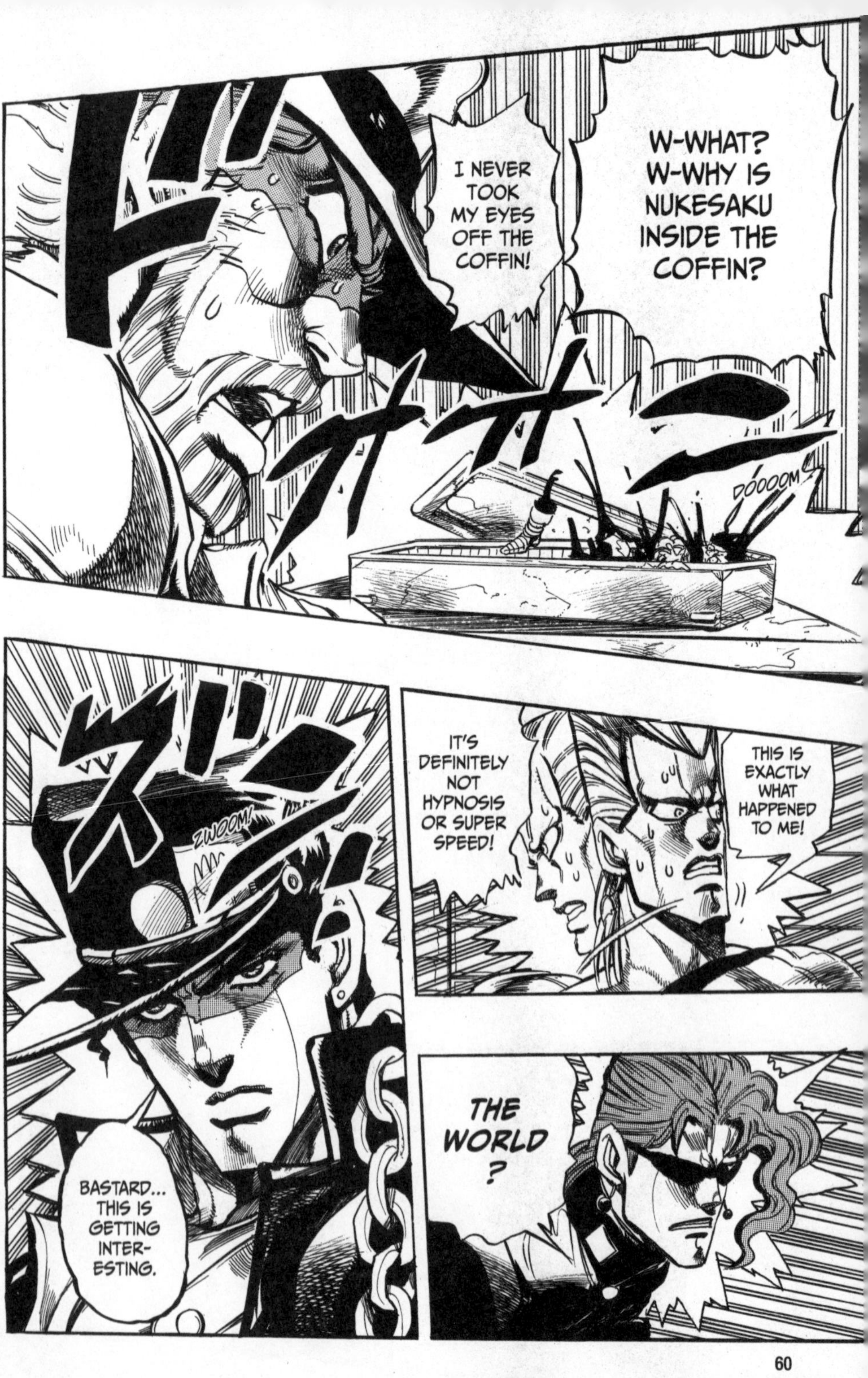
W-WHAT? W-WHY IS NUKESAKU INSIDE THE COFFIN?
I NEVER TOOK MY EYES OFF THE COFFIN!
DOOOOM
THIS IS EXACTLY WHAT HAPPENED TO ME!
IT'S DEFINITELY NOT HYPNOSIS OR SUPER SPEED!
THE WORLD ?
ZWOOM!
BASTARD... THIS IS GETTING INTER-ESTING.

CHAPTER 137: DIO's World PART 4

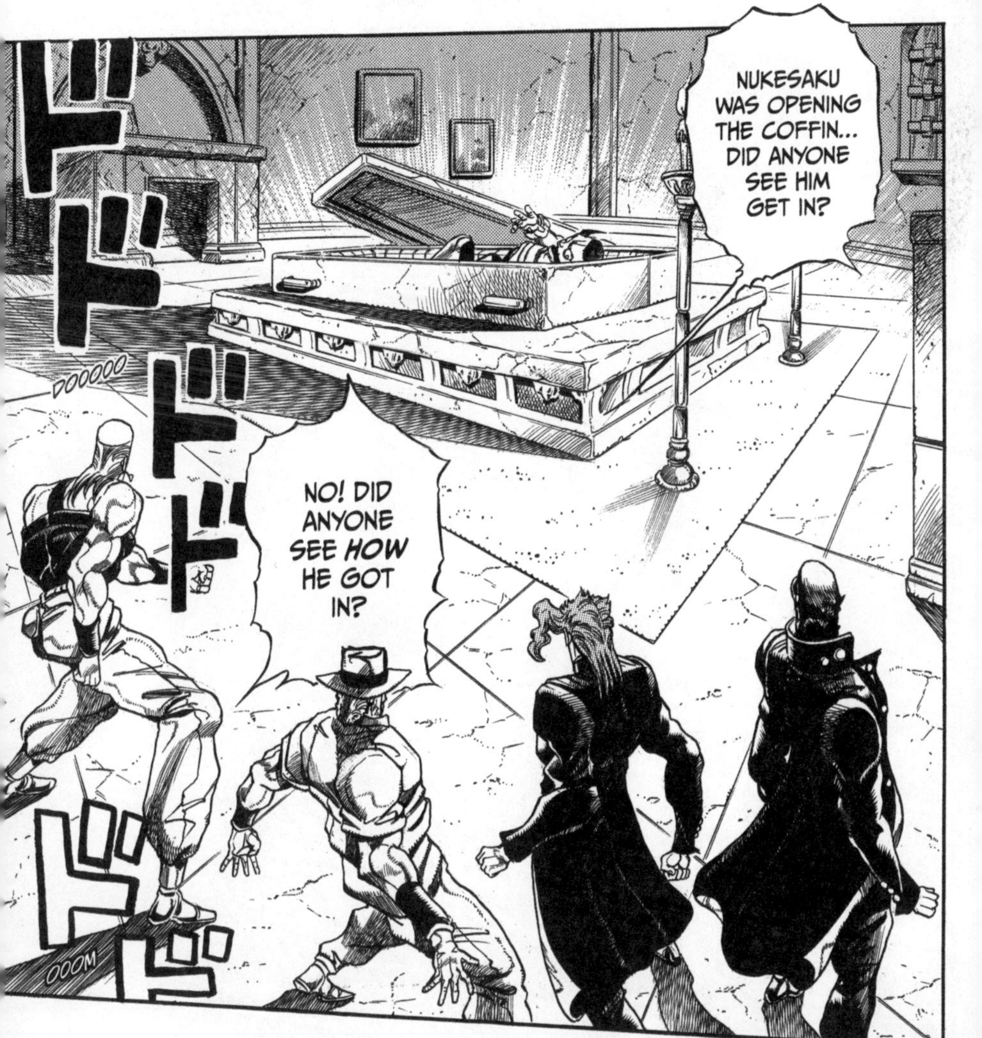
NUKESAKU WAS OPENING THE COFFIN... DID ANYONE SEE HIM GET IN?
NO! DID ANYONE SEE *HOW* HE GOT IN?
ドドドドドドド
DOOOOO
ドドド
OOOM

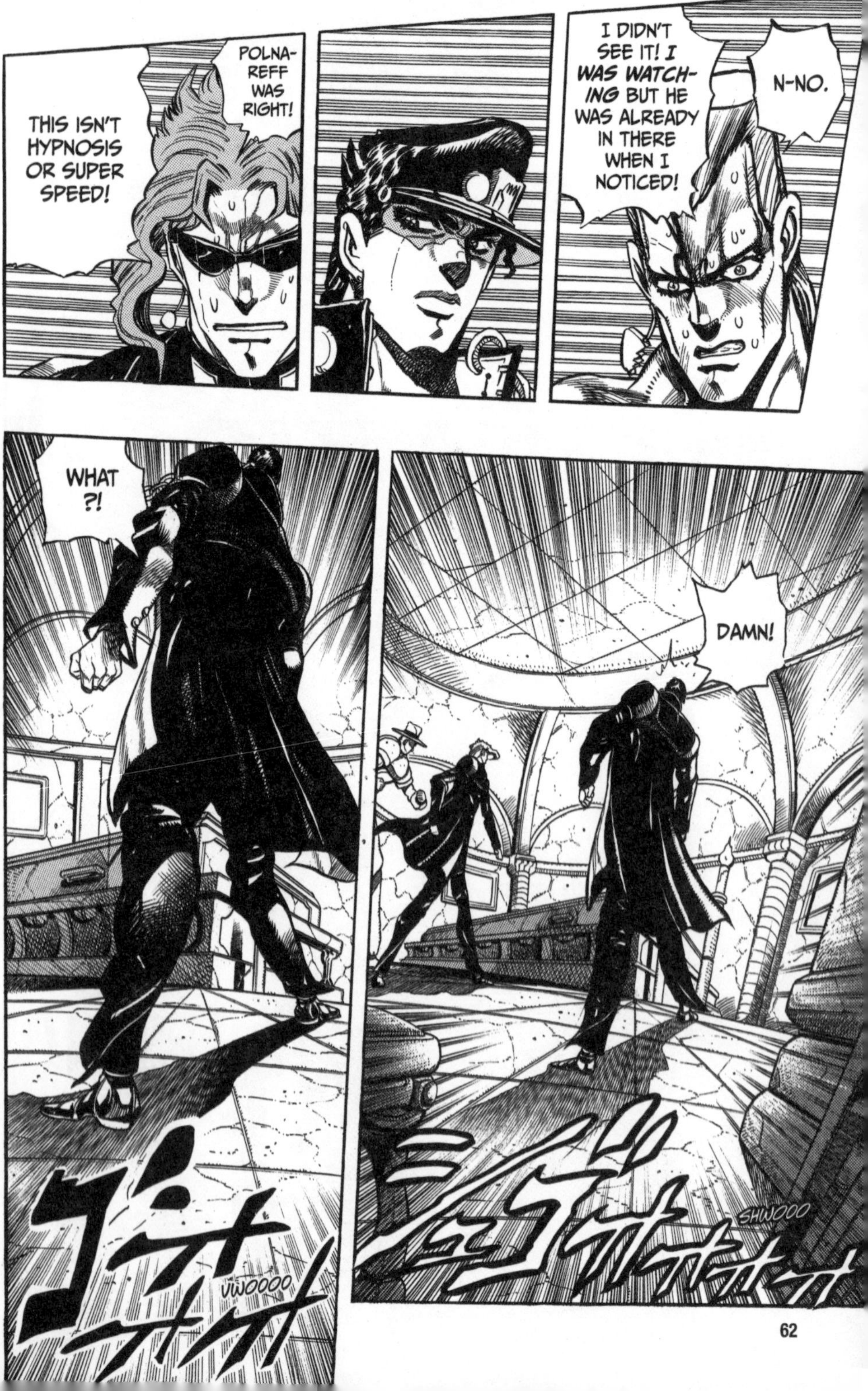
N-NO.
I DIDN'T SEE IT! I WAS WATCHING BUT HE WAS ALREADY IN THERE WHEN I NOTICED!
POLNAREFF WAS RIGHT!
THIS ISN'T HYPNOSIS OR SUPER SPEED!
DAMN!
SHWOOO
WHAT?!
VWOOOO

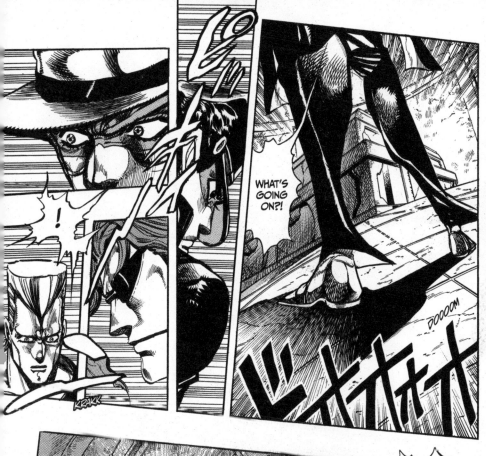

WHAT'S GOING ON?!

DOOOOM

KRAKK

RUN!

DASH

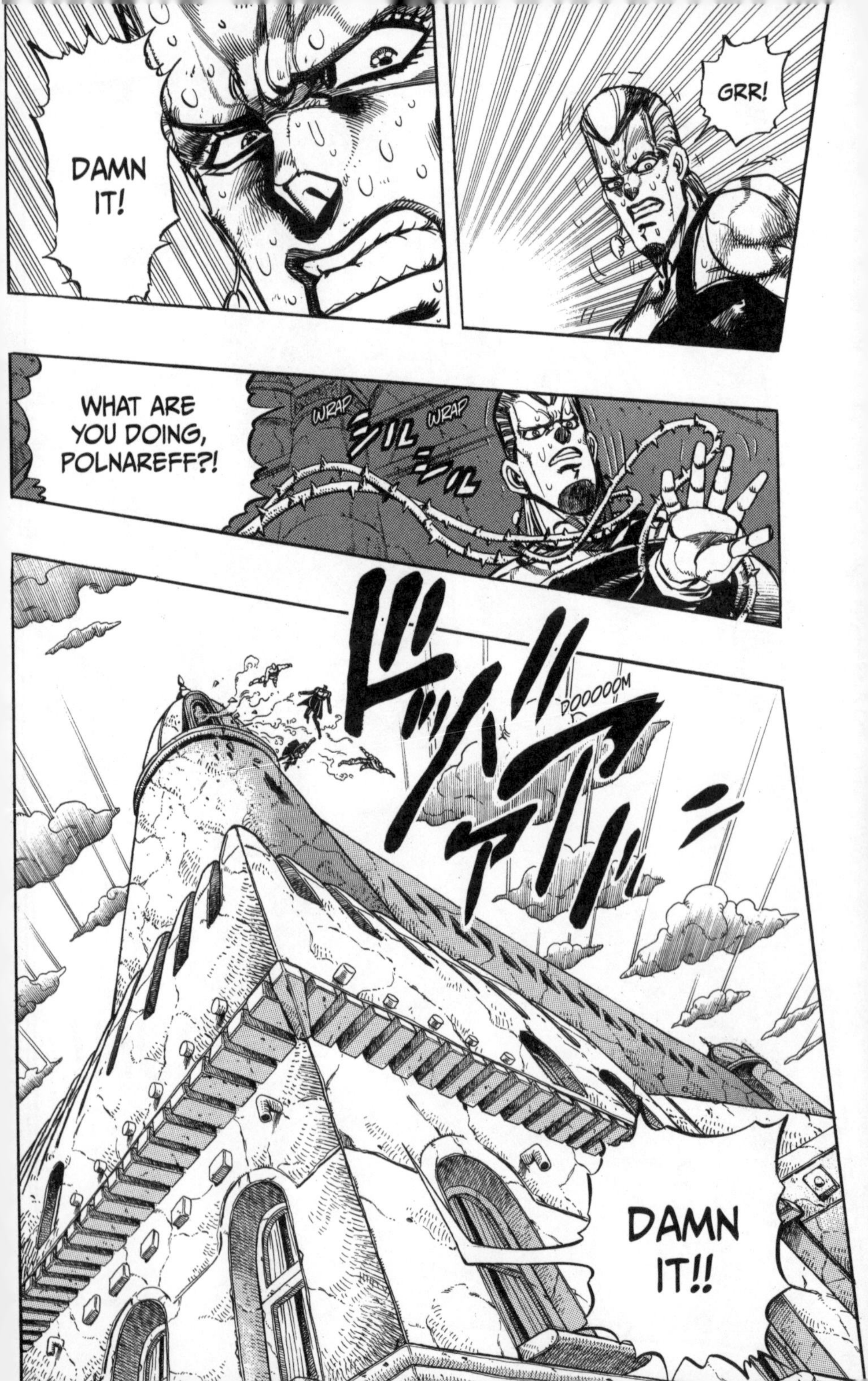
GRR!
DAMN IT!
WHAT ARE YOU DOING, POLNAREFF?!
WRAP
WRAP
DOOOOOM
DAMN IT!!

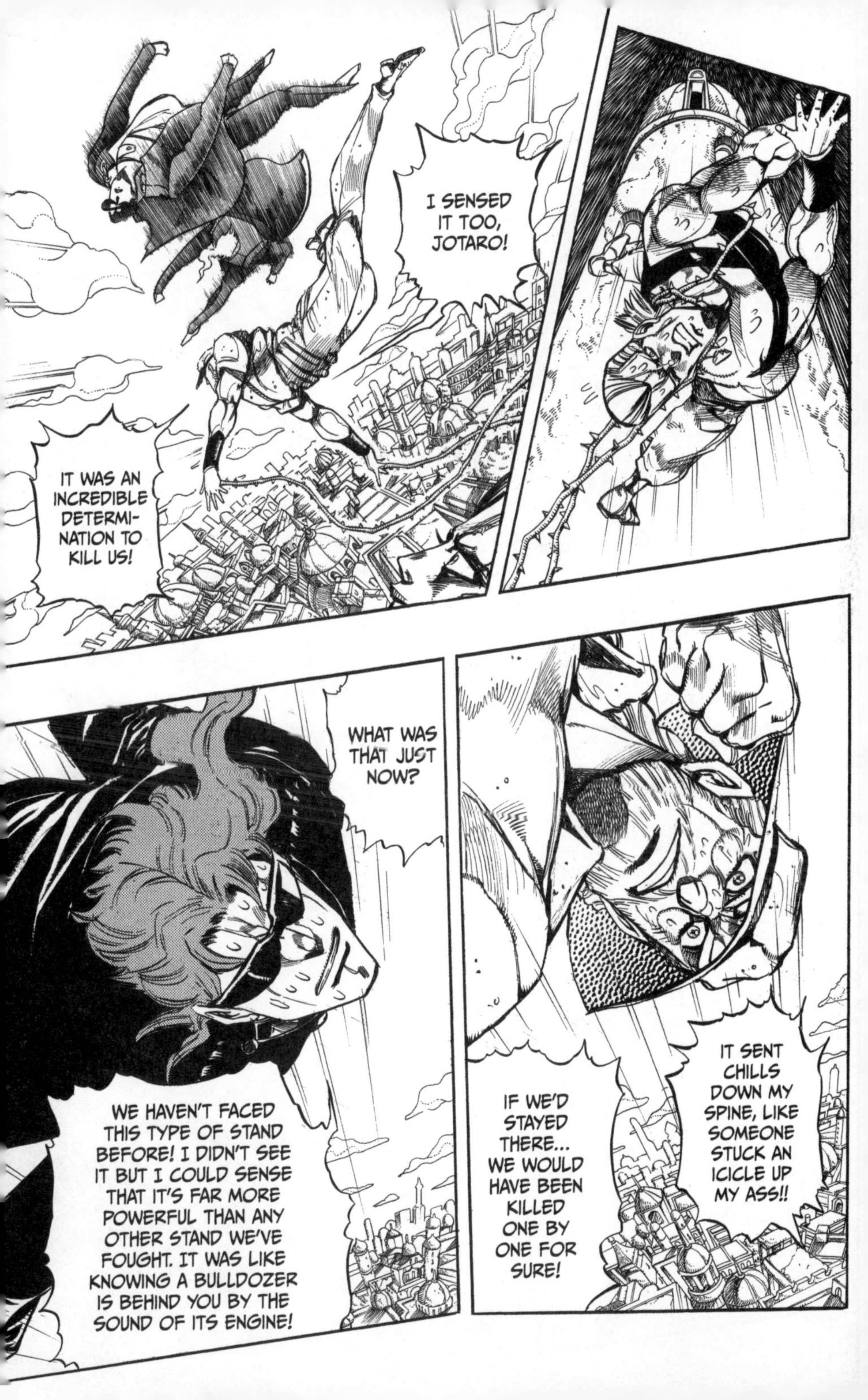
I SENSED IT TOO, JOTARO!
IT WAS AN INCREDIBLE DETERMINATION TO KILL US!
IT SENT CHILLS DOWN MY SPINE, LIKE SOMEONE STUCK AN ICICLE UP MY ASS!!
IF WE'D STAYED THERE... WE WOULD HAVE BEEN KILLED ONE BY ONE FOR SURE!
WHAT WAS THAT JUST NOW?
WE HAVEN'T FACED THIS TYPE OF STAND BEFORE! I DIDN'T SEE IT BUT I COULD SENSE THAT IT'S FAR MORE POWERFUL THAN ANY OTHER STAND WE'VE FOUGHT. IT WAS LIKE KNOWING A BULLDOZER IS BEHIND YOU BY THE SOUND OF ITS ENGINE!

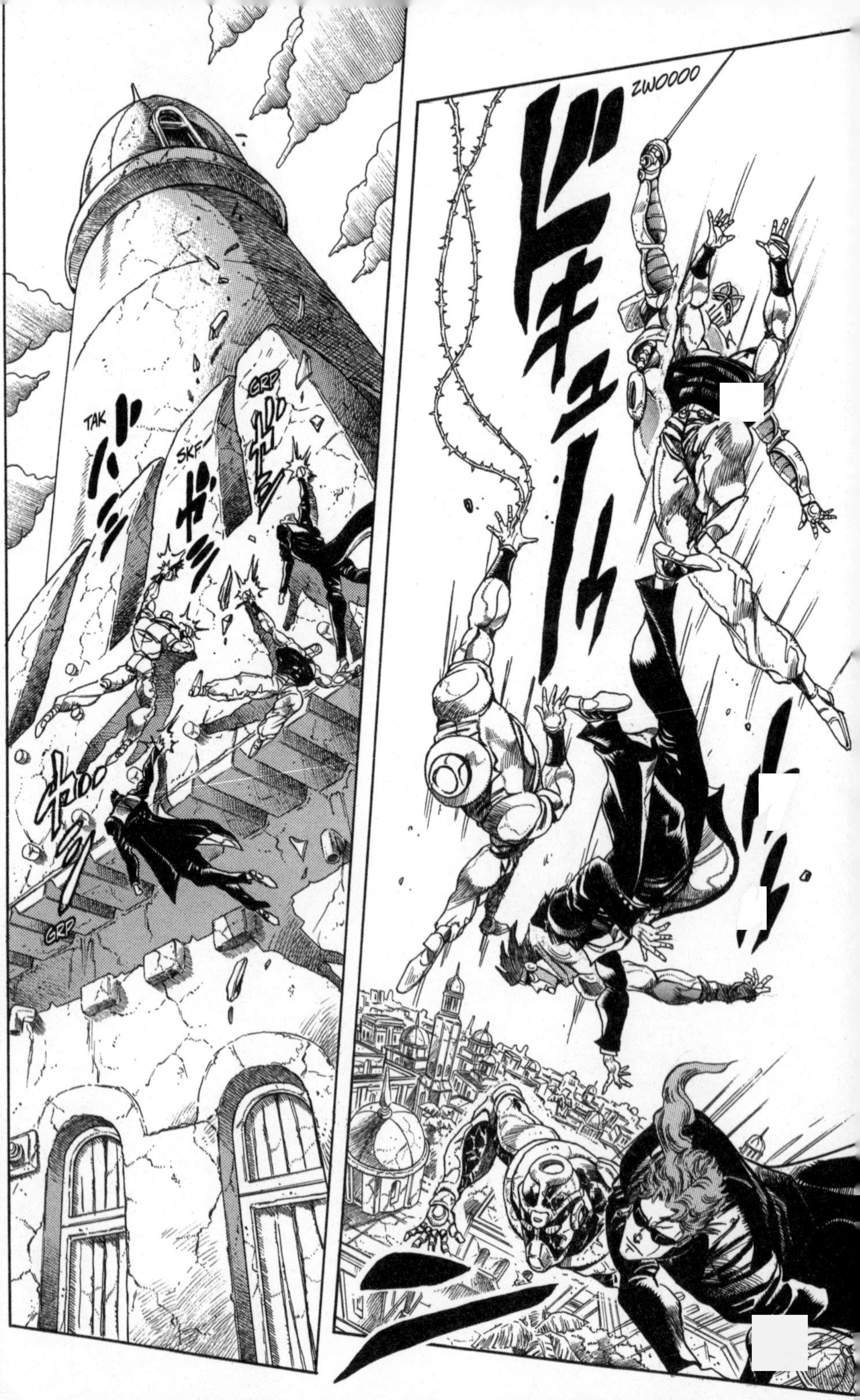
ZWOOOO
GRP
TAK
SKF
GRP

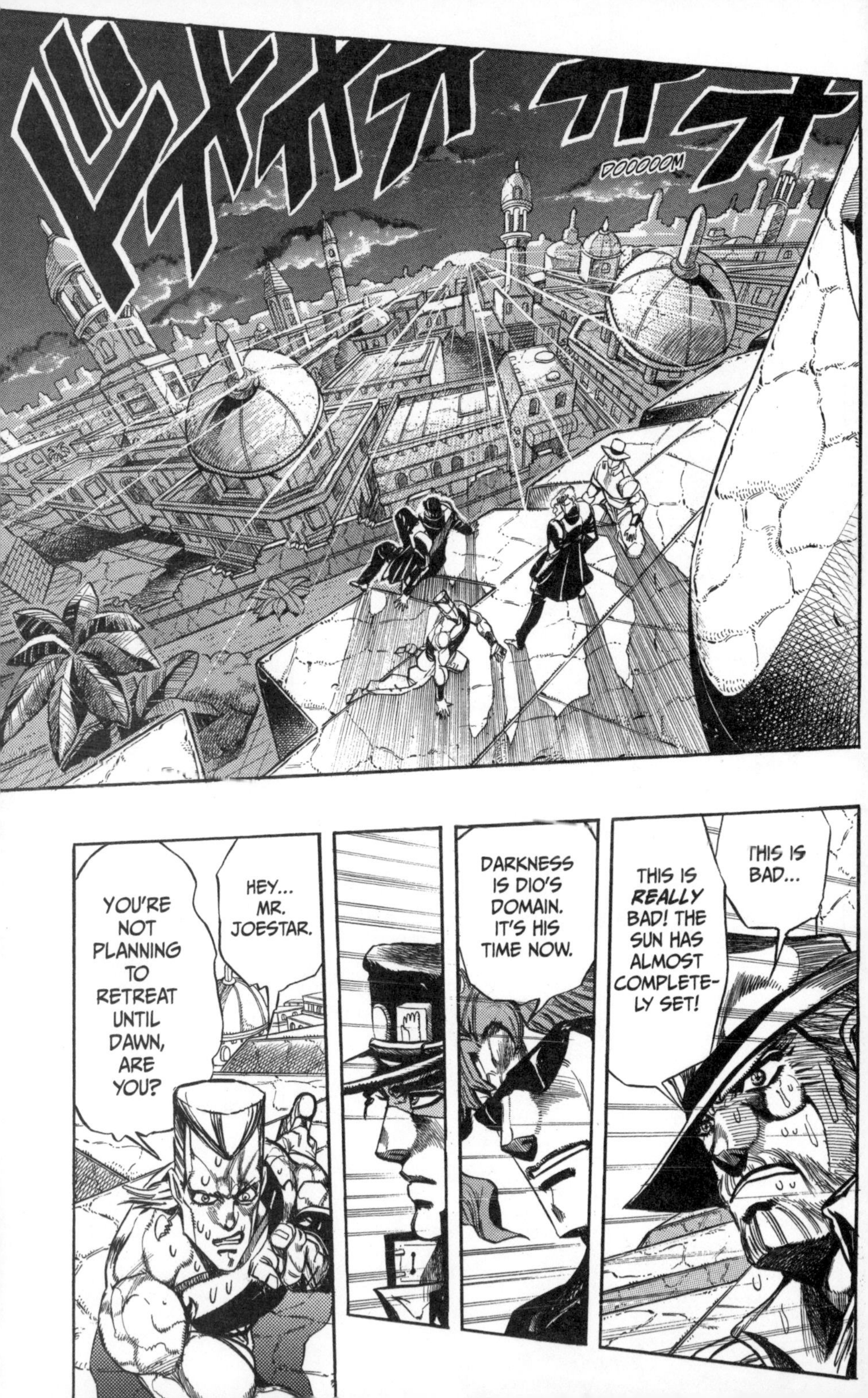
DOOOOOM
THIS IS BAD...
THIS IS REALLY BAD! THE SUN HAS ALMOST COMPLETELY SET!
DARKNESS IS DIO'S DOMAIN. IT'S HIS TIME NOW.
HEY... MR. JOESTAR.
YOU'RE NOT PLANNING TO RETREAT UNTIL DAWN, ARE YOU?

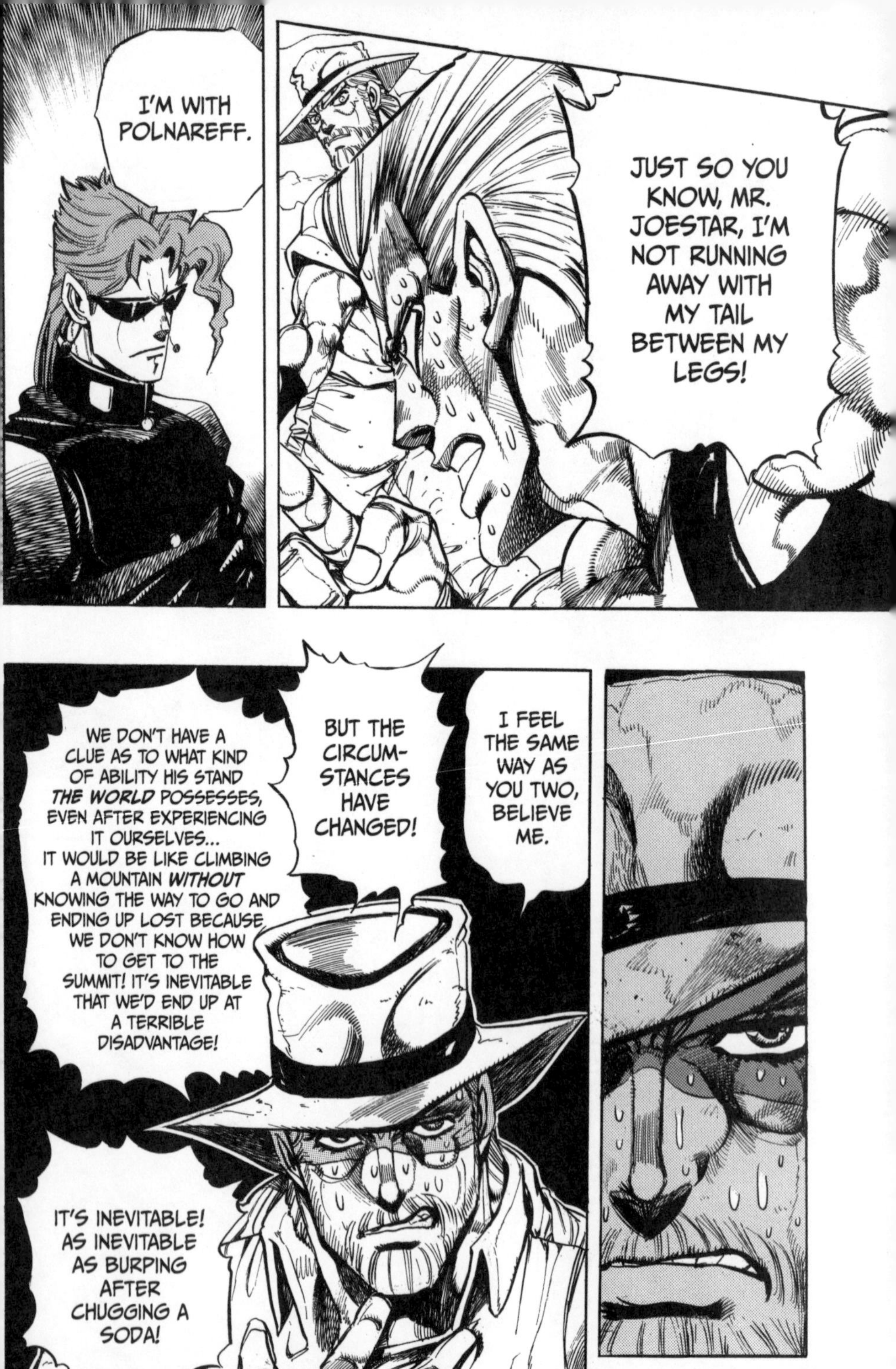
JUST SO YOU KNOW, MR. JOESTAR, I'M NOT RUNNING AWAY WITH MY TAIL BETWEEN MY LEGS!
I'M WITH POLNAREFF.
I FEEL THE SAME WAY AS YOU TWO, BELIEVE ME.
BUT THE CIRCUM-STANCES HAVE CHANGED!
WE DON'T HAVE A CLUE AS TO WHAT KIND OF ABILITY HIS STAND *THE WORLD* POSSESSES, EVEN AFTER EXPERIENCING IT OURSELVES... IT WOULD BE LIKE CLIMBING A MOUNTAIN *WITHOUT* KNOWING THE WAY TO GO AND ENDING UP LOST BECAUSE WE DON'T KNOW HOW TO GET TO THE SUMMIT! IT'S INEVITABLE THAT WE'D END UP AT A TERRIBLE DISADVANTAGE!
IT'S INEVITABLE! AS INEVITABLE AS BURPING AFTER CHUGGING A SODA!

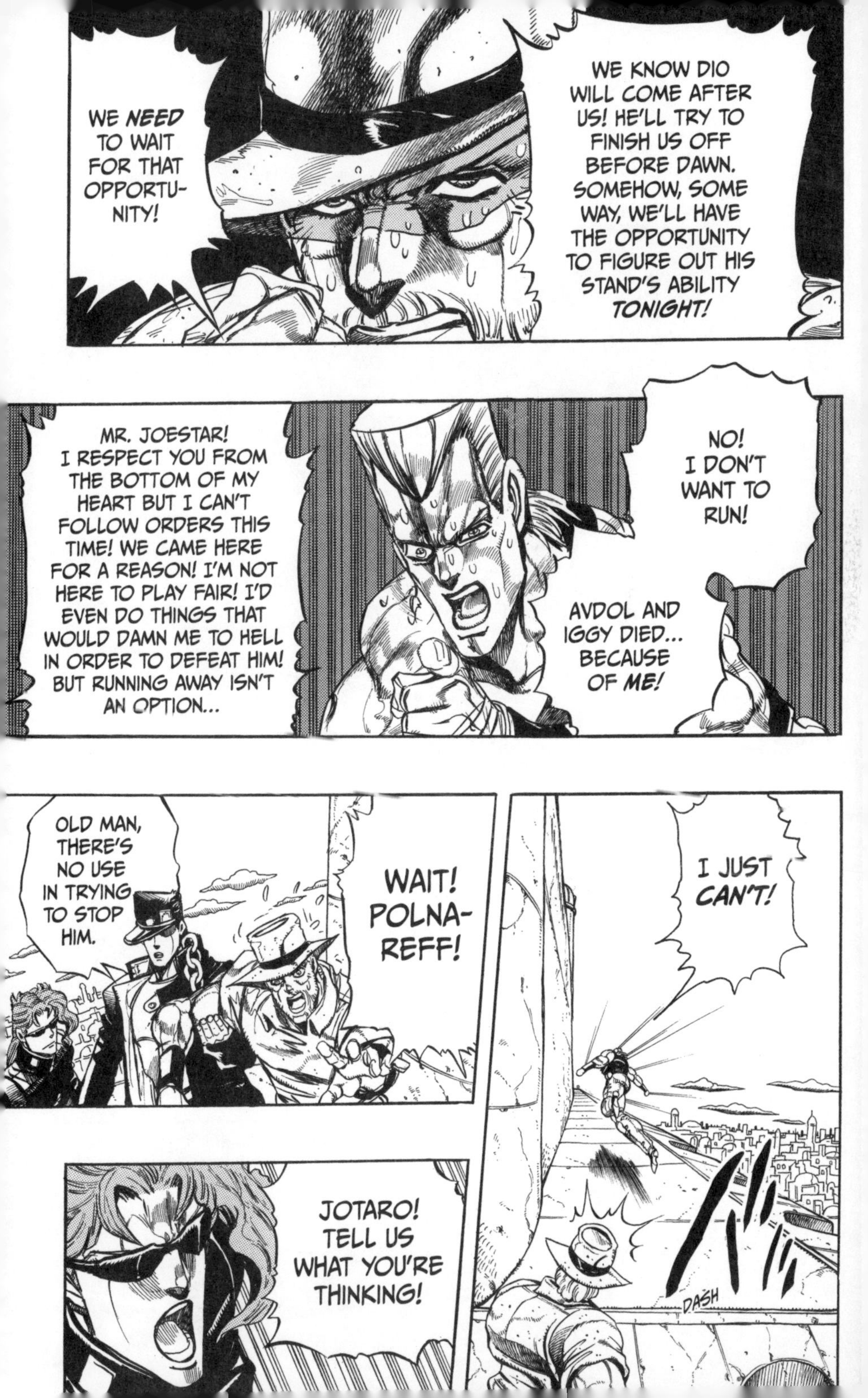
WE KNOW DIO WILL COME AFTER US! HE'LL TRY TO FINISH US OFF BEFORE DAWN. SOMEHOW, SOME WAY, WE'LL HAVE THE OPPORTUNITY TO FIGURE OUT HIS STAND'S ABILITY *TONIGHT!*
WE *NEED* TO WAIT FOR THAT OPPORTU-NITY!
NO! I DON'T WANT TO RUN!
MR. JOESTAR! I RESPECT YOU FROM THE BOTTOM OF MY HEART BUT I CAN'T FOLLOW ORDERS THIS TIME! WE CAME HERE FOR A REASON! I'M NOT HERE TO PLAY FAIR! I'D EVEN DO THINGS THAT WOULD DAMN ME TO HELL IN ORDER TO DEFEAT HIM! BUT RUNNING AWAY ISN'T AN OPTION...
AVDOL AND IGGY DIED... BECAUSE OF *ME!*
I JUST *CAN'T!*
DASH
WAIT! POLNA-REFF!
OLD MAN, THERE'S NO USE IN TRYING TO STOP HIM.
JOTARO! TELL US WHAT YOU'RE THINKING!

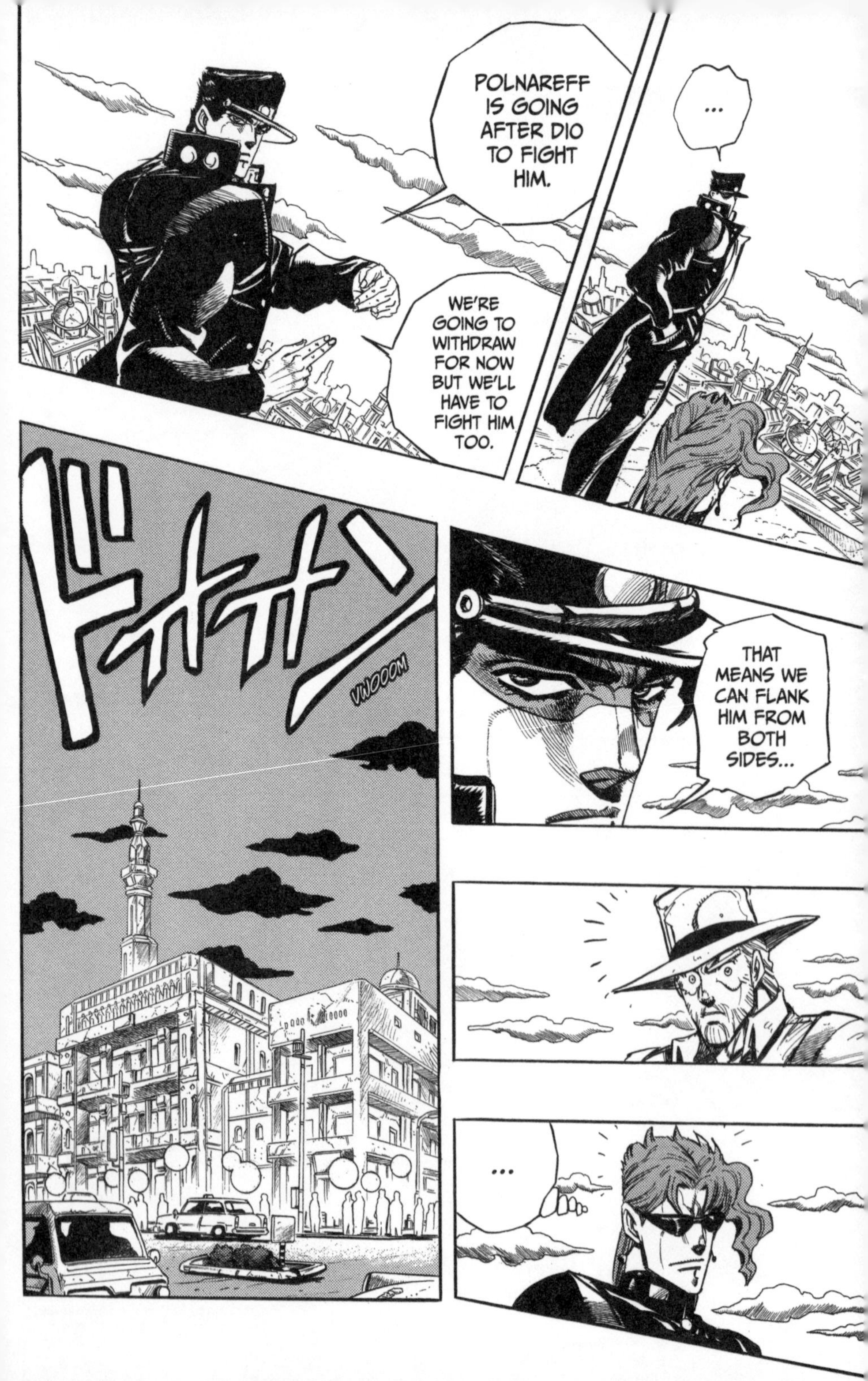
...
POLNAREFF IS GOING AFTER DIO TO FIGHT HIM.
WE'RE GOING TO WITHDRAW FOR NOW BUT WE'LL HAVE TO FIGHT HIM TOO.
THAT MEANS WE CAN FLANK HIM FROM BOTH SIDES...
...
ドォォン
VWOOOM

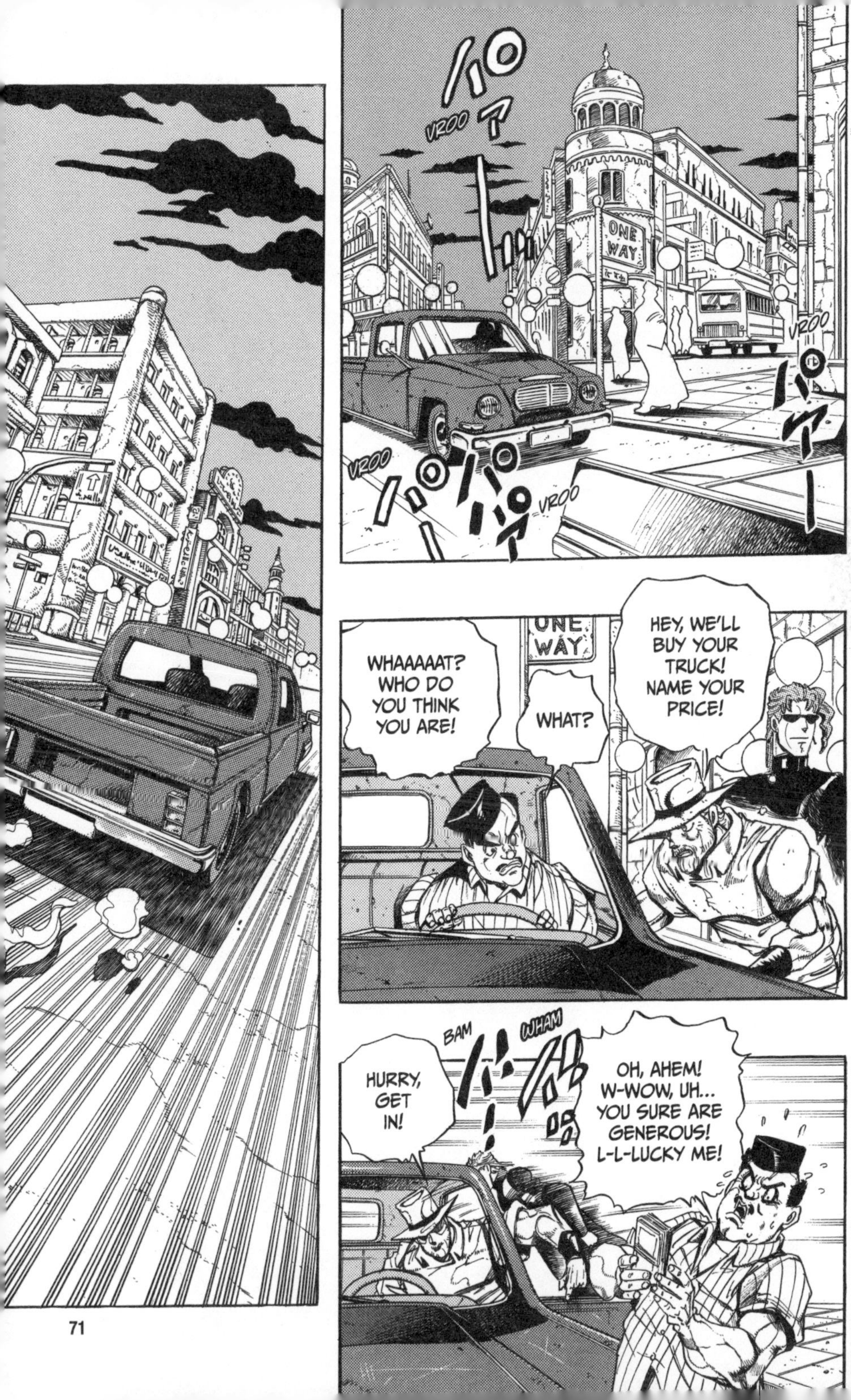
VROO
ONE WAY
VROO
VROO
VROO
HEY, WE'LL BUY YOUR TRUCK! NAME YOUR PRICE!
WHAT?
ONE WAY
WHAAAAAT? WHO DO YOU THINK YOU ARE!
OH, AHEM! W-WOW, UH... YOU SURE ARE GENEROUS! L-L-LUCKY ME!
WHAM
BAM
HURRY, GET IN!

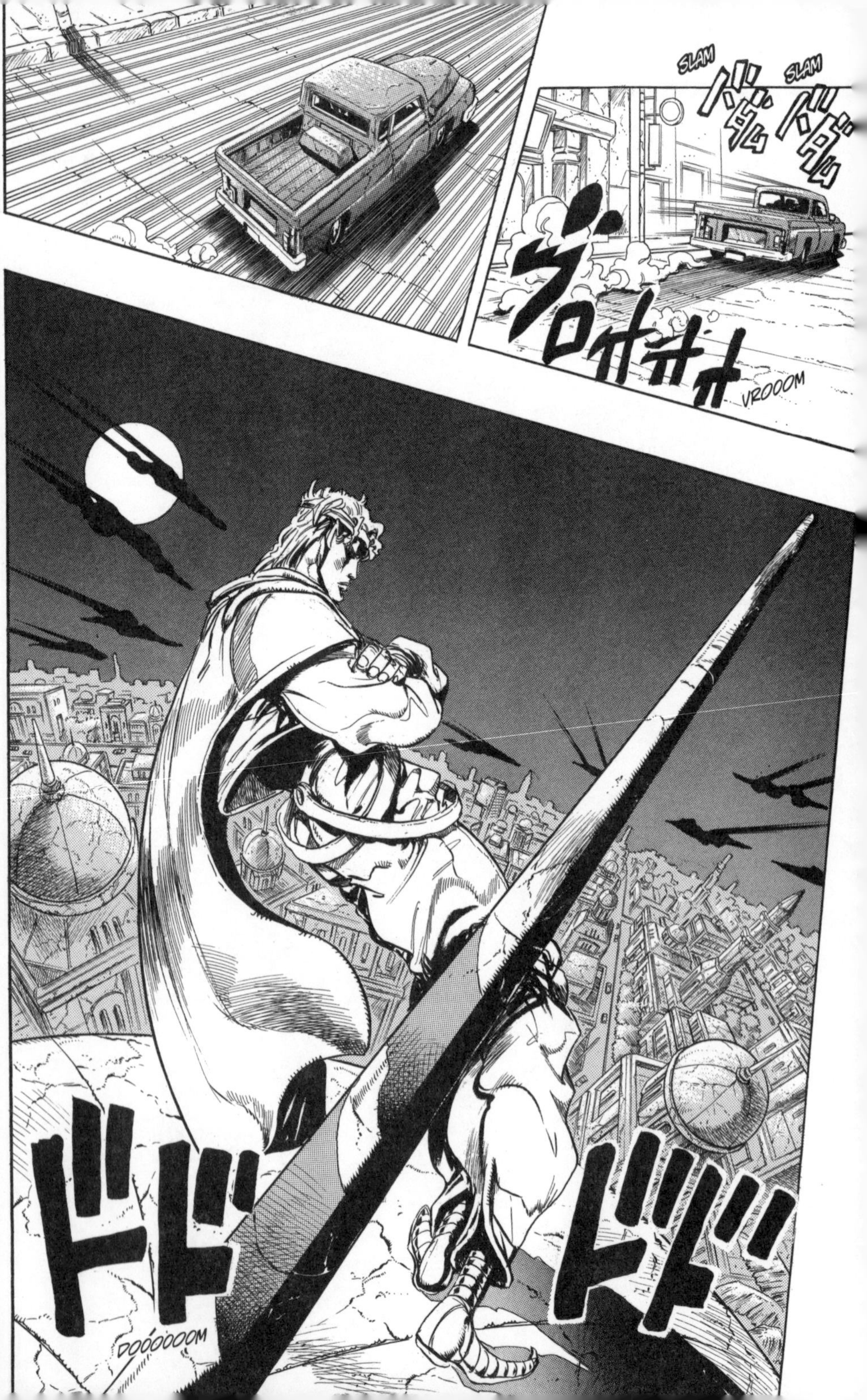
SLAM
SLAM
VROOOM
DOOOOOOM

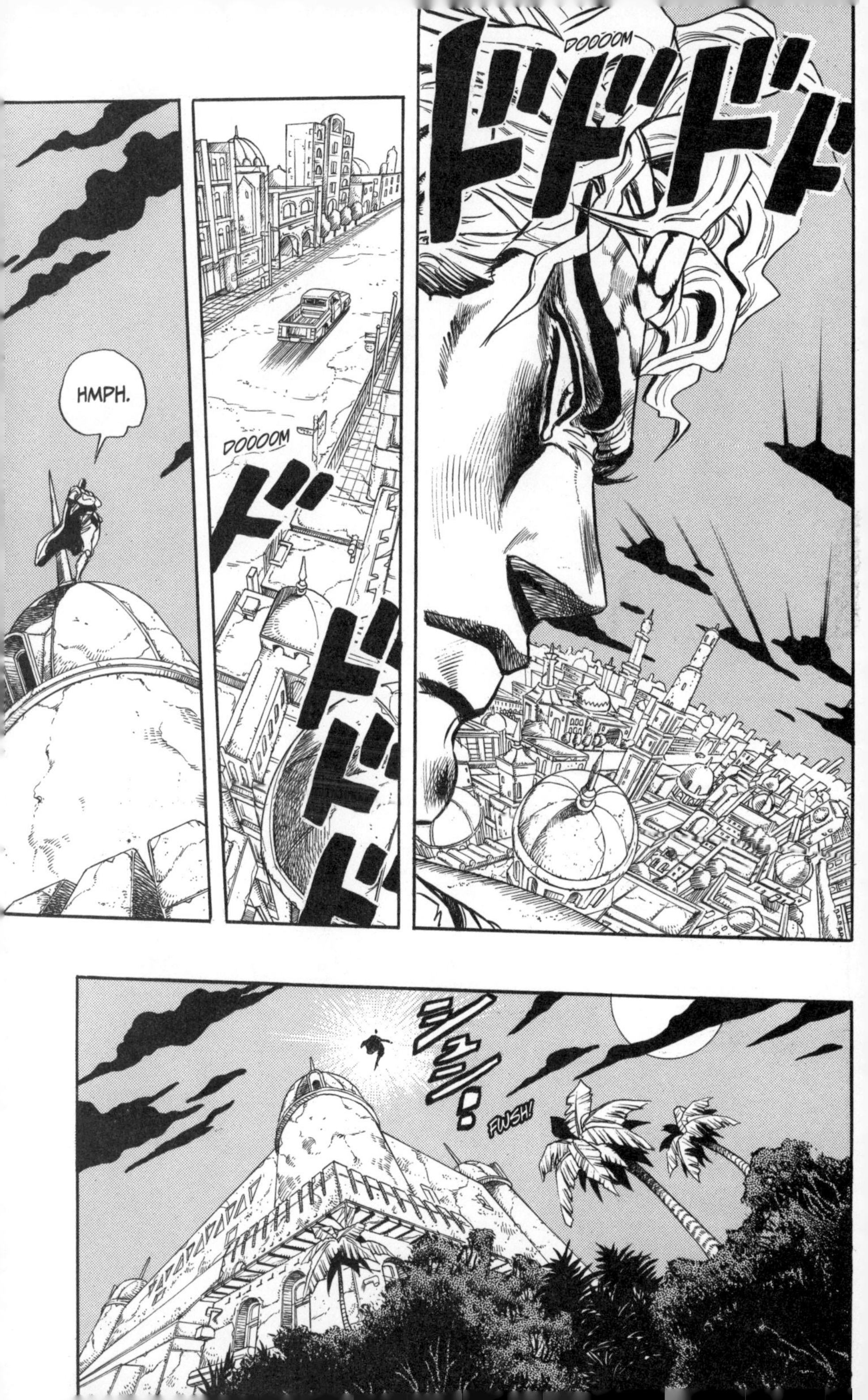
DOOOOM
ドドドド
DOOOOM
ドドドド
HMPH.
シュン!
FWSH!

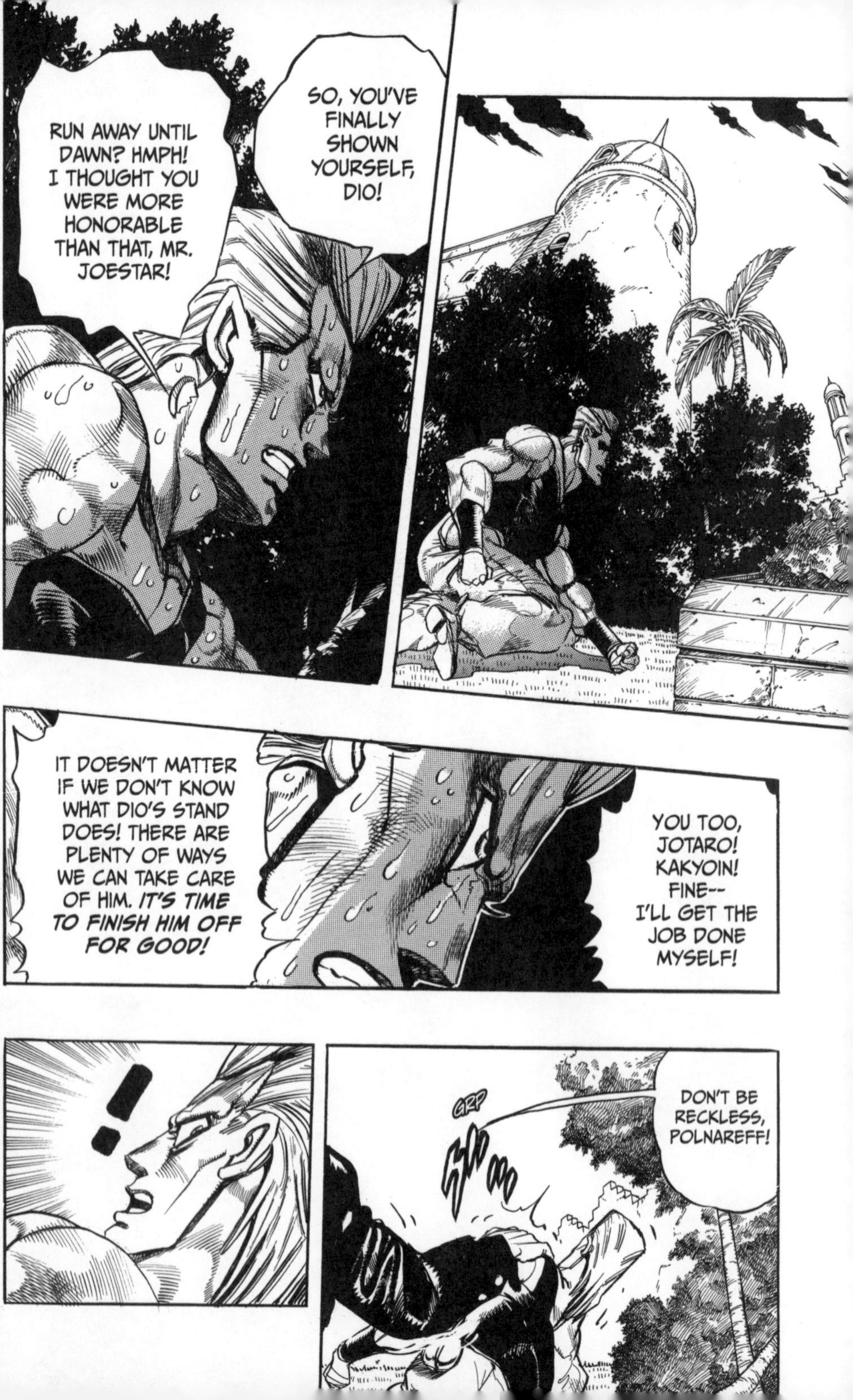
SO, YOU'VE FINALLY SHOWN YOURSELF, DIO!
RUN AWAY UNTIL DAWN? HMPH! I THOUGHT YOU WERE MORE HONORABLE THAN THAT, MR. JOESTAR!
YOU TOO, JOTARO! KAKYOIN! FINE-- I'LL GET THE JOB DONE MYSELF!
IT DOESN'T MATTER IF WE DON'T KNOW WHAT DIO'S STAND DOES! THERE ARE PLENTY OF WAYS WE CAN TAKE CARE OF HIM. *IT'S TIME TO FINISH HIM OFF FOR GOOD!*
DON'T BE RECKLESS, POLNAREFF!
GRP
!!

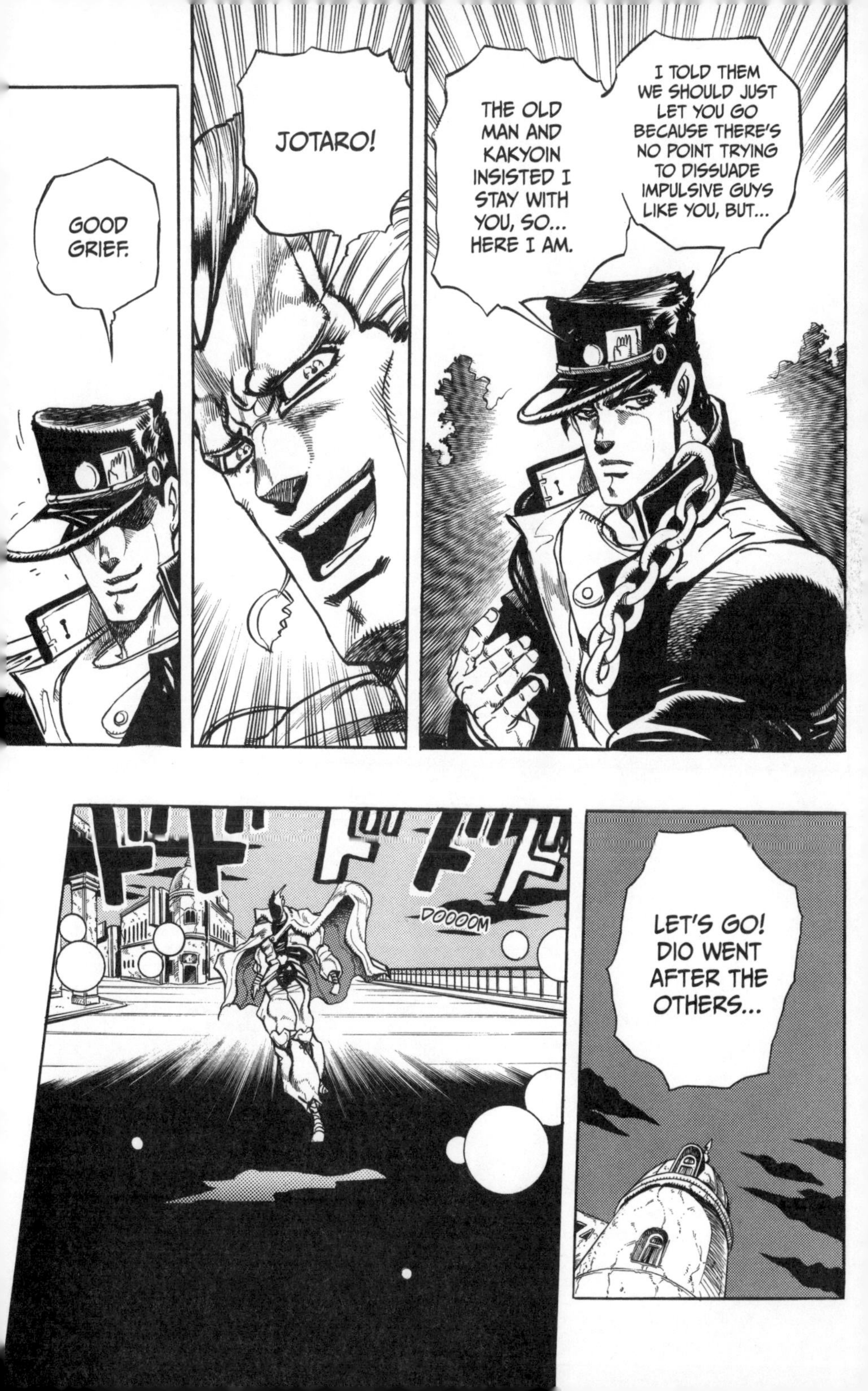
I TOLD THEM WE SHOULD JUST LET YOU GO BECAUSE THERE'S NO POINT TRYING TO DISSUADE IMPULSIVE GUYS LIKE YOU, BUT...
THE OLD MAN AND KAKYOIN INSISTED I STAY WITH YOU, SO... HERE I AM.
JOTARO!
GOOD GRIEF.
LET'S GO! DIO WENT AFTER THE OTHERS...
DOOOOM

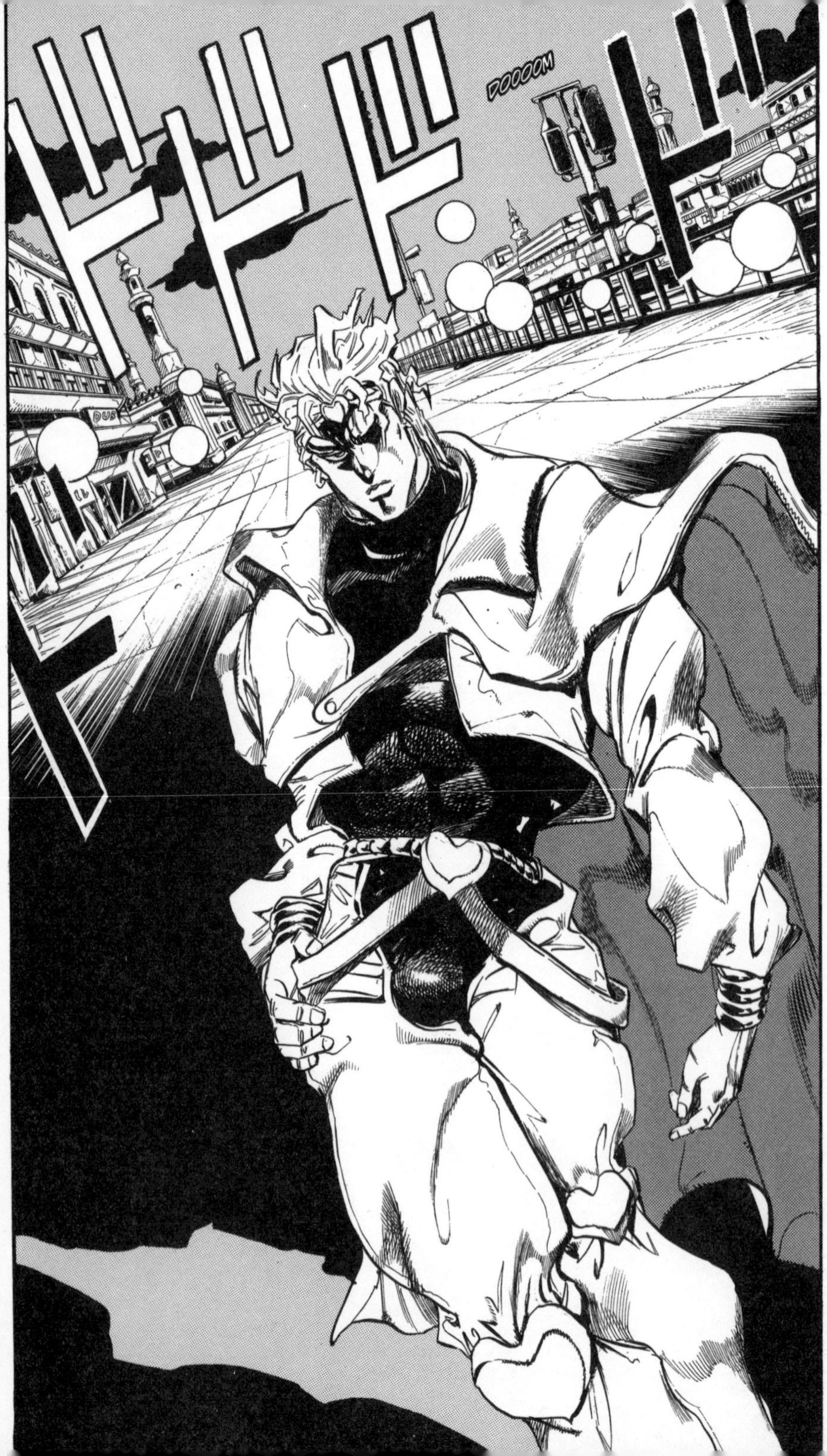
DOOOOM

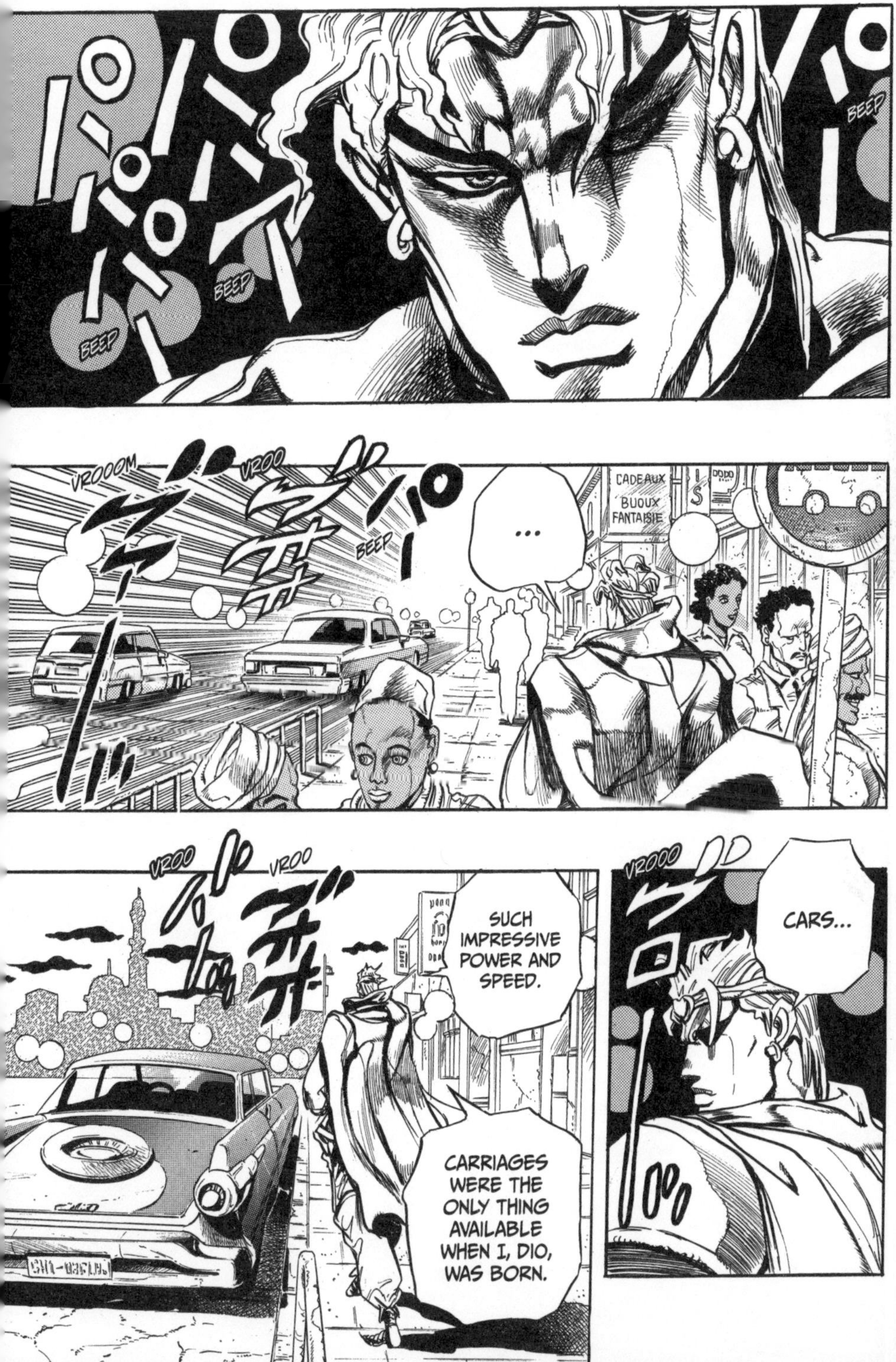
BEEP
BEEP
BEEP
...
BEEP
VROO
VROOOM
CADEAUX
BIJOUX
FANTAISIE
VROOO
CARS...
VROO
VROO
SUCH IMPRESSIVE POWER AND SPEED.
CARRIAGES WERE THE ONLY THING AVAILABLE WHEN I, DIO, WAS BORN.

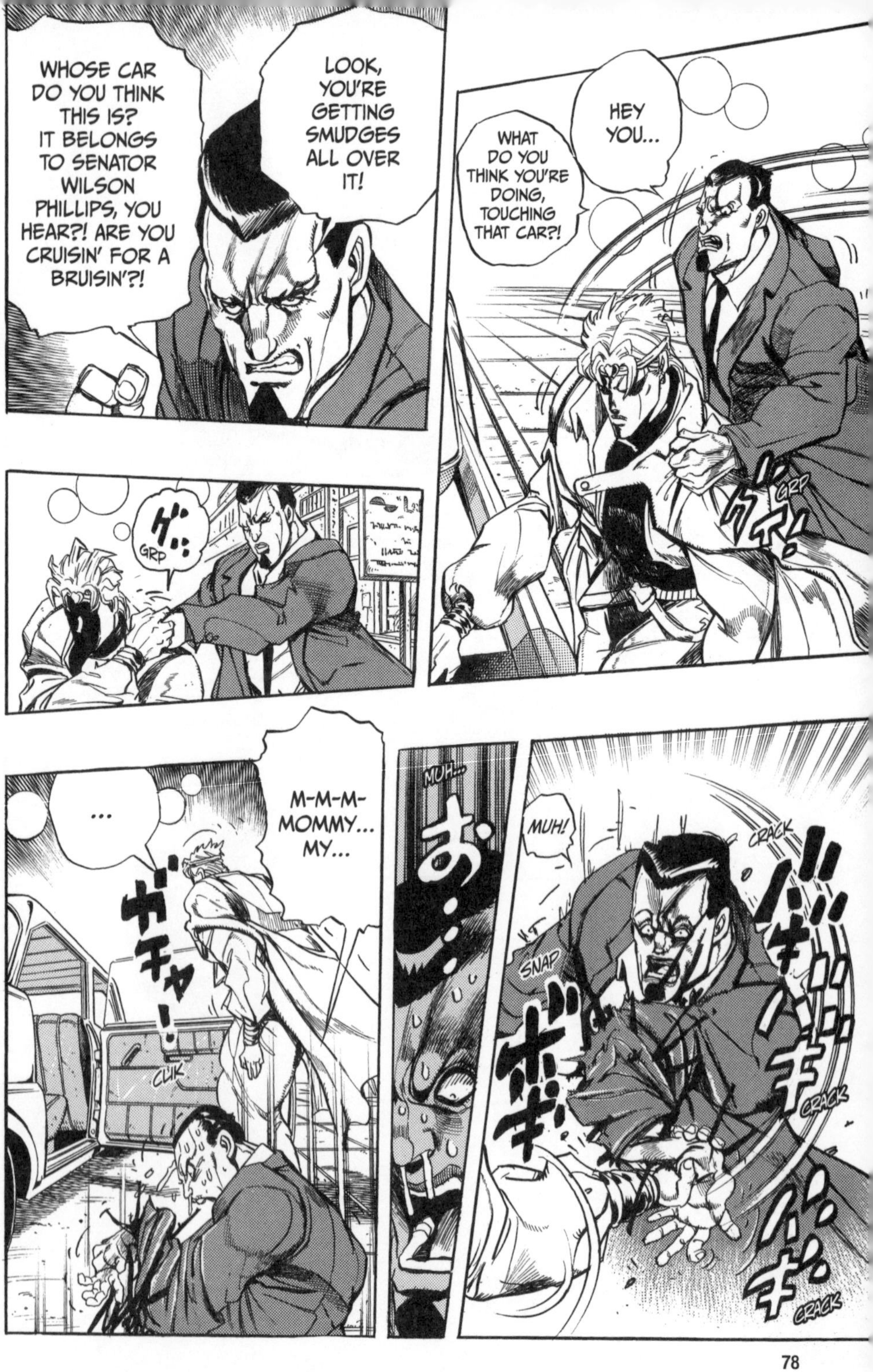
HEY YOU...
WHAT DO YOU THINK YOU'RE DOING, TOUCHING THAT CAR?!
GRP
LOOK, YOU'RE GETTING SMUDGES ALL OVER IT!
WHOSE CAR DO YOU THINK THIS IS? IT BELONGS TO SENATOR WILSON PHILLIPS, YOU HEAR?! ARE YOU CRUISIN' FOR A BRUISIN'?!
GRP
MUH!
CRACK
SNAP
CRACK
CRACK
MUH...
M-M-M-MOMMY... MY...
...
CLIK

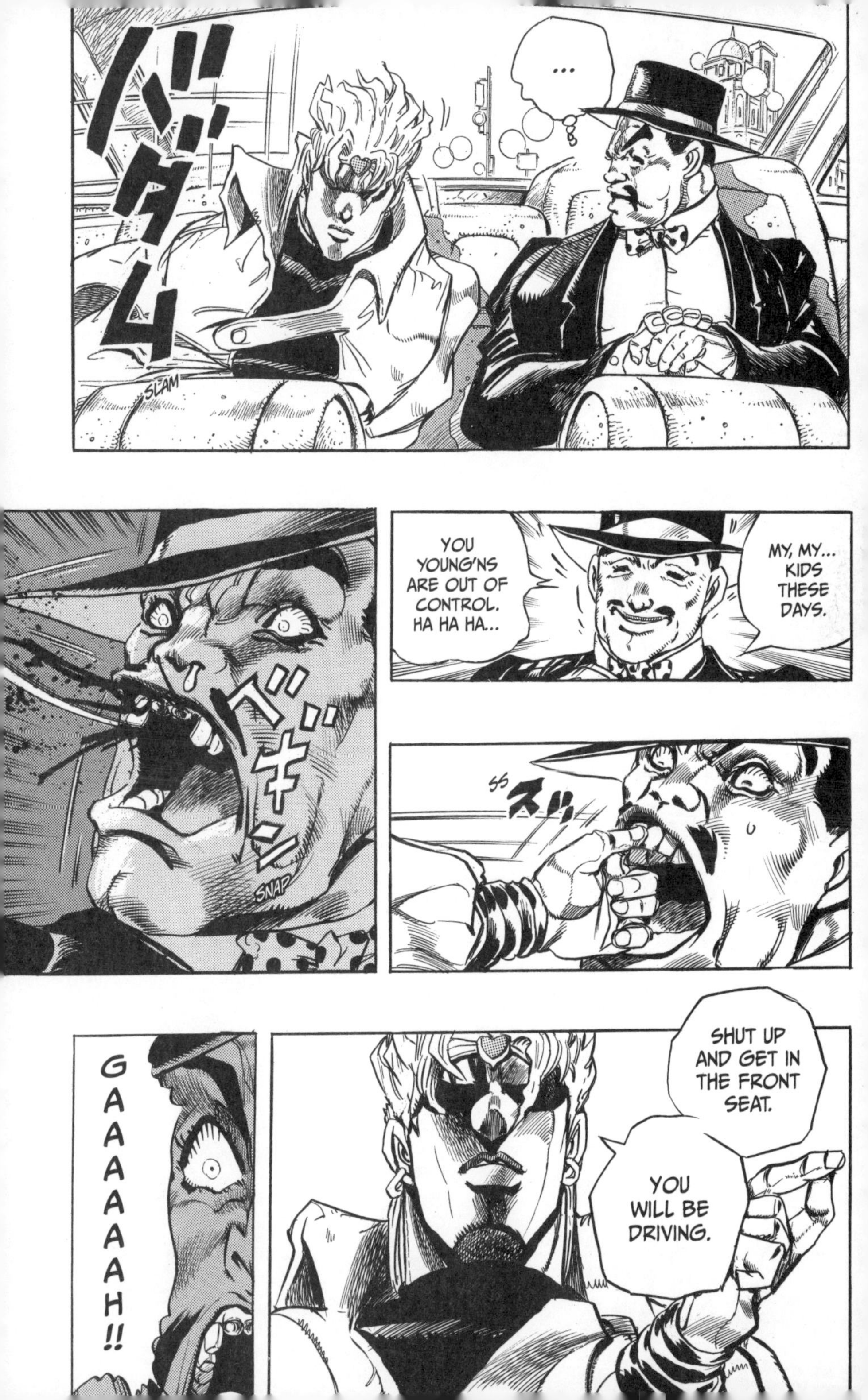

バダム
SLAM
...
MY, MY... KIDS THESE DAYS.
YOU YOUNG'NS ARE OUT OF CONTROL. HA HA HA...
SS
スッ
ベギン
SNAP
SHUT UP AND GET IN THE FRONT SEAT.
YOU WILL BE DRIVING.
GAAAAAAAH!!

CHAPTER 138: DIO's World PART 5

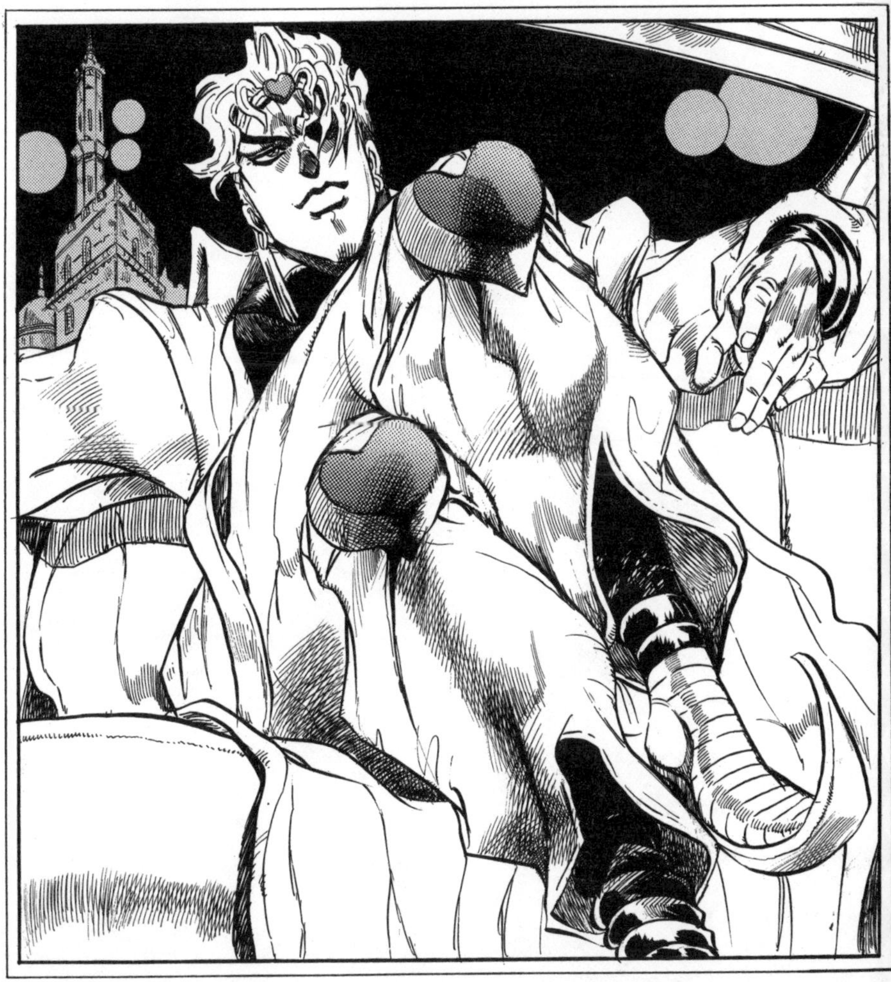

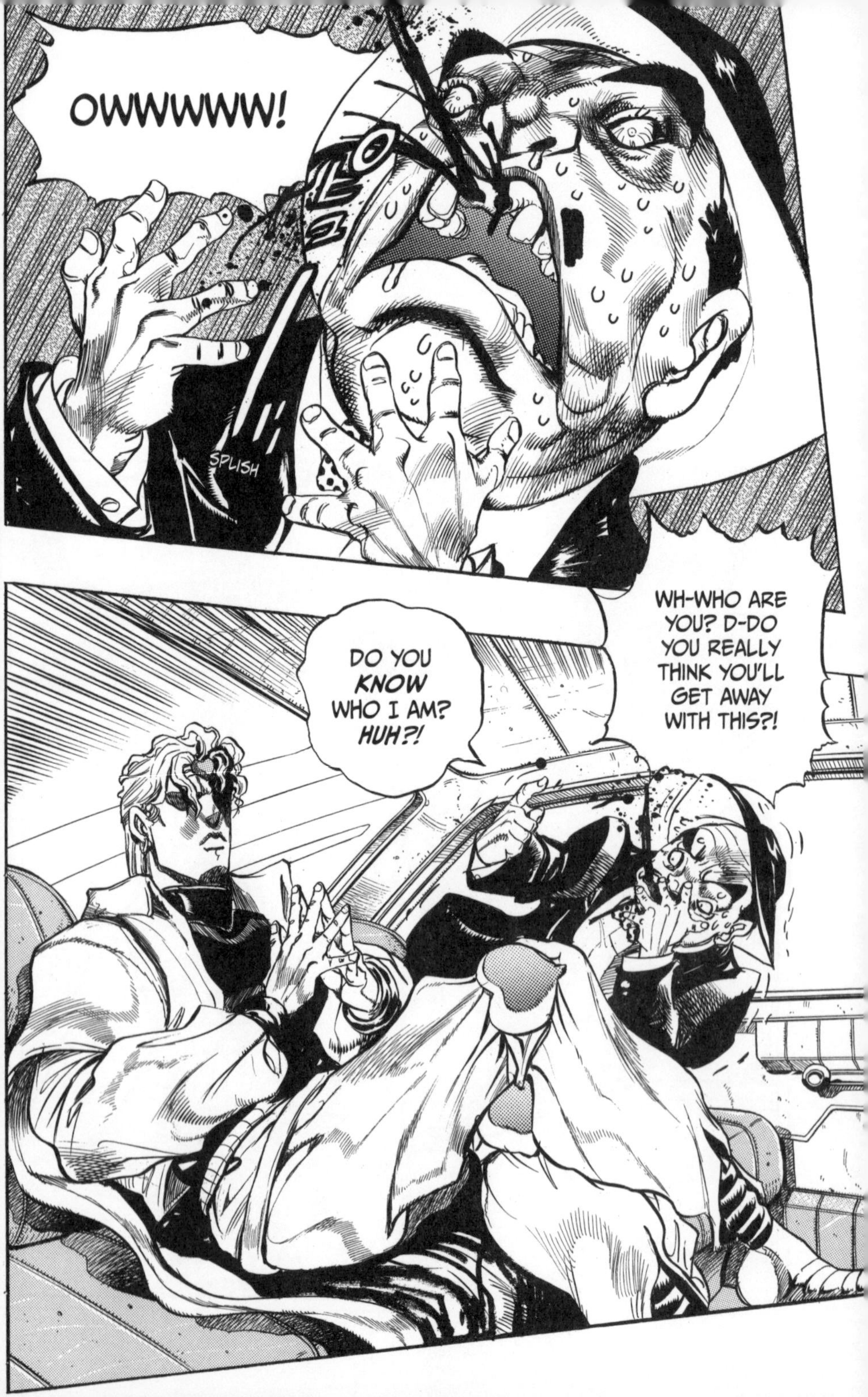
OWWWWW!
SPLISH
WH-WHO ARE YOU? D-DO YOU REALLY THINK YOU'LL GET AWAY WITH THIS?!
DO YOU *KNOW* WHO I AM? *HUH?!*

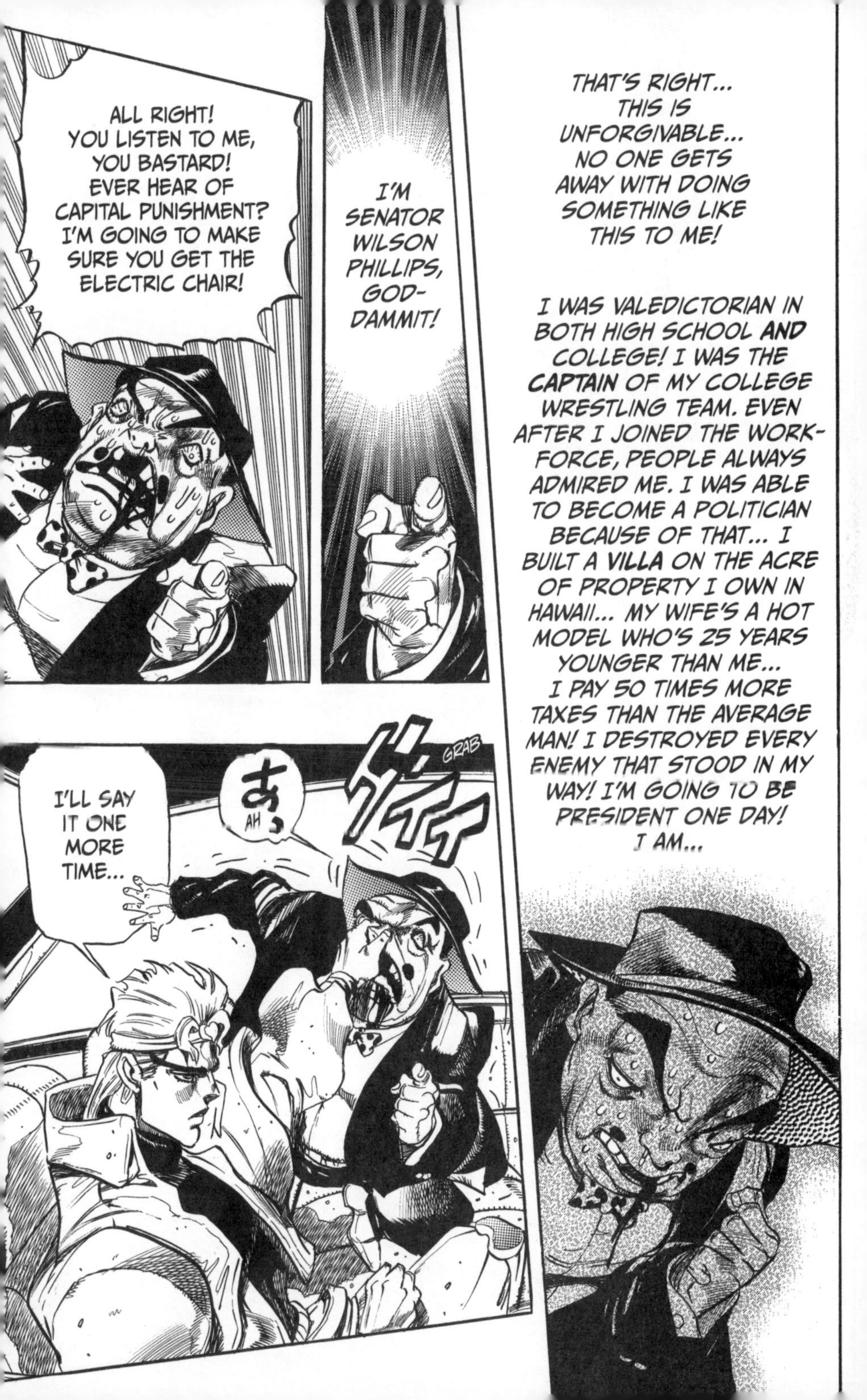

THAT'S RIGHT... THIS IS UNFORGIVABLE... NO ONE GETS AWAY WITH DOING SOMETHING LIKE THIS TO ME!
I WAS VALEDICTORIAN IN BOTH HIGH SCHOOL **AND** COLLEGE! I WAS THE **CAPTAIN** OF MY COLLEGE WRESTLING TEAM. EVEN AFTER I JOINED THE WORK-FORCE, PEOPLE ALWAYS ADMIRED ME. I WAS ABLE TO BECOME A POLITICIAN BECAUSE OF THAT... I BUILT A **VILLA** ON THE ACRE OF PROPERTY I OWN IN HAWAII... MY WIFE'S A HOT MODEL WHO'S 25 YEARS YOUNGER THAN ME... I PAY 50 TIMES MORE TAXES THAN THE AVERAGE MAN! I DESTROYED EVERY ENEMY THAT STOOD IN MY WAY! I'M GOING TO BE PRESIDENT ONE DAY! I AM...
I'M SENATOR WILSON PHILLIPS, GOD-DAMMIT!
ALL RIGHT! YOU LISTEN TO ME, YOU BASTARD! EVER HEAR OF CAPITAL PUNISHMENT? I'M GOING TO MAKE SURE YOU GET THE ELECTRIC CHAIR!
GRAB
あ
AH
I'LL SAY IT ONE MORE TIME...

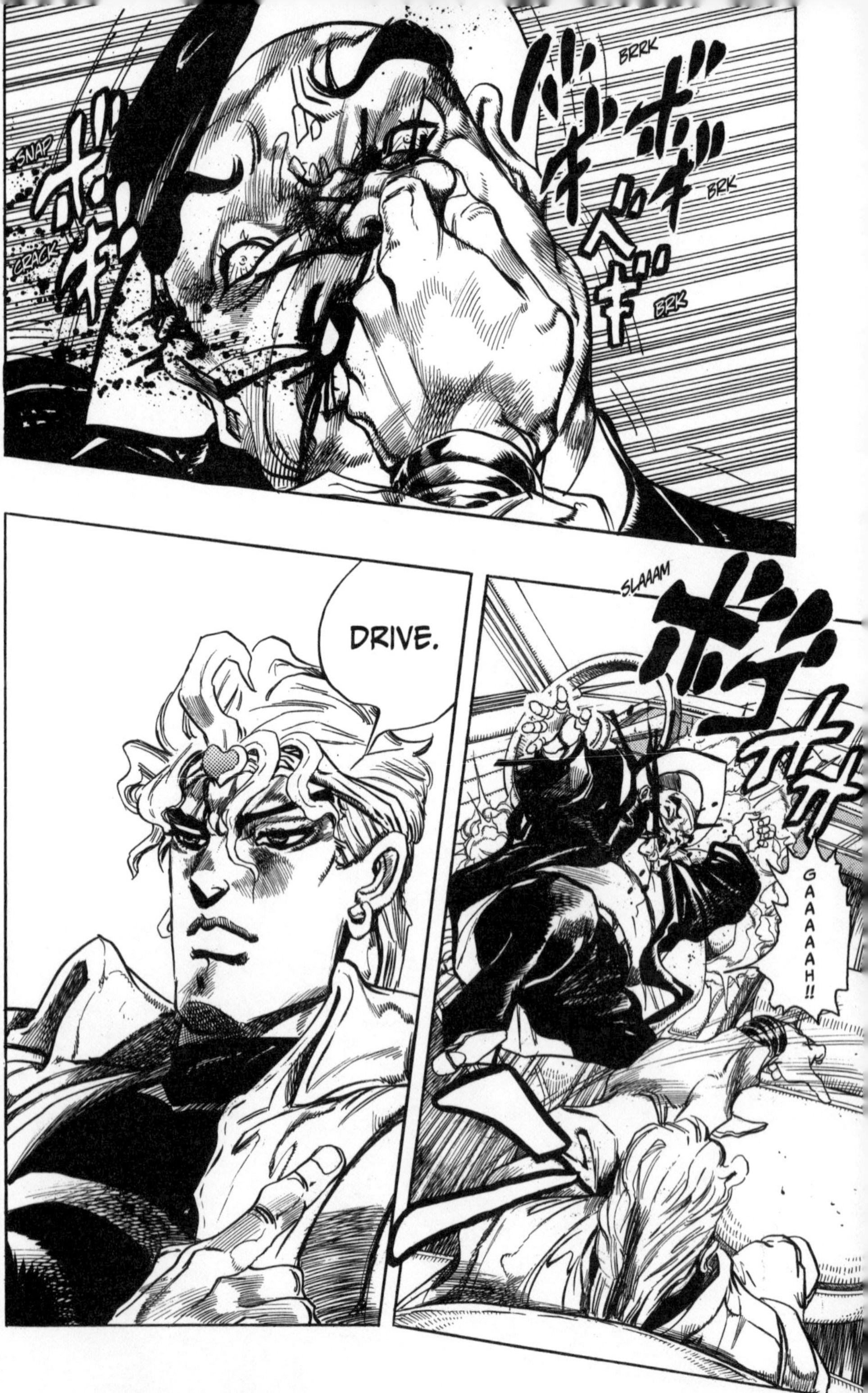
BRRK
BRK
BRK
SNAP
CRACK
SLAAAM
GAAAAAAH!!
DRIVE.

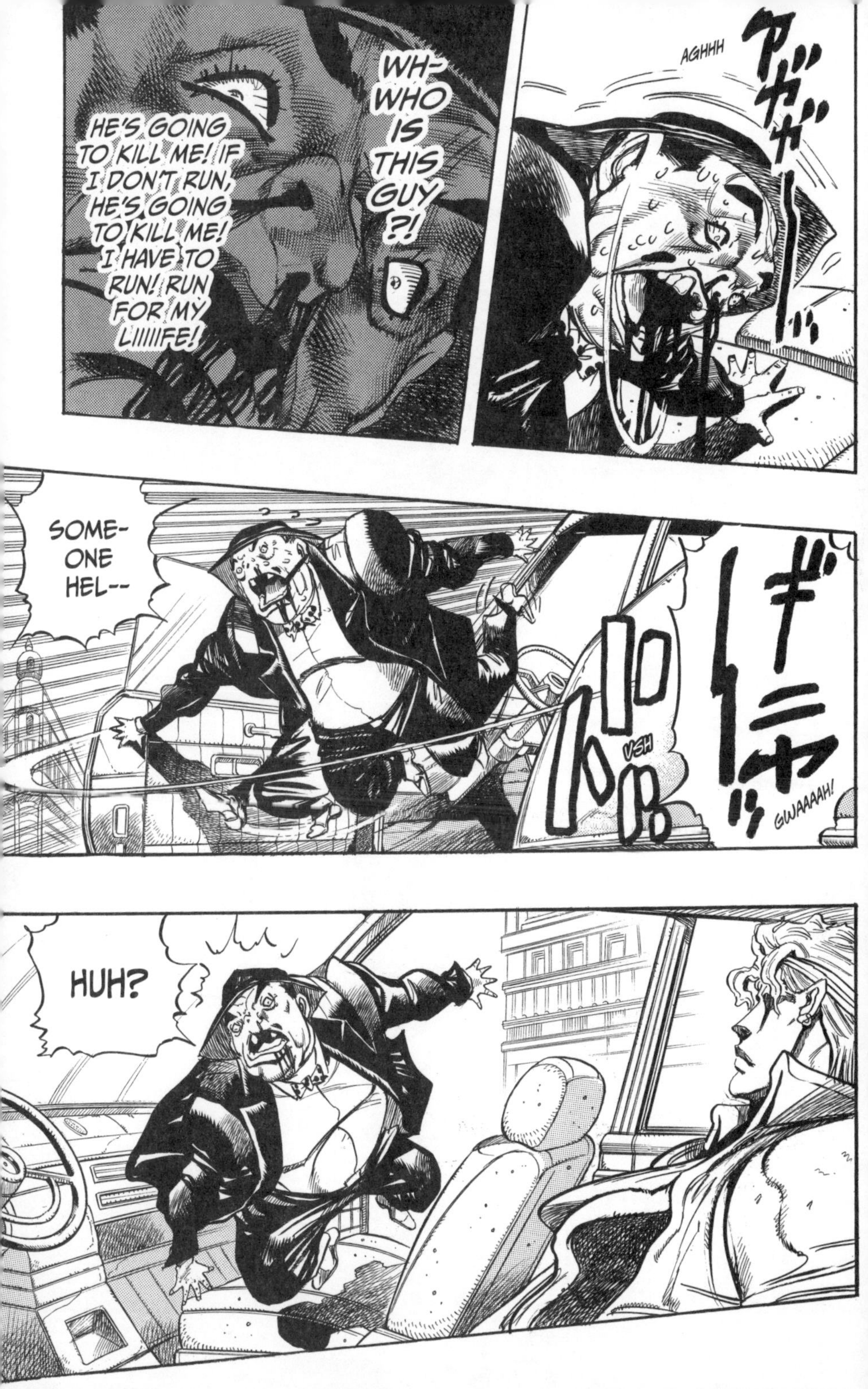
AGHHH
WH-WHO IS THIS GUY?!
HE'S GOING TO KILL ME! IF I DON'T RUN, HE'S GOING TO KILL ME! I HAVE TO RUN! RUN FOR MY LIIIIIFE!
GWAAAAH!
SOME-ONE HEL--
VSH
HUH?

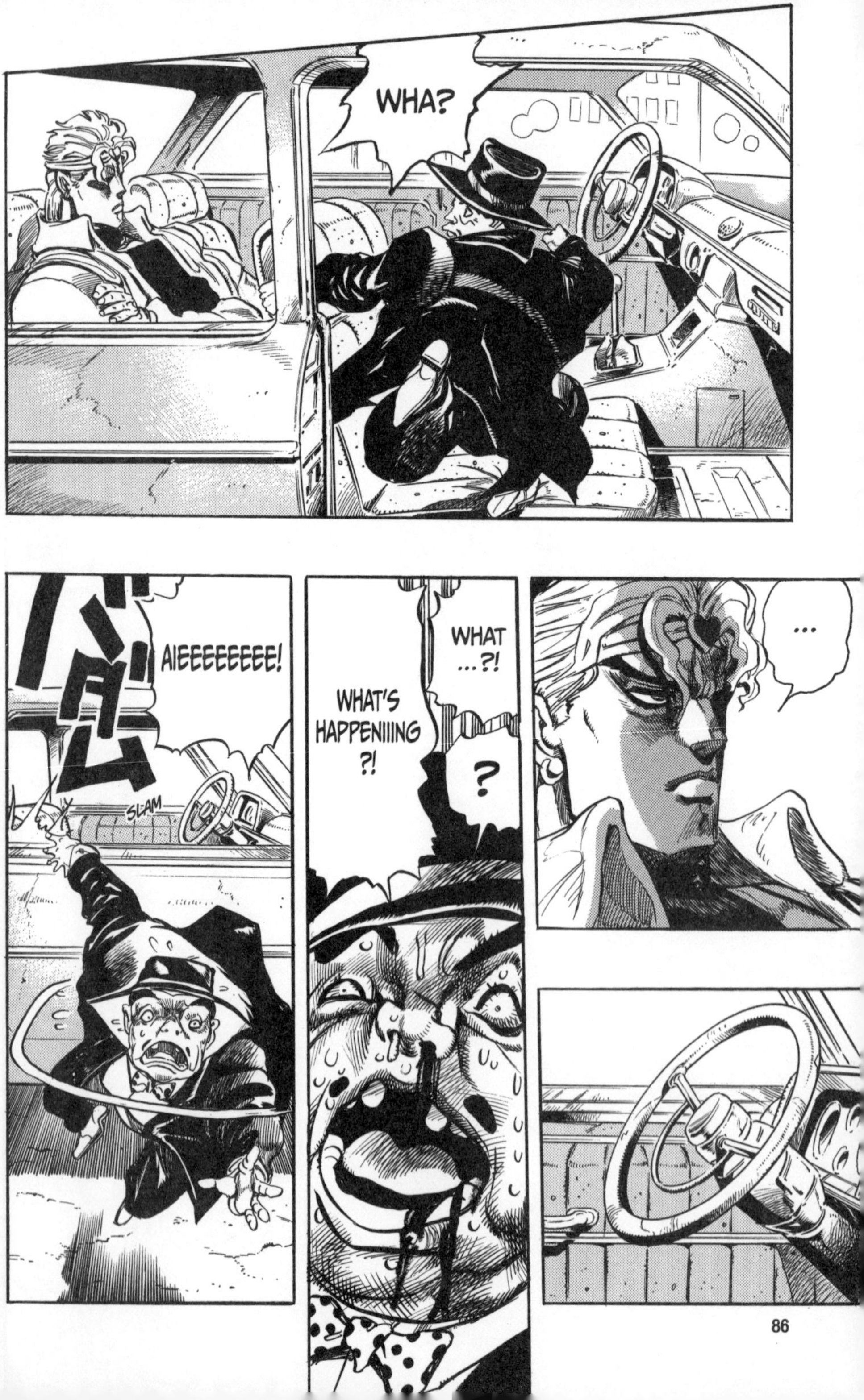
WHA?
...
WHAT ...?!
?
WHAT'S HAPPENIIING ?!
AIEEEEEEEEE!
SLAM

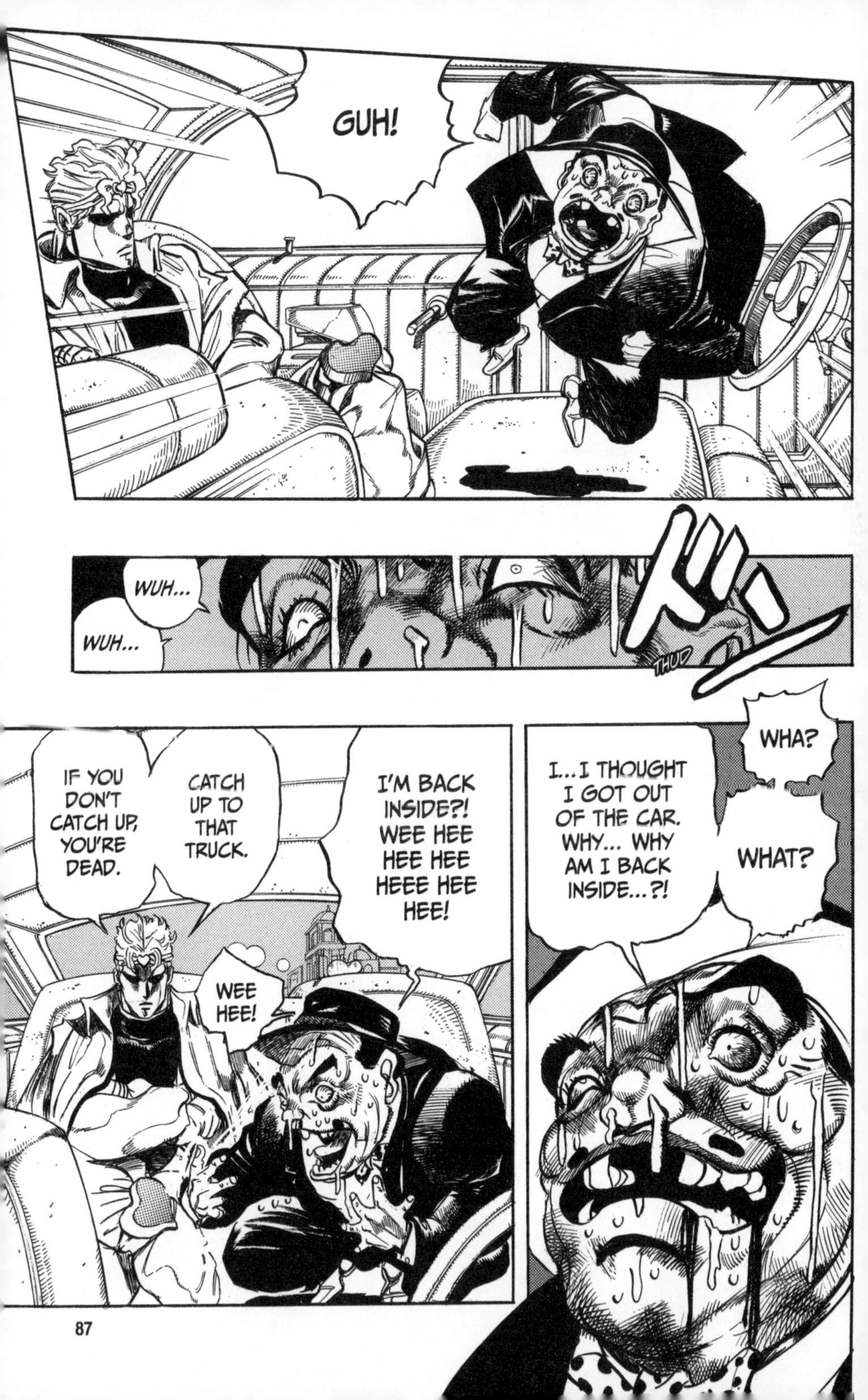
GUH!
THUD
WUH...
WUH...
WHA?
WHAT?
I...I THOUGHT I GOT OUT OF THE CAR. WHY... WHY AM I BACK INSIDE...?!
I'M BACK INSIDE?! WEE HEE HEE HEE HEEE HEE HEE!
WEE HEE!
CATCH UP TO THAT TRUCK.
IF YOU DON'T CATCH UP, YOU'RE DEAD.

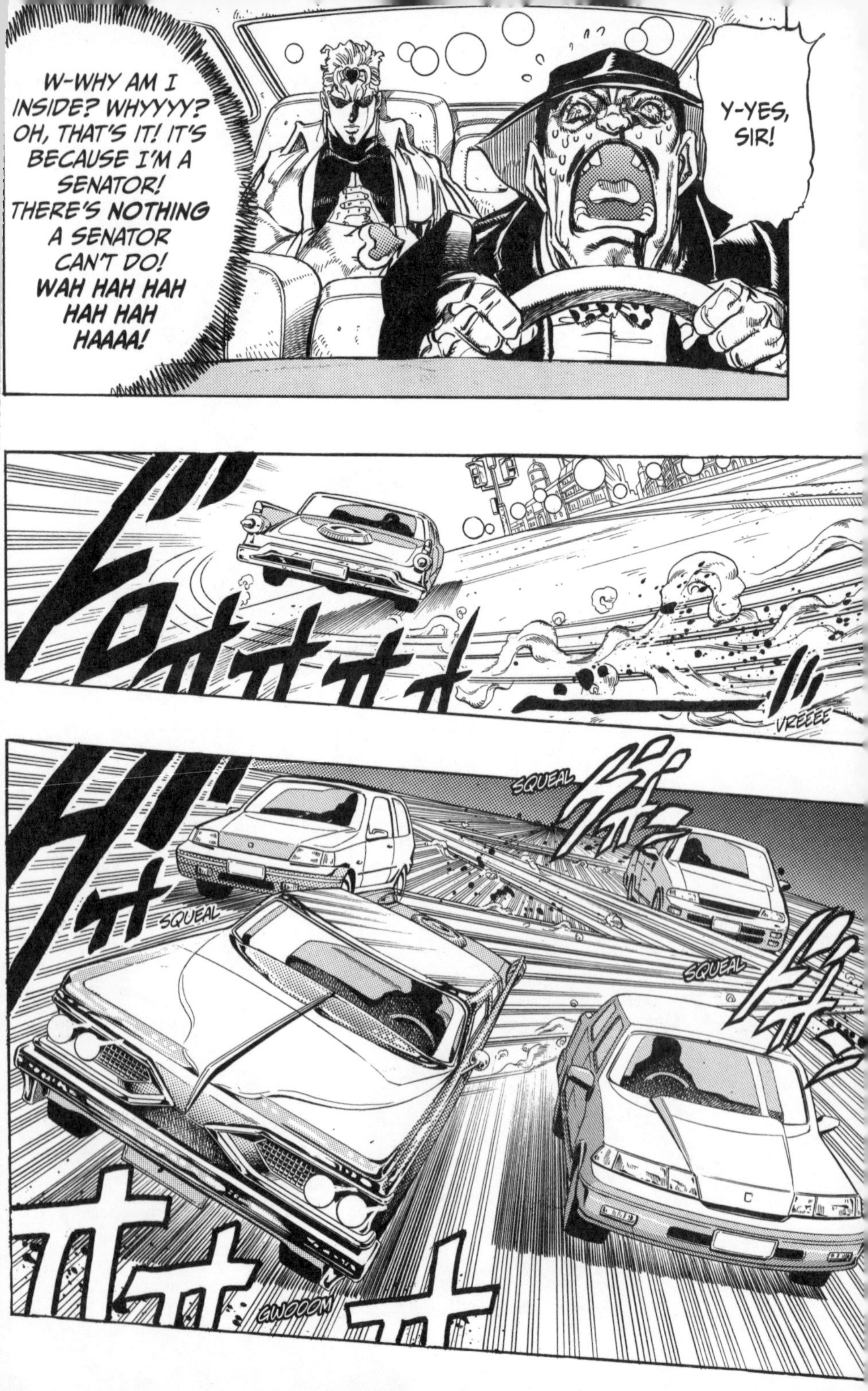
Y-YES, SIR!
W-WHY AM I INSIDE? WHYYYY? OH, THAT'S IT! IT'S BECAUSE I'M A SENATOR! THERE'S NOTHING A SENATOR CAN'T DO! WAH HAH HAH HAH HAH HAAAA!
VREEEE
SQUEAL
SQUEAL
SQUEAL
GWOOOM

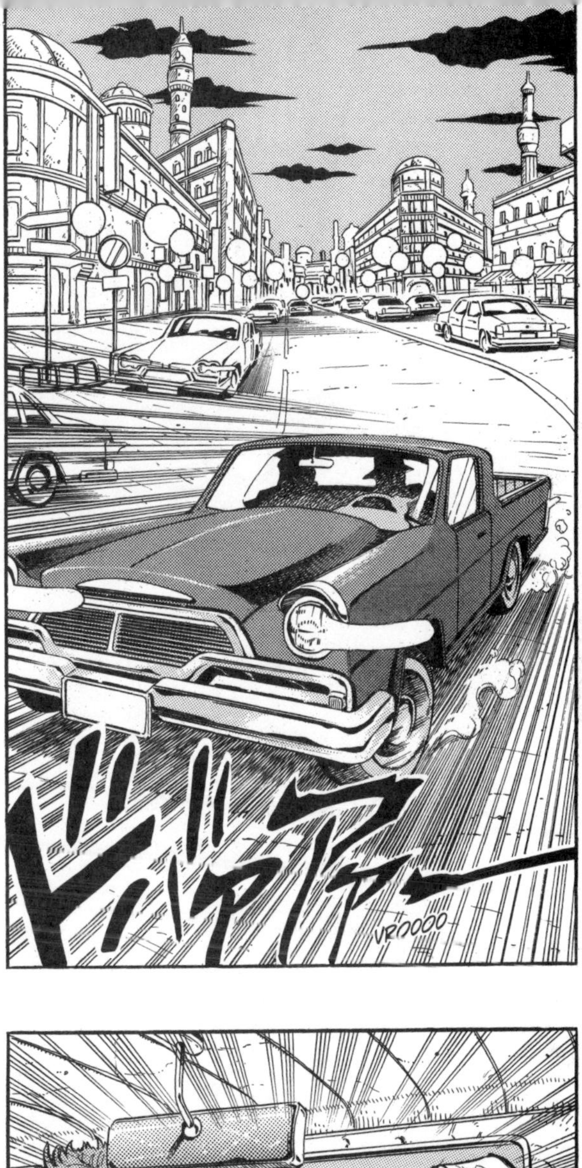
VROOOO
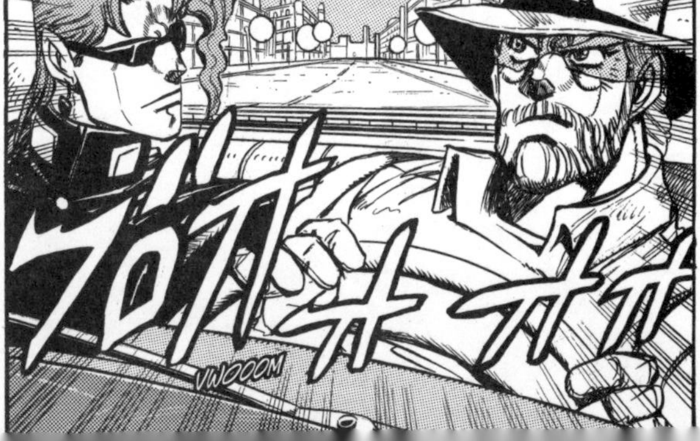
VWOOOM
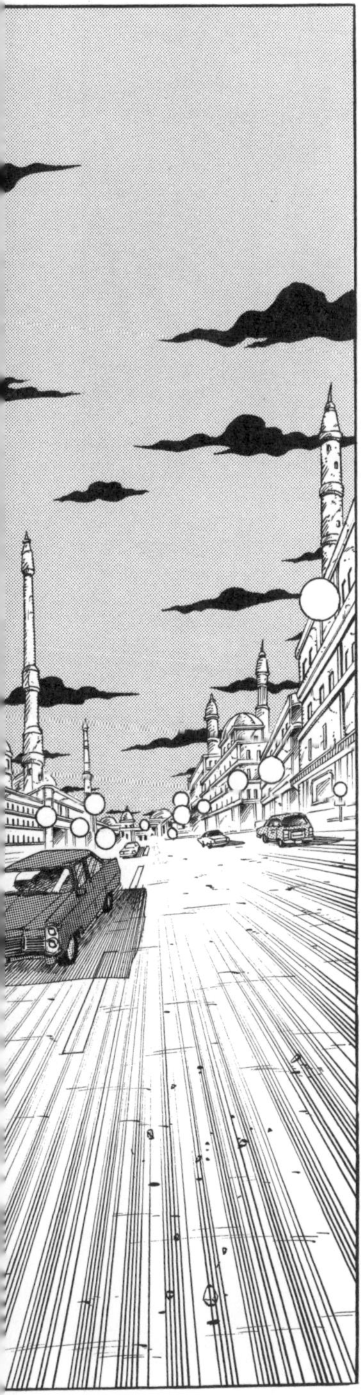

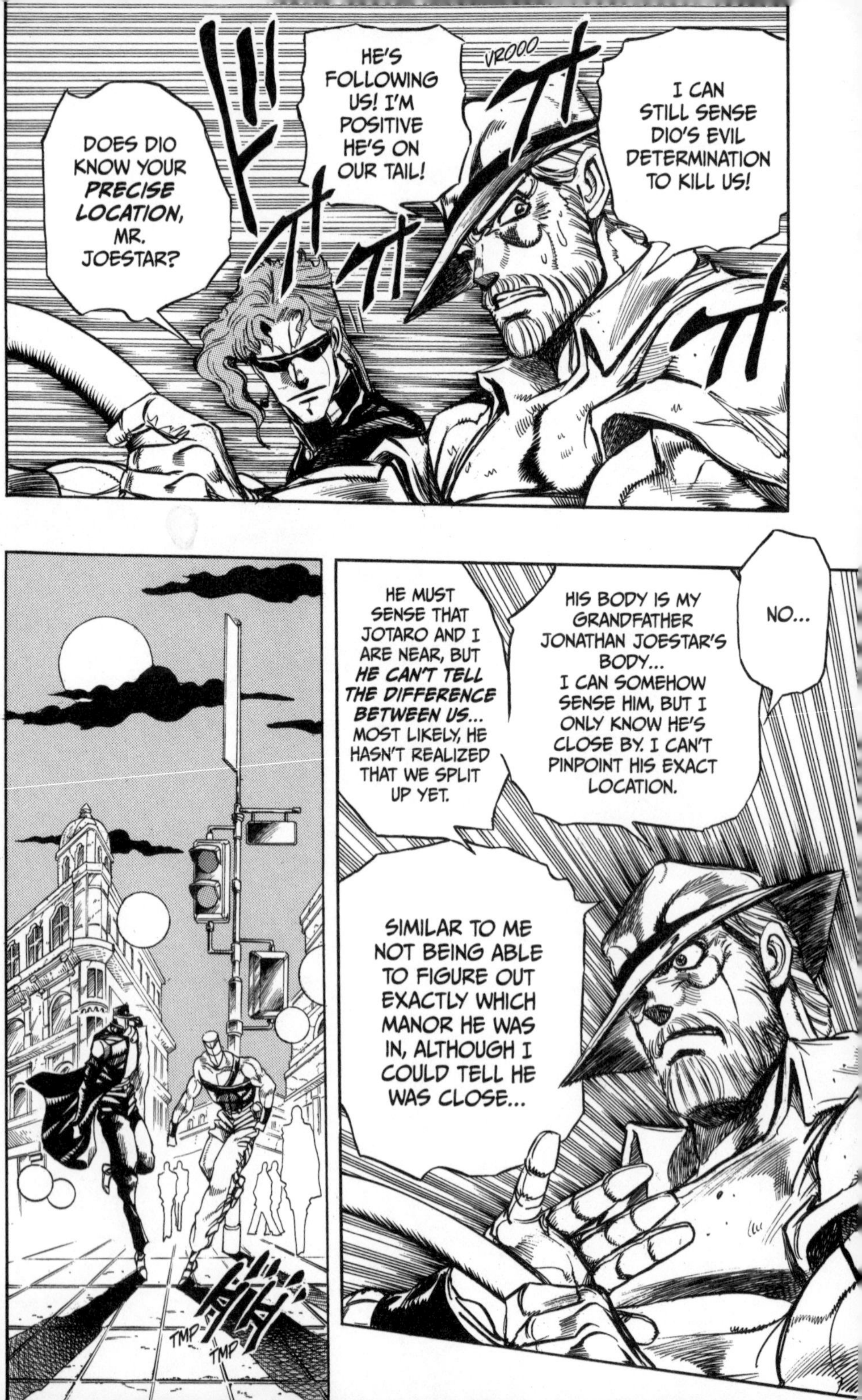
I CAN STILL SENSE DIO'S EVIL DETERMINATION TO KILL US!
VROOO
HE'S FOLLOWING US! I'M POSITIVE HE'S ON OUR TAIL!
DOES DIO KNOW YOUR *PRECISE LOCATION,* MR. JOESTAR?
NO...
HIS BODY IS MY GRANDFATHER JONATHAN JOESTAR'S BODY... I CAN SOMEHOW SENSE HIM, BUT I ONLY KNOW HE'S CLOSE BY. I CAN'T PINPOINT HIS EXACT LOCATION.
HE MUST SENSE THAT JOTARO AND I ARE NEAR, BUT *HE CAN'T TELL THE DIFFERENCE BETWEEN US...* MOST LIKELY, HE HASN'T REALIZED THAT WE SPLIT UP YET.
SIMILAR TO ME NOT BEING ABLE TO FIGURE OUT EXACTLY WHICH MANOR HE WAS IN, ALTHOUGH I COULD TELL HE WAS CLOSE...
TMP
TMP

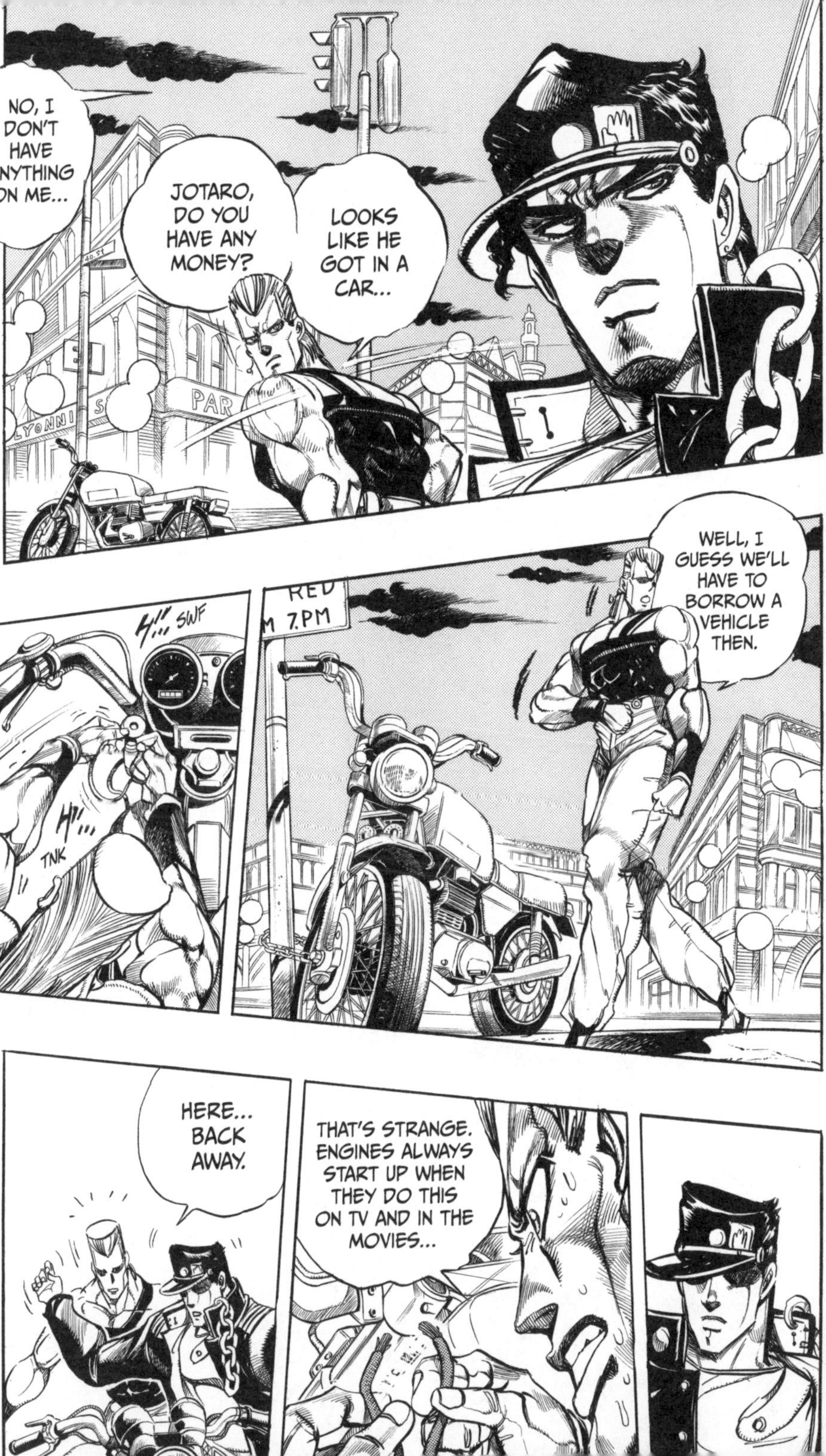
LOOKS LIKE HE GOT IN A CAR...
JOTARO, DO YOU HAVE ANY MONEY?
NO, I DON'T HAVE ANYTHING ON ME...
WELL, I GUESS WE'LL HAVE TO BORROW A VEHICLE THEN.
RED
M 7.PM
SWF
TNK
THAT'S STRANGE. ENGINES ALWAYS START UP WHEN THEY DO THIS ON TV AND IN THE MOVIES...
HERE... BACK AWAY.

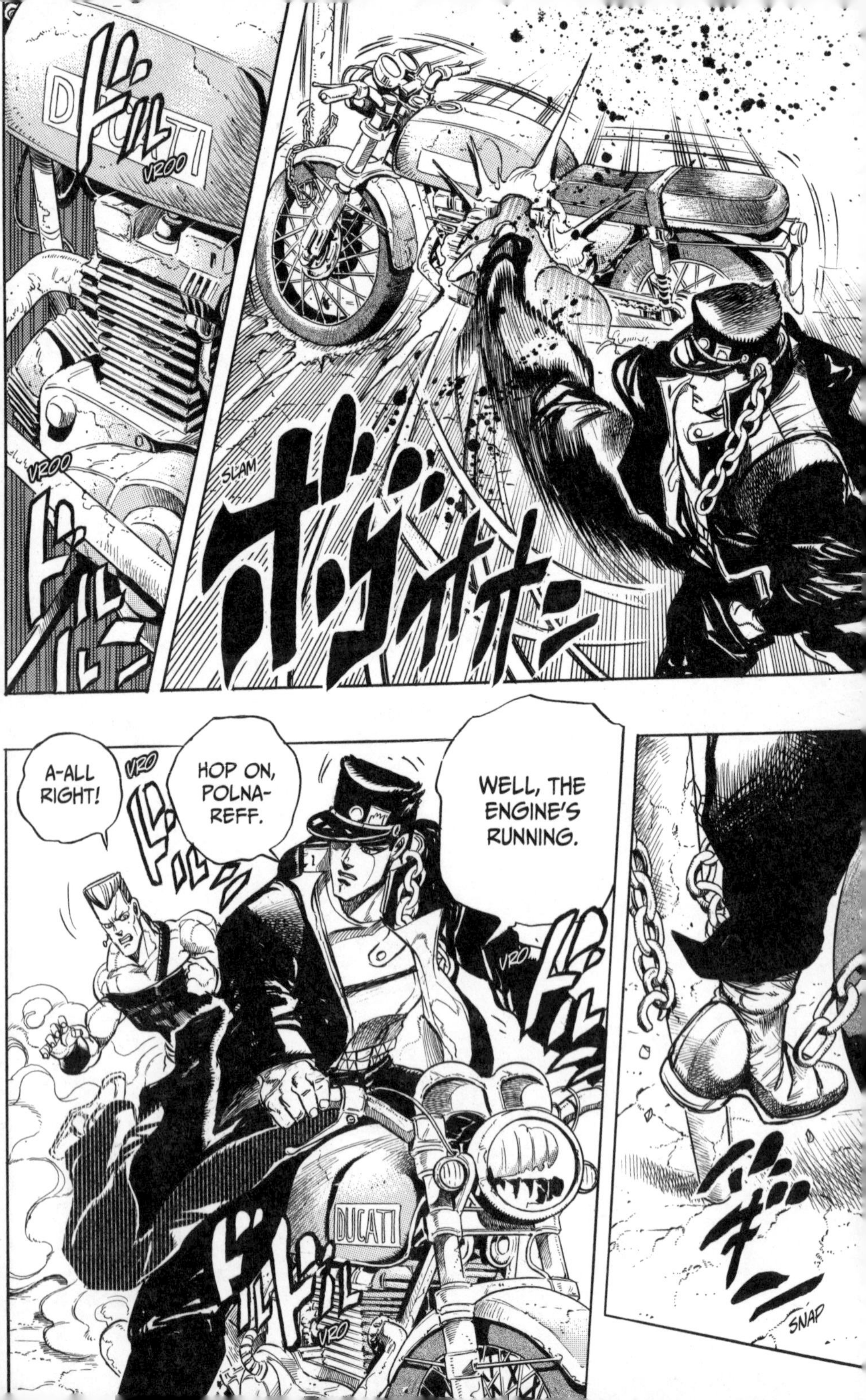
SLAM
DUCATI
VROO
VROO
SNAP
WELL, THE ENGINE'S RUNNING.
VRO
HOP ON, POLNAREFF.
VRO
A-ALL RIGHT!
DUCATI
VRO

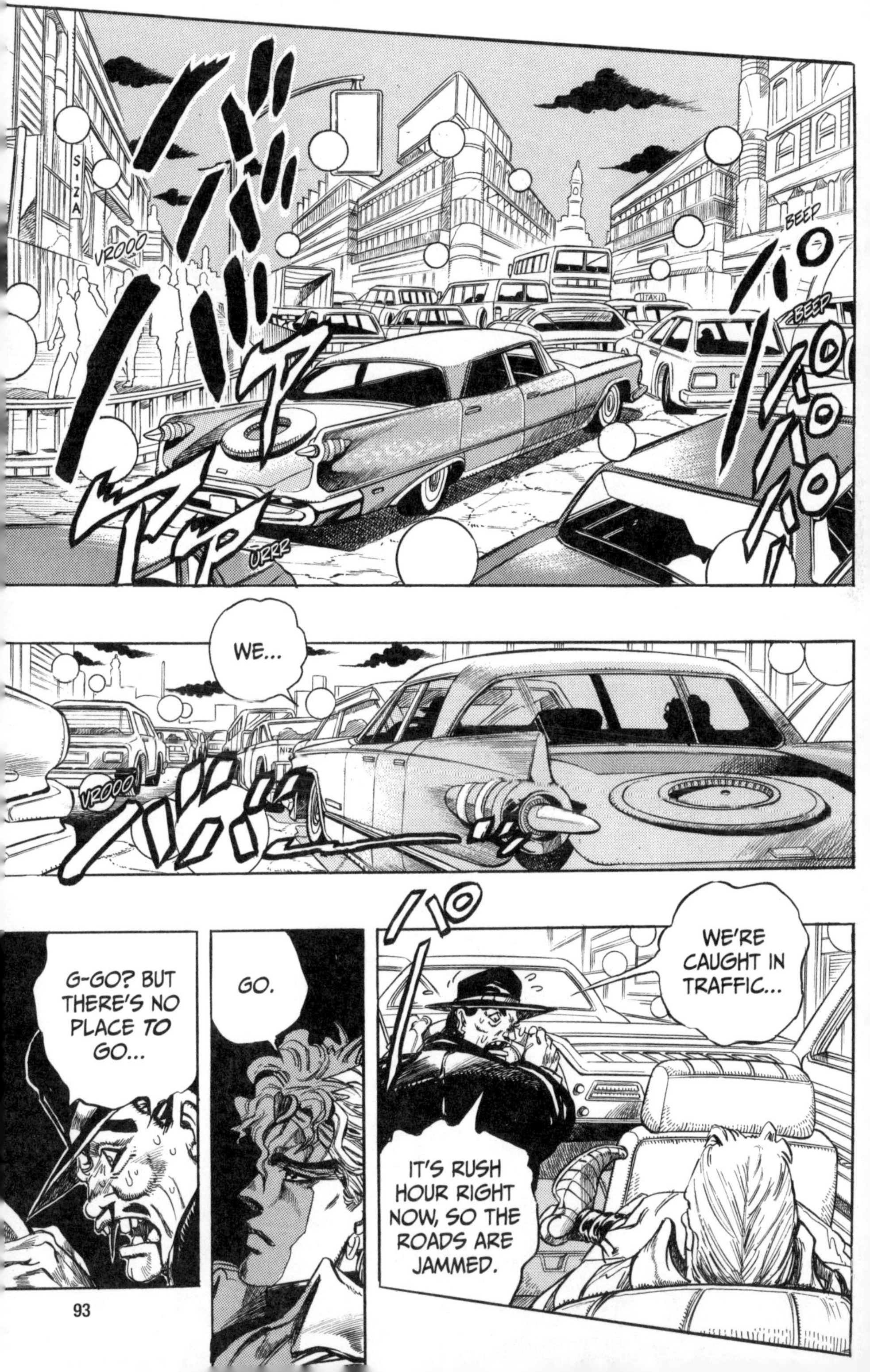
BEEP
BEEP
VROOO
URRR
WE...
VROOO
WE'RE CAUGHT IN TRAFFIC...
IT'S RUSH HOUR RIGHT NOW, SO THE ROADS ARE JAMMED.
GO.
G-GO? BUT THERE'S NO PLACE TO GO...

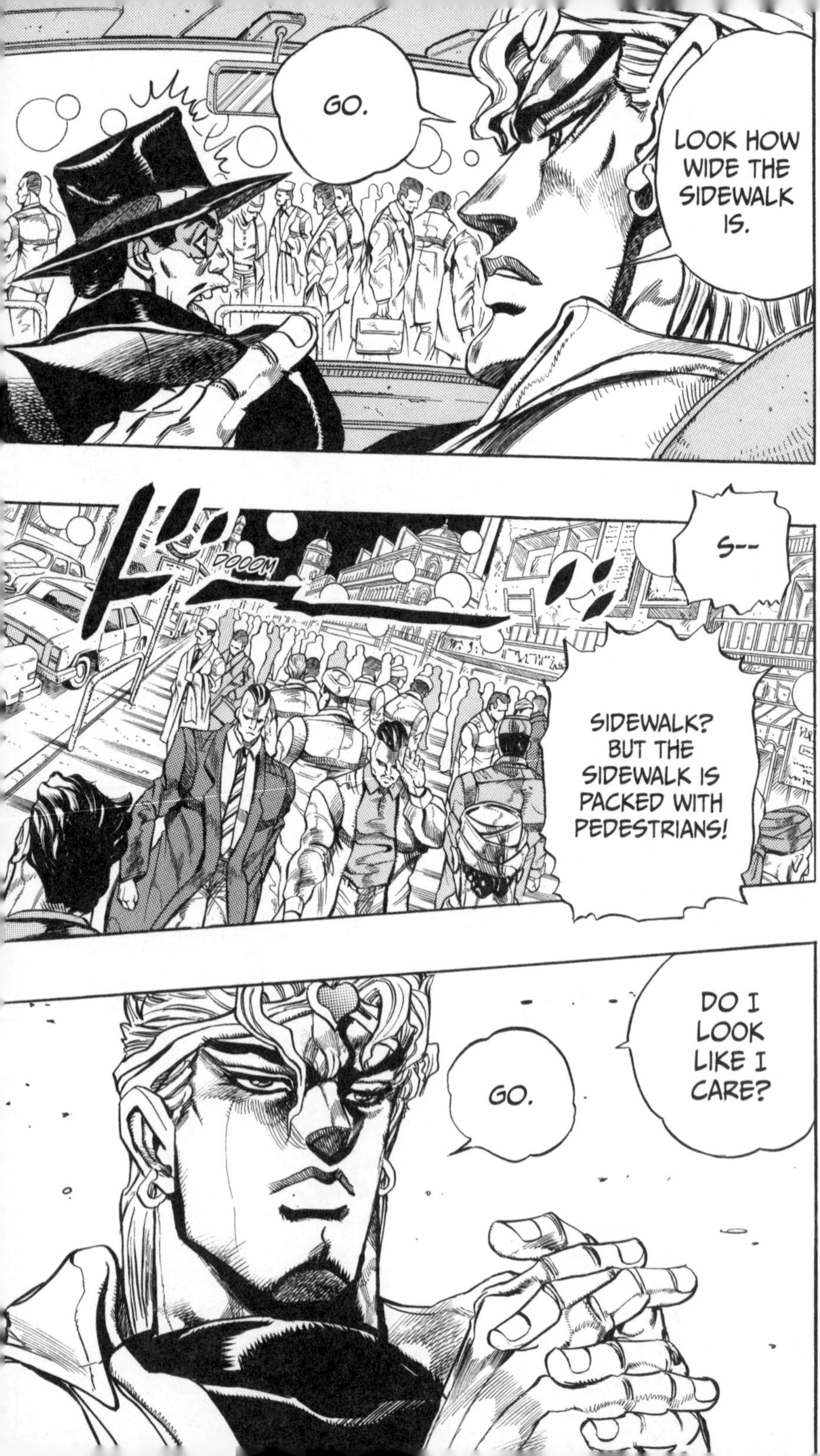
LOOK HOW WIDE THE SIDEWALK IS.
GO.
S--
DOOOM
SIDEWALK? BUT THE SIDEWALK IS PACKED WITH PEDESTRIANS!
DO I LOOK LIKE I CARE?
GO.

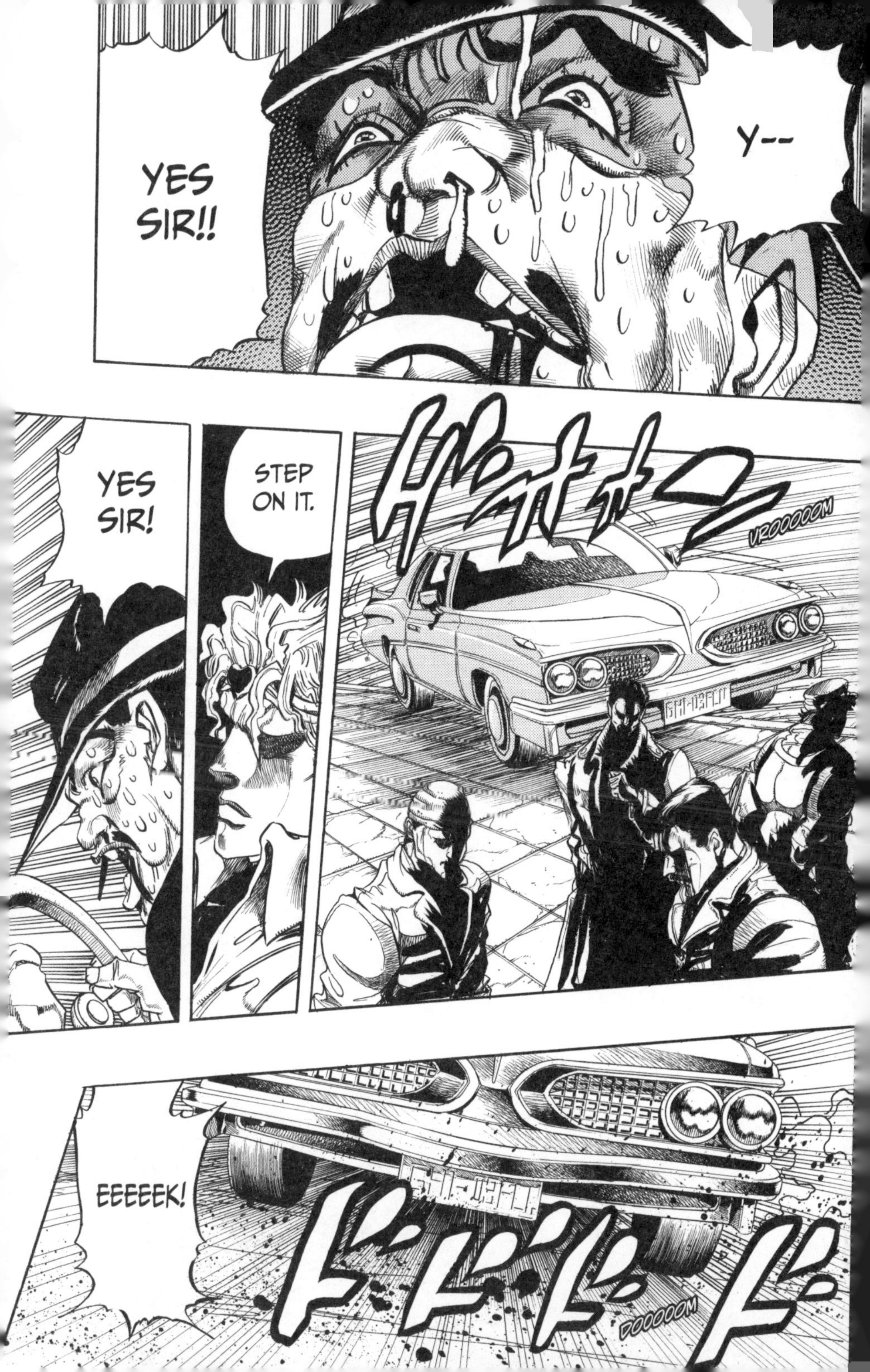
Y--
YES SIR!!
VROOOOOM
STEP ON IT.
YES SIR!
EEEEEK!
DOOOOOM

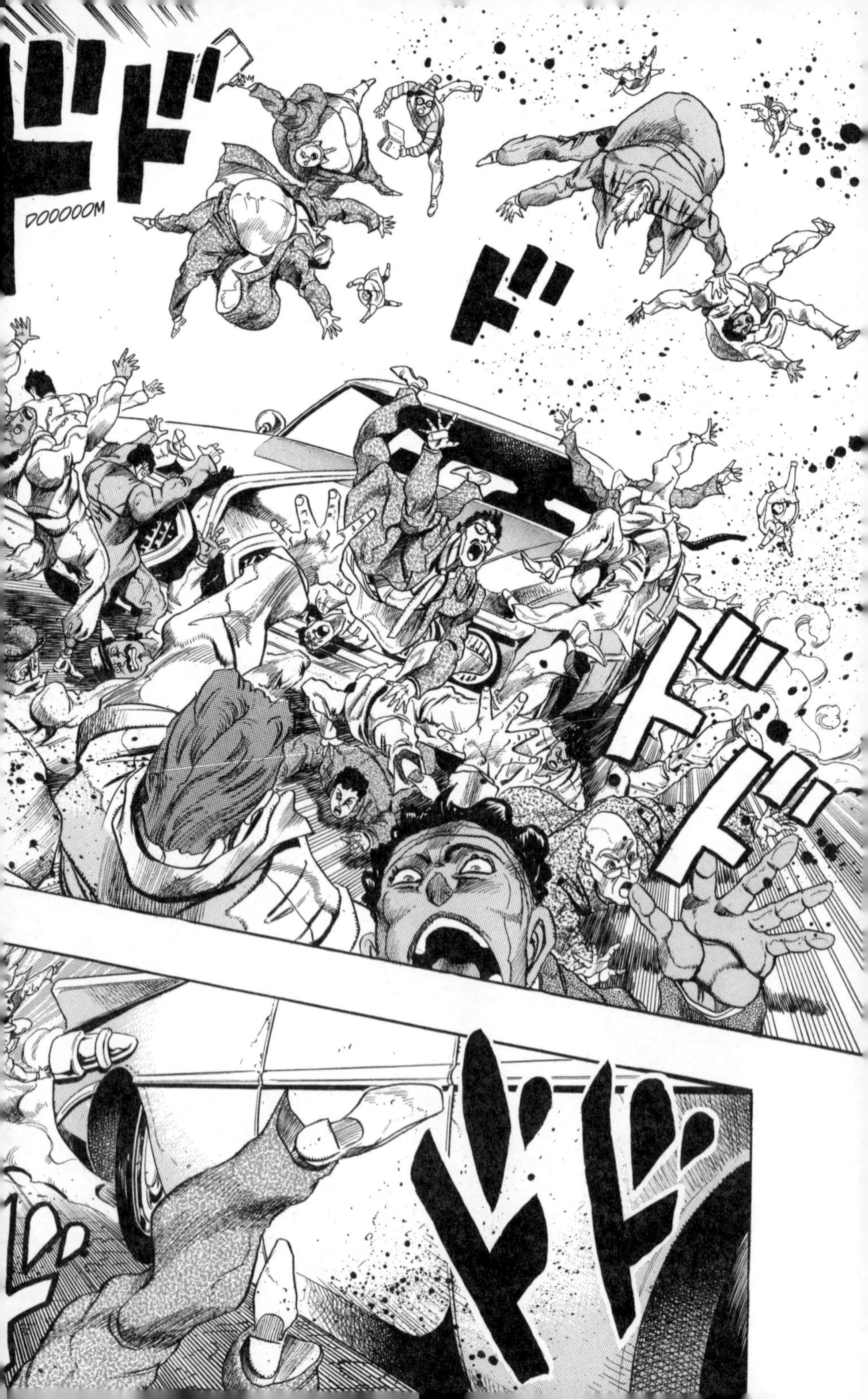
ド
ドド
DOOOOOM
ドド
ドド

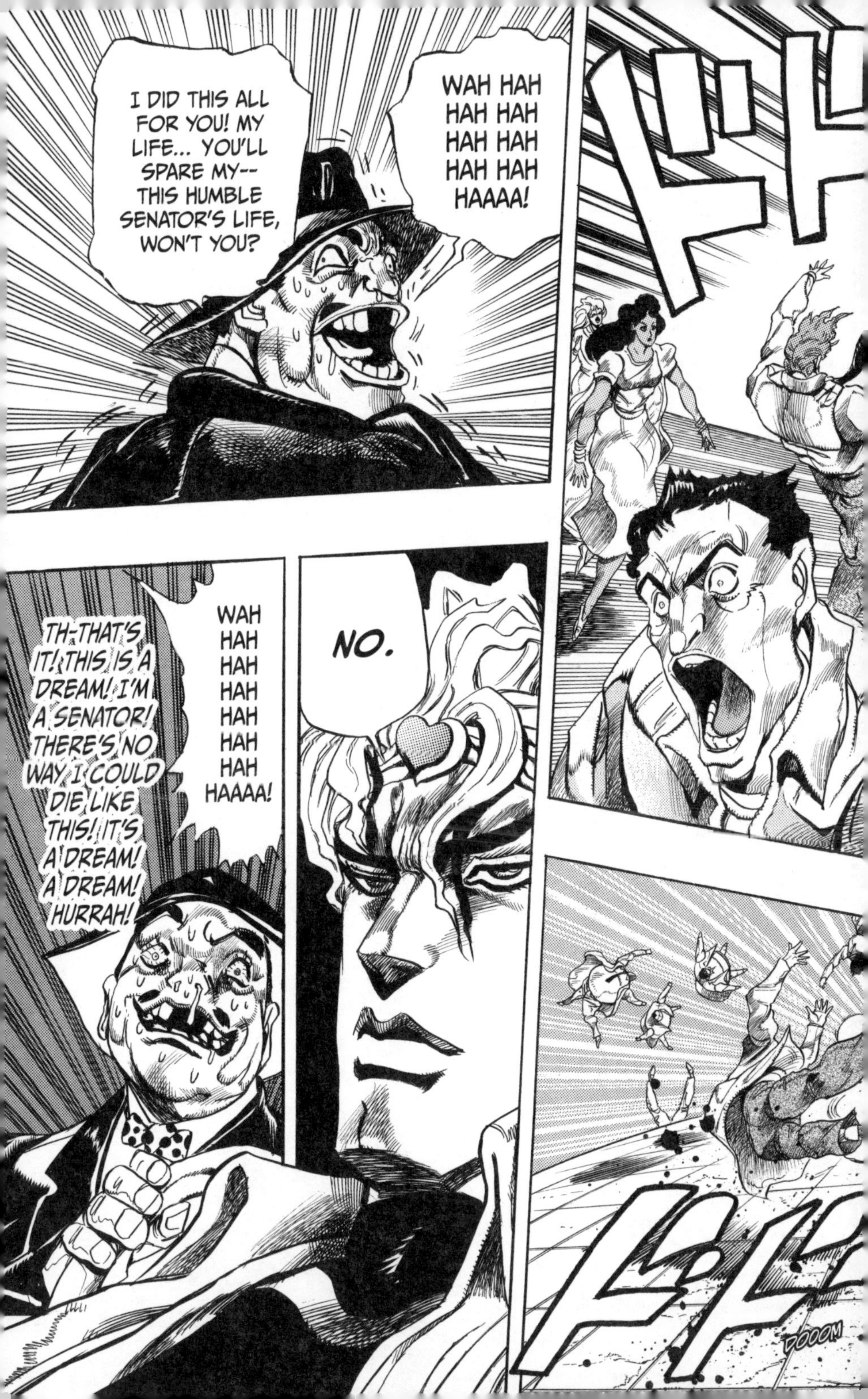
ドドド
WAH HAH HAH HAH HAH HAH HAH HAH HAAAA!
I DID THIS ALL FOR YOU! MY LIFE... YOU'LL SPARE MY-- THIS HUMBLE SENATOR'S LIFE, WON'T YOU?
NO.
WAH HAH HAH HAH HAH HAH HAH HAAAA!
TH-THAT'S IT! THIS IS A DREAM! I'M A SENATOR! THERE'S NO WAY I COULD DIE LIKE THIS! IT'S A DREAM! A DREAM! HURRAH!
ドド
DOOOM

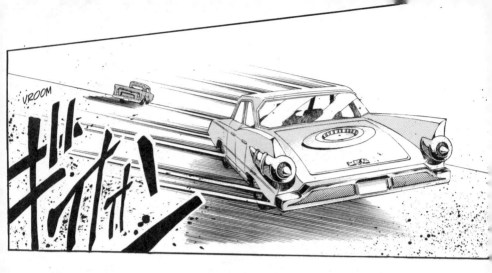

VROOM

GWOOOOO

DOOOM

THERE THEY ARE.

CATCH UP... GET CLOSER.

I CAN'T USE *THE WORLD* UNLESS I GET CLOSE TO THEM...

DOOOOM

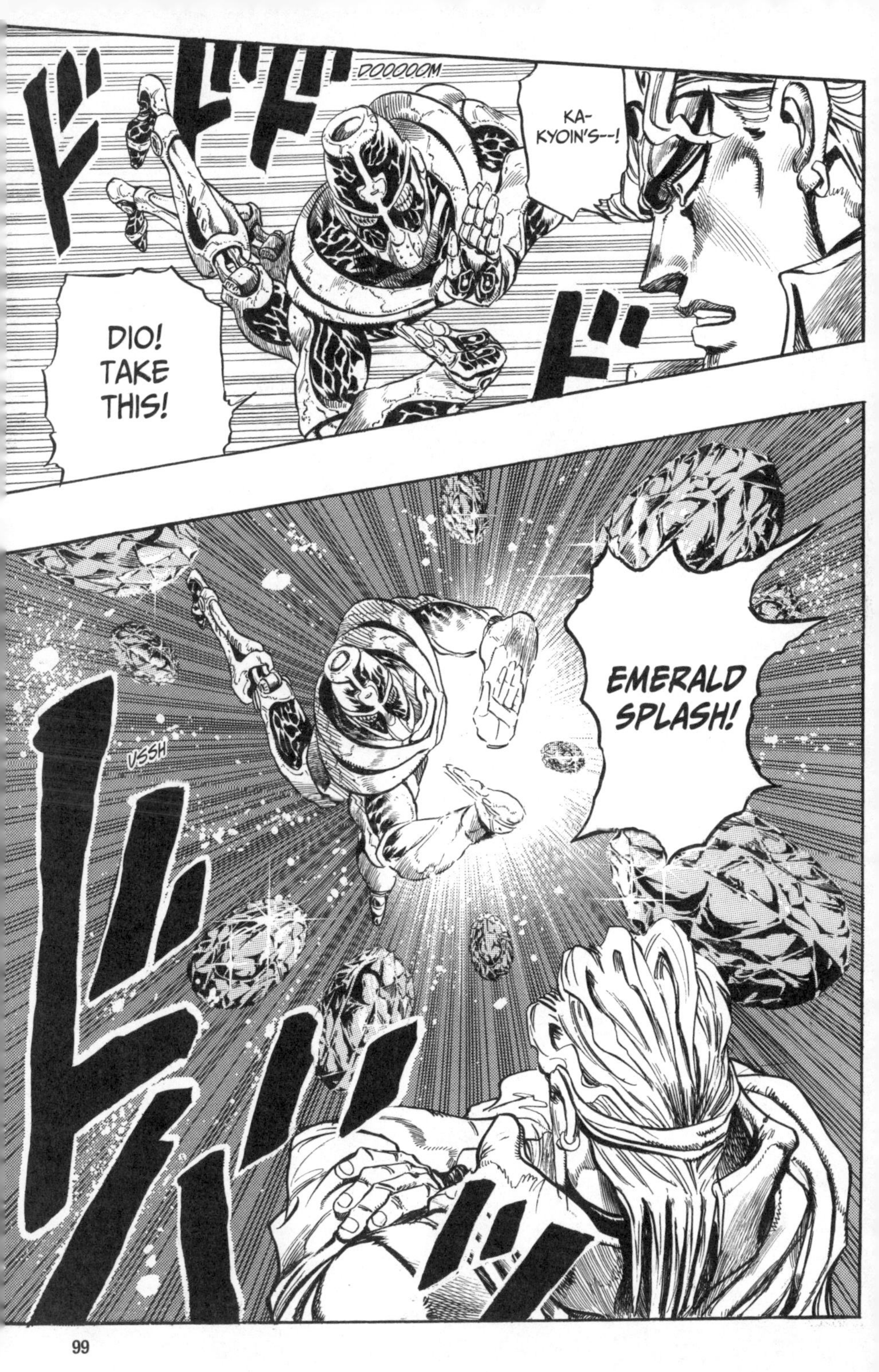
KA-KYOIN'S--!
DOOOOOM
DIO! TAKE THIS!
EMERALD SPLASH!
VSSH

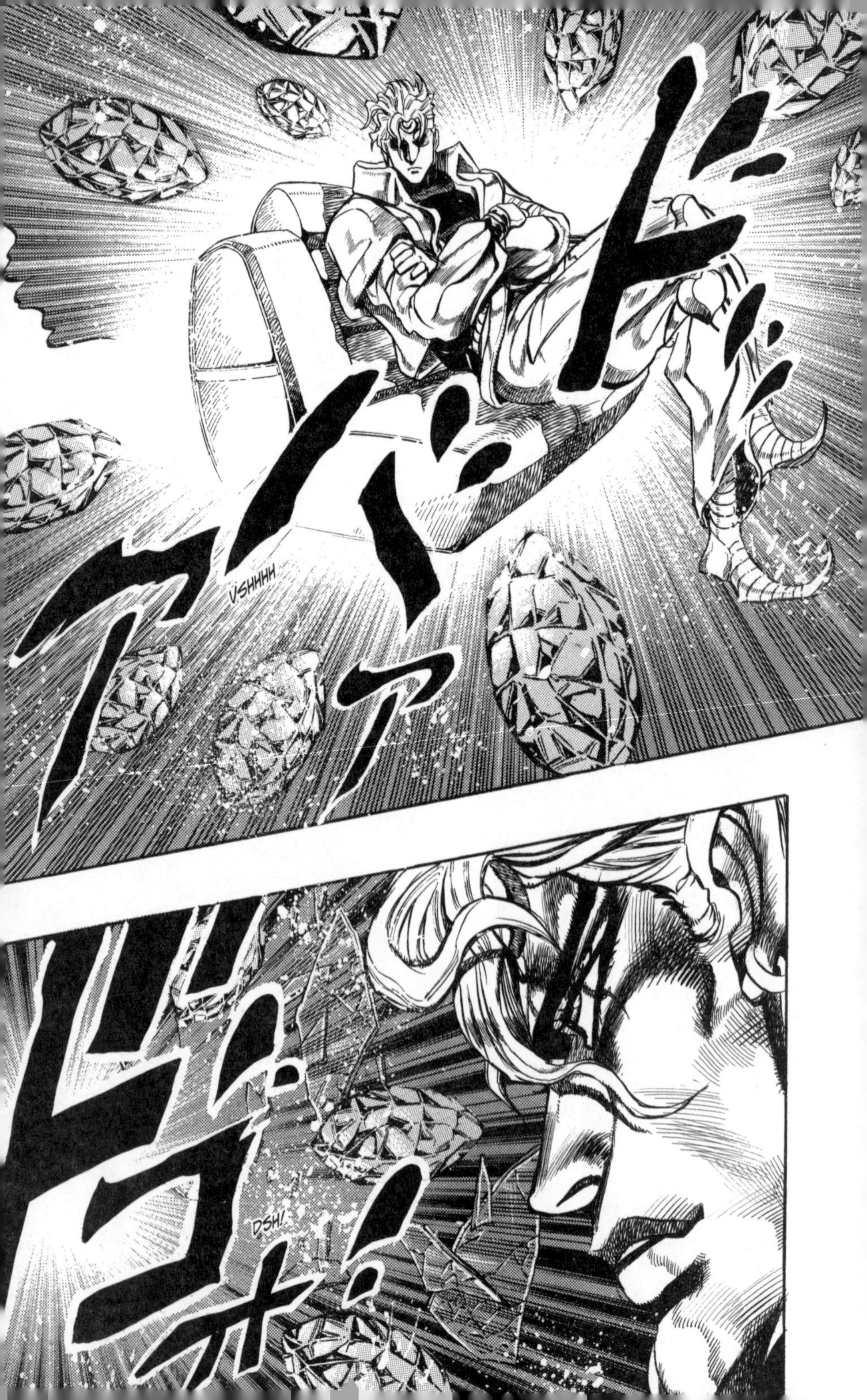

V'SHHHH
DSH!

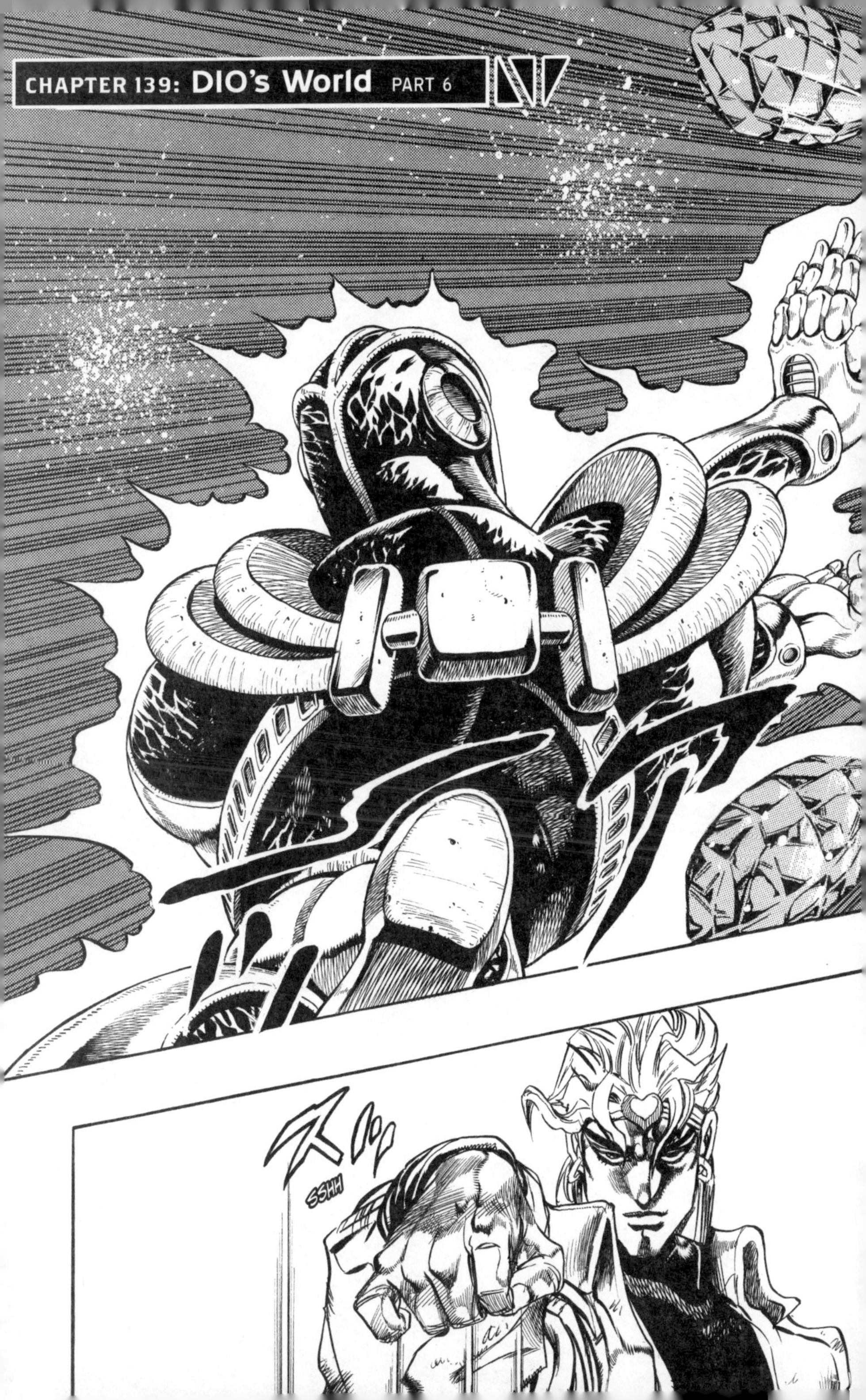

CHAPTER 139: DIO's World PART 6
SSHH

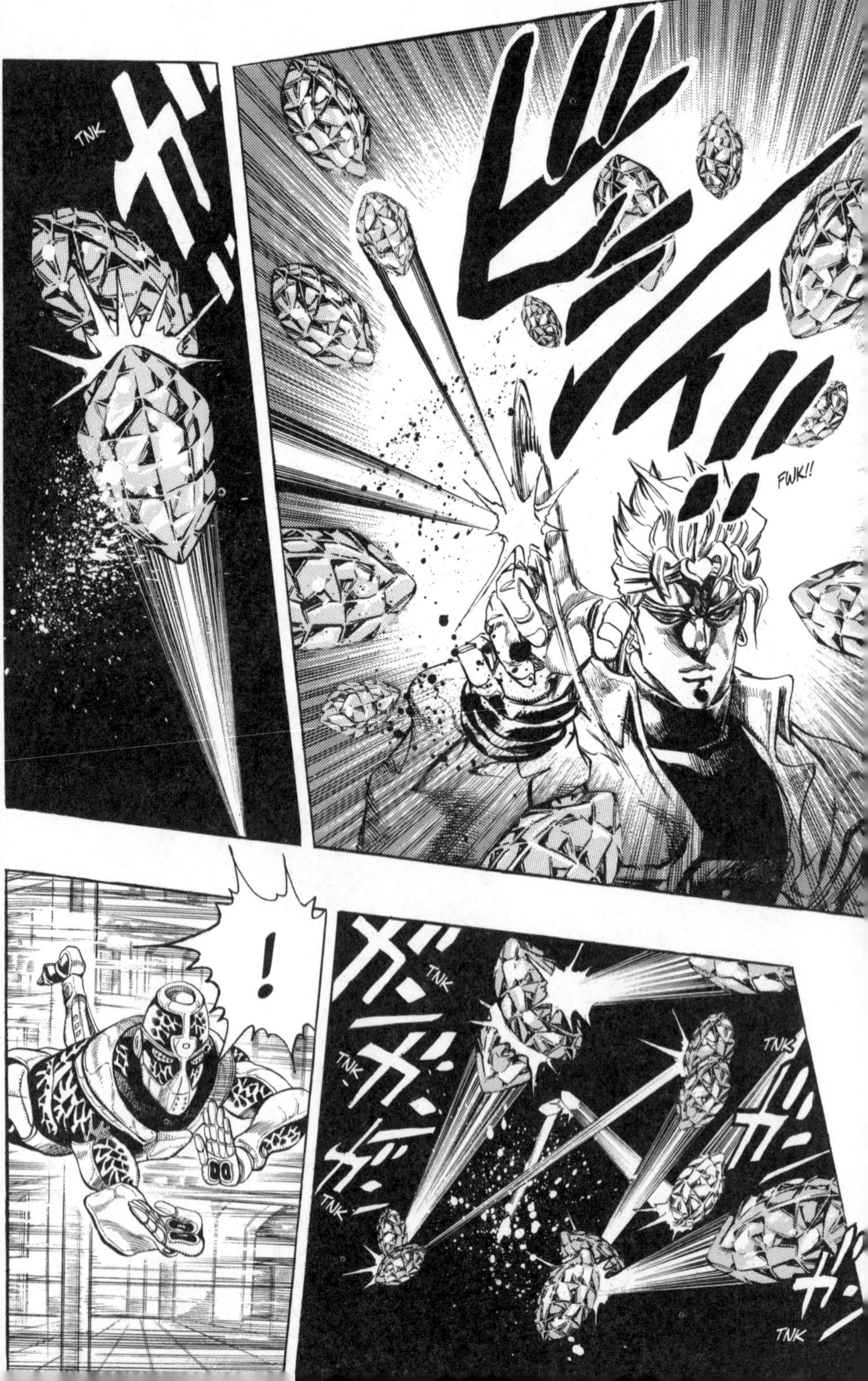
FWK!!
TNK
TNK
TNK
TNK
TNK
TNK
!

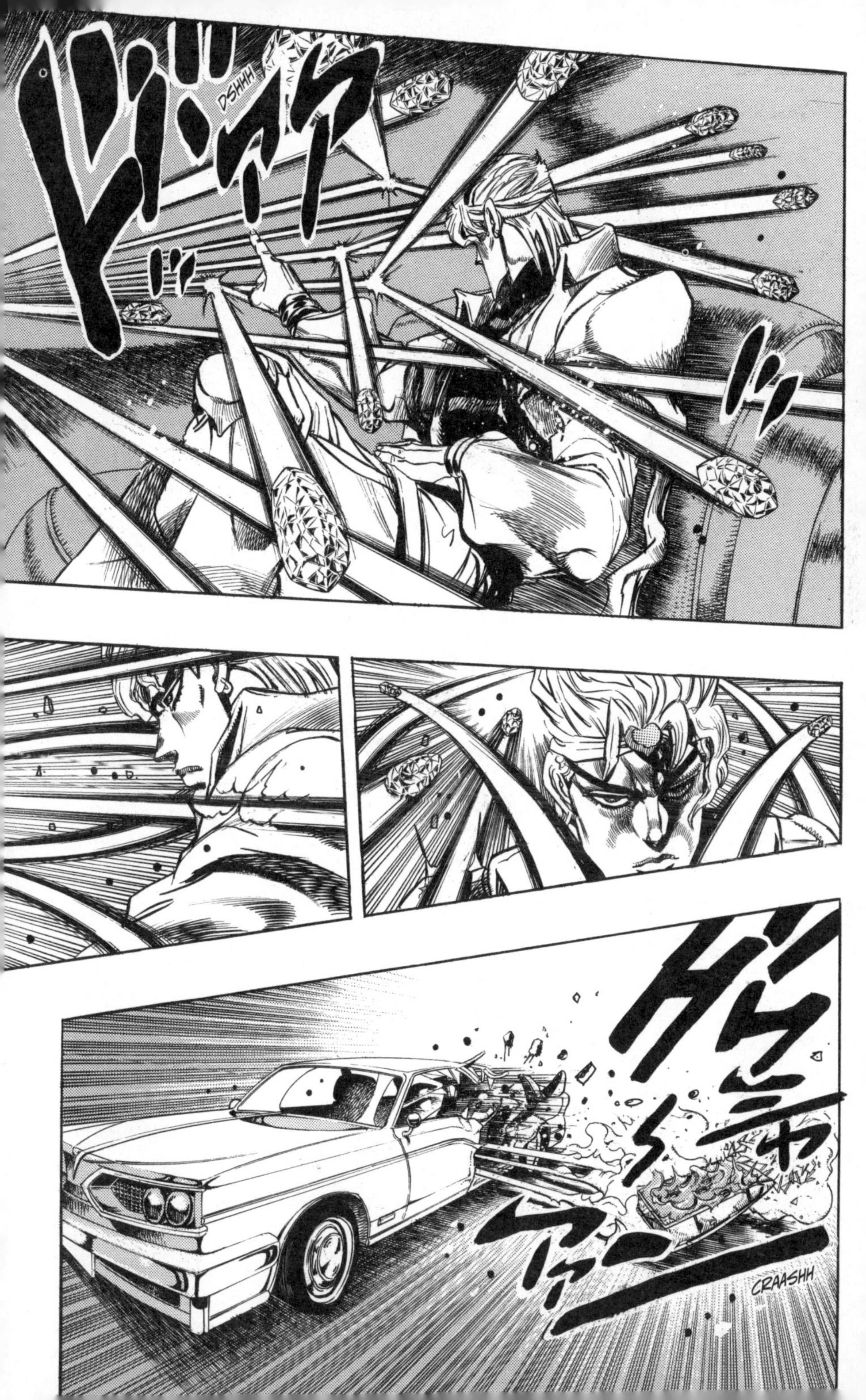
DSHHH
CRAASHH

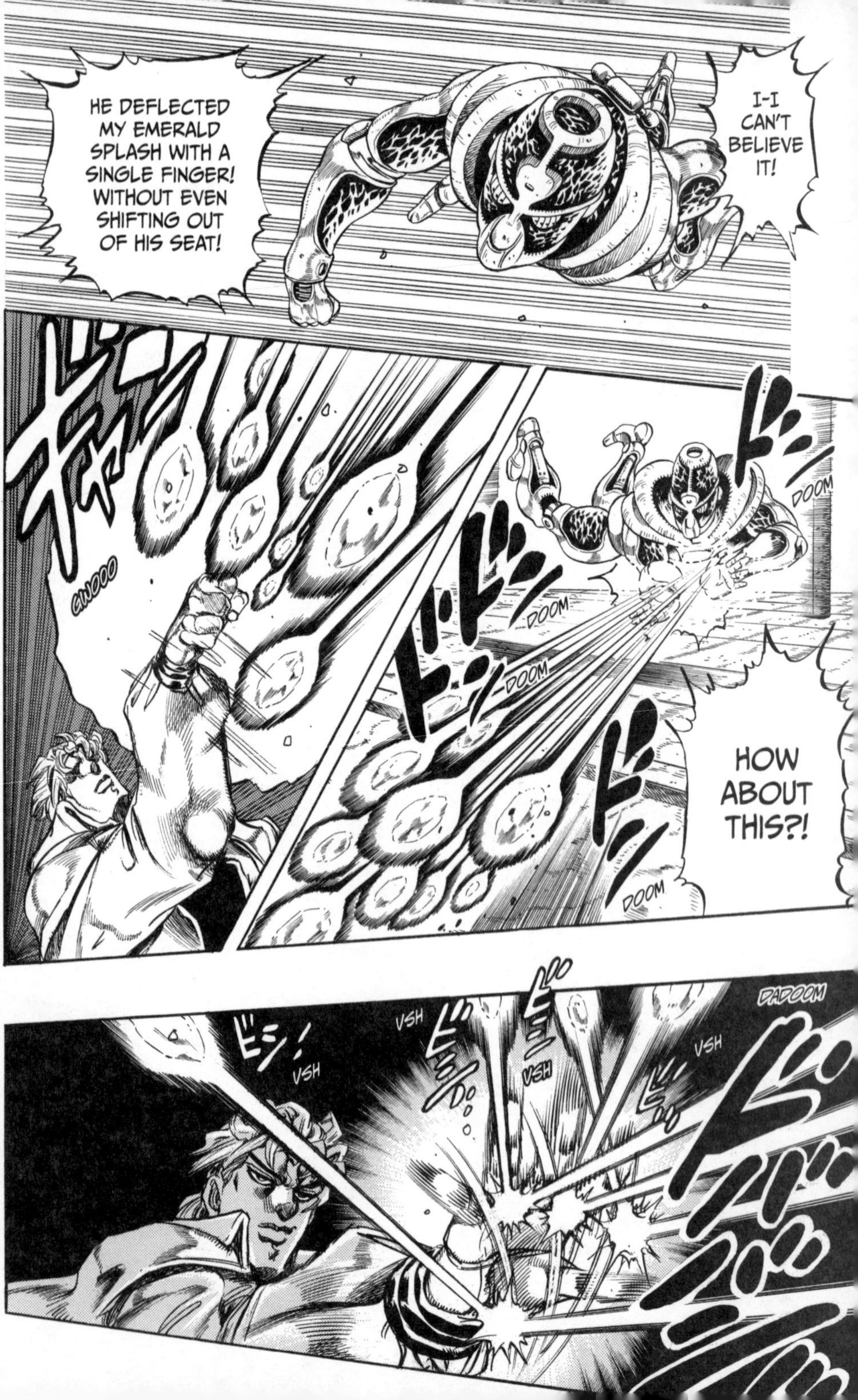
I-I CAN'T BELIEVE IT!
HE DEFLECTED MY EMERALD SPLASH WITH A SINGLE FINGER! WITHOUT EVEN SHIFTING OUT OF HIS SEAT!
DOOM
DOOM
DOOM
HOW ABOUT THIS?!
DOOM
GWOOO
DADOOM
VSH
VSH
VSH
VSH

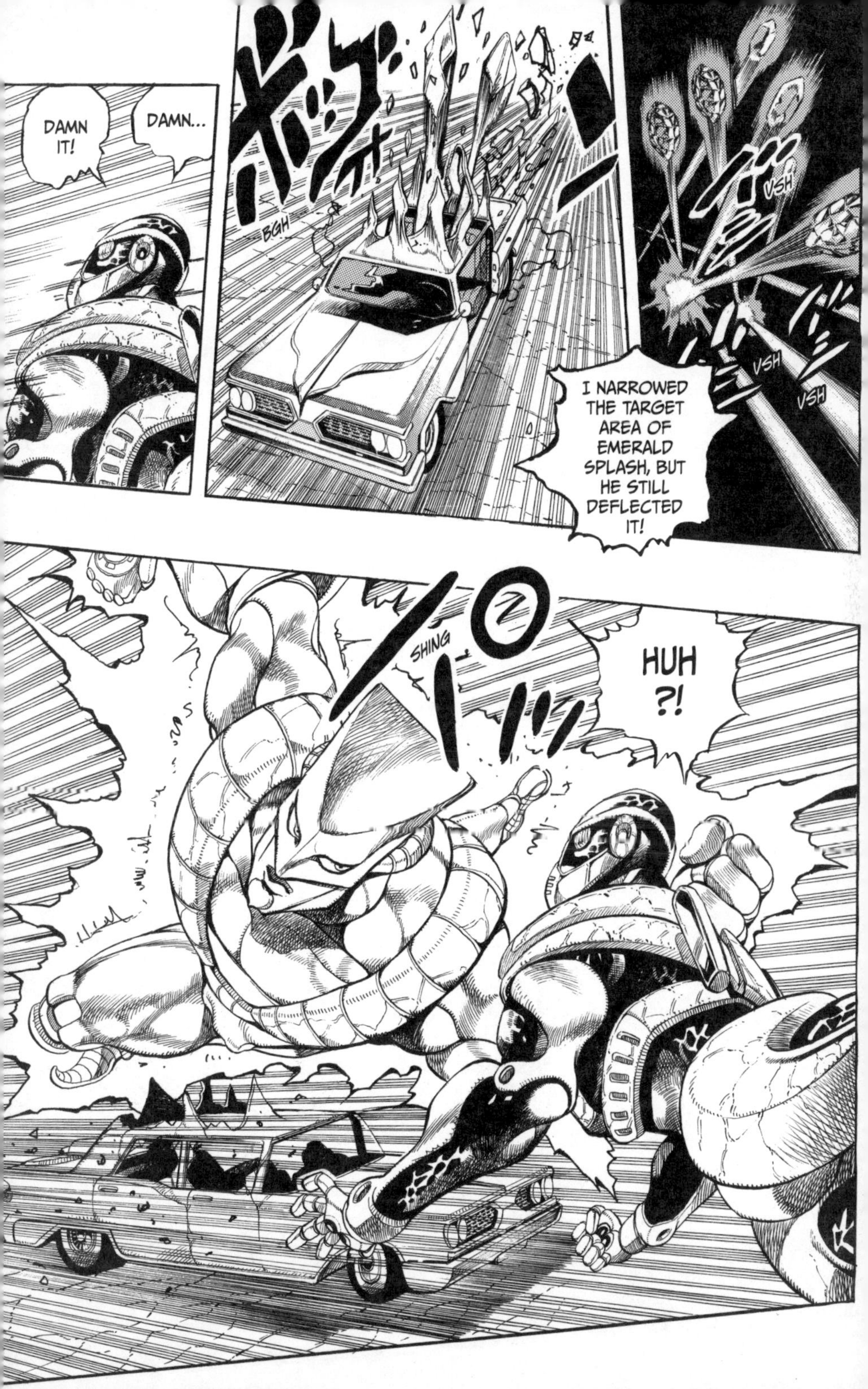
VSH
VSH
VSH
I NARROWED THE TARGET AREA OF EMERALD SPLASH, BUT HE STILL DEFLECTED IT!
BGH
DAMN...
DAMN IT!
HUH ?!
SHING

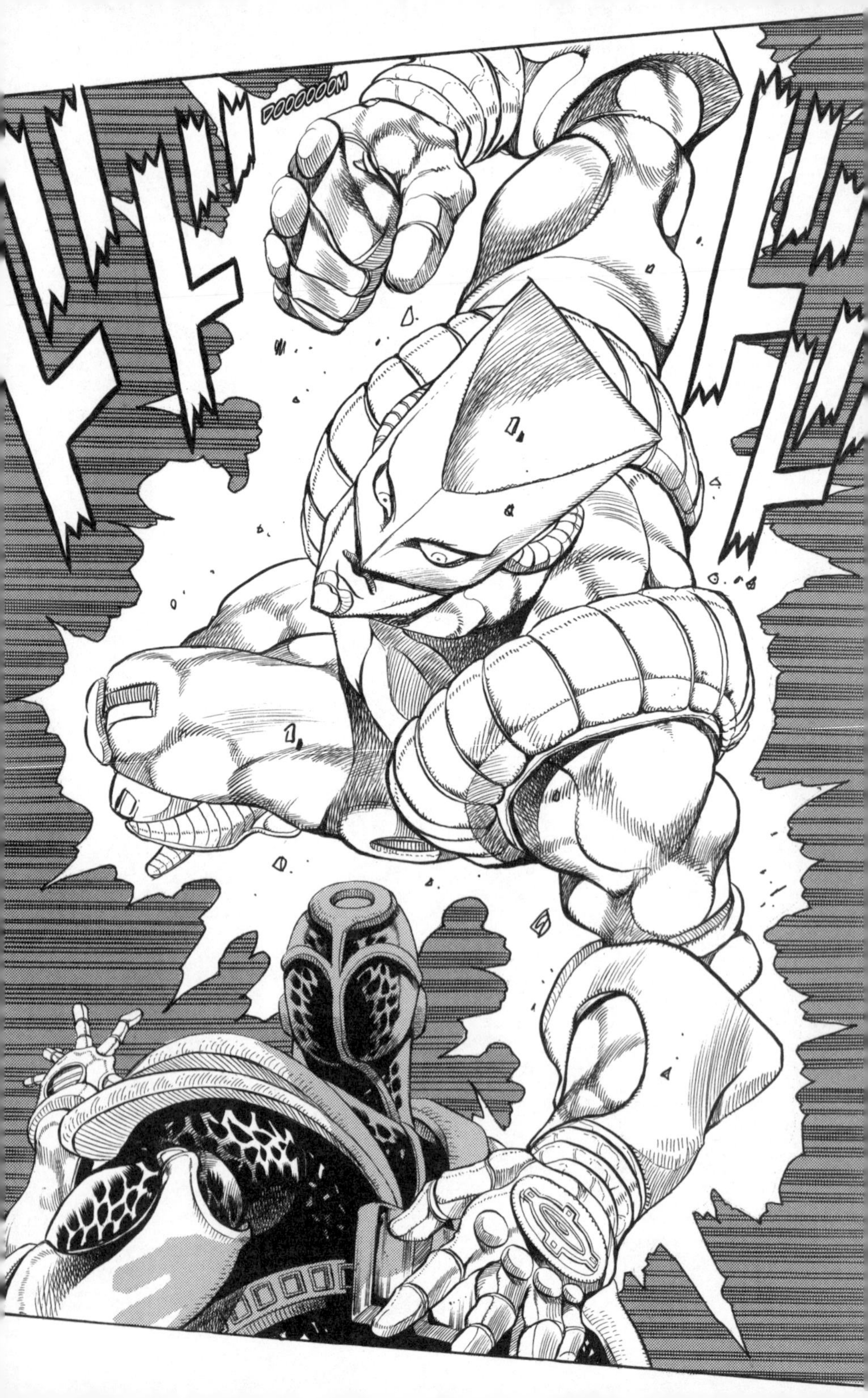
DOOOOOOM

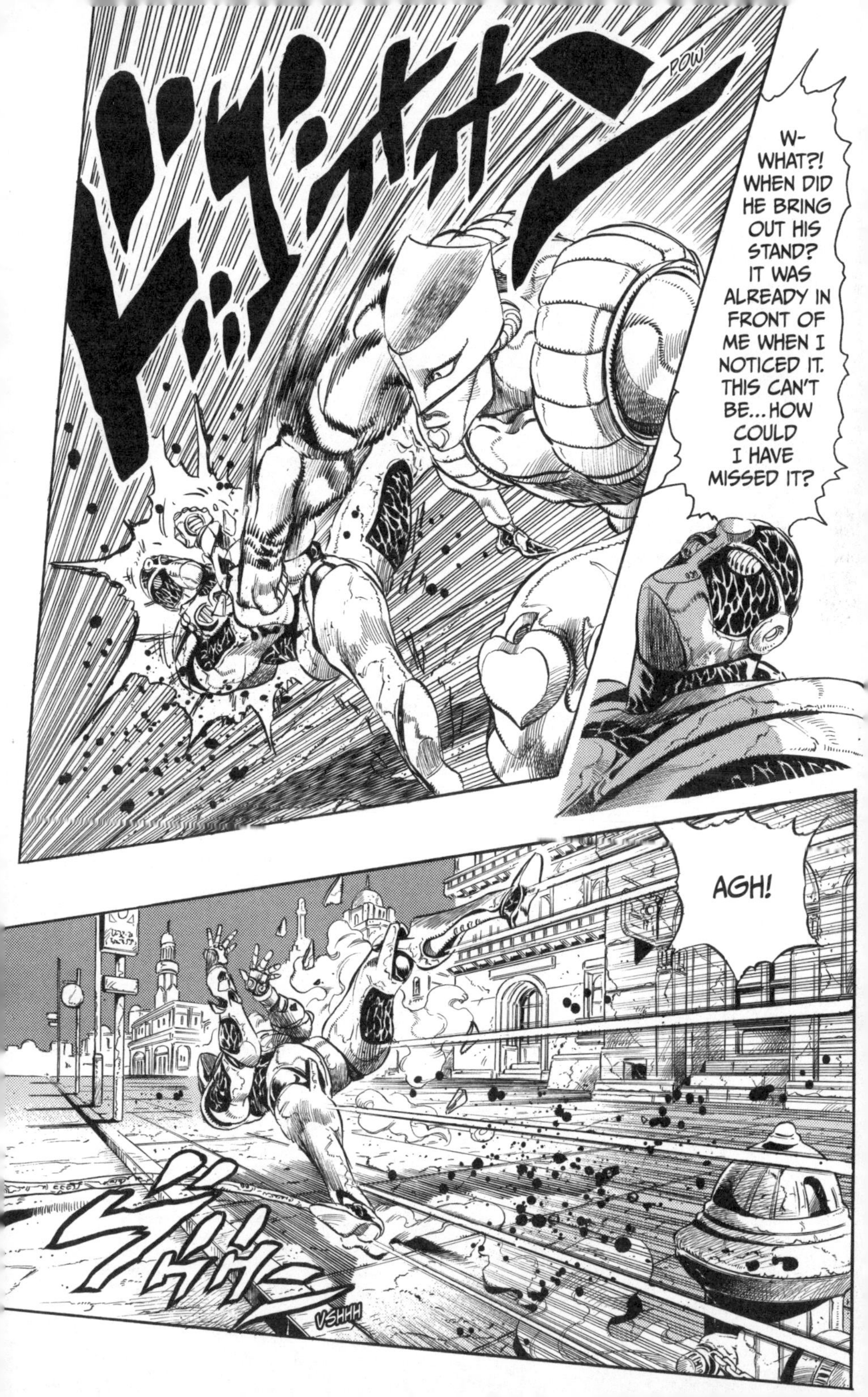
POW
W-WHAT?! WHEN DID HE BRING OUT HIS STAND? IT WAS ALREADY IN FRONT OF ME WHEN I NOTICED IT. THIS CAN'T BE...HOW COULD I HAVE MISSED IT?
AGH!
VSHHH

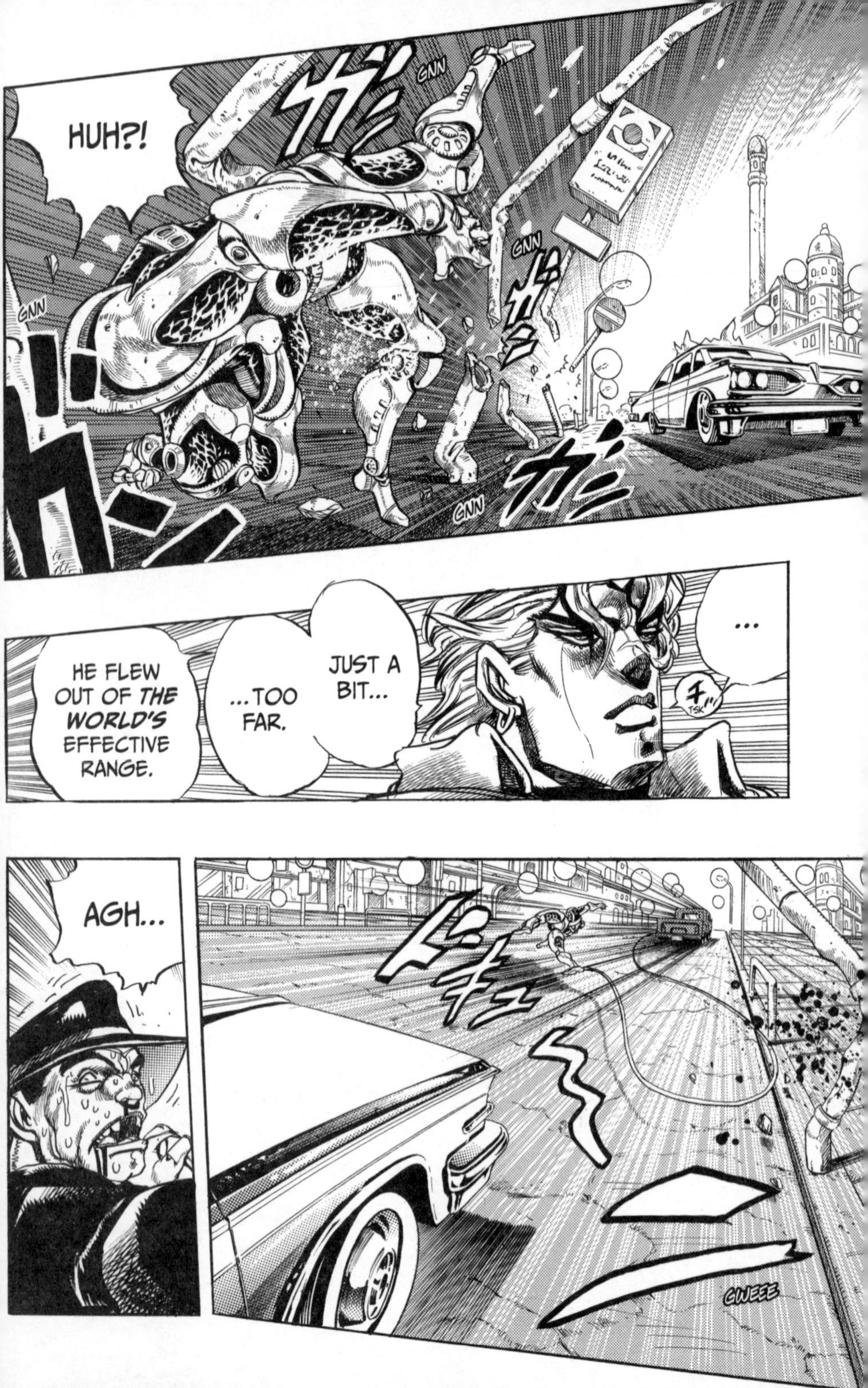
GNN
HUH?!
GNN
GNN
GNN
...
TSK
JUST A BIT...
...TOO FAR.
HE FLEW OUT OF *THE WORLD'S* EFFECTIVE RANGE.
GWEEE
AGH...

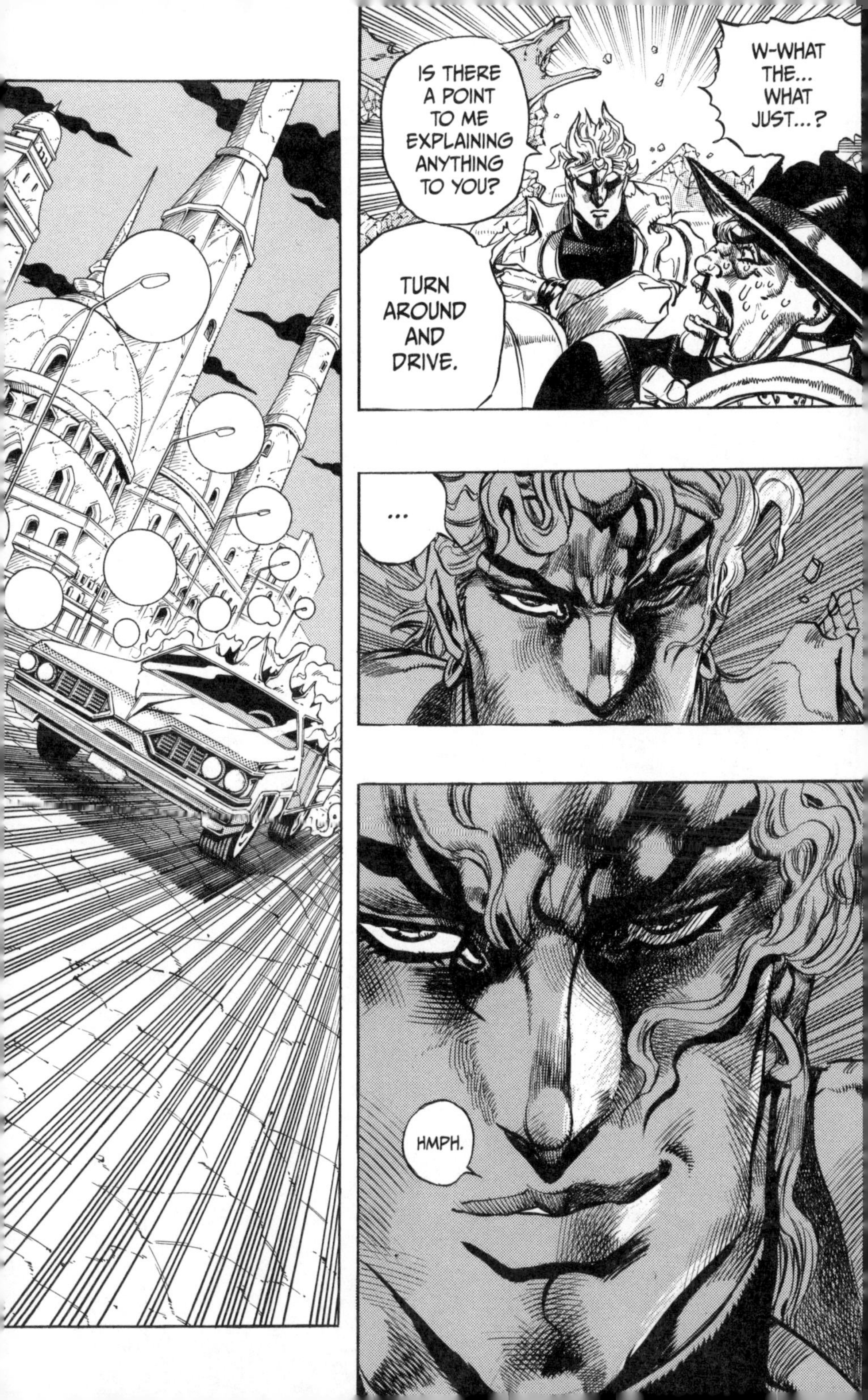
W-WHAT THE... WHAT JUST...?
IS THERE A POINT TO ME EXPLAINING ANYTHING TO YOU?
TURN AROUND AND DRIVE.
...
HMPH.

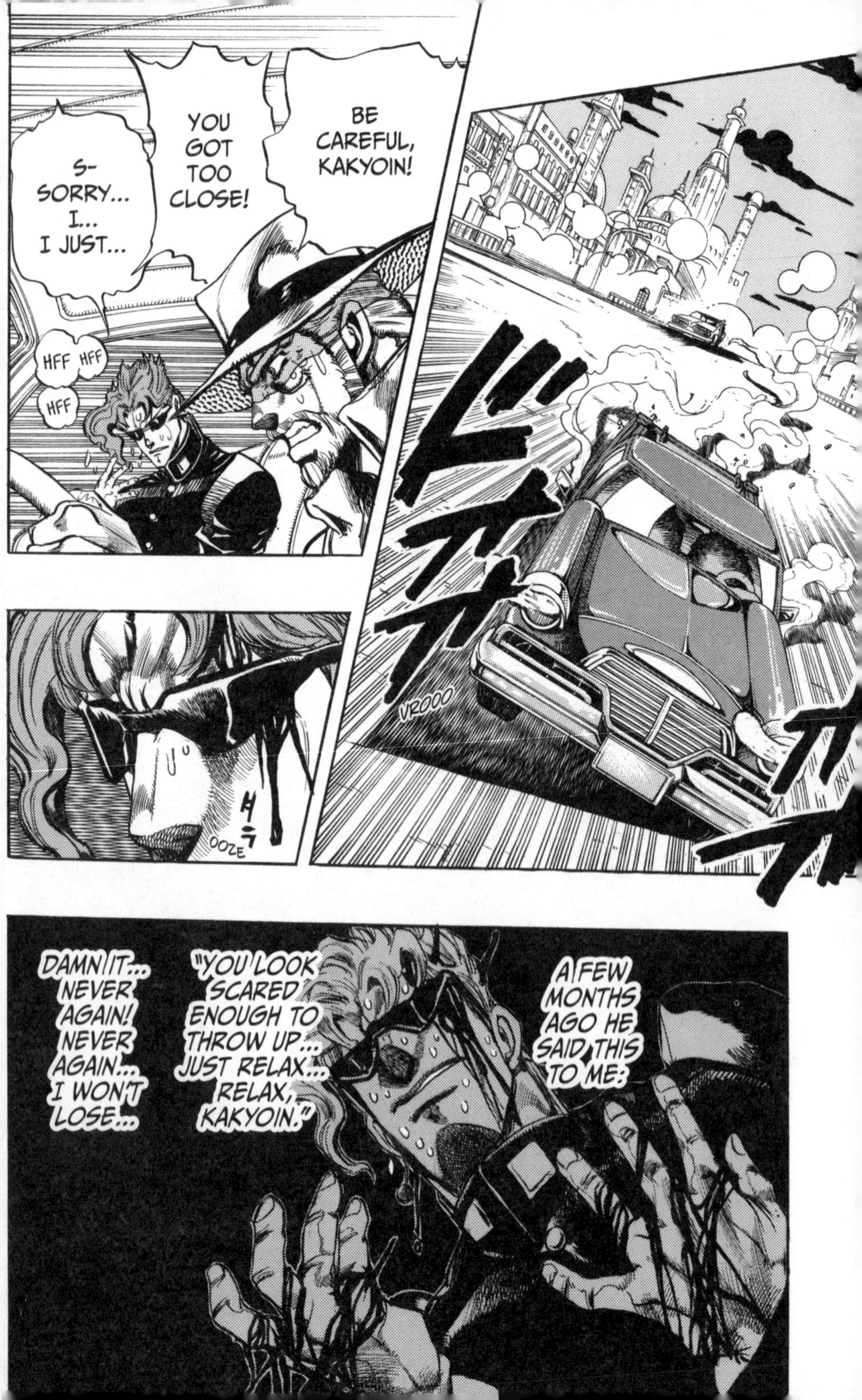
VROOO
BE CAREFUL, KAKYOIN!
YOU GOT TOO CLOSE!
S-SORRY... I... I JUST...
HFF HFF
HFF
OOZE
A FEW MONTHS AGO HE SAID THIS TO ME:
"YOU LOOK SCARED ENOUGH TO THROW UP... JUST RELAX... RELAX, KAKYOIN."
DAMN IT... NEVER AGAIN! NEVER AGAIN... I WON'T LOSE...

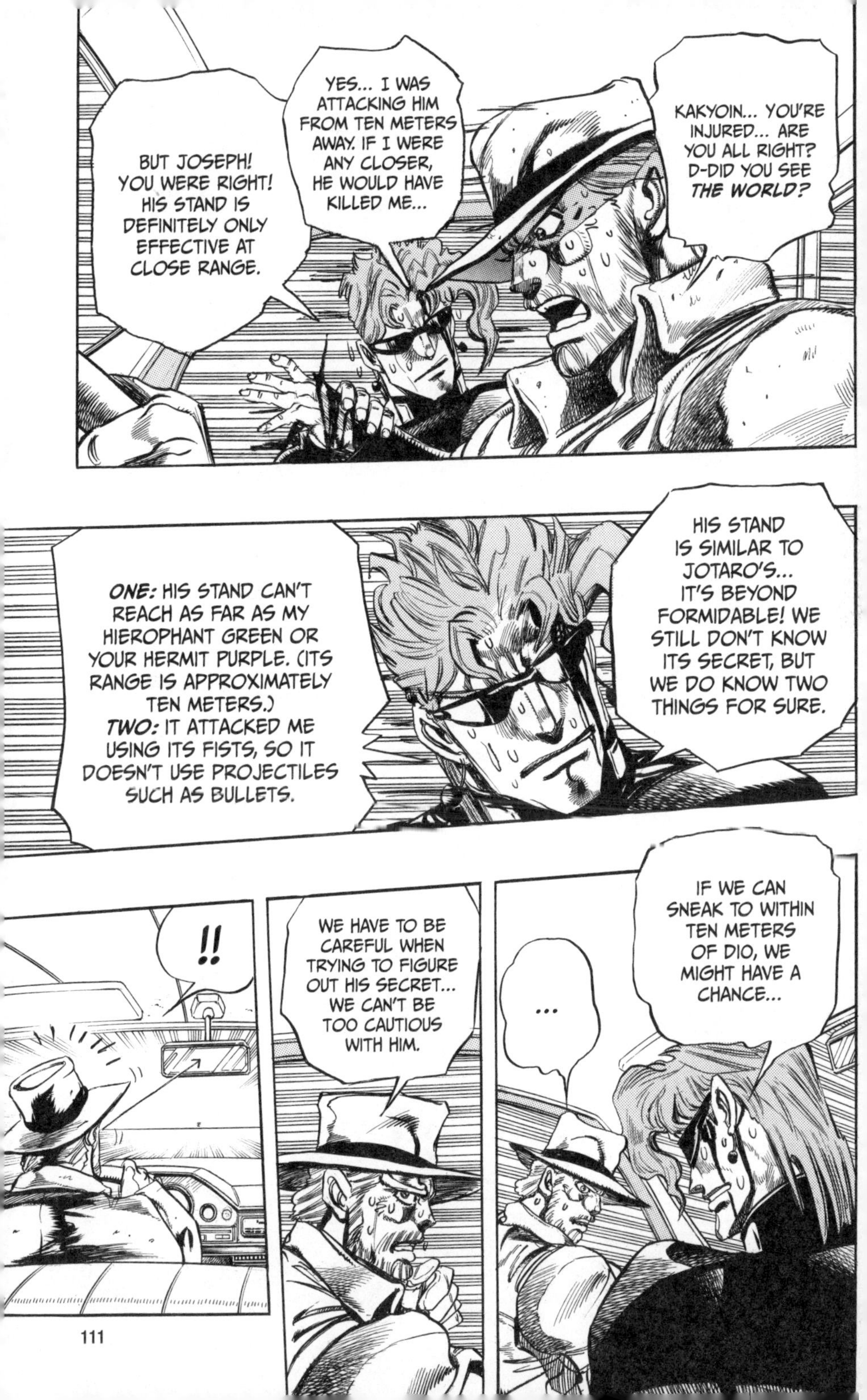
KAKYOIN... YOU'RE INJURED... ARE YOU ALL RIGHT? D-DID YOU SEE *THE WORLD?*
YES... I WAS ATTACKING HIM FROM TEN METERS AWAY. IF I WERE ANY CLOSER, HE WOULD HAVE KILLED ME...
BUT JOSEPH! YOU WERE RIGHT! HIS STAND IS DEFINITELY ONLY EFFECTIVE AT CLOSE RANGE.
HIS STAND IS SIMILAR TO JOTARO'S... IT'S BEYOND FORMIDABLE! WE STILL DON'T KNOW ITS SECRET, BUT WE DO KNOW TWO THINGS FOR SURE.
ONE: HIS STAND CAN'T REACH AS FAR AS MY HIEROPHANT GREEN OR YOUR HERMIT PURPLE. (ITS RANGE IS APPROXIMATELY TEN METERS.) *TWO:* IT ATTACKED ME USING ITS FISTS, SO IT DOESN'T USE PROJECTILES SUCH AS BULLETS.
IF WE CAN SNEAK TO WITHIN TEN METERS OF DIO, WE MIGHT HAVE A CHANCE...
...
WE HAVE TO BE CAREFUL WHEN TRYING TO FIGURE OUT HIS SECRET... WE CAN'T BE TOO CAUTIOUS WITH HIM.
!!

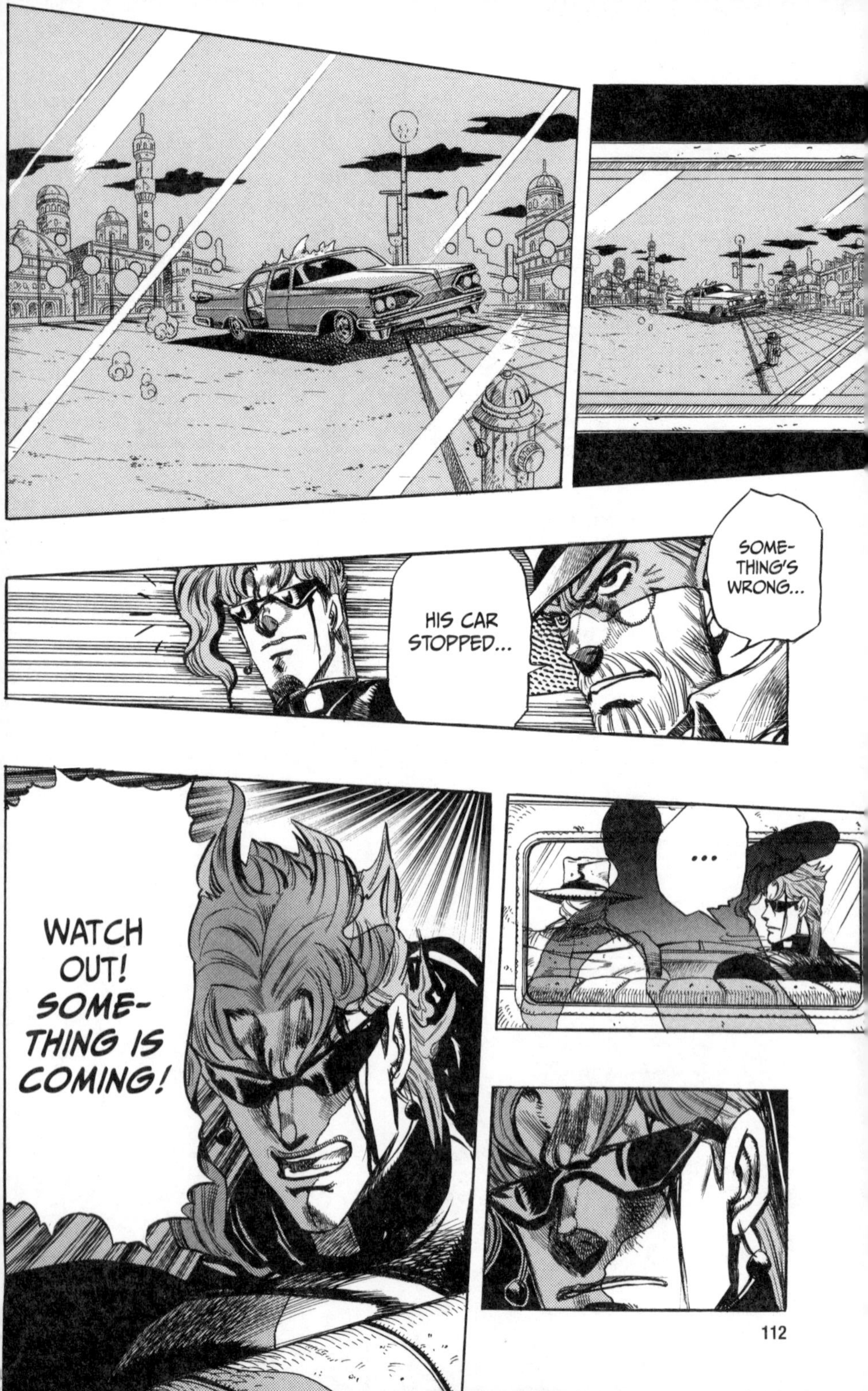
SOME-THING'S WRONG...
HIS CAR STOPPED...
...
WATCH OUT! SOME-THING IS COMING!

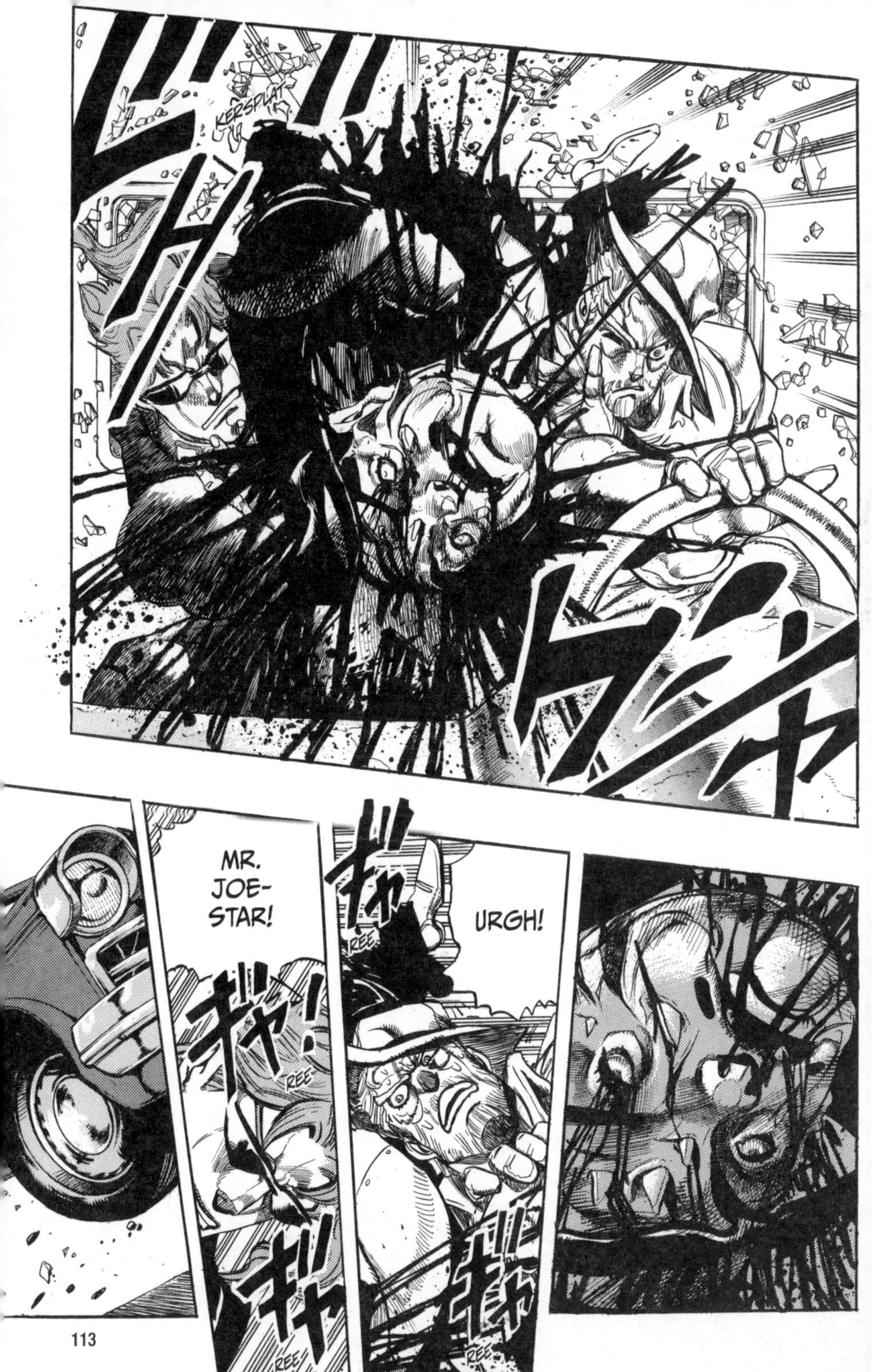
KERSPLAT
URGH!
REE
REE
MR. JOE-STAR!
REE
REE

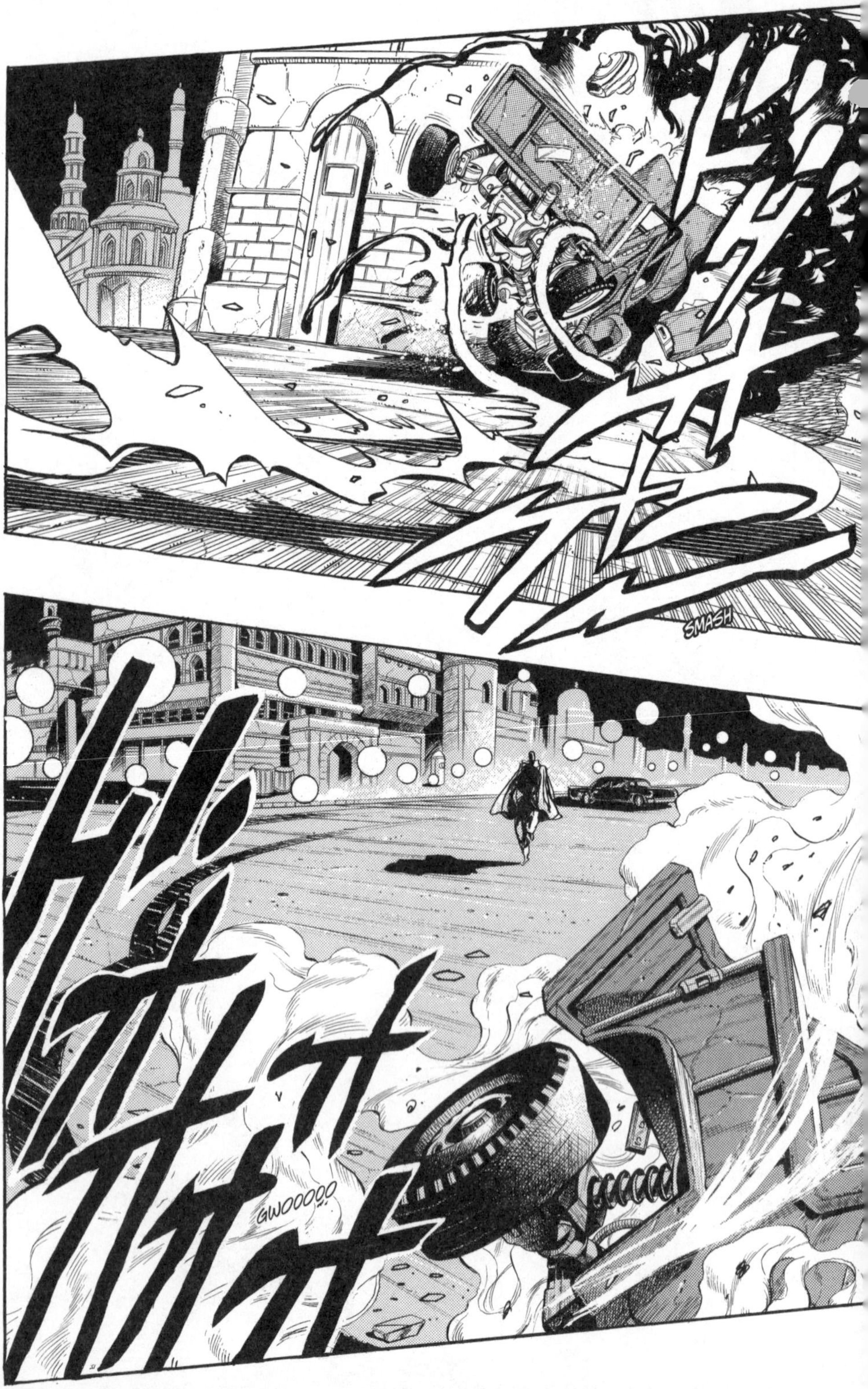
SMASH
GWOOOOO

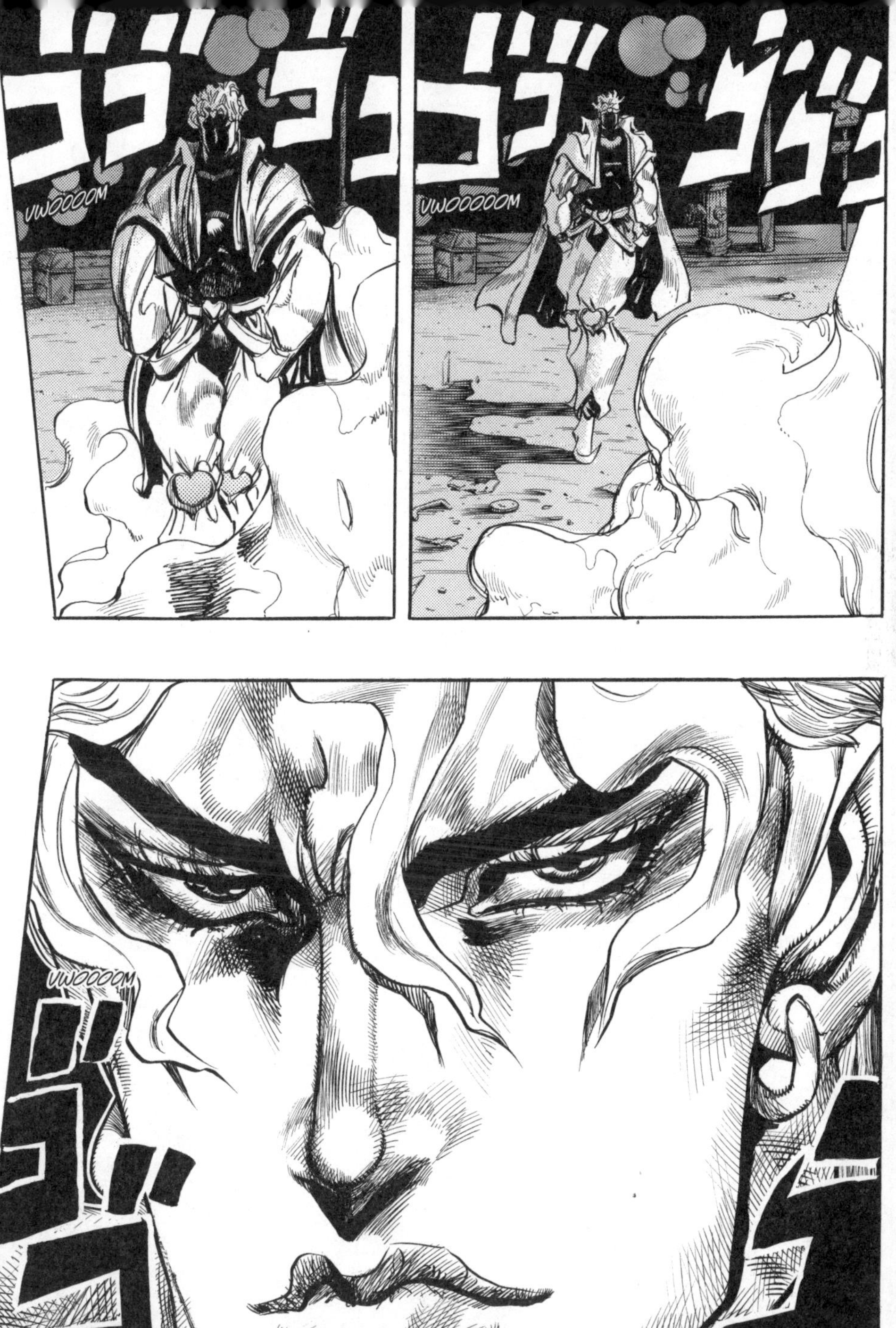
ゴゴゴゴ
VWOOOOOM
ゴゴゴゴ
VWOOOOM
VWOOOOM
ゴゴゴ

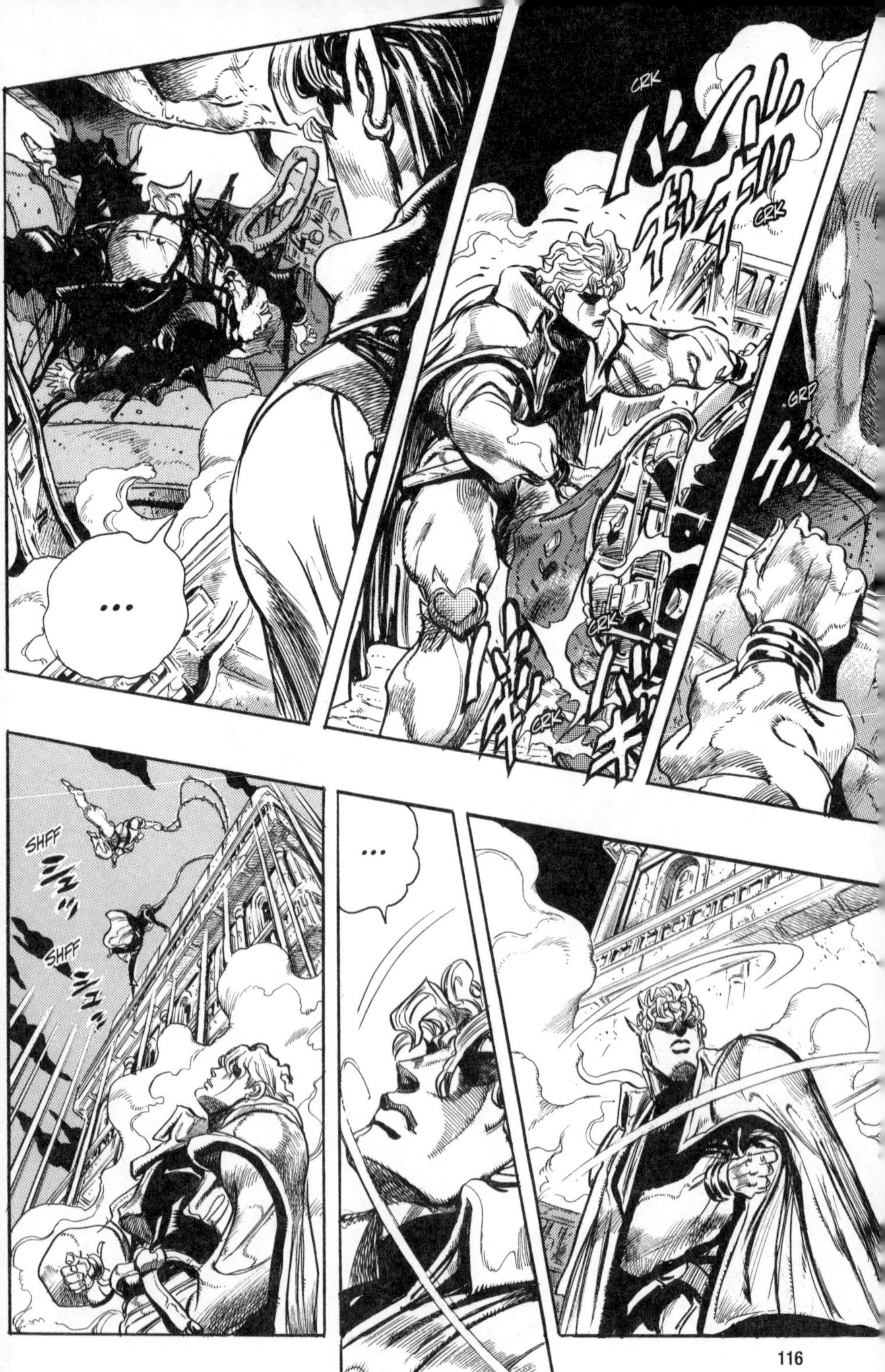
GRP
CRK
CRK
CRK
CRK
...
...
SHFF
SHFF

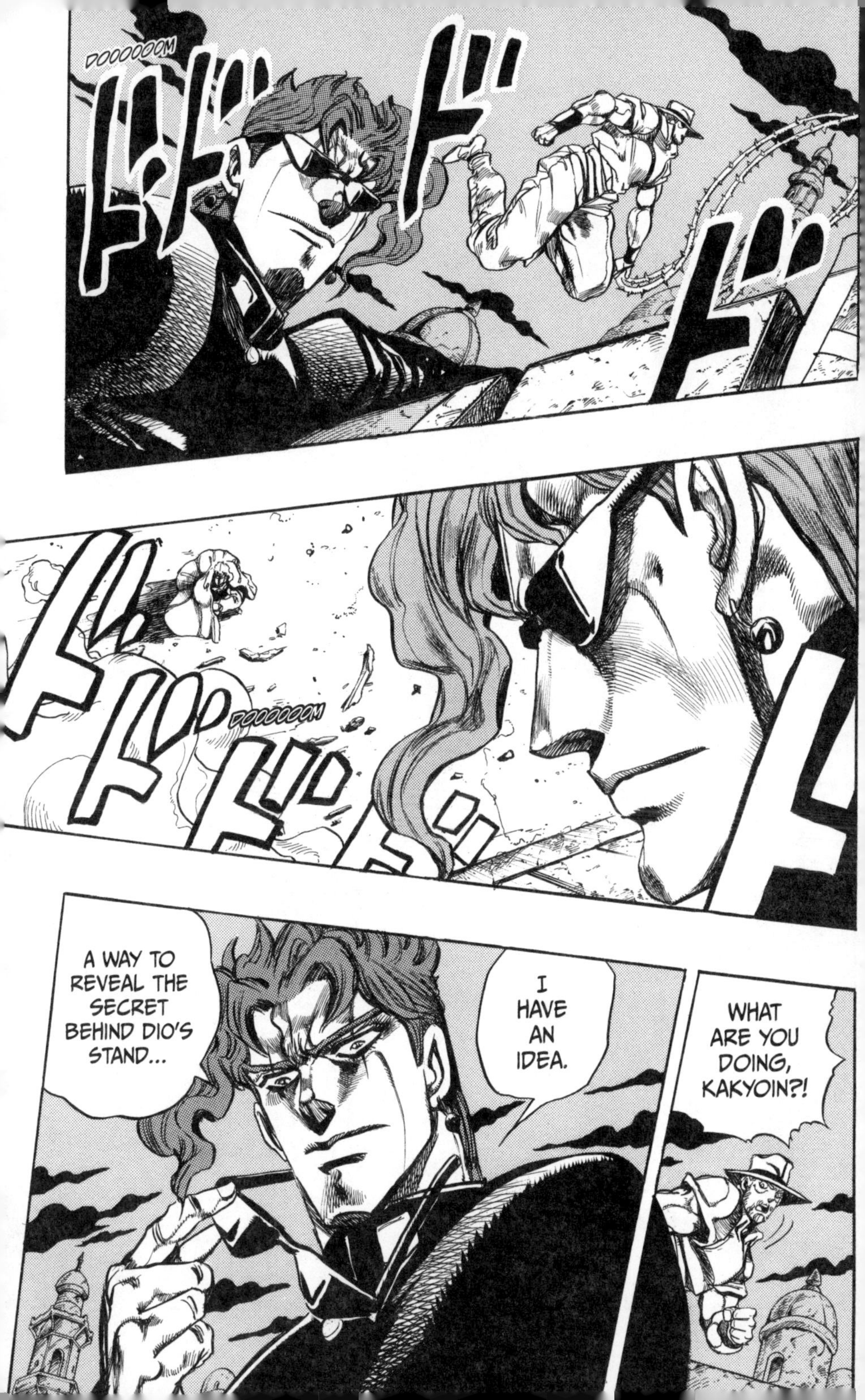
DOOOOOOM
DOOOOOOOM
WHAT ARE YOU DOING, KAKYOIN?!
I HAVE AN IDEA.
A WAY TO REVEAL THE SECRET BEHIND DIO'S STAND...

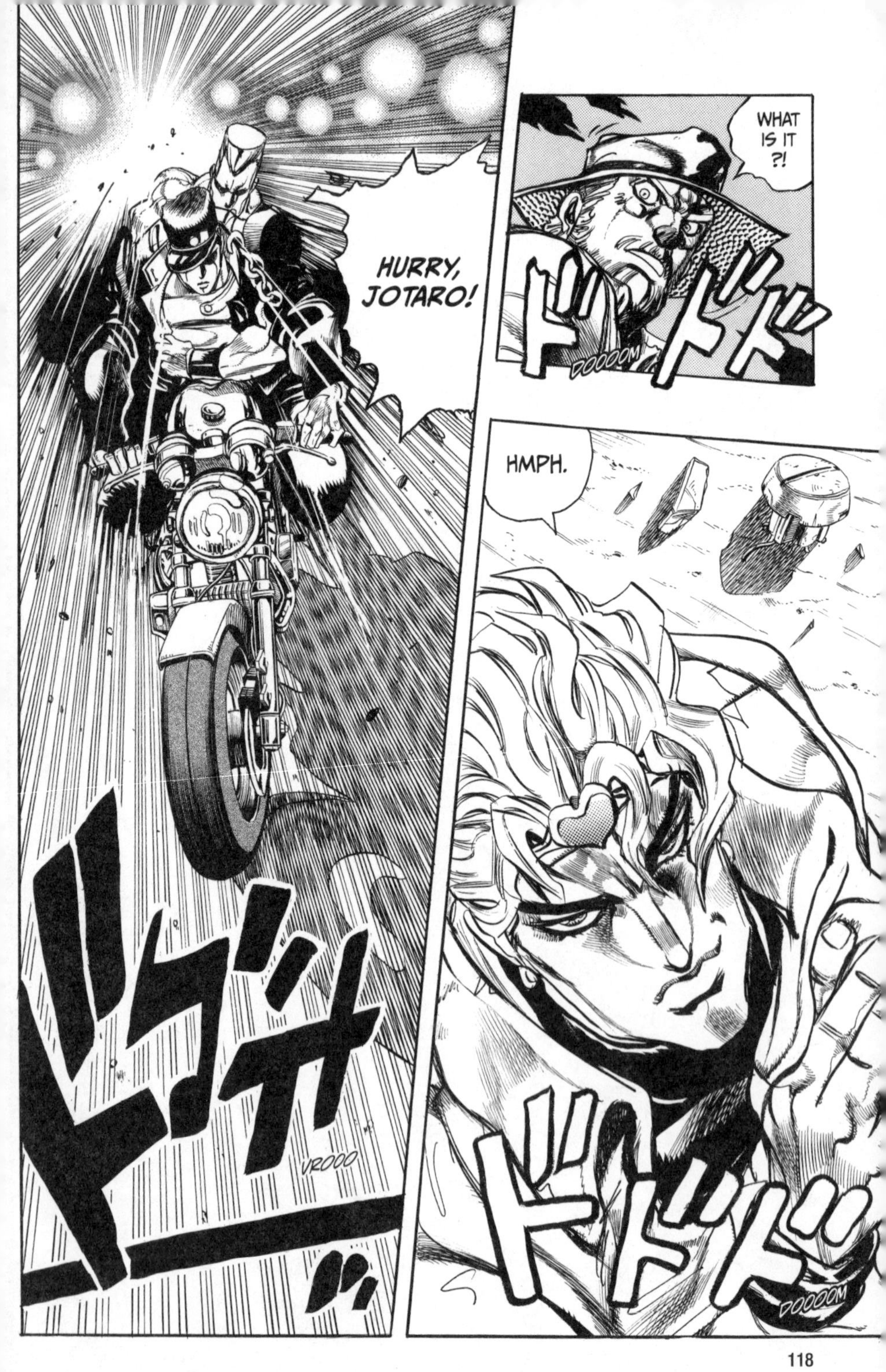
WHAT IS IT ?!
DOOOOM
HMPH.
DOOOOM
HURRY, JOTARO!
VROOO

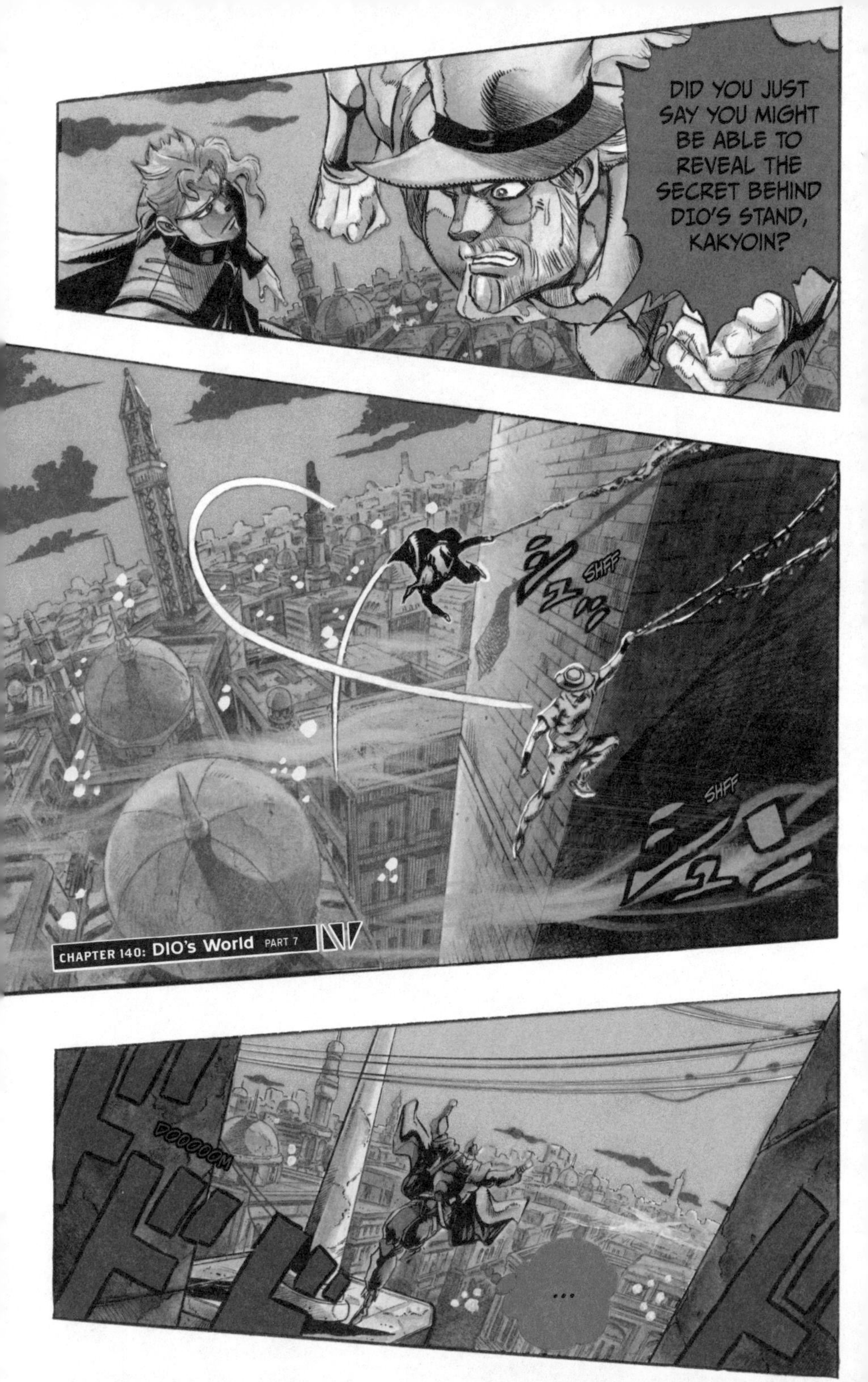
DID YOU JUST SAY YOU MIGHT BE ABLE TO REVEAL THE SECRET BEHIND DIO'S STAND, KAKYOIN?
SHFF
SHFF
CHAPTER 140: DIO's World PART 7
DOOOOOM
...

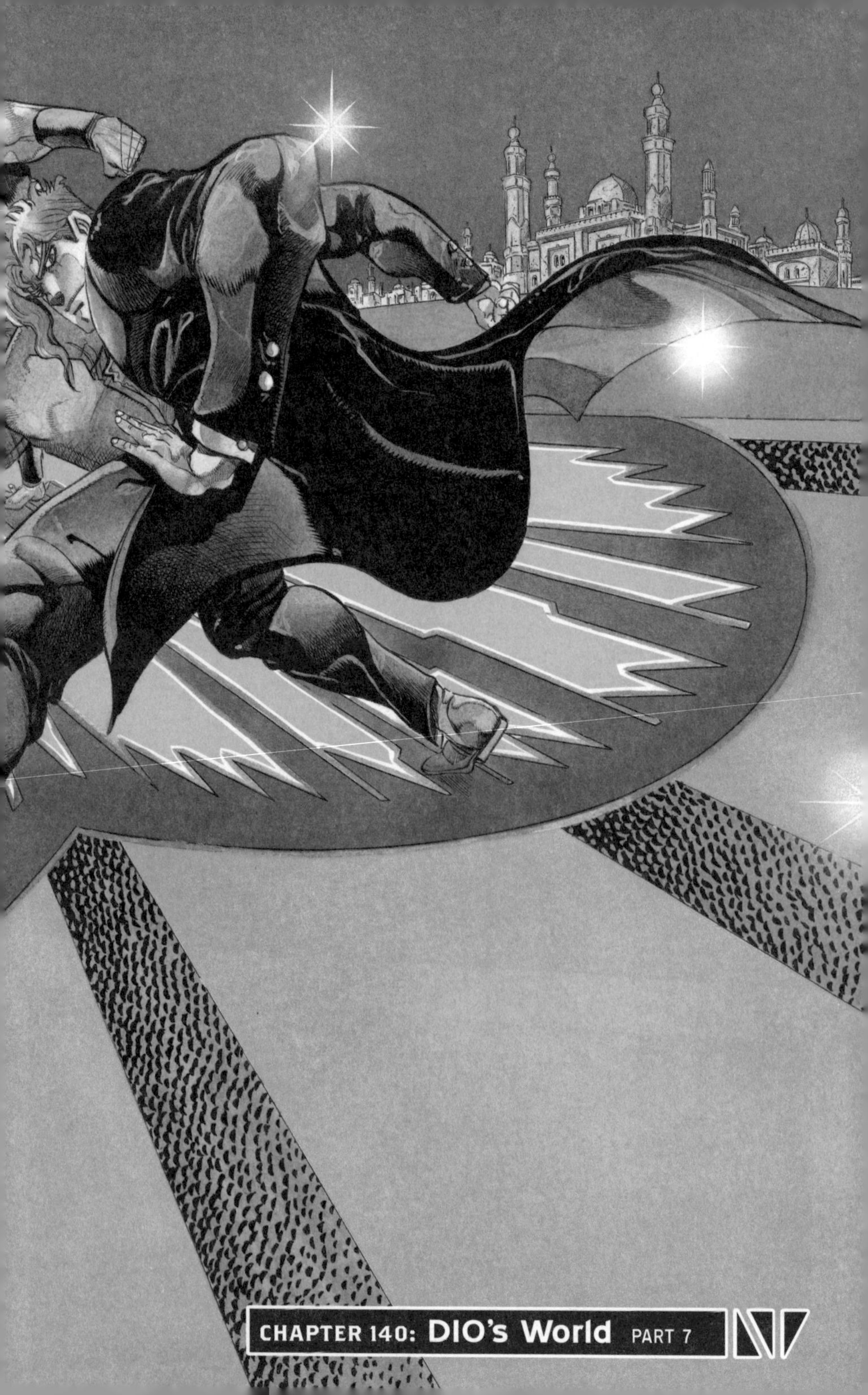
CHAPTER 140: DIO's World PART 7

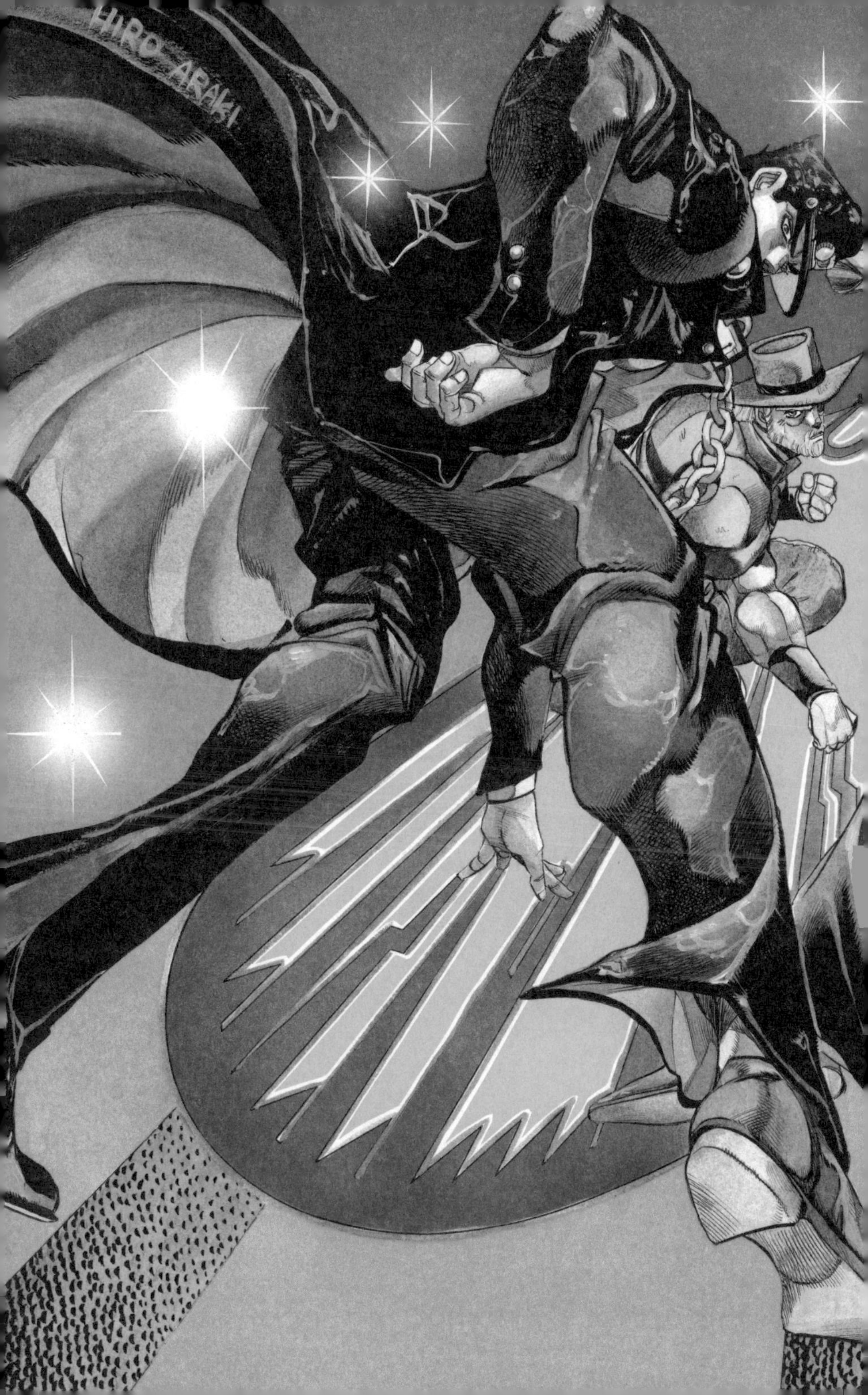
HIRO ARAKI

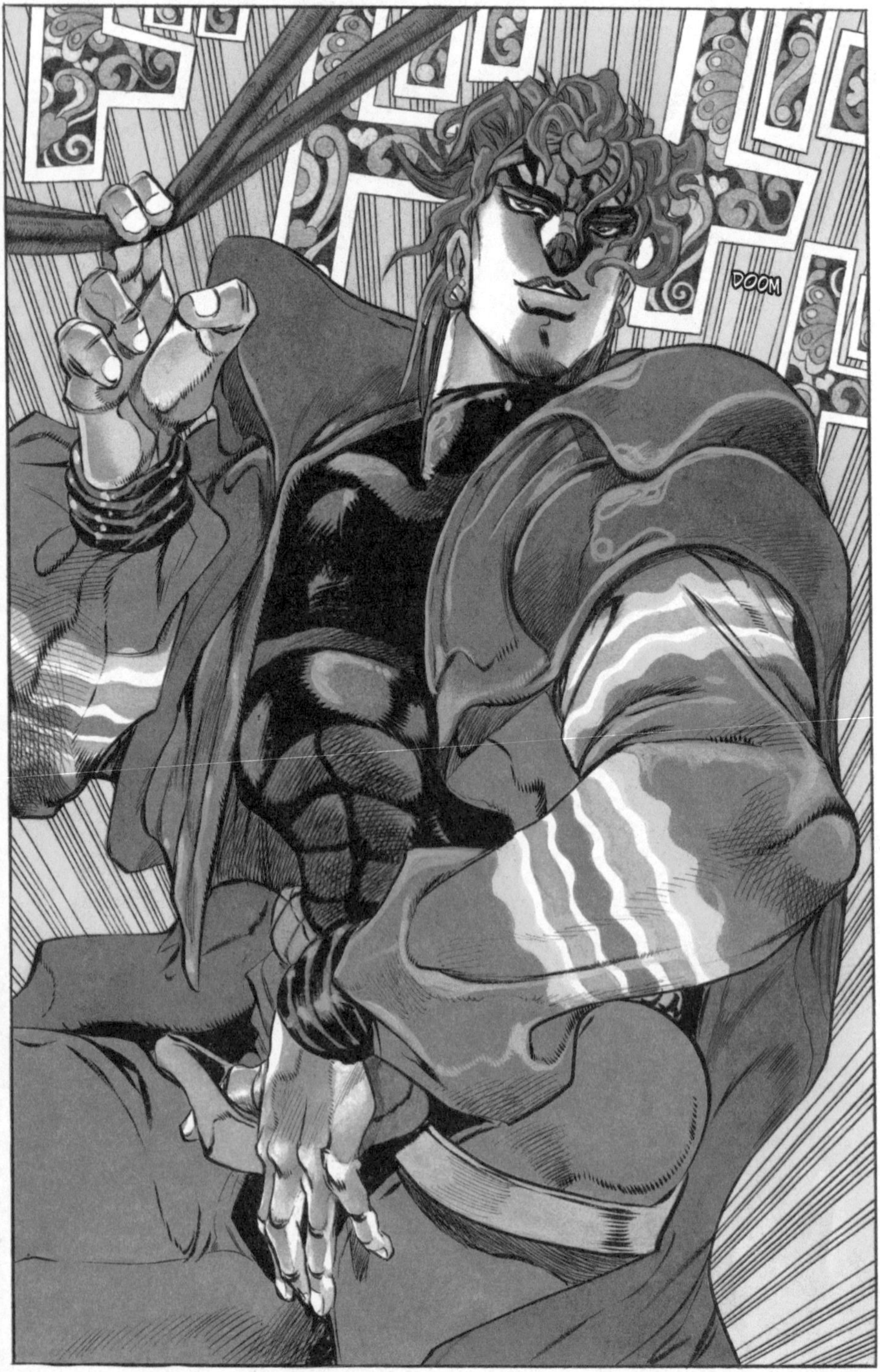
DOOM

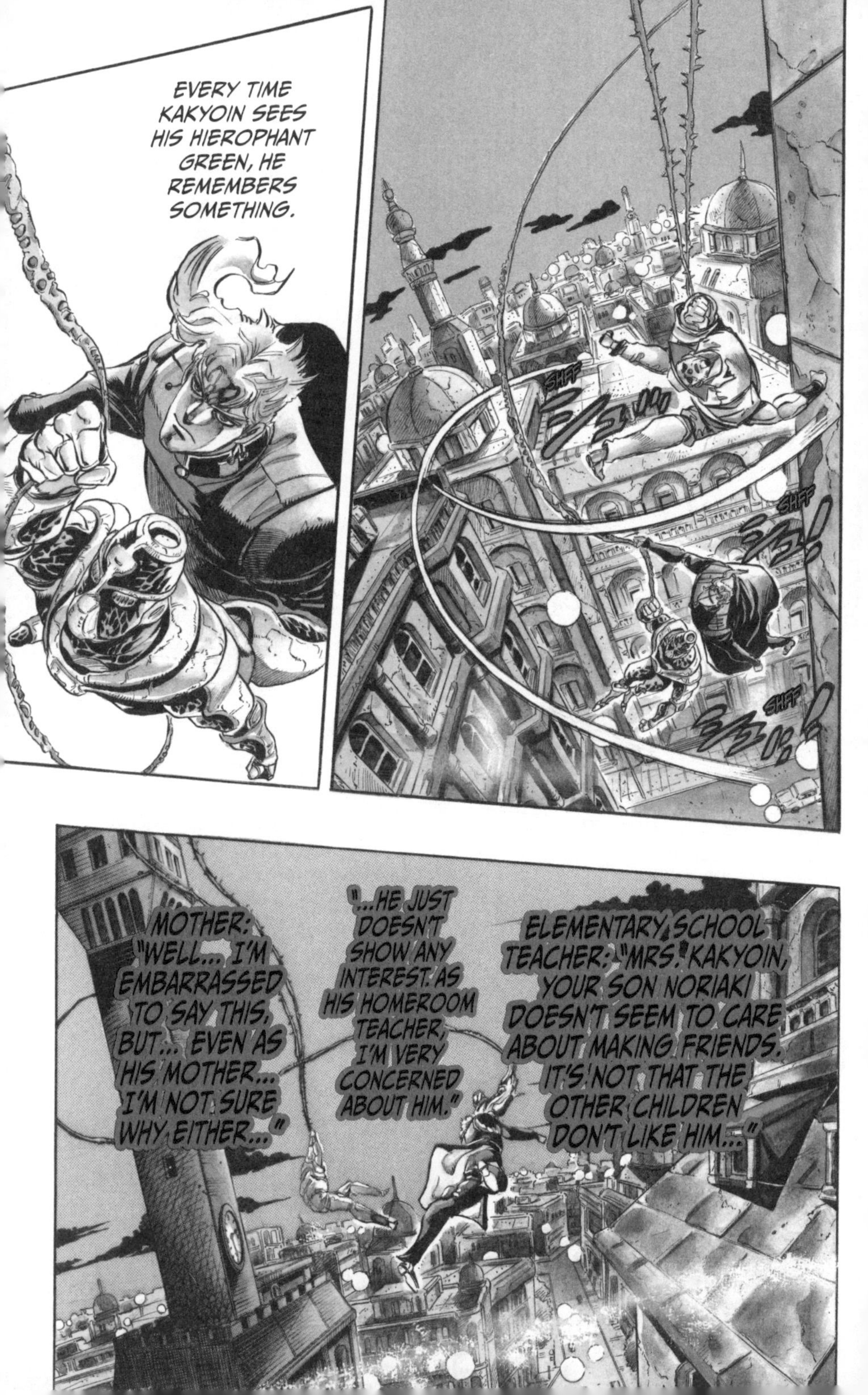
SHFF
SHFF
SHFF
EVERY TIME KAKYOIN SEES HIS HIEROPHANT GREEN, HE REMEMBERS SOMETHING.
ELEMENTARY SCHOOL TEACHER: "MRS. KAKYOIN, YOUR SON NORIAKI DOESN'T SEEM TO CARE ABOUT MAKING FRIENDS. IT'S NOT THAT THE OTHER CHILDREN DON'T LIKE HIM..."
"...HE JUST DOESN'T SHOW ANY INTEREST. AS HIS HOMEROOM TEACHER, I'M VERY CONCERNED ABOUT HIM."
MOTHER: "WELL... I'M EMBARRASSED TO SAY THIS, BUT... EVEN AS HIS MOTHER... I'M NOT SURE WHY EITHER..."

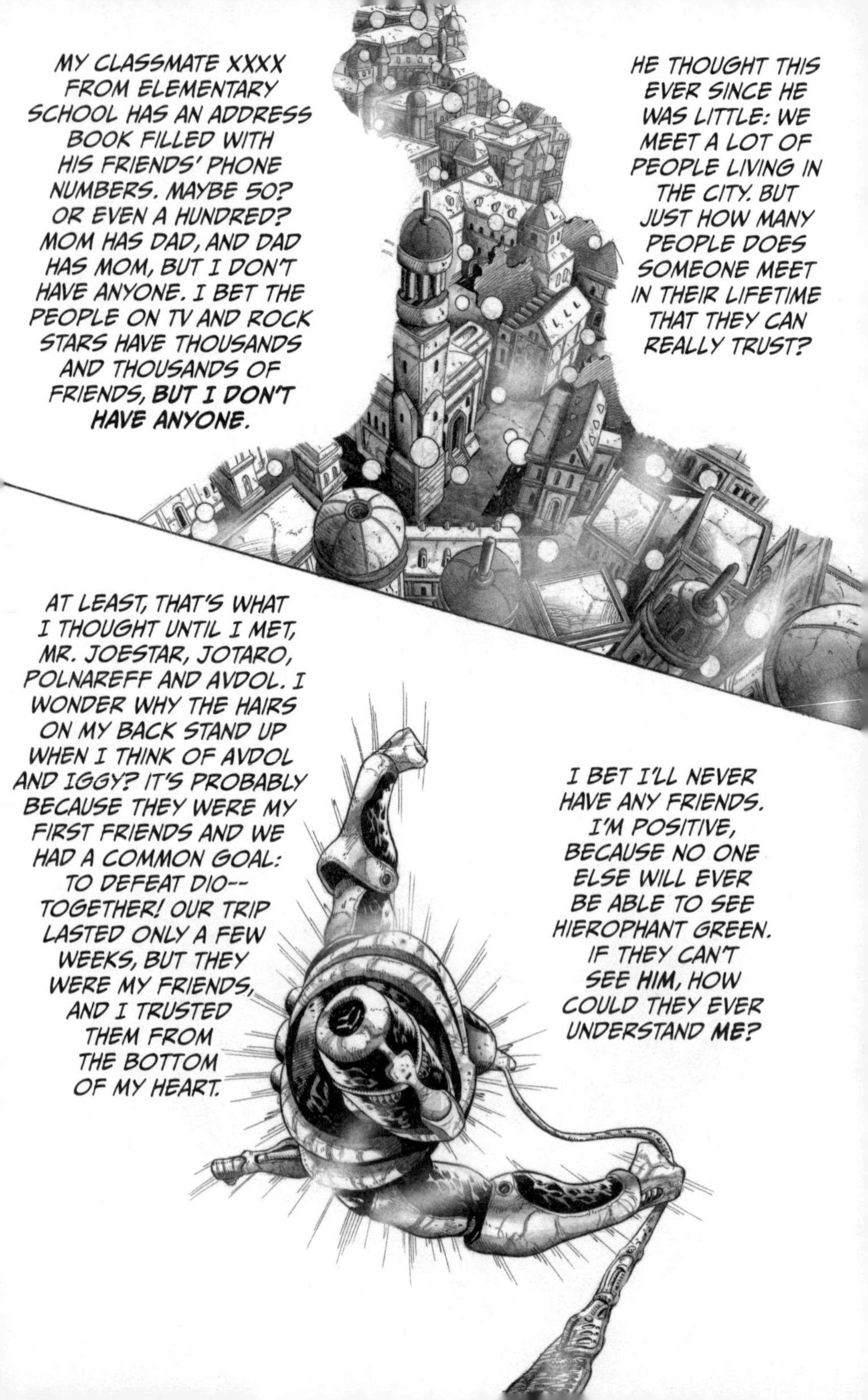
HE THOUGHT THIS EVER SINCE HE WAS LITTLE: WE MEET A LOT OF PEOPLE LIVING IN THE CITY. BUT JUST HOW MANY PEOPLE DOES SOMEONE MEET IN THEIR LIFETIME THAT THEY CAN REALLY TRUST?
MY CLASSMATE XXXX FROM ELEMENTARY SCHOOL HAS AN ADDRESS BOOK FILLED WITH HIS FRIENDS' PHONE NUMBERS. MAYBE 50? OR EVEN A HUNDRED? MOM HAS DAD, AND DAD HAS MOM, BUT I DON'T HAVE ANYONE. I BET THE PEOPLE ON TV AND ROCK STARS HAVE THOUSANDS AND THOUSANDS OF FRIENDS, **BUT I DON'T HAVE ANYONE.**
I BET I'LL NEVER HAVE ANY FRIENDS. I'M POSITIVE, BECAUSE NO ONE ELSE WILL EVER BE ABLE TO SEE HIEROPHANT GREEN. IF THEY CAN'T SEE **HIM**, HOW COULD THEY EVER UNDERSTAND **ME**?
AT LEAST, THAT'S WHAT I THOUGHT UNTIL I MET, MR. JOESTAR, JOTARO, POLNAREFF AND AVDOL. I WONDER WHY THE HAIRS ON MY BACK STAND UP WHEN I THINK OF AVDOL AND IGGY? IT'S PROBABLY BECAUSE THEY WERE MY FIRST FRIENDS AND WE HAD A COMMON GOAL: TO DEFEAT DIO-- TOGETHER! OUR TRIP LASTED ONLY A FEW WEEKS, BUT THEY WERE MY FRIENDS, AND I TRUSTED THEM FROM THE BOTTOM OF MY HEART.

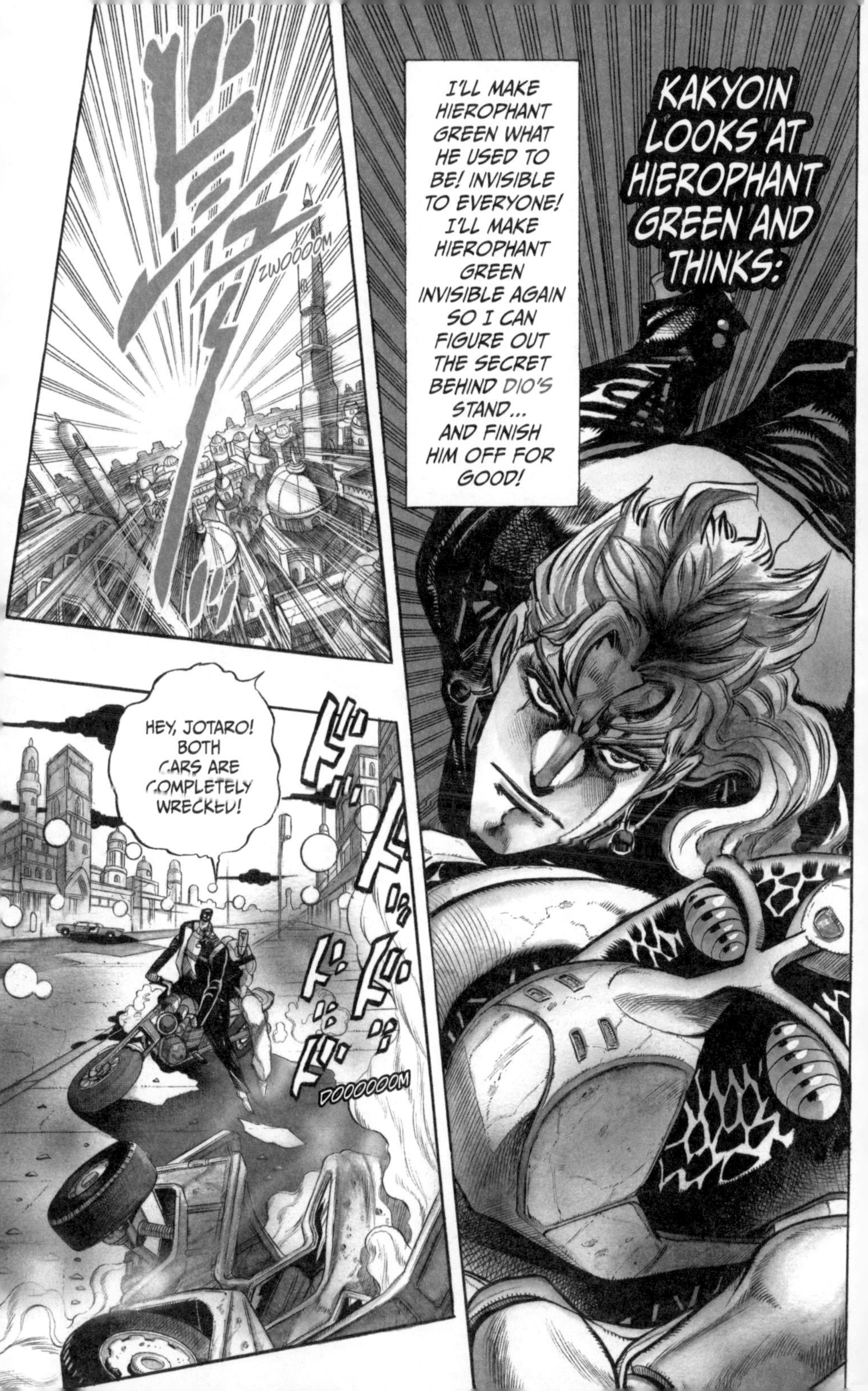
KAKYOIN LOOKS AT HIEROPHANT GREEN AND THINKS:
I'LL MAKE HIEROPHANT GREEN WHAT HE USED TO BE! INVISIBLE TO EVERYONE! I'LL MAKE HIEROPHANT GREEN INVISIBLE AGAIN SO I CAN FIGURE OUT THE SECRET BEHIND DIO'S STAND... AND FINISH HIM OFF FOR GOOD!
ZWOOOOM
HEY, JOTARO! BOTH CARS ARE COMPLETELY WRECKED!
DOOOOOOM

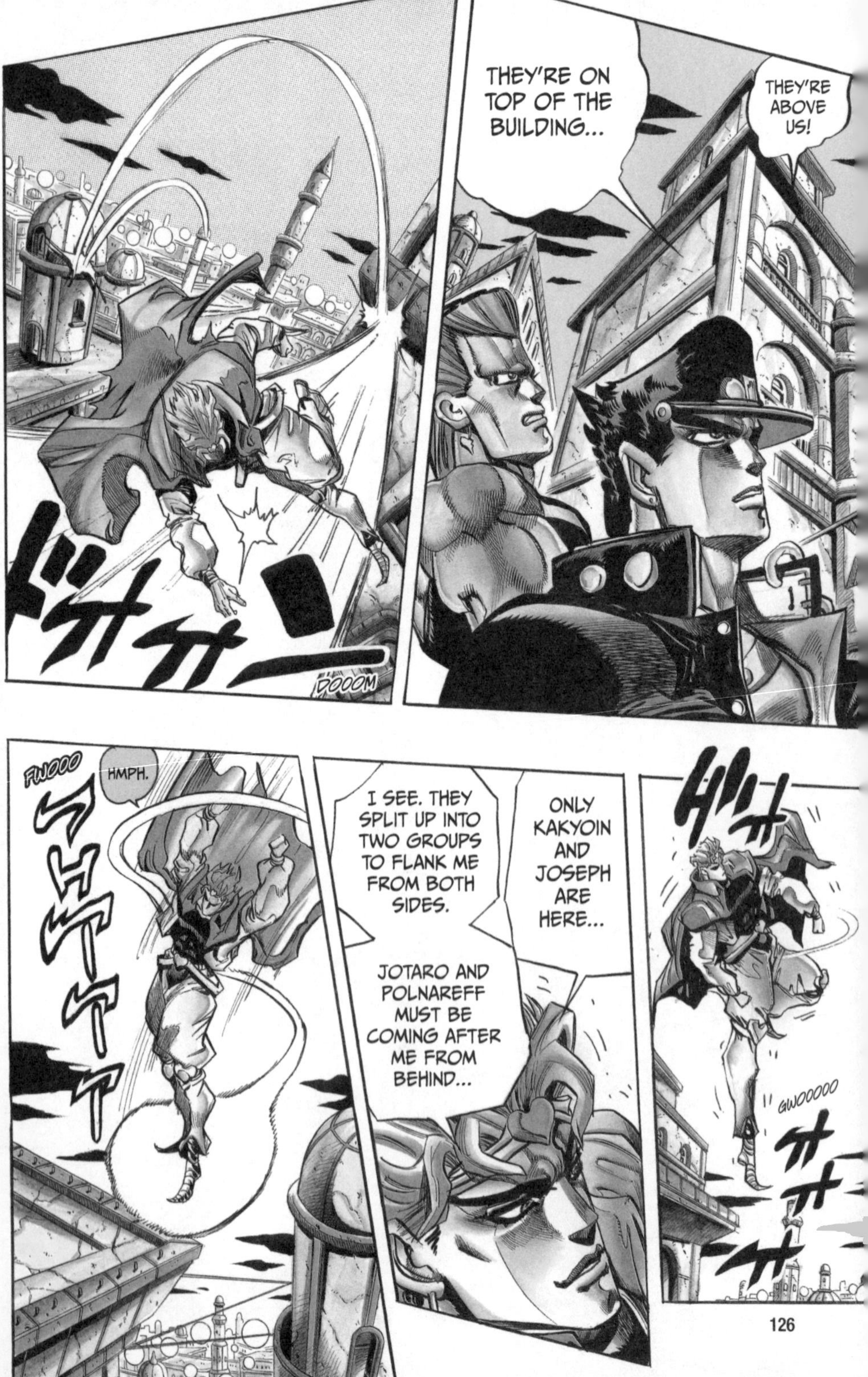
THEY'RE ABOVE US!
THEY'RE ON TOP OF THE BUILDING...
DOOOM
GWOOOOO
ONLY KAKYOIN AND JOSEPH ARE HERE...
I SEE. THEY SPLIT UP INTO TWO GROUPS TO FLANK ME FROM BOTH SIDES.
JOTARO AND POLNAREFF MUST BE COMING AFTER ME FROM BEHIND...
HMPH.
FWOOO

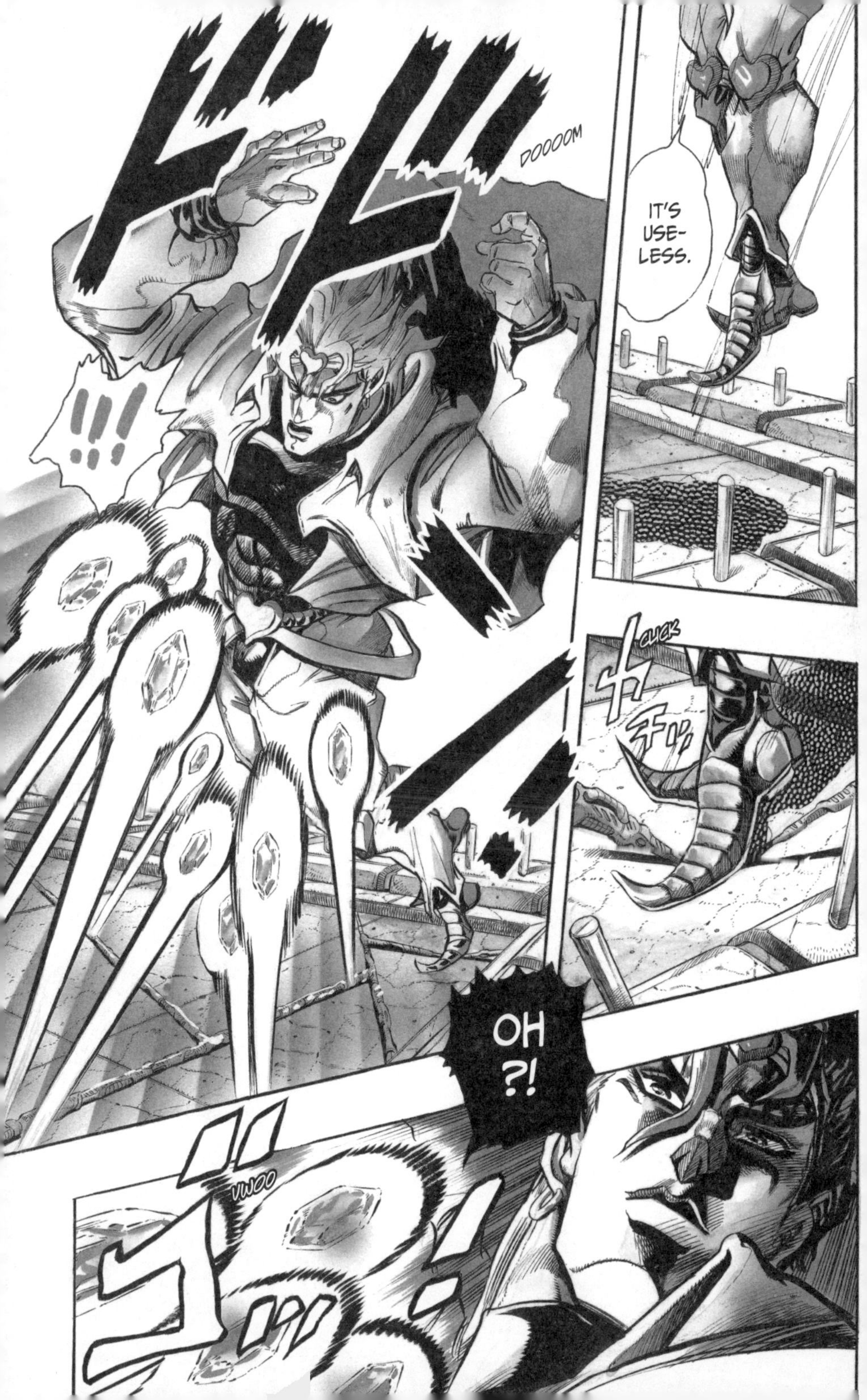
IT'S USE- LESS.
CLICK
DOOOOM
!!!
OH ?!
VWOO

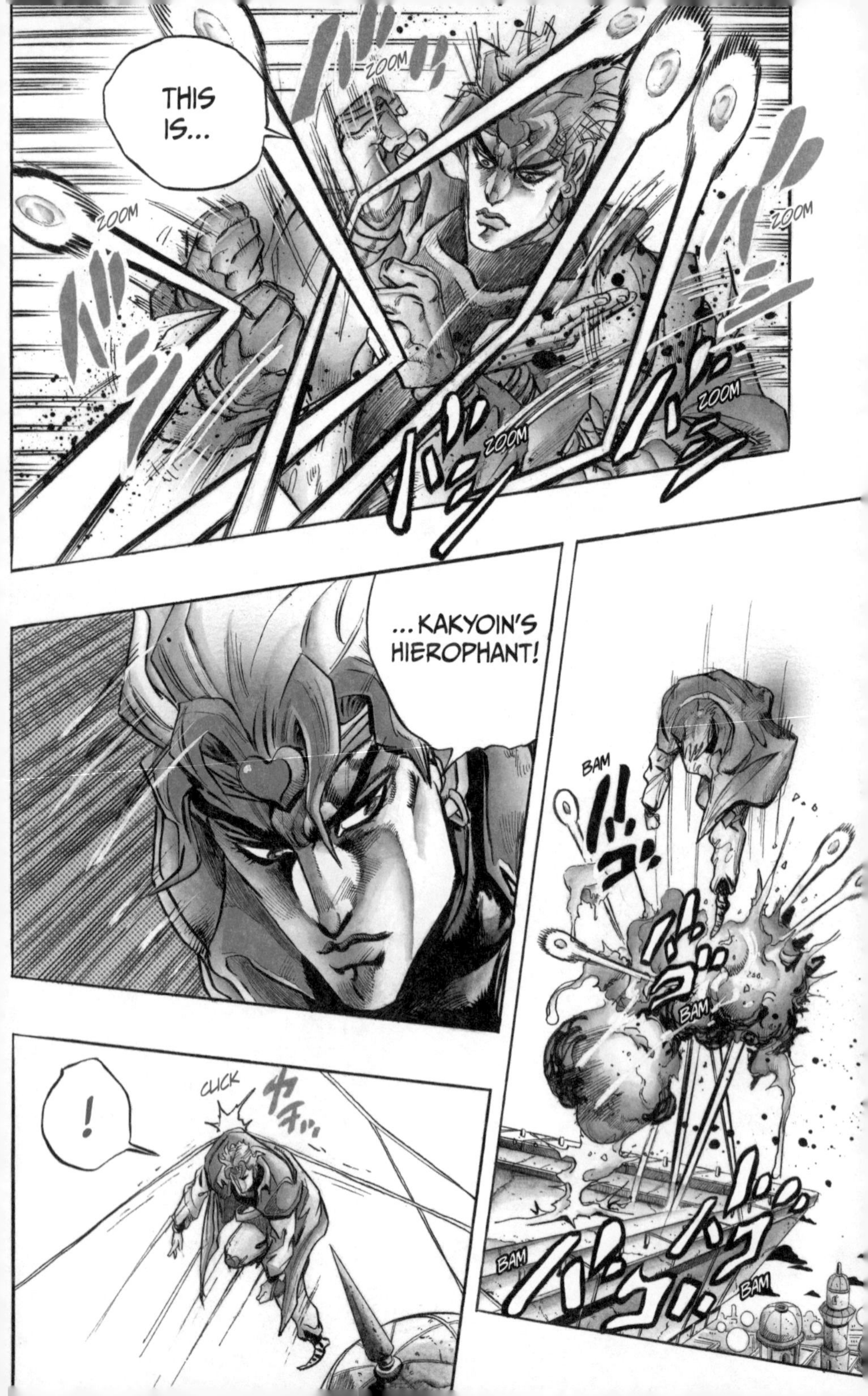
ZOOM
ZOOM
THIS IS...
ZOOM
ZOOM
ZOOM
ZOOM
BAM
BAM
BAM
BAM
...KAKYOIN'S HIEROPHANT!
CLICK
!

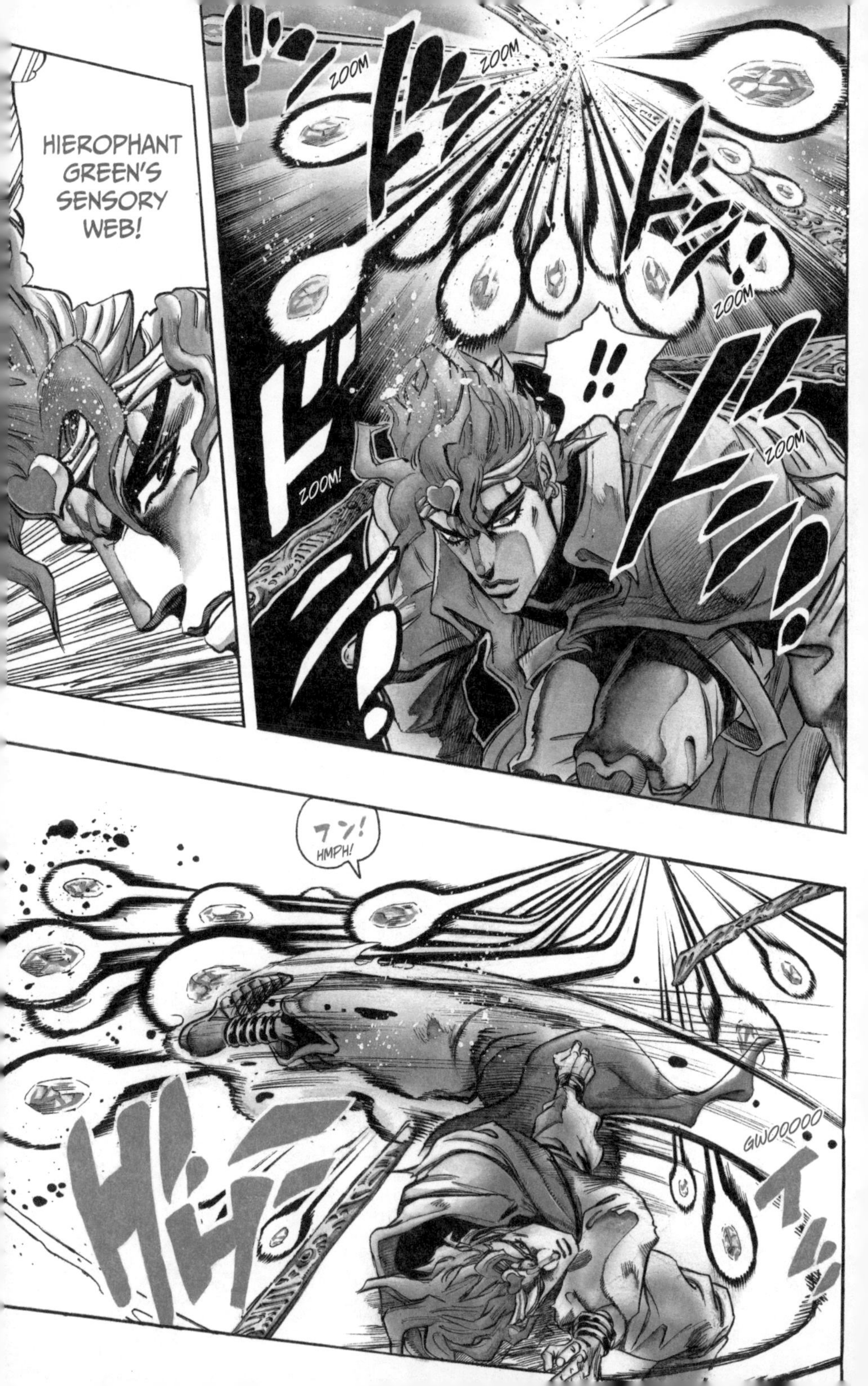
ZOOM
ZOOM
ZOOM
!!
ZOOM
ZOOM!
HIEROPHANT GREEN'S SENSORY WEB!
フン!
HMPH!
GWOOOOO

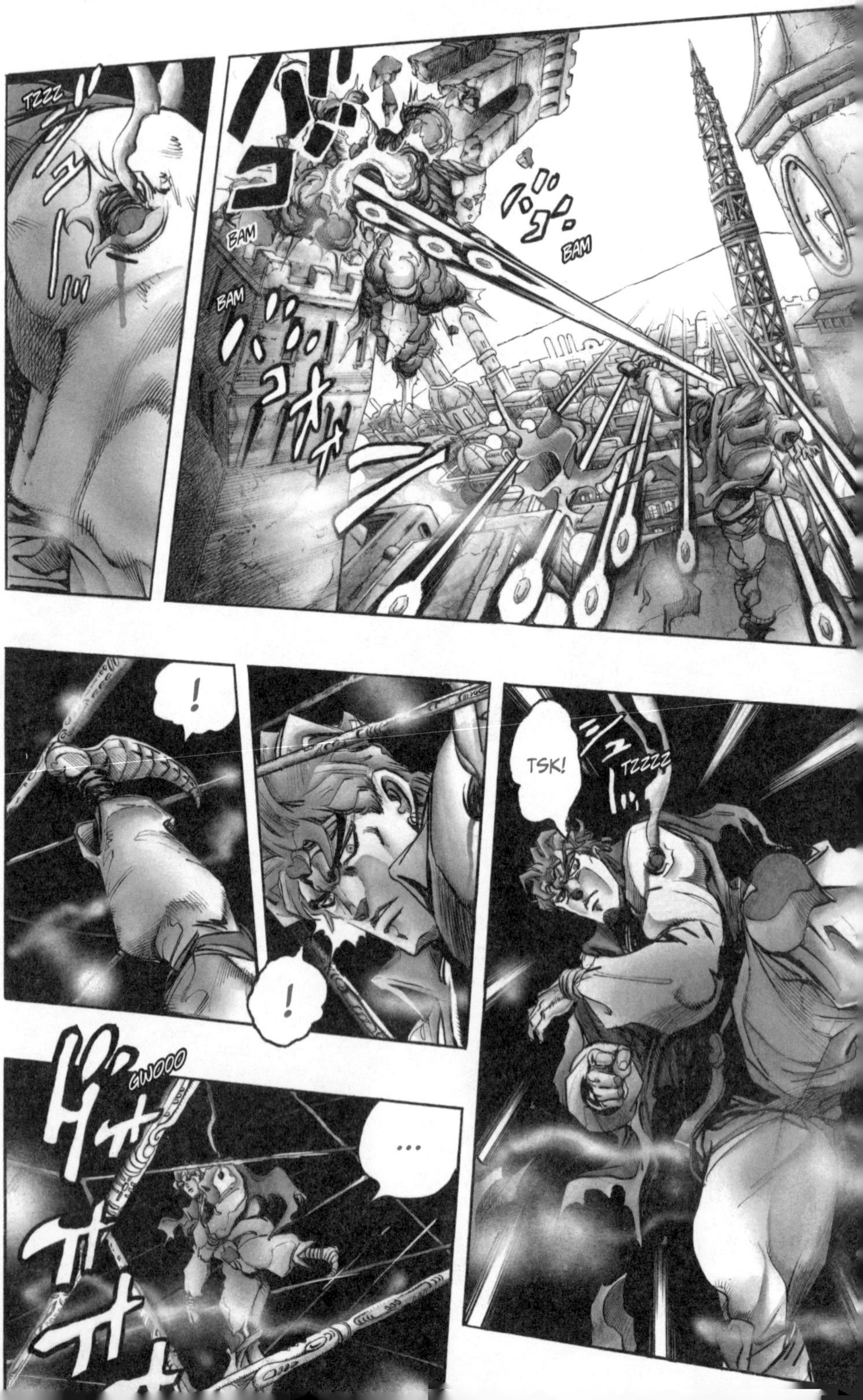
BAM
BAM
BAM
TZZZ
TSK!
TZZZZ
!
!
GWOOO
...

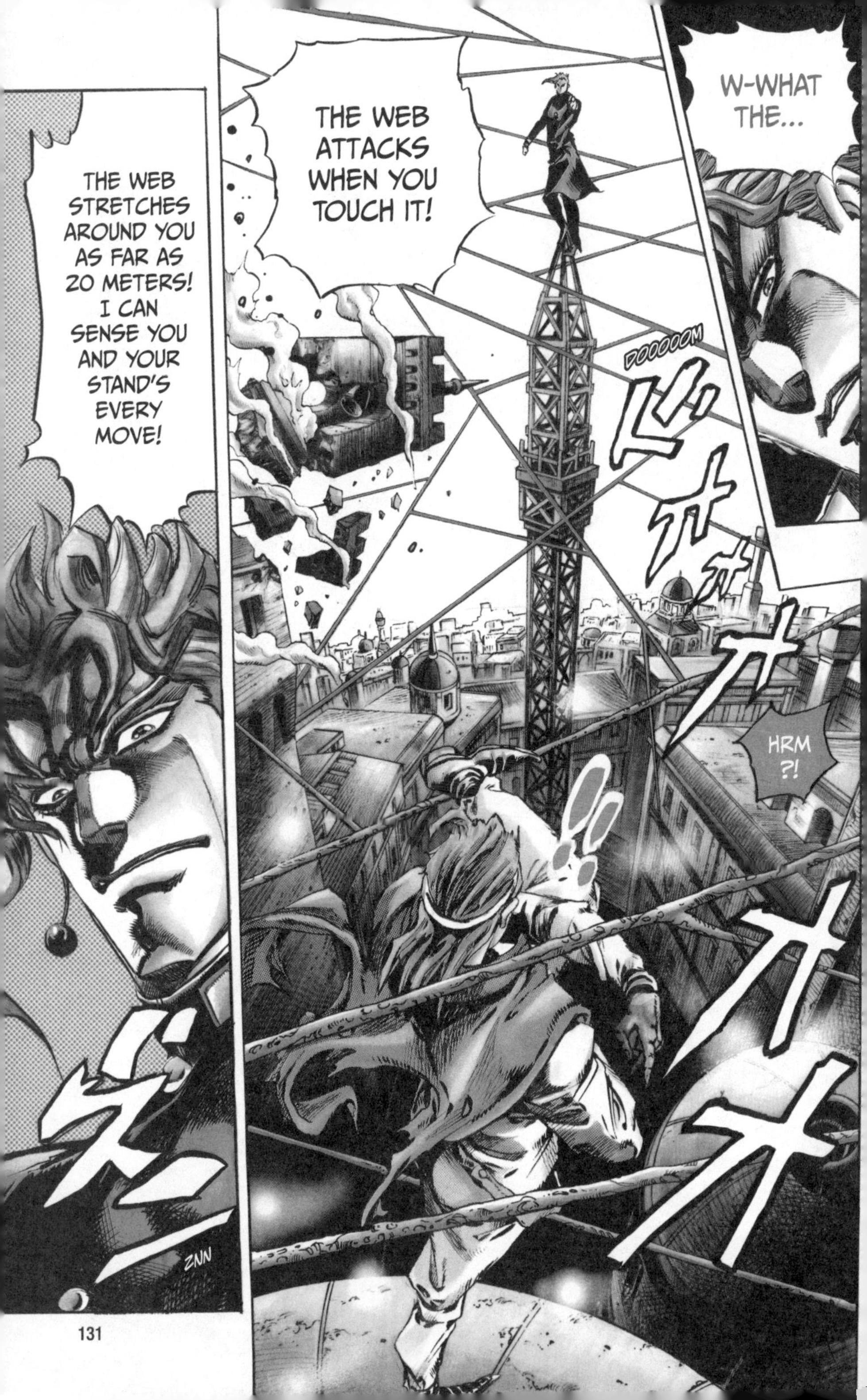
W-WHAT THE...
THE WEB ATTACKS WHEN YOU TOUCH IT!
DOOOOOM
HRM ?!
THE WEB STRETCHES AROUND YOU AS FAR AS 20 METERS! I CAN SENSE YOU AND YOUR STAND'S EVERY MOVE!
ZNN

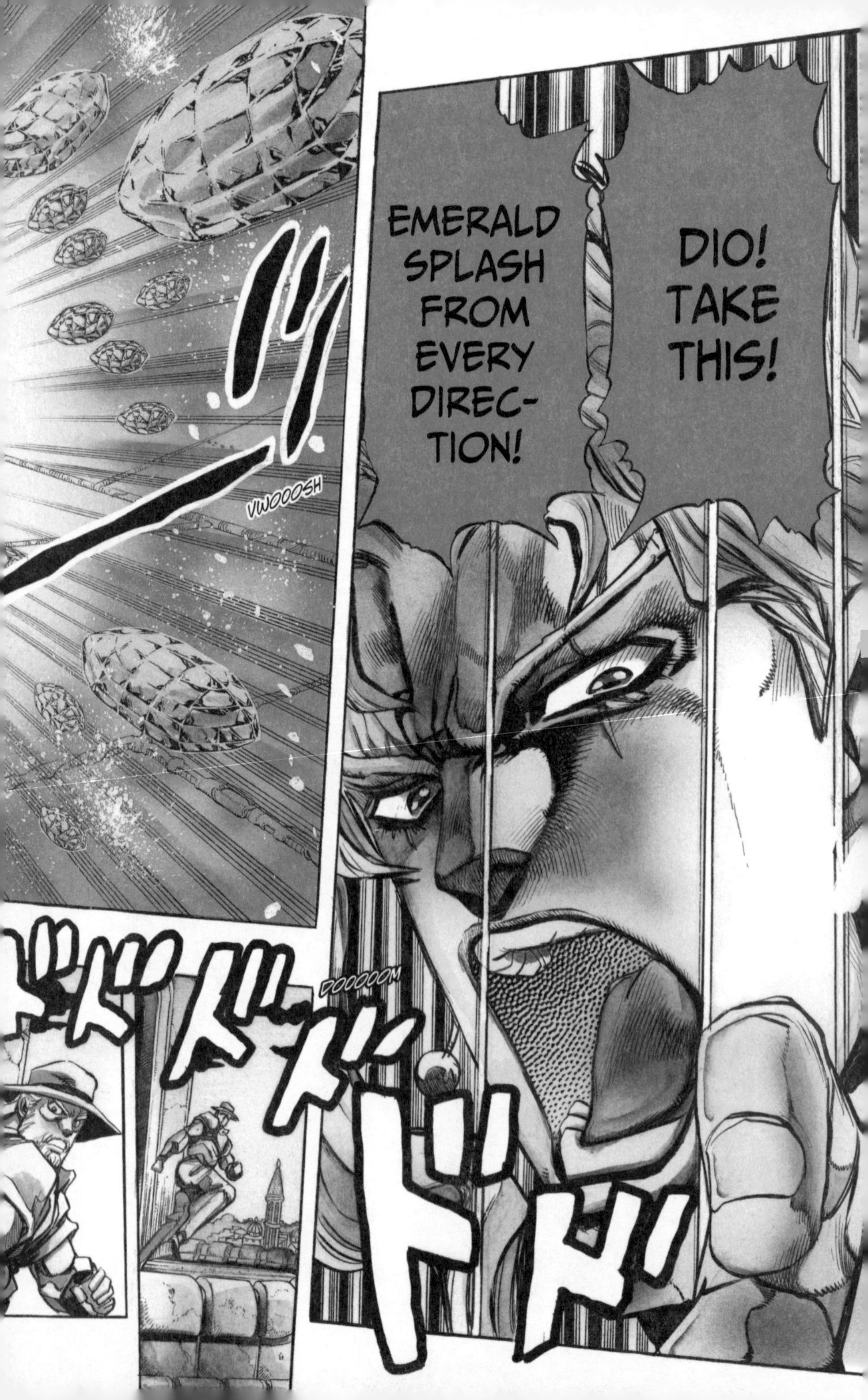
DIO! TAKE THIS!
EMERALD SPLASH FROM EVERY DIREC-TION!
VWOOOSH
DOOOOOM

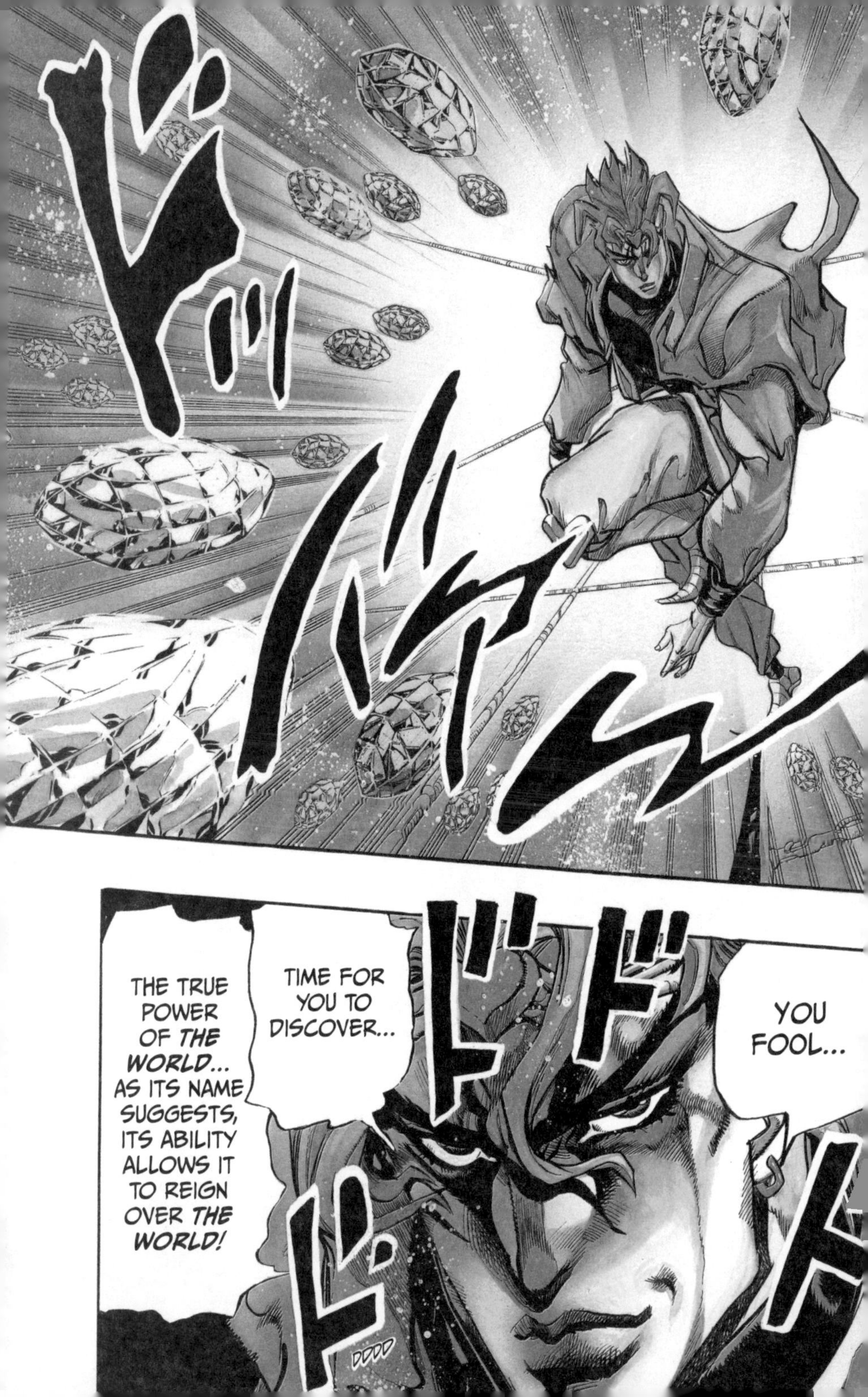
YOU FOOL...
TIME FOR YOU TO DISCOVER...
THE TRUE POWER OF *THE WORLD*... AS ITS NAME SUGGESTS, ITS ABILITY ALLOWS IT TO REIGN OVER *THE WORLD*!
DDDD

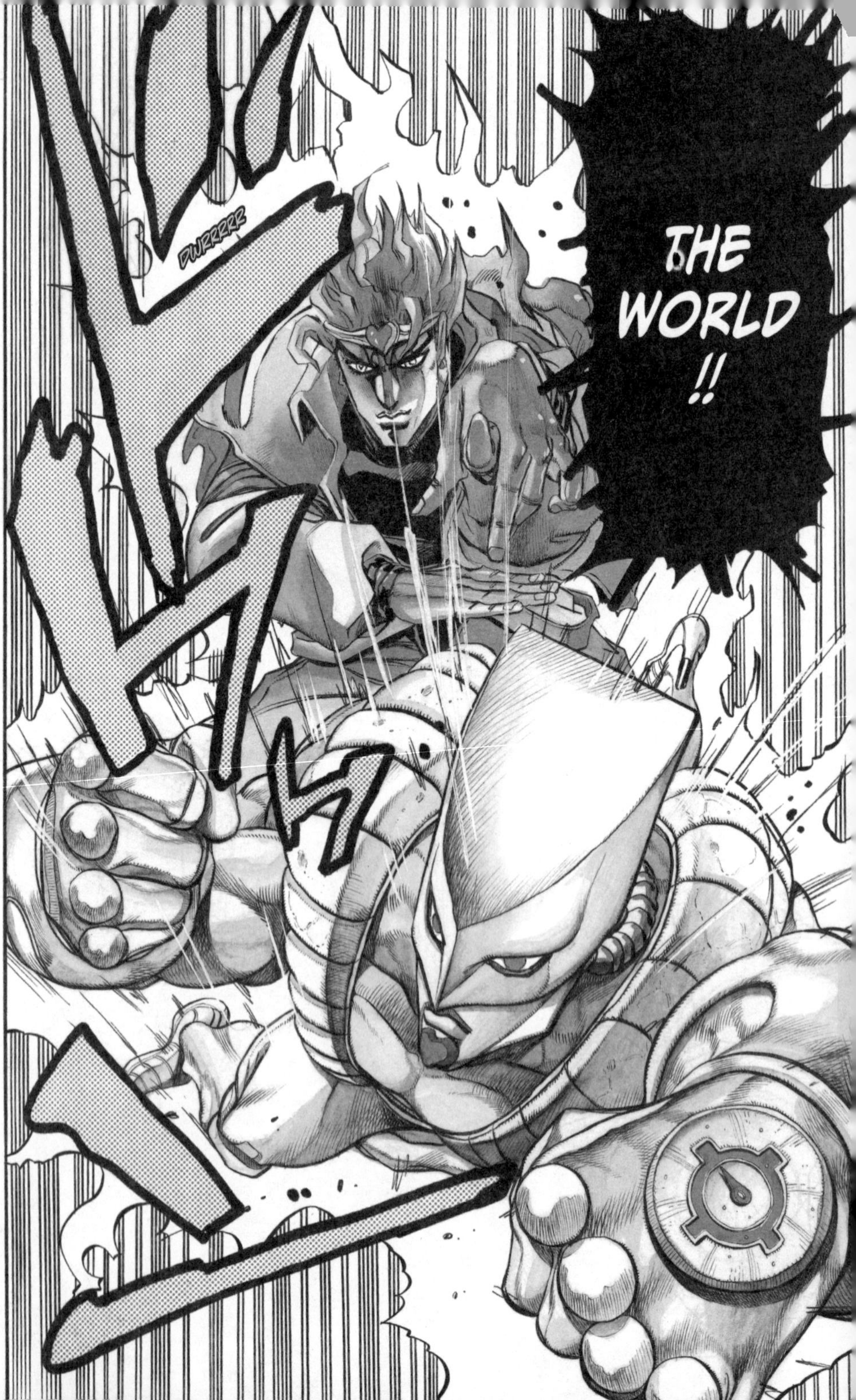
THE WORLD !!
DWRRRRR

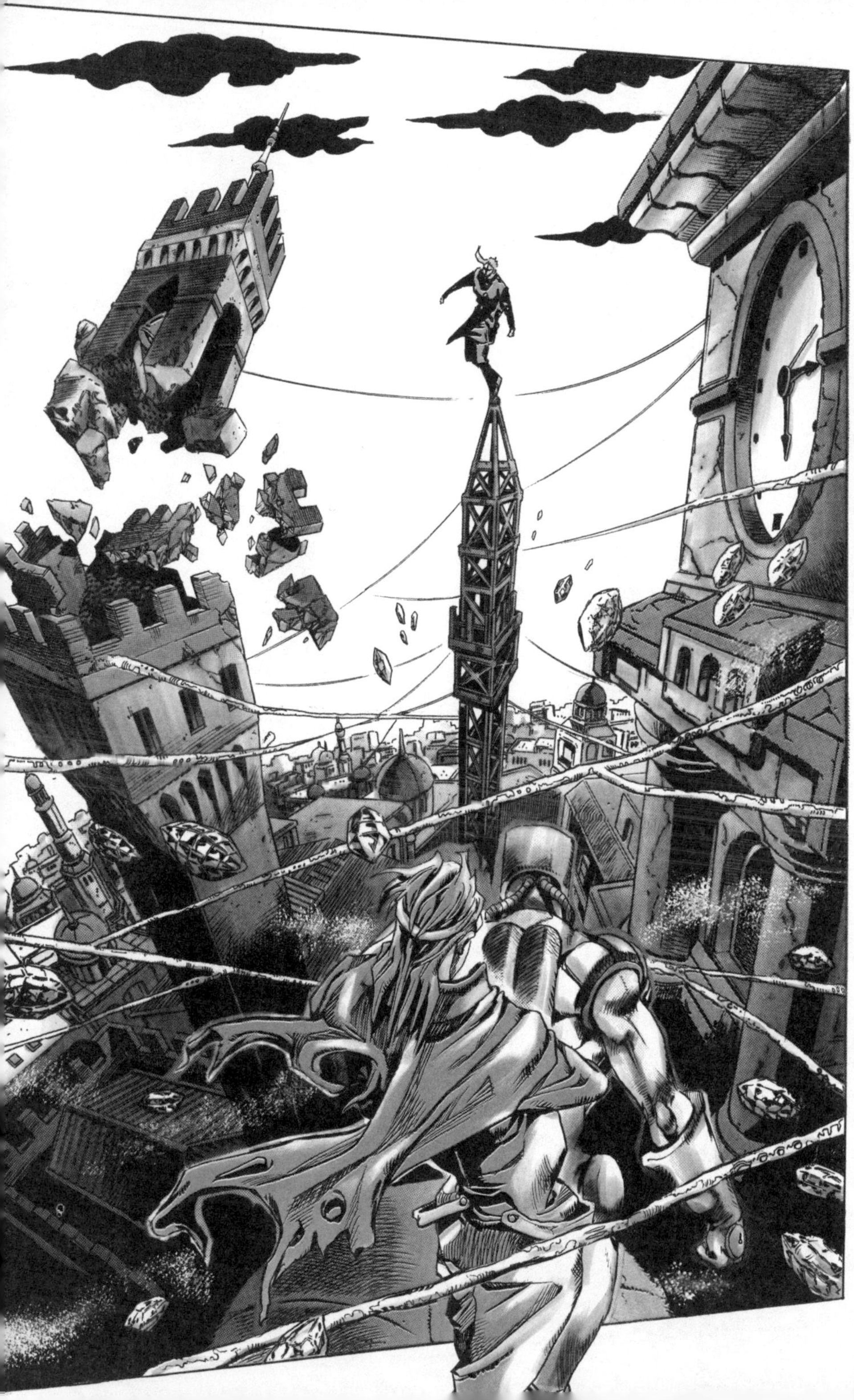

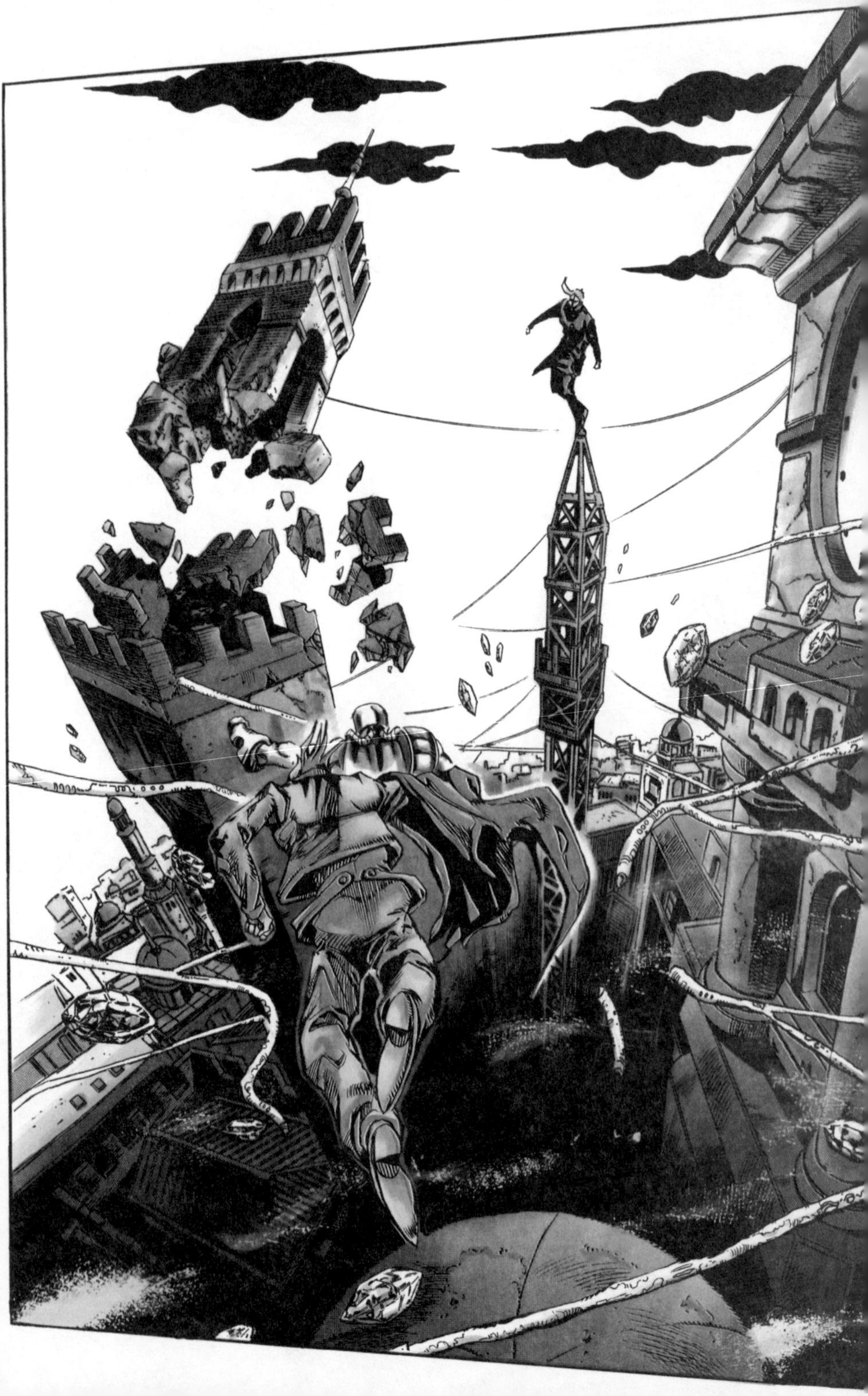

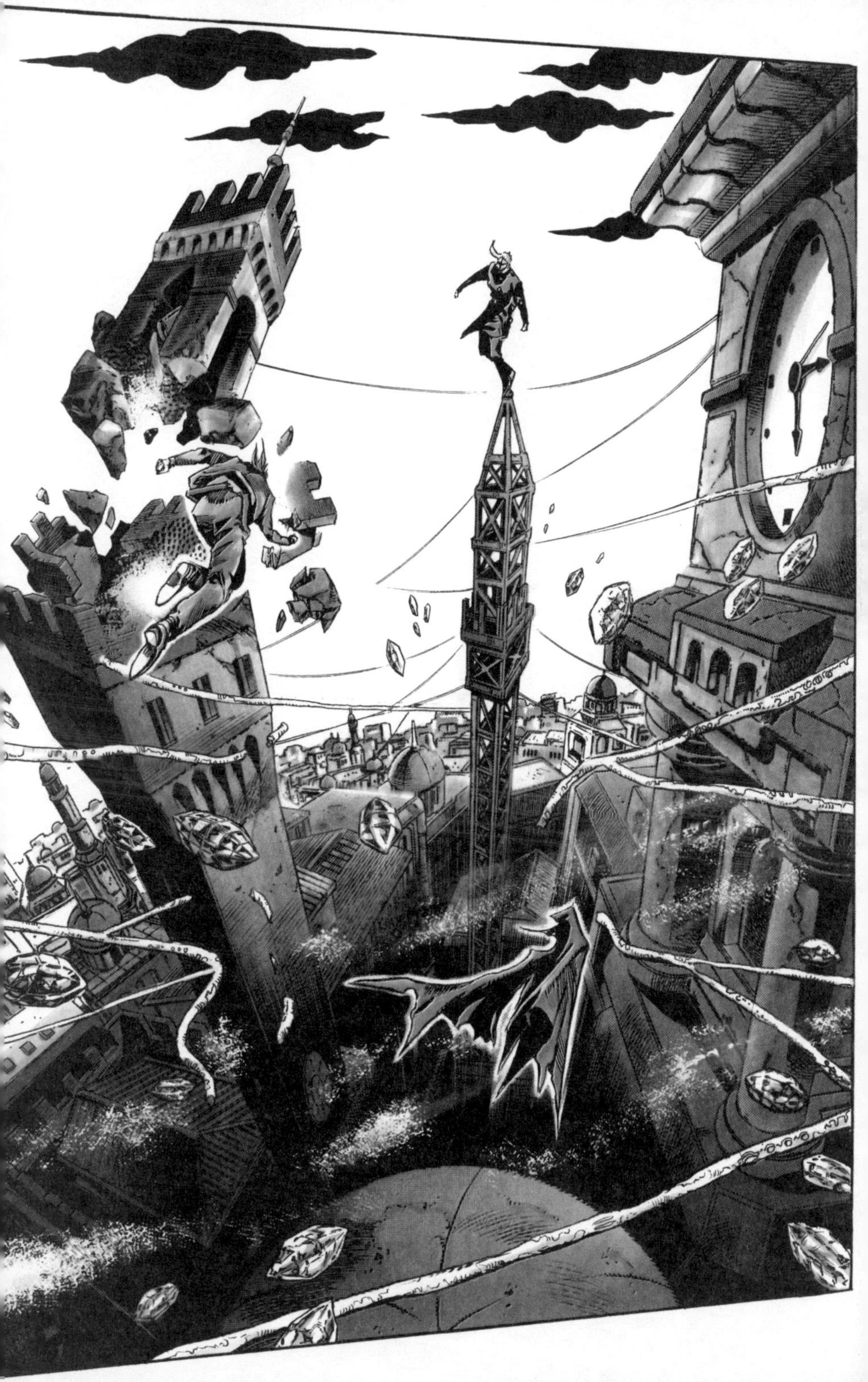

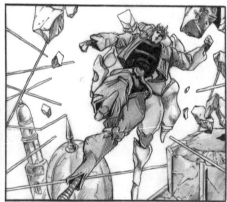

SINCE TIME HAS STOPPED FOR YOU, YOU PROBABLY CAN'T SEE OR SENSE ANYTHING DIFFERENT, BUT...

THE WORLD!

THIS IS...

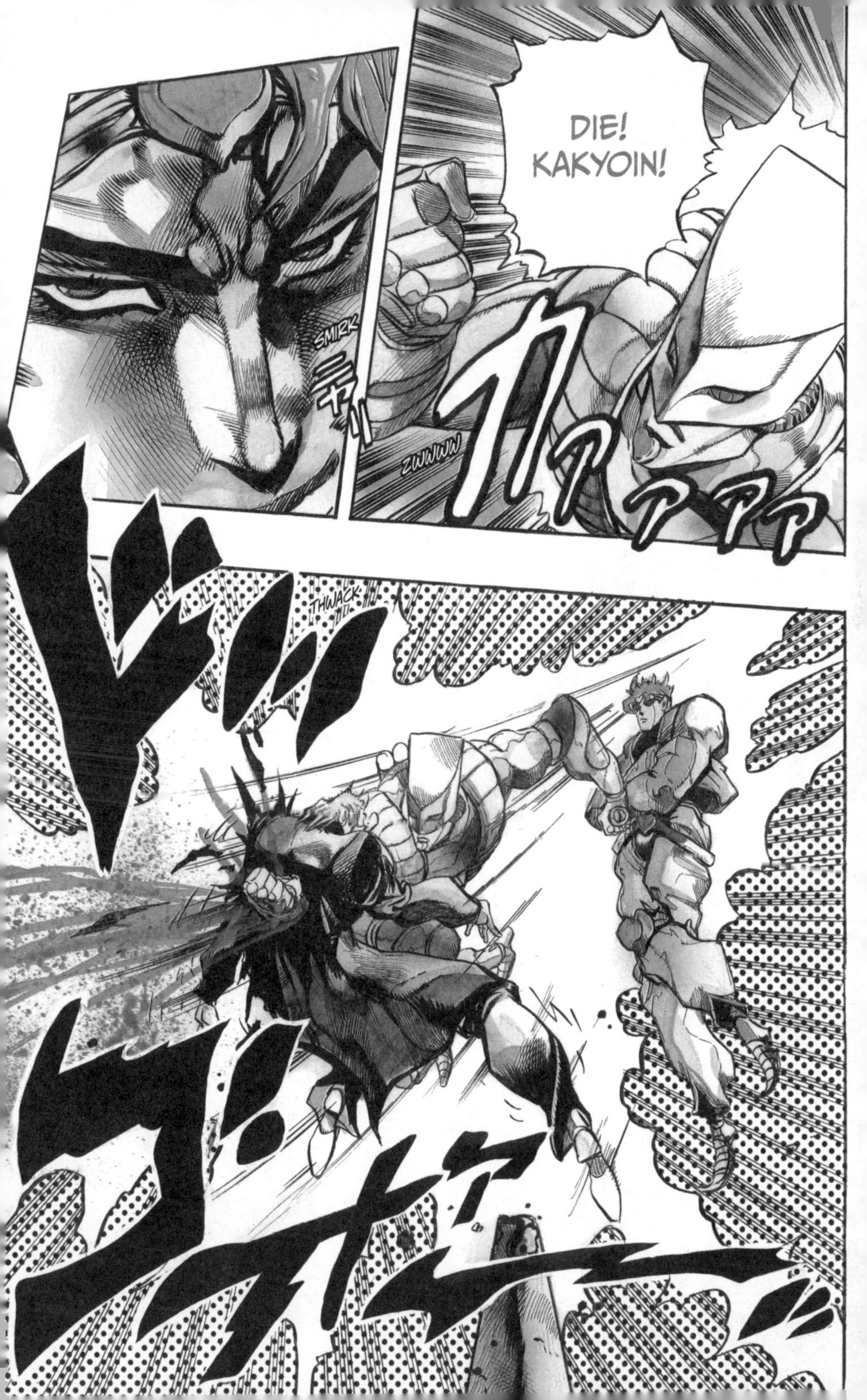
DIE! KAKYOIN!
ZWWWW
SMIRK
THWACK

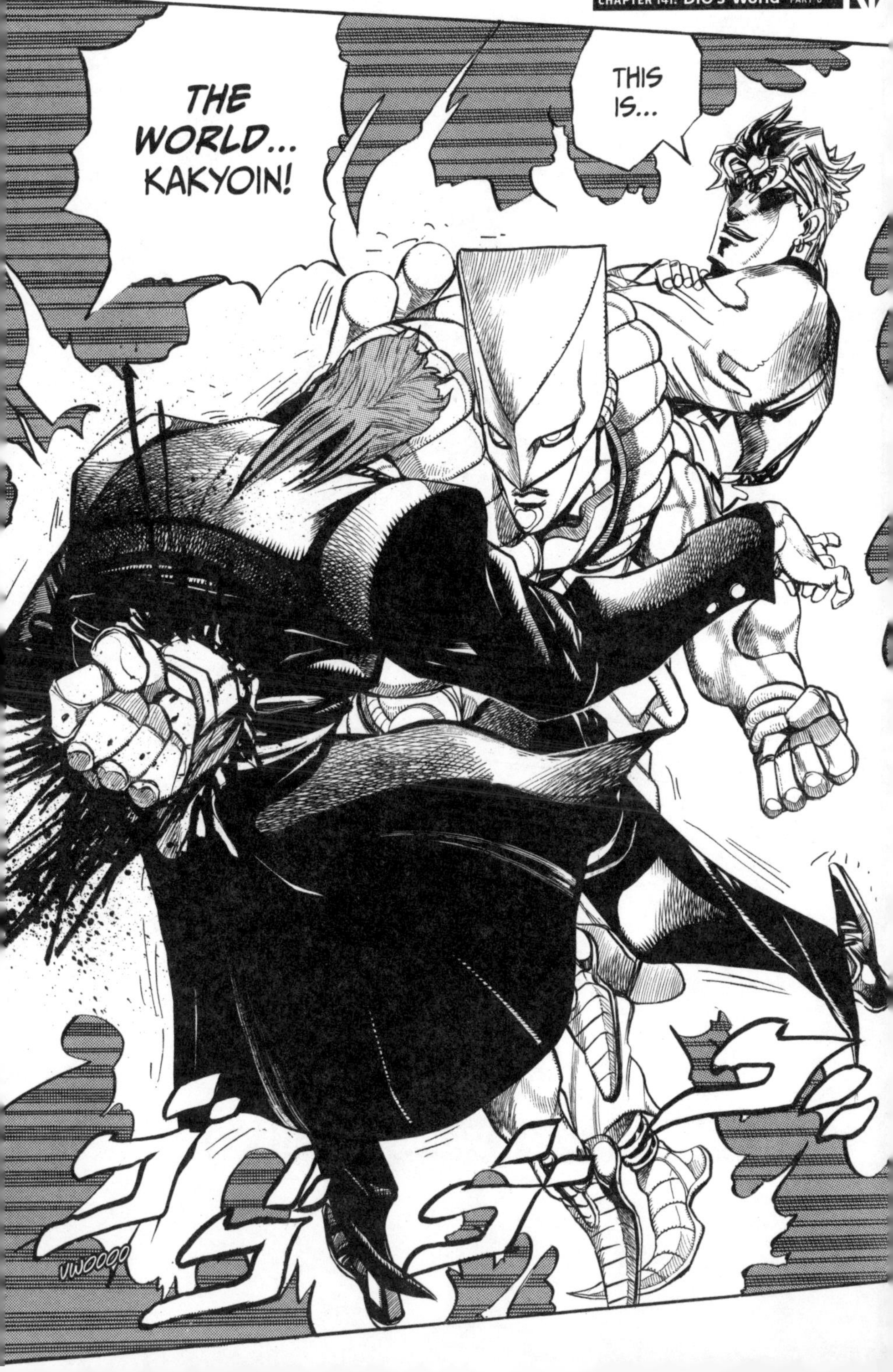
THIS IS...
THE WORLD... KAKYOIN!
VWOOOO

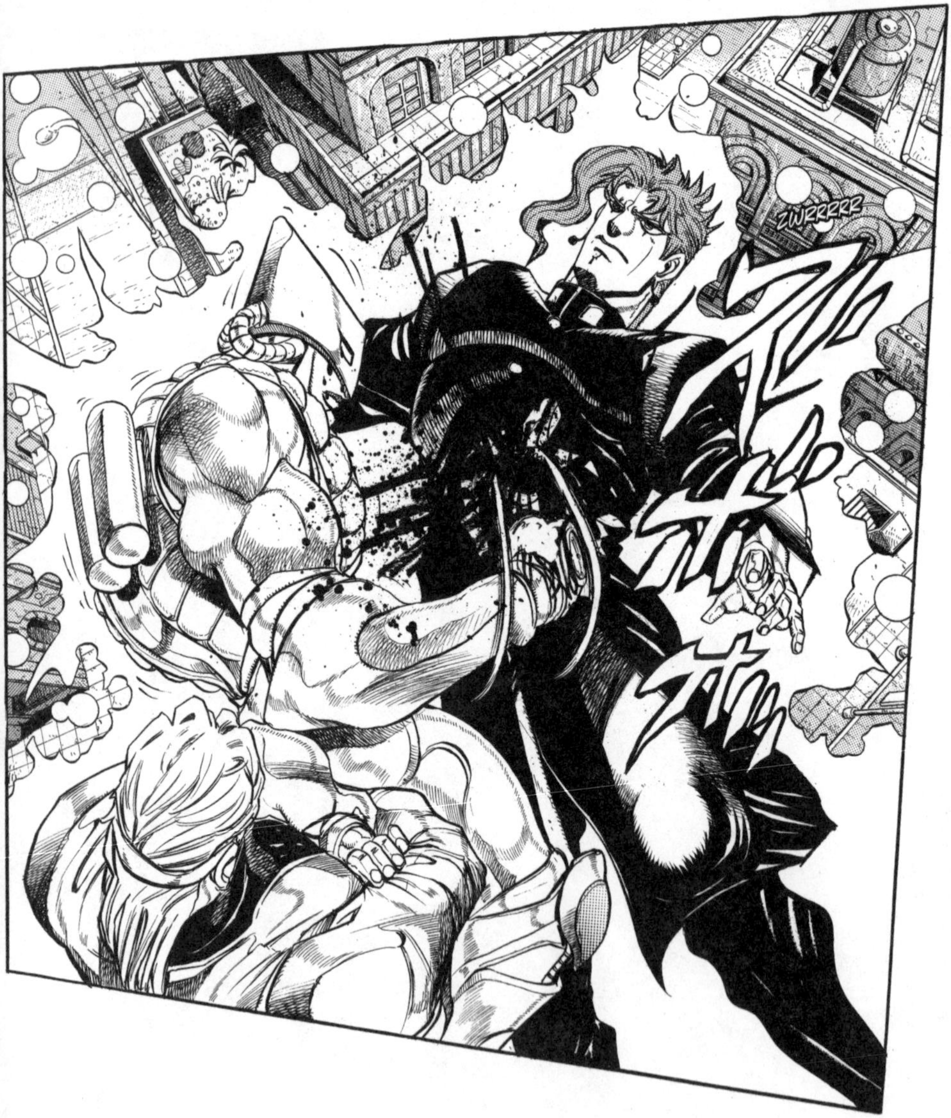
ZWRRRRR

CHAPTER 141: DIO's World PART 8

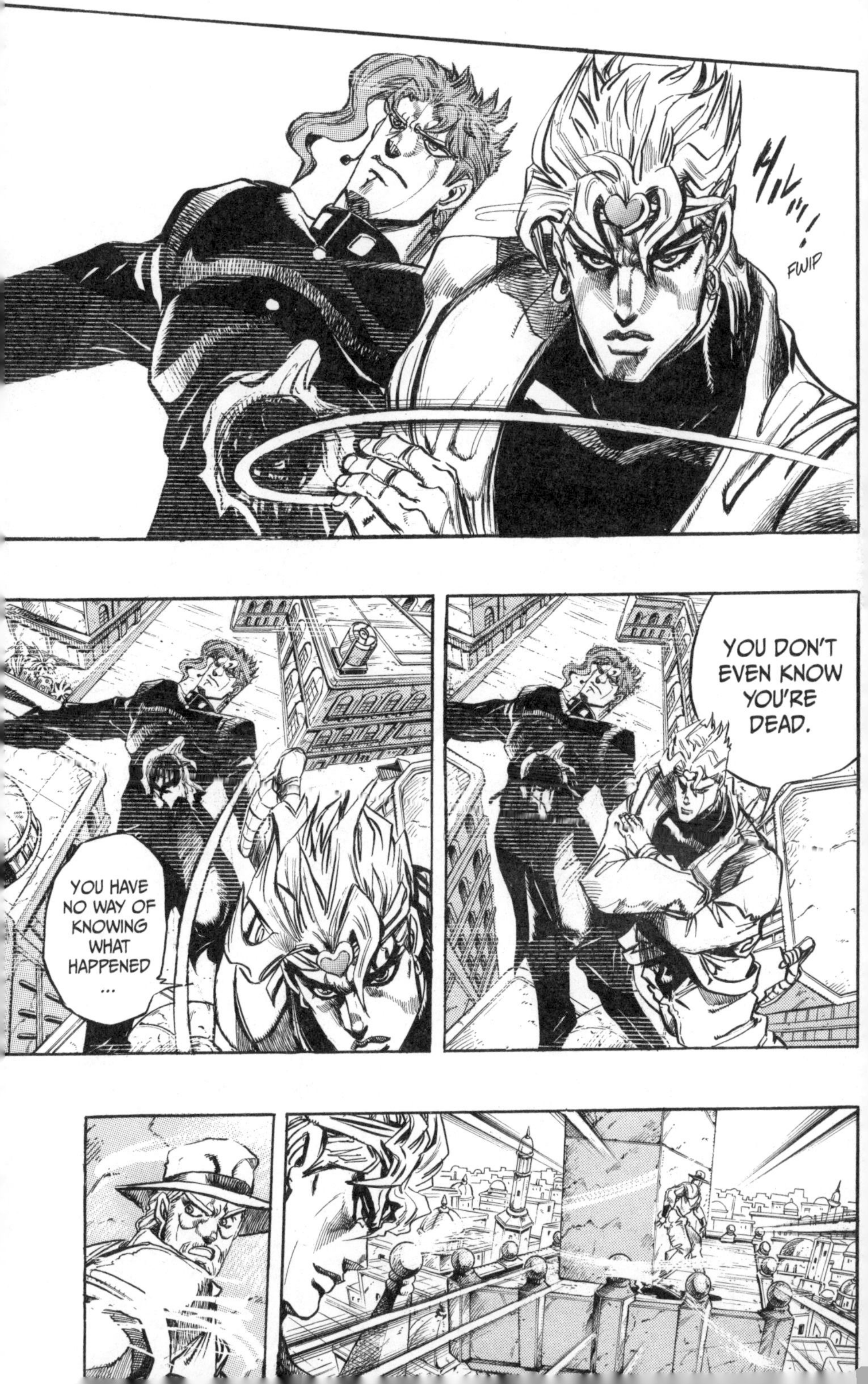
FWIP
YOU DON'T EVEN KNOW YOU'RE DEAD.
YOU HAVE NO WAY OF KNOWING WHAT HAPPENED ...

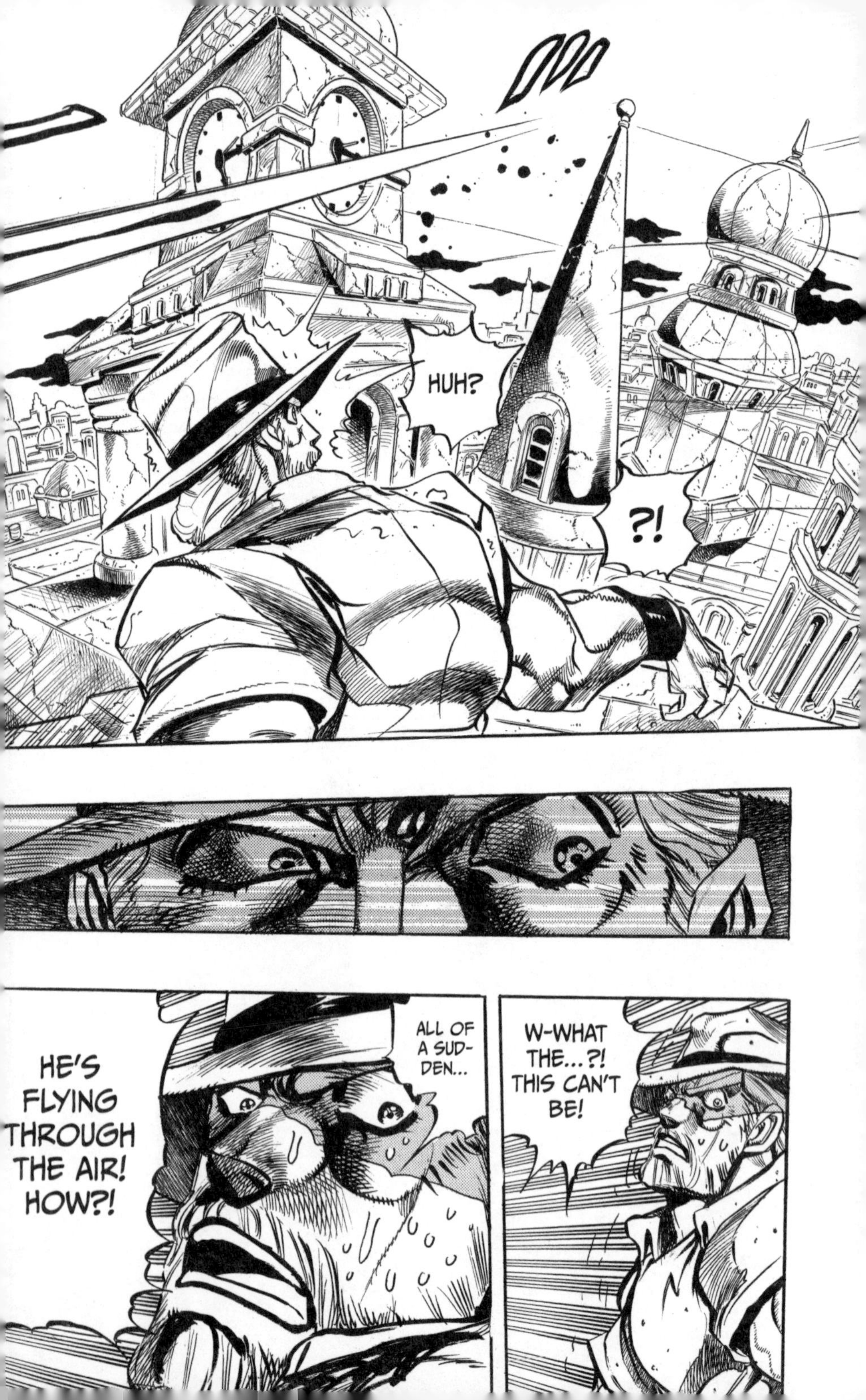
HUH?
?!
W-WHAT THE...?! THIS CAN'T BE!
ALL OF A SUD-DEN...
HE'S FLYING THROUGH THE AIR! HOW?!

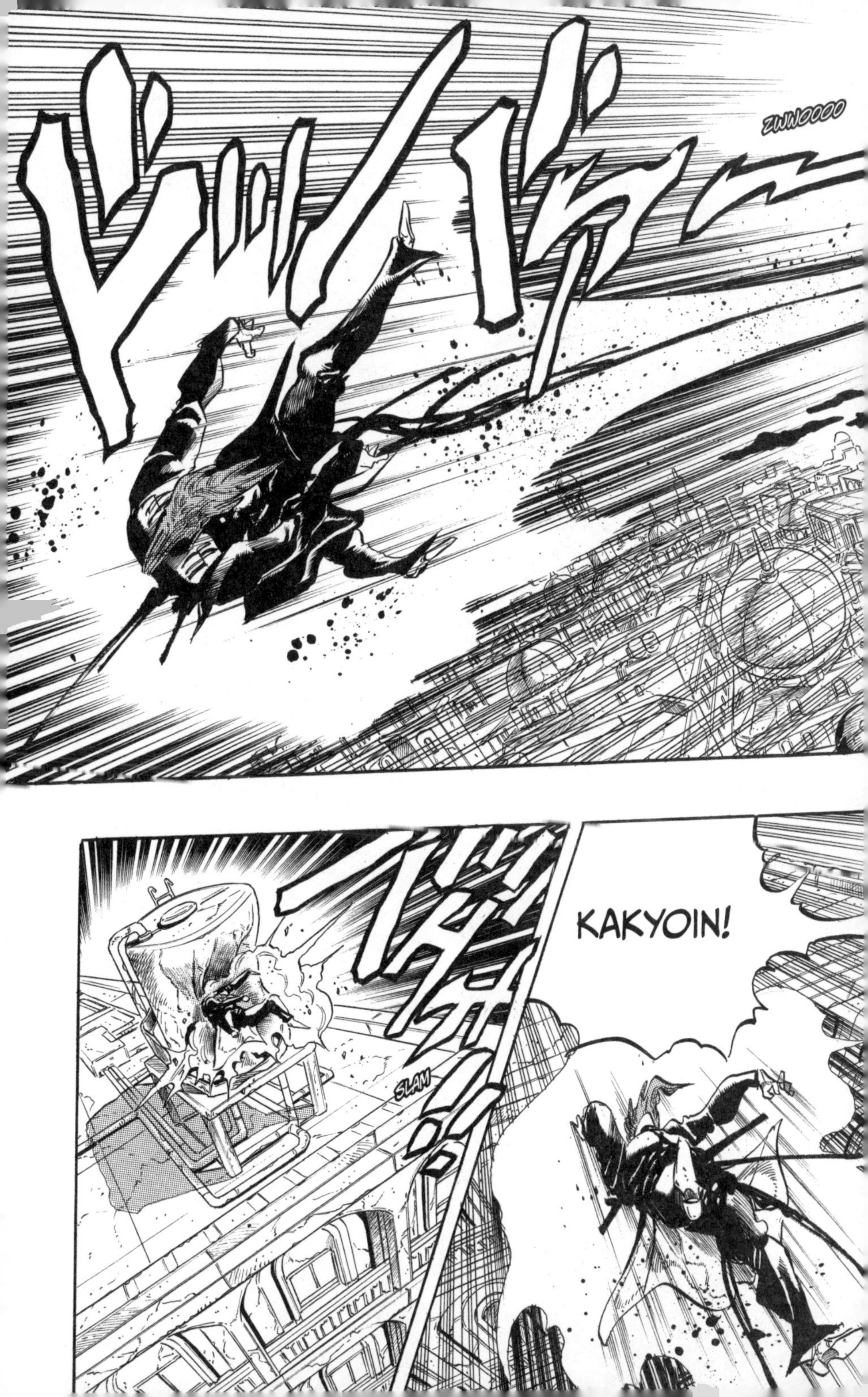
ZWWOOOO
KAKYOIN!
SLAM

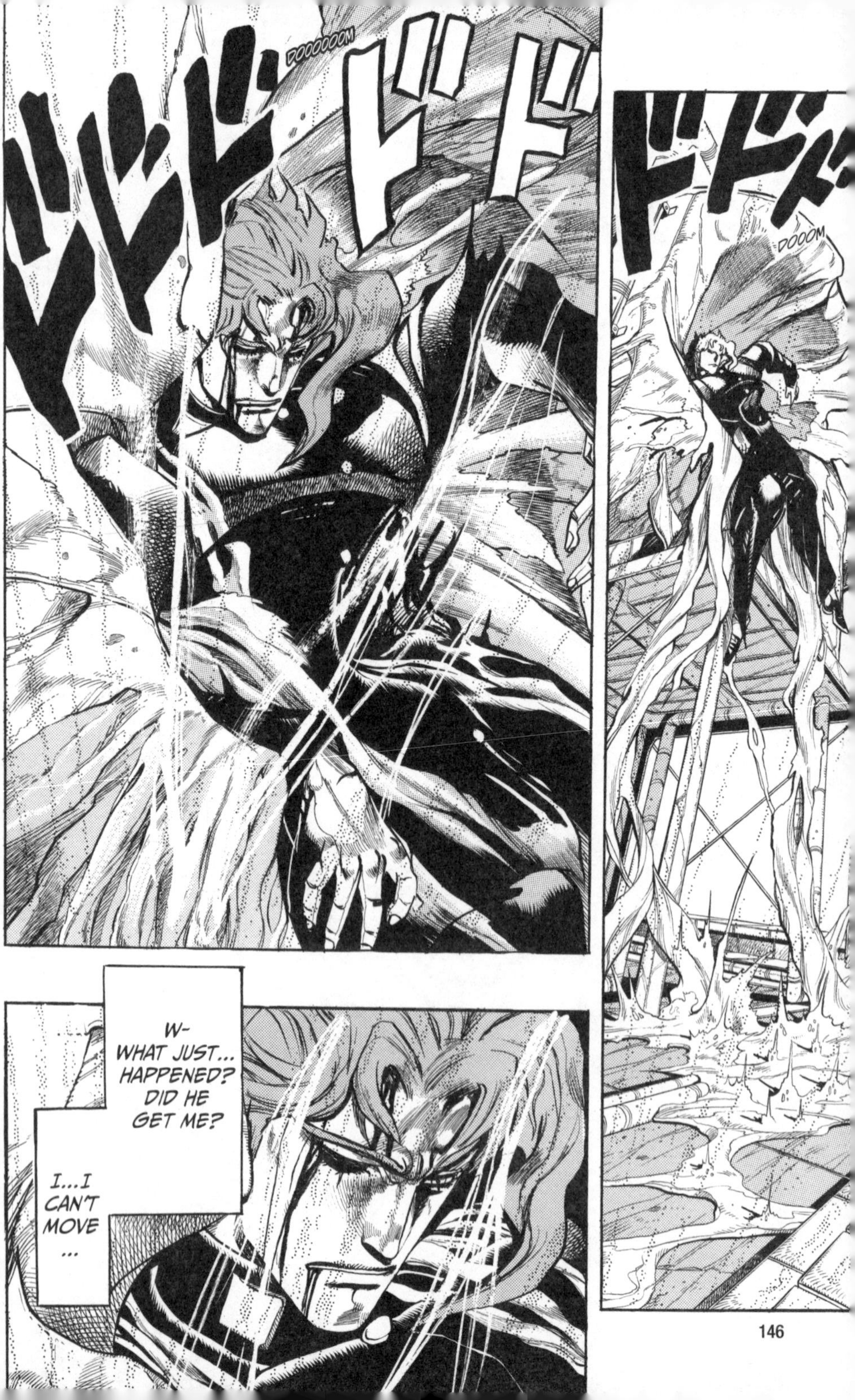
DOOOM
DOOOOOOM
W- WHAT JUST... HAPPENED? DID HE GET ME?
I...I CAN'T MOVE ...

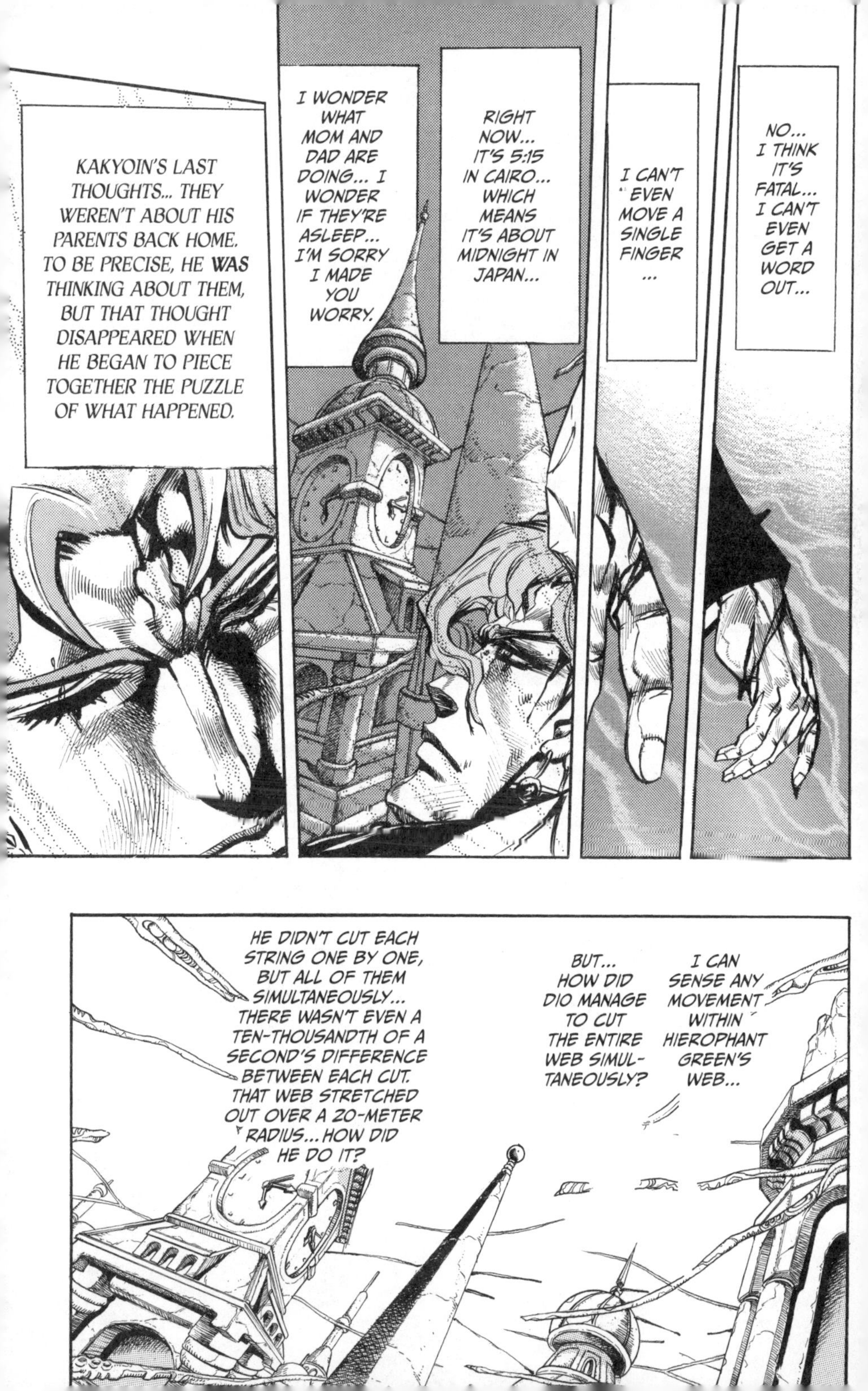
NO... I THINK IT'S FATAL... I CAN'T EVEN GET A WORD OUT...
I CAN'T EVEN MOVE A SINGLE FINGER ...
RIGHT NOW... IT'S 5:15 IN CAIRO... WHICH MEANS IT'S ABOUT MIDNIGHT IN JAPAN...
I WONDER WHAT MOM AND DAD ARE DOING... I WONDER IF THEY'RE ASLEEP... I'M SORRY I MADE YOU WORRY.
KAKYOIN'S LAST THOUGHTS... THEY WEREN'T ABOUT HIS PARENTS BACK HOME. TO BE PRECISE, HE **WAS** THINKING ABOUT THEM, BUT THAT THOUGHT DISAPPEARED WHEN HE BEGAN TO PIECE TOGETHER THE PUZZLE OF WHAT HAPPENED.
I CAN SENSE ANY MOVEMENT WITHIN HIEROPHANT GREEN'S WEB...
BUT... HOW DID DIO MANAGE TO CUT THE ENTIRE WEB SIMUL-TANEOUSLY?
HE DIDN'T CUT EACH STRING ONE BY ONE, BUT ALL OF THEM SIMULTANEOUSLY... THERE WASN'T EVEN A TEN-THOUSANDTH OF A SECOND'S DIFFERENCE BETWEEN EACH CUT. THAT WEB STRETCHED OUT OVER A 20-METER RADIUS... HOW DID HE DO IT?

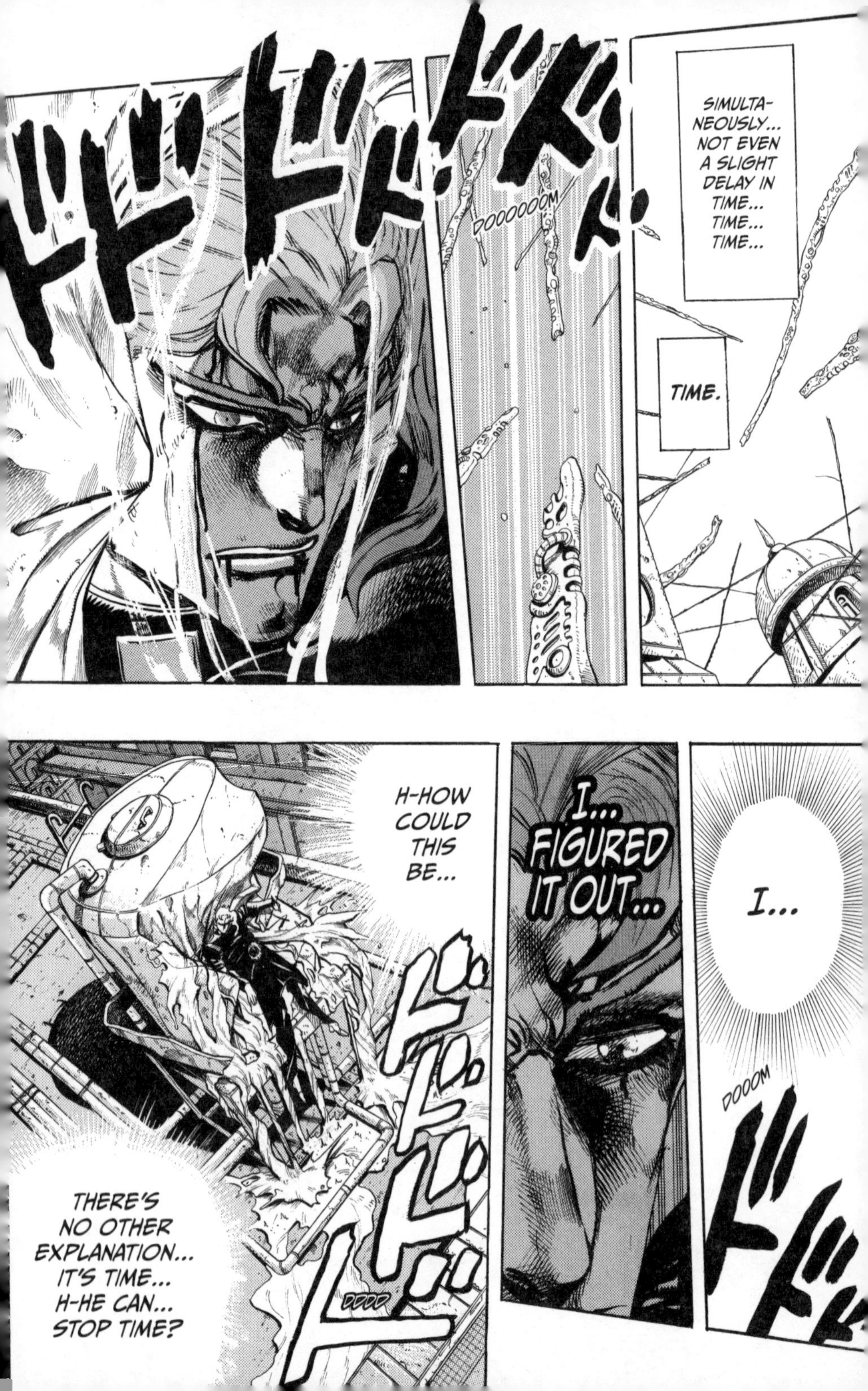
SIMULTA-NEOUSLY... NOT EVEN A SLIGHT DELAY IN TIME... TIME... TIME...
TIME.
DOOOOOOOM
I...
DOOOM
I... FIGURED IT OUT...
H-HOW COULD THIS BE...
THERE'S NO OTHER EXPLANATION... IT'S TIME... H-HE CAN... STOP TIME?
DDDD

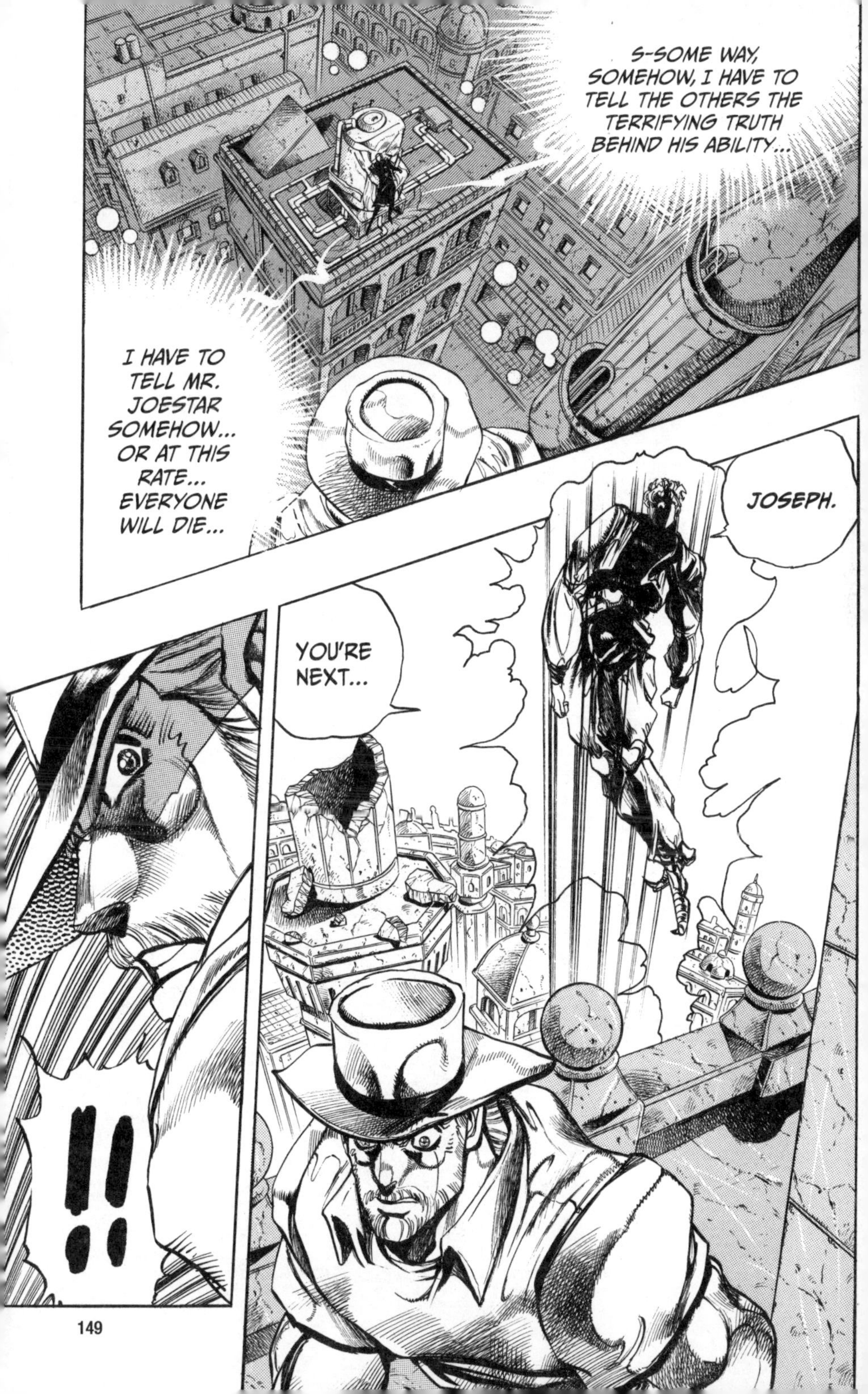
S-SOME WAY, SOMEHOW, I HAVE TO TELL THE OTHERS THE TERRIFYING TRUTH BEHIND HIS ABILITY...
I HAVE TO TELL MR. JOESTAR SOMEHOW... OR AT THIS RATE... EVERYONE WILL DIE...
JOSEPH.
YOU'RE NEXT...
!!

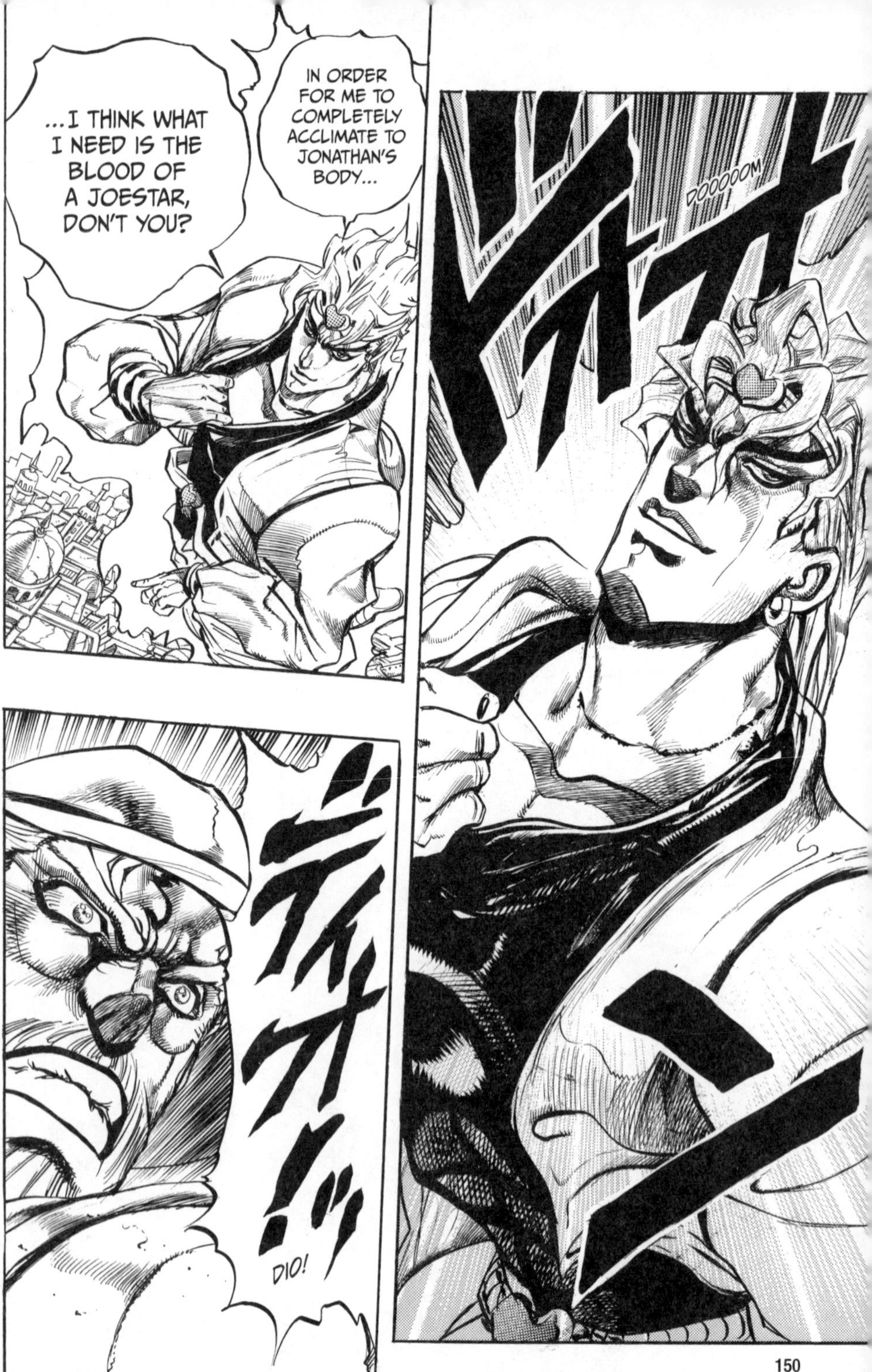
IN ORDER FOR ME TO COMPLETELY ACCLIMATE TO JONATHAN'S BODY...
...I THINK WHAT I NEED IS THE BLOOD OF A JOESTAR, DON'T YOU?
DOOOOOM
DIO!

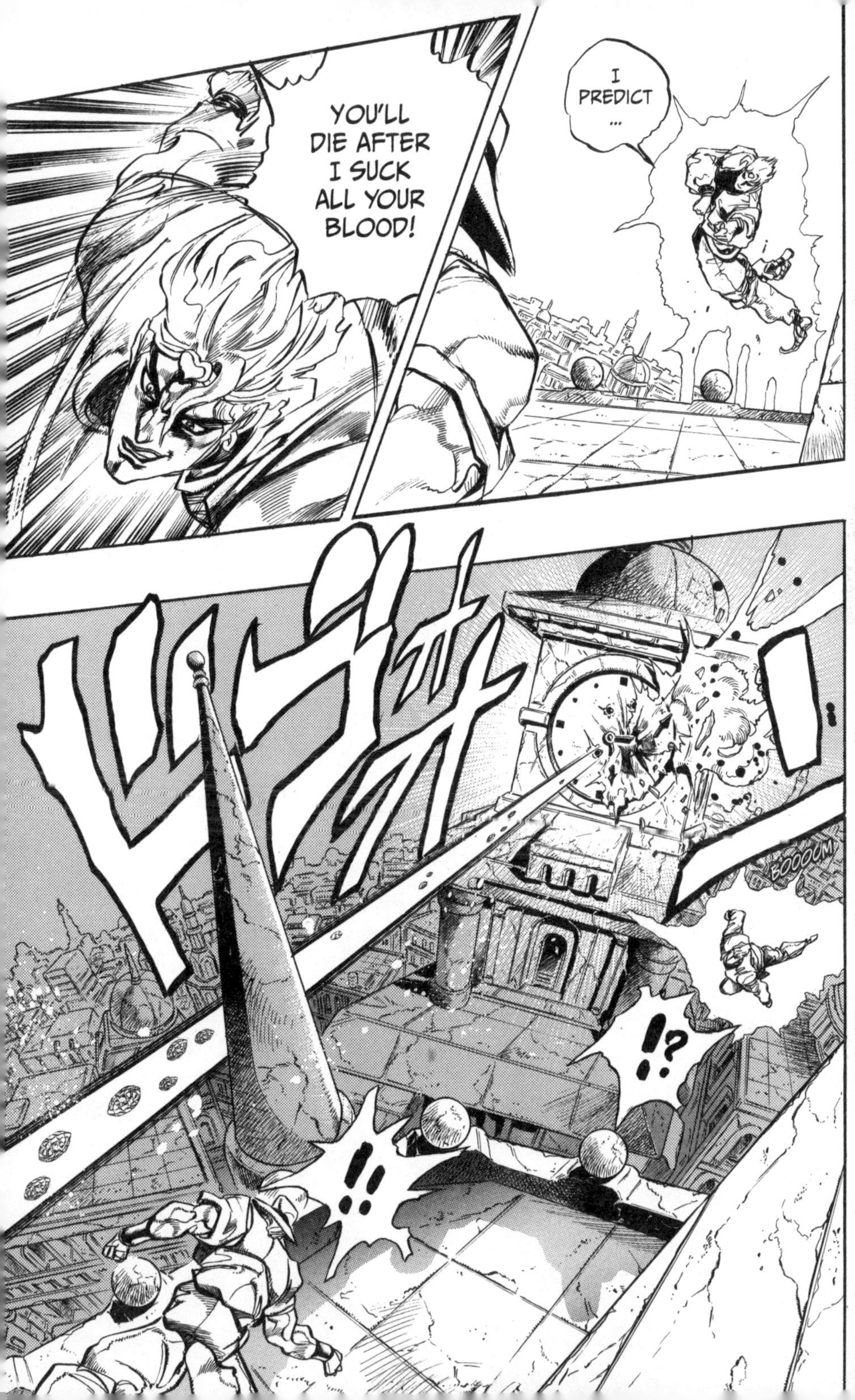
I PREDICT ...
YOU'LL DIE AFTER I SUCK ALL YOUR BLOOD!
BOOOOOM
!?
!!

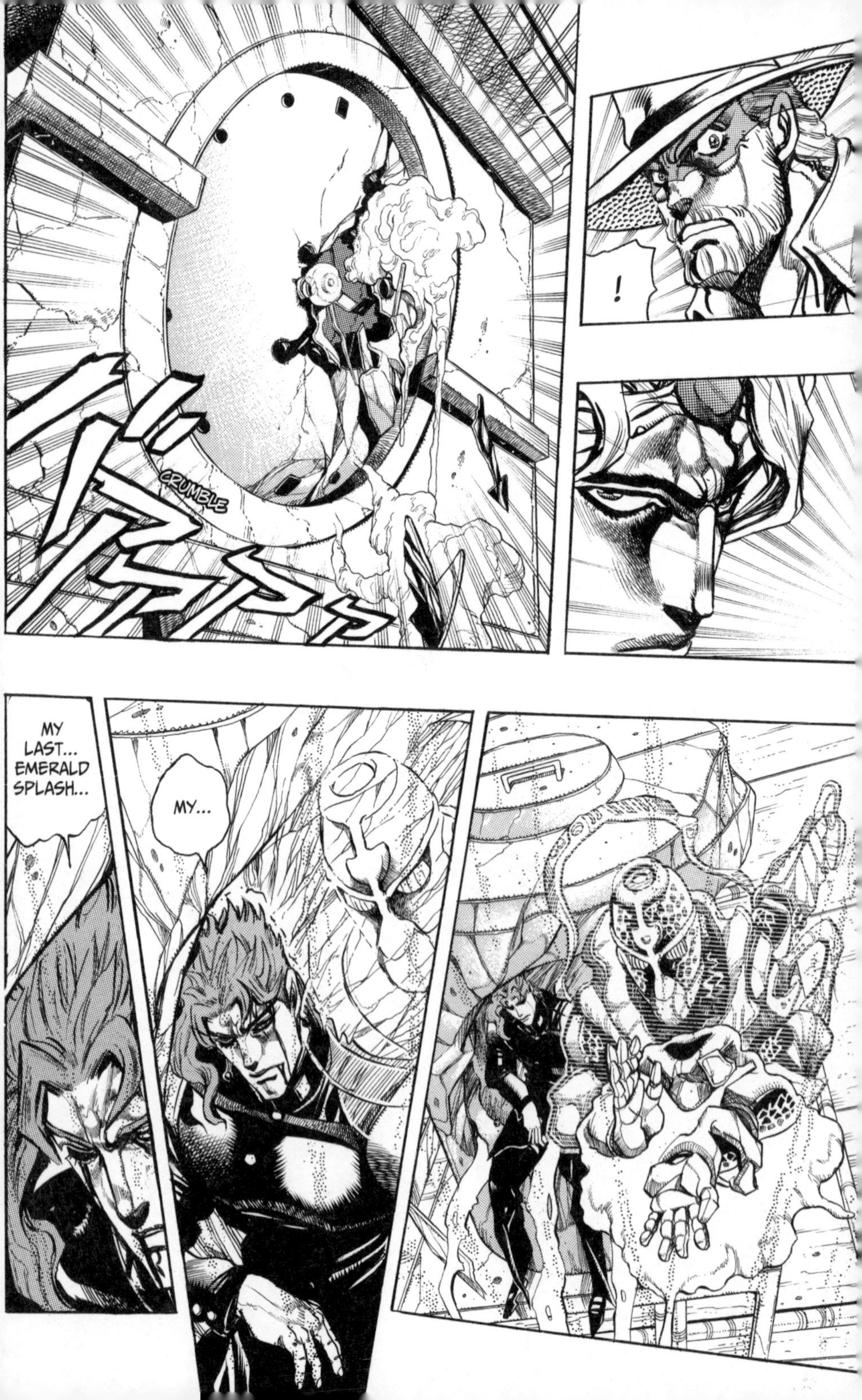
!
CRUMBLE
MY...
MY LAST... EMERALD SPLASH...

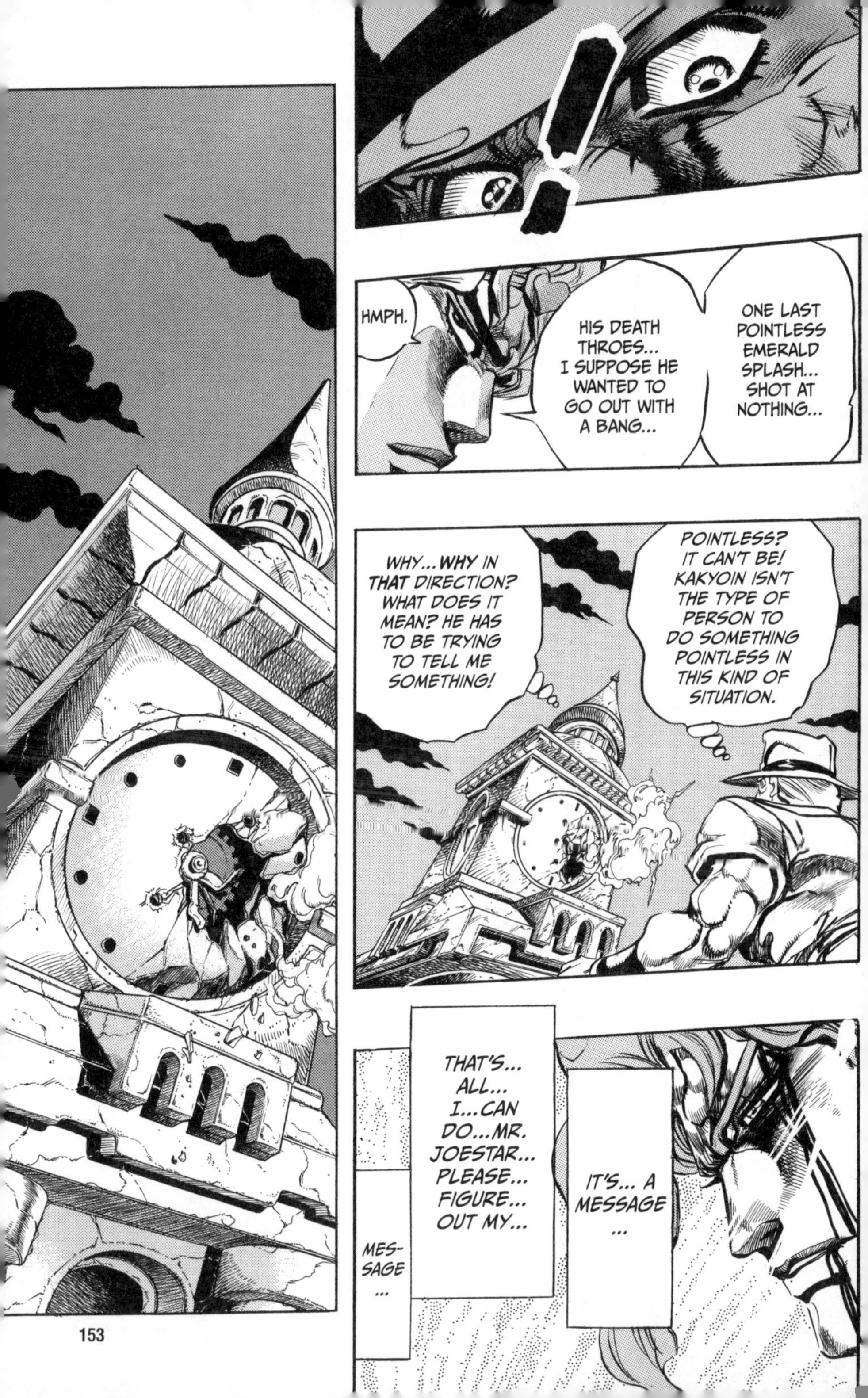
ONE LAST POINTLESS EMERALD SPLASH... SHOT AT NOTHING...
HIS DEATH THROES... I SUPPOSE HE WANTED TO GO OUT WITH A BANG...
HMPH.
POINTLESS? IT CAN'T BE! KAKYOIN ISN'T THE TYPE OF PERSON TO DO SOMETHING POINTLESS IN THIS KIND OF SITUATION.
WHY... WHY IN THAT DIRECTION? WHAT DOES IT MEAN? HE HAS TO BE TRYING TO TELL ME SOMETHING!
IT'S... A MESSAGE ...
THAT'S... ALL... I...CAN DO...MR. JOESTAR... PLEASE... FIGURE... OUT MY...
MES-SAGE ...

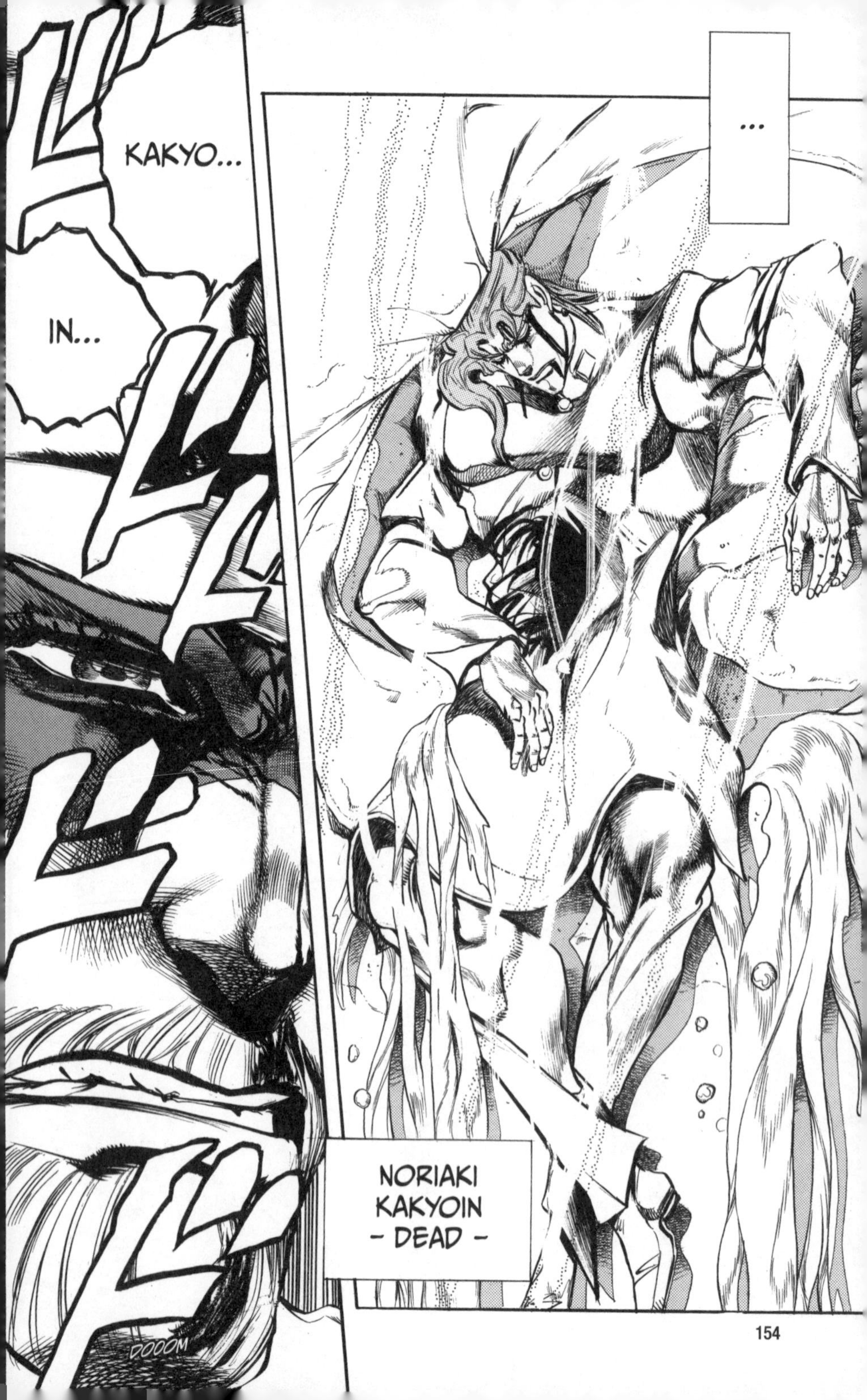
...
NORIAKI KAKYOIN - DEAD -
KAKYO...
IN...
DOOOM

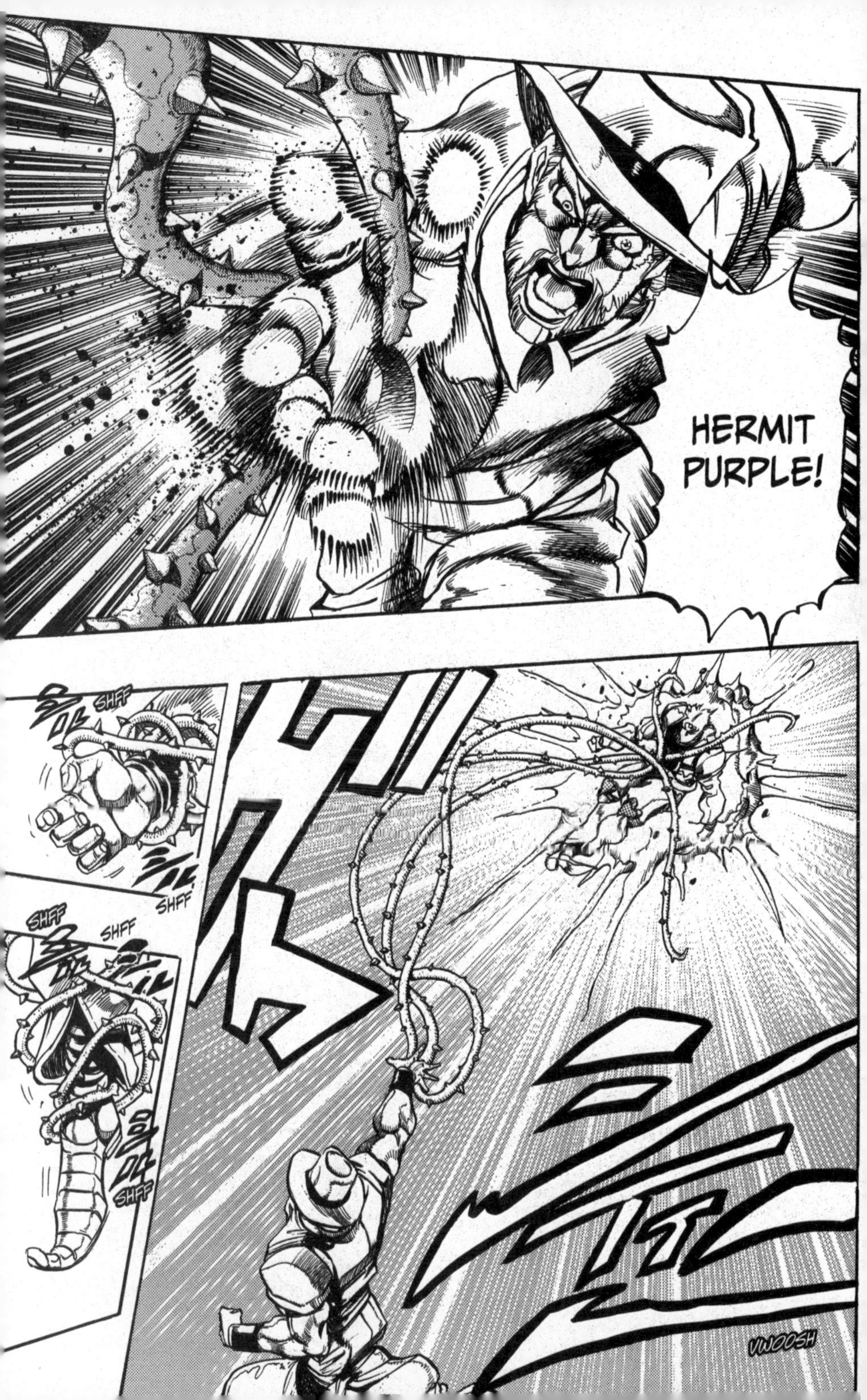
HERMIT PURPLE!
VWOOSH
SHFF
SHFF
SHFF
SHFF
SHFF

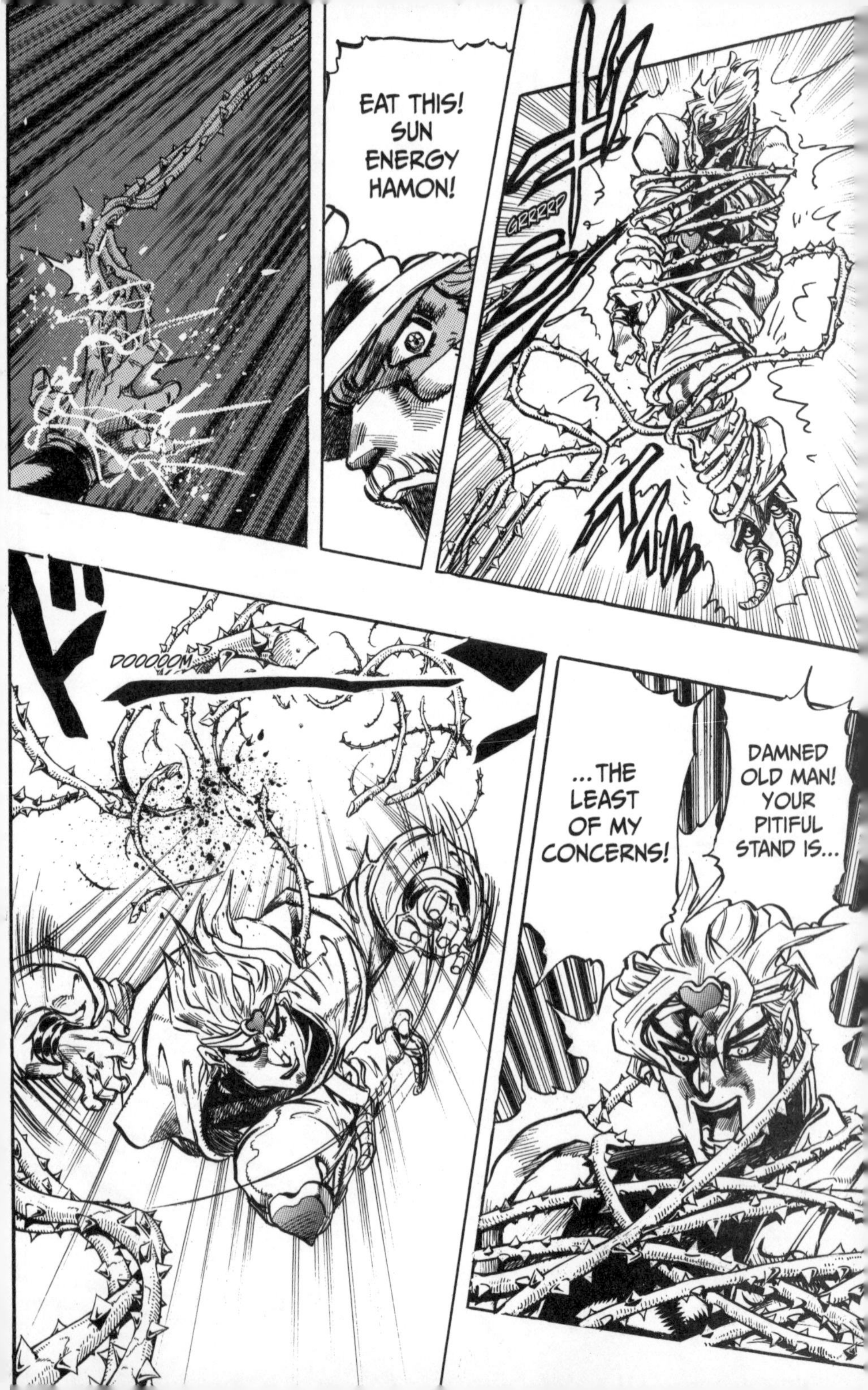
GRRRRP
EAT THIS! SUN ENERGY HAMON!
DAMNED OLD MAN! YOUR PITIFUL STAND IS...
...THE LEAST OF MY CONCERNS!
DOOOOOM

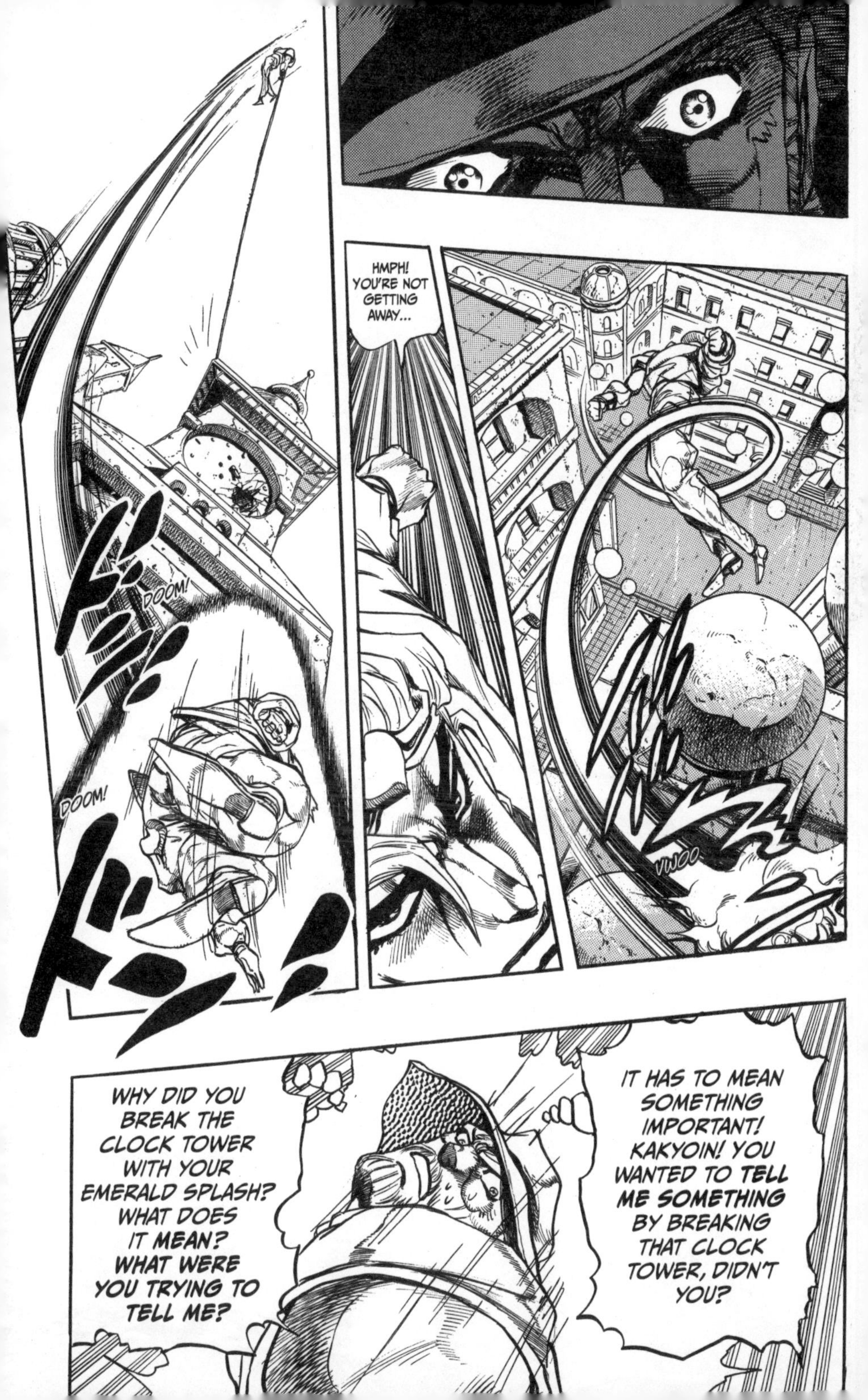
VWOO
HMPH! YOU'RE NOT GETTING AWAY...
DOOM!
DOOM!
IT HAS TO MEAN SOMETHING IMPORTANT! KAKYOIN! YOU WANTED TO TELL ME SOMETHING BY BREAKING THAT CLOCK TOWER, DIDN'T YOU?
WHY DID YOU BREAK THE CLOCK TOWER WITH YOUR EMERALD SPLASH? WHAT DOES IT MEAN? WHAT WERE YOU TRYING TO TELL ME?

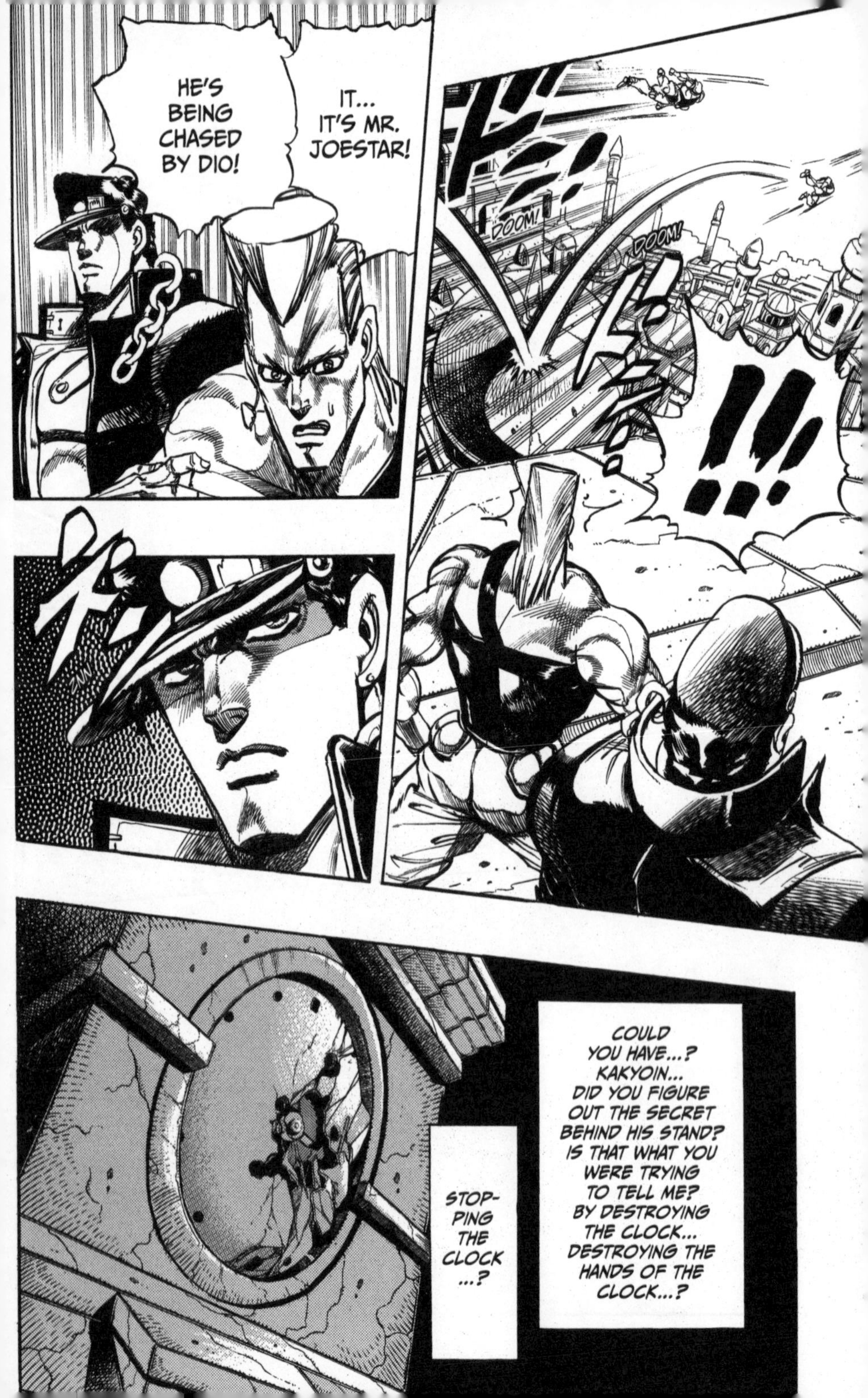
DOOM!
DOOM!
IT... IT'S MR. JOESTAR!
HE'S BEING CHASED BY DIO!
COULD YOU HAVE...? KAKYOIN... DID YOU FIGURE OUT THE SECRET BEHIND HIS STAND? IS THAT WHAT YOU WERE TRYING TO TELL ME? BY DESTROYING THE CLOCK... DESTROYING THE HANDS OF THE CLOCK...?
STOP-PING THE CLOCK ...?

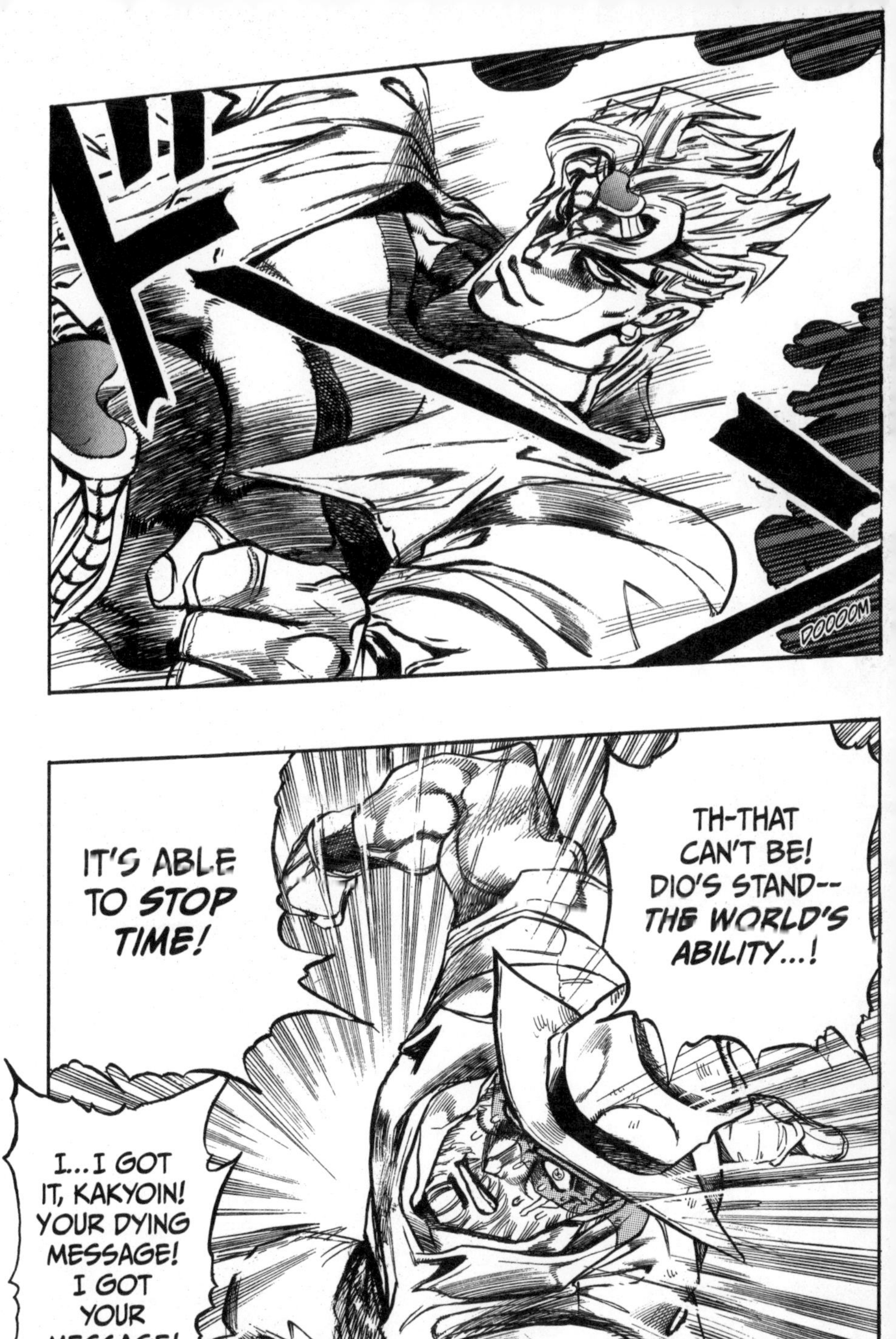
DOOOOM
TH-THAT CAN'T BE! DIO'S STAND-- *THE WORLD'S* ABILITY...!
IT'S ABLE TO *STOP TIME!*
I...I GOT IT, KAKYOIN! YOUR DYING MESSAGE! I GOT YOUR MESSAGE!

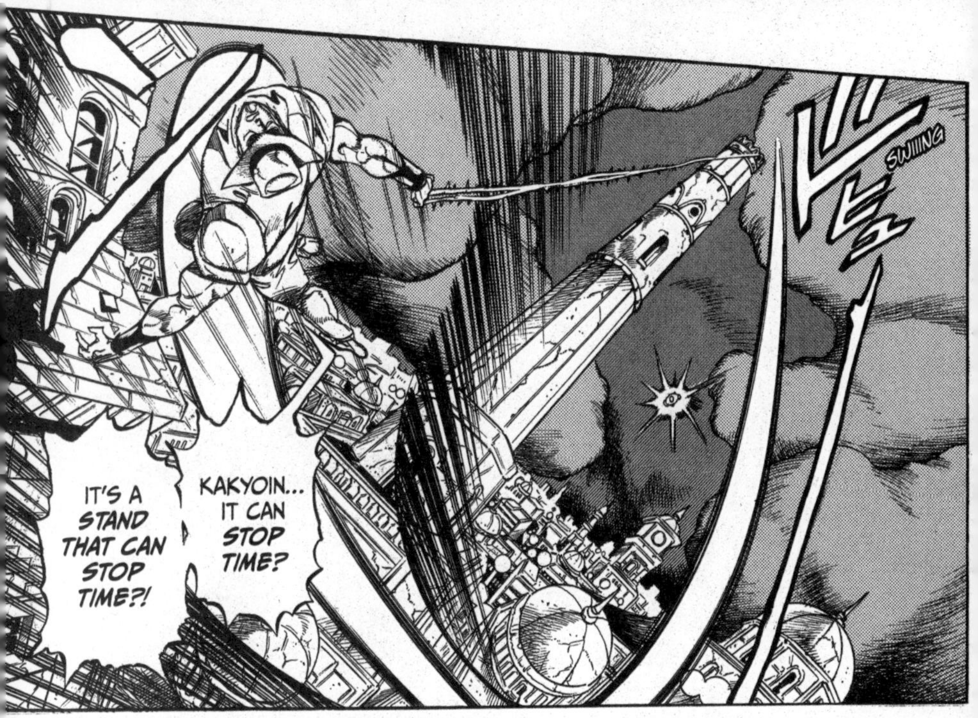
SWIIING
KAKYOIN... IT CAN STOP TIME?
IT'S A STAND THAT CAN STOP TIME?!

CHAPTER 142: DIO's World PART 9

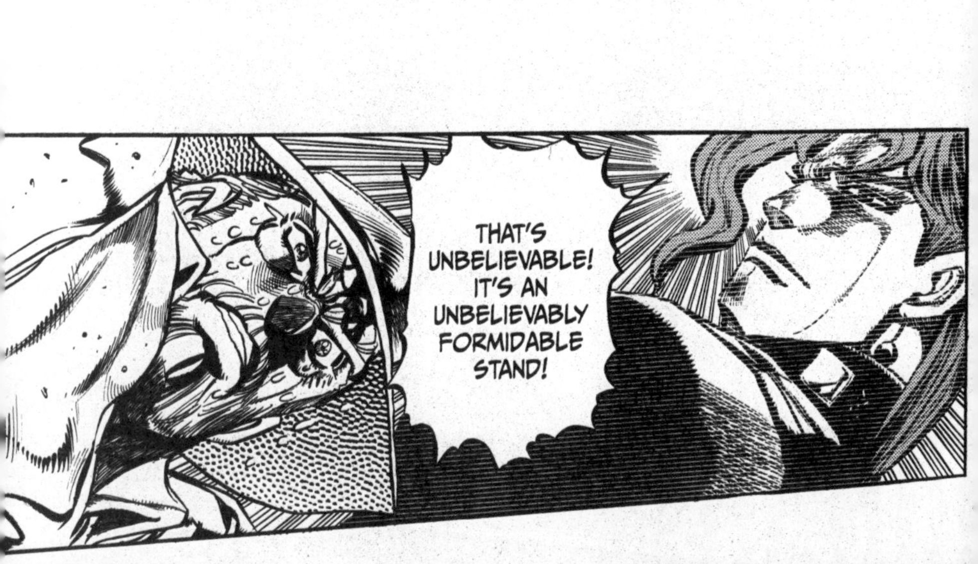
THAT'S UNBELIEVABLE! IT'S AN UNBELIEVABLY FORMIDABLE STAND!

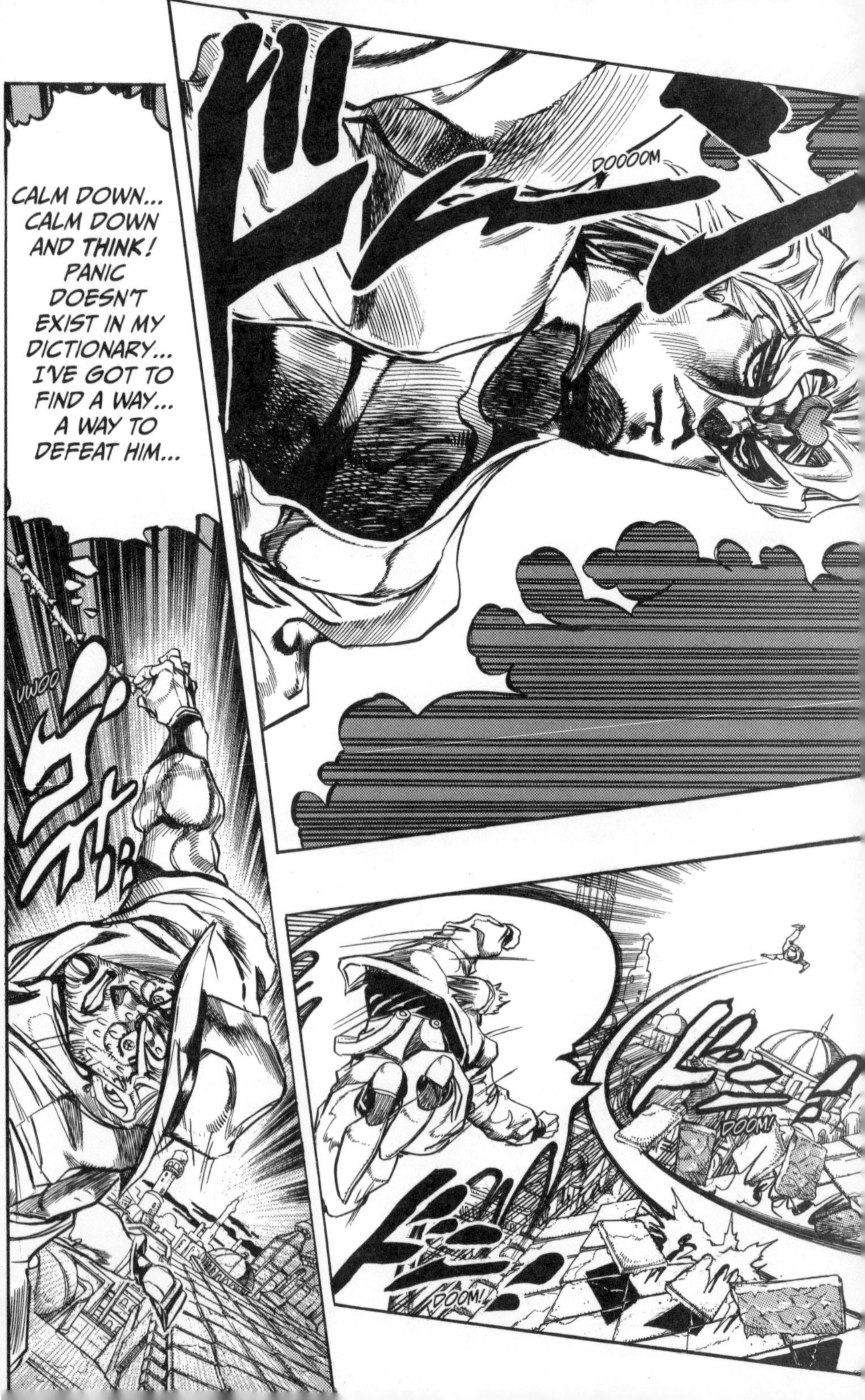
DOOOOM
DOOM!
DOOM!
CALM DOWN... CALM DOWN AND THINK! PANIC DOESN'T EXIST IN MY DICTIONARY... I'VE GOT TO FIND A WAY... A WAY TO DEFEAT HIM...
UWOO

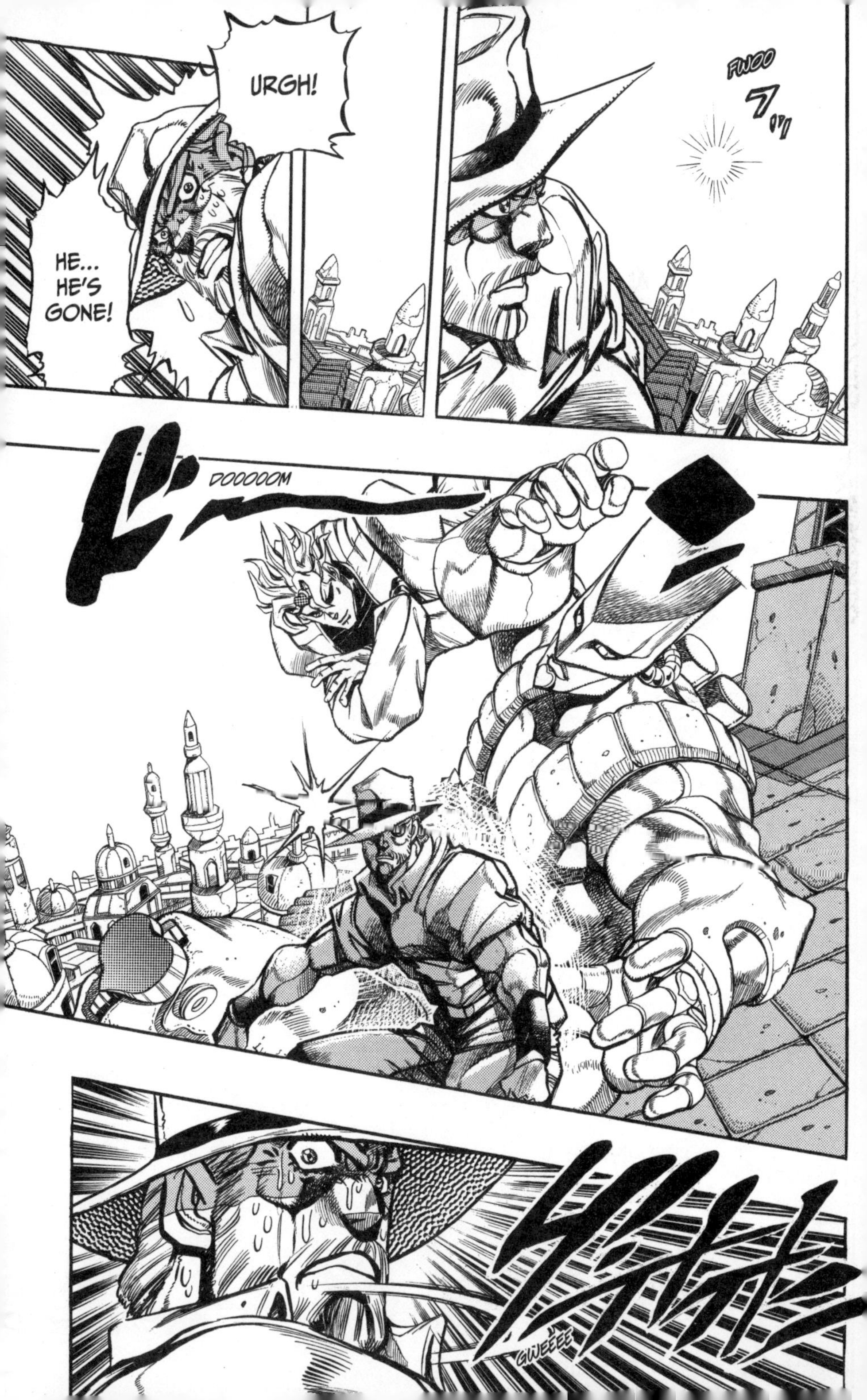
FWOO
URGH!
HE... HE'S GONE!
DOOOOOM
GWEEEE

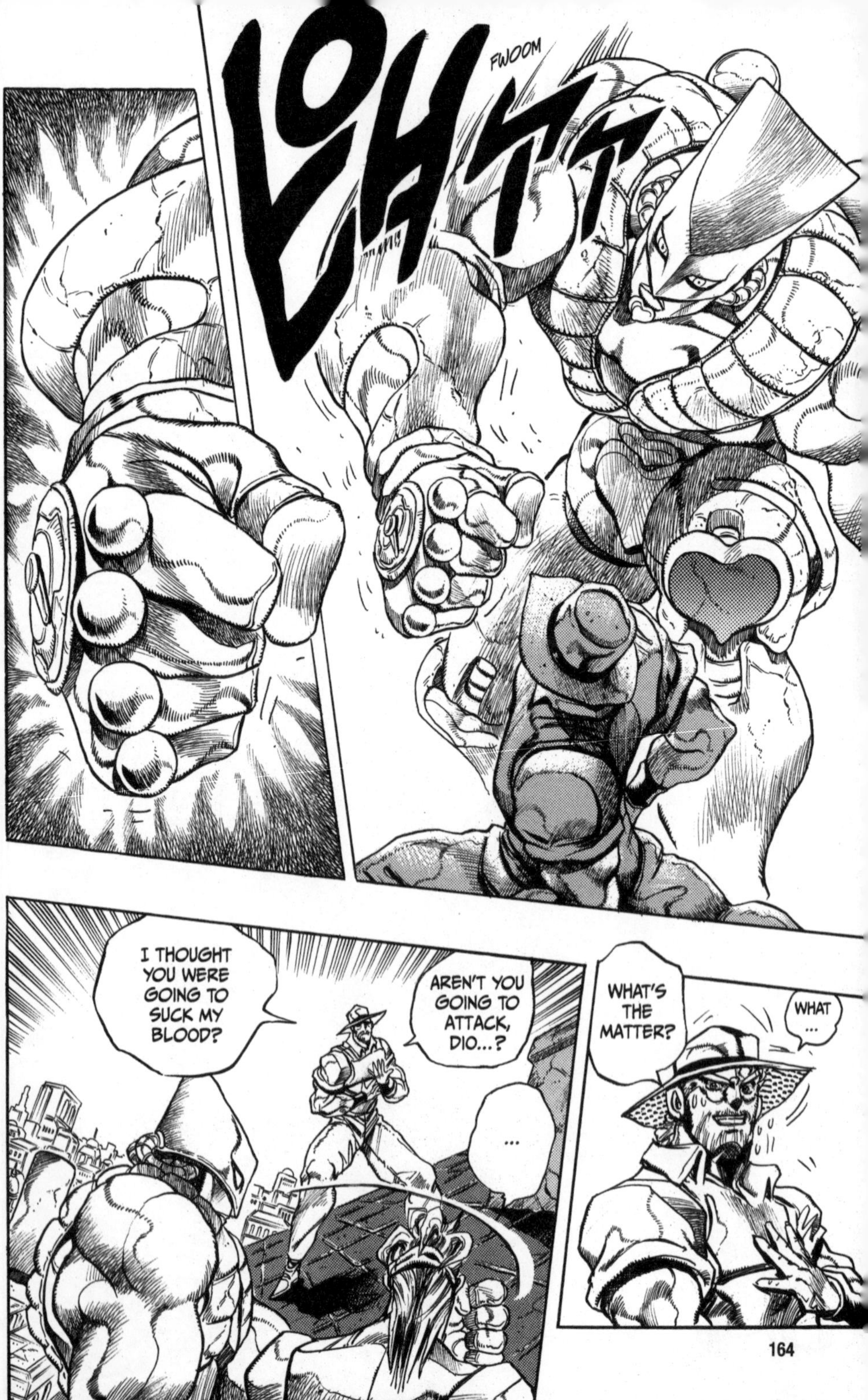
FWOOM
WHAT ...
WHAT'S THE MATTER?
AREN'T YOU GOING TO ATTACK, DIO...?
I THOUGHT YOU WERE GOING TO SUCK MY BLOOD?
...

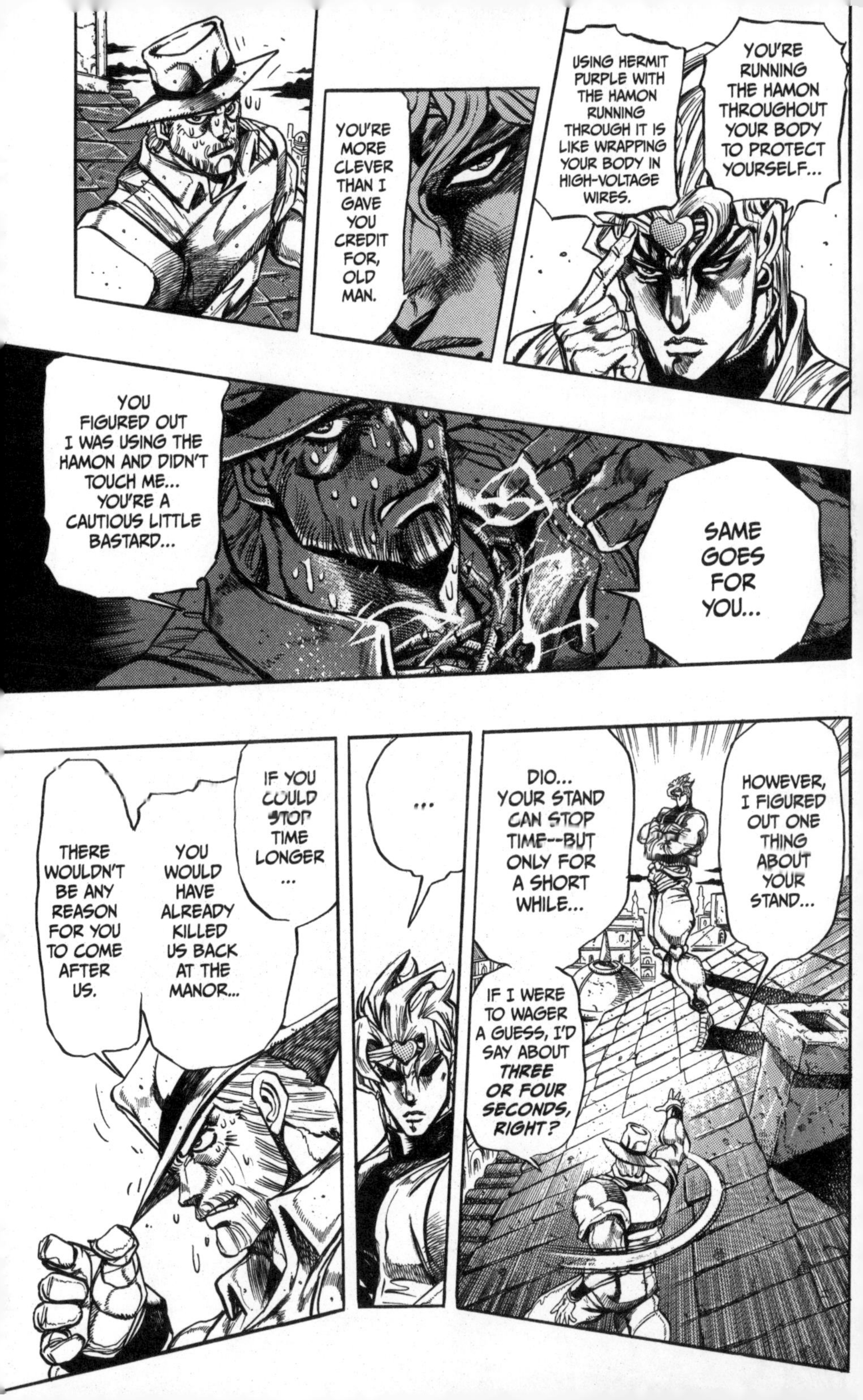
YOU'RE RUNNING THE HAMON THROUGHOUT YOUR BODY TO PROTECT YOURSELF...
USING HERMIT PURPLE WITH THE HAMON RUNNING THROUGH IT IS LIKE WRAPPING YOUR BODY IN HIGH-VOLTAGE WIRES.
YOU'RE MORE CLEVER THAN I GAVE YOU CREDIT FOR, OLD MAN.
YOU FIGURED OUT I WAS USING THE HAMON AND DIDN'T TOUCH ME... YOU'RE A CAUTIOUS LITTLE BASTARD...
SAME GOES FOR YOU...
HOWEVER, I FIGURED OUT ONE THING ABOUT YOUR STAND...
DIO... YOUR STAND CAN STOP TIME--BUT ONLY FOR A SHORT WHILE...
IF I WERE TO WAGER A GUESS, I'D SAY ABOUT THREE OR FOUR SECONDS, RIGHT?
...
IF YOU COULD STOP TIME LONGER...
YOU WOULD HAVE ALREADY KILLED US BACK AT THE MANOR...
THERE WOULDN'T BE ANY REASON FOR YOU TO COME AFTER US.

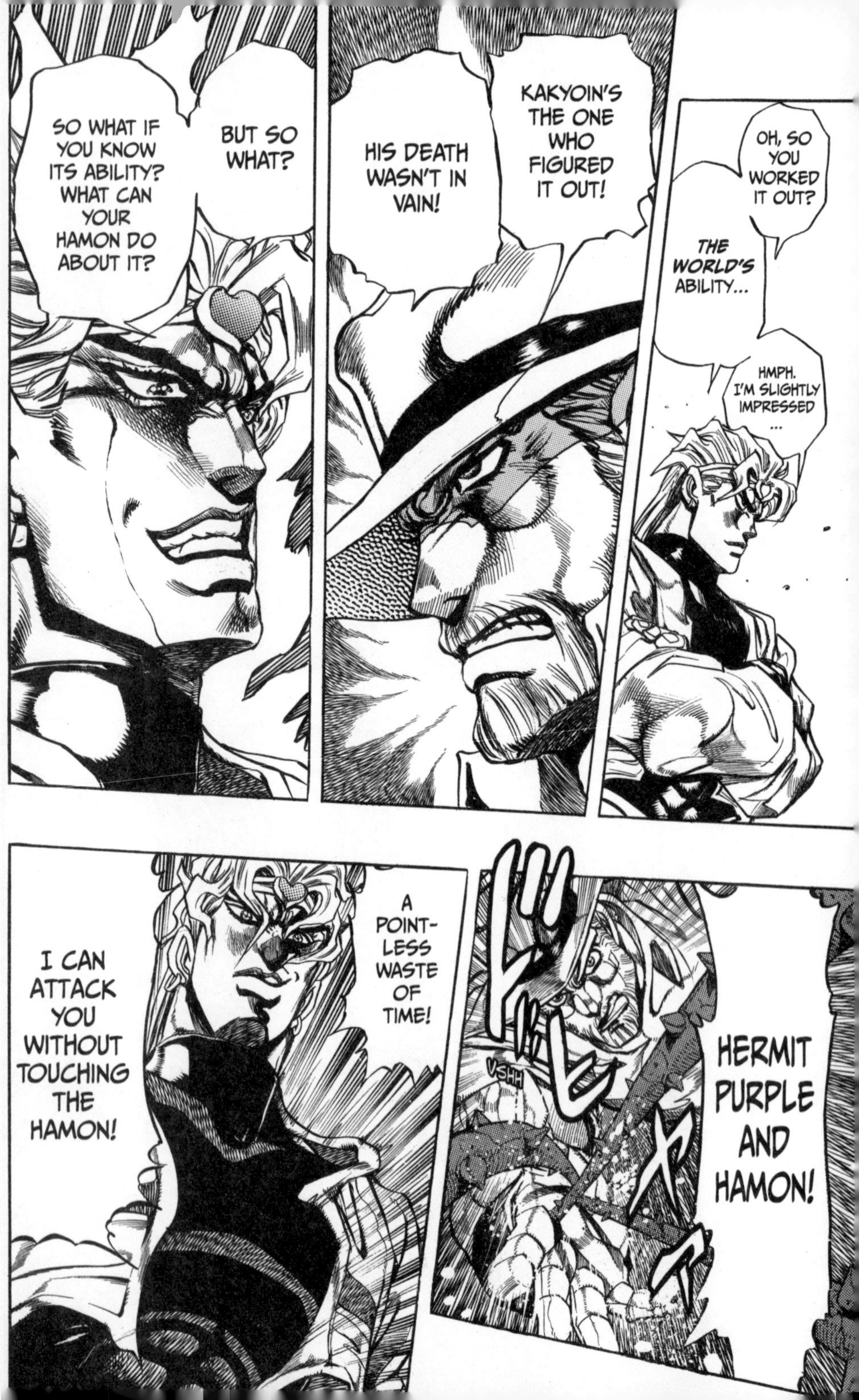
OH, SO YOU WORKED IT OUT?
THE WORLD'S ABILITY...
HMPH. I'M SLIGHTLY IMPRESSED ...
KAKYOIN'S THE ONE WHO FIGURED IT OUT!
HIS DEATH WASN'T IN VAIN!
BUT SO WHAT?
SO WHAT IF YOU KNOW ITS ABILITY? WHAT CAN YOUR HAMON DO ABOUT IT?
HERMIT PURPLE AND HAMON!
VSHH
A POINT-LESS WASTE OF TIME!
I CAN ATTACK YOU WITHOUT TOUCHING THE HAMON!

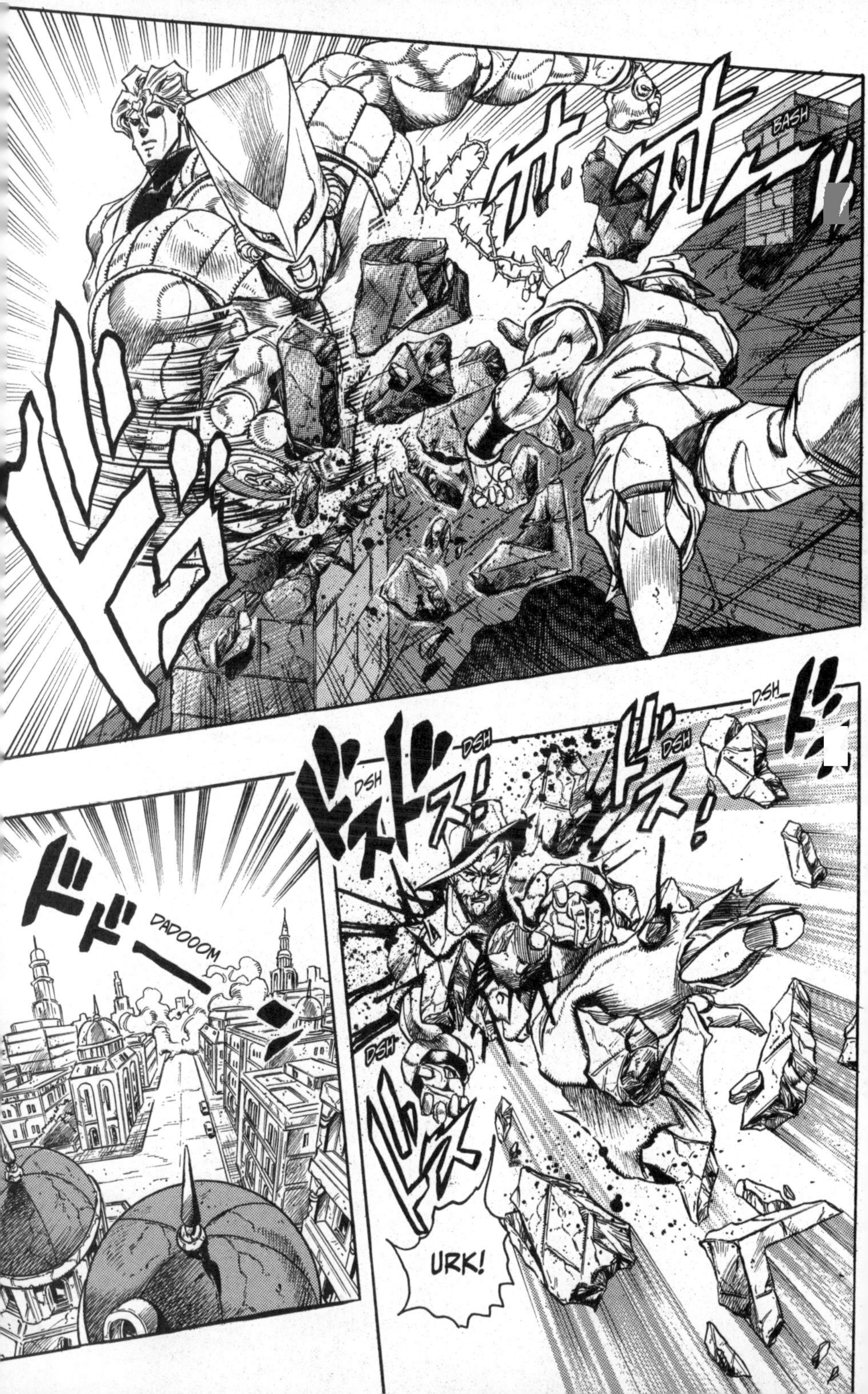
BASH
DSH
DSH
DSH
DSH
DSH
URK!
DADOOOM

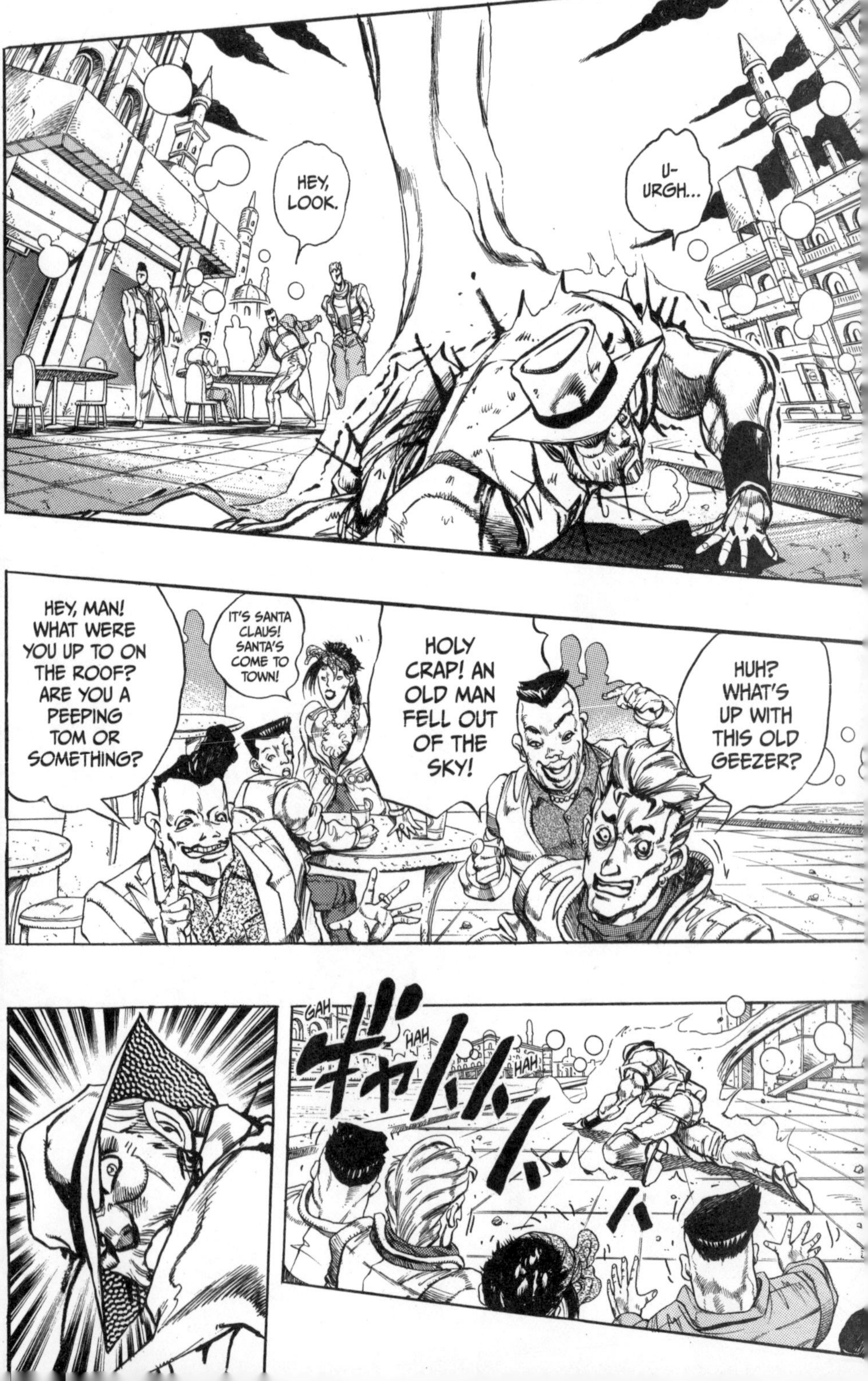
U-
URGH...
HEY, LOOK.
HUH? WHAT'S UP WITH THIS OLD GEEZER?
HOLY CRAP! AN OLD MAN FELL OUT OF THE SKY!
IT'S SANTA CLAUS! SANTA'S COME TO TOWN!
HEY, MAN! WHAT WERE YOU UP TO ON THE ROOF? ARE YOU A PEEPING TOM OR SOMETHING?
GAH
HAH
HAH

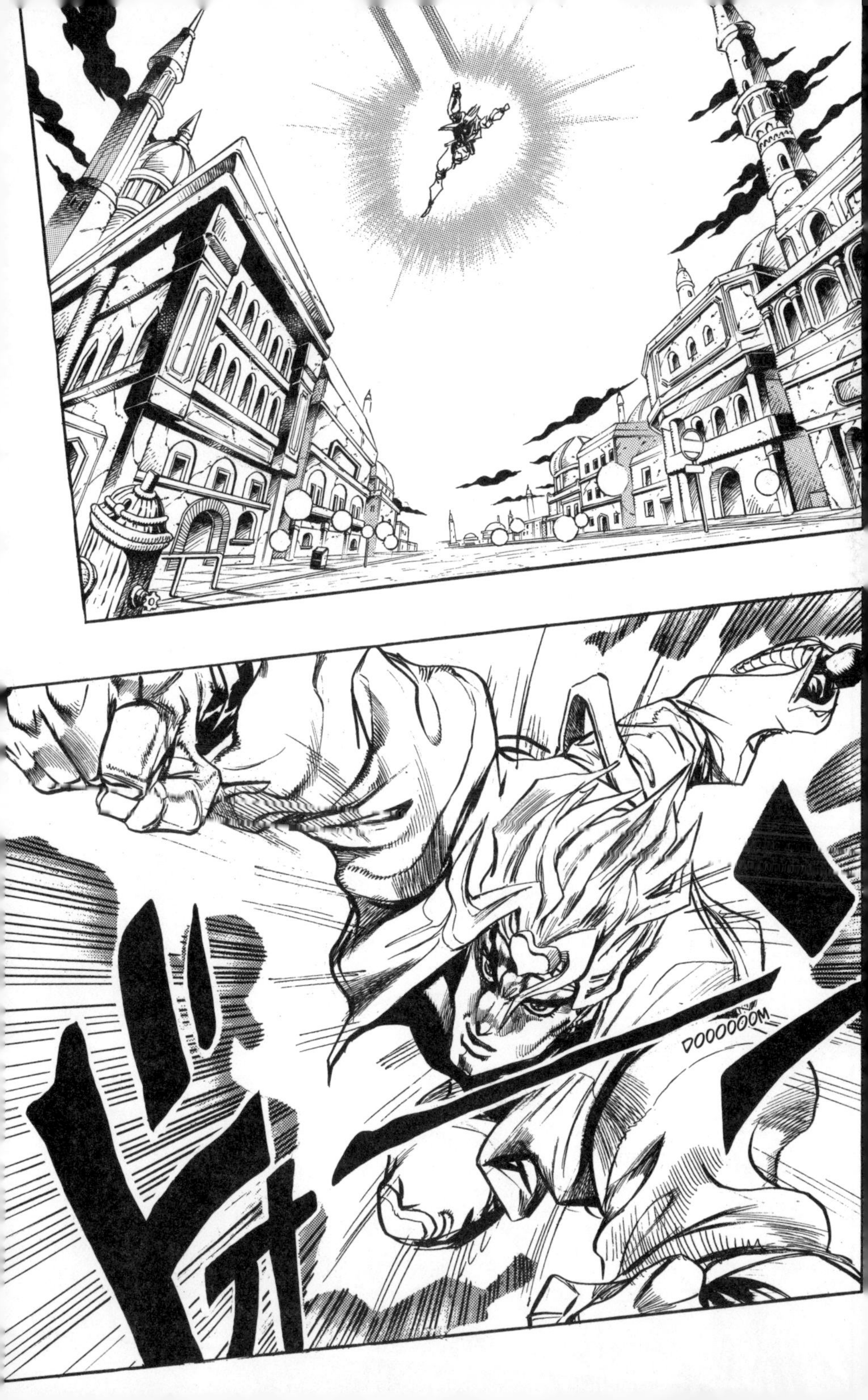
DOOOOOOM

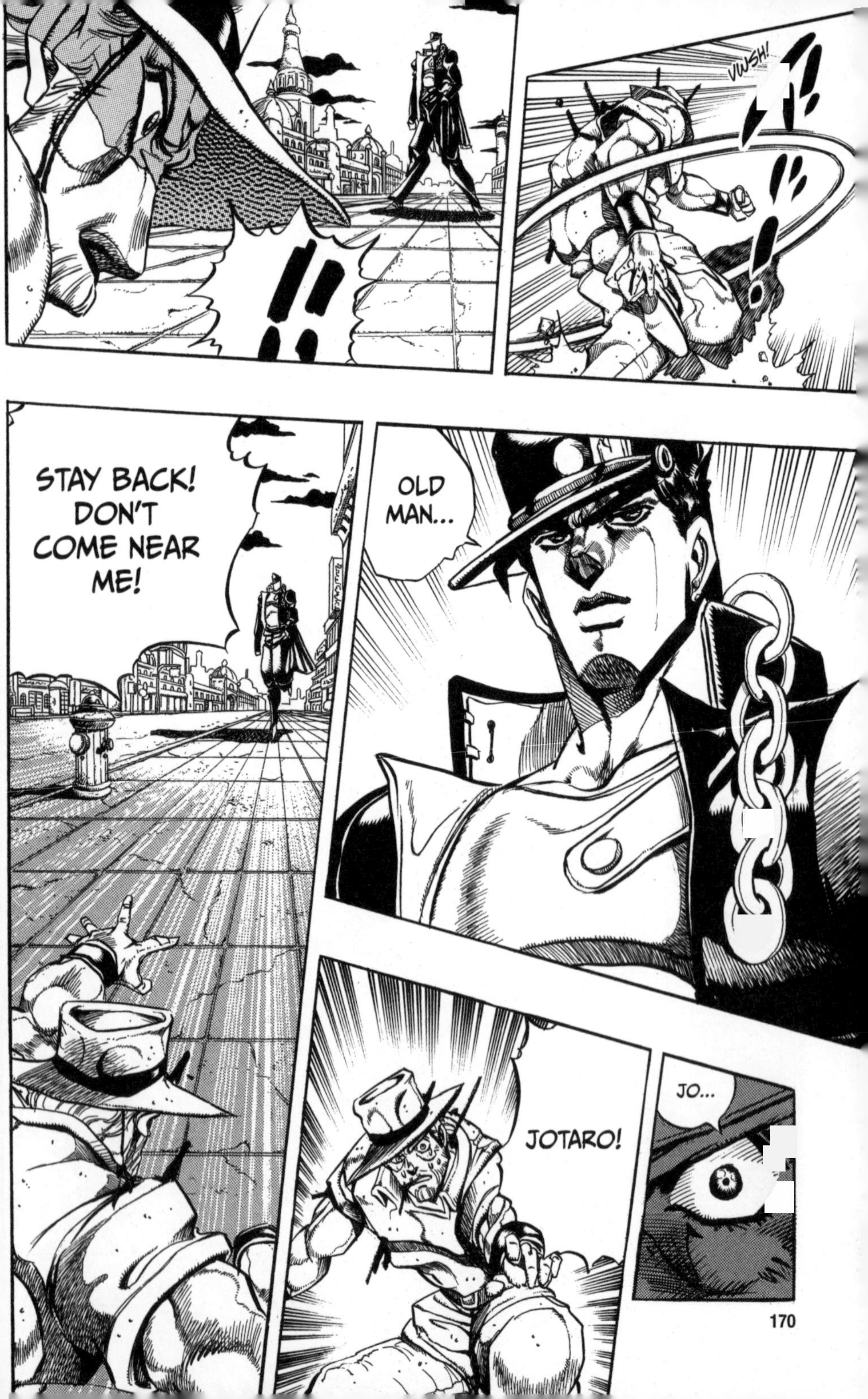
VWSH!
OLD MAN...
STAY BACK! DON'T COME NEAR ME!
JO...
JOTARO!

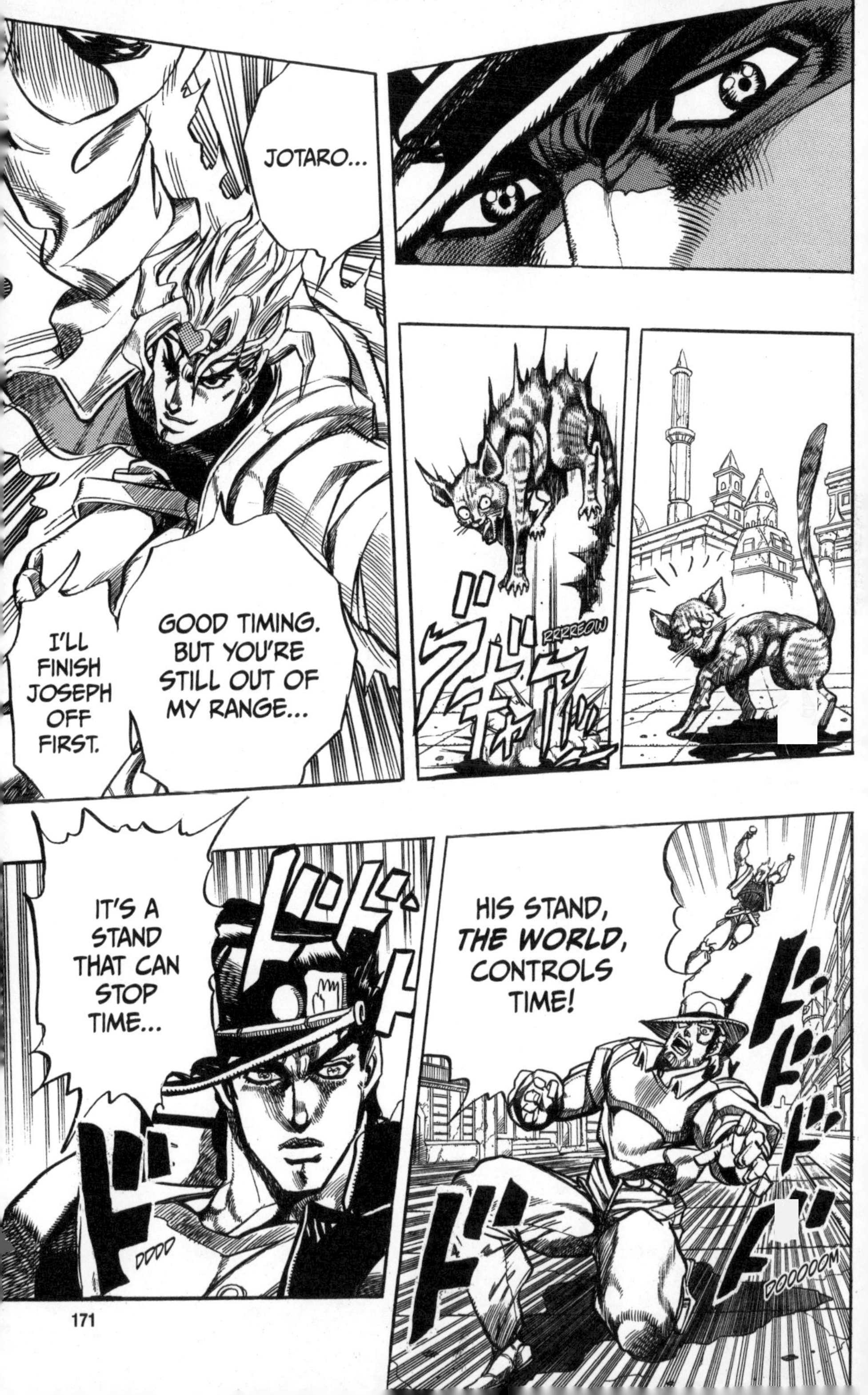
RRRREOW
JOTARO...
GOOD TIMING. BUT YOU'RE STILL OUT OF MY RANGE...
I'LL FINISH JOSEPH OFF FIRST.
HIS STAND, *THE WORLD*, CONTROLS TIME!
DOOOOOM
IT'S A STAND THAT CAN STOP TIME...
DDDD

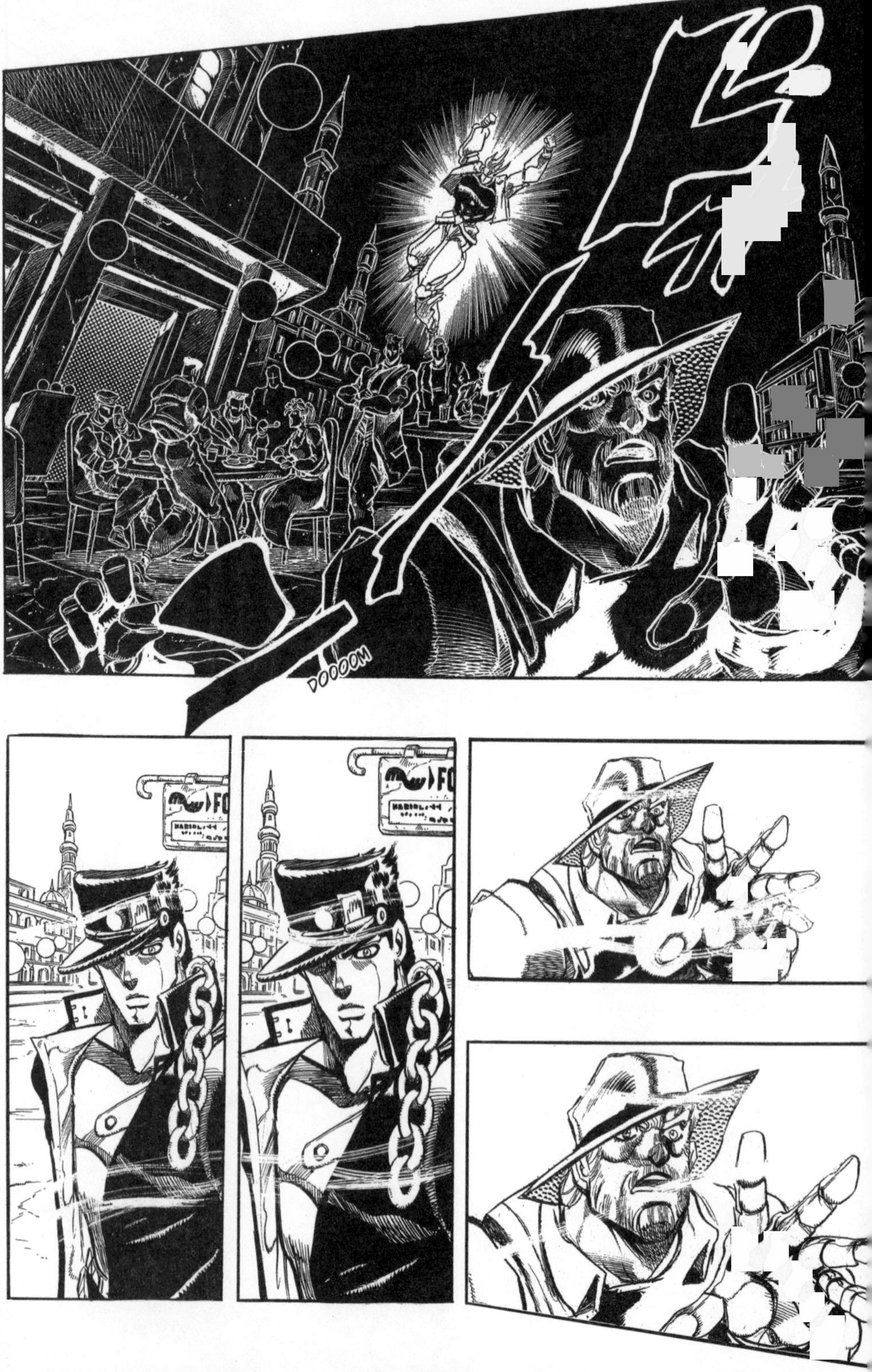
DOOOOM

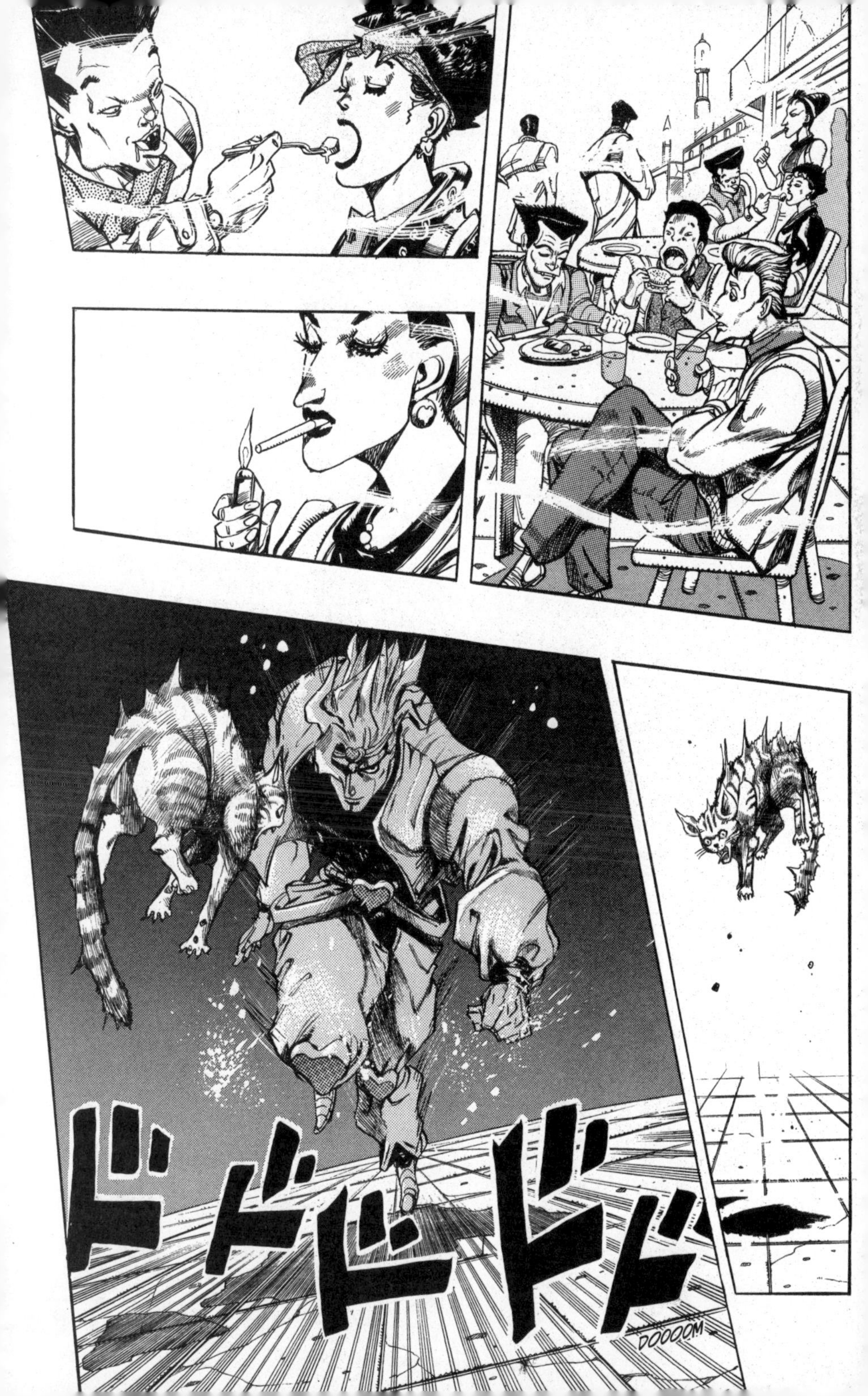
ドドドドド
DOOOOM

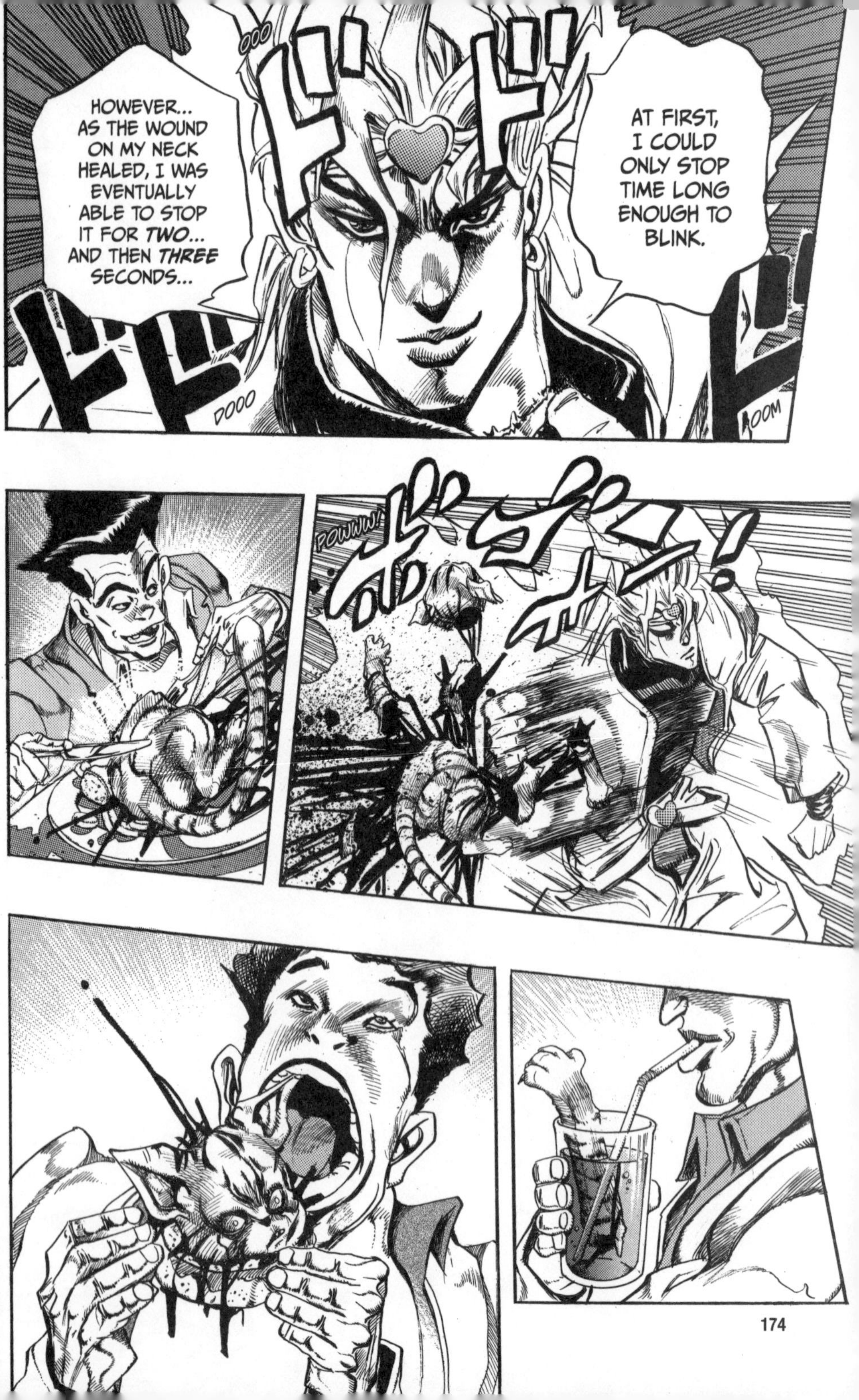
OOO
AT FIRST, I COULD ONLY STOP TIME LONG ENOUGH TO BLINK.
HOWEVER... AS THE WOUND ON MY NECK HEALED, I WAS EVENTUALLY ABLE TO STOP IT FOR *TWO*... AND THEN *THREE* SECONDS...
OOM
DOOO
POWWW!

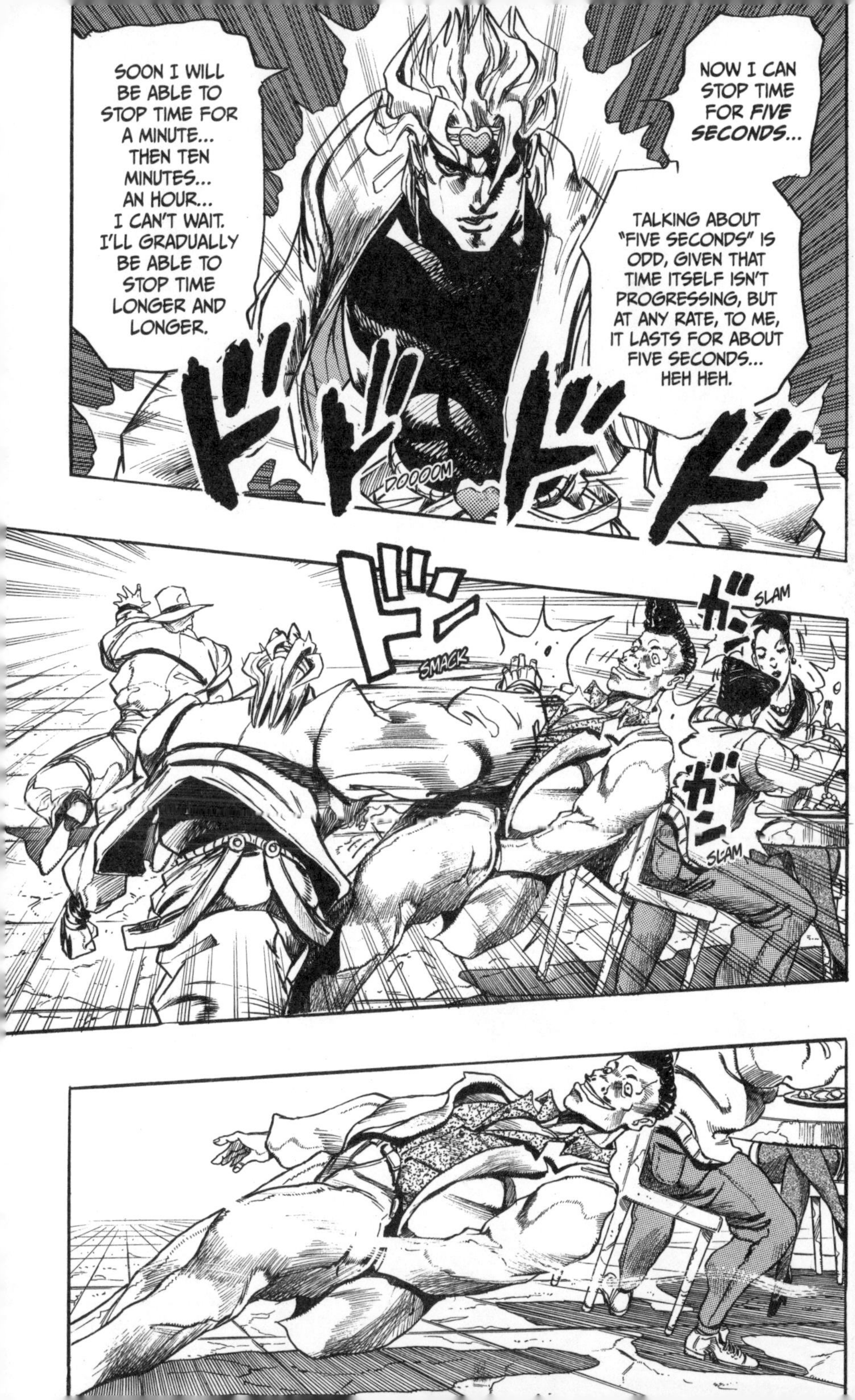
NOW I CAN STOP TIME FOR *FIVE SECONDS*...
TALKING ABOUT "FIVE SECONDS" IS ODD, GIVEN THAT TIME ITSELF ISN'T PROGRESSING, BUT AT ANY RATE, TO ME, IT LASTS FOR ABOUT FIVE SECONDS... HEH HEH.
SOON I WILL BE ABLE TO STOP TIME FOR A MINUTE... THEN TEN MINUTES... AN HOUR... I CAN'T WAIT. I'LL GRADUALLY BE ABLE TO STOP TIME LONGER AND LONGER.
DOOOOM
SLAM
SMACK
SLAM

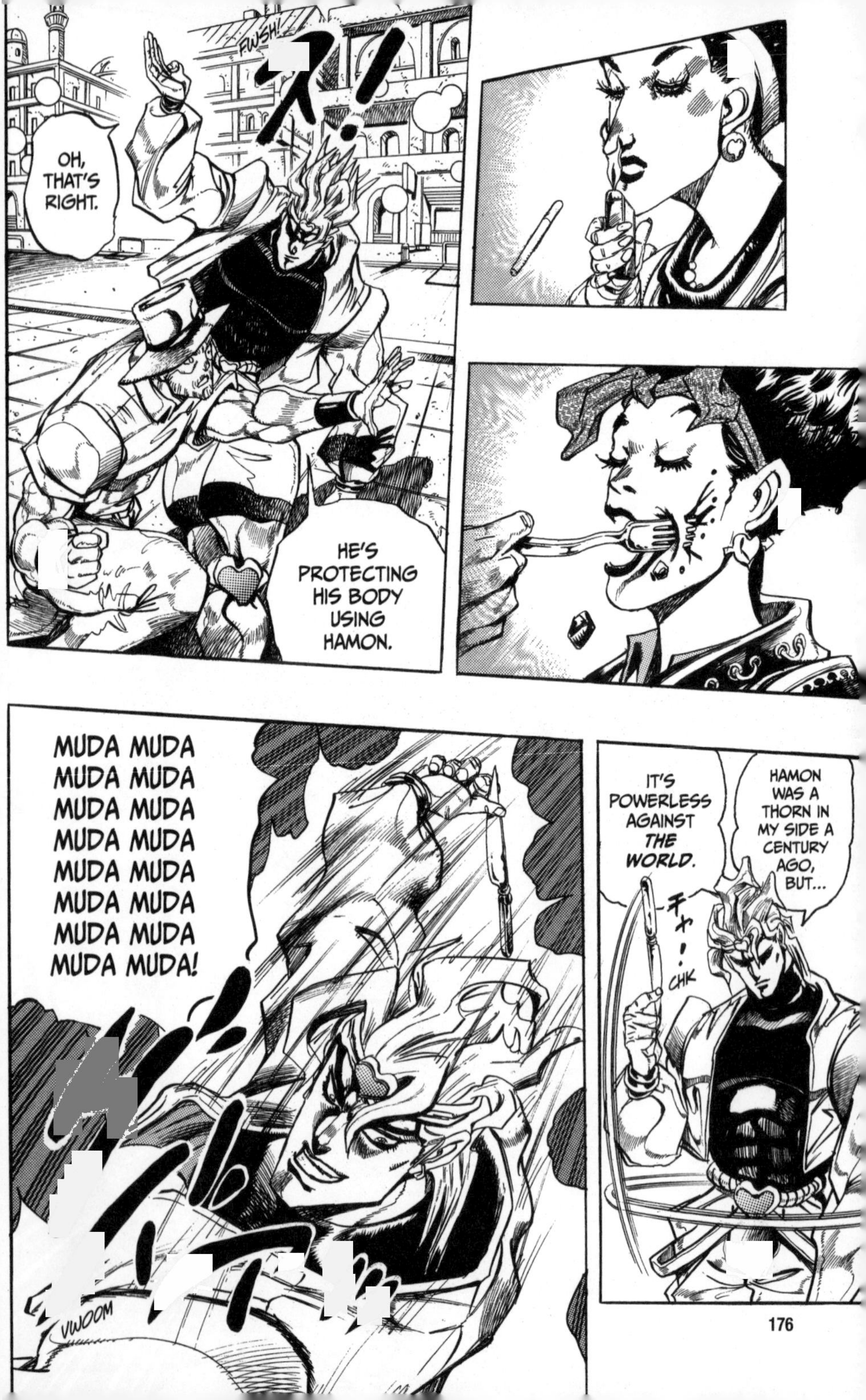
FWSH!
OH, THAT'S RIGHT.
HE'S PROTECTING HIS BODY USING HAMON.
HAMON WAS A THORN IN MY SIDE A CENTURY AGO, BUT...
IT'S POWERLESS AGAINST *THE WORLD*.
チャ!
CHK
MUDA MUDA MUDA MUDA MUDA MUDA MUDA MUDA MUDA MUDA MUDA MUDA MUDA MUDA MUDA MUDA!
VWOOM

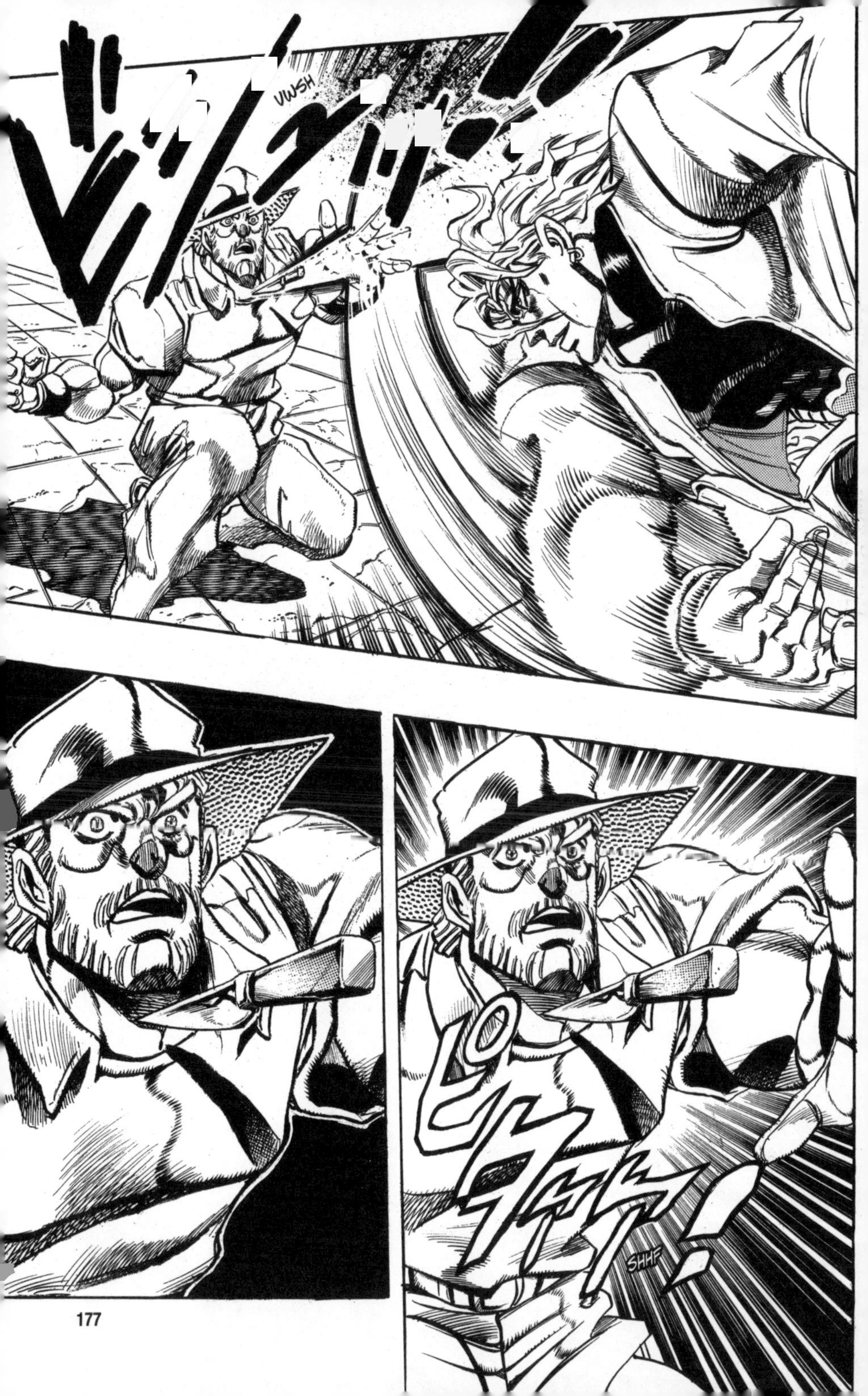
VWSH
SHHF

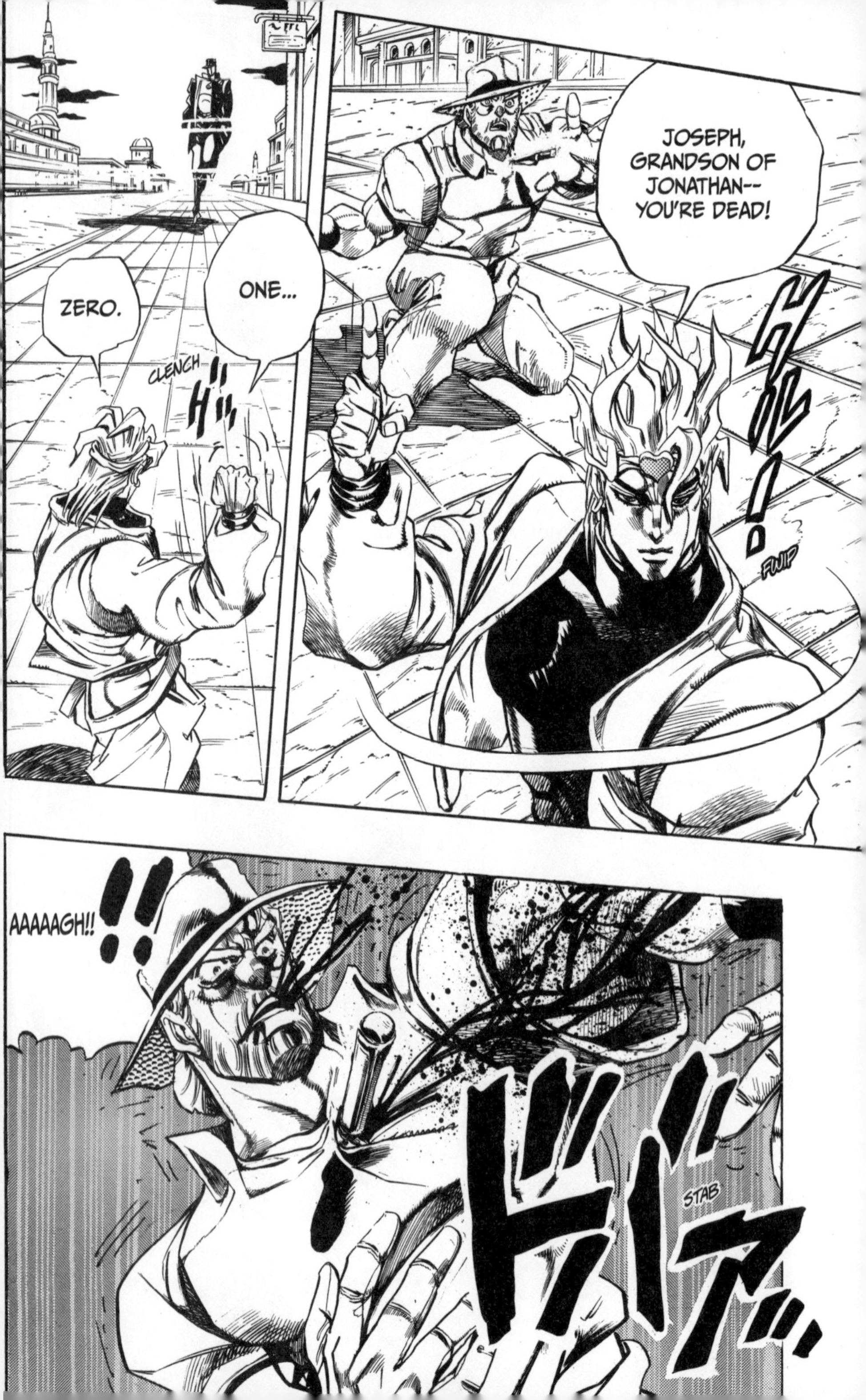
JOSEPH, GRANDSON OF JONATHAN-- YOU'RE DEAD!
FWIP
ONE...
ZERO.
CLENCH
AAAAAGH!!
STAB

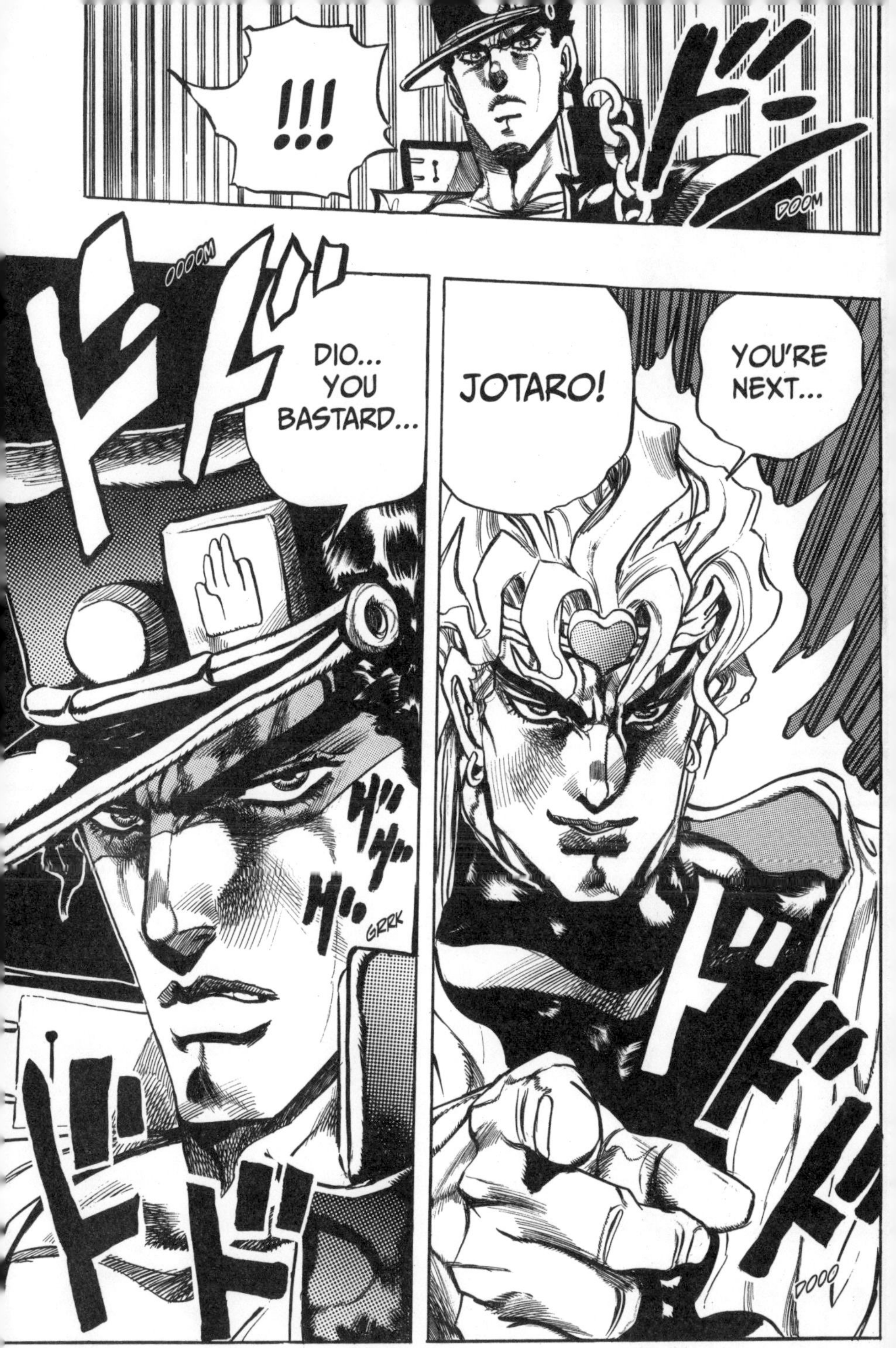
!!!
DOOM
YOU'RE NEXT...
JOTARO!
DOOO
DIO... YOU BASTARD...
OOOOM
GRRK

JoJo's
BIZARRE ADVENTURE

CHAPTER 143: DIO's World PART 10

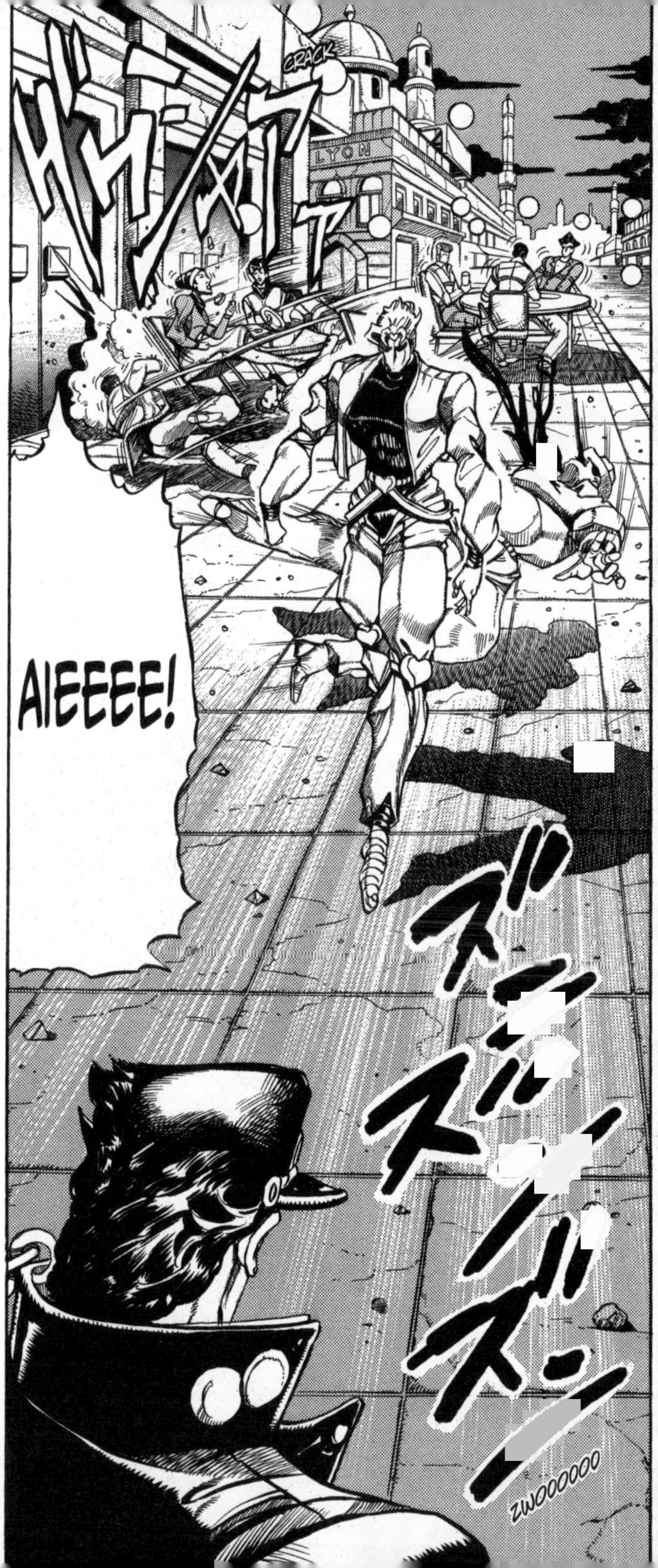

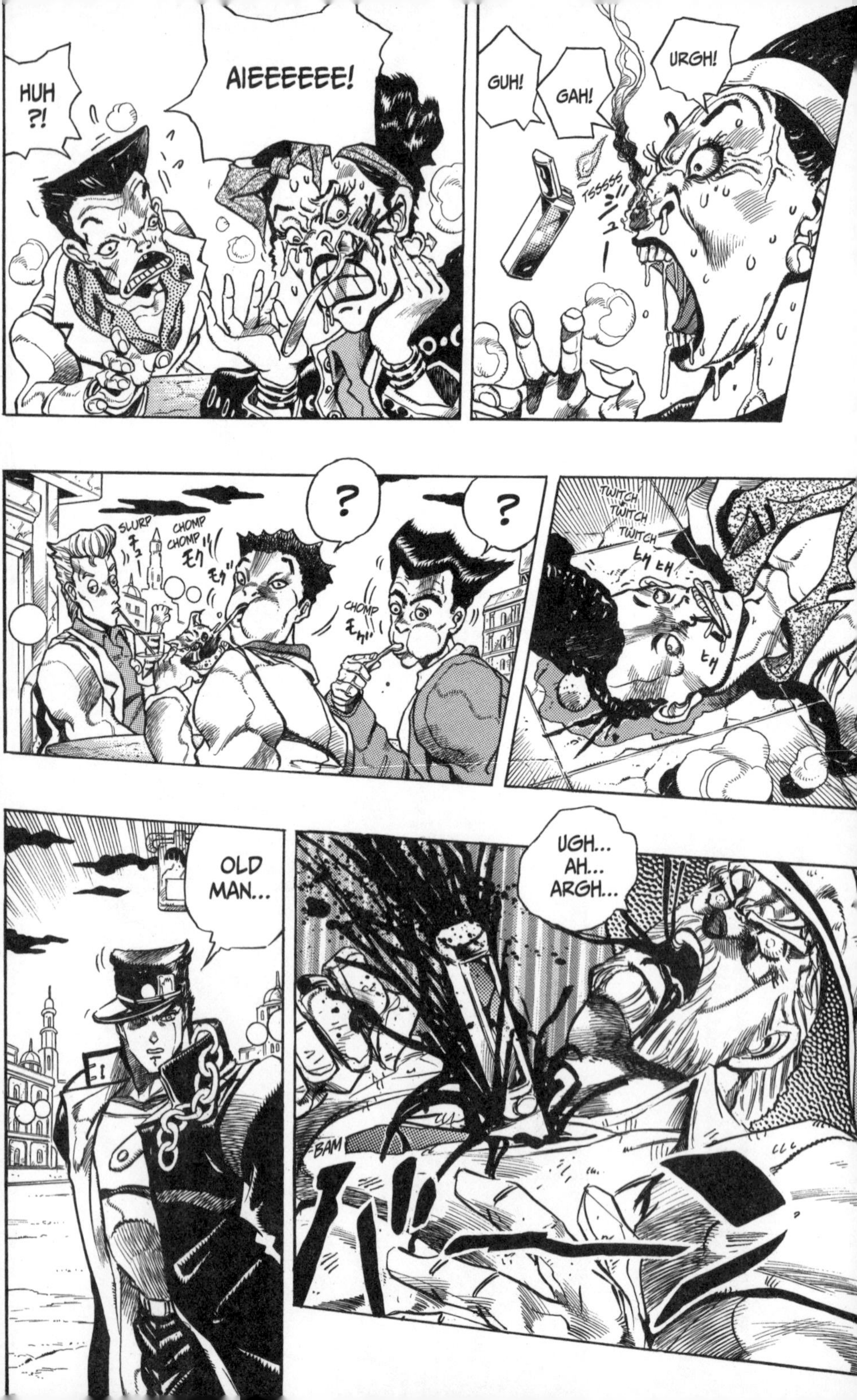
URGH!
GAH!
GUH!
TSSSSS
AIEEEEEE!
HUH ?!
TWITCH TWITCH TWITCH
?
?
CHOMP
CHOMP CHOMP
SLURP
UGH... AH... ARGH...
BAM
OLD MAN...

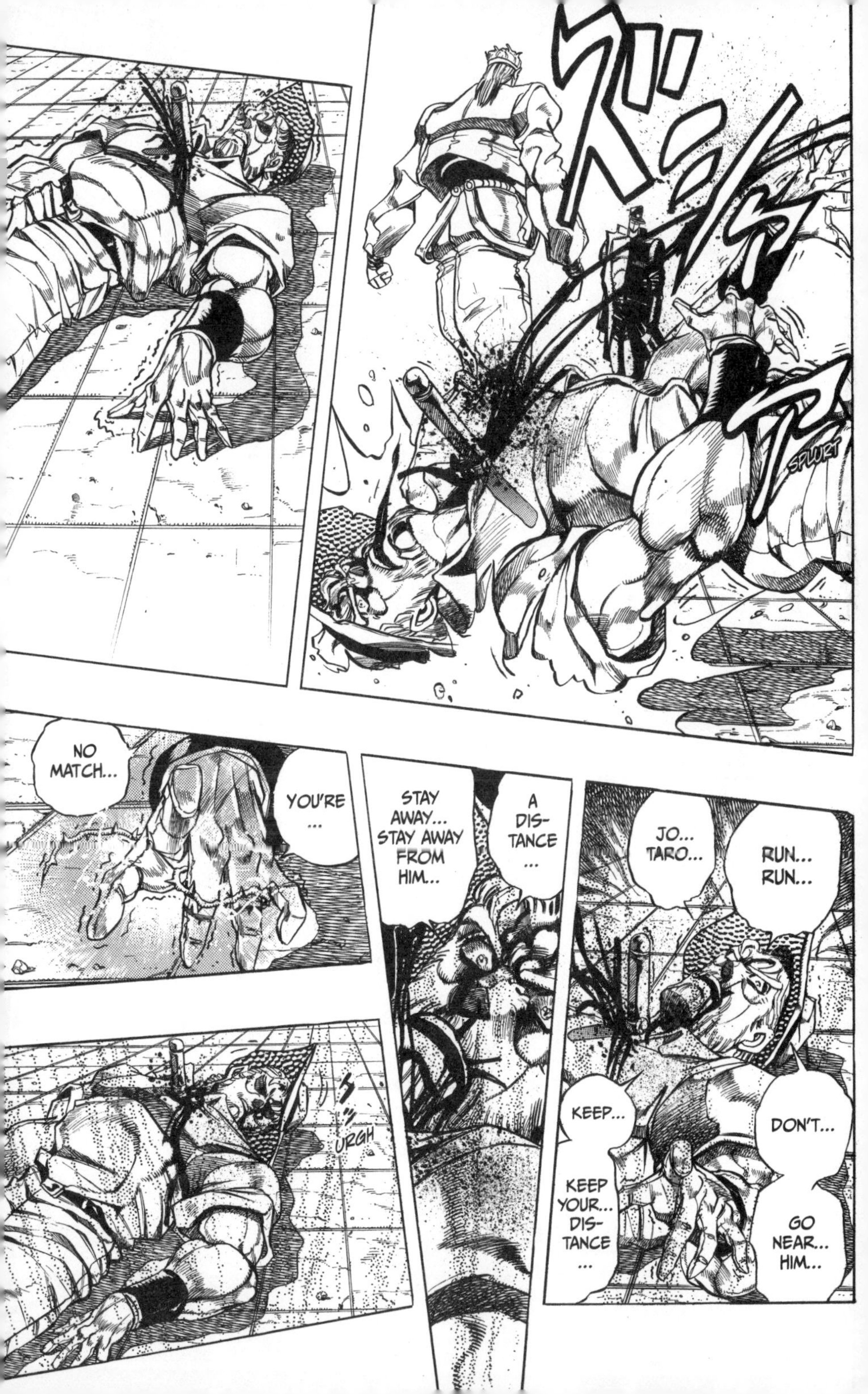

SPLURT
RUN... RUN...
JO... TARO...
DON'T...
GO NEAR... HIM...
KEEP...
KEEP YOUR... DIS-TANCE ...
A DIS-TANCE ...
STAY AWAY... STAY AWAY FROM HIM...
YOU'RE ...
NO MATCH...
URGH

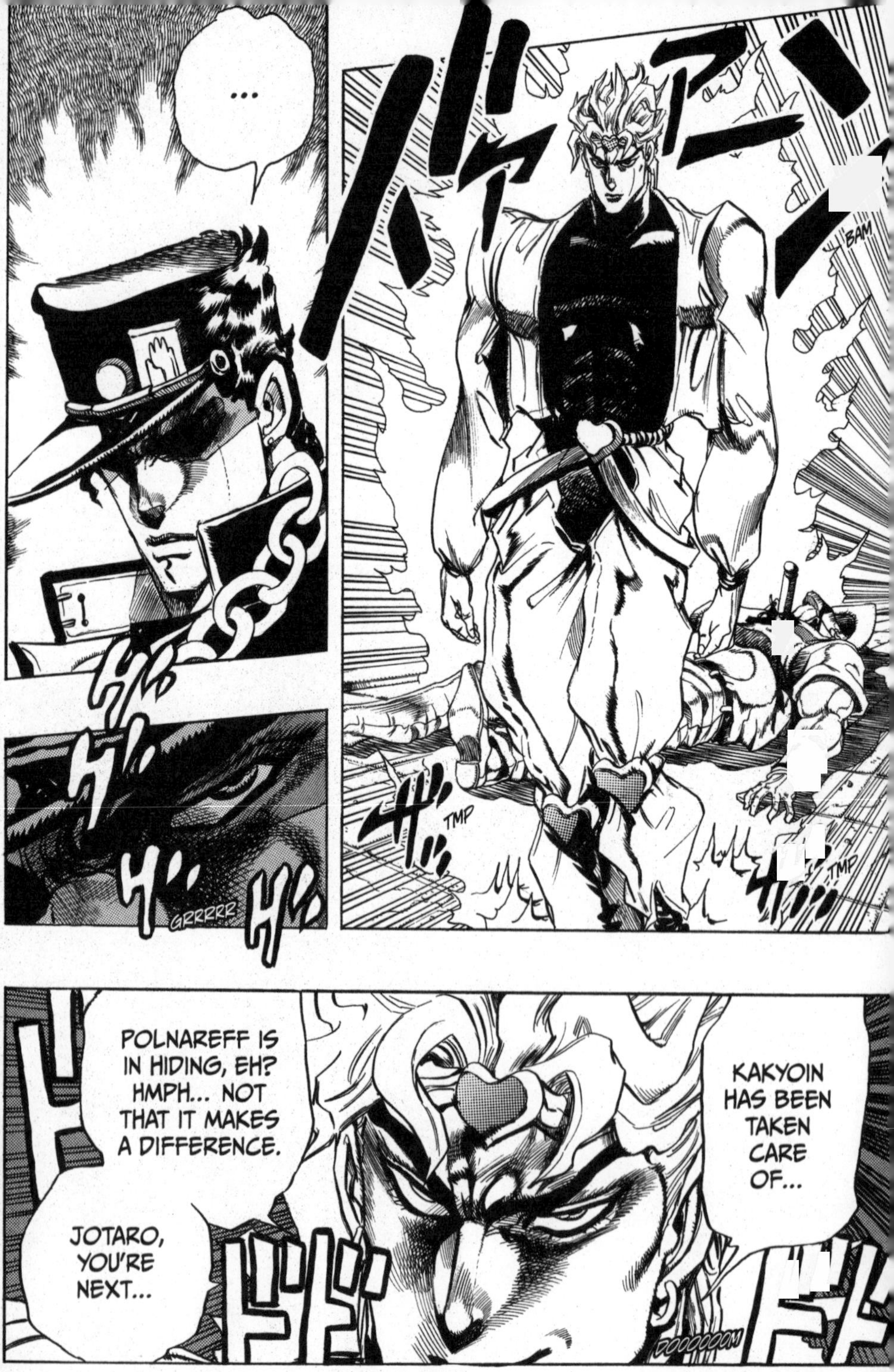
BAM
TMP
TMP
...
GRRRRR
KAKYOIN HAS BEEN TAKEN CARE OF...
POLNAREFF IS IN HIDING, EH? HMPH... NOT THAT IT MAKES A DIFFERENCE.
JOTARO, YOU'RE NEXT...
DOOOOOOM

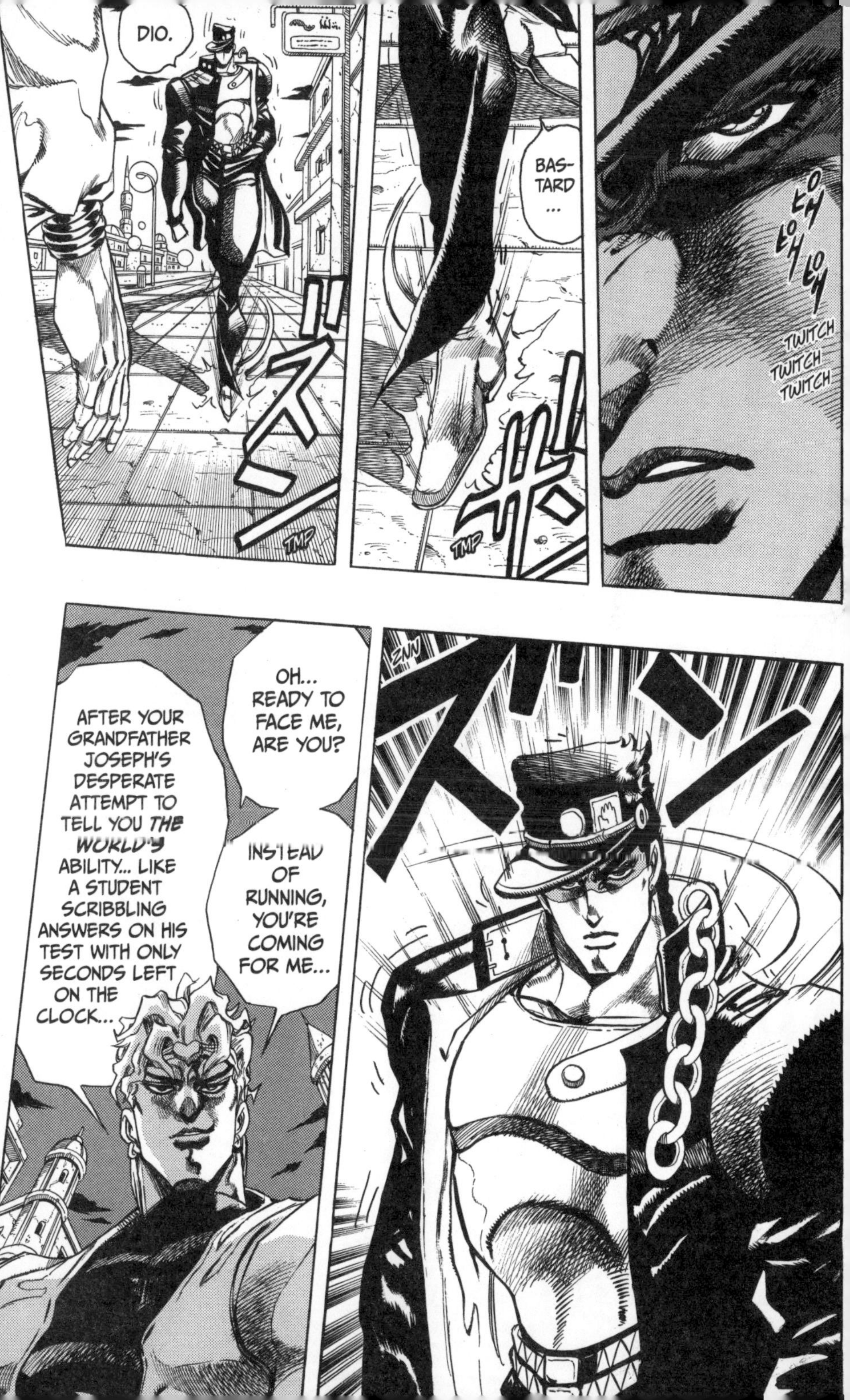
TWITCH TWITCH TWITCH
BAS-TARD...
TMP
DIO.
TMP
ZNN
OH... READY TO FACE ME, ARE YOU?
INSTEAD OF RUNNING, YOU'RE COMING FOR ME...
AFTER YOUR GRANDFATHER JOSEPH'S DESPERATE ATTEMPT TO TELL YOU *THE WORLD'S* ABILITY... LIKE A STUDENT SCRIBBLING ANSWERS ON HIS TEST WITH ONLY SECONDS LEFT ON THE CLOCK...

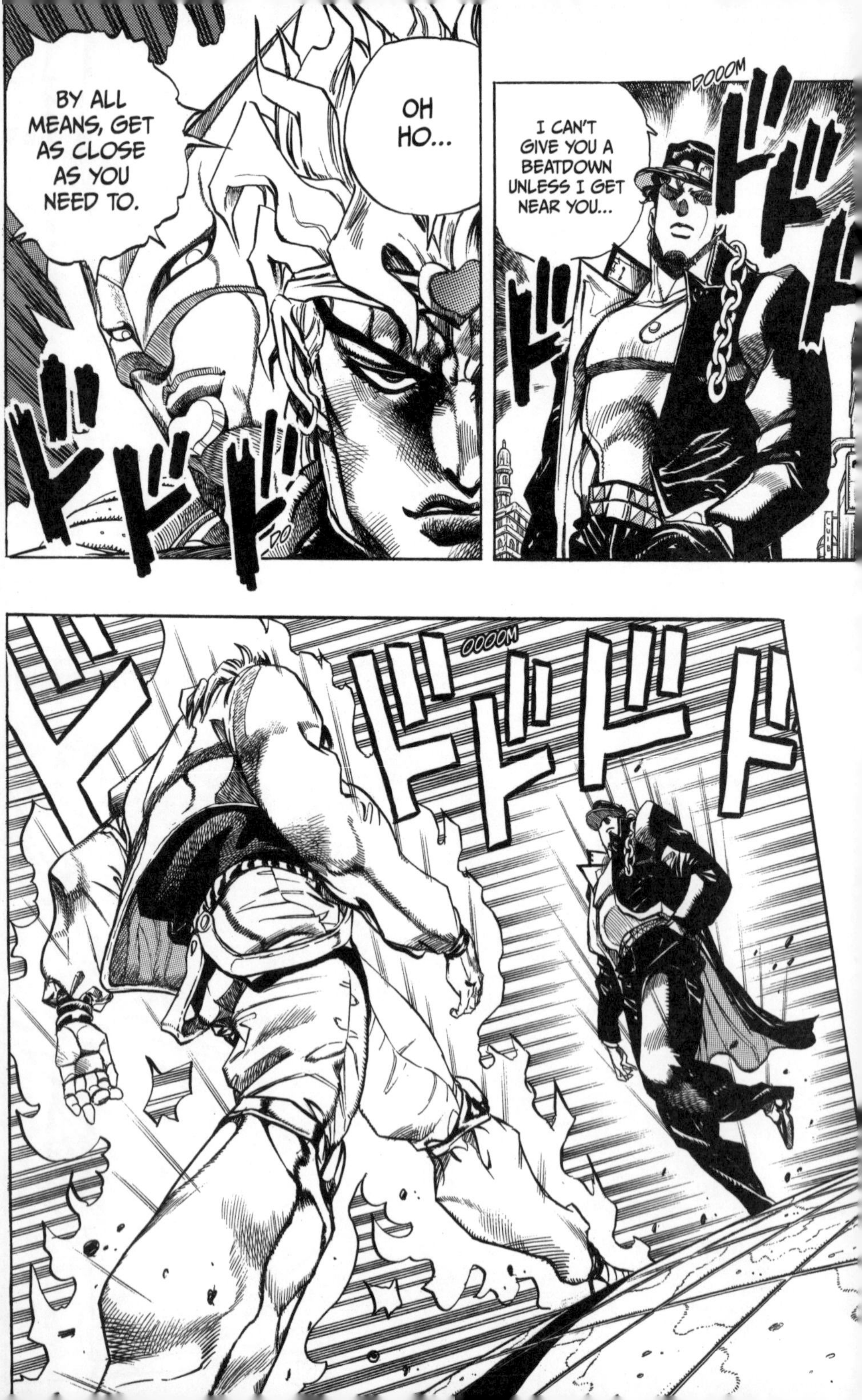
DOOOM
I CAN'T GIVE YOU A BEATDOWN UNLESS I GET NEAR YOU...
OH HO...
BY ALL MEANS, GET AS CLOSE AS YOU NEED TO.
DO
OOOOM

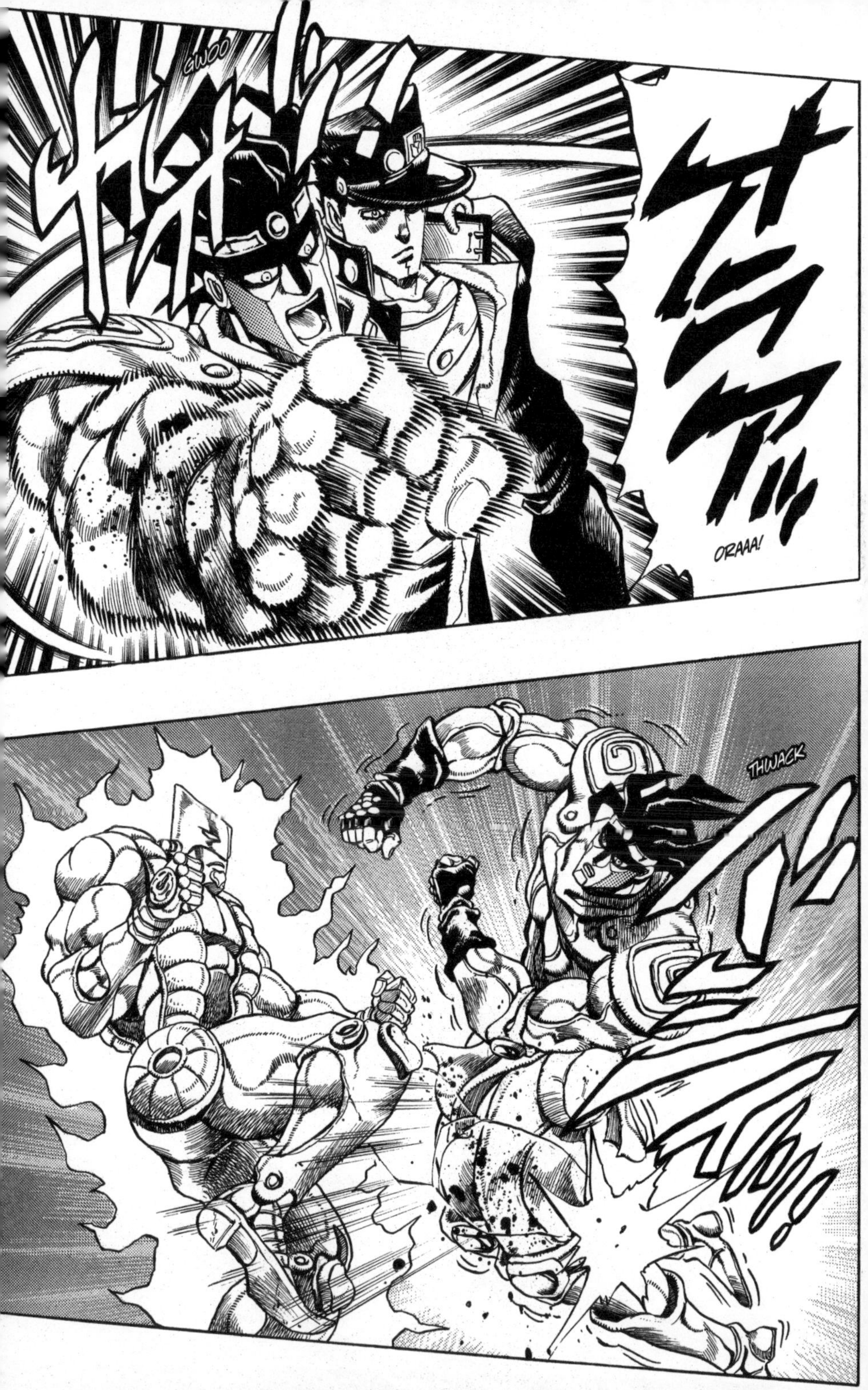
GWOO
ORAAA!
THWACK

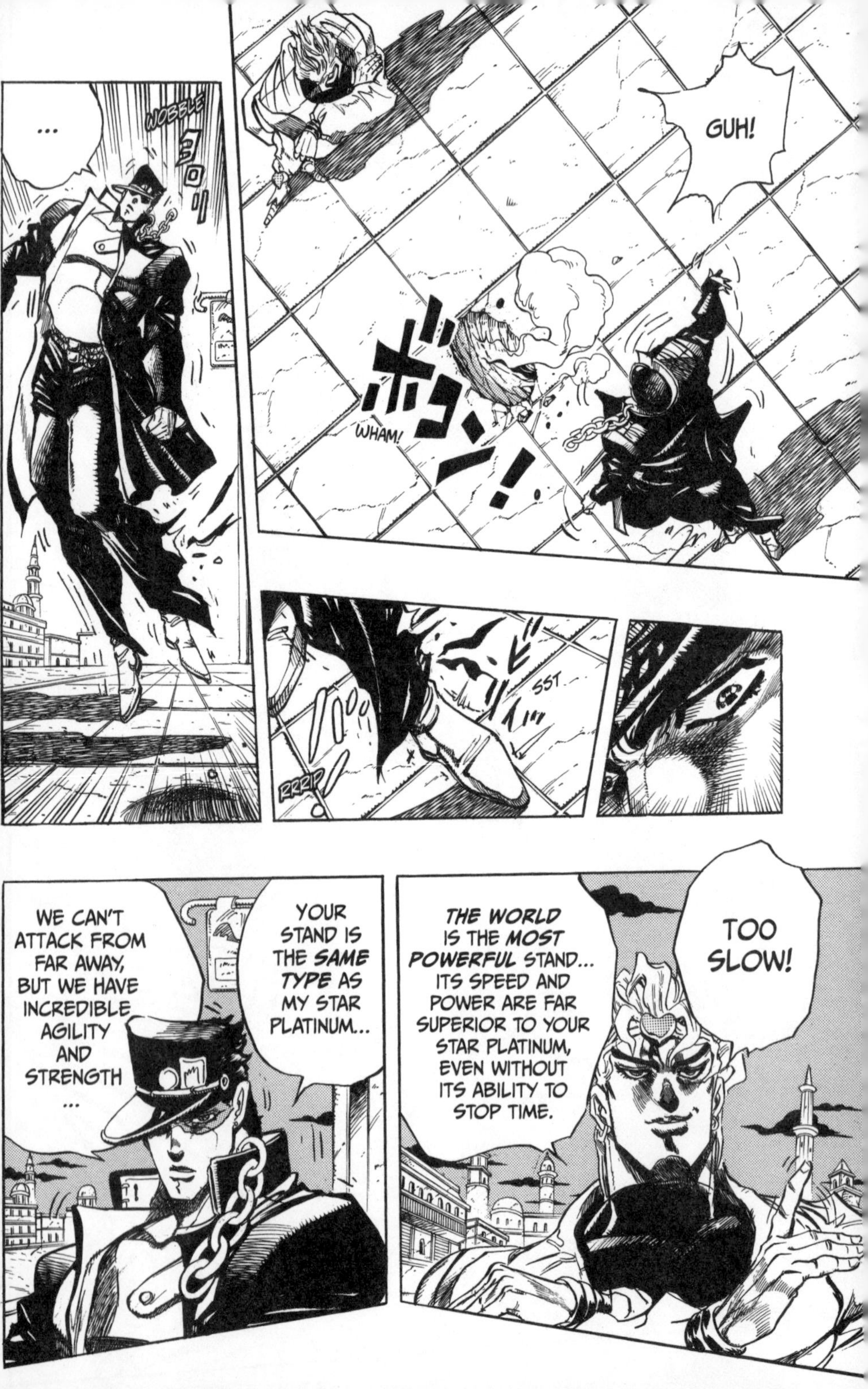
GUH!
WHAM!
...
WOBBLE
SST
RRRIP
TOO SLOW!
THE WORLD IS THE MOST POWERFUL STAND... ITS SPEED AND POWER ARE FAR SUPERIOR TO YOUR STAR PLATINUM, EVEN WITHOUT ITS ABILITY TO STOP TIME.
YOUR STAND IS THE SAME TYPE AS MY STAR PLATINUM...
WE CAN'T ATTACK FROM FAR AWAY, BUT WE HAVE INCREDIBLE AGILITY AND STRENGTH ...

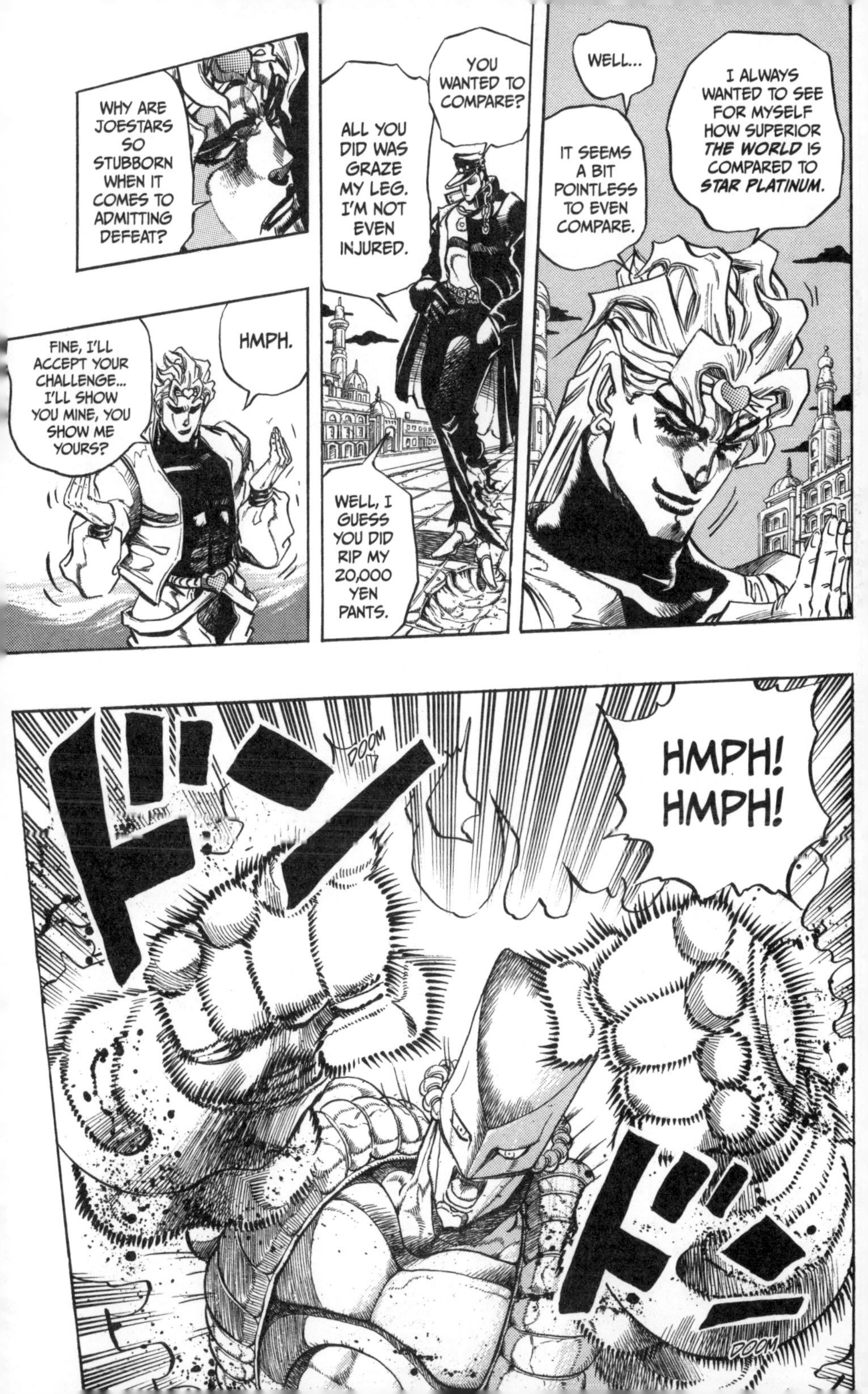
I ALWAYS WANTED TO SEE FOR MYSELF HOW SUPERIOR *THE WORLD* IS COMPARED TO *STAR PLATINUM*.
WELL...
IT SEEMS A BIT POINTLESS TO EVEN COMPARE.
YOU WANTED TO COMPARE?
ALL YOU DID WAS GRAZE MY LEG. I'M NOT EVEN INJURED.
WELL, I GUESS YOU DID RIP MY 20,000 YEN PANTS.
WHY ARE JOESTARS SO STUBBORN WHEN IT COMES TO ADMITTING DEFEAT?
HMPH.
FINE, I'LL ACCEPT YOUR CHALLENGE... I'LL SHOW YOU MINE, YOU SHOW ME YOURS?
HMPH! HMPH!
DOOM
DOOM

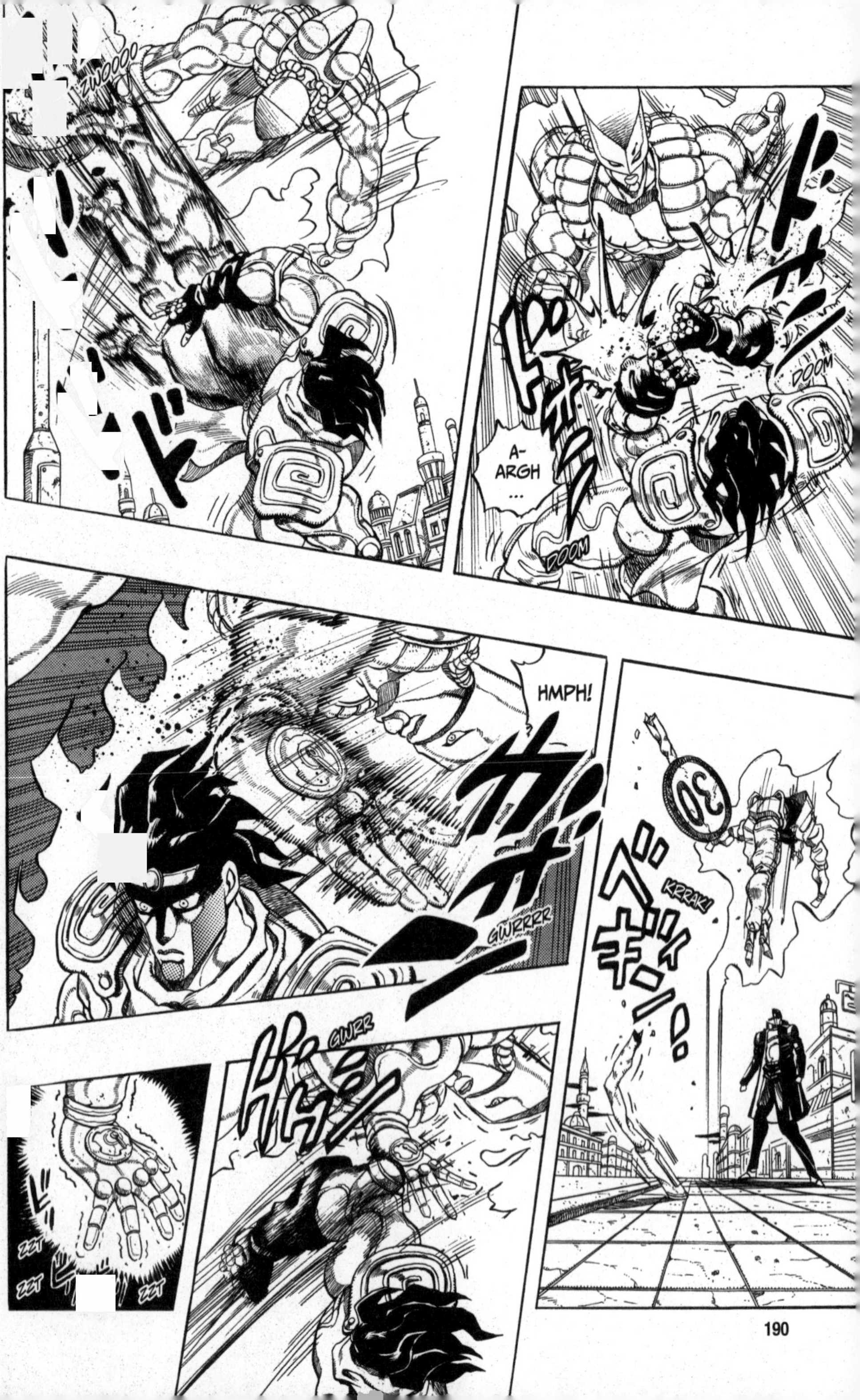
DOOM
A-ARGH ...
DOOM
ZWOOOO
KRRAK!
HMPH!
GWRRRR
GWRR
ZZT
ZZT
ZZT

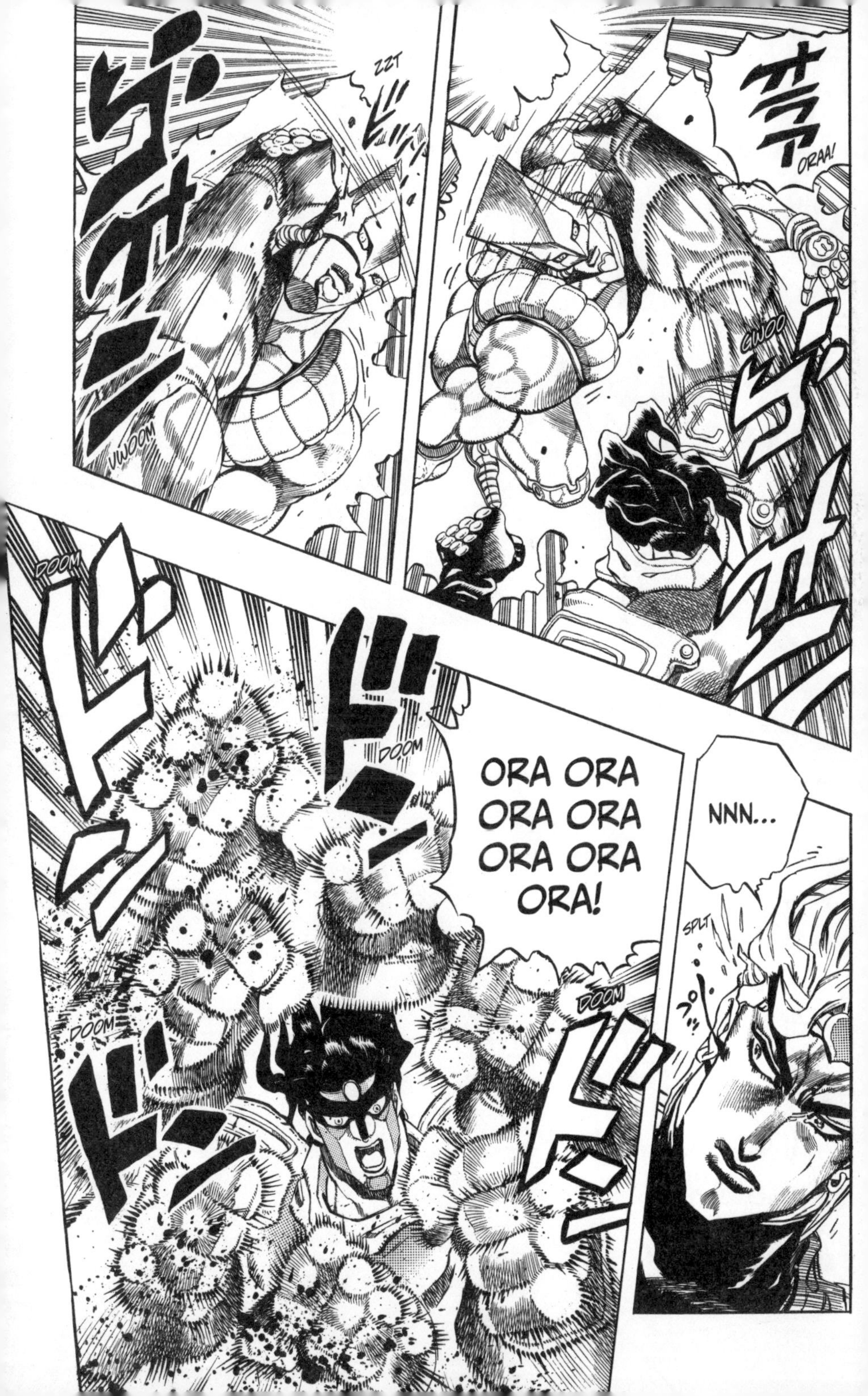

オラァ
ORAA!
GWOO
ZZT
VWOOM
NNN...
SPLT
ORA ORA
ORA ORA
ORA ORA
ORA!
DOOM
DOOM
DOOM
DOOM

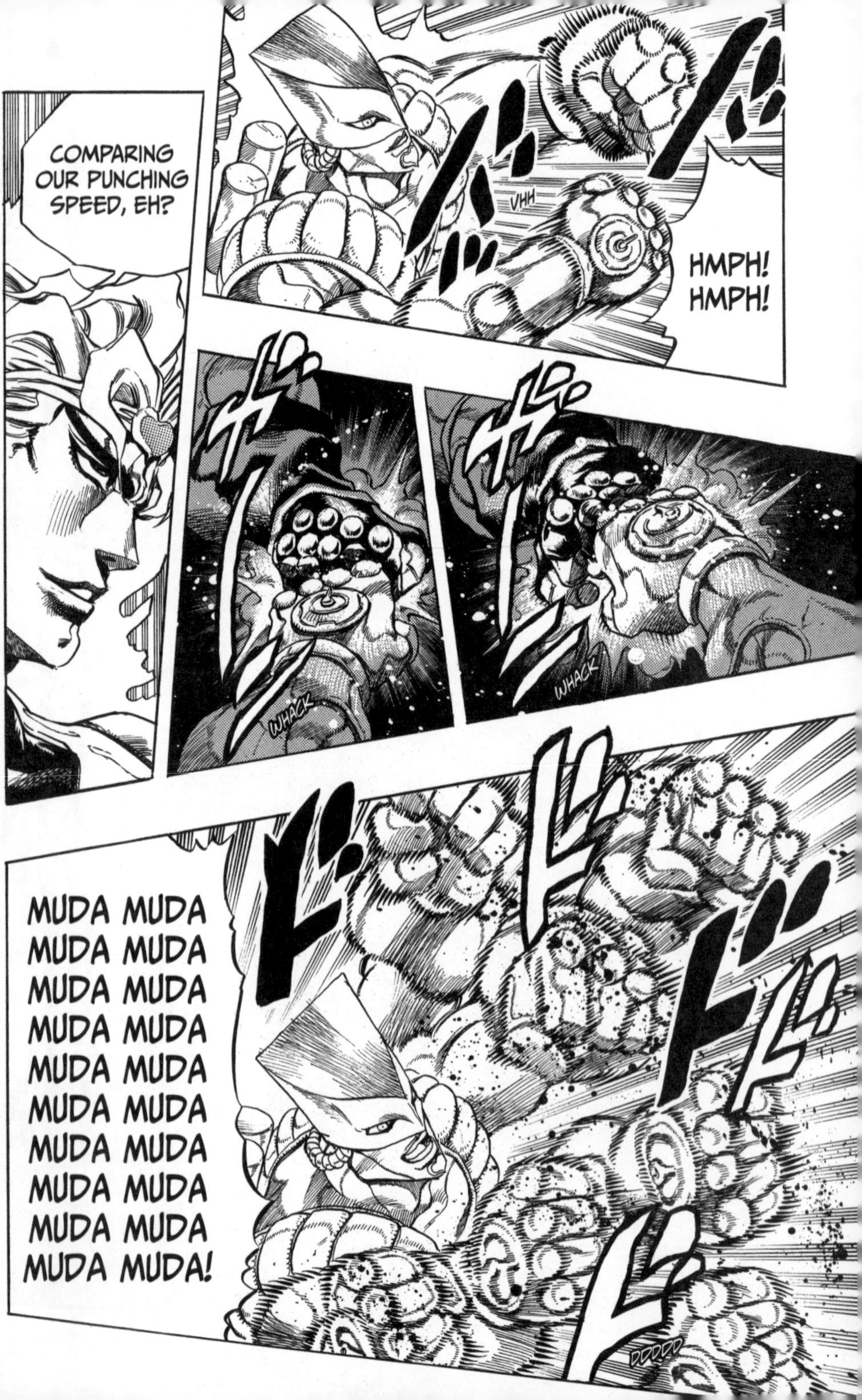
VHH
HMPH! HMPH!
WHACK
WHACK
COMPARING OUR PUNCHING SPEED, EH?
MUDA MUDA MUDA MUDA MUDA MUDA MUDA MUDA MUDA MUDA MUDA MUDA MUDA MUDA MUDA MUDA MUDA MUDA MUDA MUDA!
DDDDD

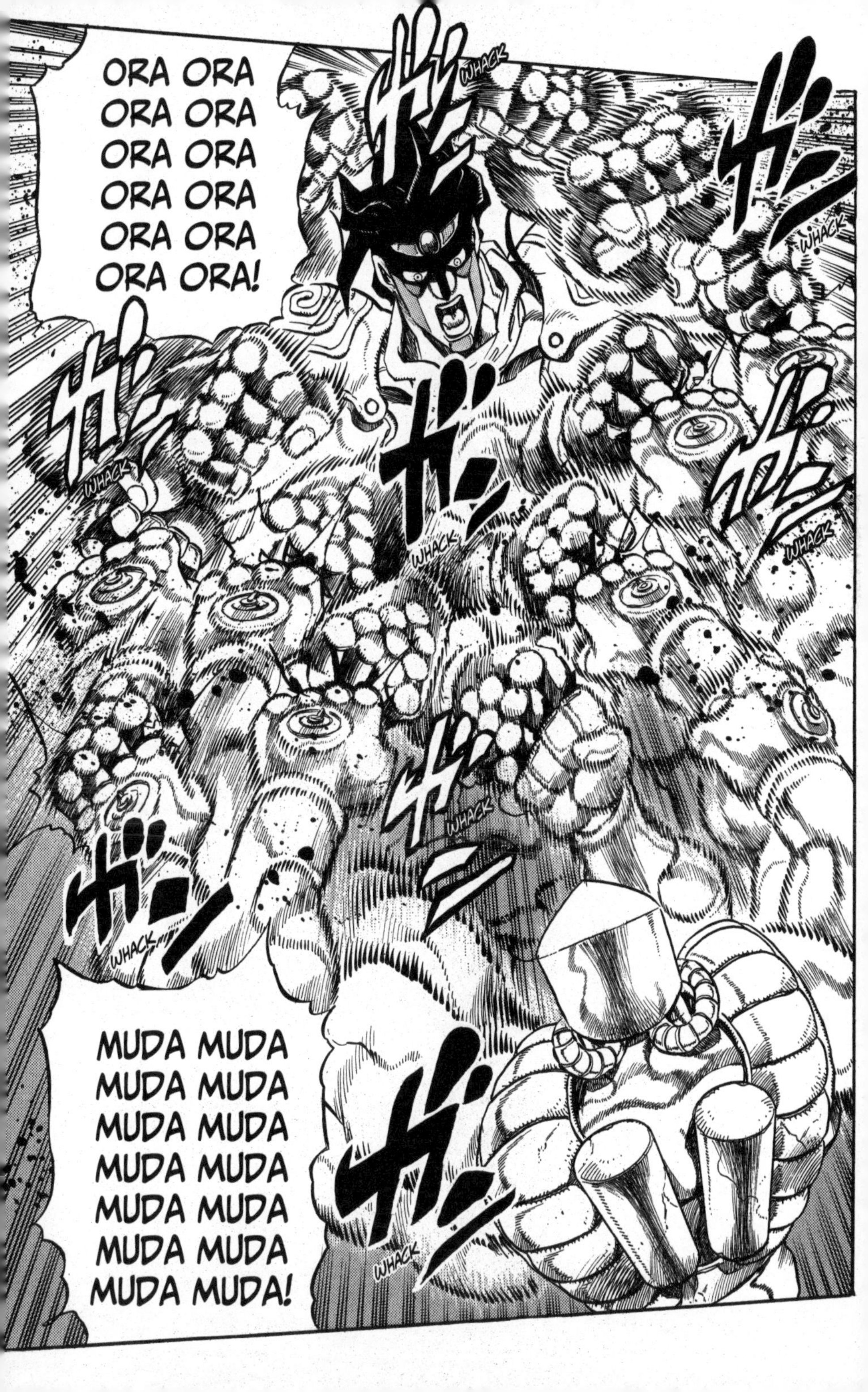
ORA ORA ORA ORA ORA ORA ORA ORA ORA ORA ORA ORA!
WHACK
WHACK
WHACK
WHACK
WHACK
WHACK
WHACK
MUDA MUDA MUDA MUDA MUDA MUDA MUDA MUDA MUDA MUDA MUDA MUDA MUDA MUDA!
WHACK

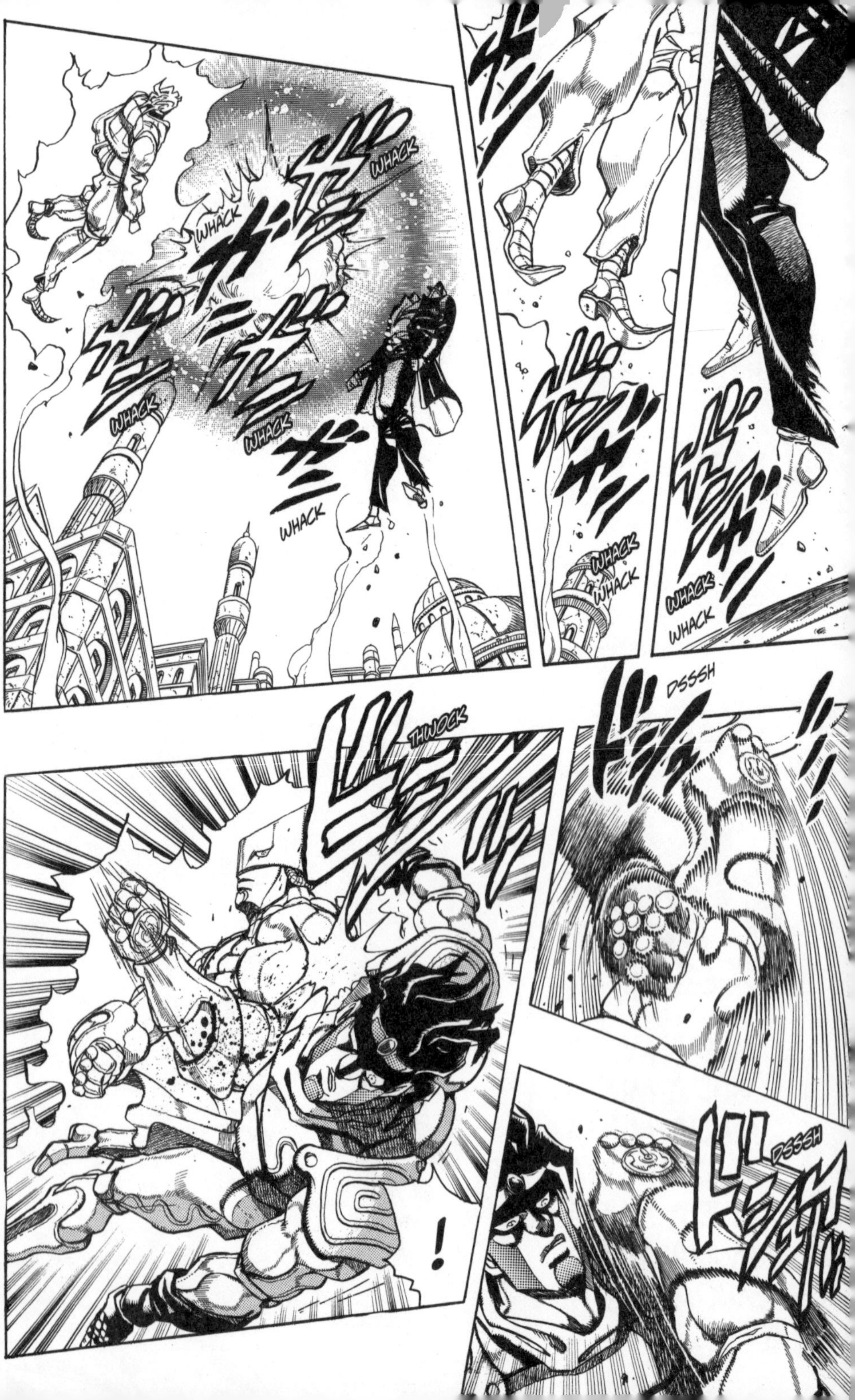
WHACK
WHACK
WHACK
WHACK
WHACK
WHACK
WHACK
WHACK
WHACK
DSSSH
DSSSH
THWOCK
!

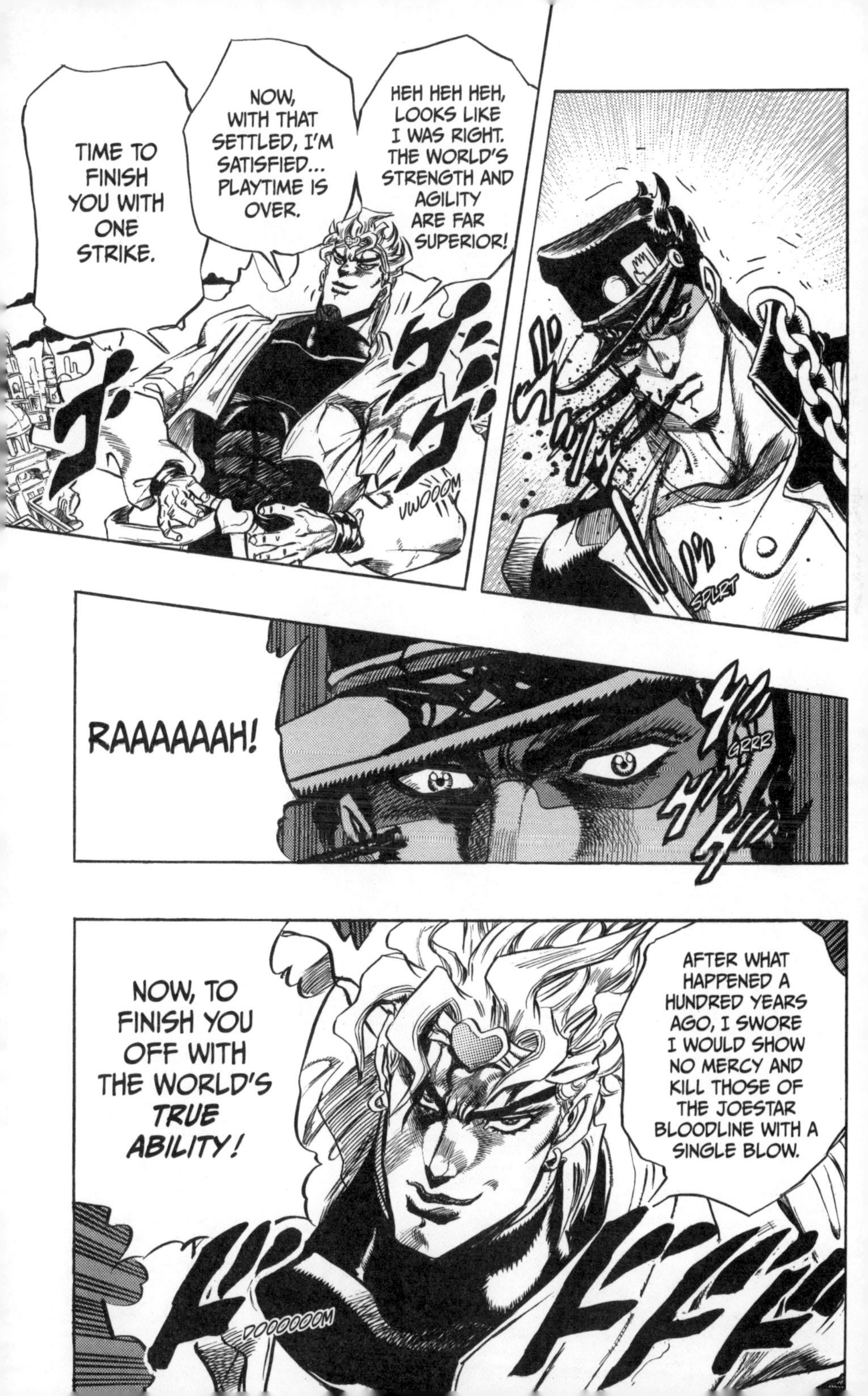
SPLRT
HEH HEH HEH, LOOKS LIKE I WAS RIGHT. THE WORLD'S STRENGTH AND AGILITY ARE FAR SUPERIOR!
NOW, WITH THAT SETTLED, I'M SATISFIED... PLAYTIME IS OVER.
TIME TO FINISH YOU WITH ONE STRIKE.
VWOOOM
RAAAAAAH!
GRRR
AFTER WHAT HAPPENED A HUNDRED YEARS AGO, I SWORE I WOULD SHOW NO MERCY AND KILL THOSE OF THE JOESTAR BLOODLINE WITH A SINGLE BLOW.
NOW, TO FINISH YOU OFF WITH THE WORLD'S *TRUE ABILITY*!
DOOOOOOM

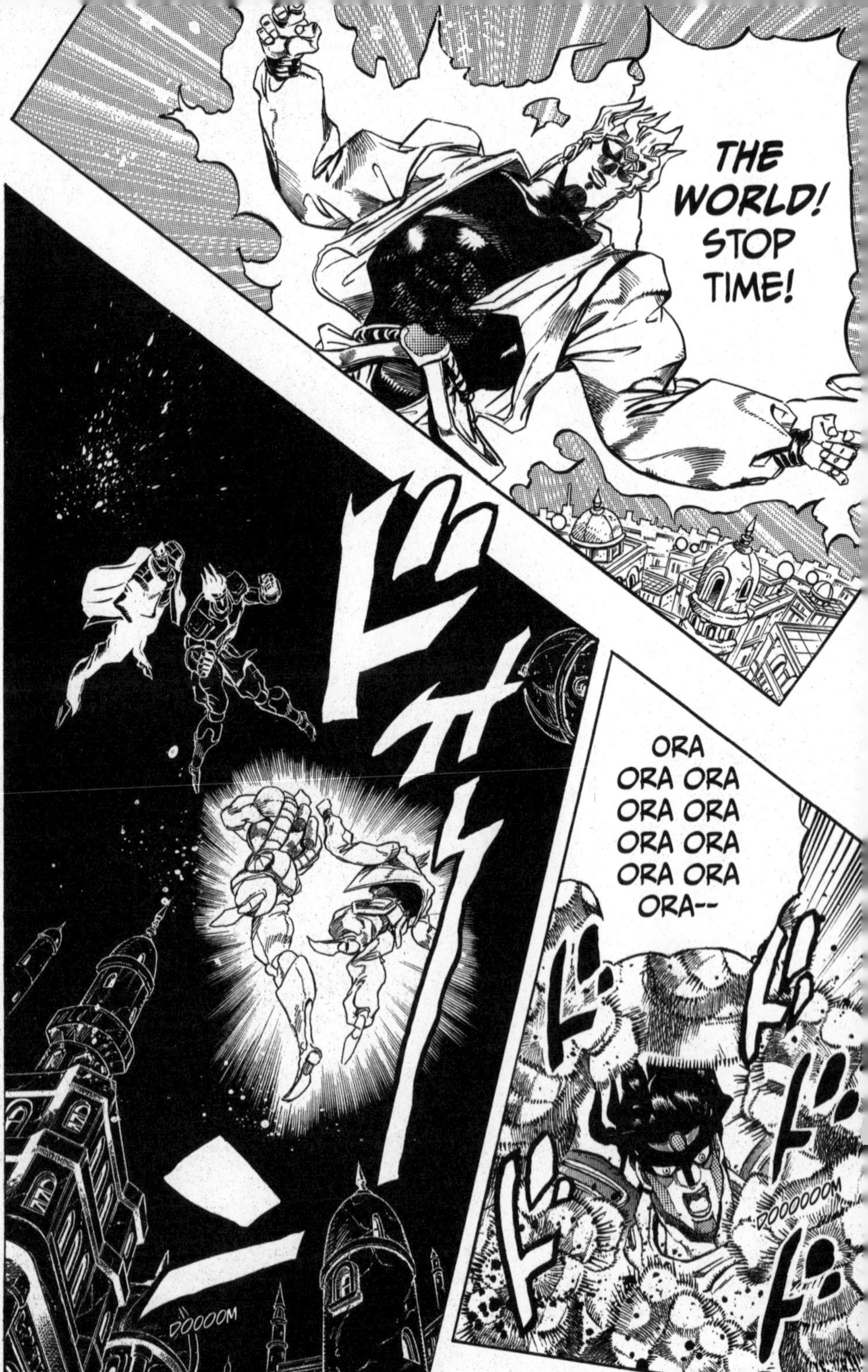
THE WORLD! STOP TIME!
ORA ORA ORA ORA ORA ORA ORA ORA ORA ORA ORA--
DOOOOOOM
DOOOOM

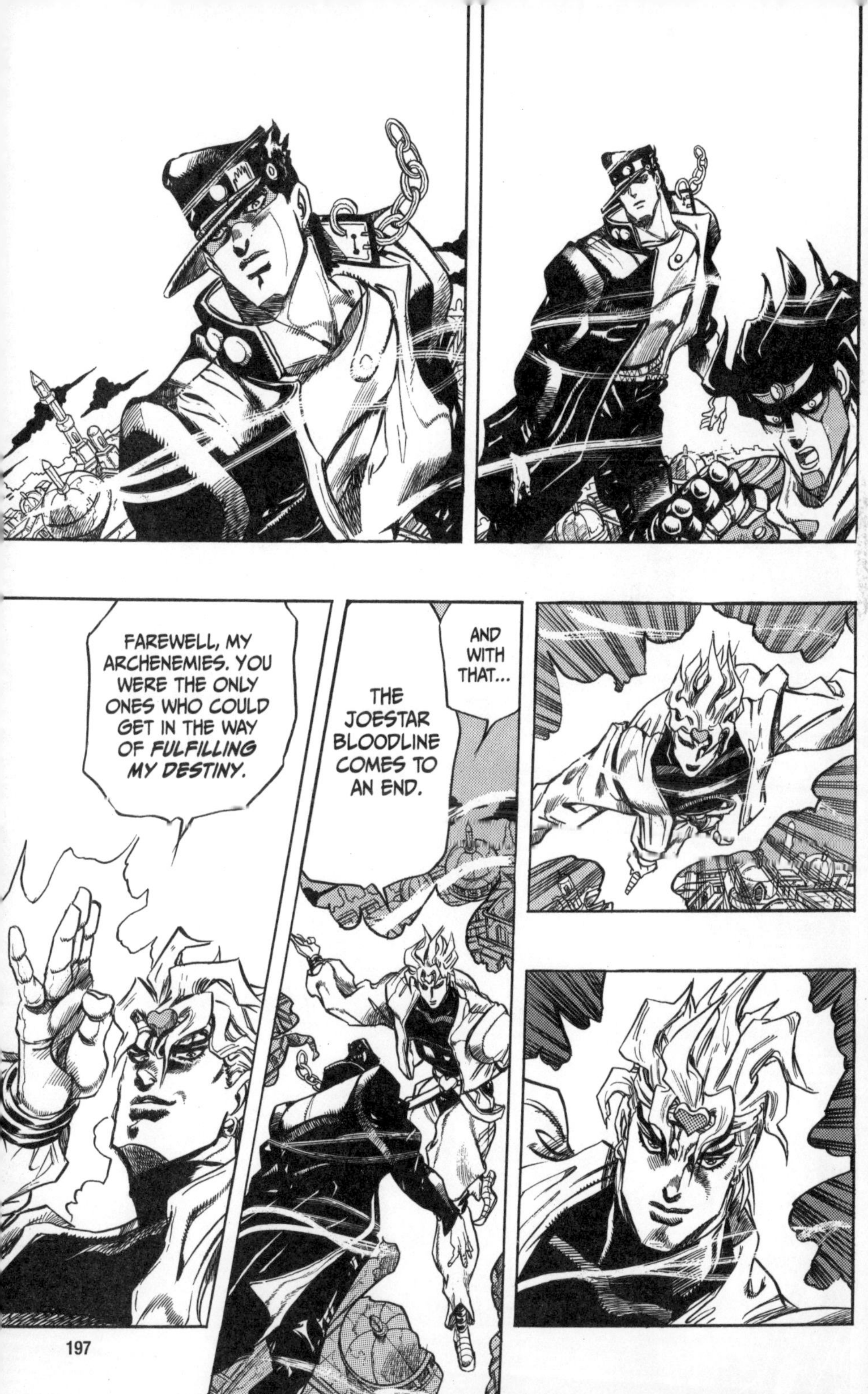
AND WITH THAT...
THE JOESTAR BLOODLINE COMES TO AN END.
FAREWELL, MY ARCHENEMIES. YOU WERE THE ONLY ONES WHO COULD GET IN THE WAY OF *FULFILLING MY DESTINY.*

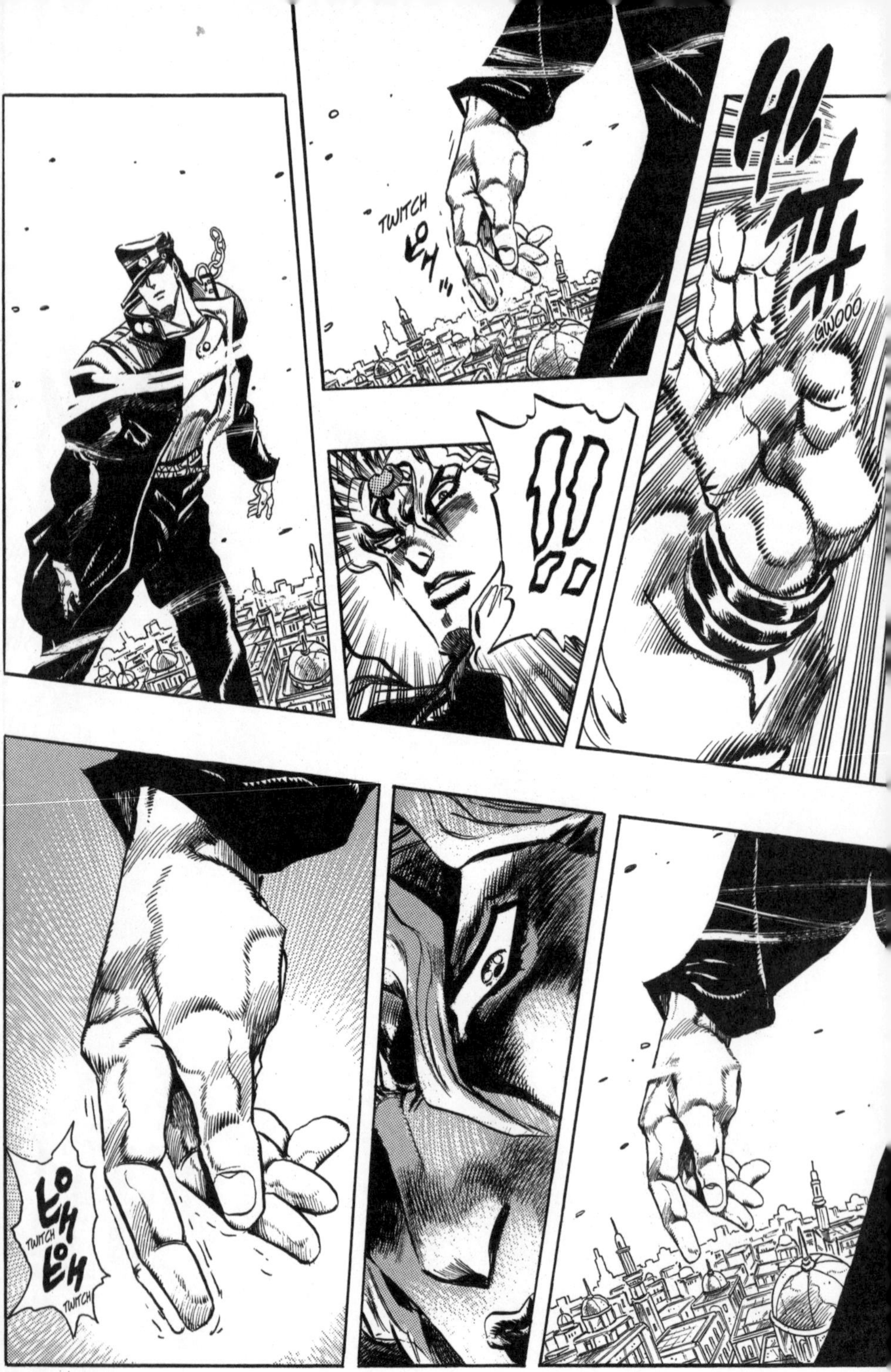
GWOOO
TWITCH
!!
TWITCH
TWITCH

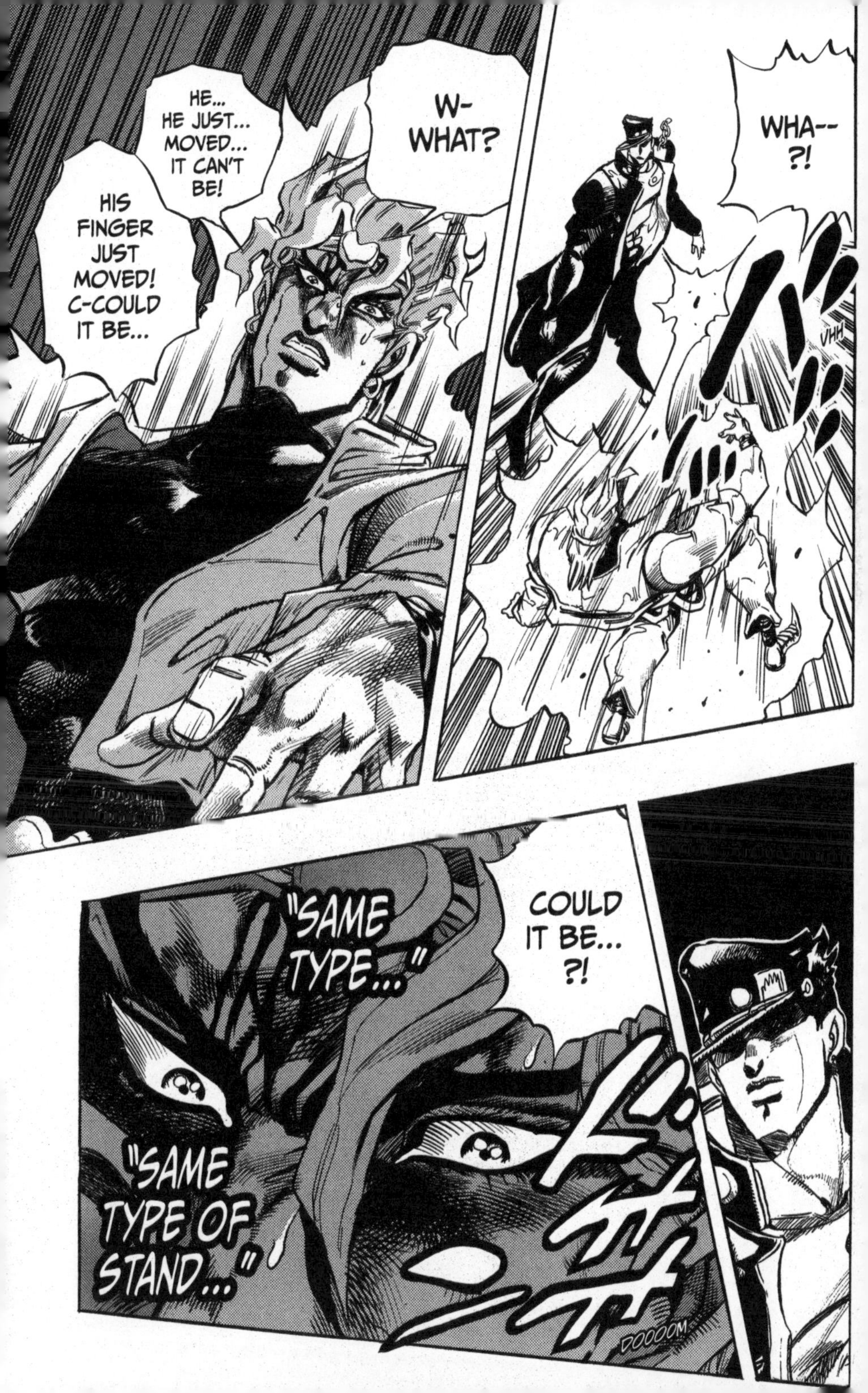
WHA-- ?!
VHH
W- WHAT?
HE... HE JUST... MOVED... IT CAN'T BE!
HIS FINGER JUST MOVED! C-COULD IT BE...
COULD IT BE... ?!
DOOOOM
"SAME TYPE..."
"SAME TYPE OF STAND..."

CHAPTER 144: DIO's World PART 11

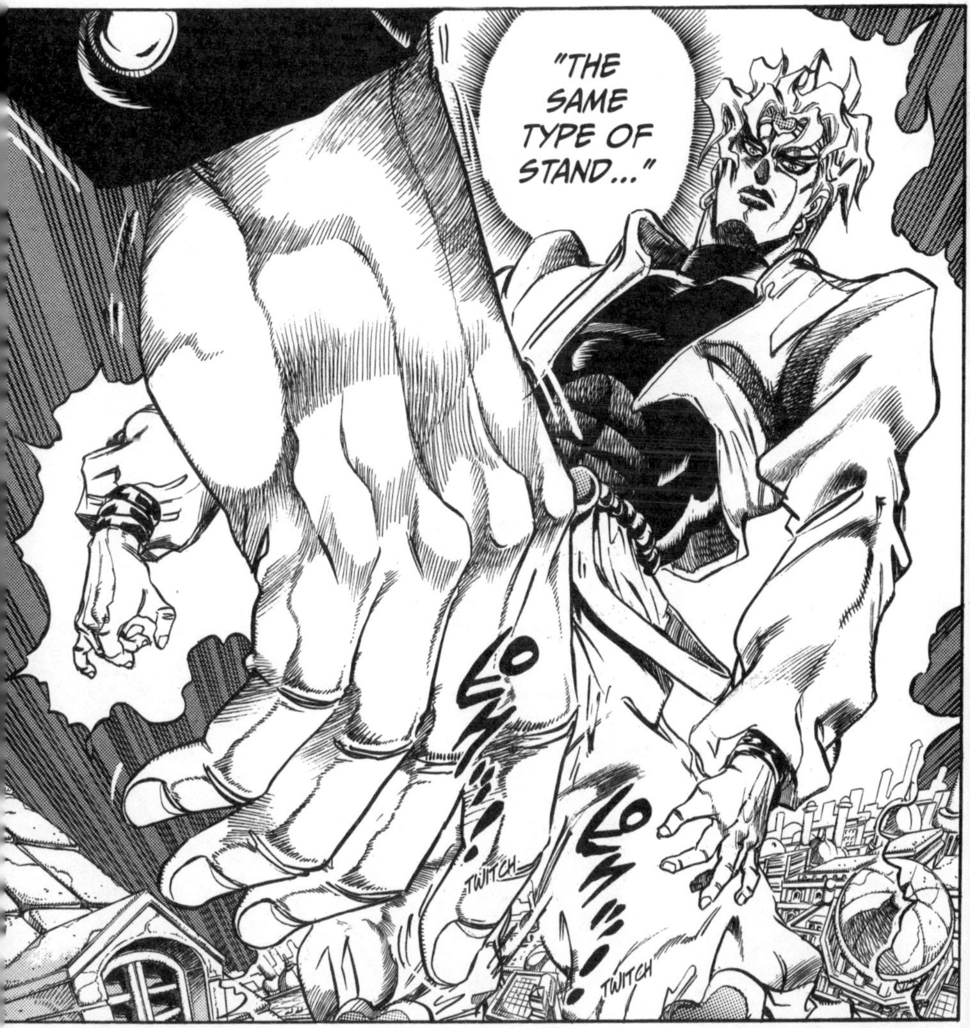
"THE SAME TYPE OF STAND..."
LOOM...!
LOOM...!
TWITCH
TWITCH

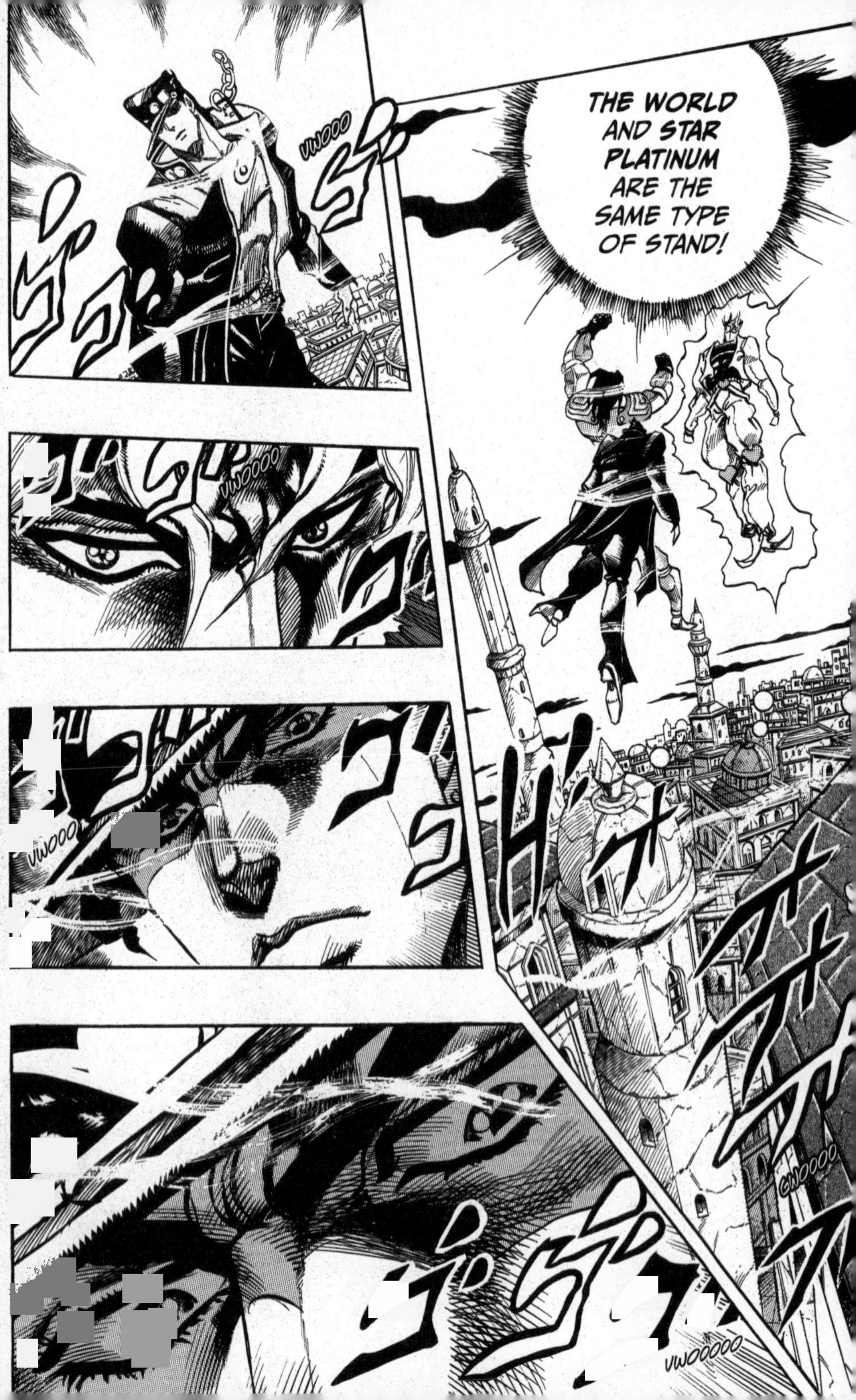
THE WORLD AND STAR PLATINUM ARE THE SAME TYPE OF STAND!
GWOOOO
VWOOO
VWOOOO
VWOOO
VWOOOOO

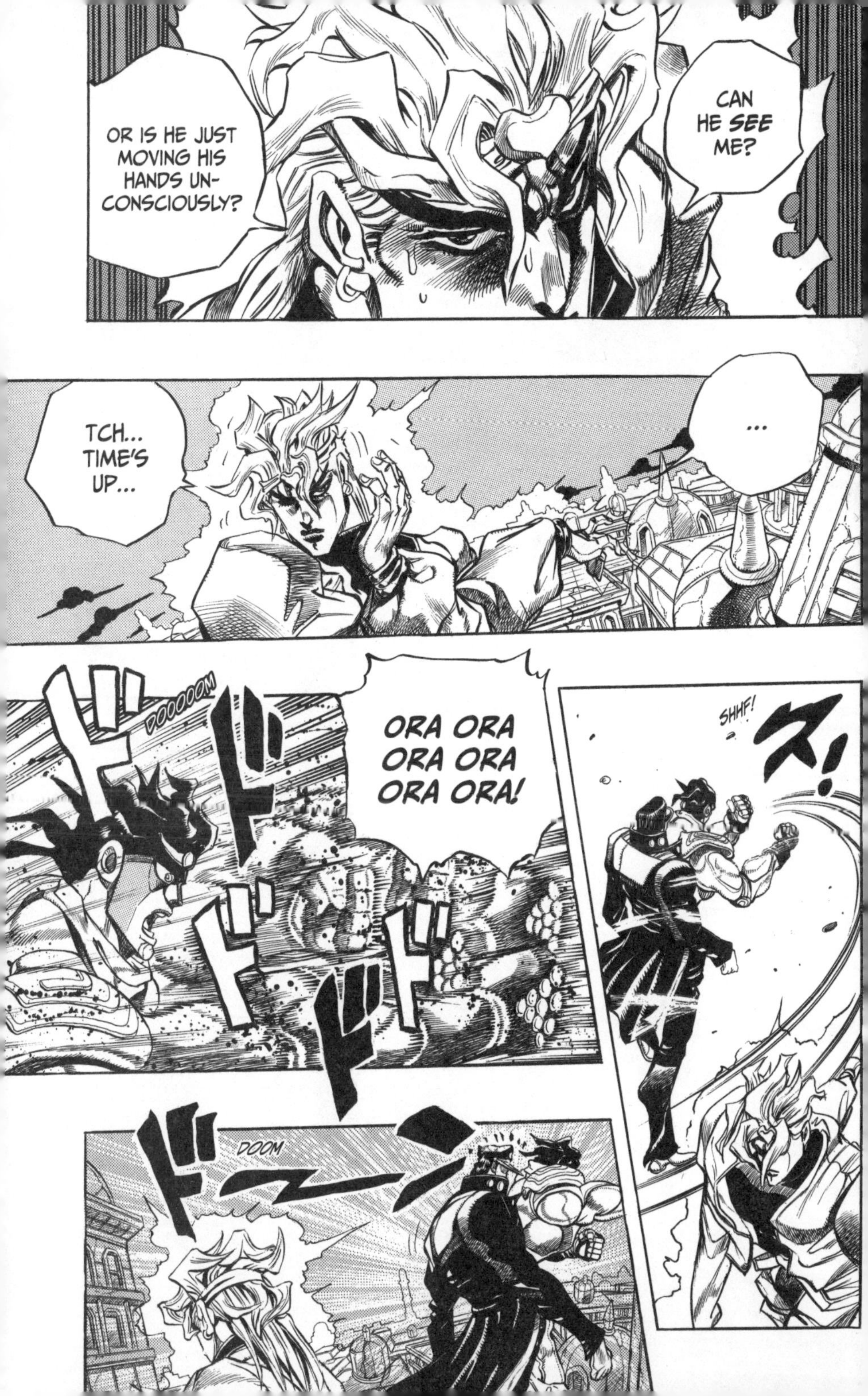
CAN HE SEE ME?
OR IS HE JUST MOVING HIS HANDS UN-CONSCIOUSLY?
...
TCH... TIME'S UP...
ス!
SHHF!
DOOOOOM
ORA ORA ORA ORA ORA ORA!
DOOM

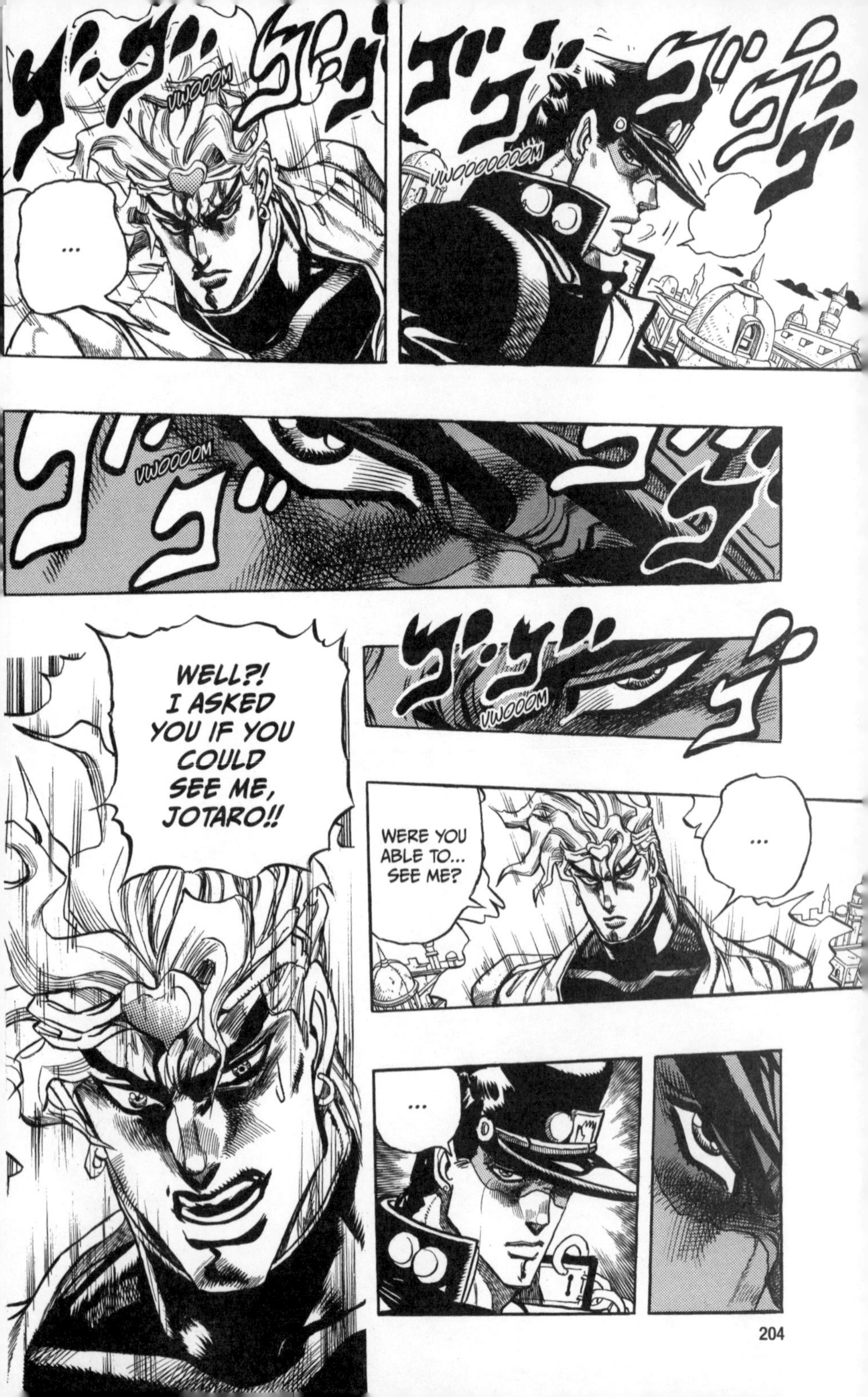
VWOOOOOOOOM
VWOOOM
...
VWOOOOM
VWOOOM
...
WERE YOU ABLE TO... SEE ME?
...
WELL?! I ASKED YOU IF YOU COULD SEE ME, JOTARO!!

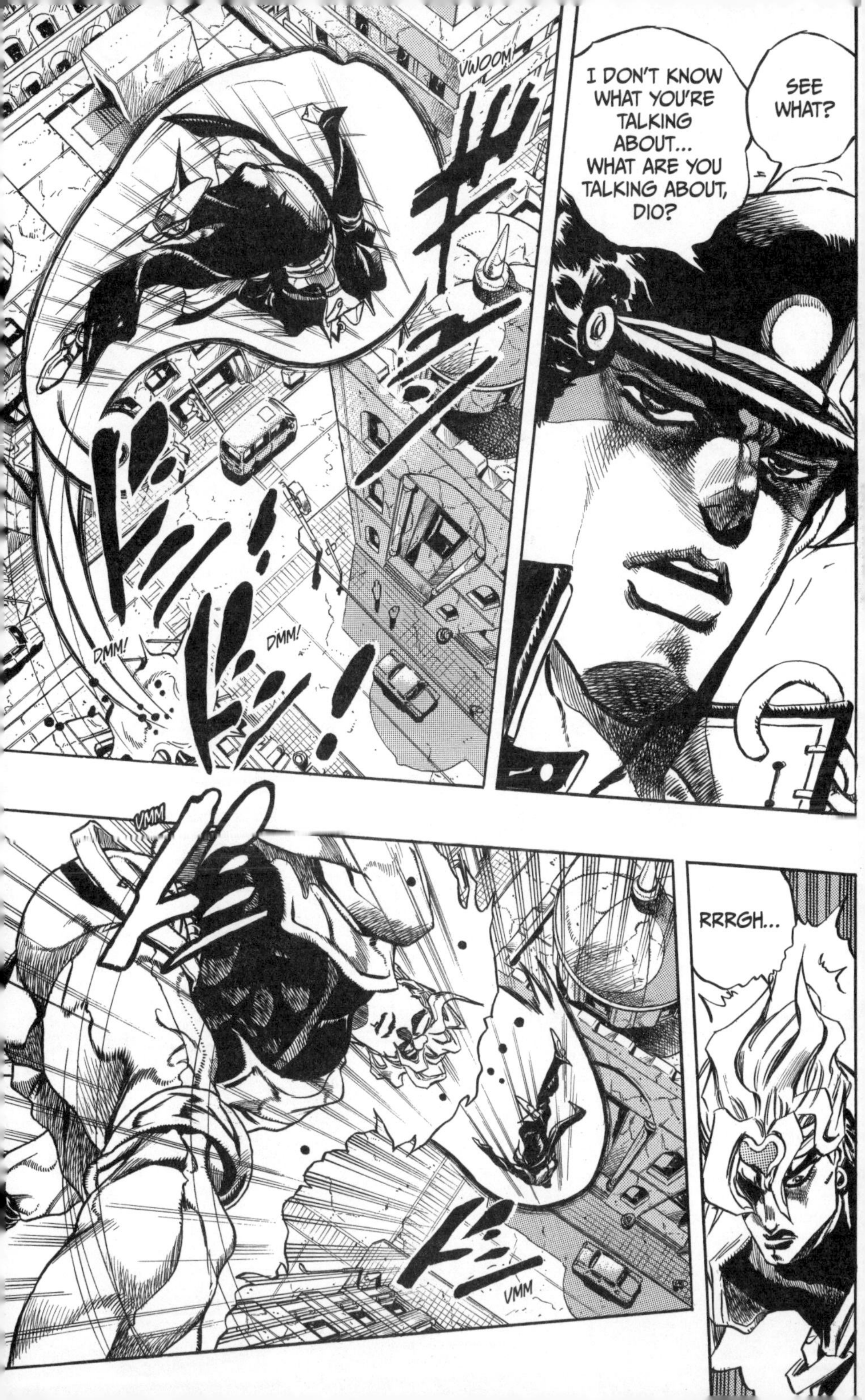
SEE WHAT?
I DON'T KNOW WHAT YOU'RE TALKING ABOUT... WHAT ARE YOU TALKING ABOUT, DIO?
VWOOM
DMM!
DMM!
RRRGH...
VMM
VMM

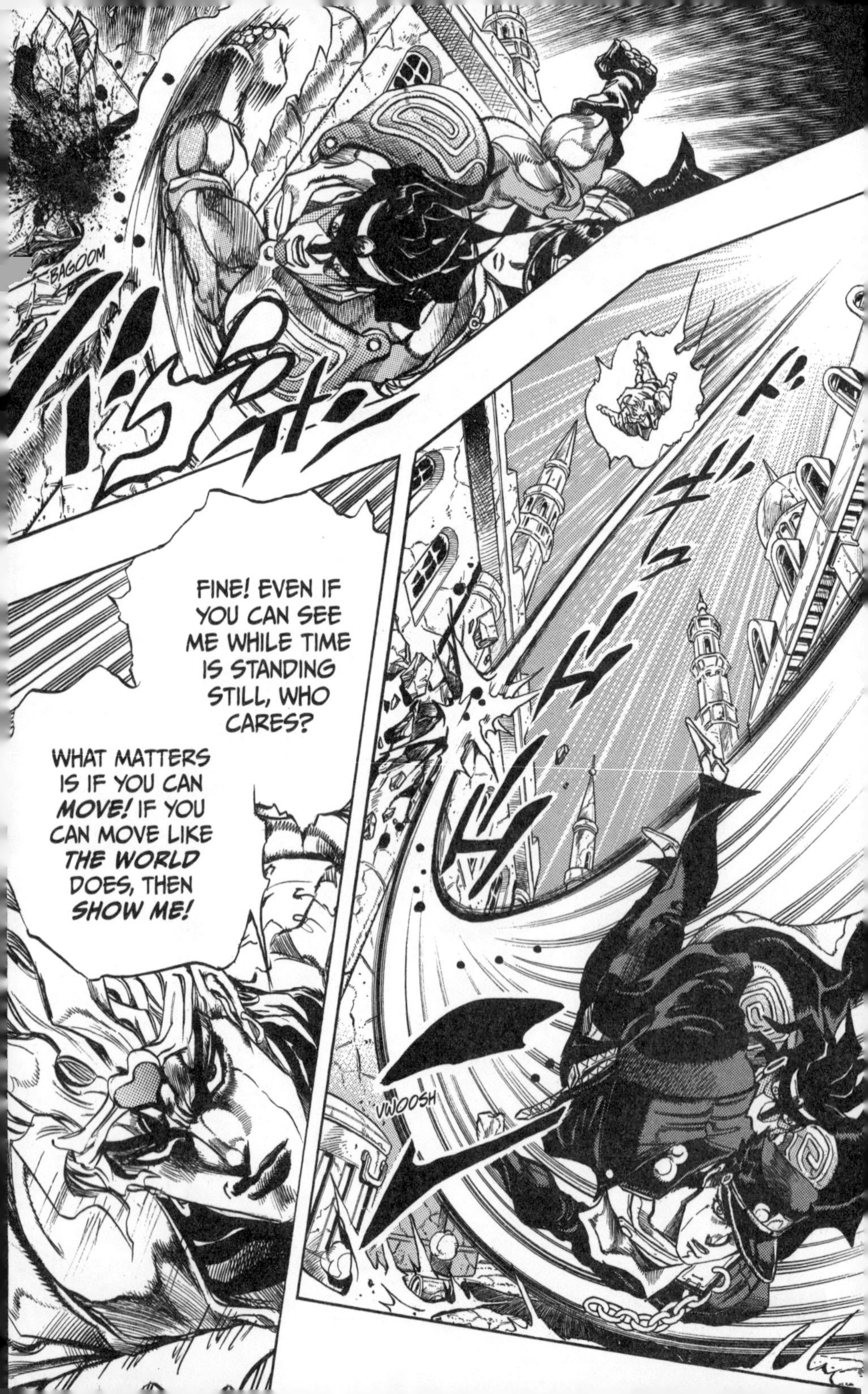
BAGOOM
VWOOSH
FINE! EVEN IF YOU CAN SEE ME WHILE TIME IS STANDING STILL, WHO CARES?
WHAT MATTERS IS IF YOU CAN *MOVE!* IF YOU CAN MOVE LIKE *THE WORLD* DOES, THEN *SHOW ME!*

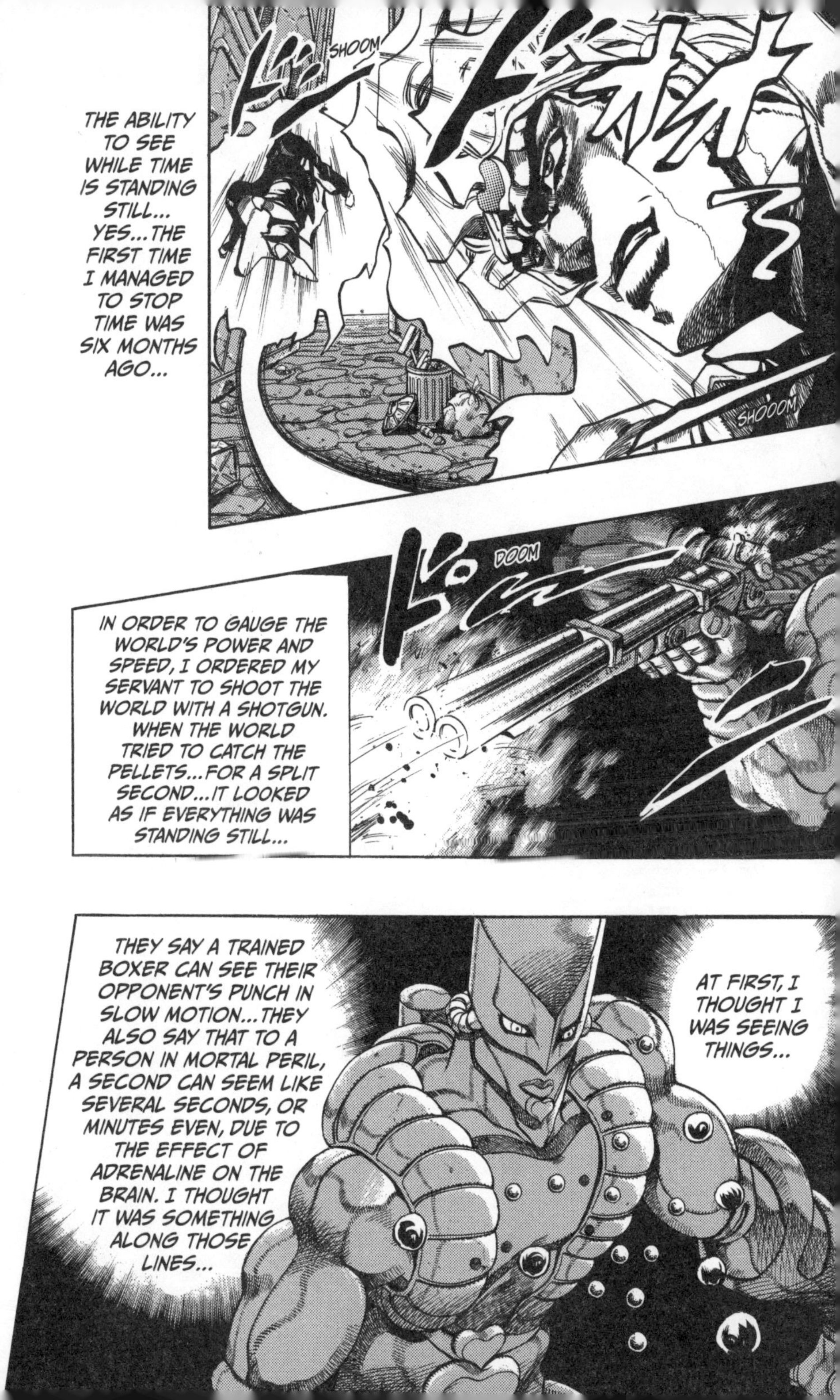
SHOOM
SHOOOM
THE ABILITY TO SEE WHILE TIME IS STANDING STILL... YES...THE FIRST TIME I MANAGED TO STOP TIME WAS SIX MONTHS AGO...
DOOM
IN ORDER TO GAUGE THE WORLD'S POWER AND SPEED, I ORDERED MY SERVANT TO SHOOT THE WORLD WITH A SHOTGUN. WHEN THE WORLD TRIED TO CATCH THE PELLETS...FOR A SPLIT SECOND...IT LOOKED AS IF EVERYTHING WAS STANDING STILL...
AT FIRST, I THOUGHT I WAS SEEING THINGS...
THEY SAY A TRAINED BOXER CAN SEE THEIR OPPONENT'S PUNCH IN SLOW MOTION...THEY ALSO SAY THAT TO A PERSON IN MORTAL PERIL, A SECOND CAN SEEM LIKE SEVERAL SECONDS, OR MINUTES EVEN, DUE TO THE EFFECT OF ADRENALINE ON THE BRAIN. I THOUGHT IT WAS SOMETHING ALONG THOSE LINES...

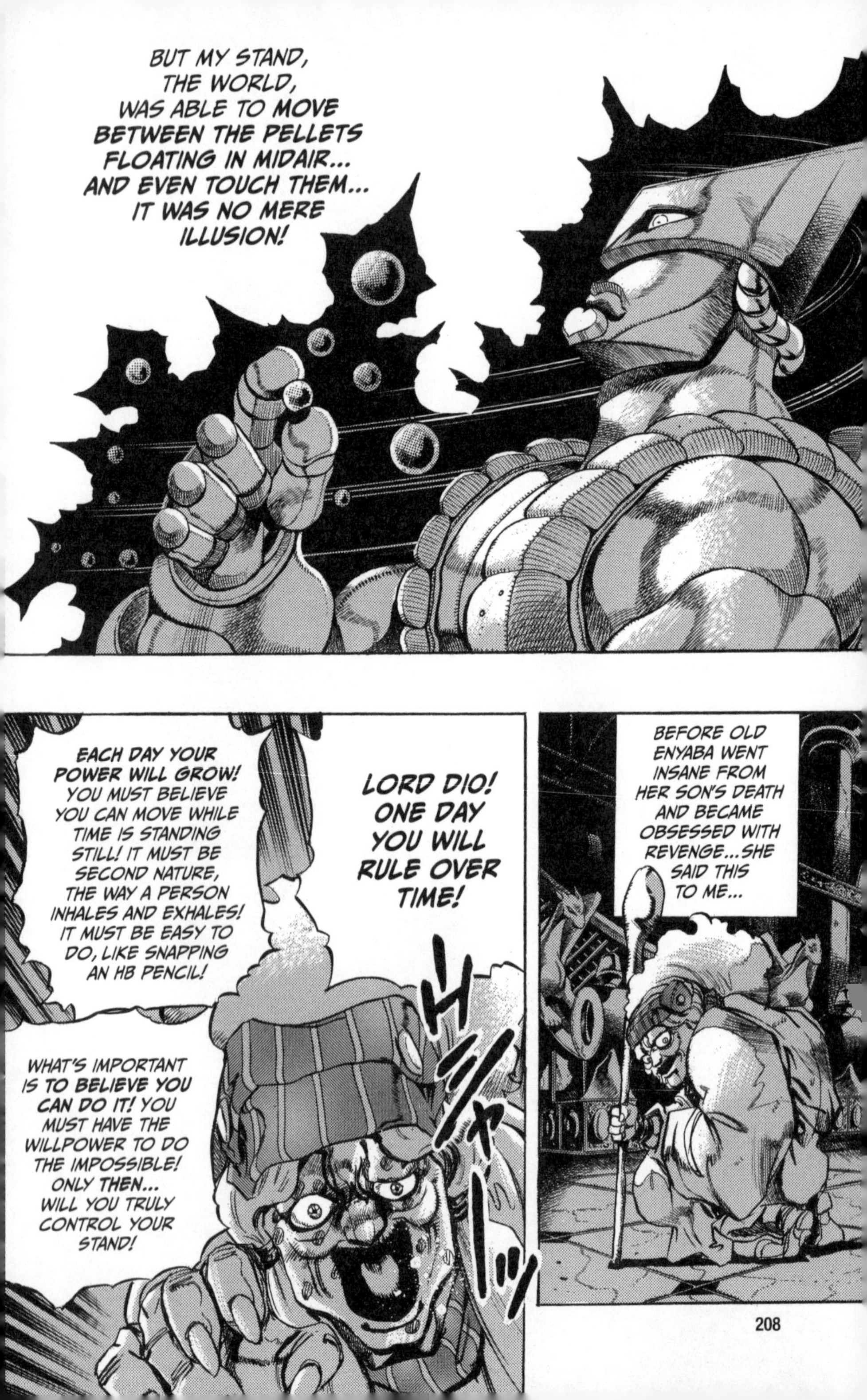
BUT MY STAND, THE WORLD, WAS ABLE TO MOVE BETWEEN THE PELLETS FLOATING IN MIDAIR... AND EVEN TOUCH THEM... IT WAS NO MERE ILLUSION!
BEFORE OLD ENYABA WENT INSANE FROM HER SON'S DEATH AND BECAME OBSESSED WITH REVENGE...SHE SAID THIS TO ME...
LORD DIO! ONE DAY YOU WILL RULE OVER TIME!
EACH DAY YOUR POWER WILL GROW! YOU MUST BELIEVE YOU CAN MOVE WHILE TIME IS STANDING STILL! IT MUST BE SECOND NATURE, THE WAY A PERSON INHALES AND EXHALES! IT MUST BE EASY TO DO, LIKE SNAPPING AN HB PENCIL!
WHAT'S IMPORTANT IS TO BELIEVE YOU CAN DO IT! YOU MUST HAVE THE WILLPOWER TO DO THE IMPOSSIBLE! ONLY THEN... WILL YOU TRULY CONTROL YOUR STAND!

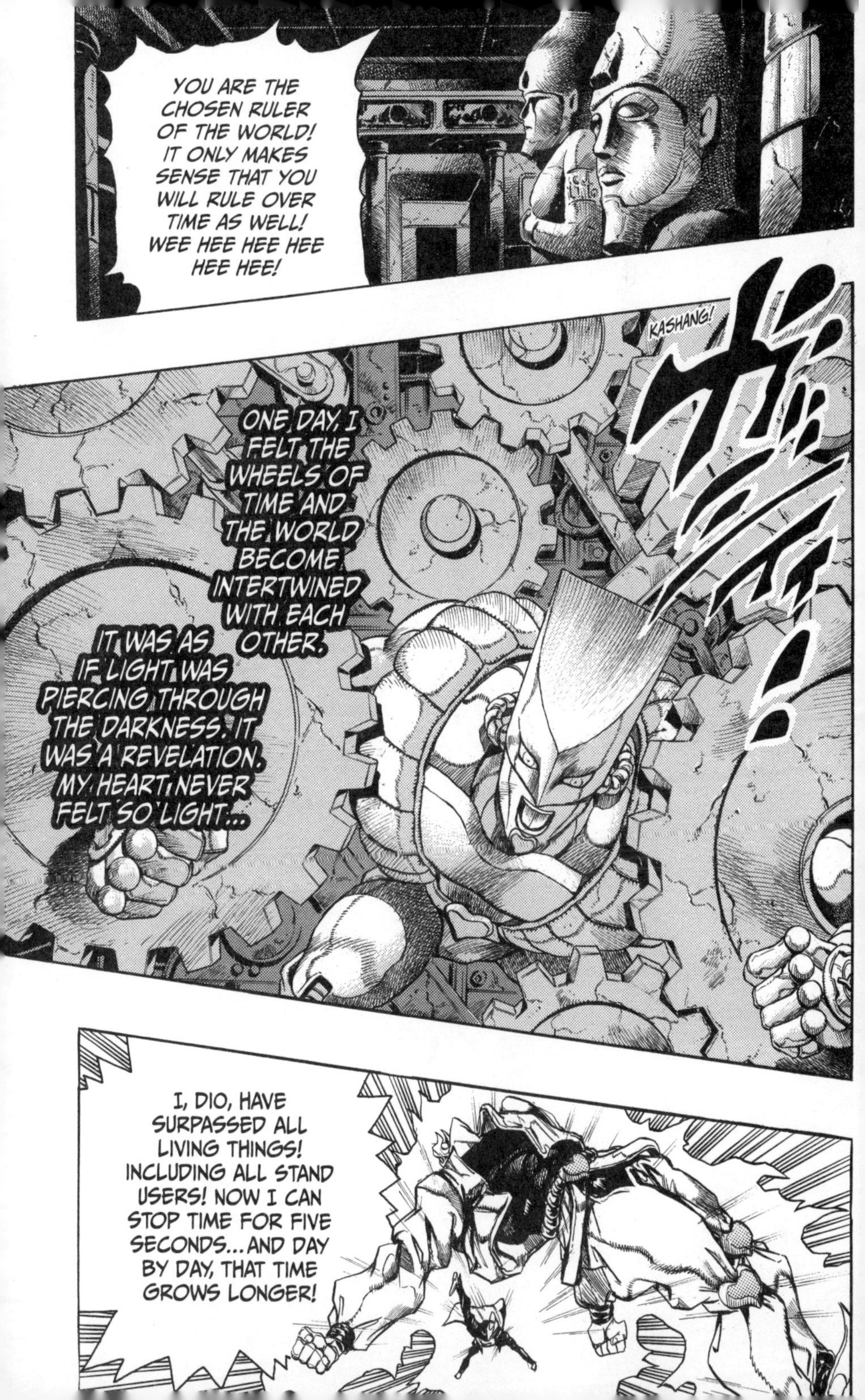
YOU ARE THE CHOSEN RULER OF THE WORLD! IT ONLY MAKES SENSE THAT YOU WILL RULE OVER TIME AS WELL! WEE HEE HEE HEE HEE HEE!
KASHANG!
ONE DAY, I FELT THE WHEELS OF TIME AND THE WORLD BECOME INTERTWINED WITH EACH OTHER.
IT WAS AS IF LIGHT WAS PIERCING THROUGH THE DARKNESS. IT WAS A REVELATION. MY HEART NEVER FELT SO LIGHT...
I, DIO, HAVE SURPASSED ALL LIVING THINGS! INCLUDING ALL STAND USERS! NOW I CAN STOP TIME FOR FIVE SECONDS...AND DAY BY DAY, THAT TIME GROWS LONGER!

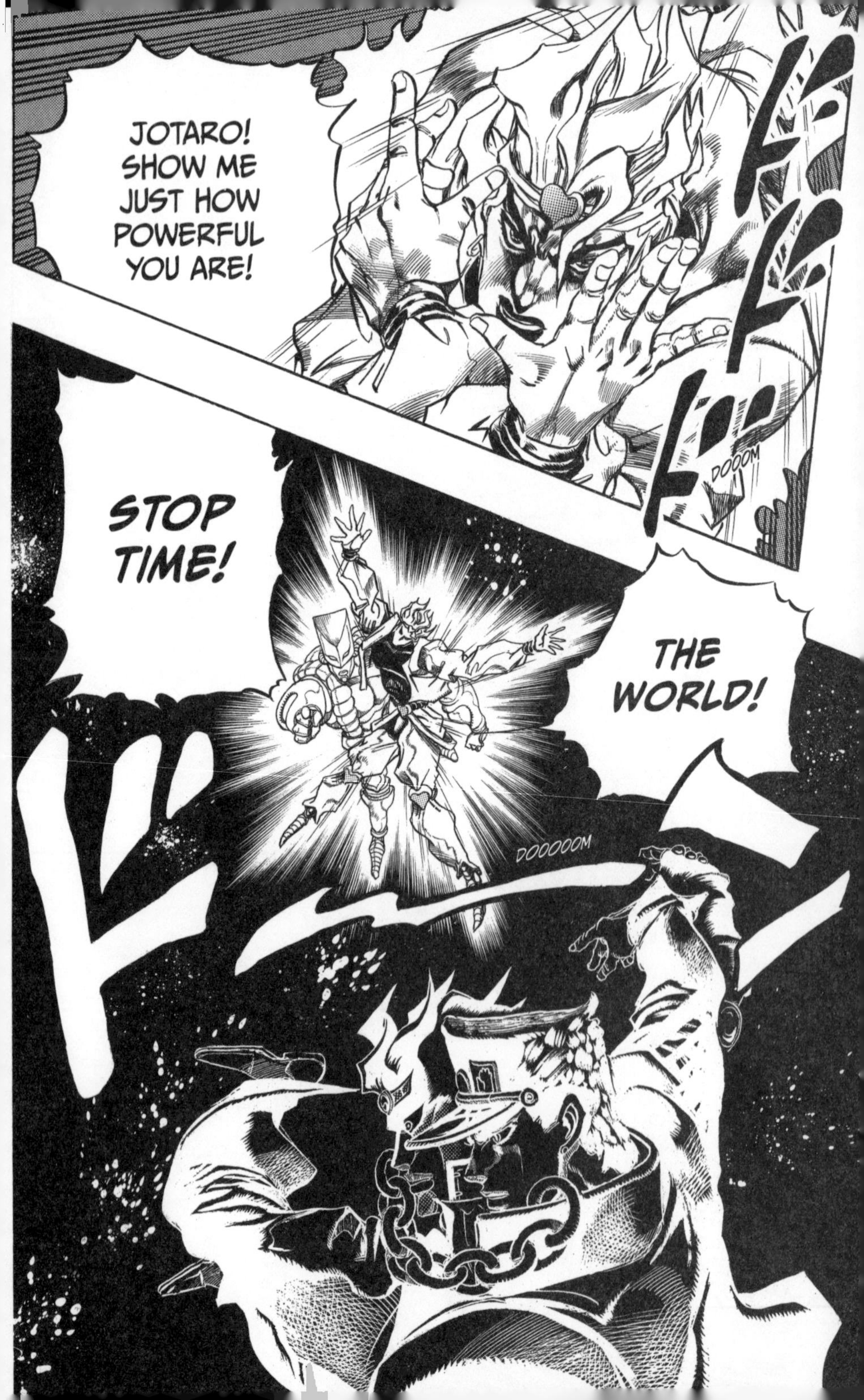
JOTARO! SHOW ME JUST HOW POWERFUL YOU ARE!
DOOOM
THE WORLD!
STOP TIME!
DOOOOOM

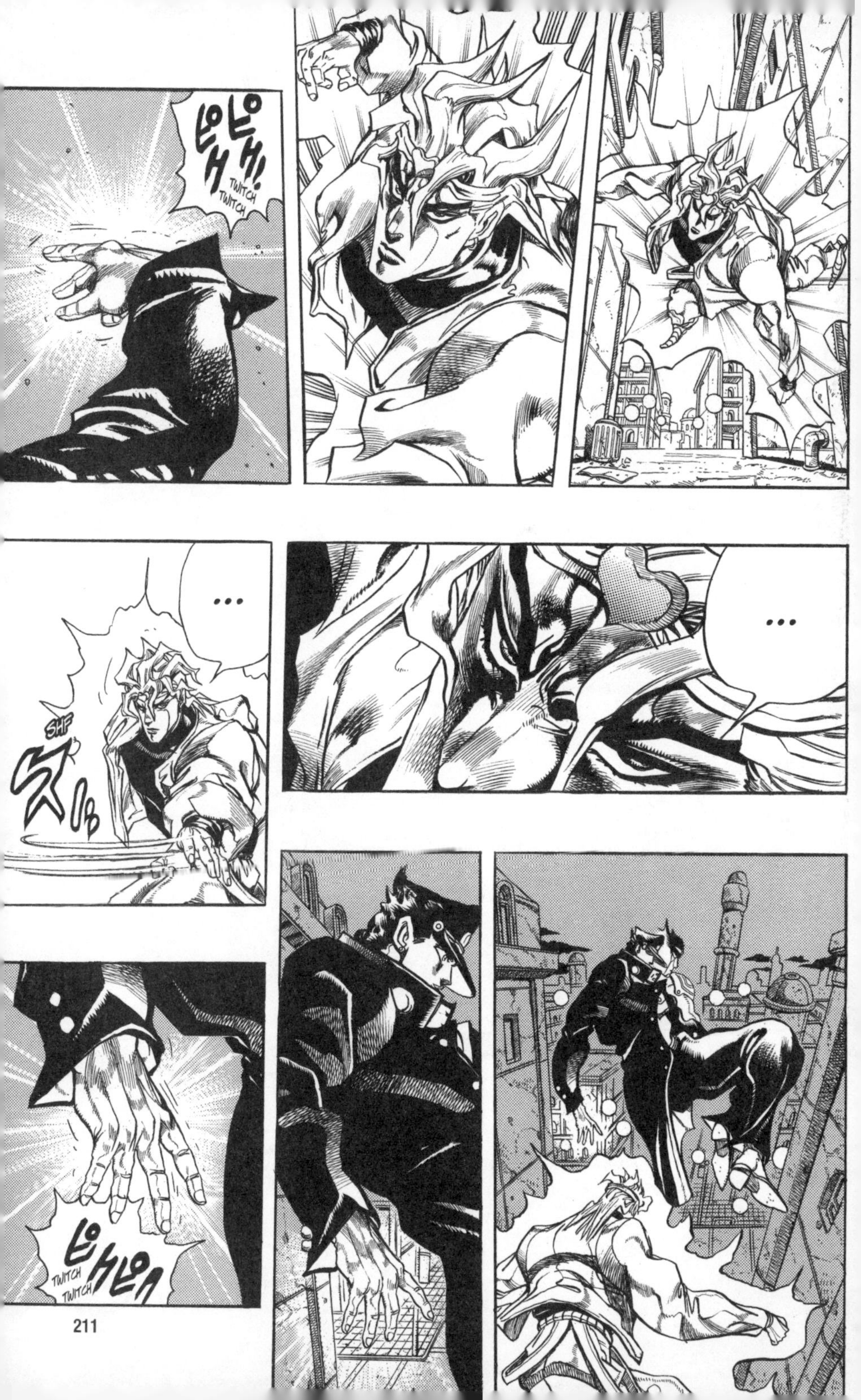
TWITCH TWITCH
...
...
SHF
TWITCH TWITCH

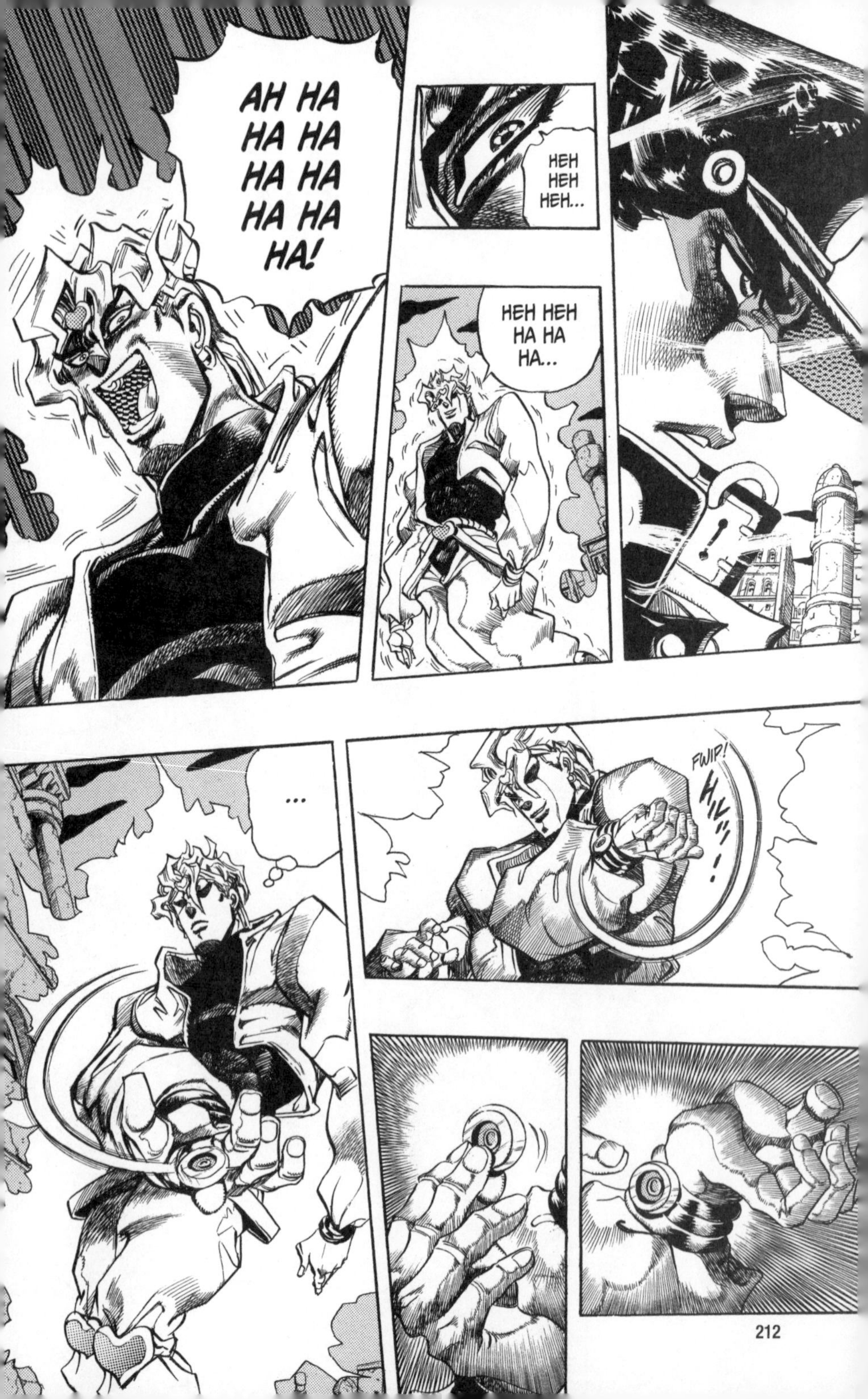
HEH HEH HEH...
HEH HEH HA HA HA...
AH HA HA HA HA HA HA HA HA!
FWIP!
...

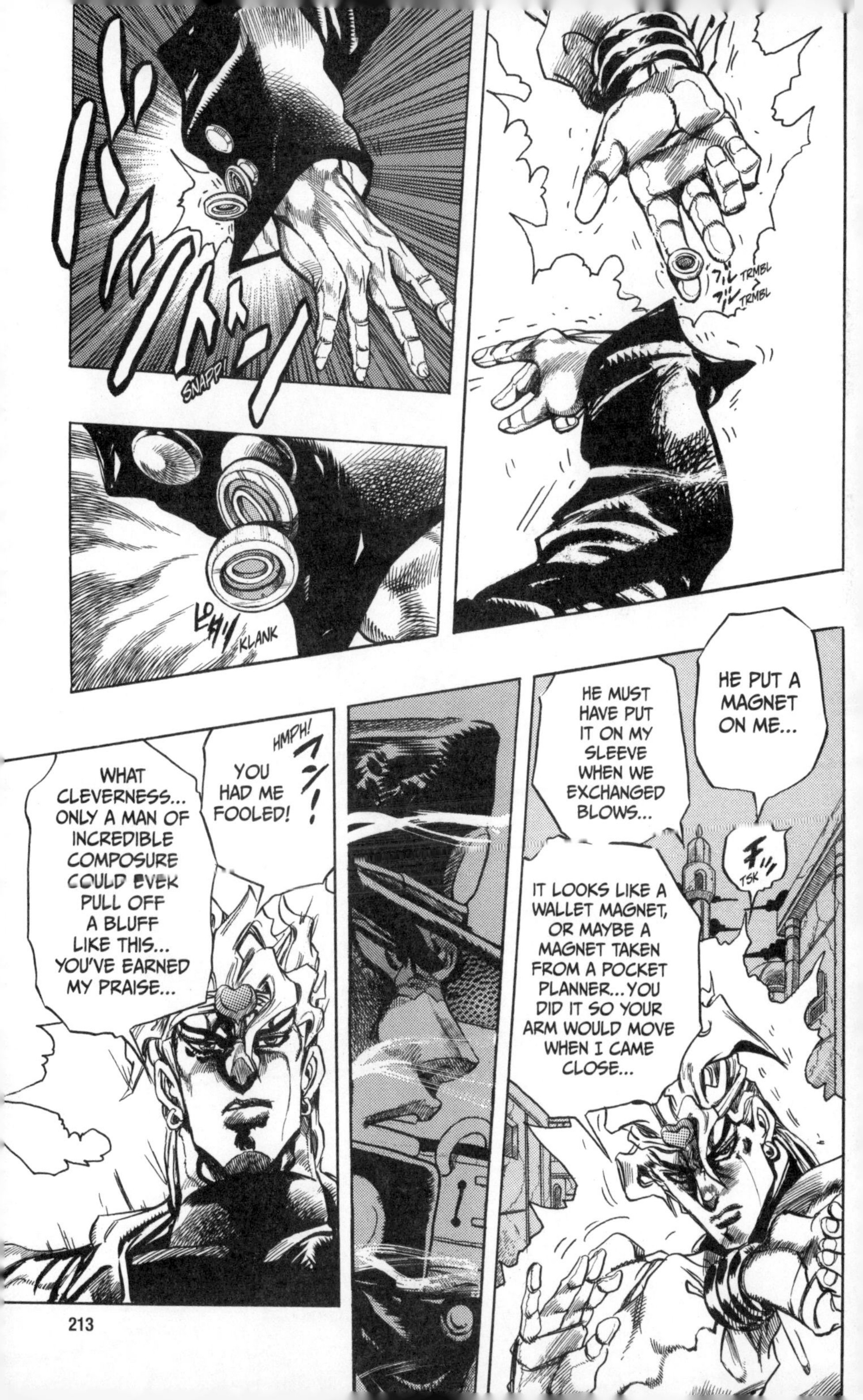
TRMBL
TRMBL
SNAPP!
KLANK
HE PUT A MAGNET ON ME...
HE MUST HAVE PUT IT ON MY SLEEVE WHEN WE EXCHANGED BLOWS...
TSK
IT LOOKS LIKE A WALLET MAGNET, OR MAYBE A MAGNET TAKEN FROM A POCKET PLANNER...YOU DID IT SO YOUR ARM WOULD MOVE WHEN I CAME CLOSE...
HMPH!
YOU HAD ME FOOLED!
WHAT CLEVERNESS... ONLY A MAN OF INCREDIBLE COMPOSURE COULD EVER PULL OFF A BLUFF LIKE THIS... YOU'VE EARNED MY PRAISE...

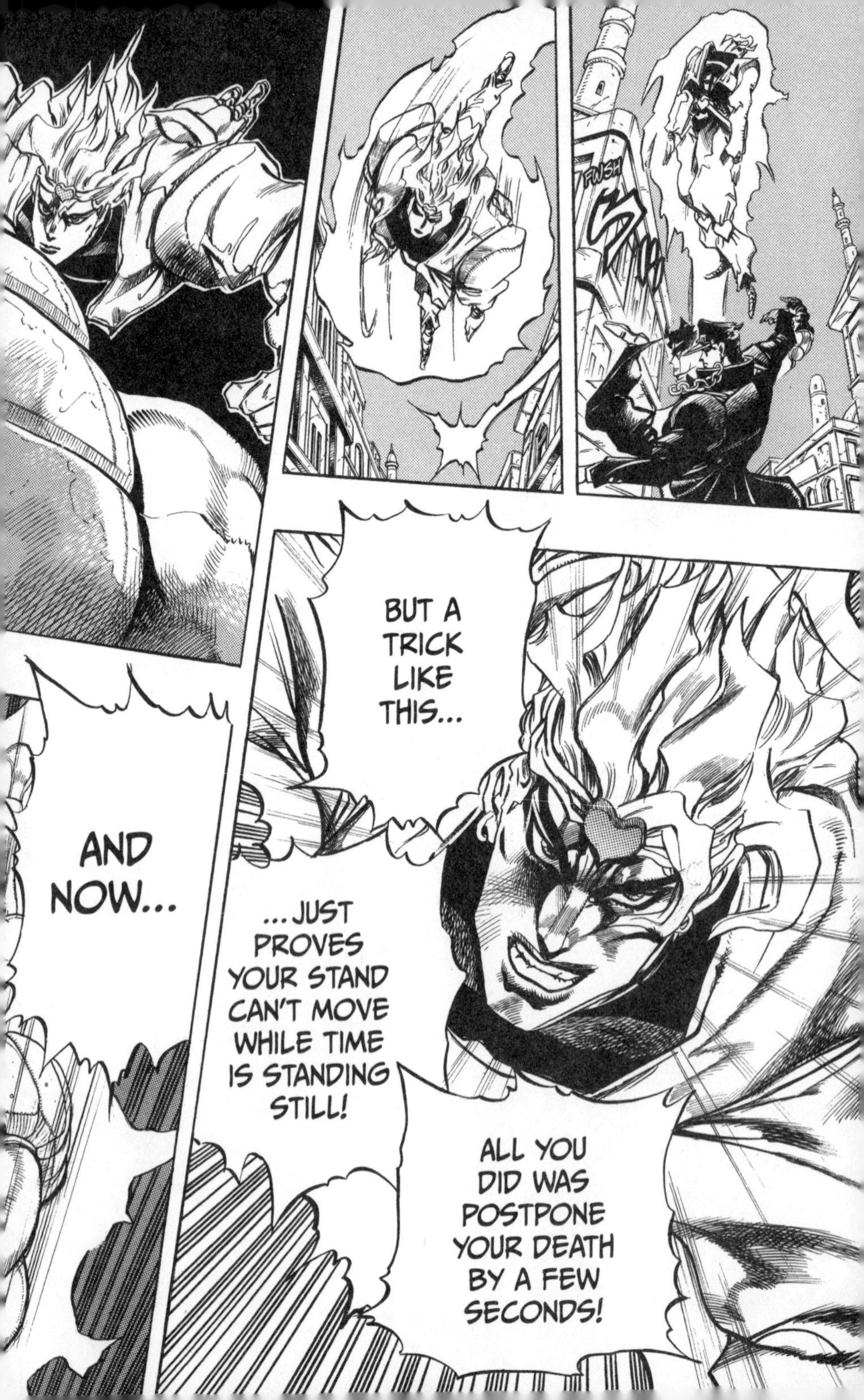
FWSH
BUT A TRICK LIKE THIS...
...JUST PROVES YOUR STAND CAN'T MOVE WHILE TIME IS STANDING STILL!
ALL YOU DID WAS POSTPONE YOUR DEATH BY A FEW SECONDS!
AND NOW...

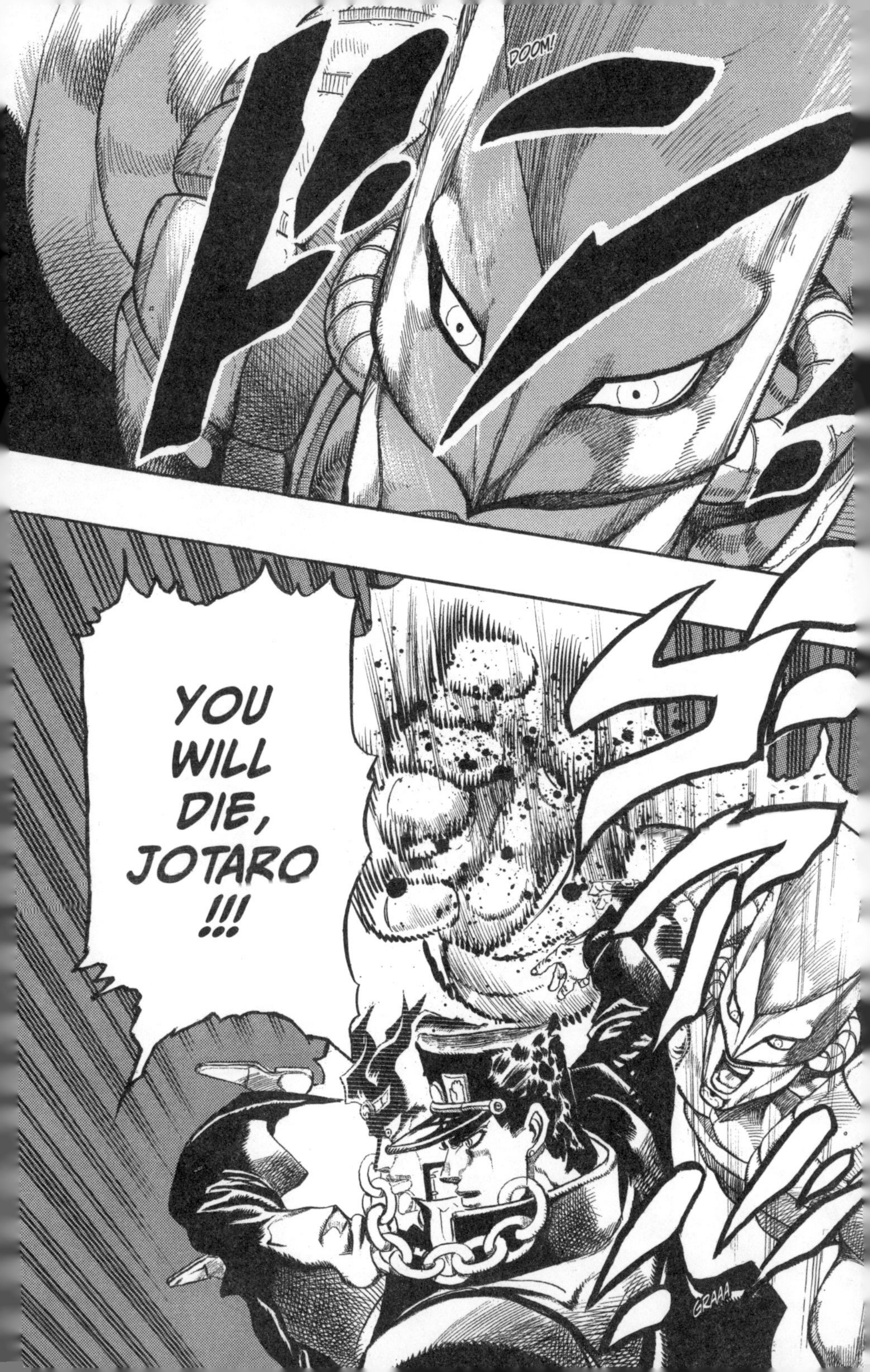
DOOM!
YOU WILL DIE, JOTARO !!!
GRAAA...

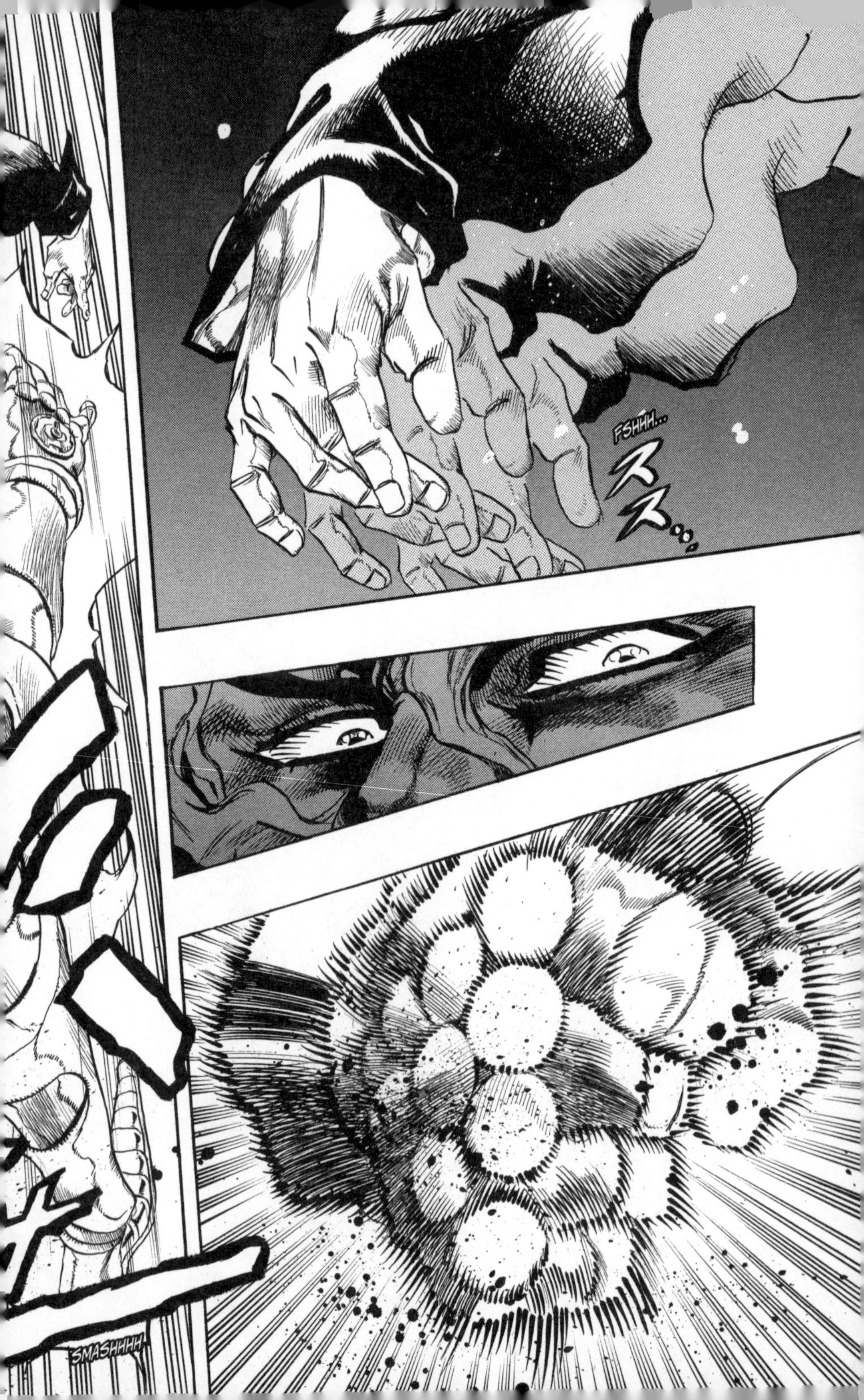
FSHHH...
スス...
SMASHHHH

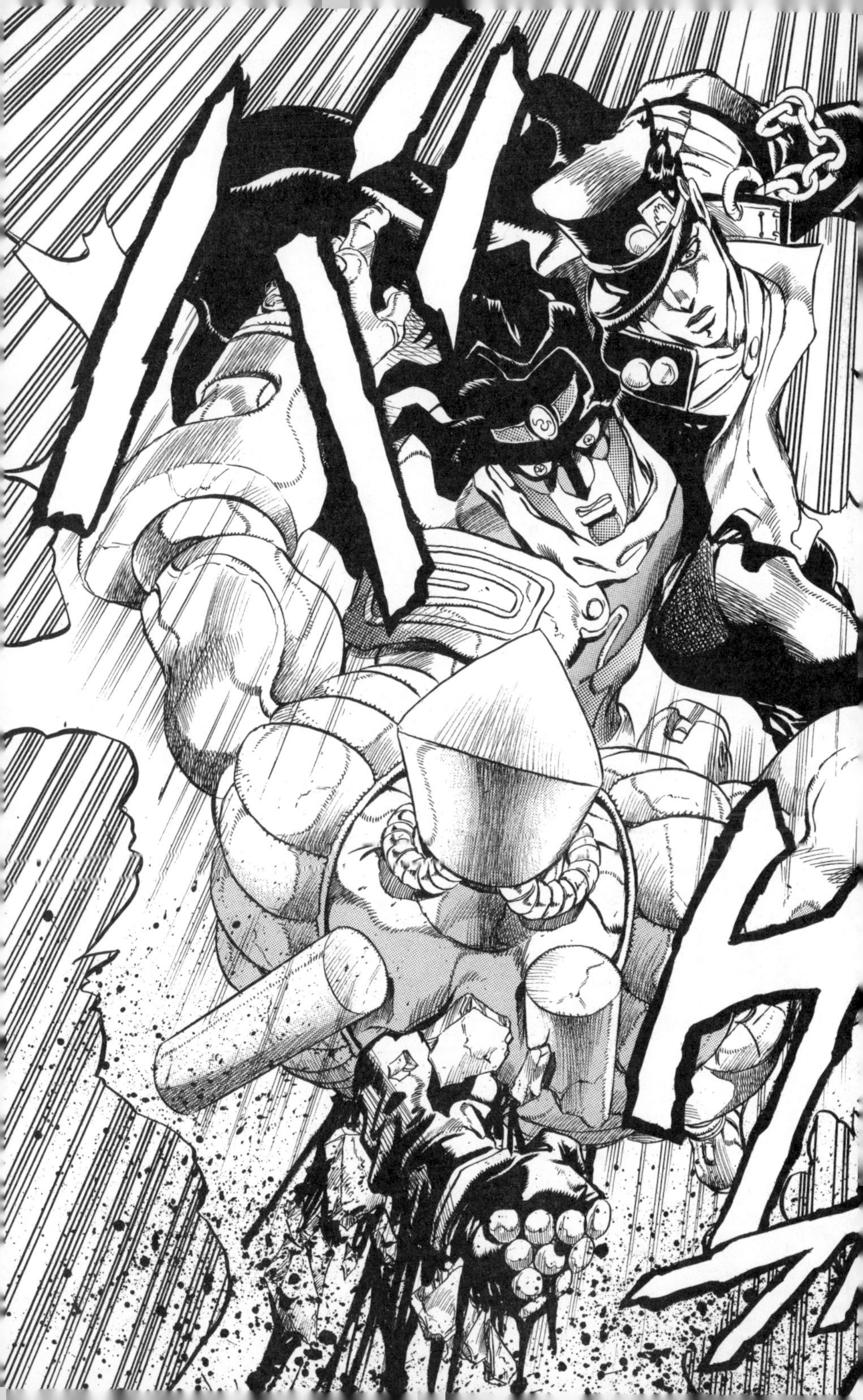

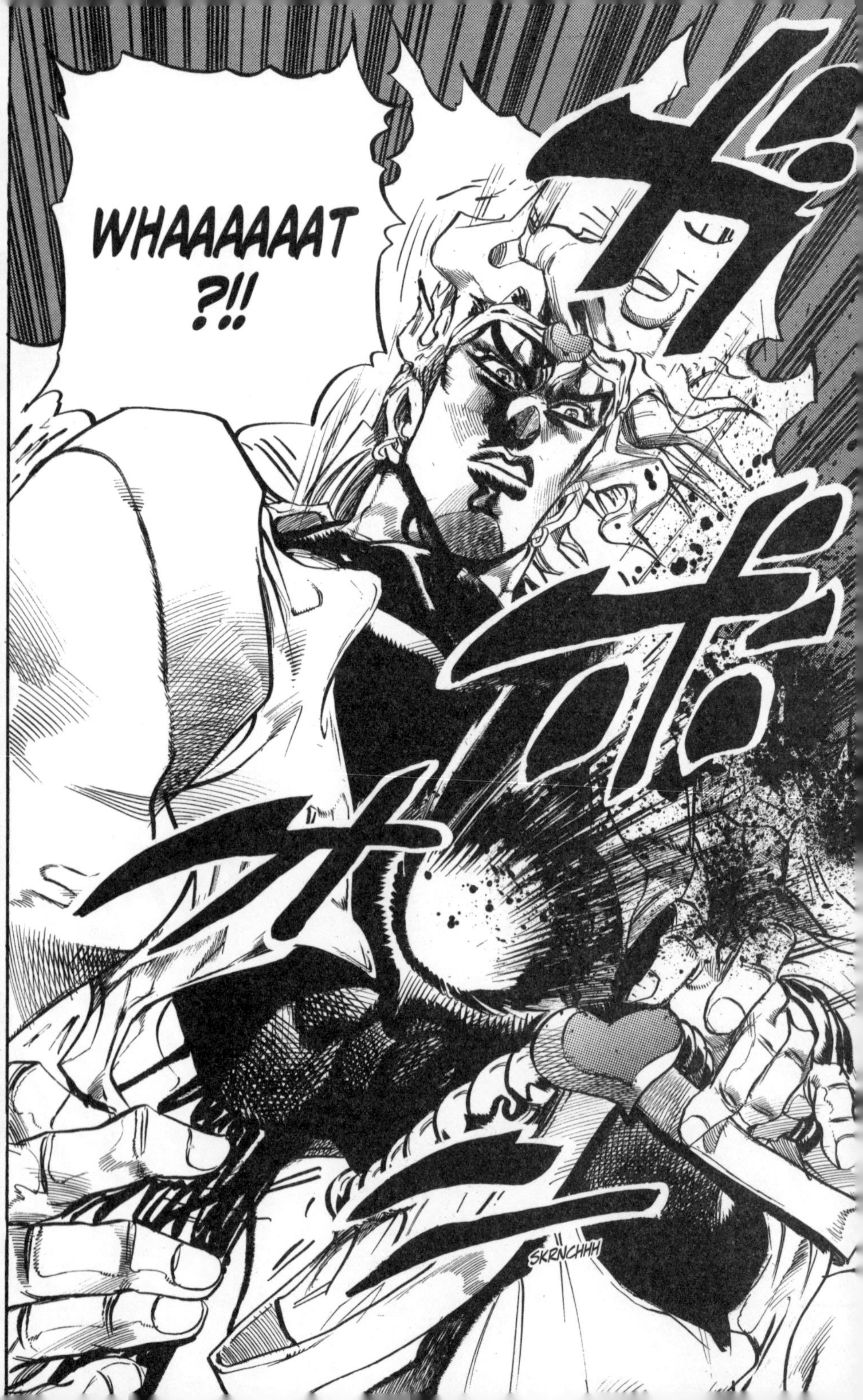
WHAAAAAAT ?!!
SKRNCHHH

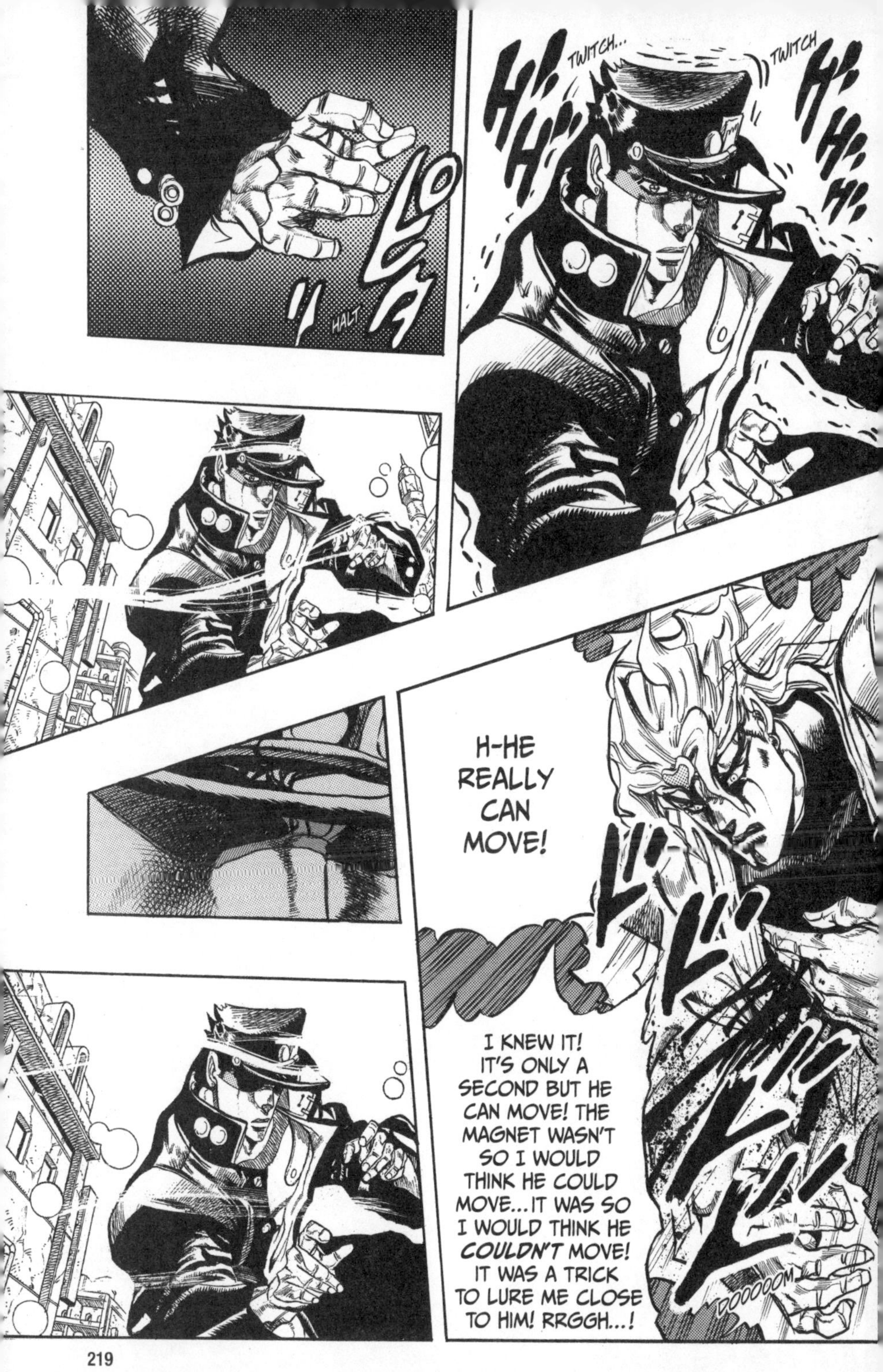
TWITCH...
TWITCH
HALT
H-HE REALLY CAN MOVE!
I KNEW IT! IT'S ONLY A SECOND BUT HE CAN MOVE! THE MAGNET WASN'T SO I WOULD THINK HE COULD MOVE...IT WAS SO I WOULD THINK HE *COULDN'T* MOVE! IT WAS A TRICK TO LURE ME CLOSE TO HIM! RRGGH...!
DOOOOOM

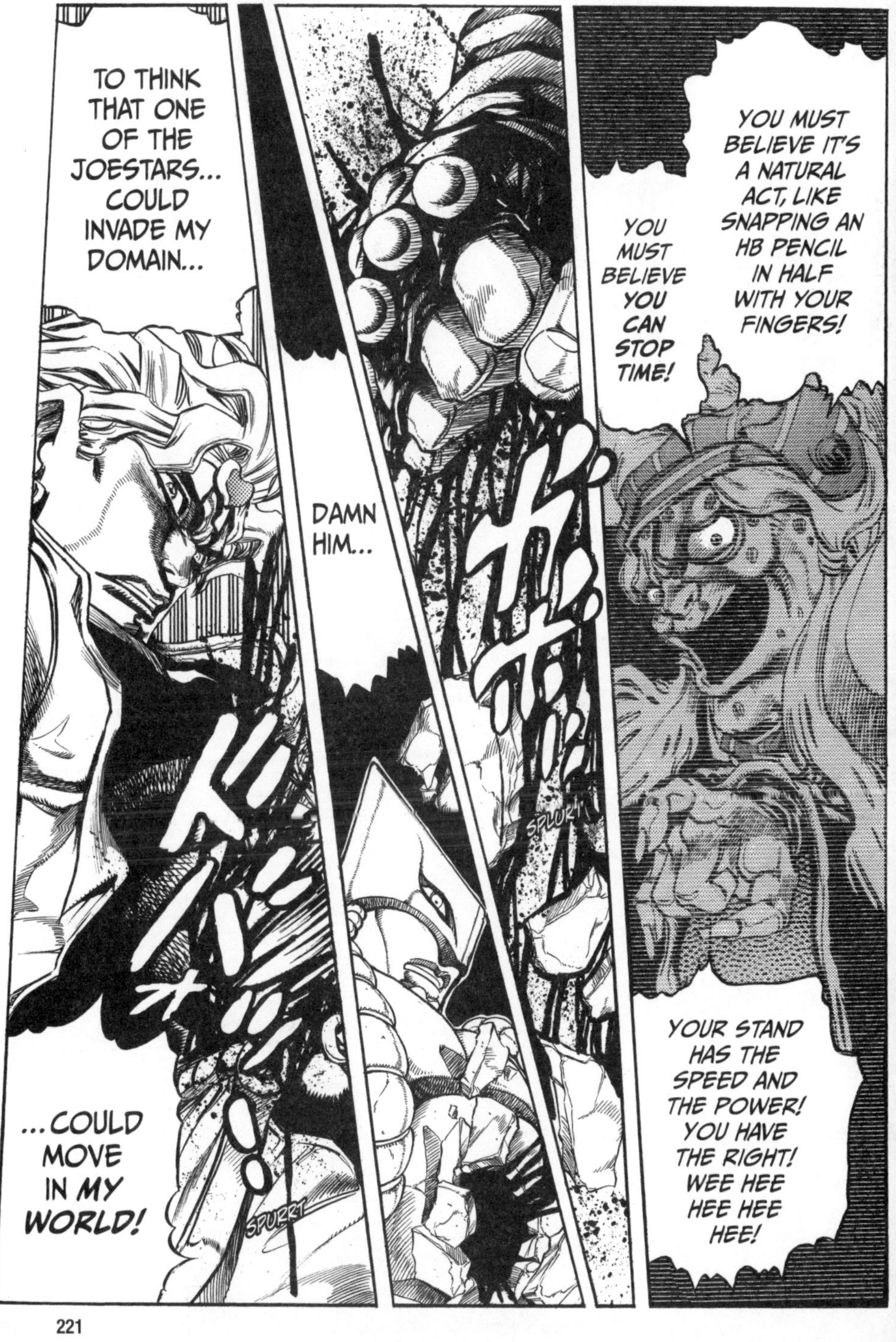
YOU MUST BELIEVE IT'S A NATURAL ACT, LIKE SNAPPING AN HB PENCIL IN HALF WITH YOUR FINGERS!
YOU MUST BELIEVE YOU CAN STOP TIME!
YOUR STAND HAS THE SPEED AND THE POWER! YOU HAVE THE RIGHT! WEE HEE HEE HEE HEE!
SPLURT
DAMN HIM...
SPURRT
TO THINK THAT ONE OF THE JOESTARS... COULD INVADE MY DOMAIN...
...COULD MOVE IN *MY* WORLD!

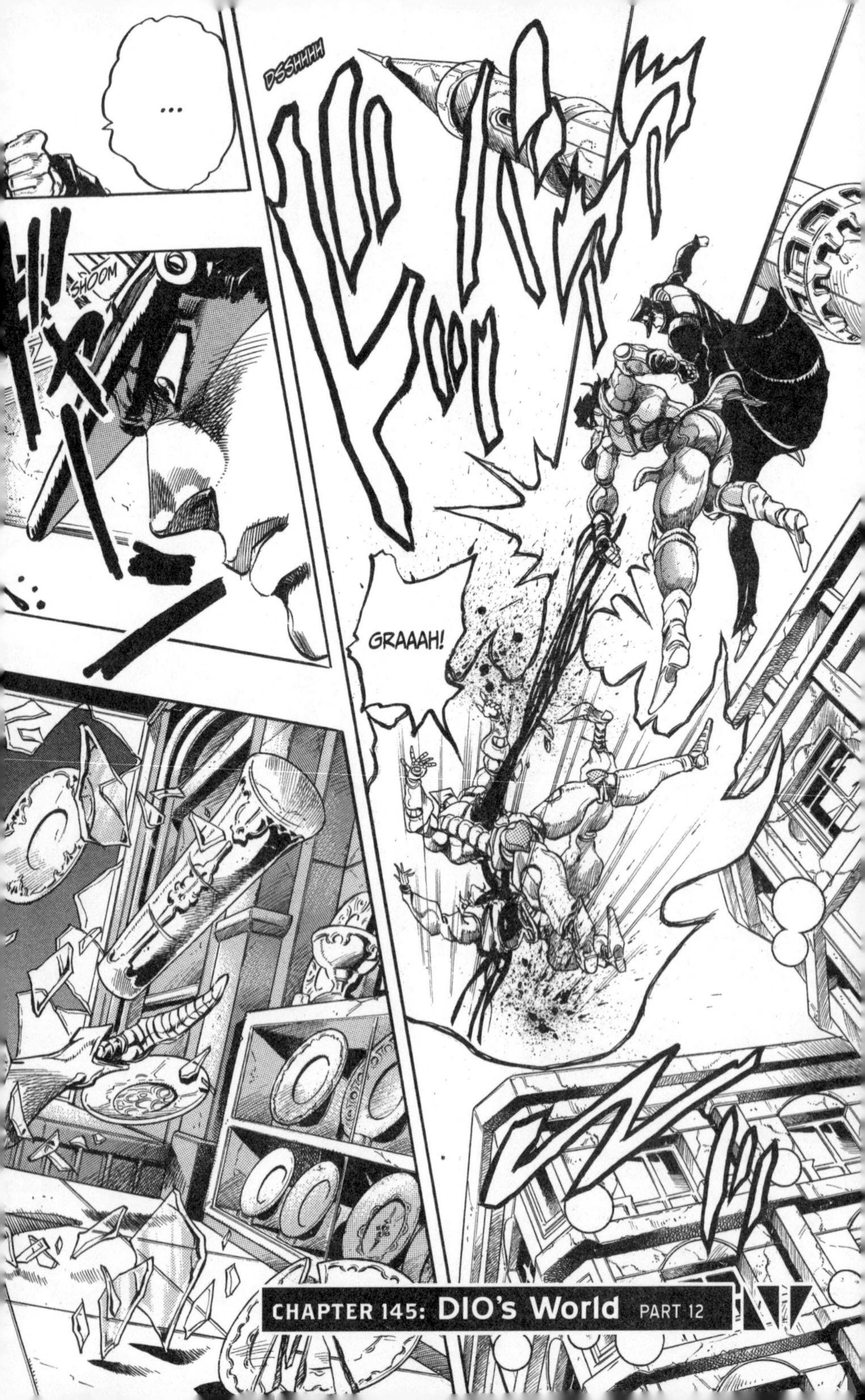
DSSHHHH
GRAAAH!
...
SHOOM
CHAPTER 145: DIO's World PART 12

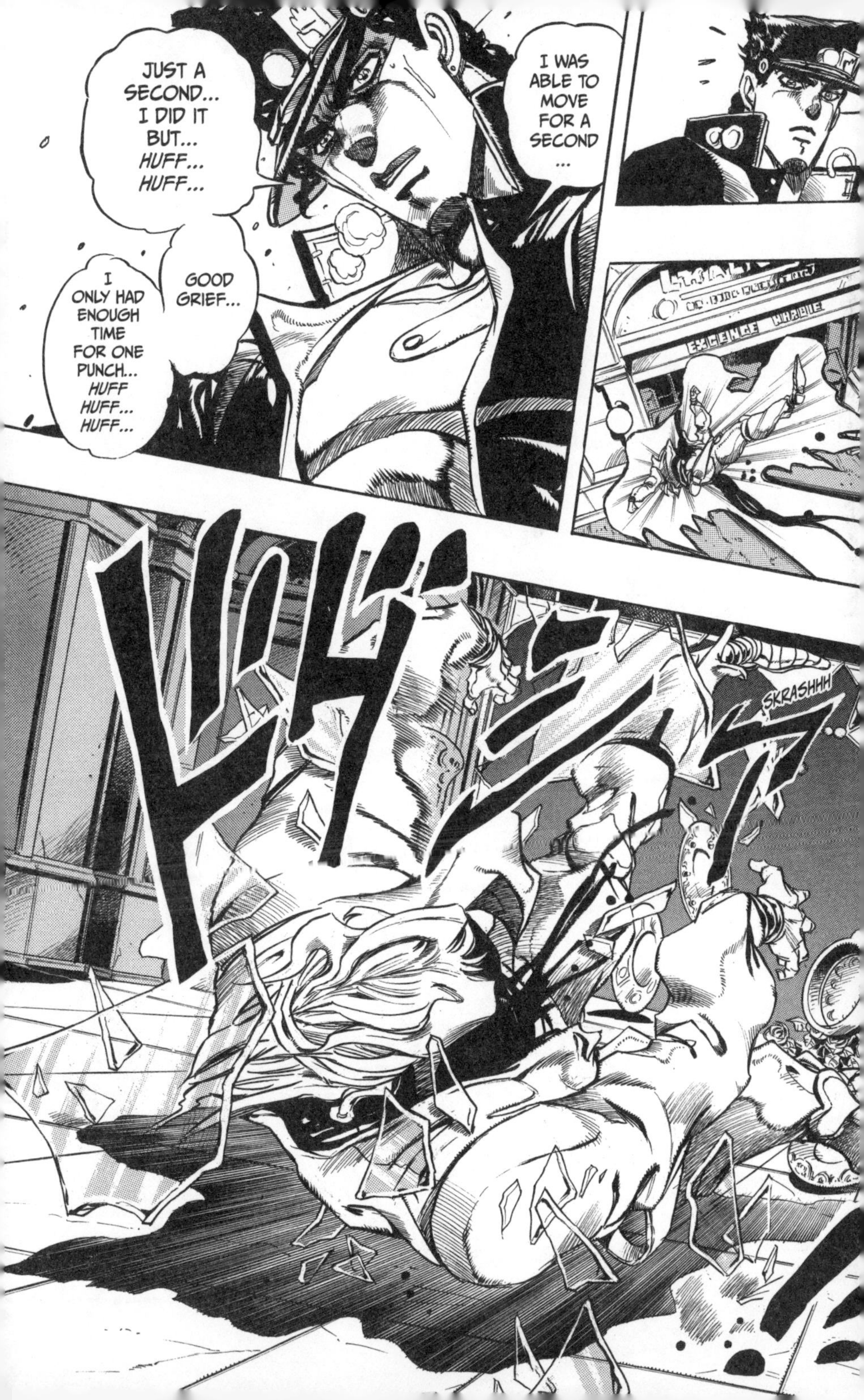
I WAS ABLE TO MOVE FOR A SECOND...
JUST A SECOND... I DID IT BUT... *HUFF... HUFF...*
GOOD GRIEF...
I ONLY HAD ENOUGH TIME FOR ONE PUNCH... *HUFF HUFF... HUFF...*
SKRASHHH

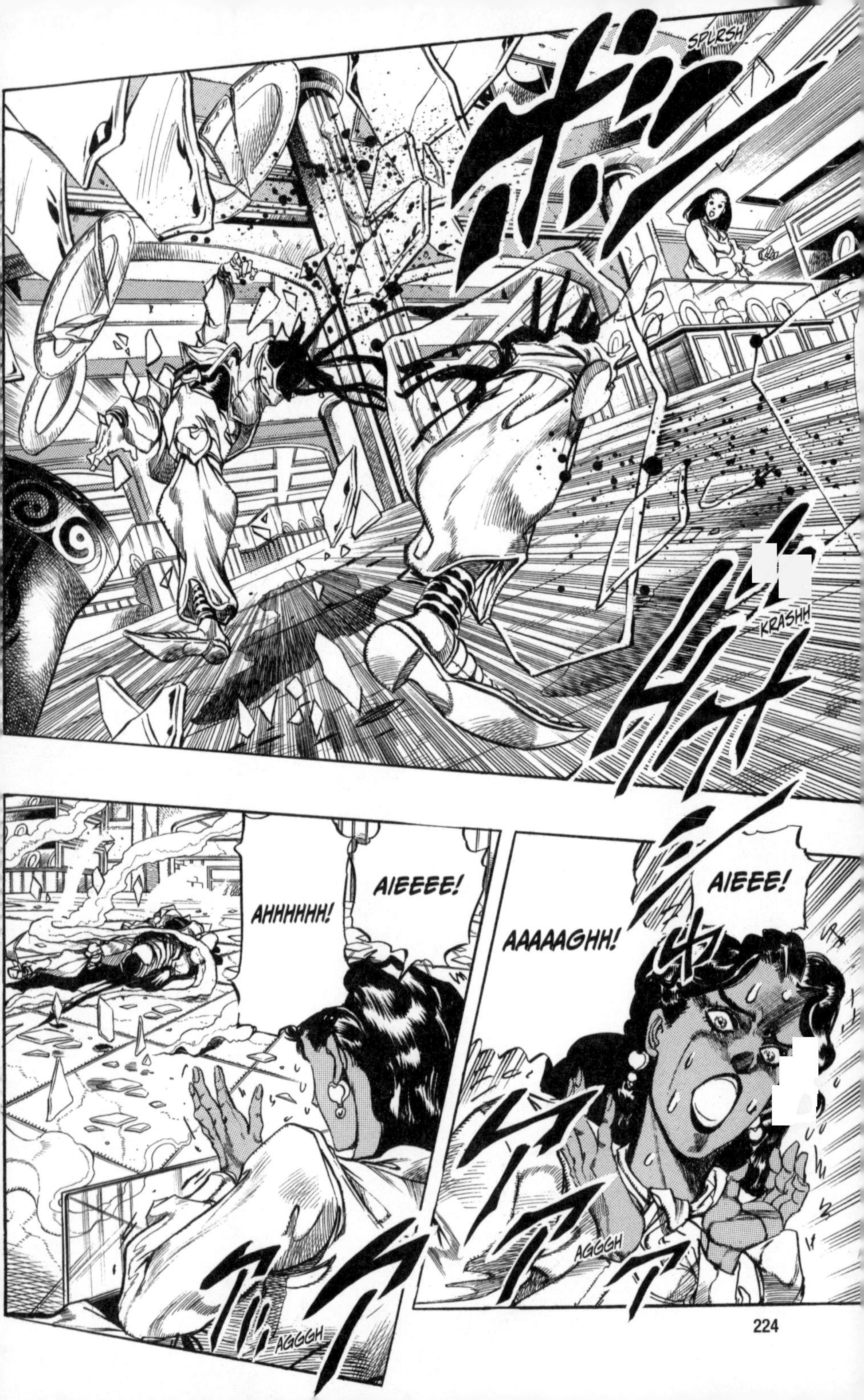
SPLRSH
KRASHH
AIEEE!
AAAAAGHH!
AGGGH
AIEEEE!
AHHHHHH!
AGGGH

TWITCH
TWITCH
!
...
FSH
!!!...??!
...?!

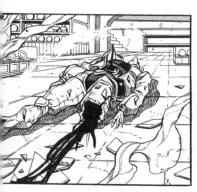

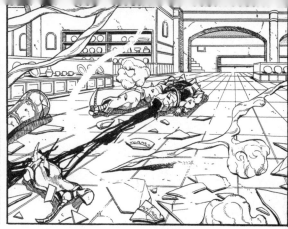

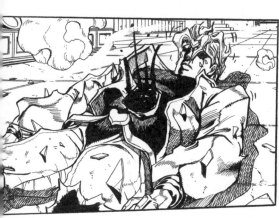

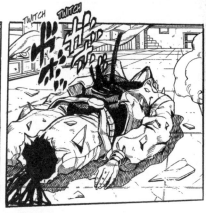

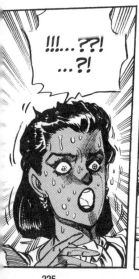

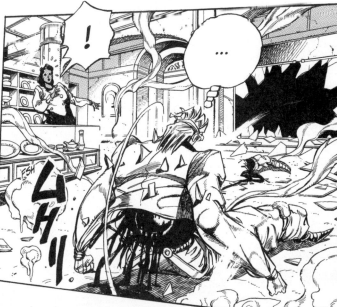

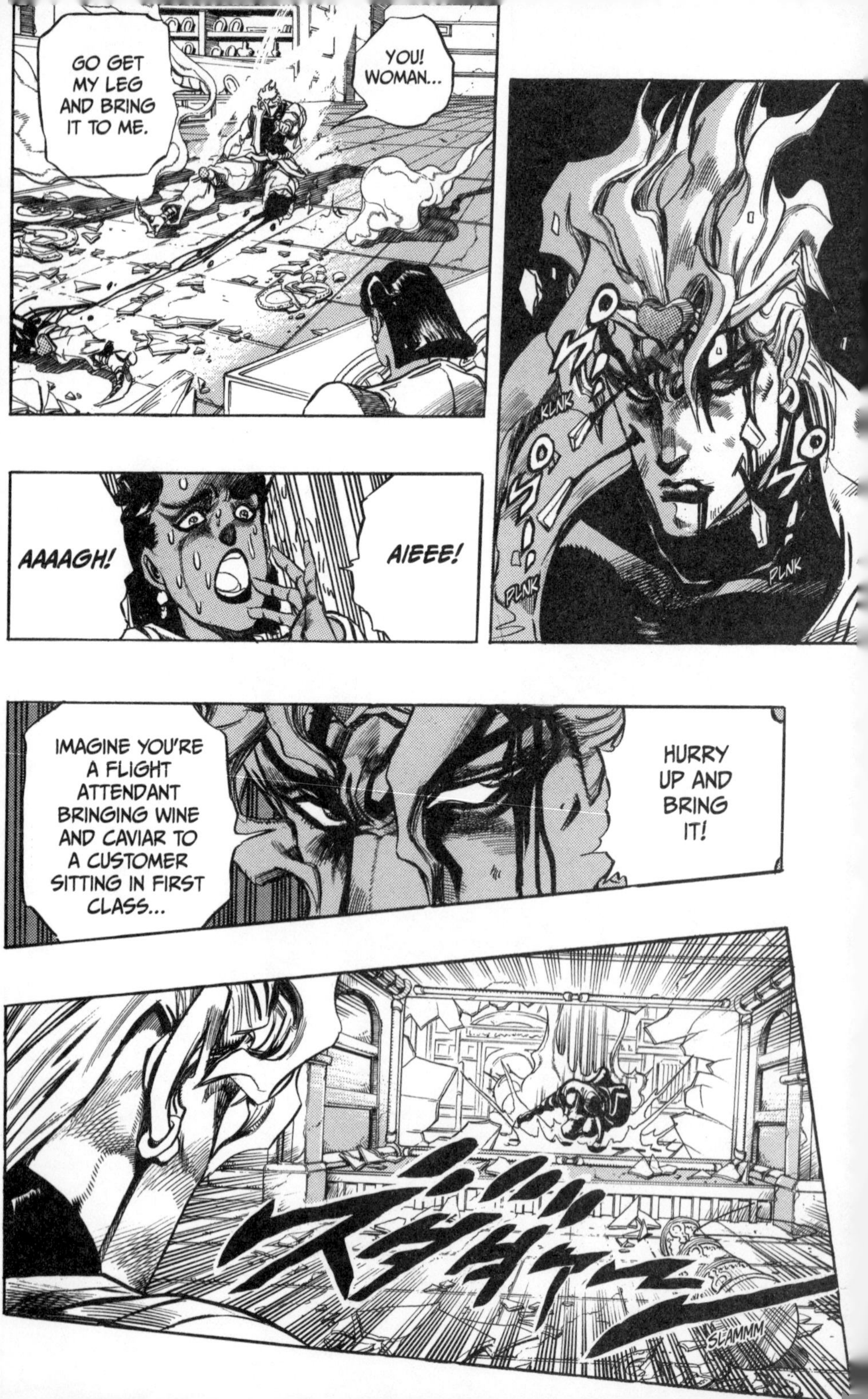
KLNK
PLNK
PLNK
YOU! WOMAN...
GO GET MY LEG AND BRING IT TO ME.
AIEEE!
AAAAGH!
HURRY UP AND BRING IT!
IMAGINE YOU'RE A FLIGHT ATTENDANT BRINGING WINE AND CAVIAR TO A CUSTOMER SITTING IN FIRST CLASS...
SLAMMM

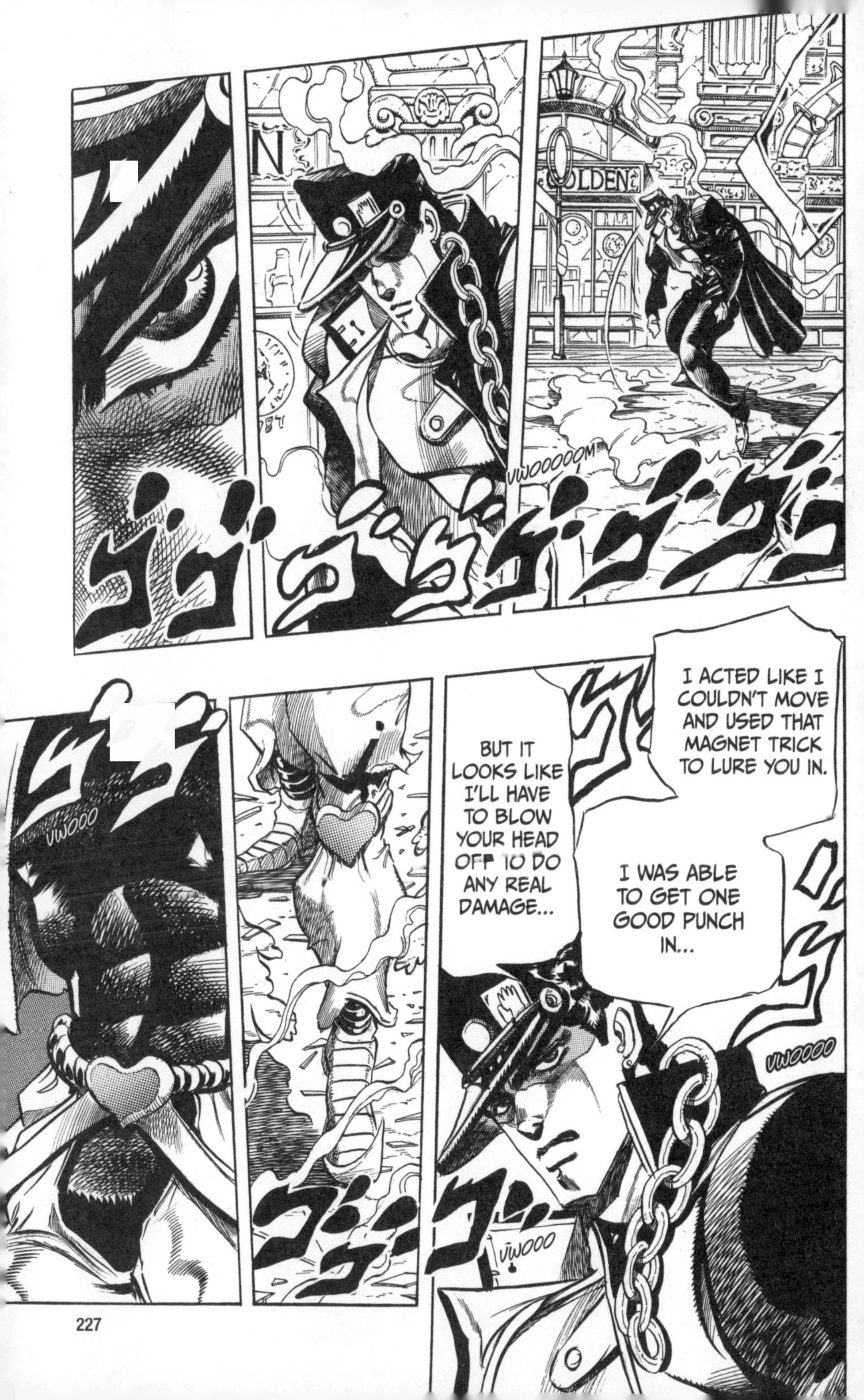
VWOOOOOM
I ACTED LIKE I COULDN'T MOVE AND USED THAT MAGNET TRICK TO LURE YOU IN.
I WAS ABLE TO GET ONE GOOD PUNCH IN...
BUT IT LOOKS LIKE I'LL HAVE TO BLOW YOUR HEAD OFF TO DO ANY REAL DAMAGE...
VWOOOO
VWOOO
VWOOO

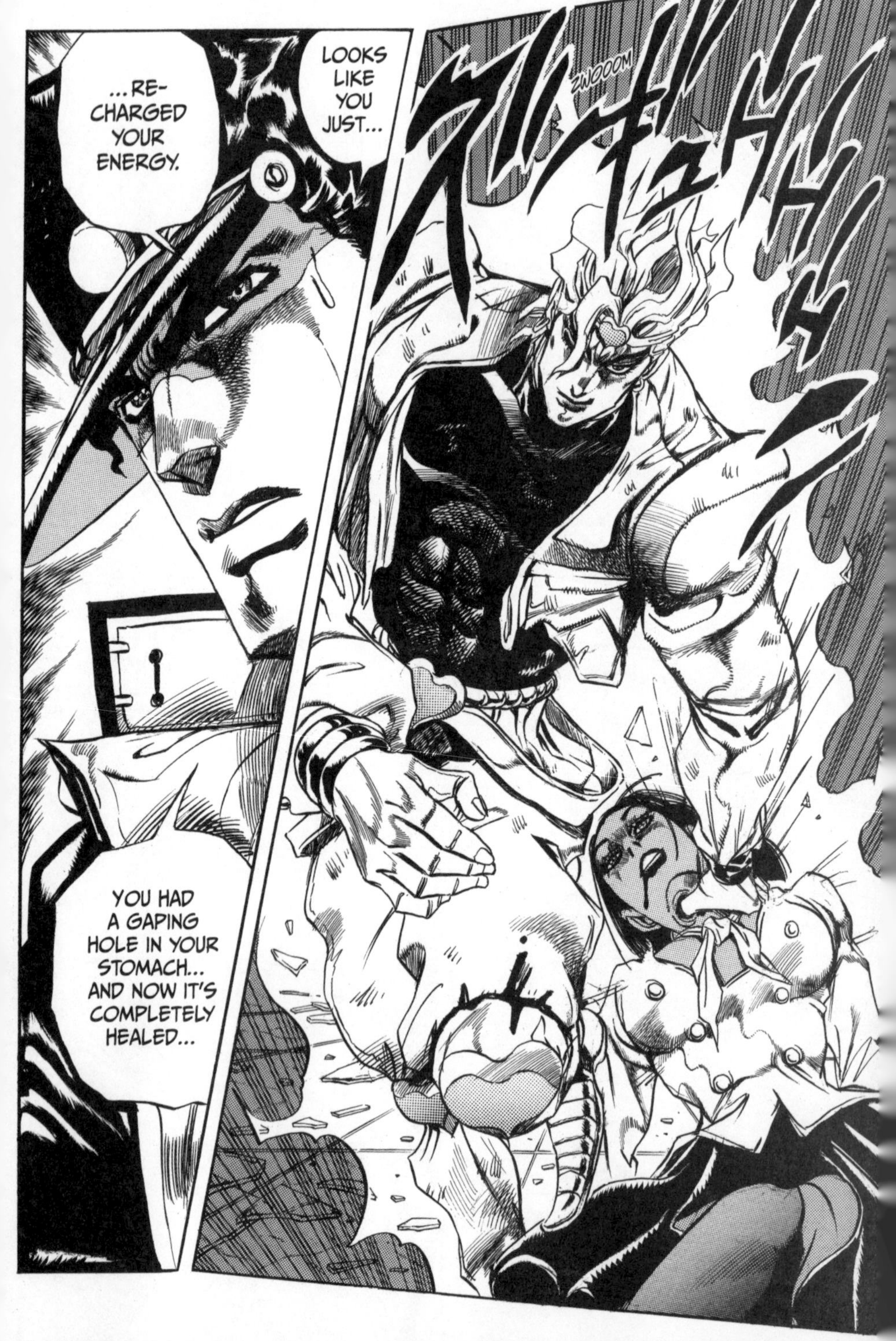
ZWOOOM
LOOKS LIKE YOU JUST...
...RE-CHARGED YOUR ENERGY.
YOU HAD A GAPING HOLE IN YOUR STOMACH... AND NOW IT'S COMPLETELY HEALED...

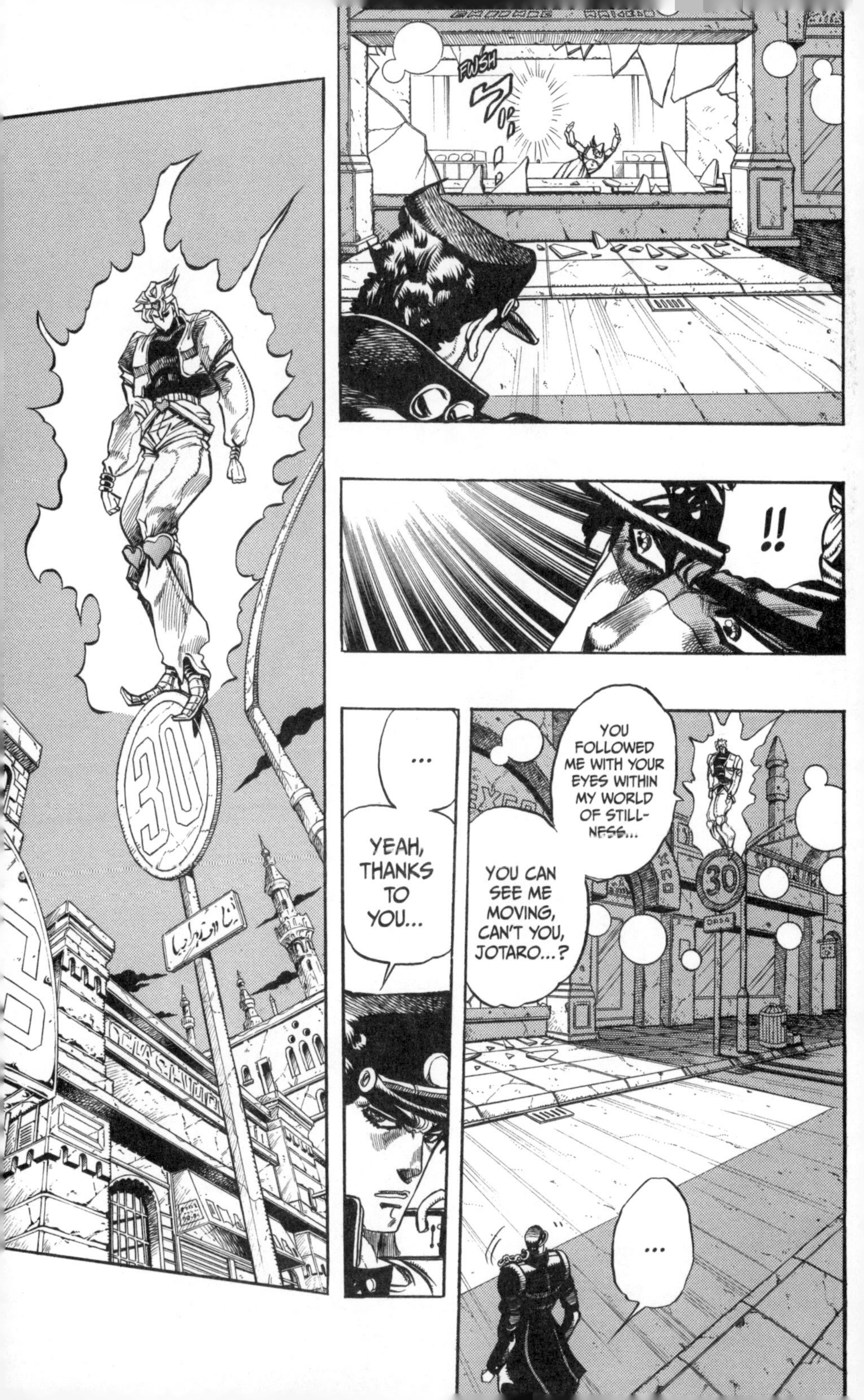
FWSH
!!
YOU FOLLOWED ME WITH YOUR EYES WITHIN MY WORLD OF STILL-NESS...
YOU CAN SEE ME MOVING, CAN'T YOU, JOTARO...?
...
...
YEAH, THANKS TO YOU...

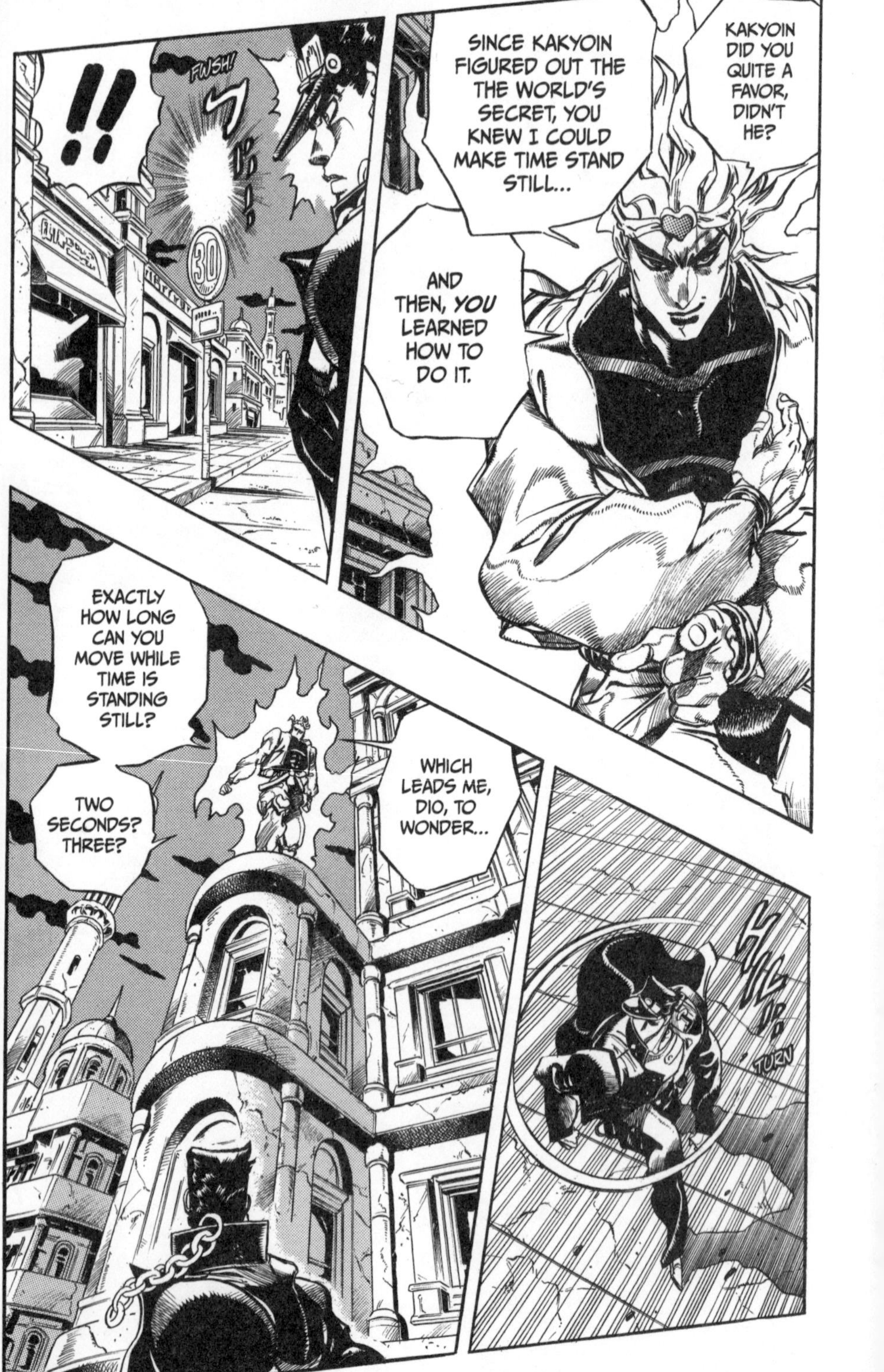
KAKYOIN DID YOU QUITE A FAVOR, DIDN'T HE?
SINCE KAKYOIN FIGURED OUT THE THE WORLD'S SECRET, YOU KNEW I COULD MAKE TIME STAND STILL...
AND THEN, *YOU* LEARNED HOW TO DO IT.
!!
FWSH!
30
TURN
WHICH LEADS ME, DIO, TO WONDER...
EXACTLY HOW LONG CAN YOU MOVE WHILE TIME IS STANDING STILL?
TWO SECONDS? THREE?

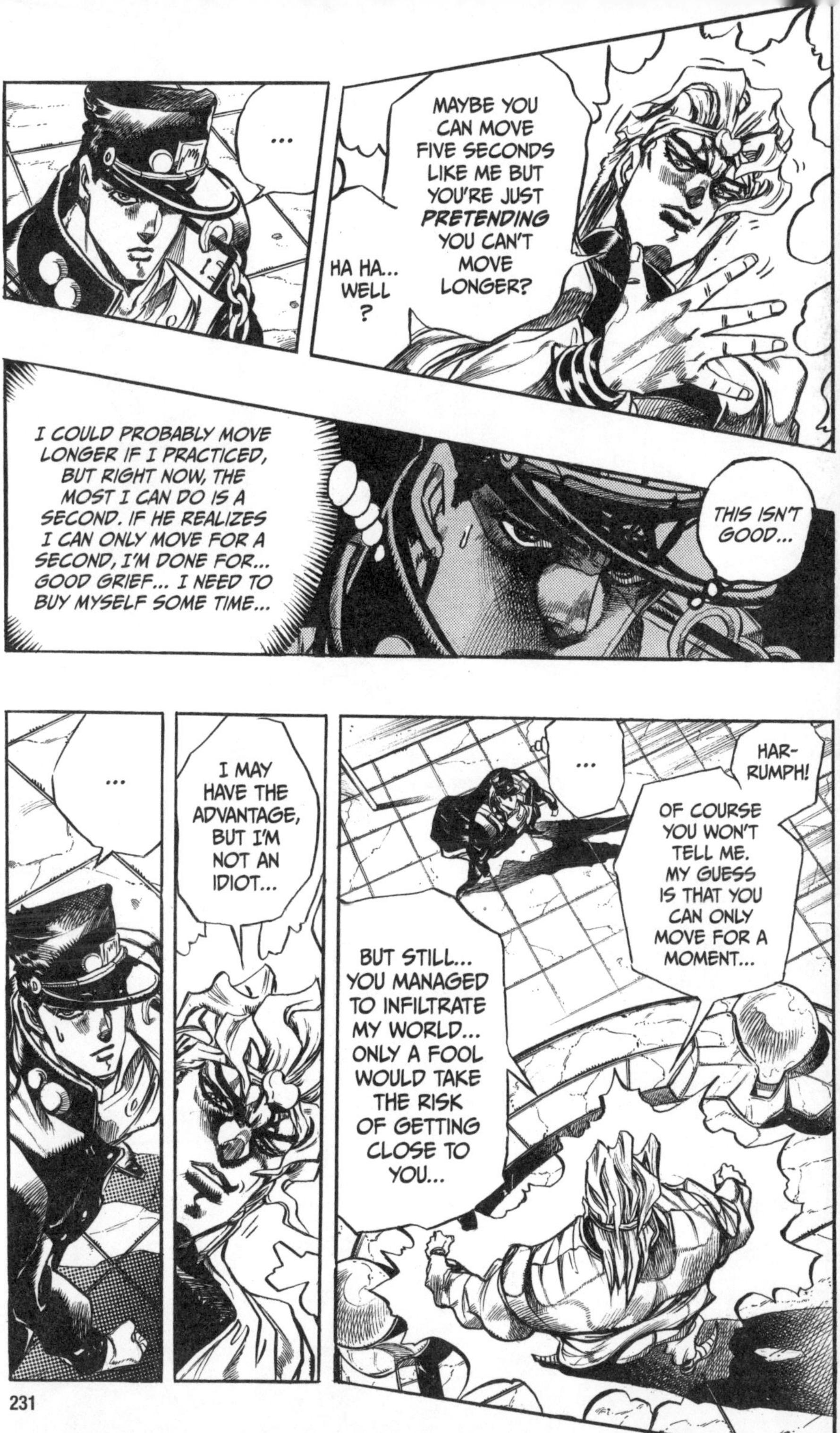
MAYBE YOU CAN MOVE FIVE SECONDS LIKE ME BUT YOU'RE JUST *PRETENDING* YOU CAN'T MOVE LONGER?
HA HA... WELL?
...
THIS ISN'T GOOD...
I COULD PROBABLY MOVE LONGER IF I PRACTICED, BUT RIGHT NOW, THE MOST I CAN DO IS A SECOND. IF HE REALIZES I CAN ONLY MOVE FOR A SECOND, I'M DONE FOR... GOOD GRIEF... I NEED TO BUY MYSELF SOME TIME...
HAR-RUMPH!
OF COURSE YOU WON'T TELL ME. MY GUESS IS THAT YOU CAN ONLY MOVE FOR A MOMENT...
...
BUT STILL... YOU MANAGED TO INFILTRATE MY WORLD... ONLY A FOOL WOULD TAKE THE RISK OF GETTING CLOSE TO YOU...
I MAY HAVE THE ADVANTAGE, BUT I'M NOT AN IDIOT...
...

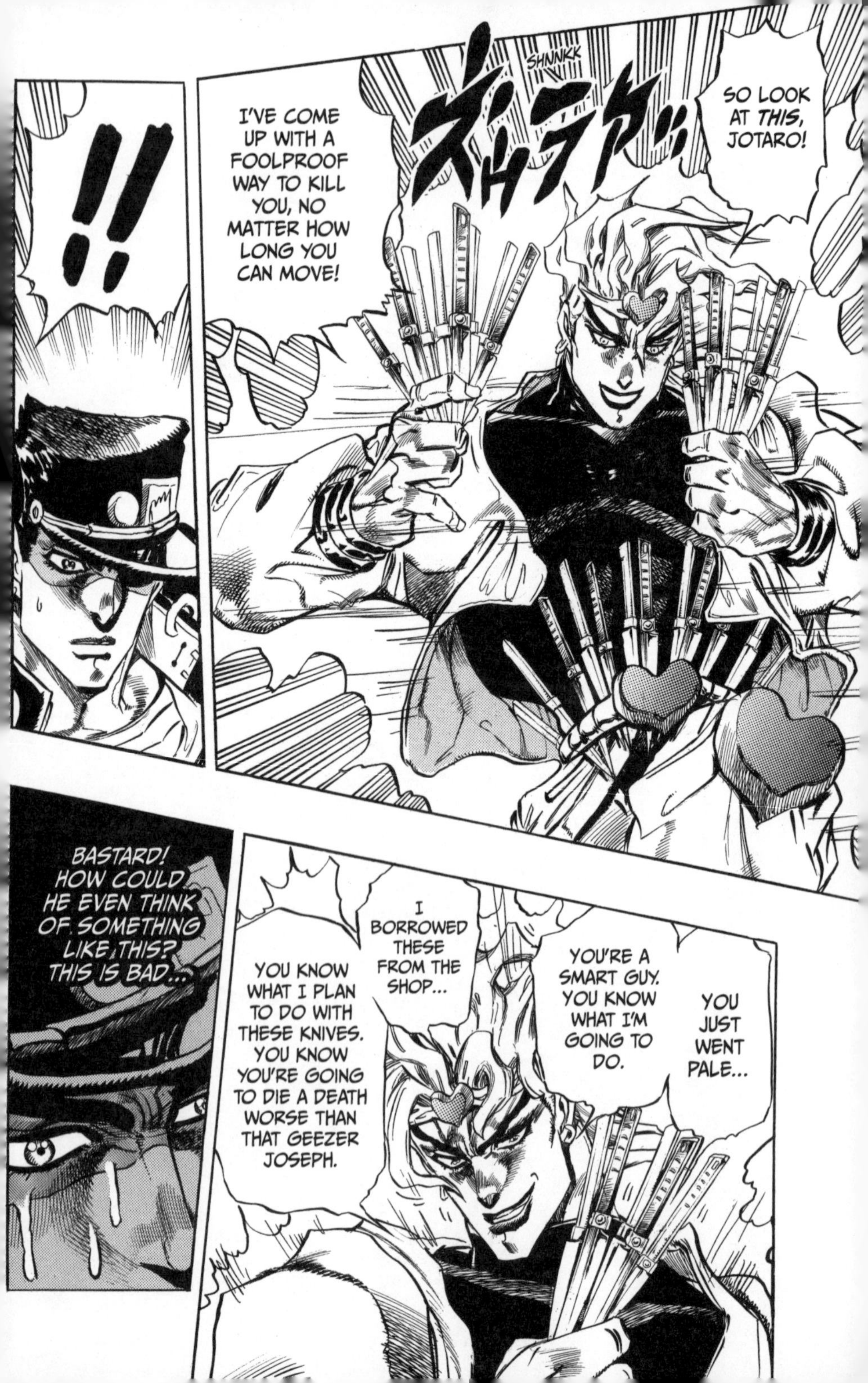
SO LOOK AT *THIS*, JOTARO!
SHNNKK
I'VE COME UP WITH A FOOLPROOF WAY TO KILL YOU, NO MATTER HOW LONG YOU CAN MOVE!
!!
YOU JUST WENT PALE...
YOU'RE A SMART GUY. YOU KNOW WHAT I'M GOING TO DO.
I BORROWED THESE FROM THE SHOP...
YOU KNOW WHAT I PLAN TO DO WITH THESE KNIVES. YOU KNOW YOU'RE GOING TO DIE A DEATH WORSE THAN THAT GEEZER JOSEPH.
BASTARD! HOW COULD HE EVEN THINK OF SOMETHING LIKE THIS? THIS IS BAD...

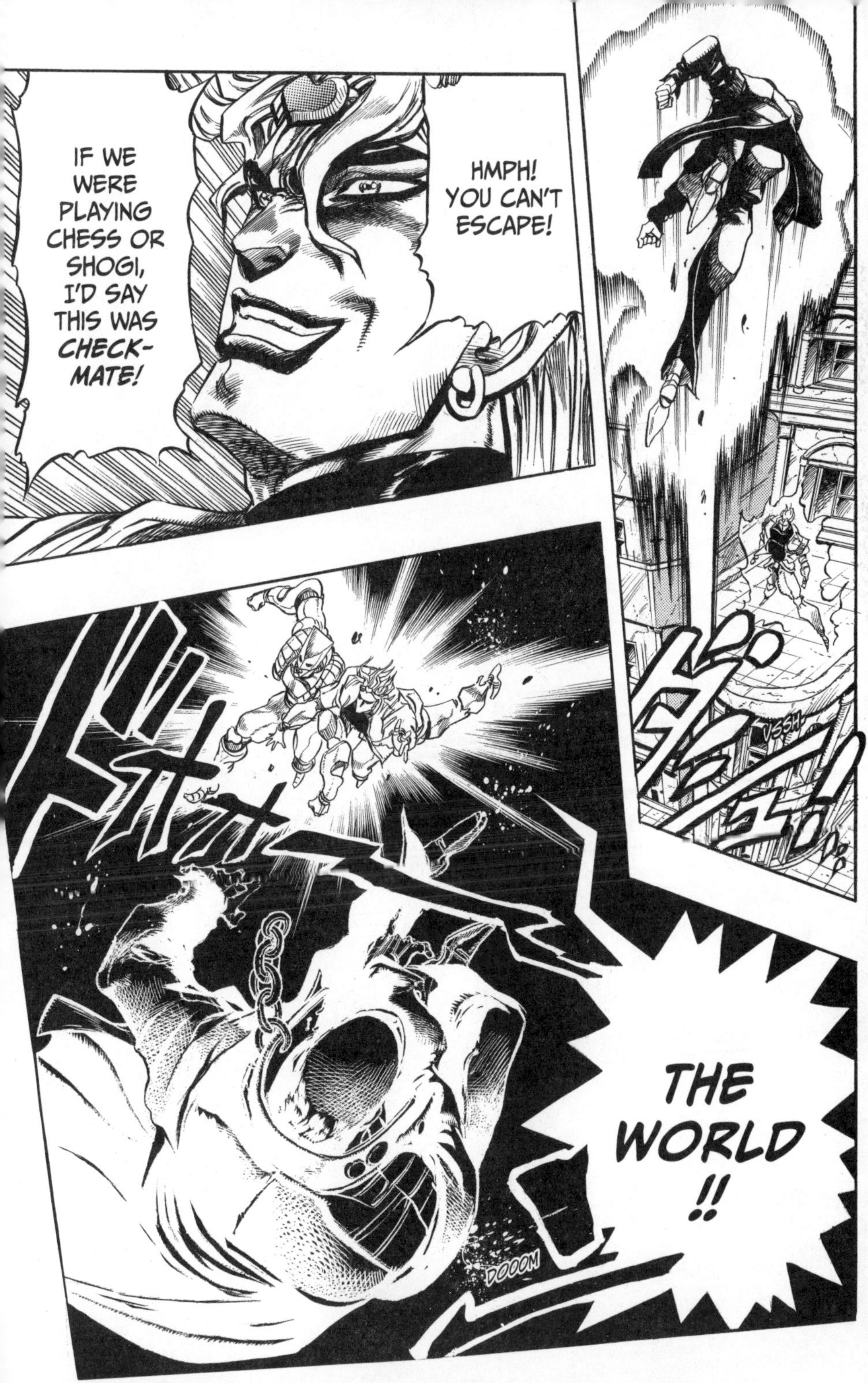
VSSH
HMPH! YOU CAN'T ESCAPE!
IF WE WERE PLAYING CHESS OR SHOGI, I'D SAY THIS WAS CHECKMATE!
THE WORLD!!
DOOOM

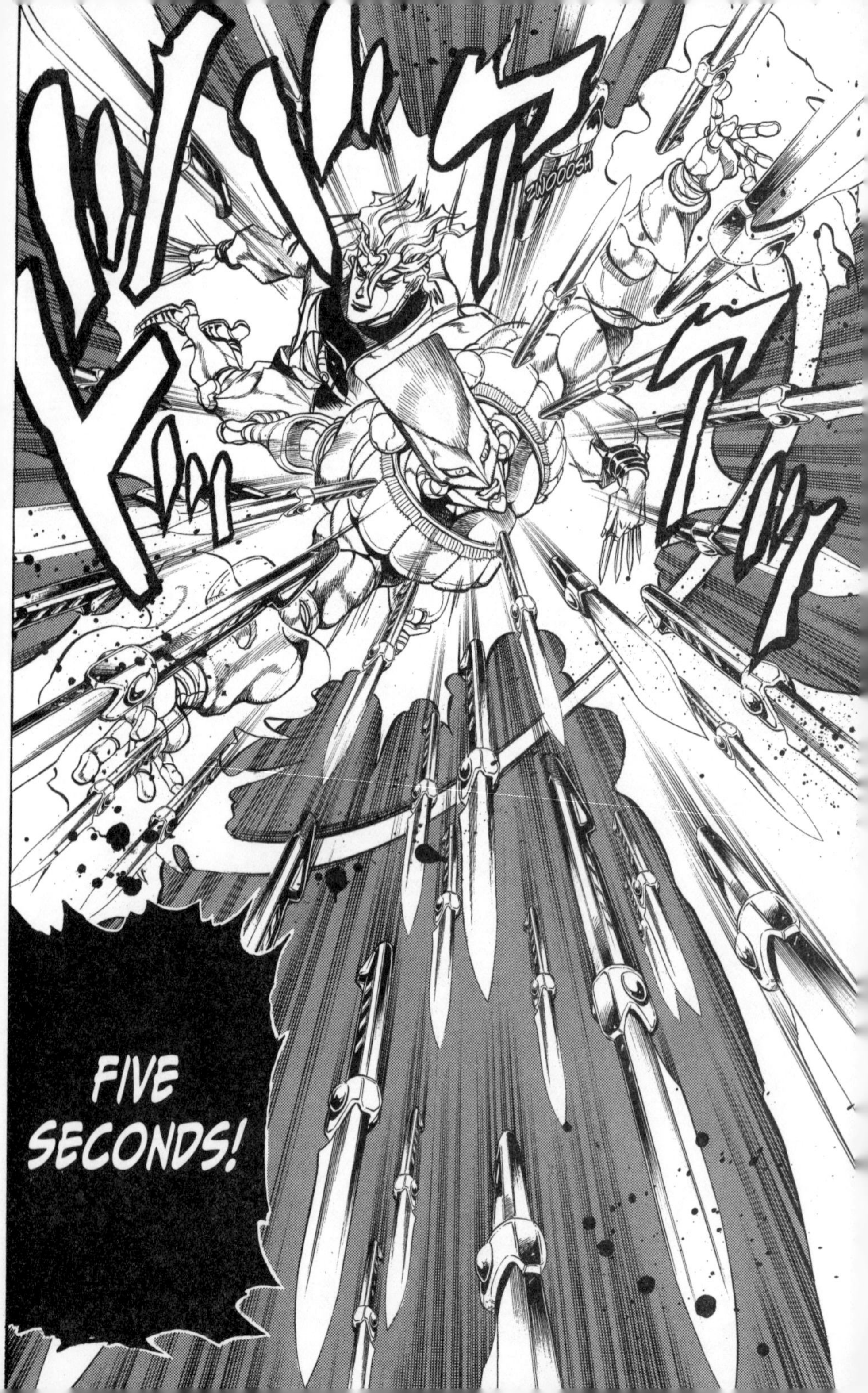
ZWOOOSH
FIVE SECONDS!

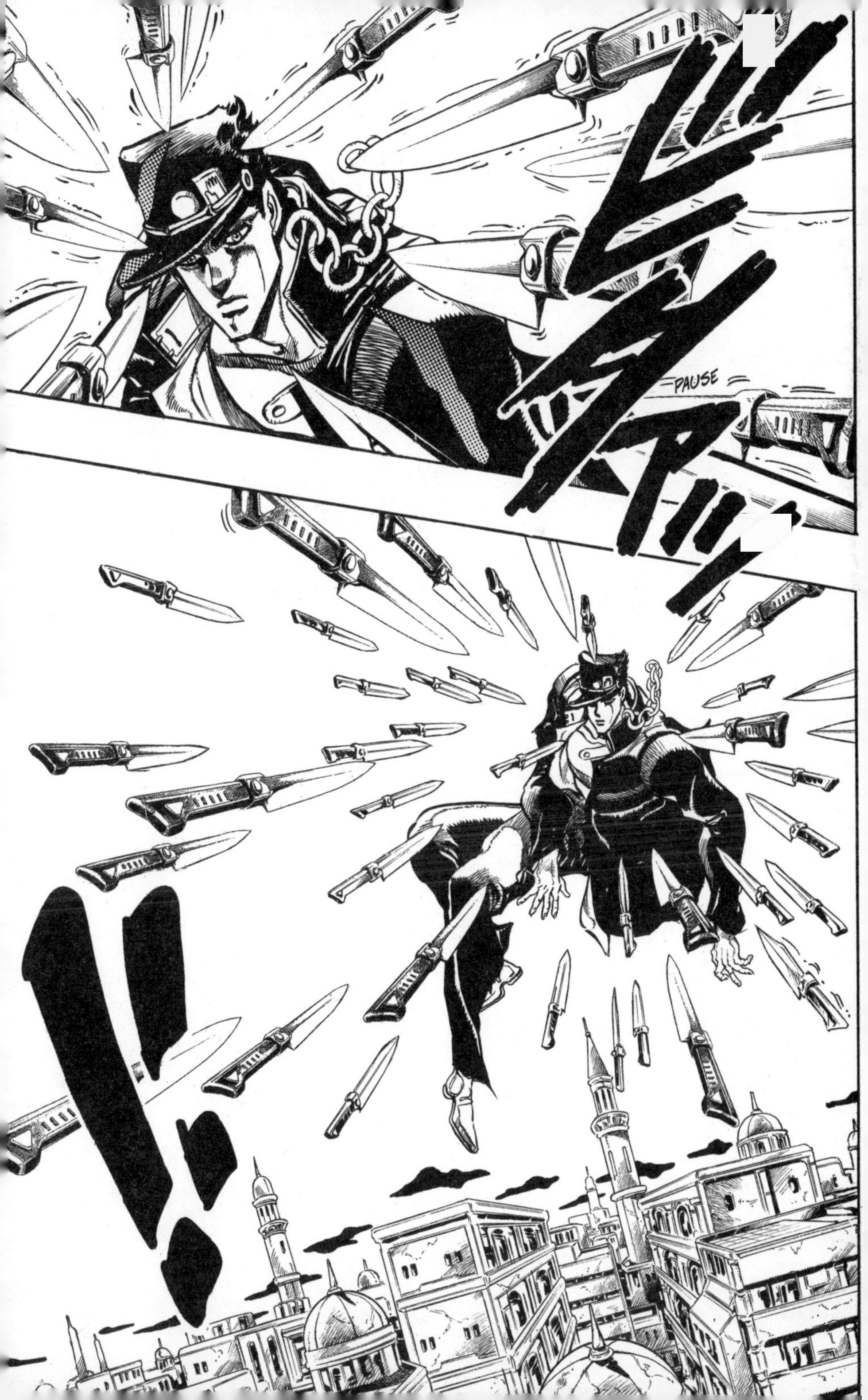
PAUSE

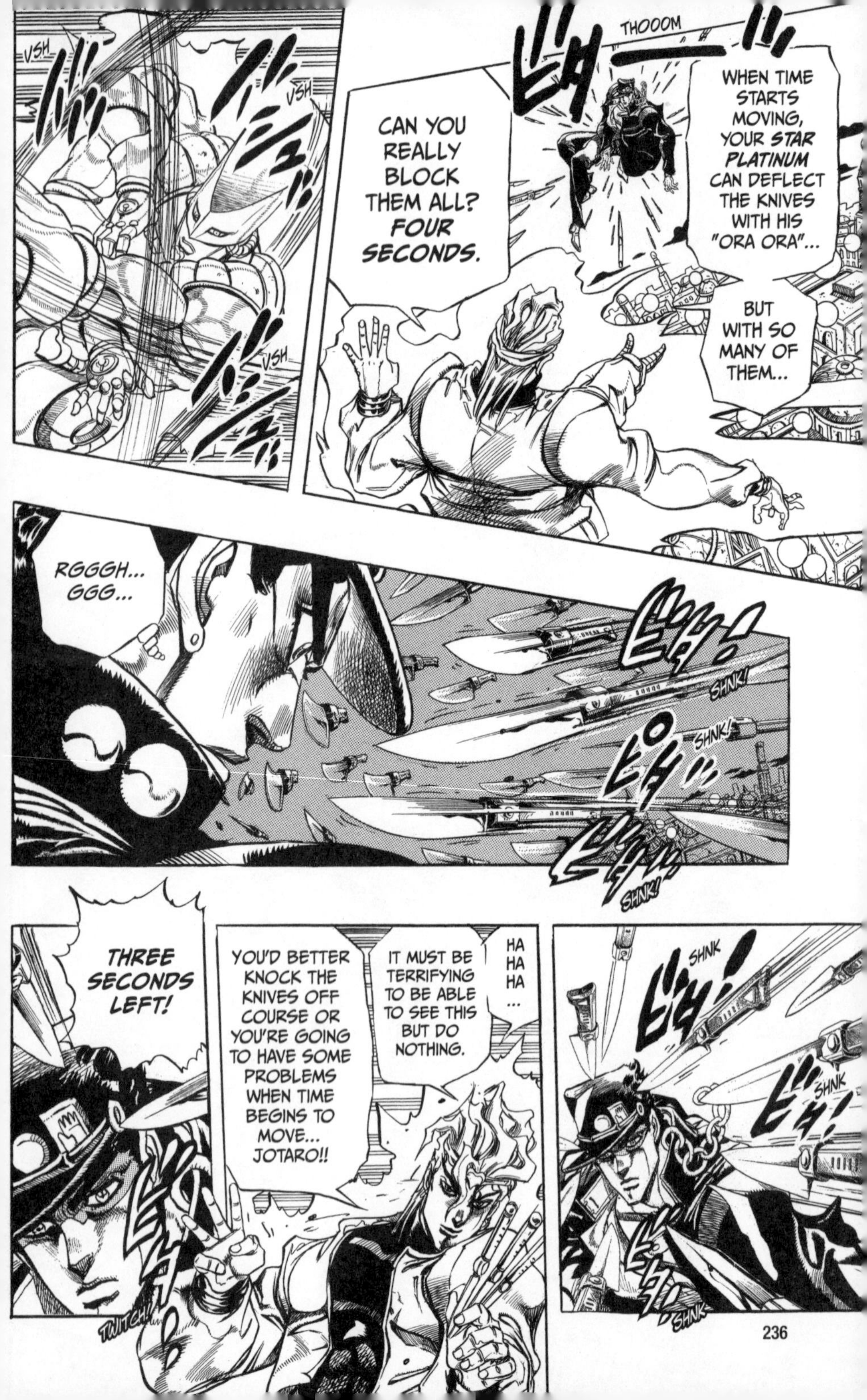
THOOOM
WHEN TIME STARTS MOVING, YOUR STAR PLATINUM CAN DEFLECT THE KNIVES WITH HIS "ORA ORA"...
BUT WITH SO MANY OF THEM...
CAN YOU REALLY BLOCK THEM ALL? FOUR SECONDS.
VSH
VSH
VSH
RGGGH... GGG...
SHNK!
SHNK!
SHNK!
SHNK
SHNK
SHNK
HA HA HA ...
IT MUST BE TERRIFYING TO BE ABLE TO SEE THIS BUT DO NOTHING.
YOU'D BETTER KNOCK THE KNIVES OFF COURSE OR YOU'RE GOING TO HAVE SOME PROBLEMS WHEN TIME BEGINS TO MOVE... JOTARO!!
THREE SECONDS LEFT!
TWITCH!

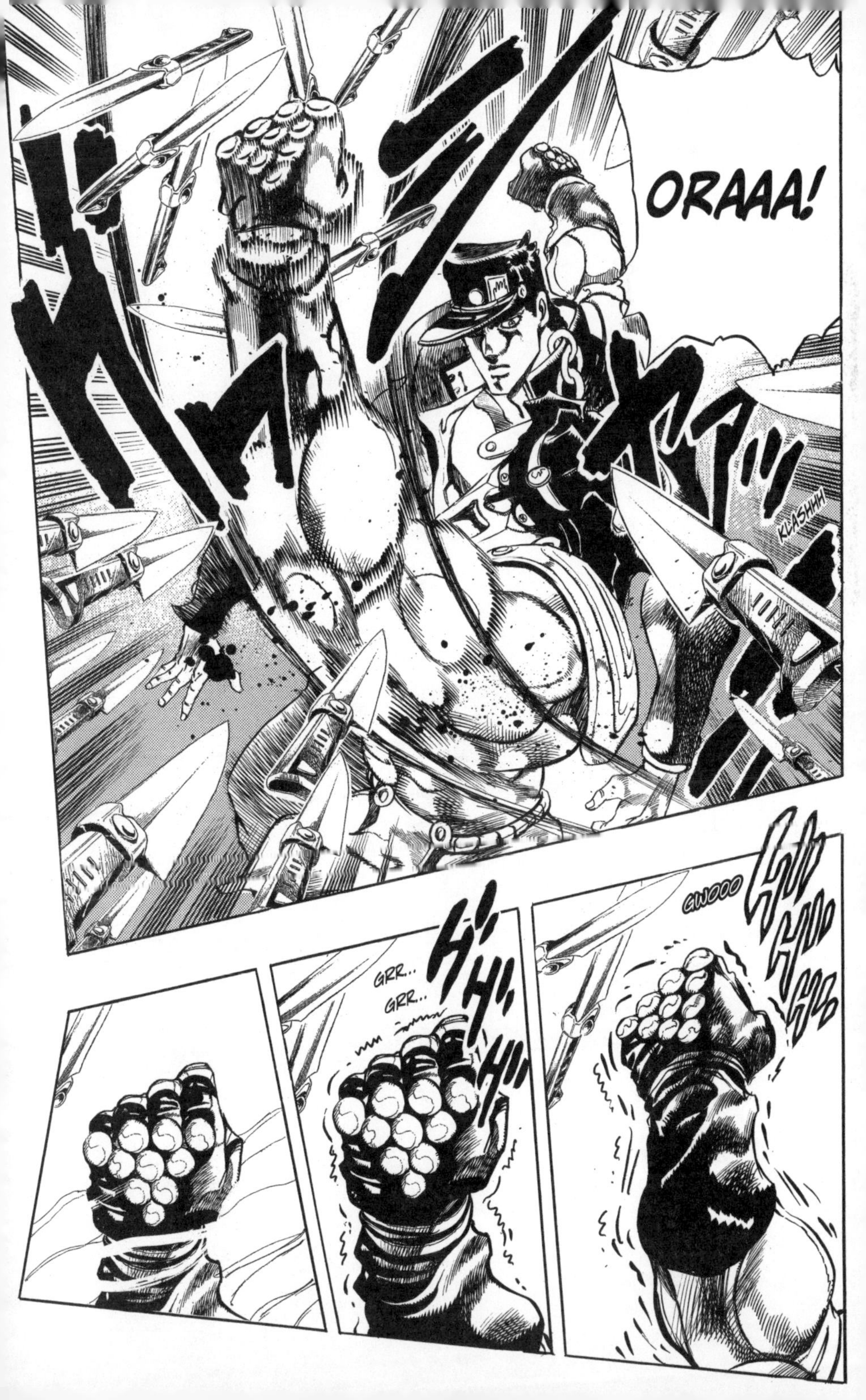
ORAAA!
KLASHHH
GWOOO
GRR...
GRR...

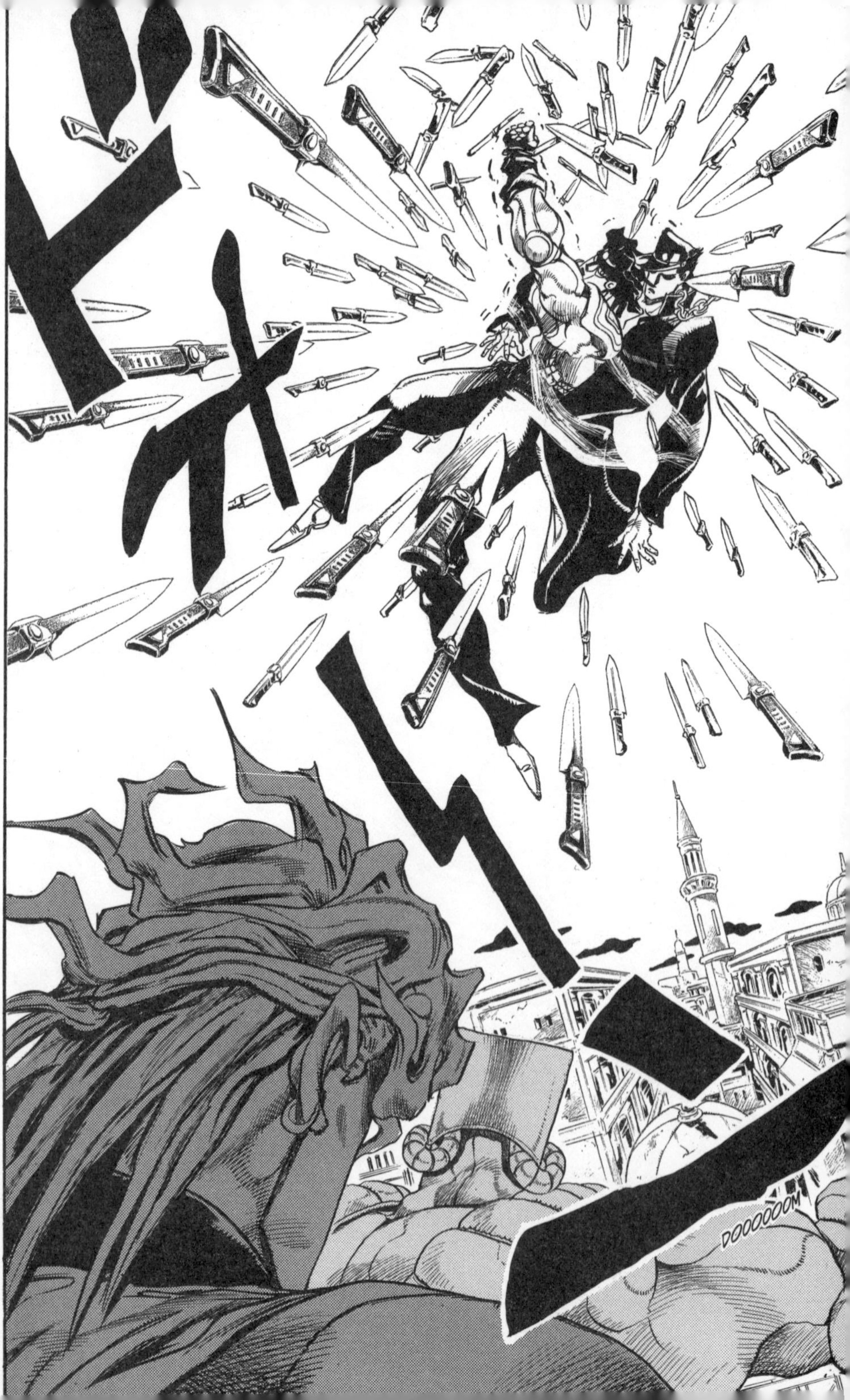
DOOOOOOM

...

...

ONE SECOND.

IS THAT ALL YOU CAN MOVE?

HA HA HA... THAT JUST PROVED YOU CAN ONLY MOVE FOR ONE SECOND.

TWO SECONDS!

AND NOW, LET TIME START ...!

ZERO.

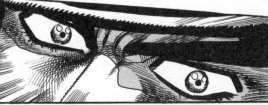

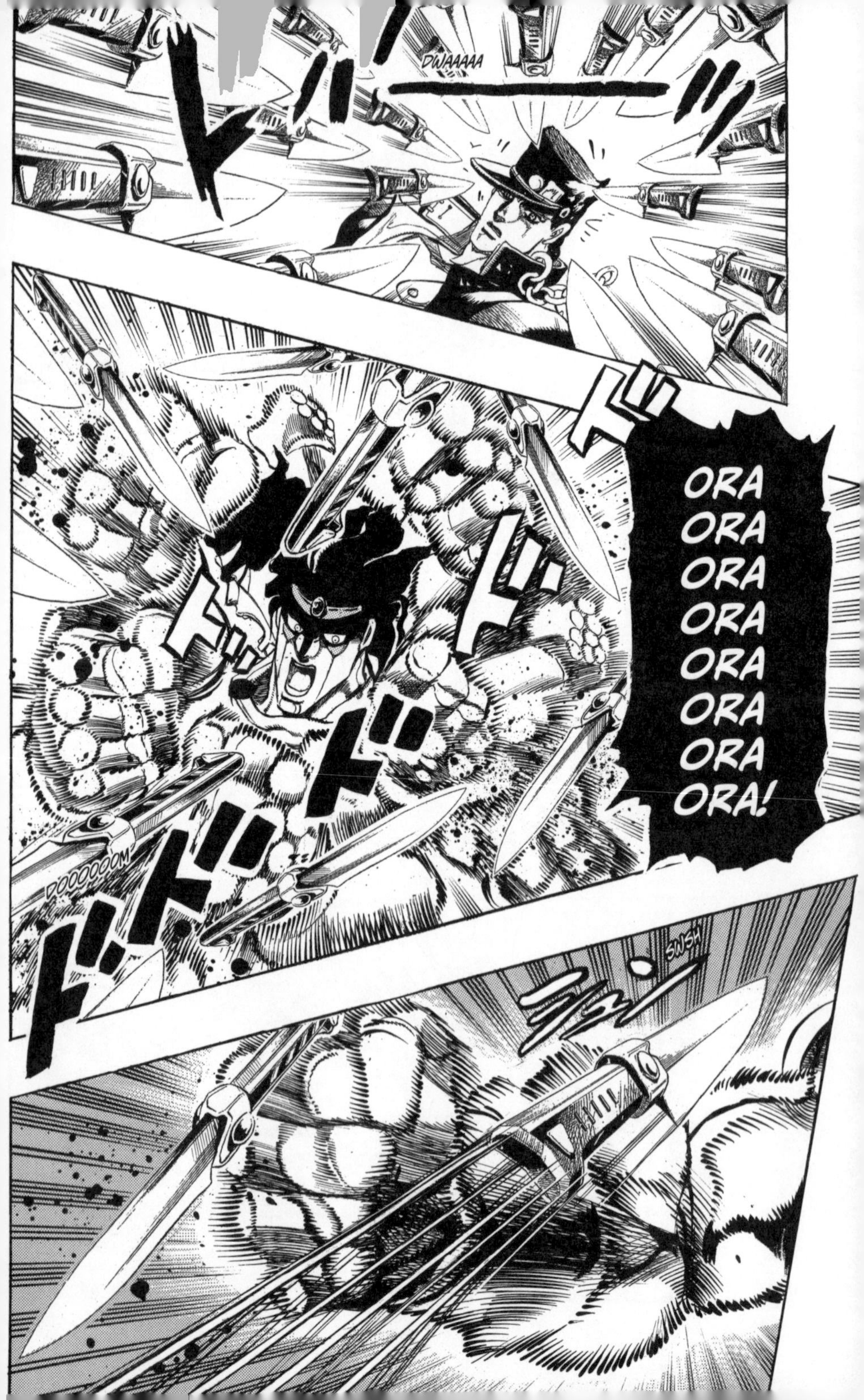
DWAAAAA
ORA ORA ORA ORA ORA ORA ORA ORA!
DOOOOOOM
SWSH

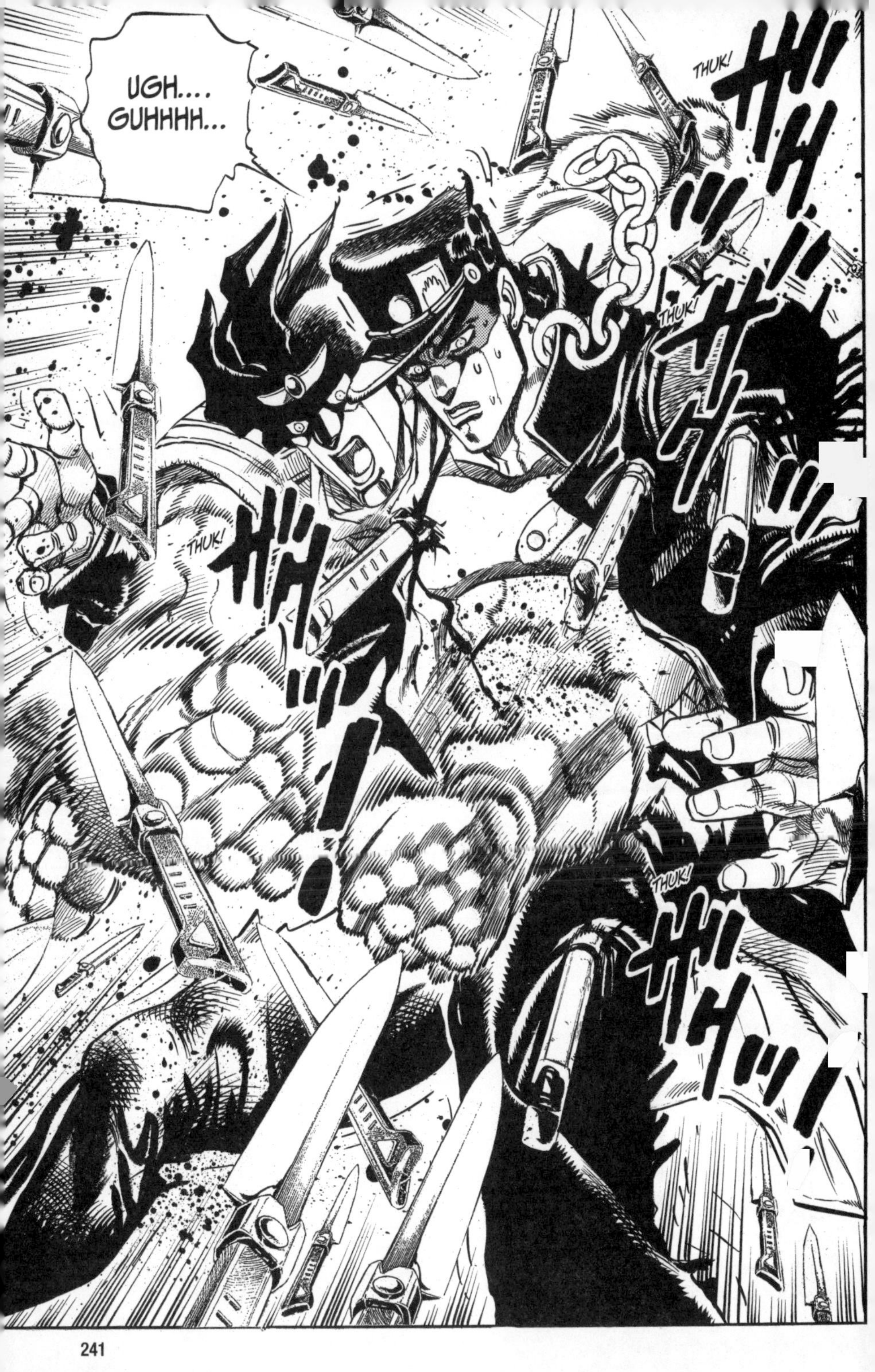
THUK!
UGH.... GUHHHH...
THUK!
THUK!
THUK!

CHAPTER 146: DIO's World PART 13

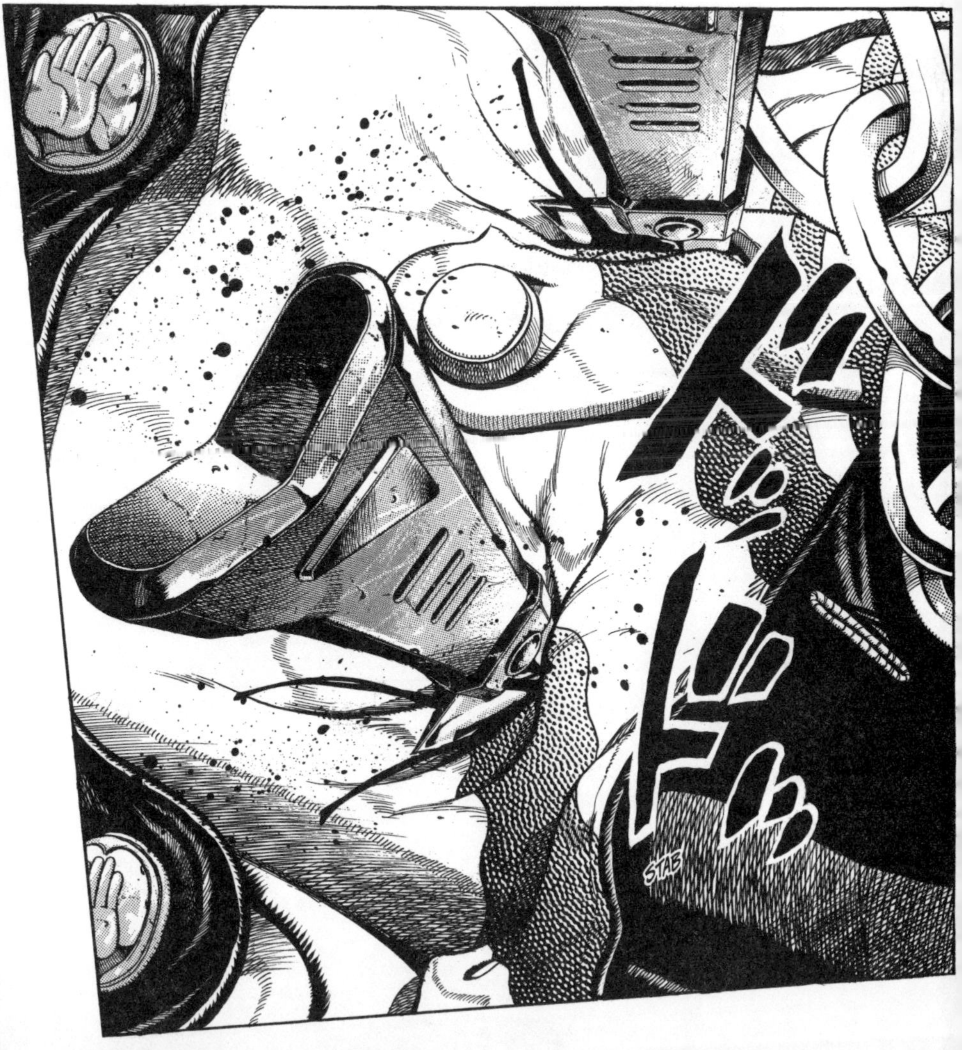
STAB

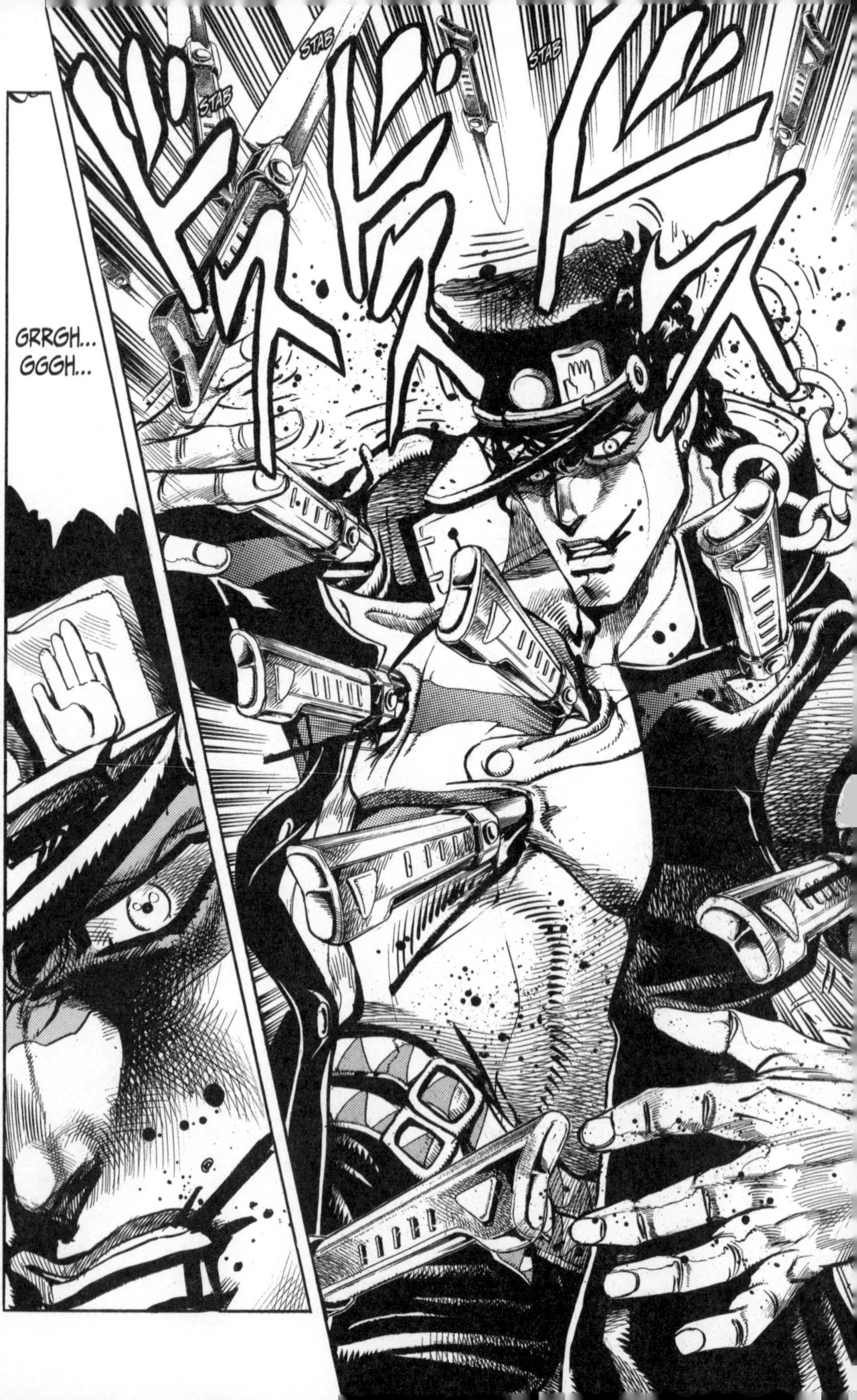
STAB
STAB
STAB
GRRGH... GGGH...

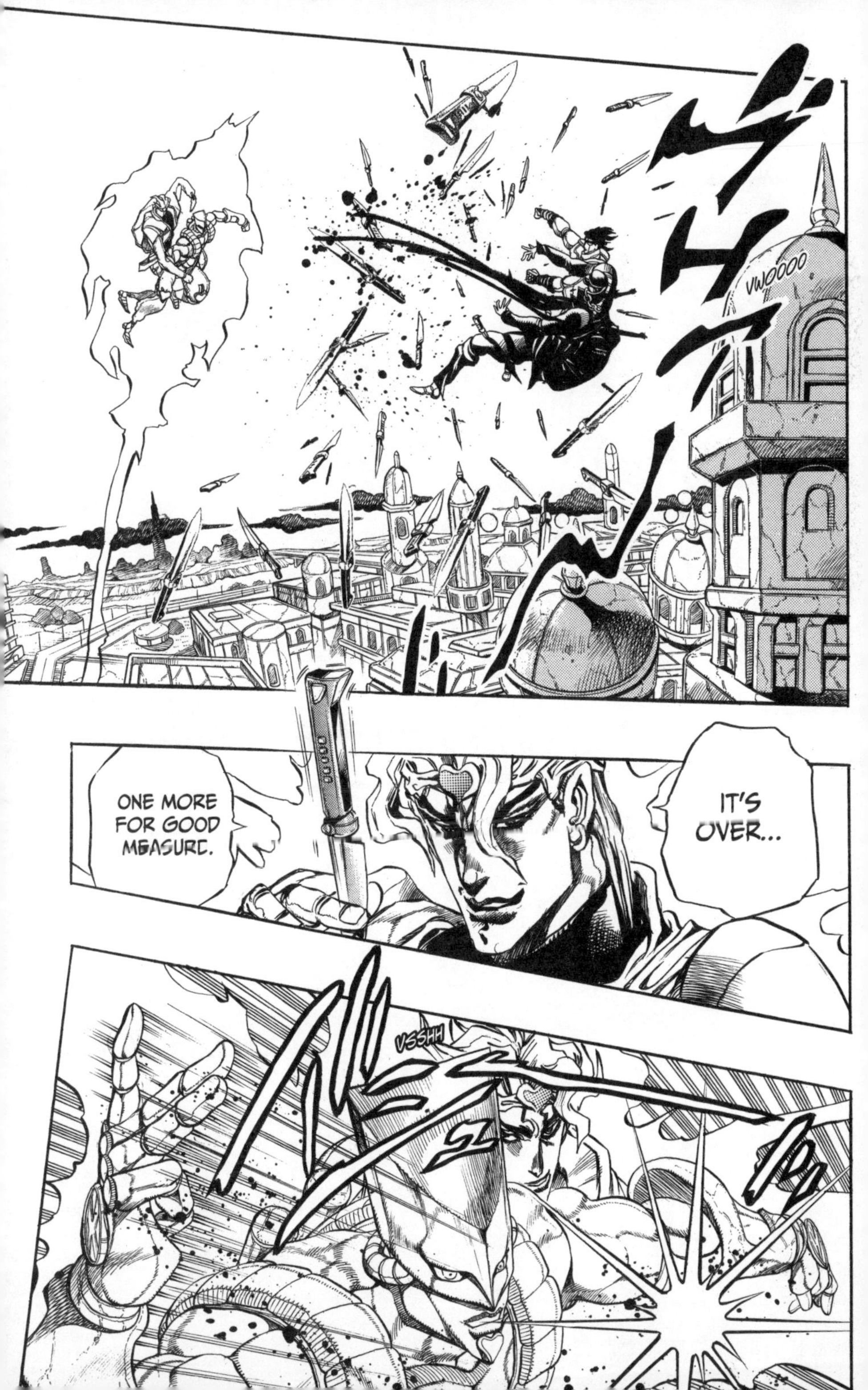
VWOOOO
IT'S OVER...
ONE MORE FOR GOOD MEASURE.
VSSHH

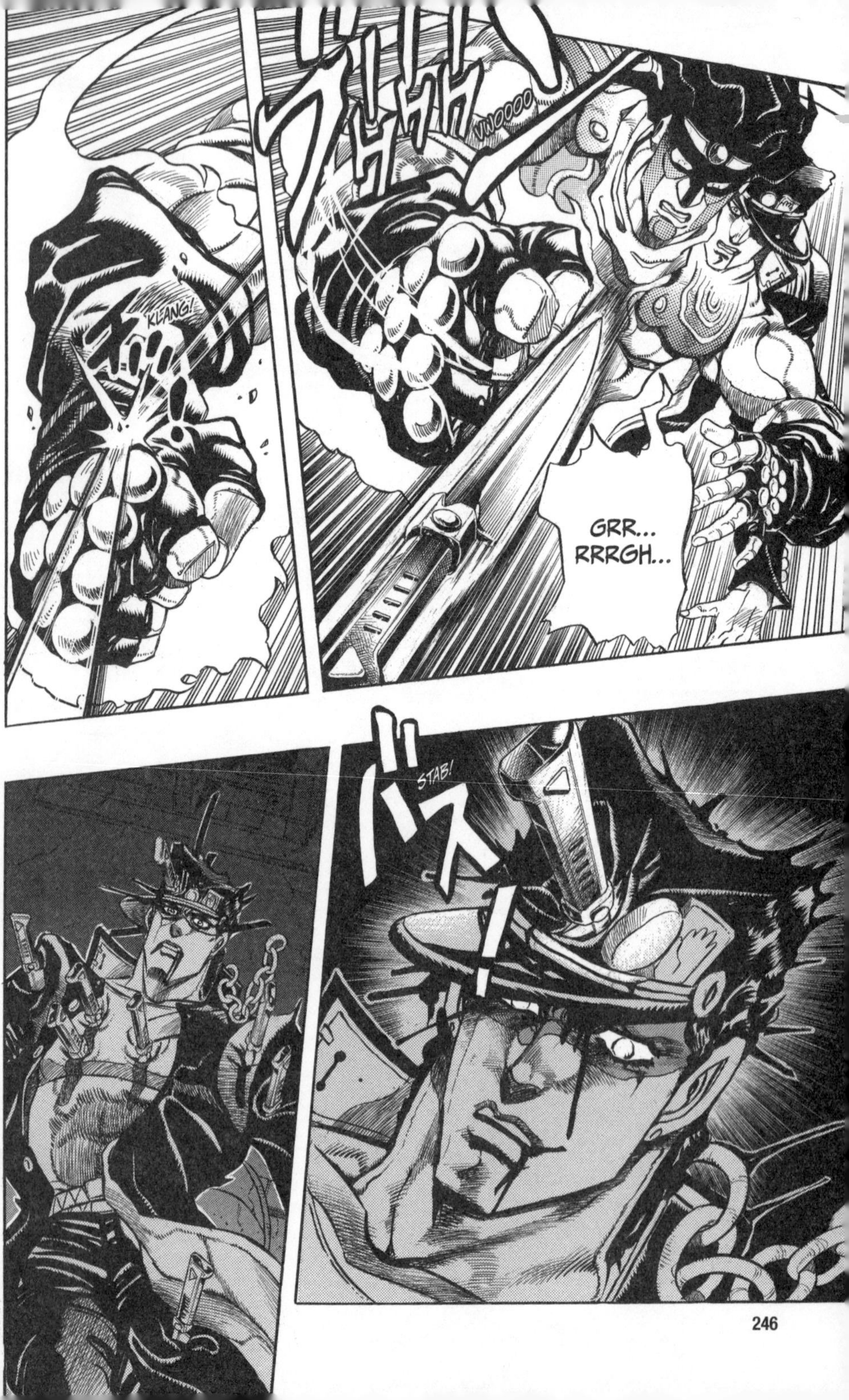
VWOOOO
GRR... RRRGH...
KLANG!
STAB!

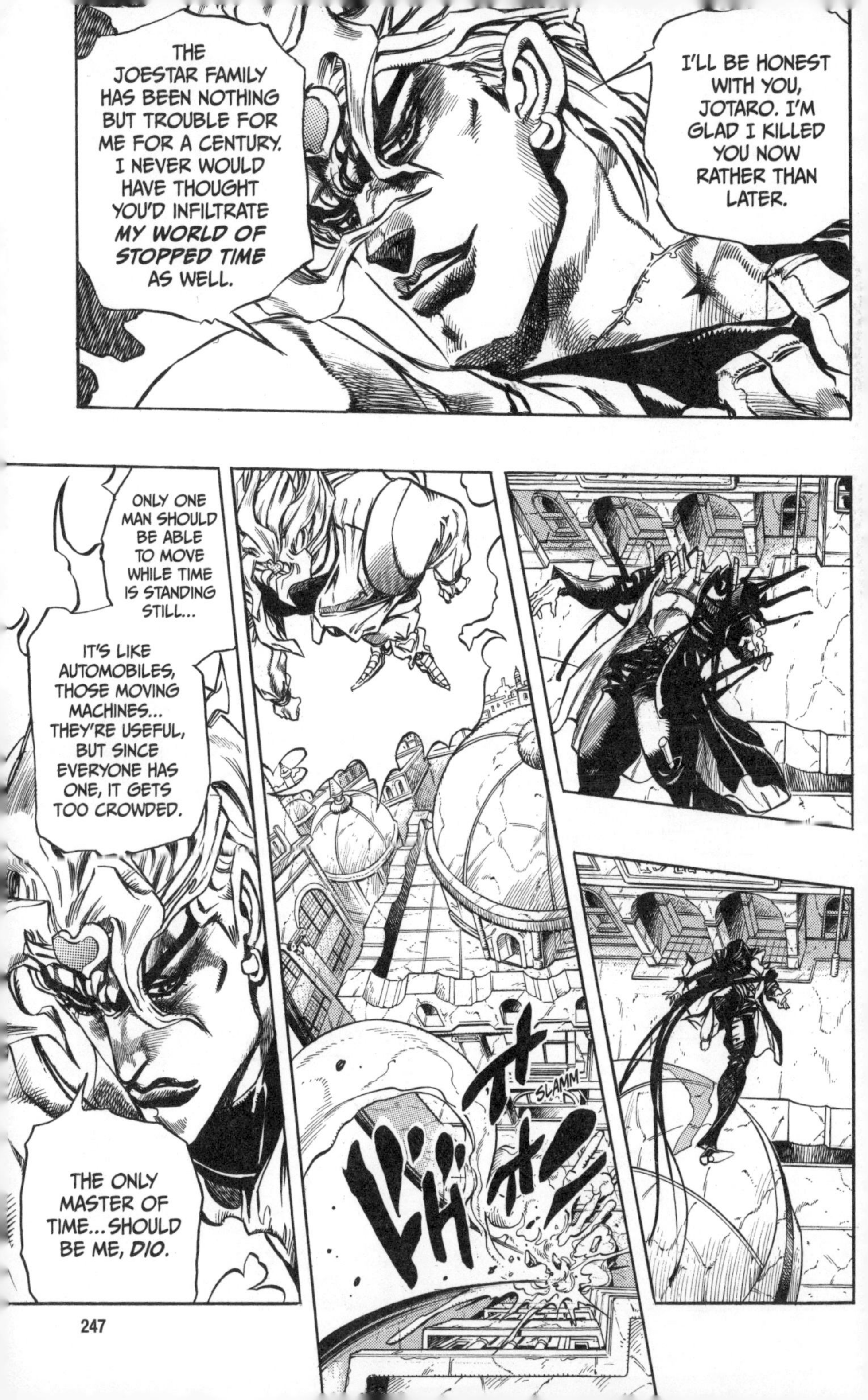
I'LL BE HONEST WITH YOU, JOTARO. I'M GLAD I KILLED YOU NOW RATHER THAN LATER.
THE JOESTAR FAMILY HAS BEEN NOTHING BUT TROUBLE FOR ME FOR A CENTURY. I NEVER WOULD HAVE THOUGHT YOU'D INFILTRATE *MY WORLD OF STOPPED TIME* AS WELL.
SLAMM
ONLY ONE MAN SHOULD BE ABLE TO MOVE WHILE TIME IS STANDING STILL...
IT'S LIKE AUTOMOBILES, THOSE MOVING MACHINES... THEY'RE USEFUL, BUT SINCE EVERYONE HAS ONE, IT GETS TOO CROWDED.
THE ONLY MASTER OF TIME... SHOULD BE ME, *DIO*.

SHAAAA

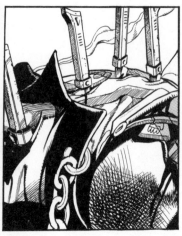

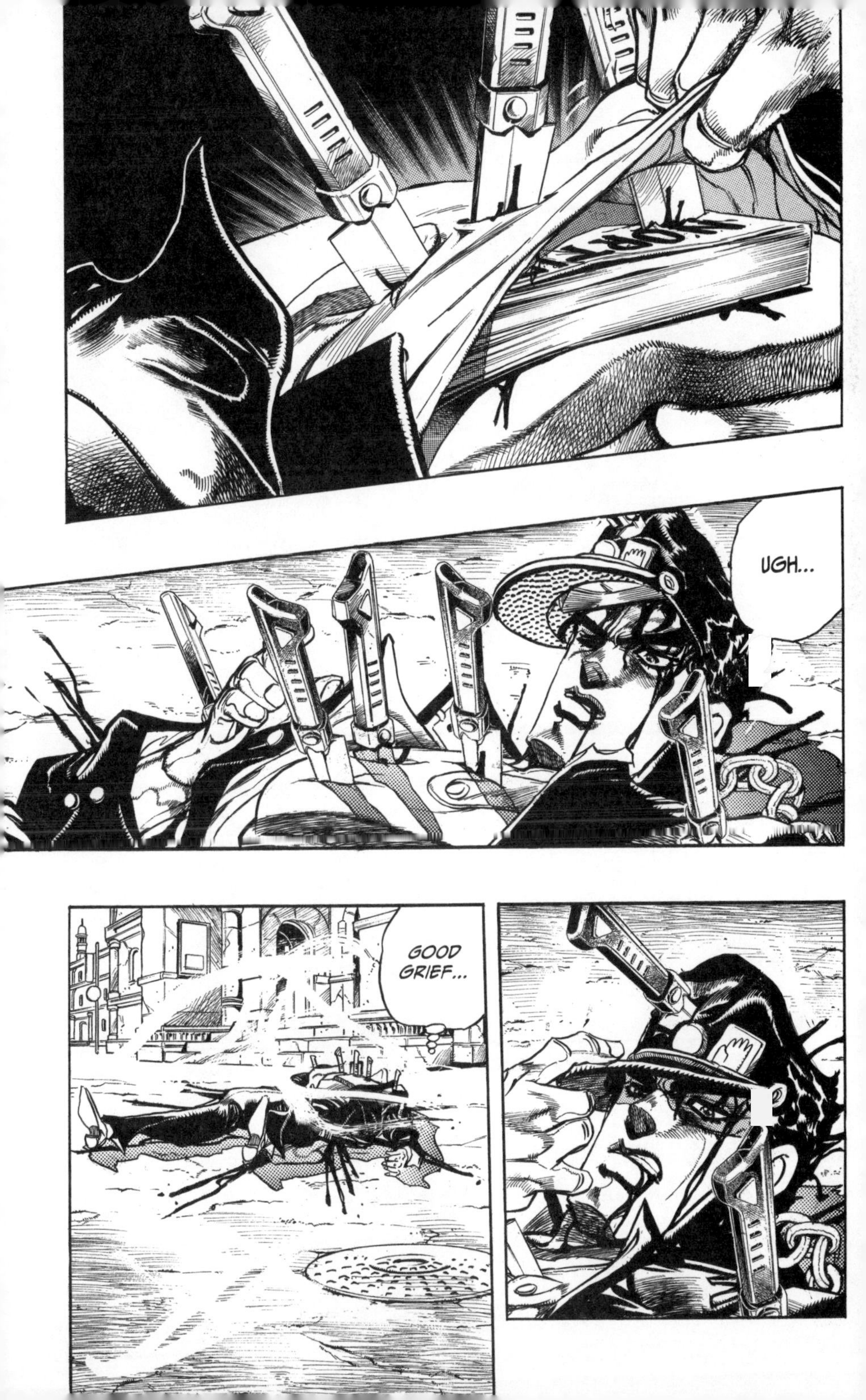
UGH...
GOOD GRIEF...

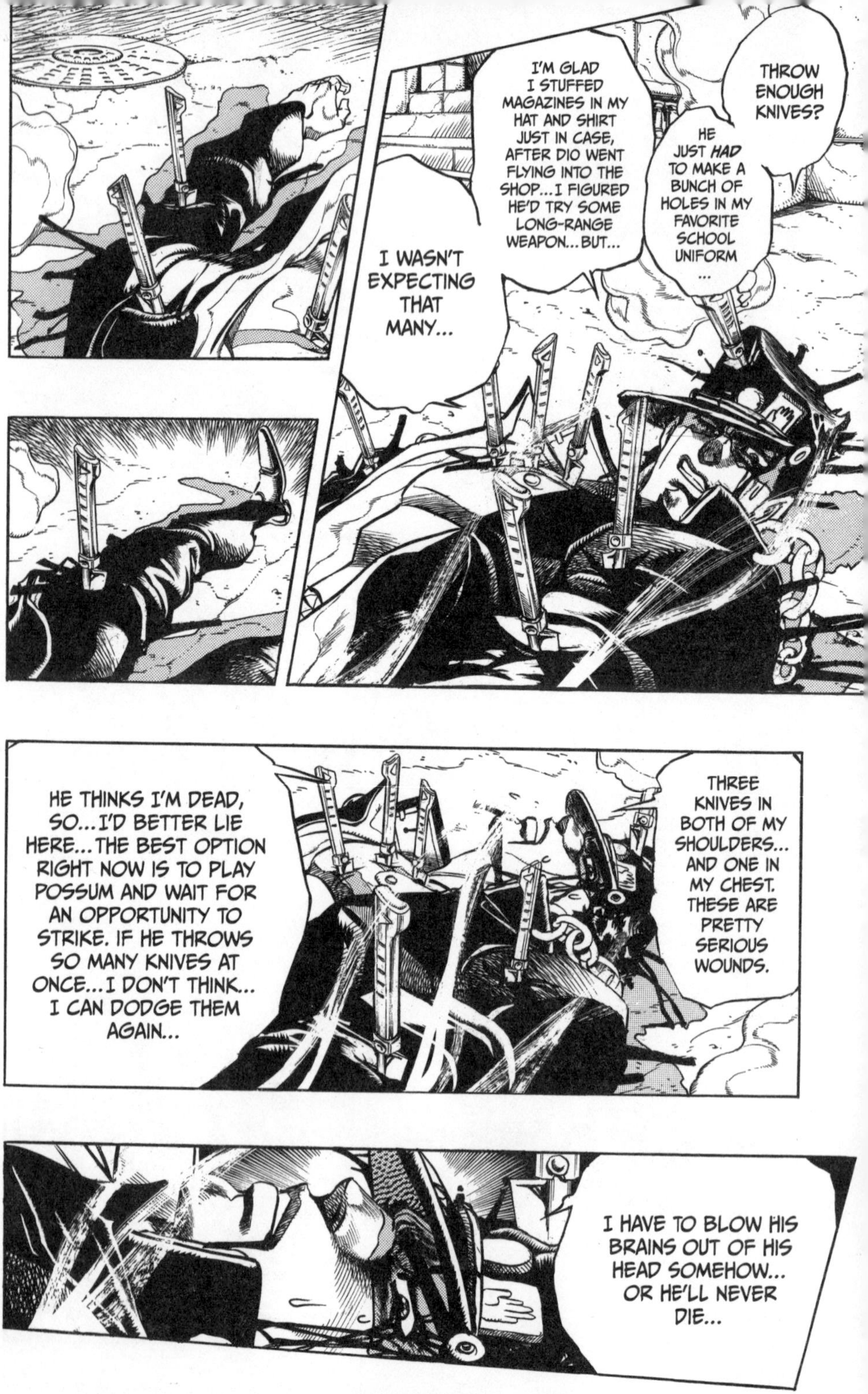
THROW ENOUGH KNIVES?
HE JUST *HAD* TO MAKE A BUNCH OF HOLES IN MY FAVORITE SCHOOL UNIFORM ...
I'M GLAD I STUFFED MAGAZINES IN MY HAT AND SHIRT JUST IN CASE, AFTER DIO WENT FLYING INTO THE SHOP...I FIGURED HE'D TRY SOME LONG-RANGE WEAPON...BUT...
I WASN'T EXPECTING THAT MANY...
THREE KNIVES IN BOTH OF MY SHOULDERS... AND ONE IN MY CHEST. THESE ARE PRETTY SERIOUS WOUNDS.
HE THINKS I'M DEAD, SO...I'D BETTER LIE HERE...THE BEST OPTION RIGHT NOW IS TO PLAY POSSUM AND WAIT FOR AN OPPORTUNITY TO STRIKE. IF HE THROWS SO MANY KNIVES AT ONCE...I DON'T THINK... I CAN DODGE THEM AGAIN...
I HAVE TO BLOW HIS BRAINS OUT OF HIS HEAD SOMEHOW... OR HE'LL NEVER DIE...

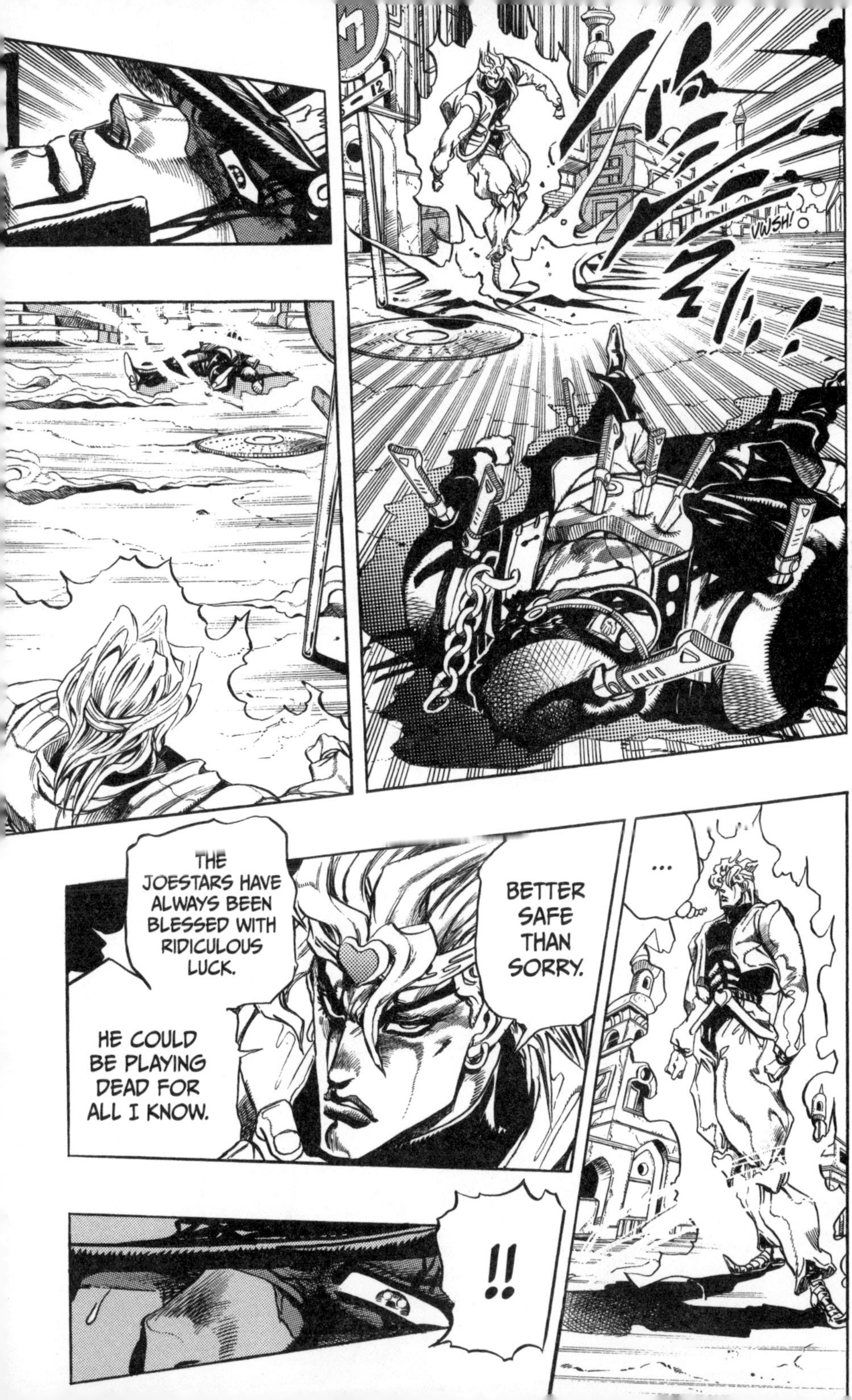
VWSH!
...
BETTER SAFE THAN SORRY.
THE JOESTARS HAVE ALWAYS BEEN BLESSED WITH RIDICULOUS LUCK.
HE COULD BE PLAYING DEAD FOR ALL I KNOW.
!!

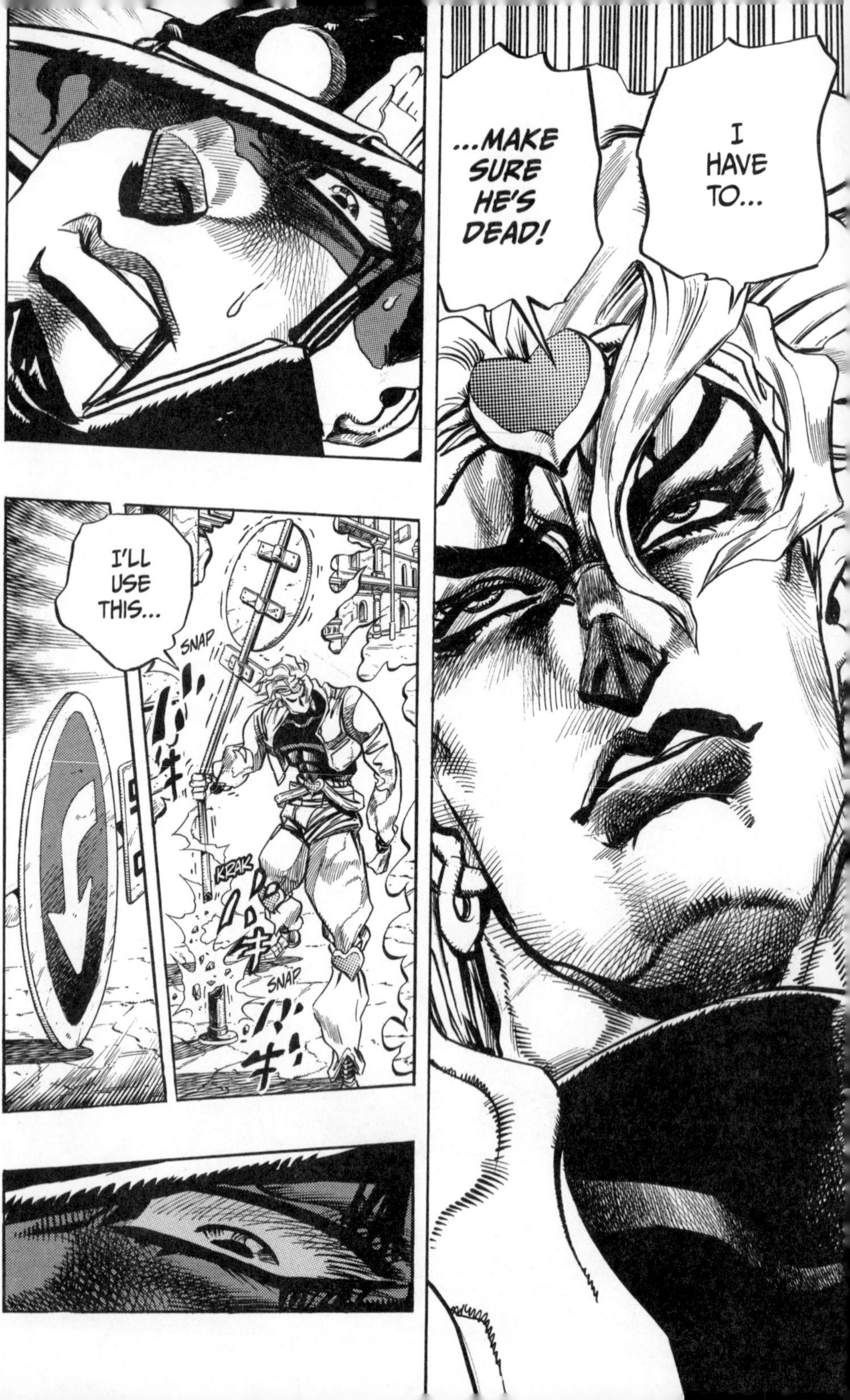
I HAVE TO...
...MAKE SURE HE'S DEAD!
I'LL USE THIS...
SNAP
KRAK
SNAP

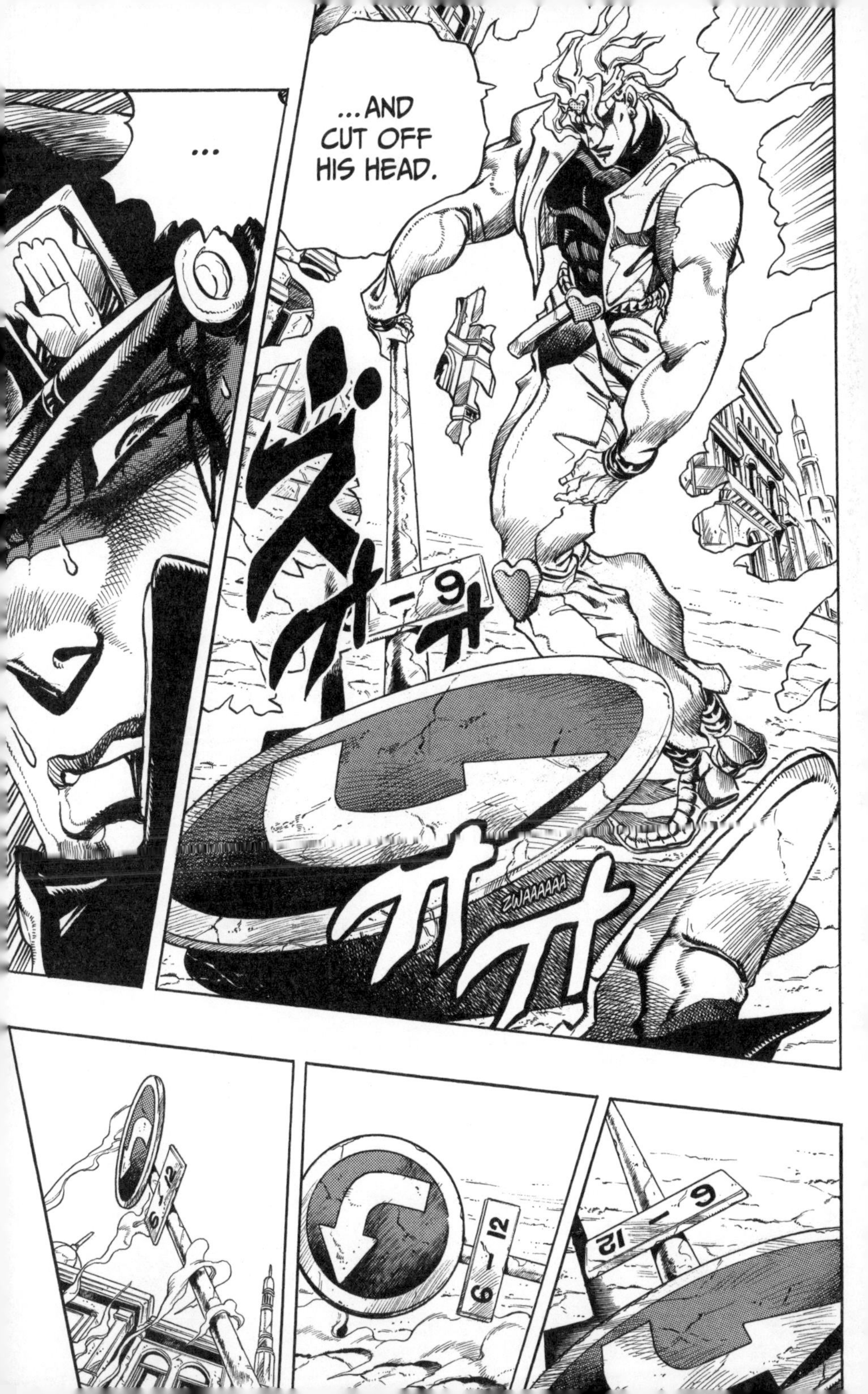
...AND CUT OFF HIS HEAD.
ZWAAAAAA
...

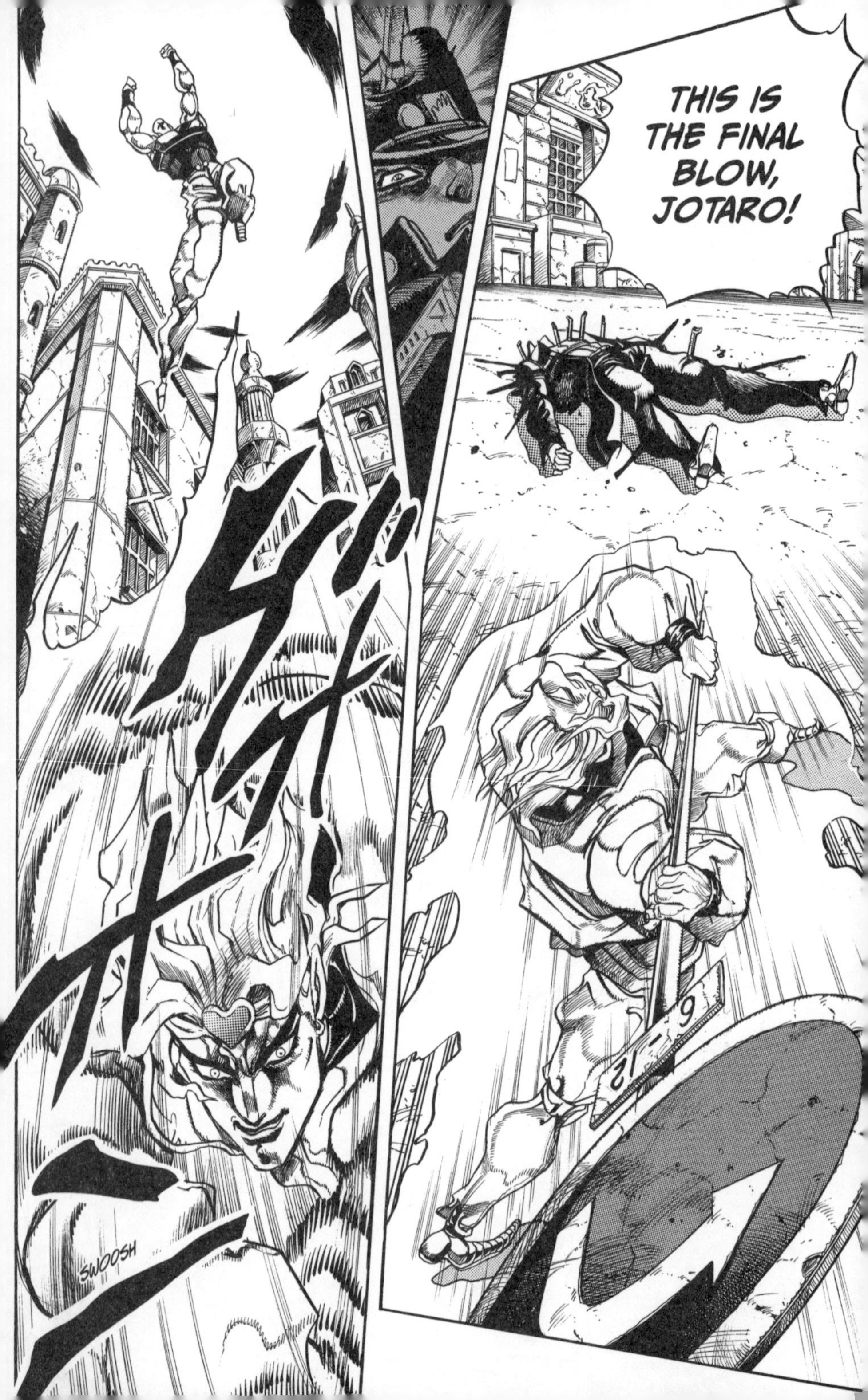
THIS IS THE FINAL BLOW, JOTARO!
SWOOSH

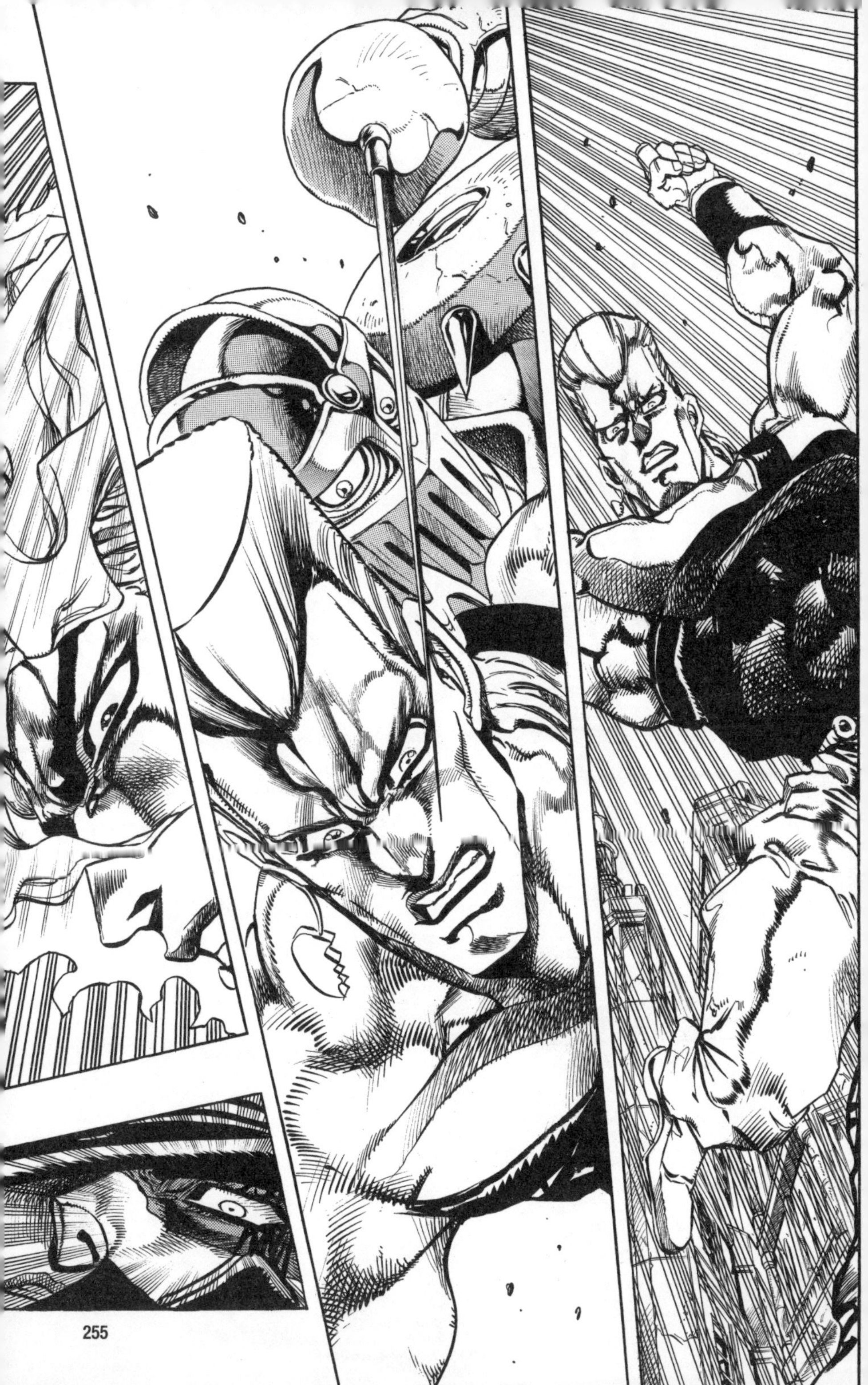

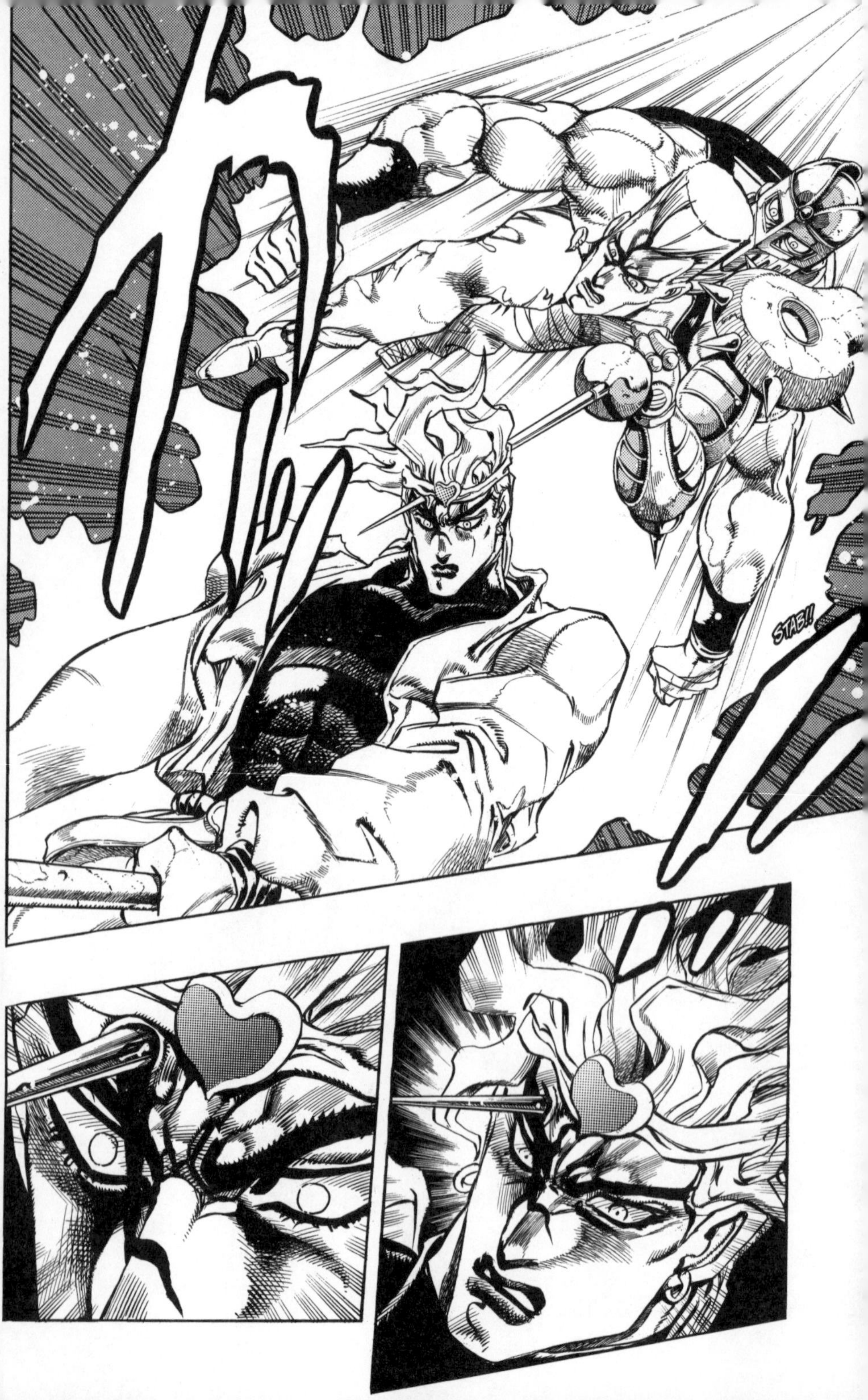
STAB!!

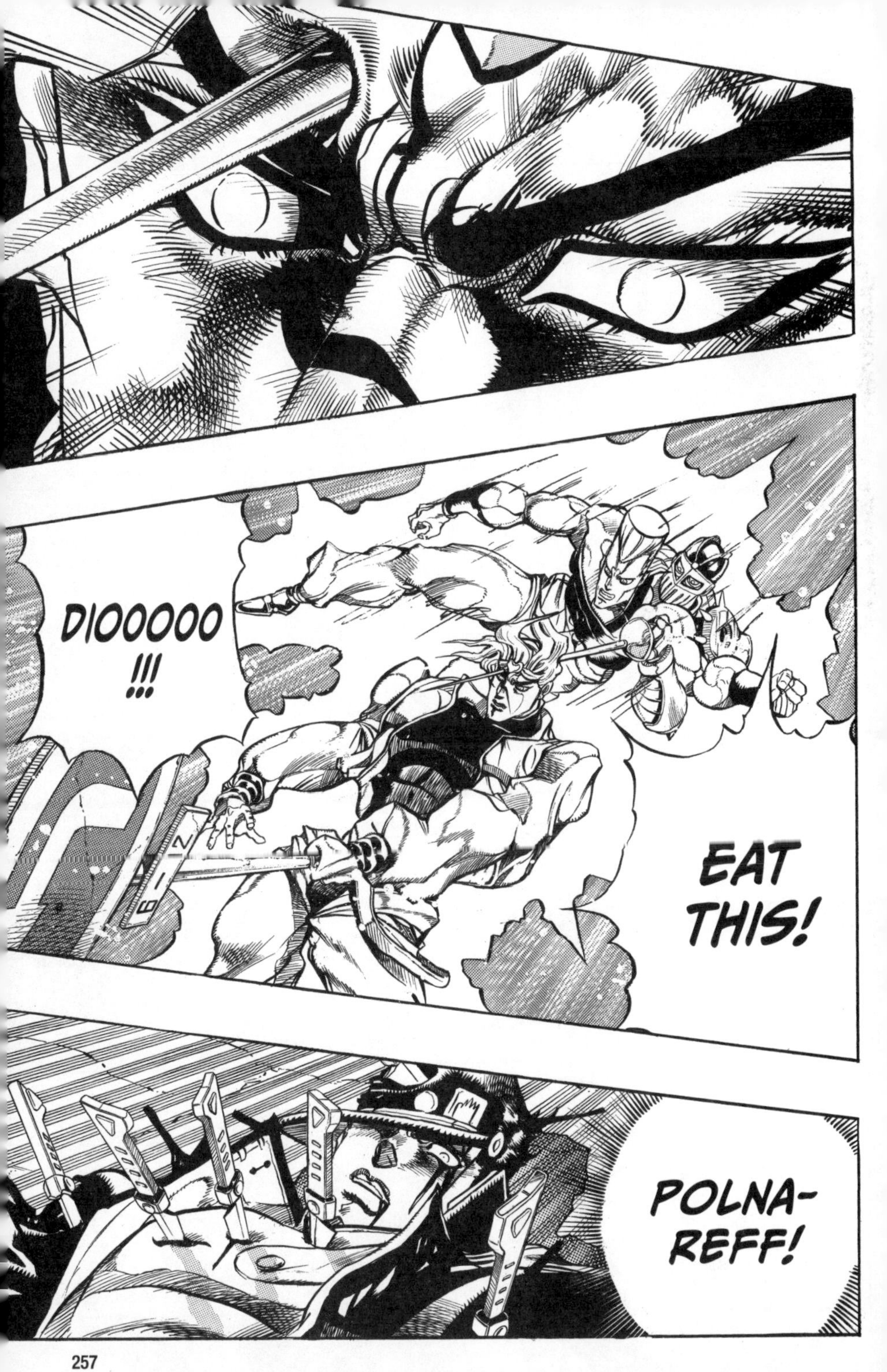
DIOOOOO !!!
EAT THIS!
POLNA-REFF!

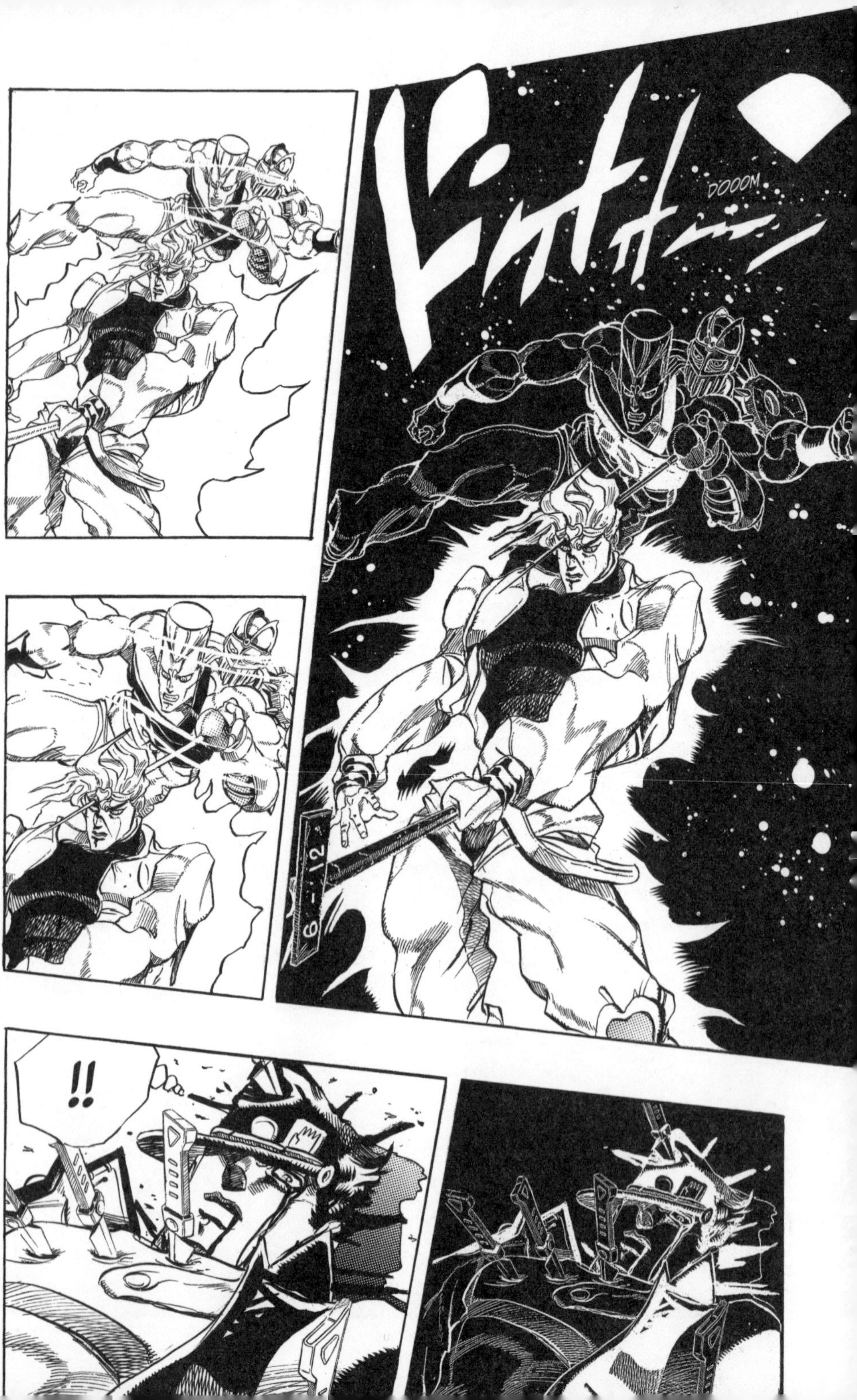
DOOOM
!!

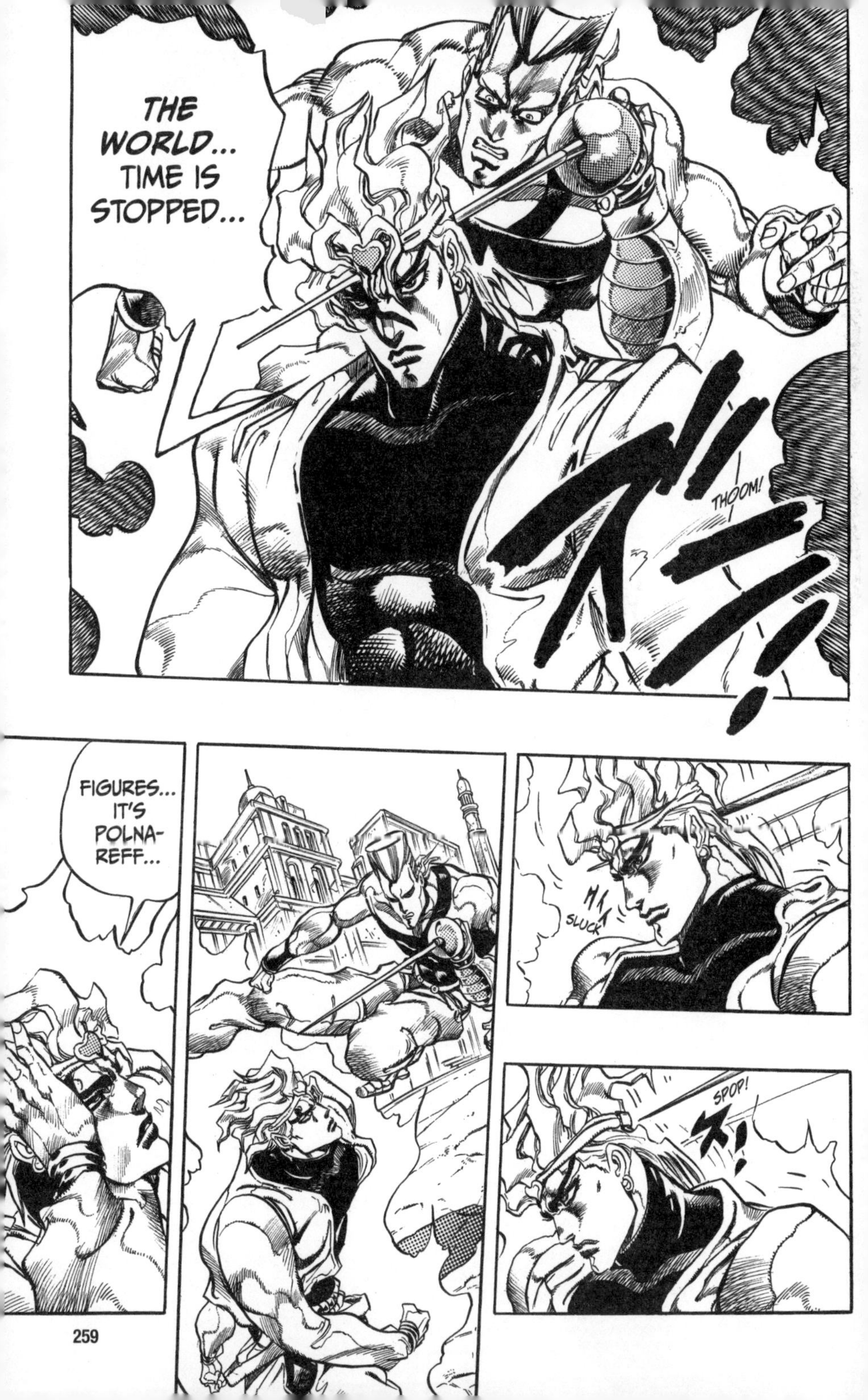
THE WORLD... TIME IS STOPPED...
THOOM!
SLUCK
SPOP!
FIGURES... IT'S POLNA-REFF...

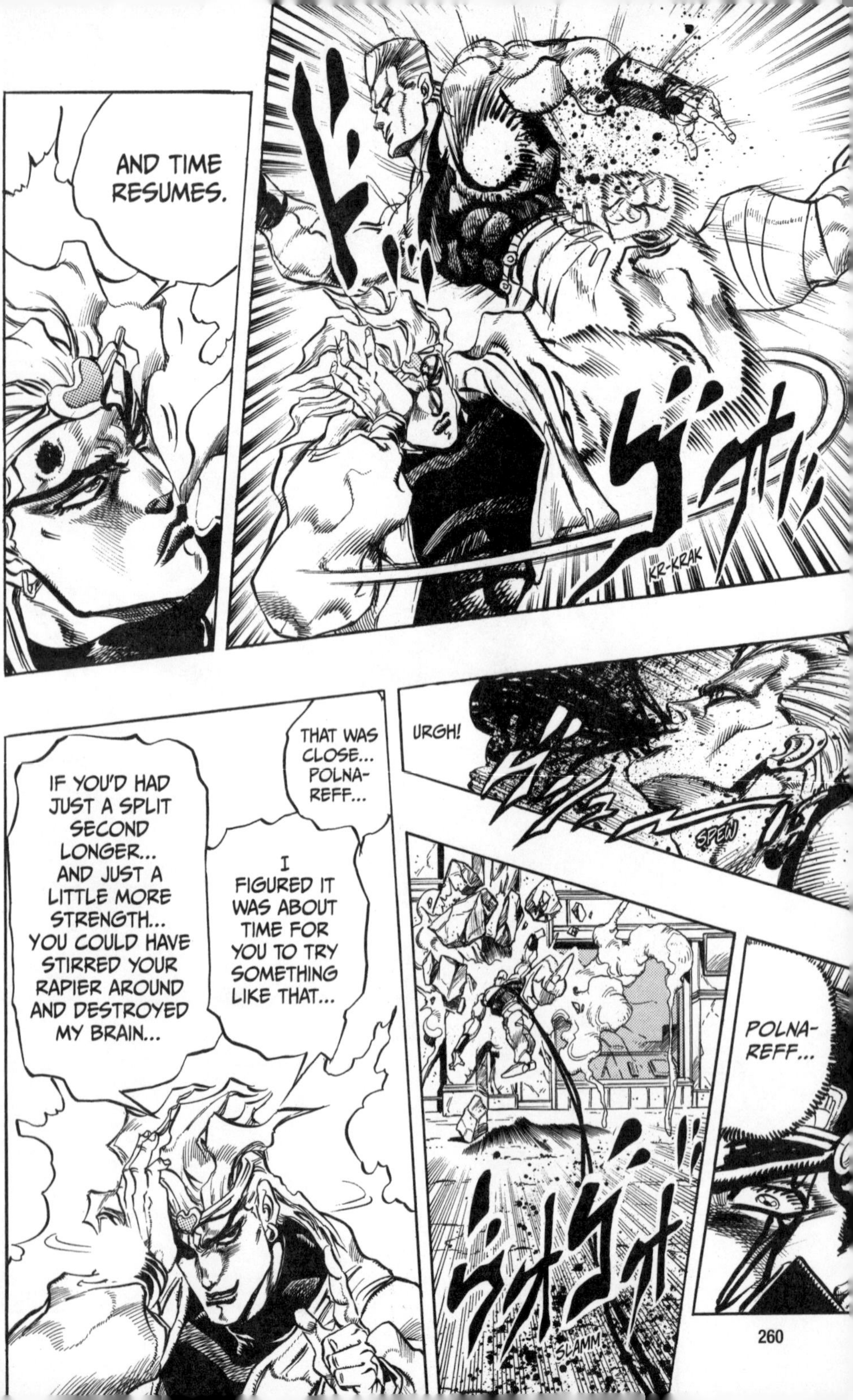
KR-KRAK
AND TIME RESUMES.
URGH!
SPEW
POLNA-REFF...
SLAMM
THAT WAS CLOSE... POLNA-REFF...
IF YOU'D HAD JUST A SPLIT SECOND LONGER... AND JUST A LITTLE MORE STRENGTH... YOU COULD HAVE STIRRED YOUR RAPIER AROUND AND DESTROYED MY BRAIN...
I FIGURED IT WAS ABOUT TIME FOR YOU TO TRY SOMETHING LIKE THAT...

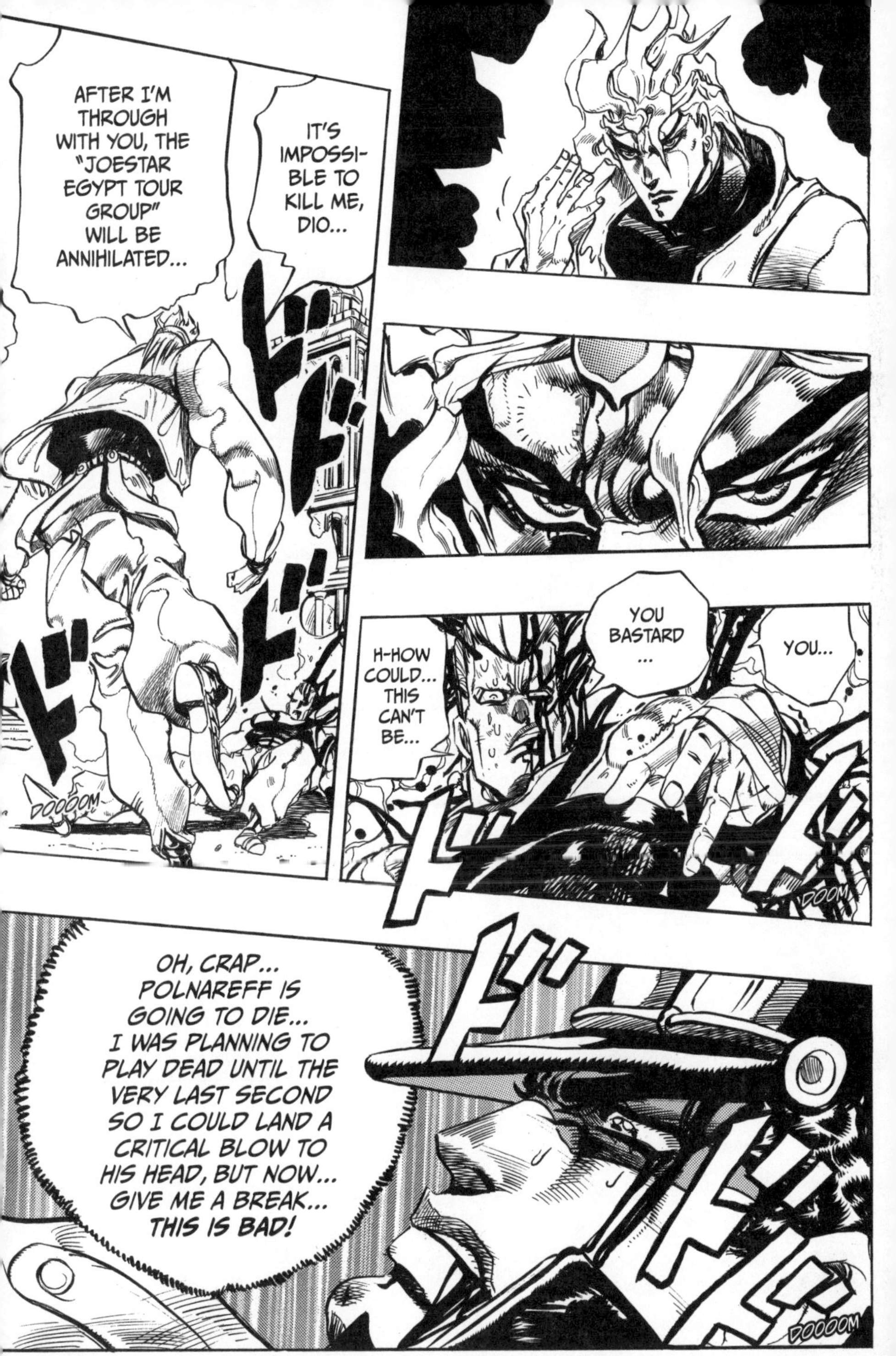

IT'S IMPOSSI-BLE TO KILL ME, DIO...
AFTER I'M THROUGH WITH YOU, THE "JOESTAR EGYPT TOUR GROUP" WILL BE ANNIHILATED...
DOOOOM
YOU...
YOU BASTARD ...
H-HOW COULD... THIS CAN'T BE...
DOOM
OH, CRAP... POLNAREFF IS GOING TO DIE... I WAS PLANNING TO PLAY DEAD UNTIL THE VERY LAST SECOND SO I COULD LAND A CRITICAL BLOW TO HIS HEAD, BUT NOW... GIVE ME A BREAK... THIS IS BAD!
DOOOOM

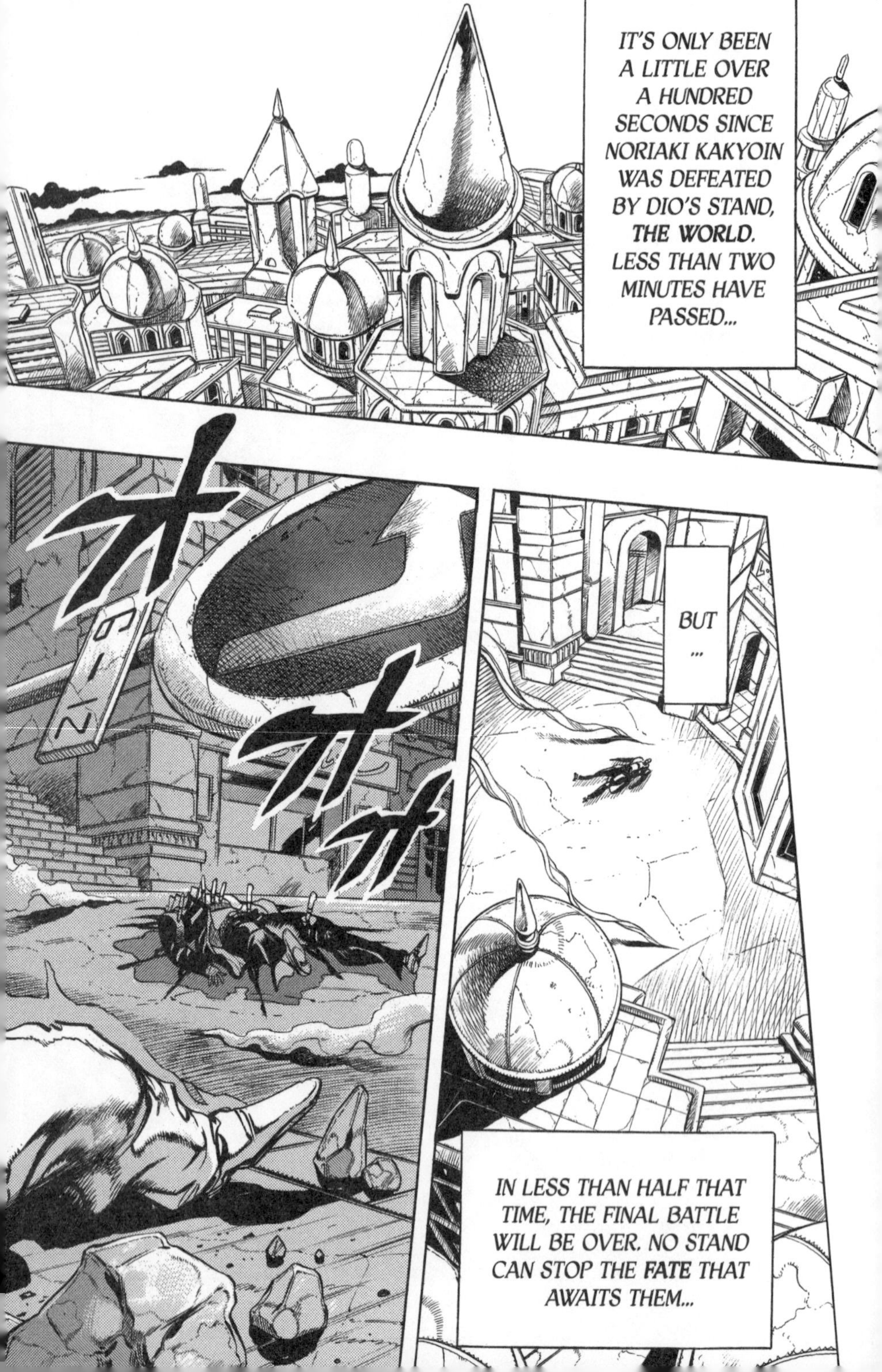
IT'S ONLY BEEN A LITTLE OVER A HUNDRED SECONDS SINCE NORIAKI KAKYOIN WAS DEFEATED BY DIO'S STAND, **THE WORLD.** LESS THAN TWO MINUTES HAVE PASSED...
BUT ...
IN LESS THAN HALF THAT TIME, THE FINAL BATTLE WILL BE OVER. NO STAND CAN STOP THE **FATE** THAT AWAITS THEM...

CHAPTER 147: DIO's World PART 14

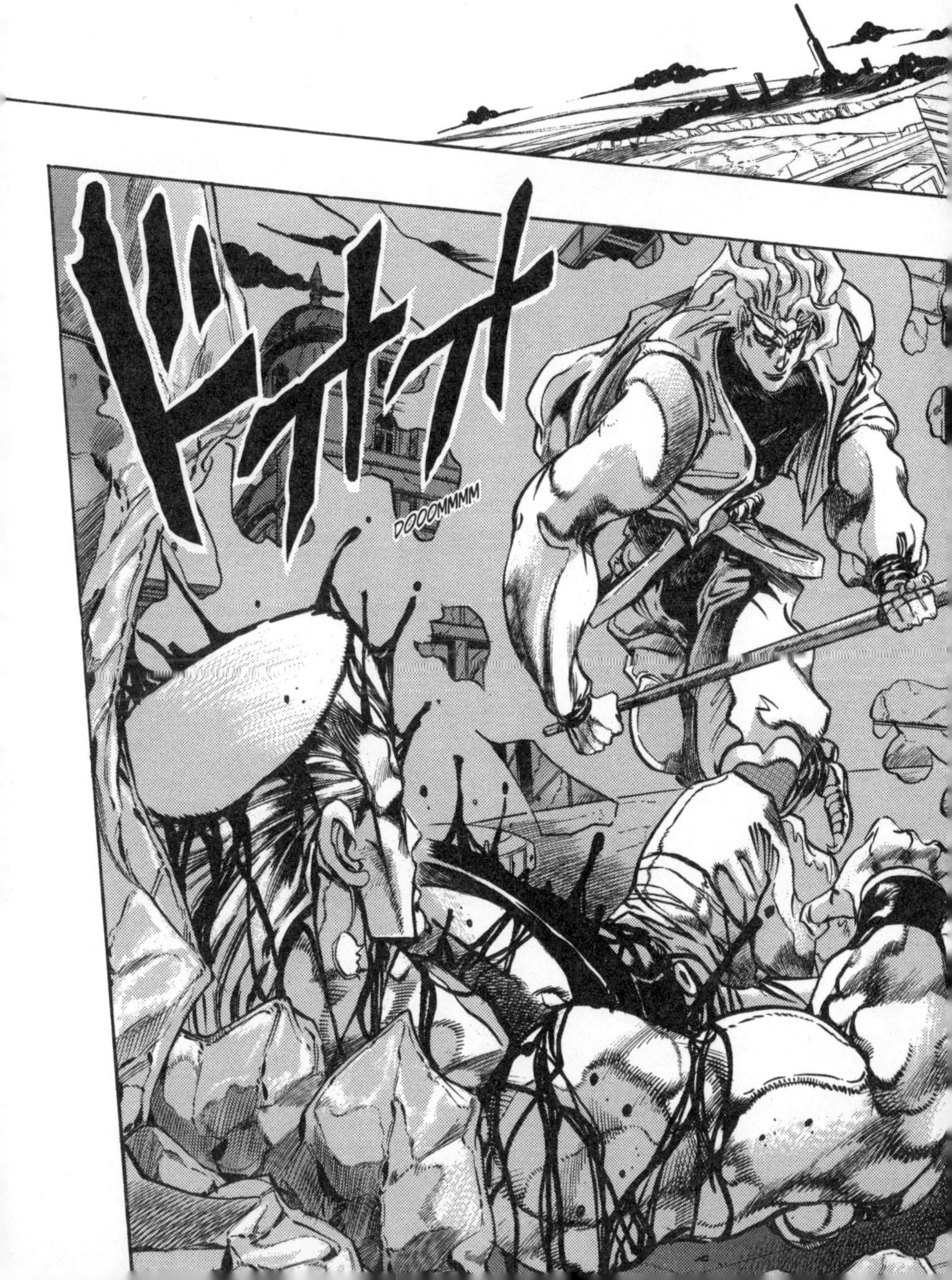
ドオオオ
DOOOMMMM

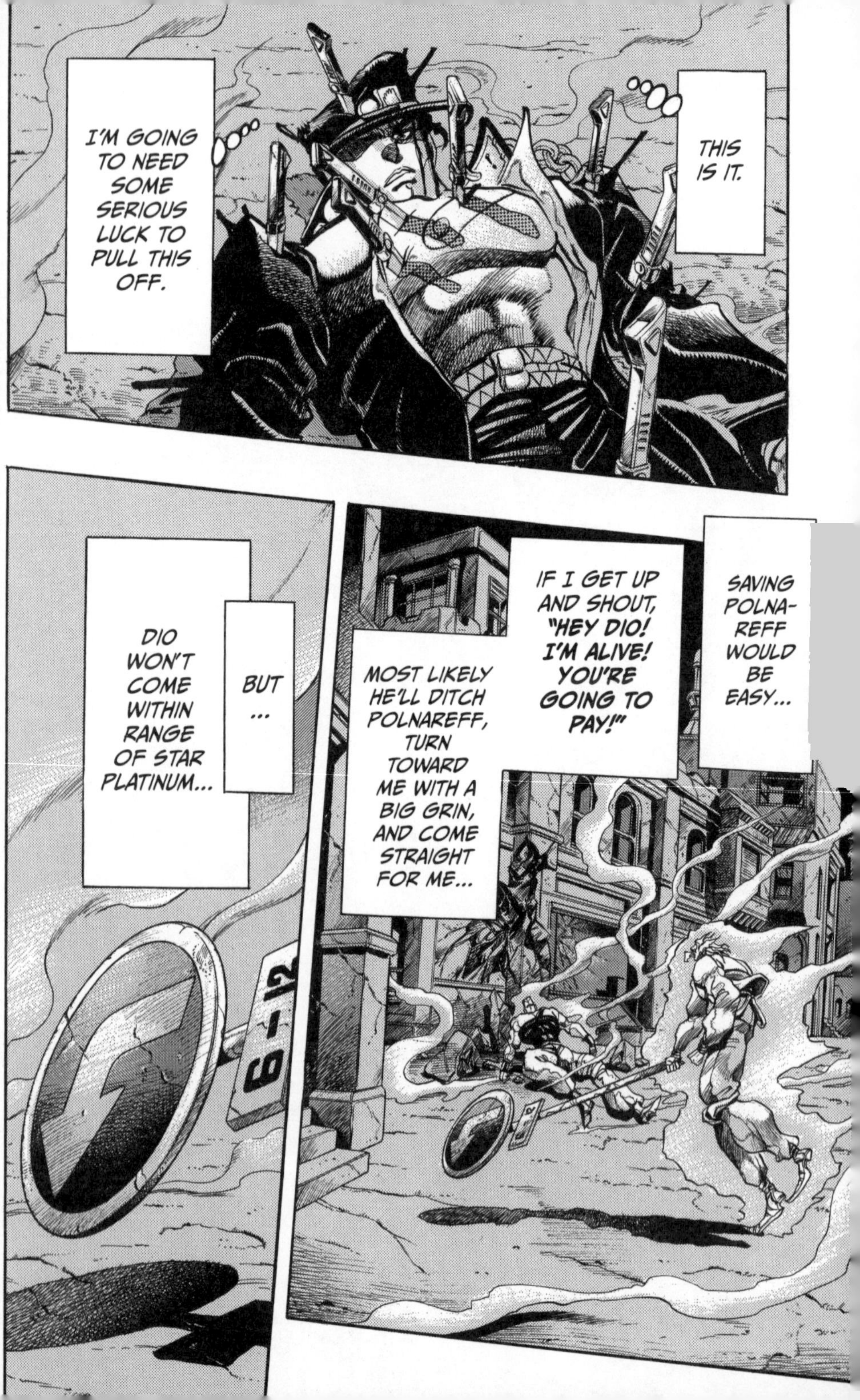
THIS IS IT.
I'M GOING TO NEED SOME SERIOUS LUCK TO PULL THIS OFF.
SAVING POLNAREFF WOULD BE EASY...
IF I GET UP AND SHOUT, "HEY DIO! I'M ALIVE! YOU'RE GOING TO PAY!"
MOST LIKELY HE'LL DITCH POLNAREFF, TURN TOWARD ME WITH A BIG GRIN, AND COME STRAIGHT FOR ME...
BUT ...
DIO WON'T COME WITHIN RANGE OF STAR PLATINUM...

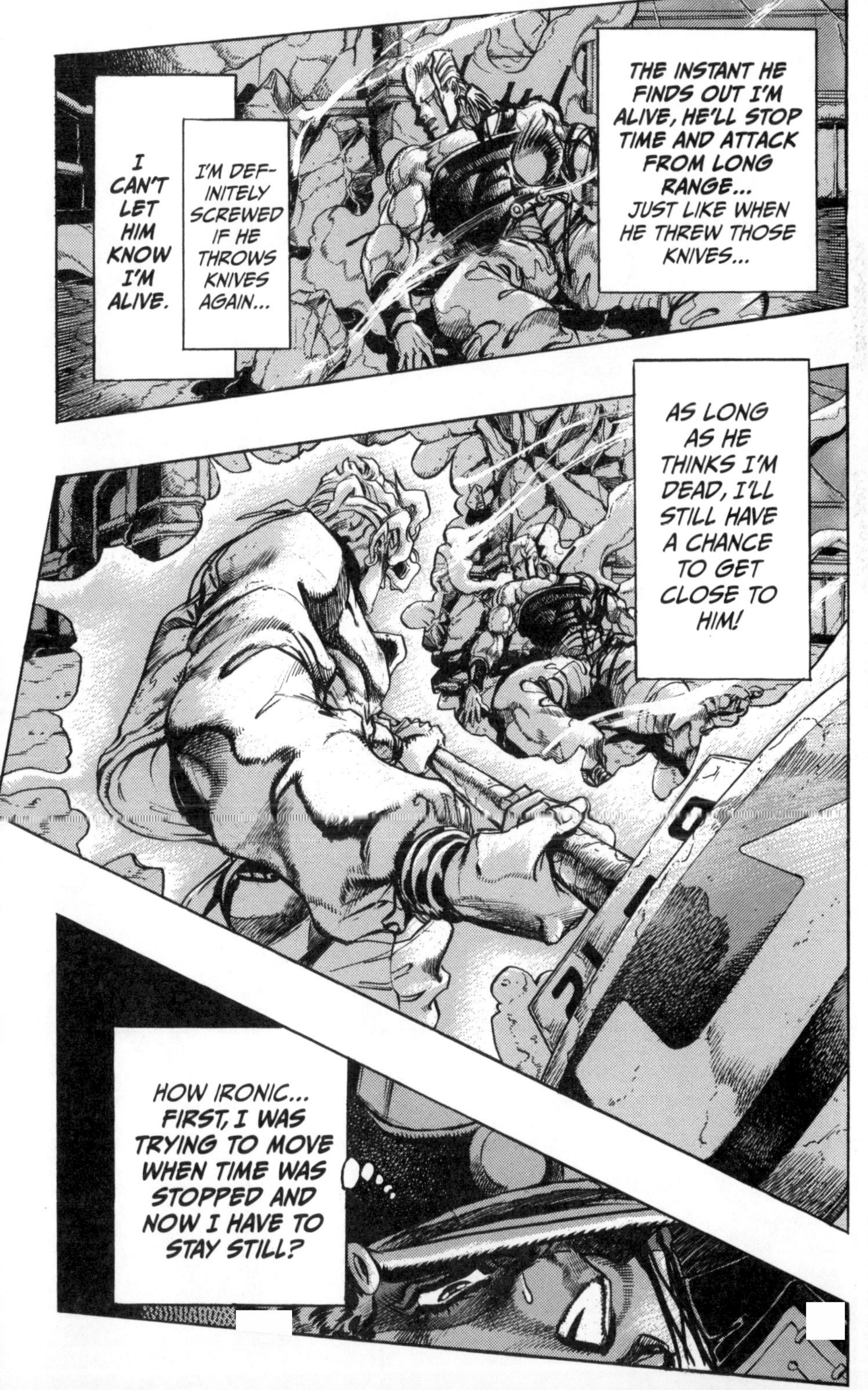
THE INSTANT HE FINDS OUT I'M ALIVE, HE'LL STOP TIME AND ATTACK FROM LONG RANGE... JUST LIKE WHEN HE THREW THOSE KNIVES...
I'M DEF-INITELY SCREWED IF HE THROWS KNIVES AGAIN...
I CAN'T LET HIM KNOW I'M ALIVE.
AS LONG AS HE THINKS I'M DEAD, I'LL STILL HAVE A CHANCE TO GET CLOSE TO HIM!
HOW IRONIC... FIRST, I WAS TRYING TO MOVE WHEN TIME WAS STOPPED AND NOW I HAVE TO STAY STILL?

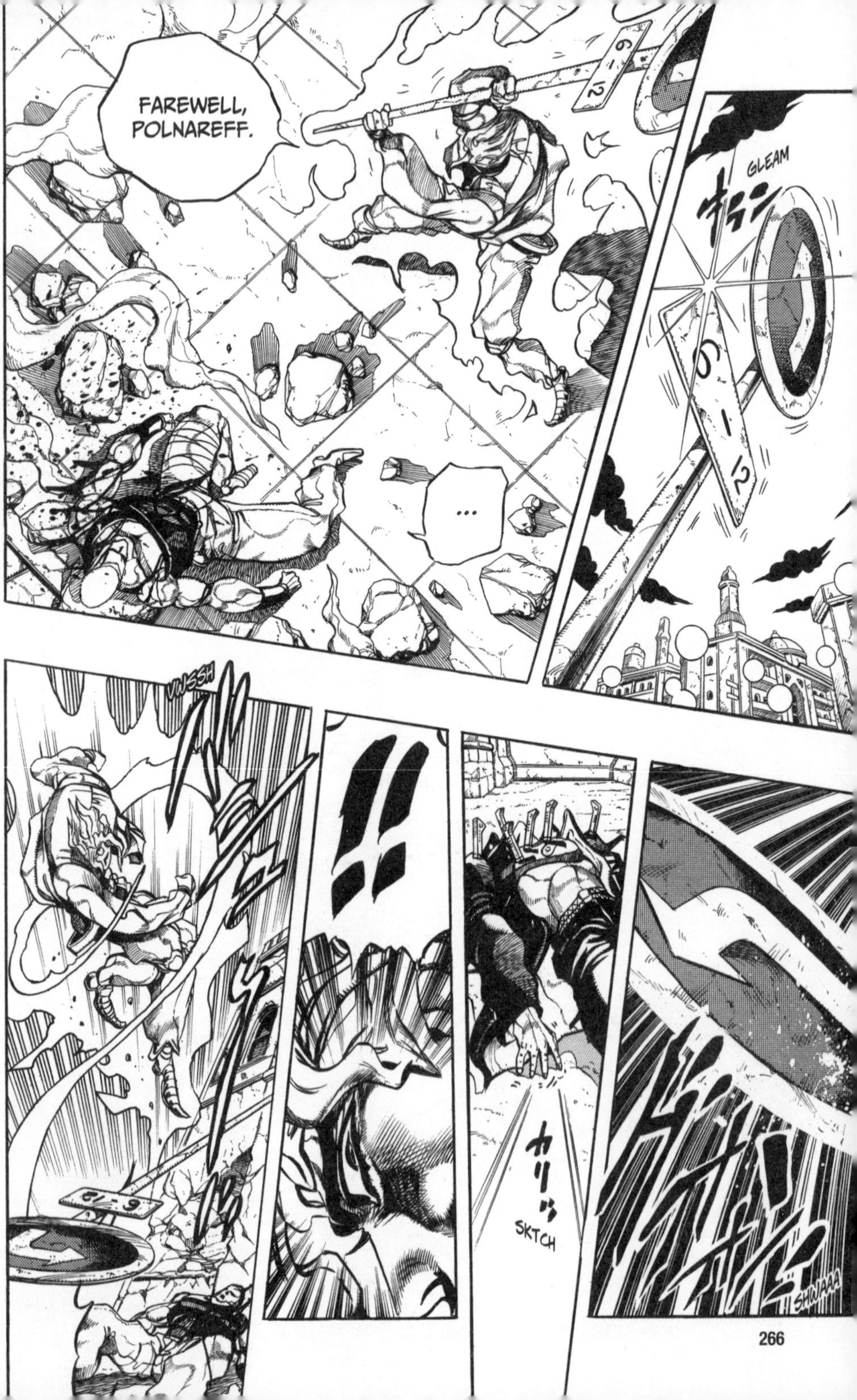
GLEAM
キラン
FAREWELL, POLNAREFF.
...
SHWAAA
SKTCH
カリッ
!!
VWSSH

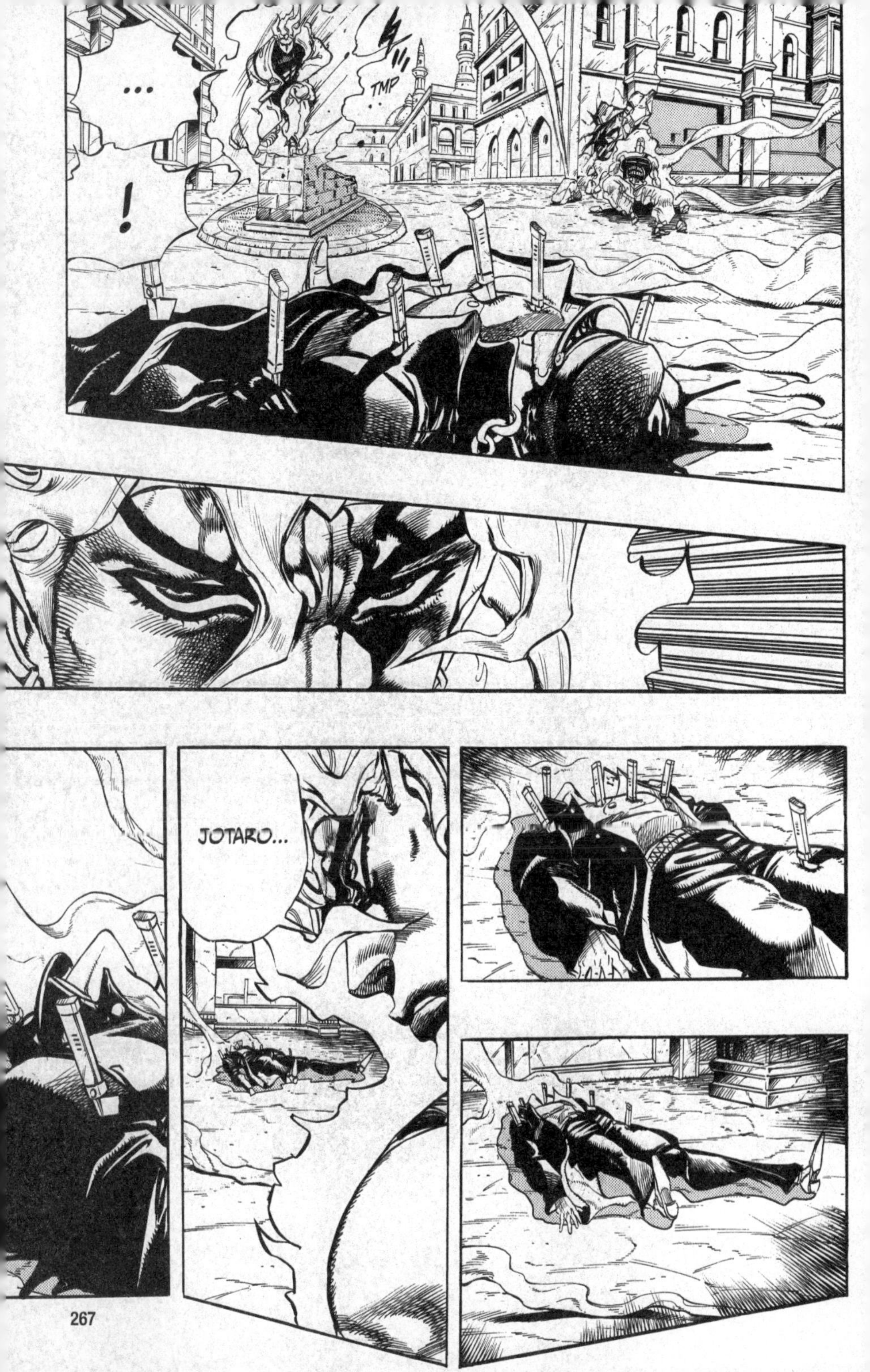
TMP
...
!
JOTARO...

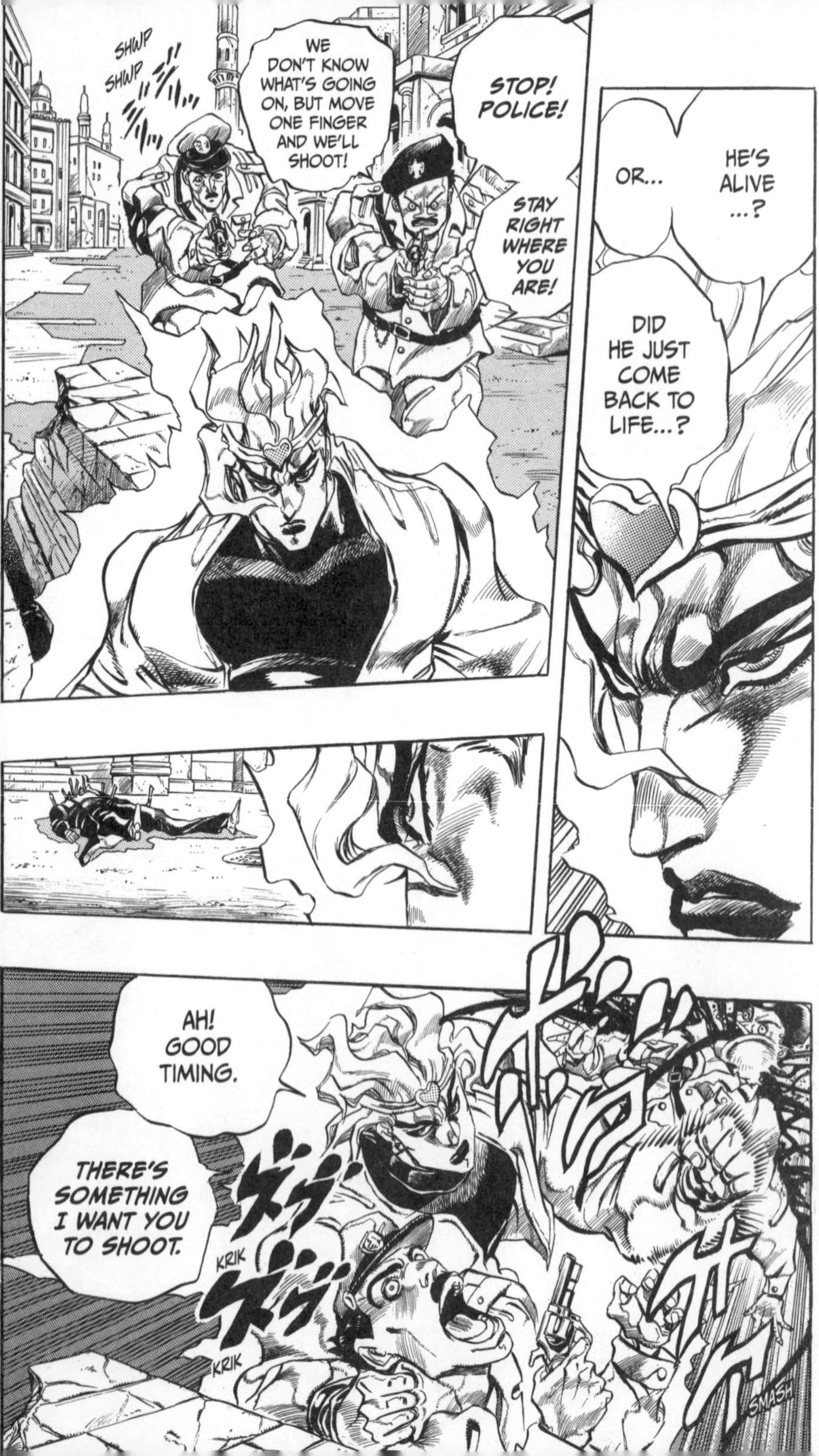
HE'S ALIVE ...?
OR...
DID HE JUST COME BACK TO LIFE...?
STOP! POLICE!
STAY RIGHT WHERE YOU ARE!
WE DON'T KNOW WHAT'S GOING ON, BUT MOVE ONE FINGER AND WE'LL SHOOT!
SHWP
SHWP
SMASH
AH! GOOD TIMING.
THERE'S SOMETHING I WANT YOU TO SHOOT.
KRIK
KRIK

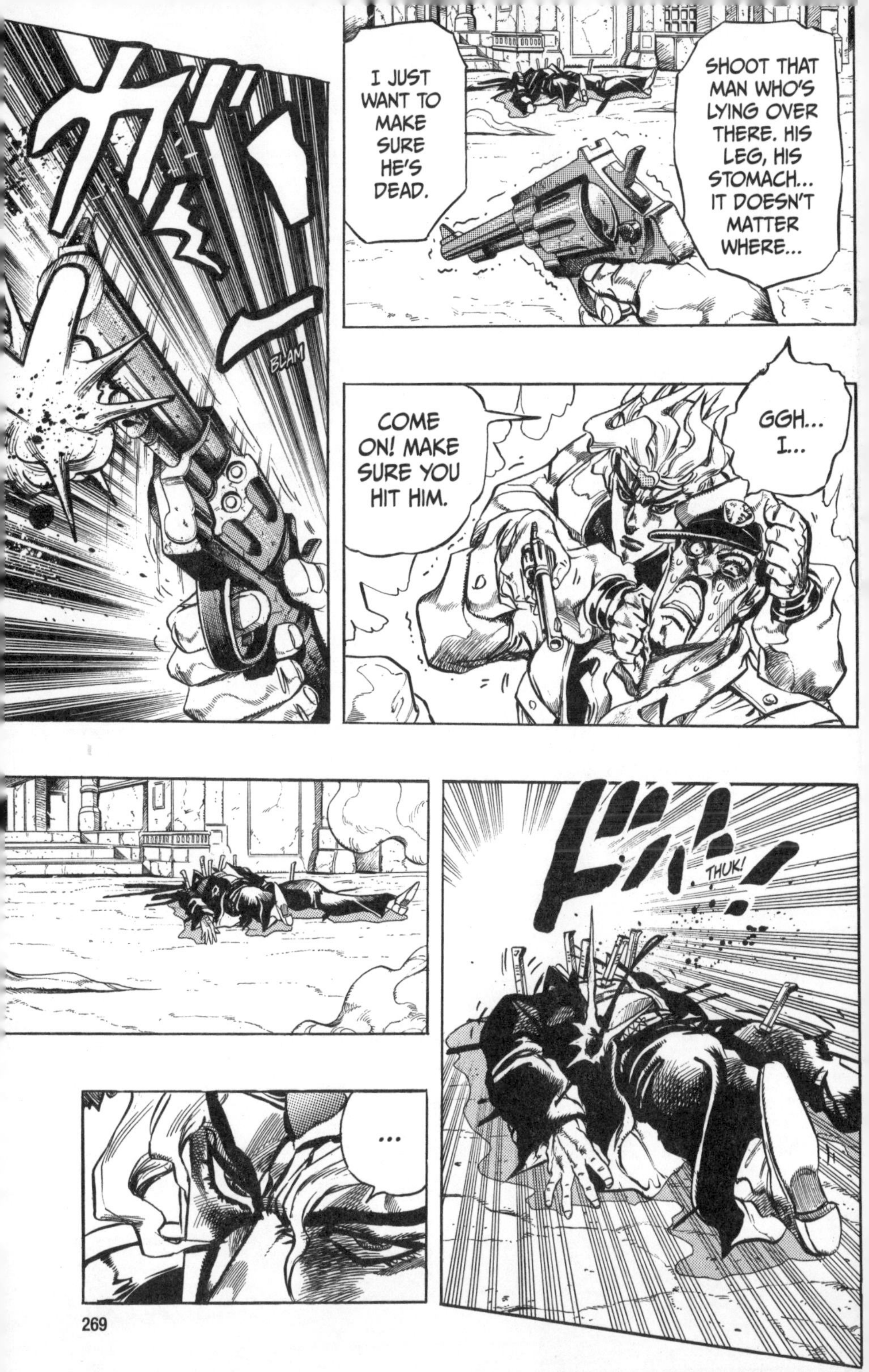
SHOOT THAT MAN WHO'S LYING OVER THERE. HIS LEG, HIS STOMACH... IT DOESN'T MATTER WHERE...
I JUST WANT TO MAKE SURE HE'S DEAD.
GGH... I...
COME ON! MAKE SURE YOU HIT HIM.
BLAM
THUK!
...

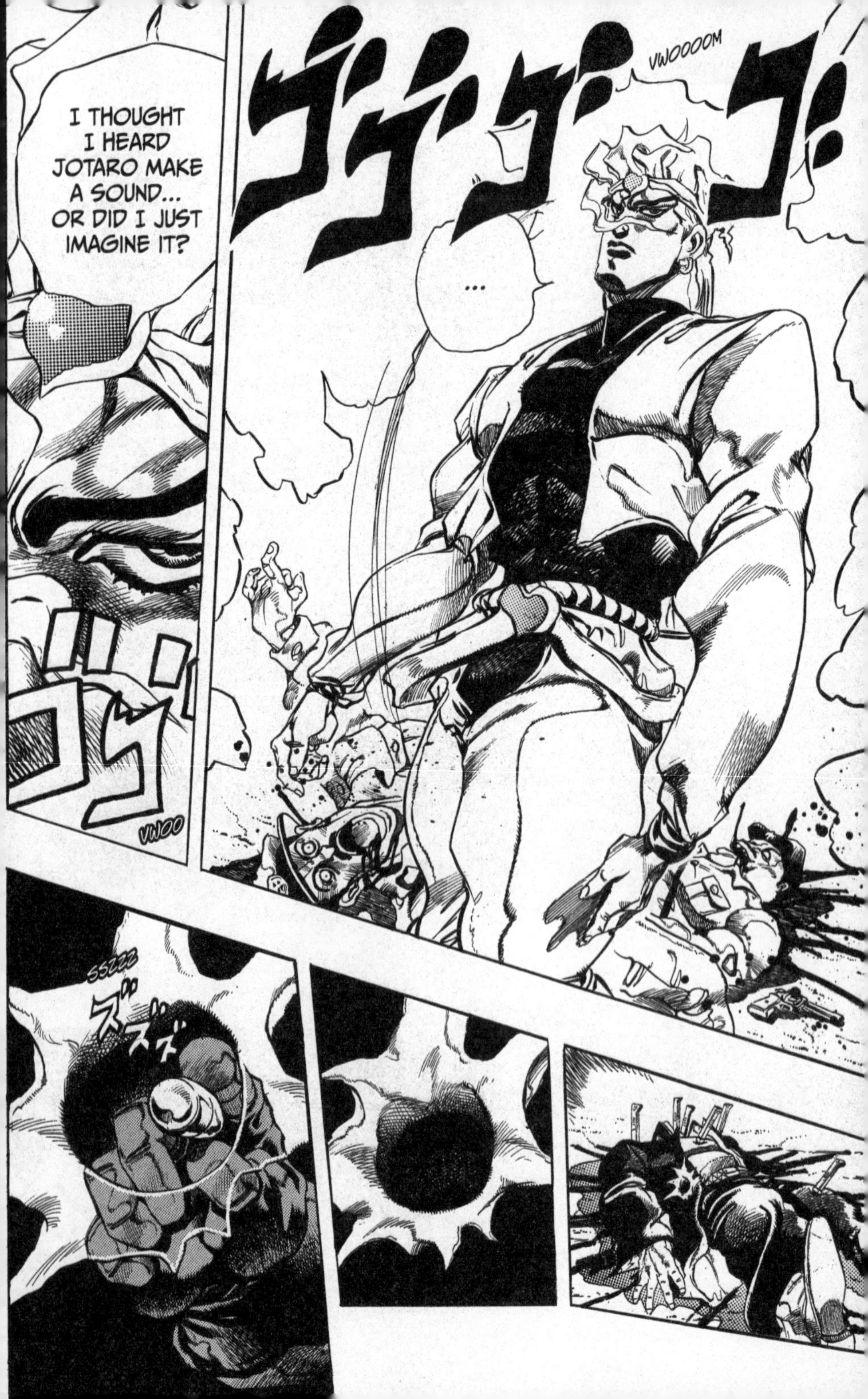
ゴゴゴゴ
VWOOOOM
...
I THOUGHT I HEARD JOTARO MAKE A SOUND... OR DID I JUST IMAGINE IT?
ゴゴ
VWOO
ズズ
SSZZZ

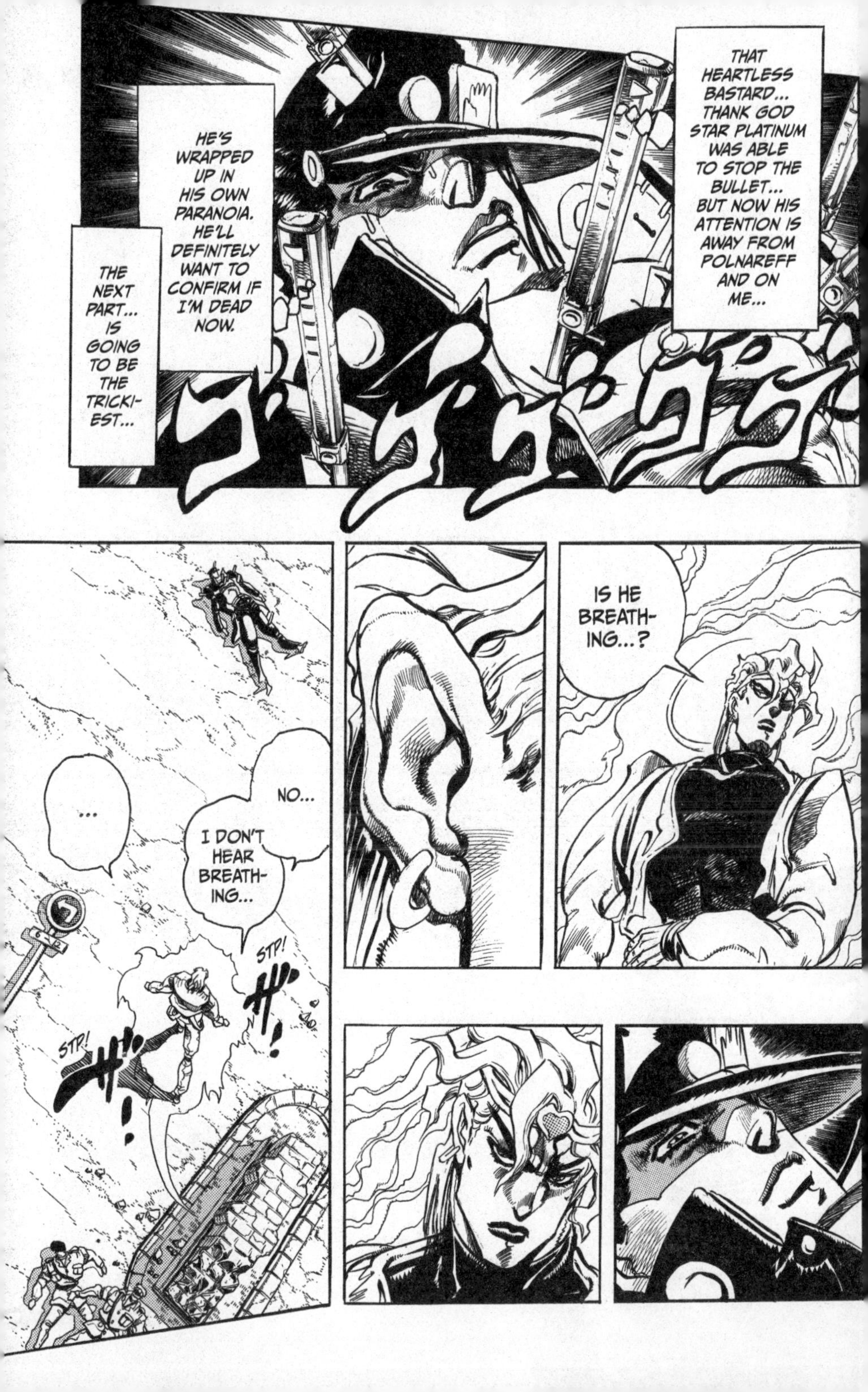

THAT HEARTLESS BASTARD... THANK GOD STAR PLATINUM WAS ABLE TO STOP THE BULLET... BUT NOW HIS ATTENTION IS AWAY FROM POLNAREFF AND ON ME...
HE'S WRAPPED UP IN HIS OWN PARANOIA. HE'LL DEFINITELY WANT TO CONFIRM IF I'M DEAD NOW.
THE NEXT PART... IS GOING TO BE THE TRICKI-EST...
IS HE BREATH-ING...?
NO...
I DON'T HEAR BREATH-ING...
...
STP!
STP!

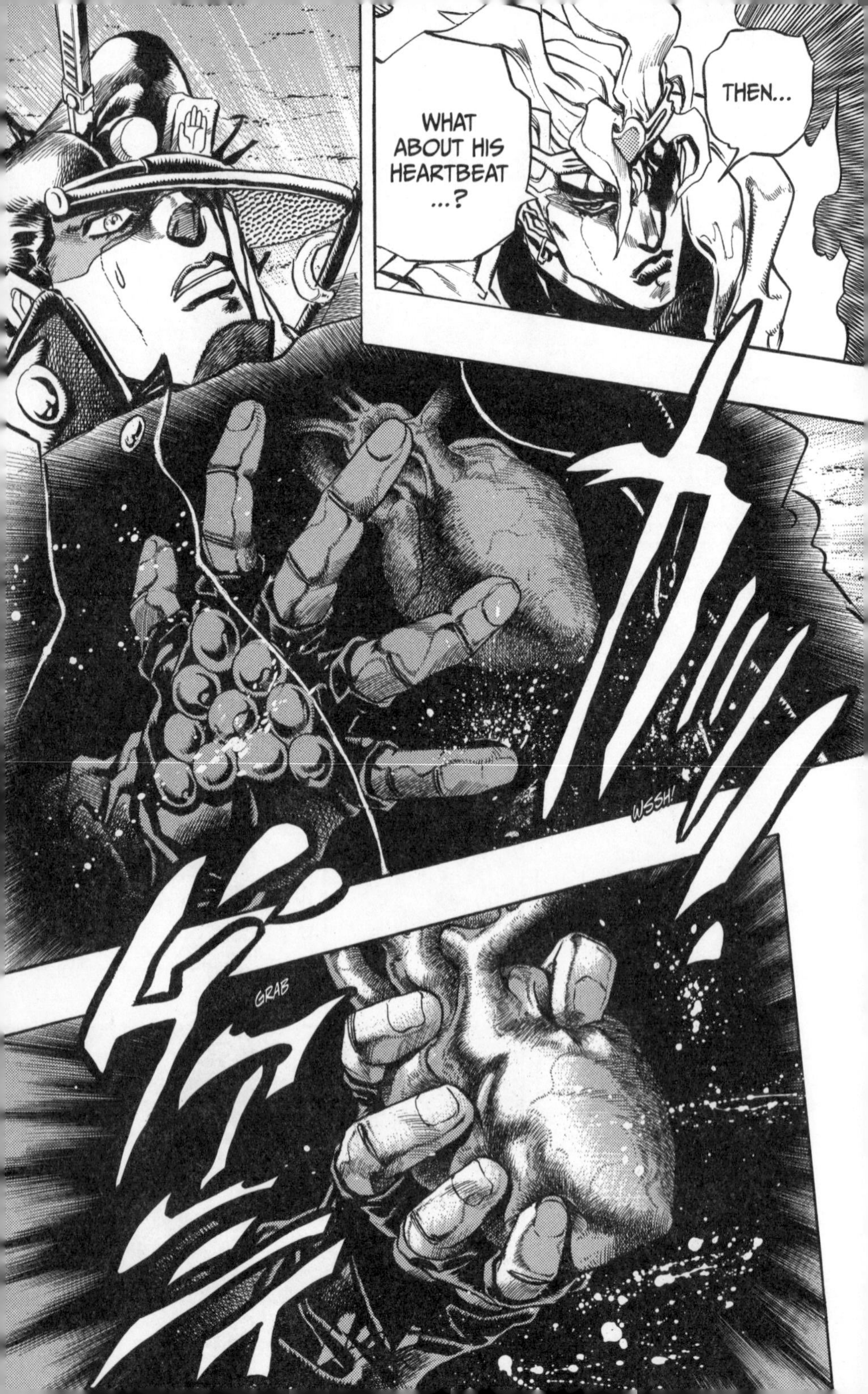
THEN...
WHAT ABOUT HIS HEARTBEAT ...?
WSSH!
GRAB

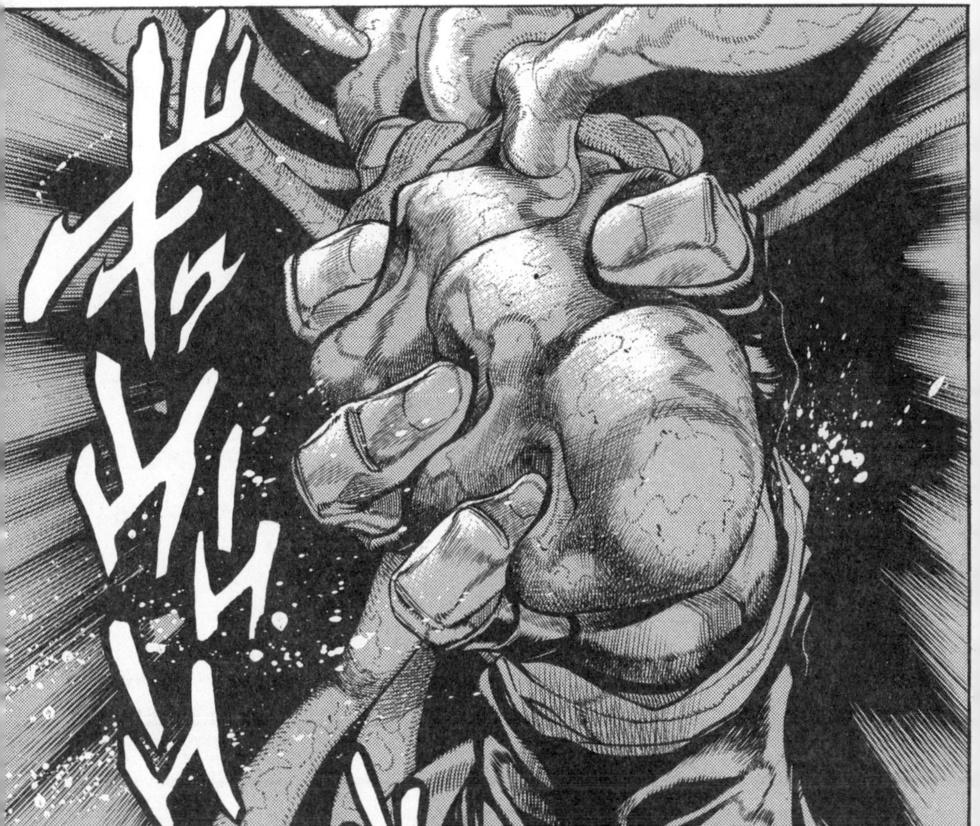
SQUEEZE
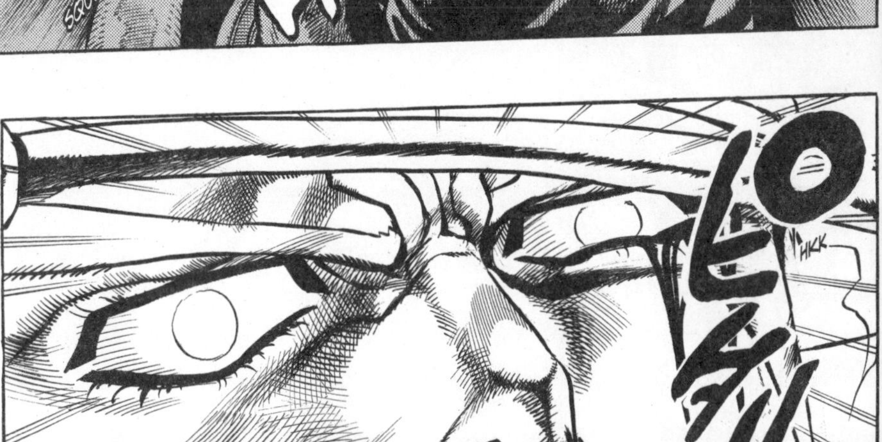
HKK

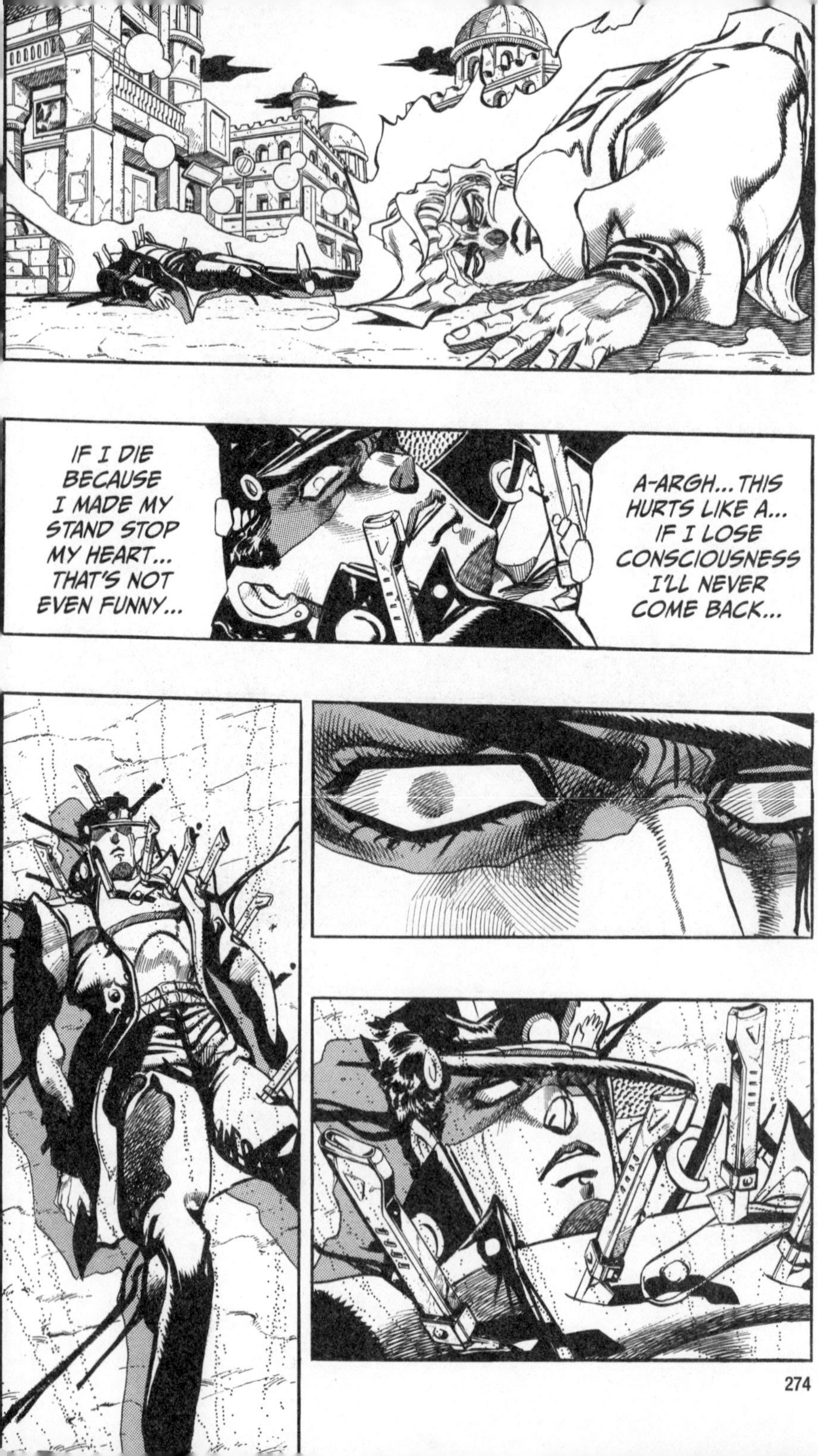
A-ARGH...THIS HURTS LIKE A... IF I LOSE CONSCIOUSNESS I'LL NEVER COME BACK...
IF I DIE BECAUSE I MADE MY STAND STOP MY HEART... THAT'S NOT EVEN FUNNY...

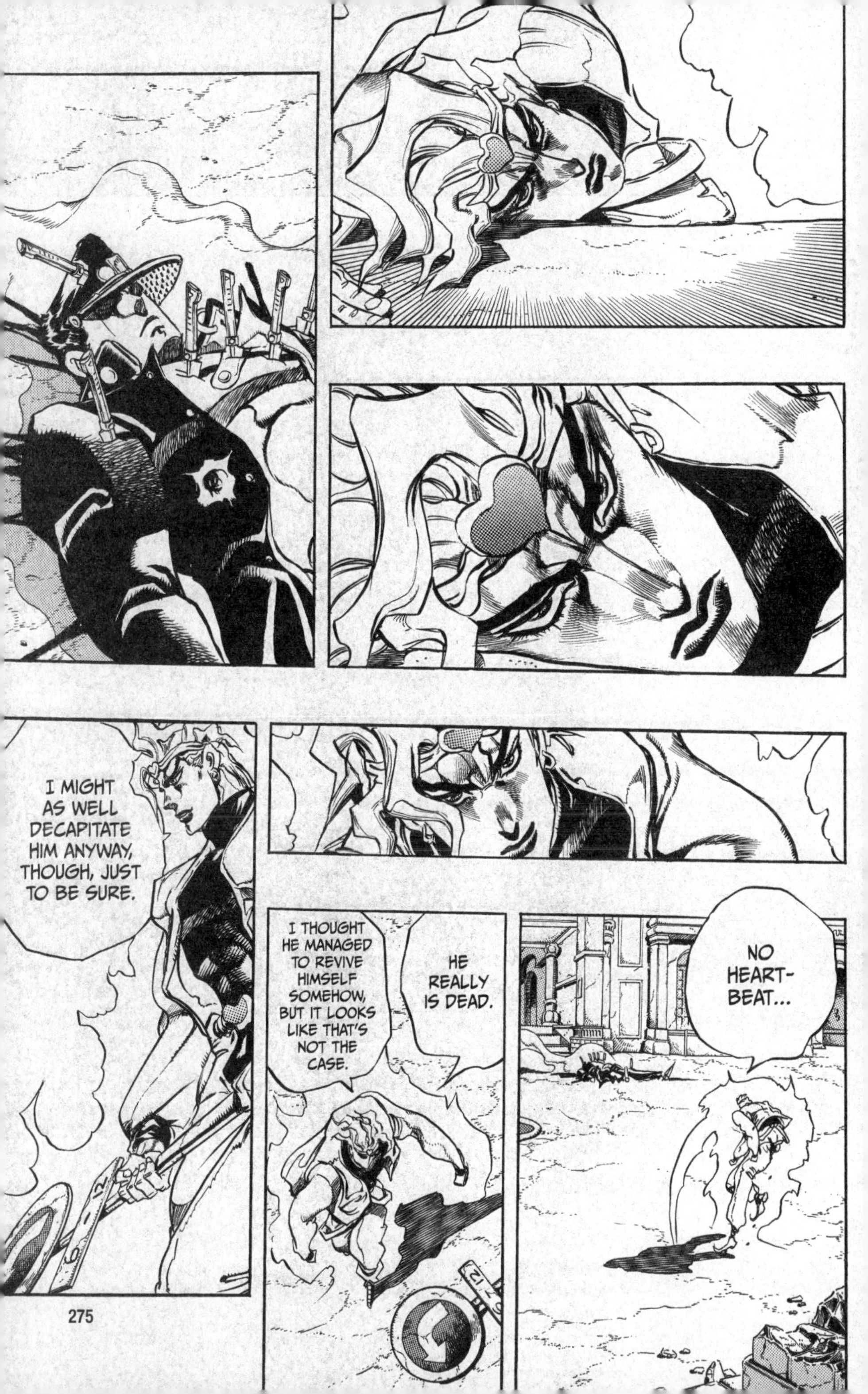
NO HEART-BEAT...
HE REALLY IS DEAD.
I THOUGHT HE MANAGED TO REVIVE HIMSELF SOMEHOW, BUT IT LOOKS LIKE THAT'S NOT THE CASE.
I MIGHT AS WELL DECAPITATE HIM ANYWAY, THOUGH, JUST TO BE SURE.

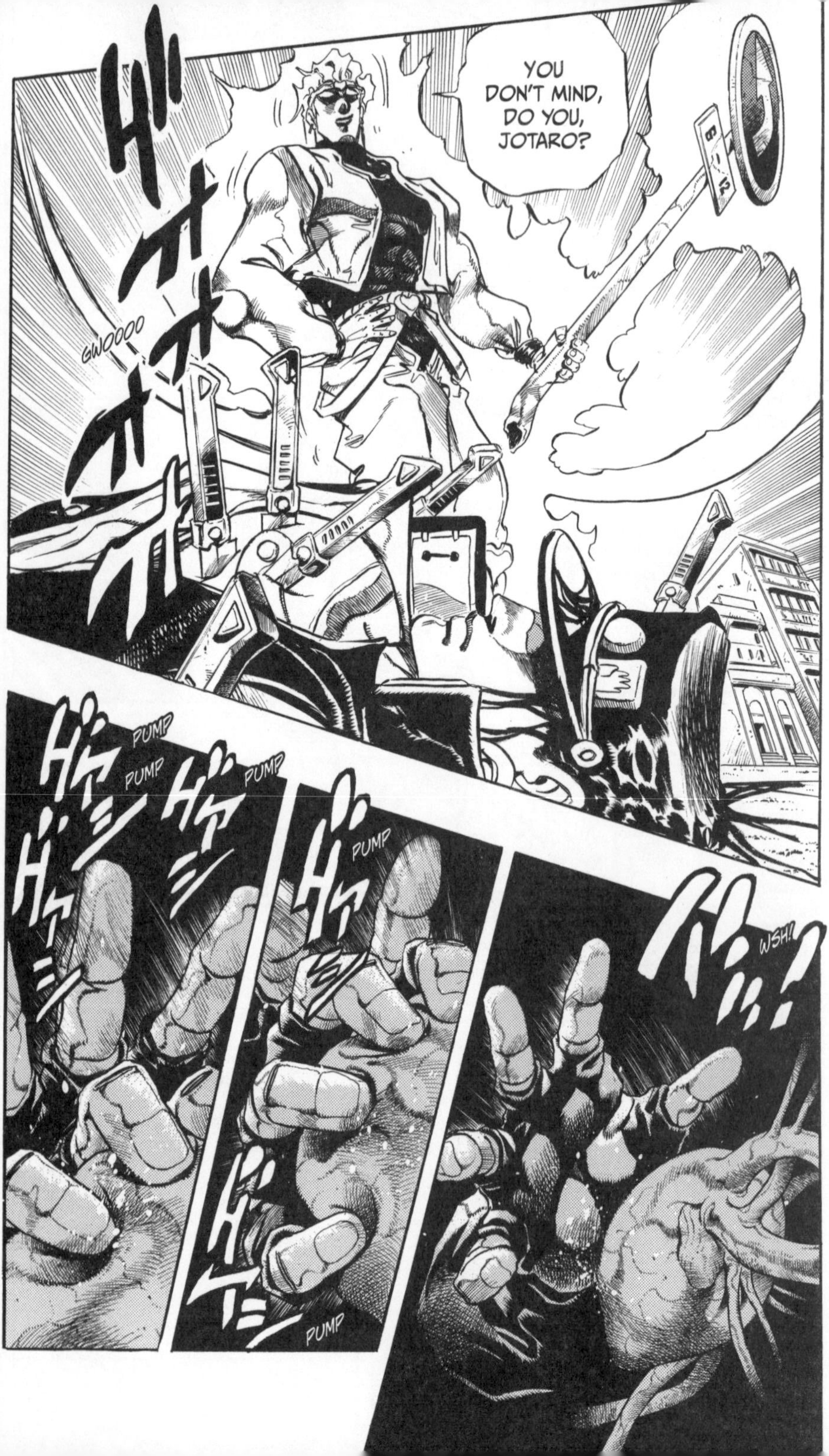
YOU DON'T MIND, DO YOU, JOTARO?
GWOOOO
WSH!
PUMP
PUMP
PUMP
PUMP
PUMP

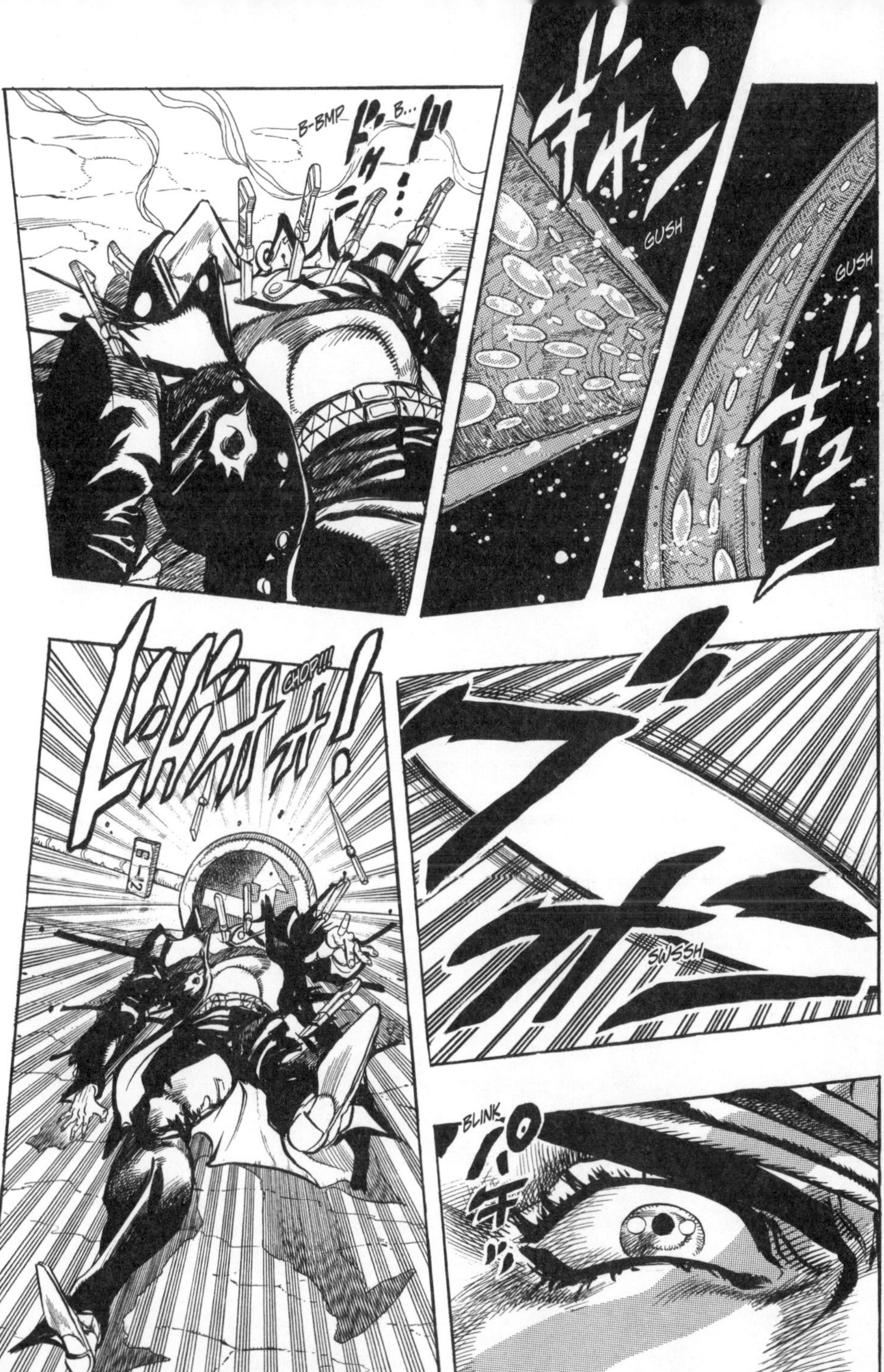
GUSH
GUSH
B-BMP
B...
SWSSH
BLINK
CHOP!!!

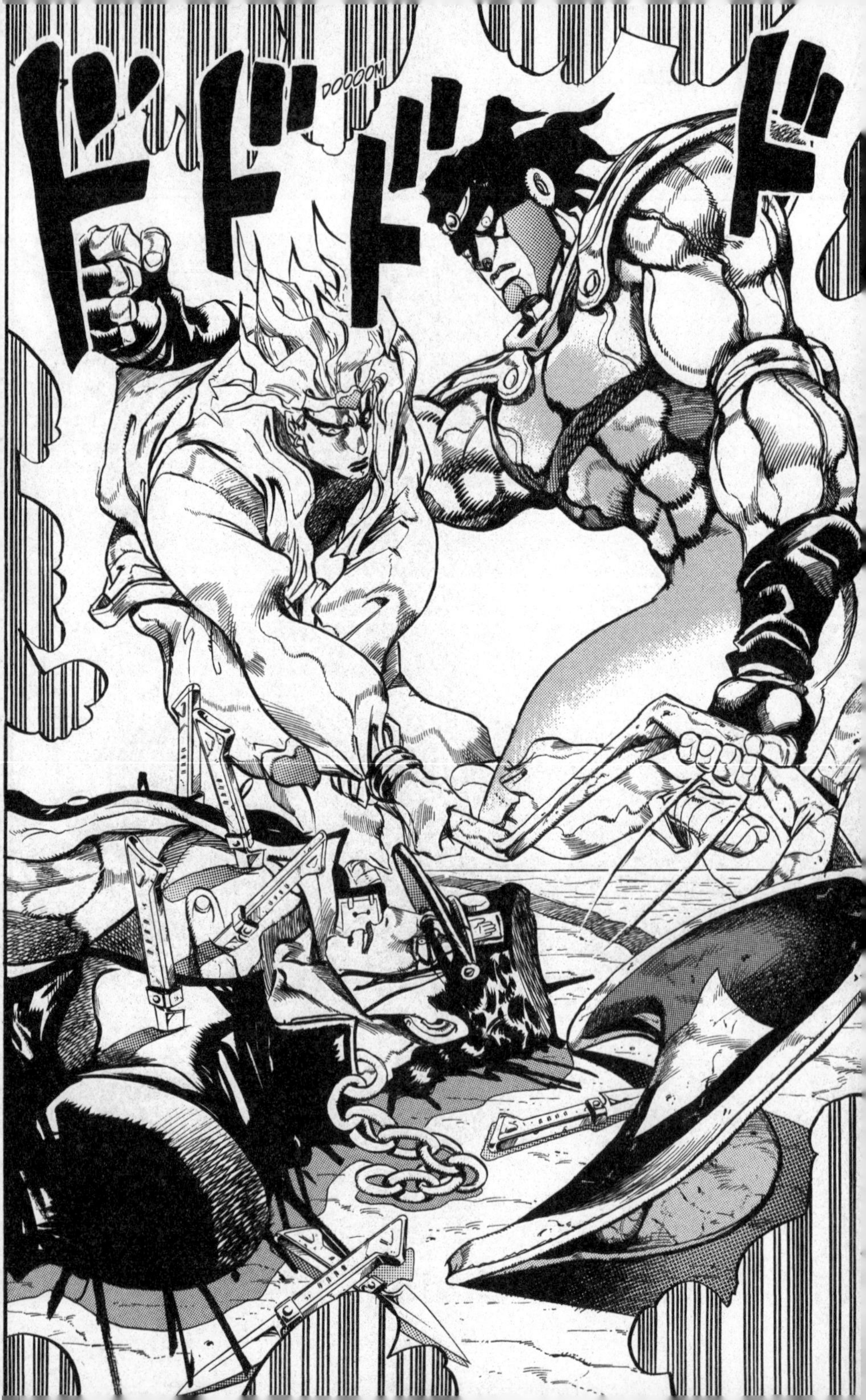
ドドドドド
DOOOOM

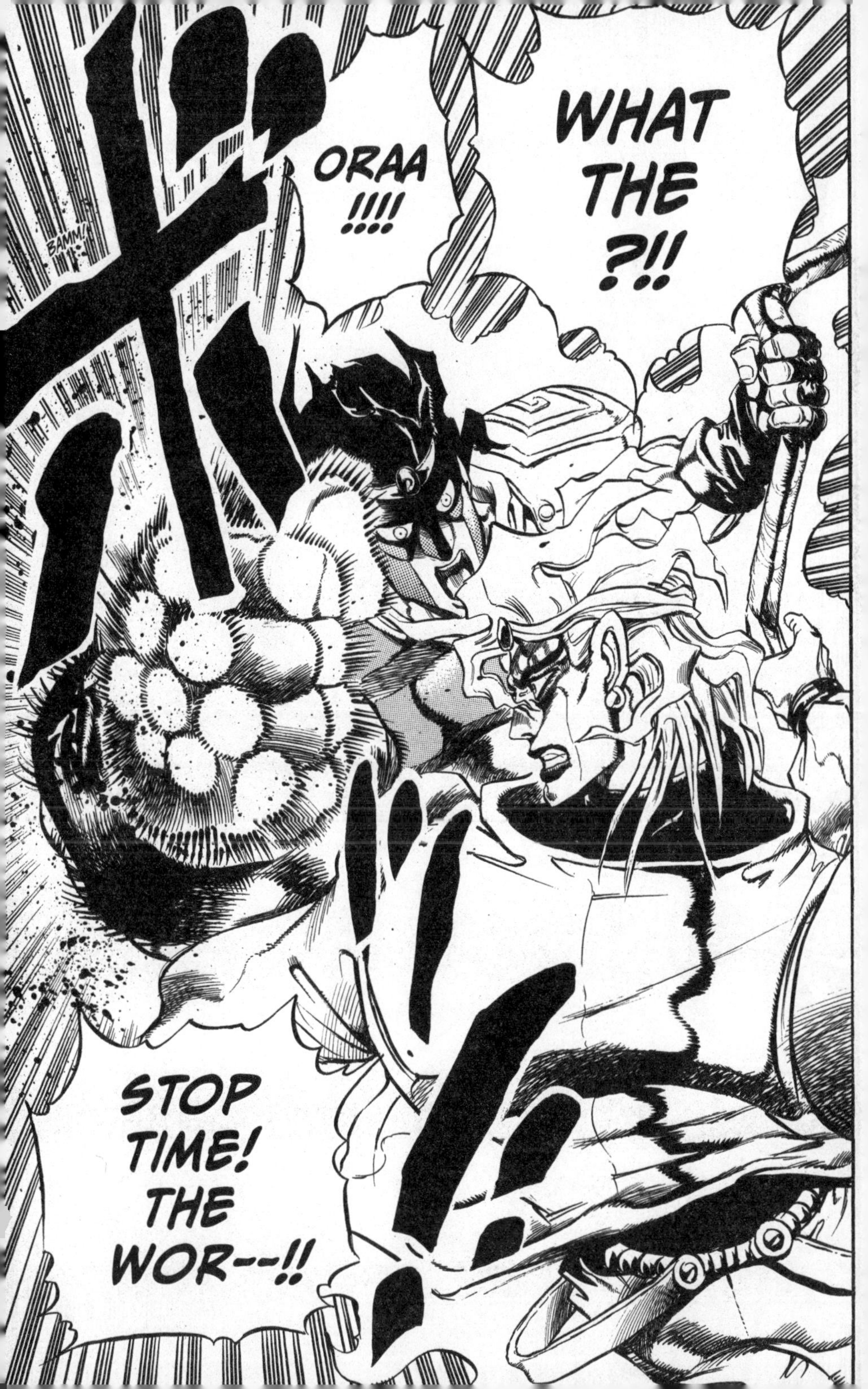

WHAT THE ?!!
ORAA !!!!
BAMM!
STOP TIME! THE WOR--!!

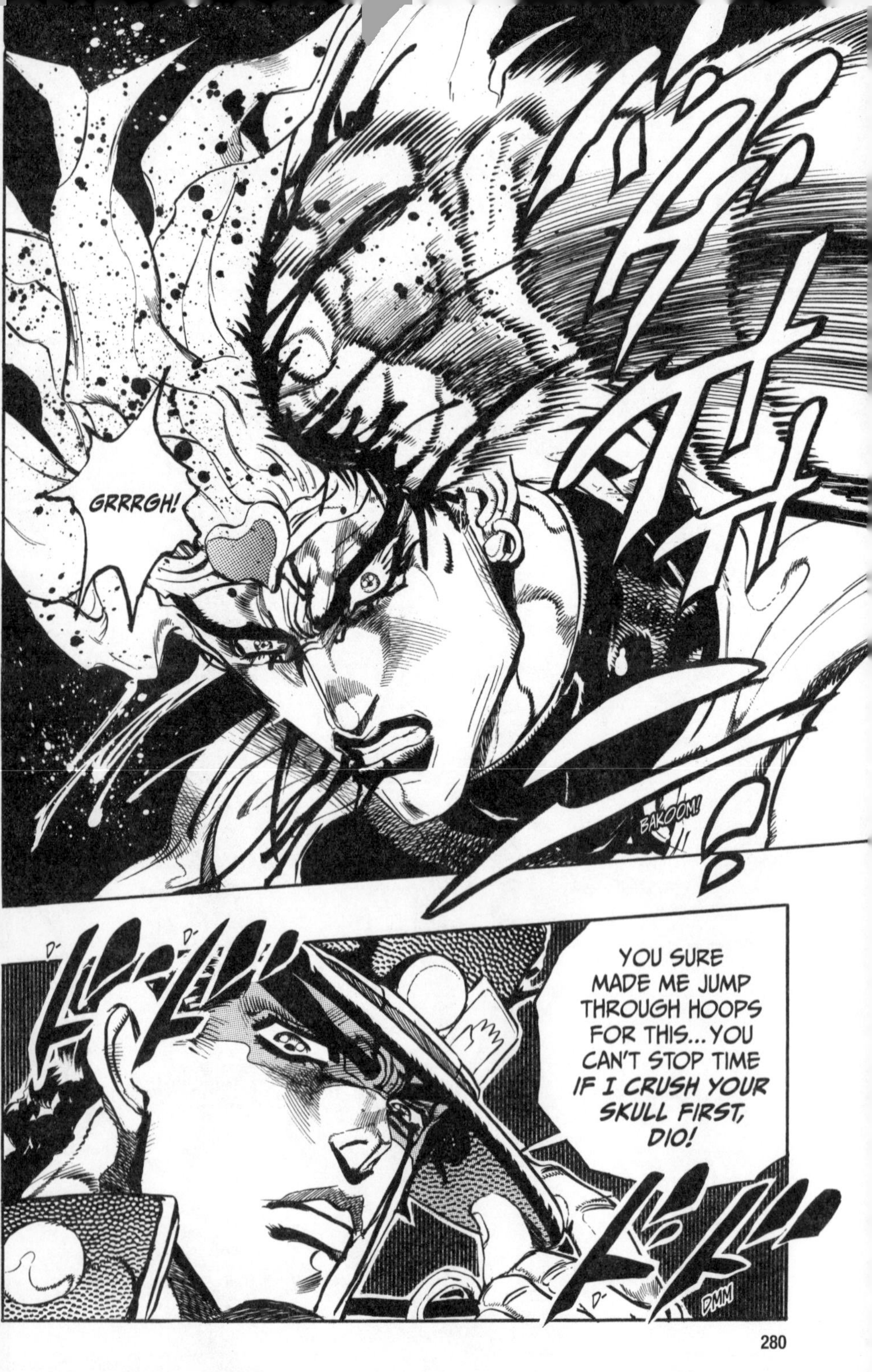
GRRRGH!
BAKOOM!
D-
D-
YOU SURE MADE ME JUMP THROUGH HOOPS FOR THIS... YOU CAN'T STOP TIME *IF I CRUSH YOUR SKULL FIRST, DIO!*
D-
DMM

CHAPTER 148: DIO's World PART 15

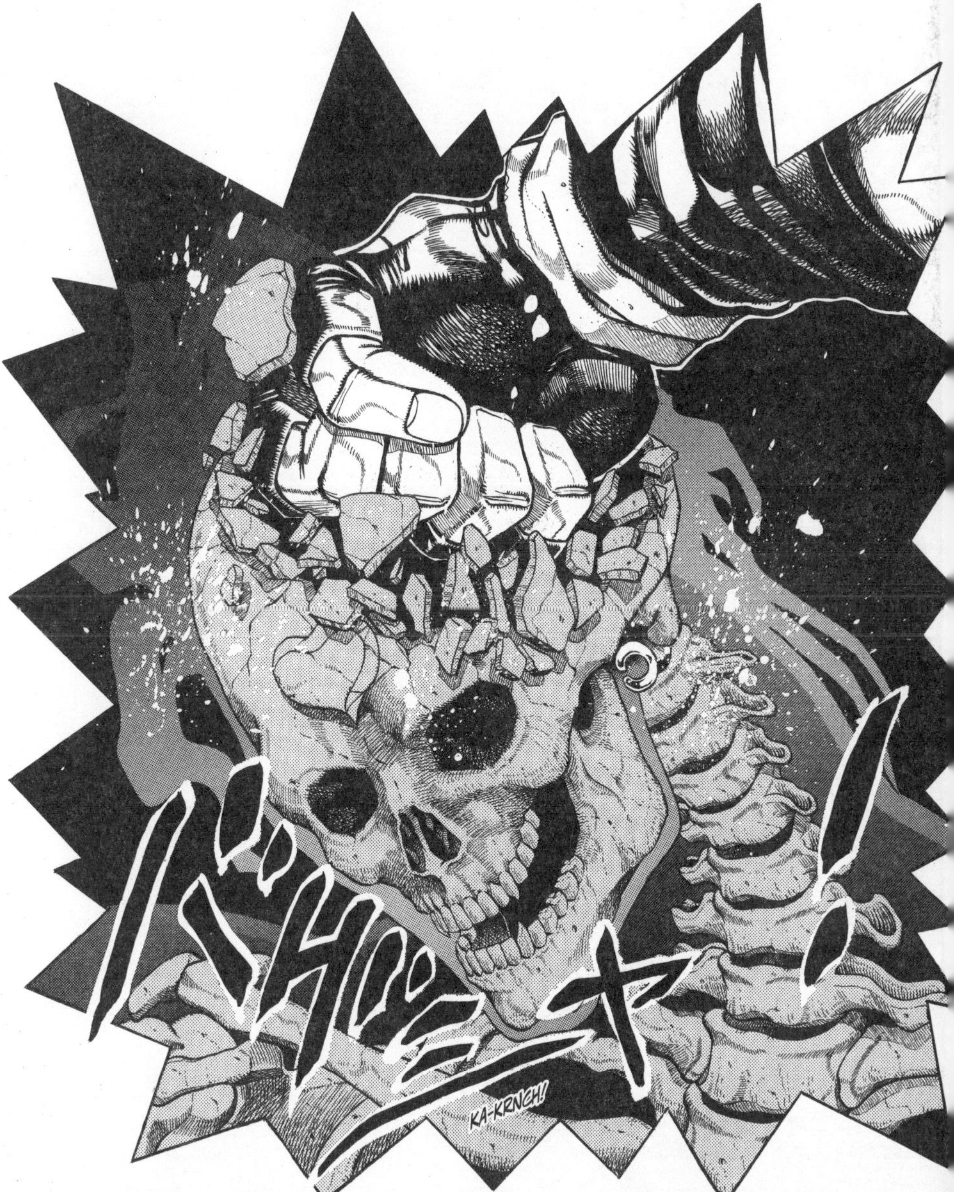

KA-KRNCH!

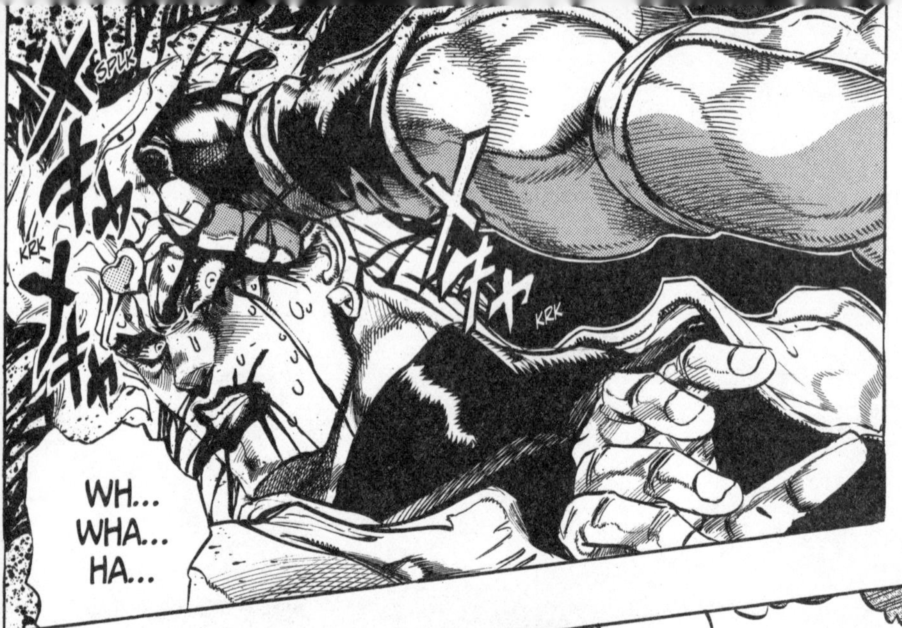
SPLK
KRK
KRK
WH... WHA... HA...
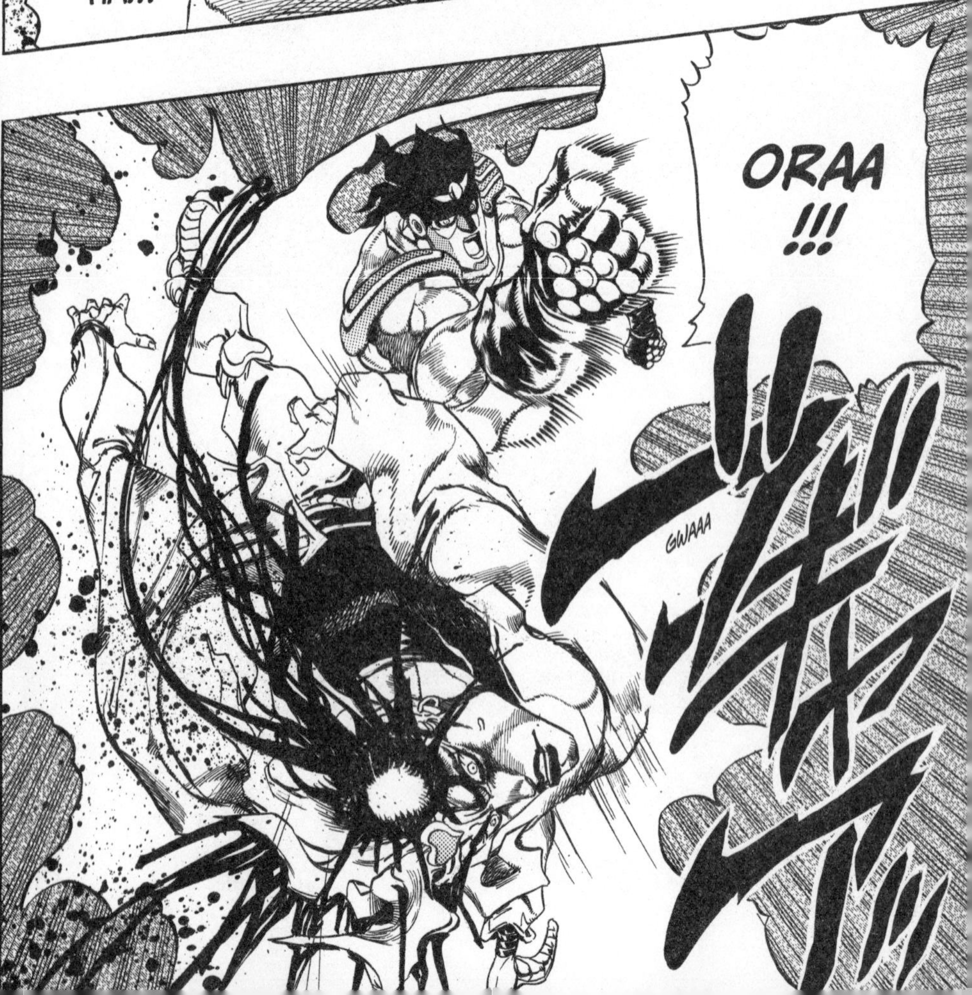
ORAA !!!
GWAAA

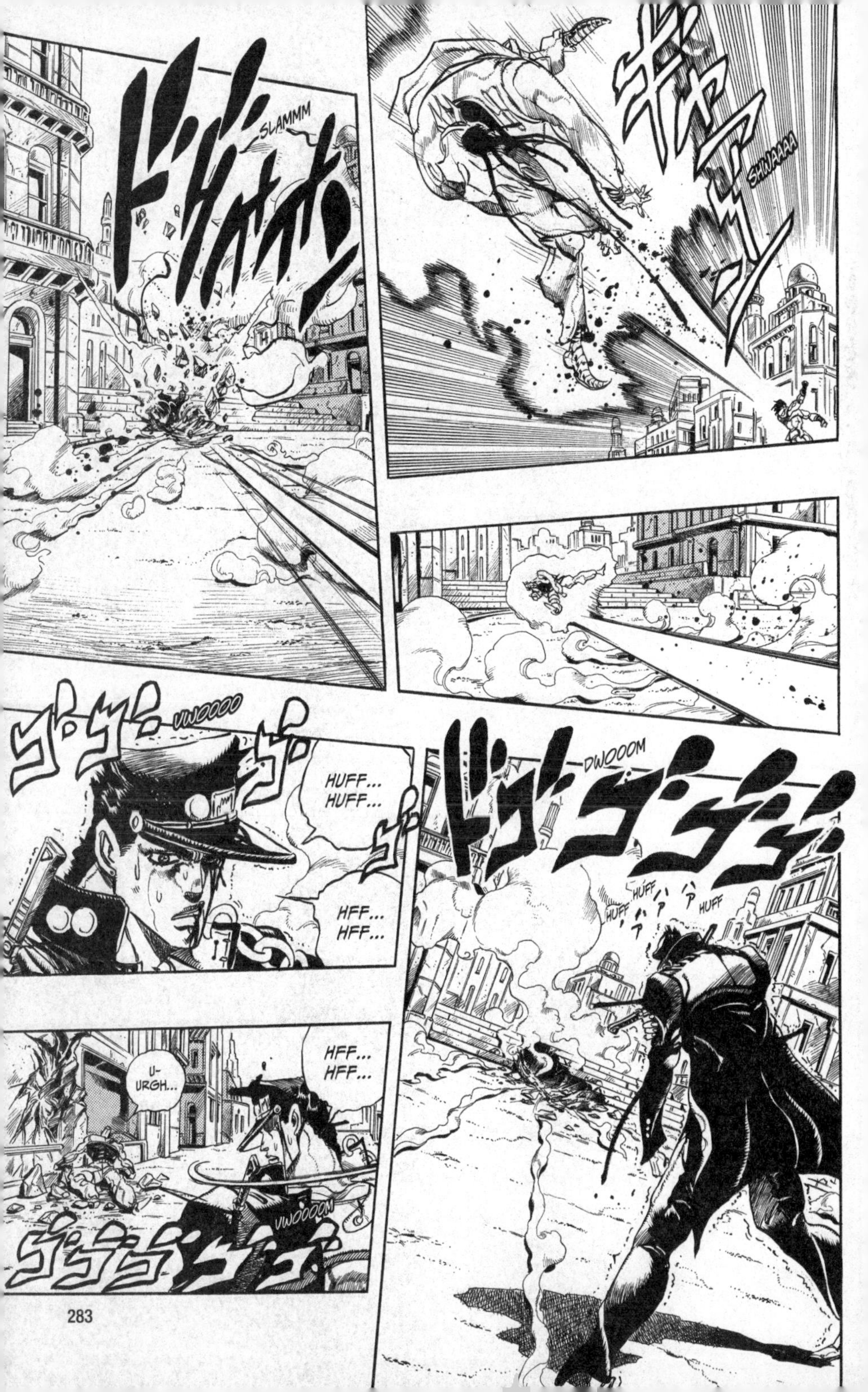
SHWAAAA
SLAMMM
DWOOOM
HUFF
HUFF
HUFF
VWOOOO
HUFF... HUFF...
HFF... HFF...
HFF... HFF...
U-URGH...
VWOOOOM

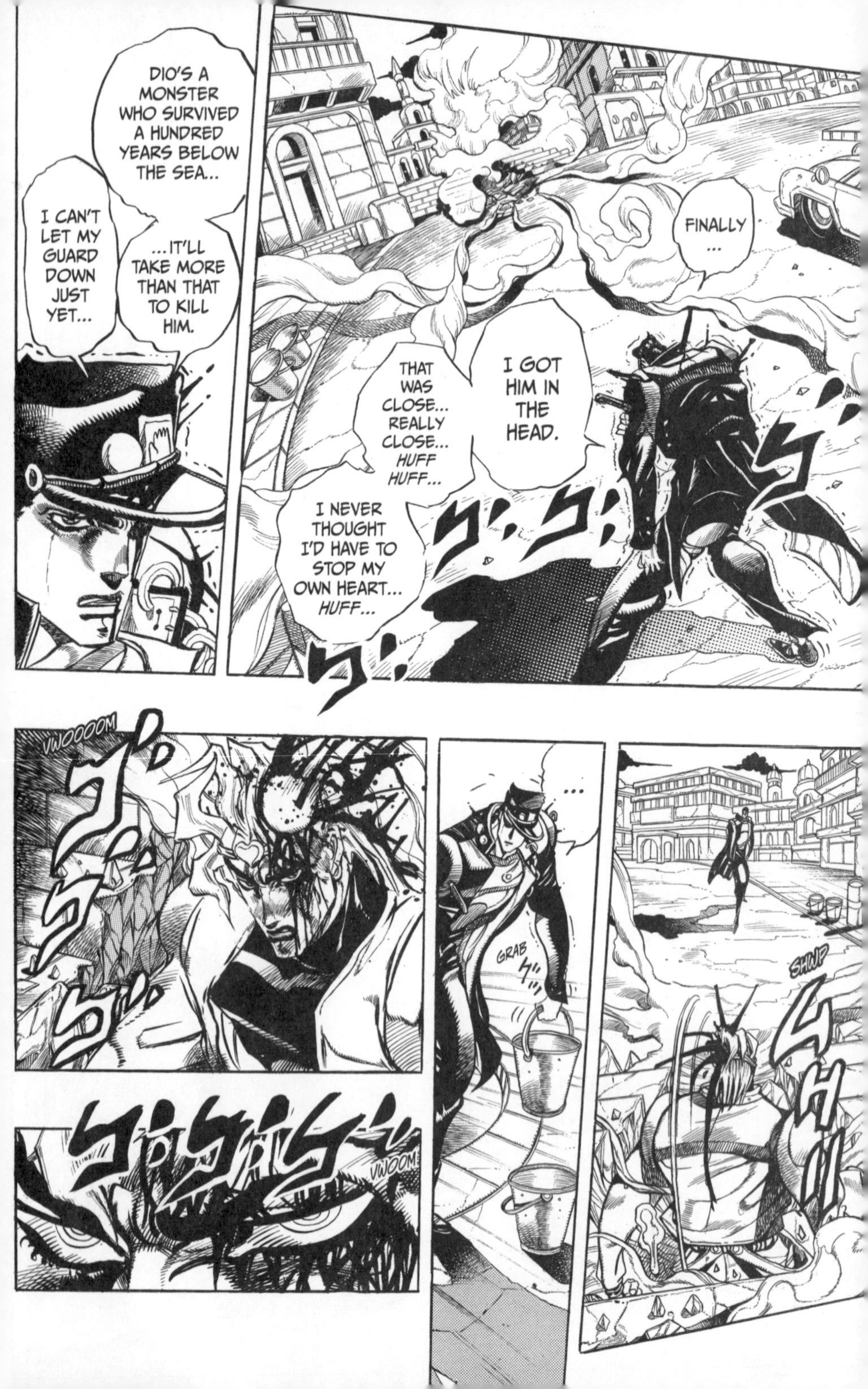
FINALLY ...
I GOT HIM IN THE HEAD.
THAT WAS CLOSE... REALLY CLOSE... *HUFF HUFF...*
I NEVER THOUGHT I'D HAVE TO STOP MY OWN HEART... *HUFF...*
DIO'S A MONSTER WHO SURVIVED A HUNDRED YEARS BELOW THE SEA...
...IT'LL TAKE MORE THAN THAT TO KILL HIM.
I CAN'T LET MY GUARD DOWN JUST YET...
SHWP
...
GRAB
VWOOOOM
VWOOM

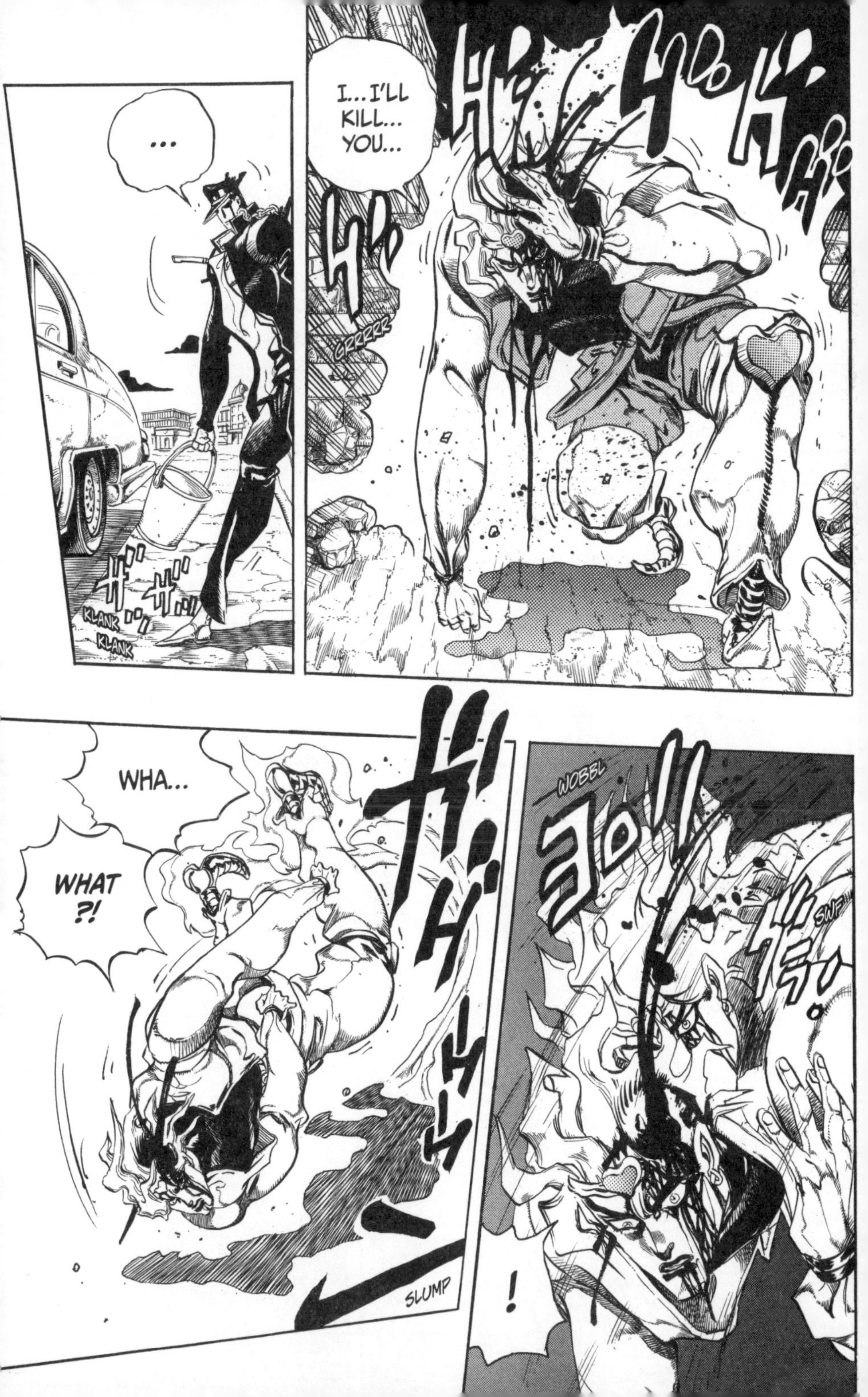
I...I'LL KILL... YOU...
GRRRRR
...
KLANK
KLANK
WOBBL
SWF
!
WHA...
WHAT ?!
SLUMP

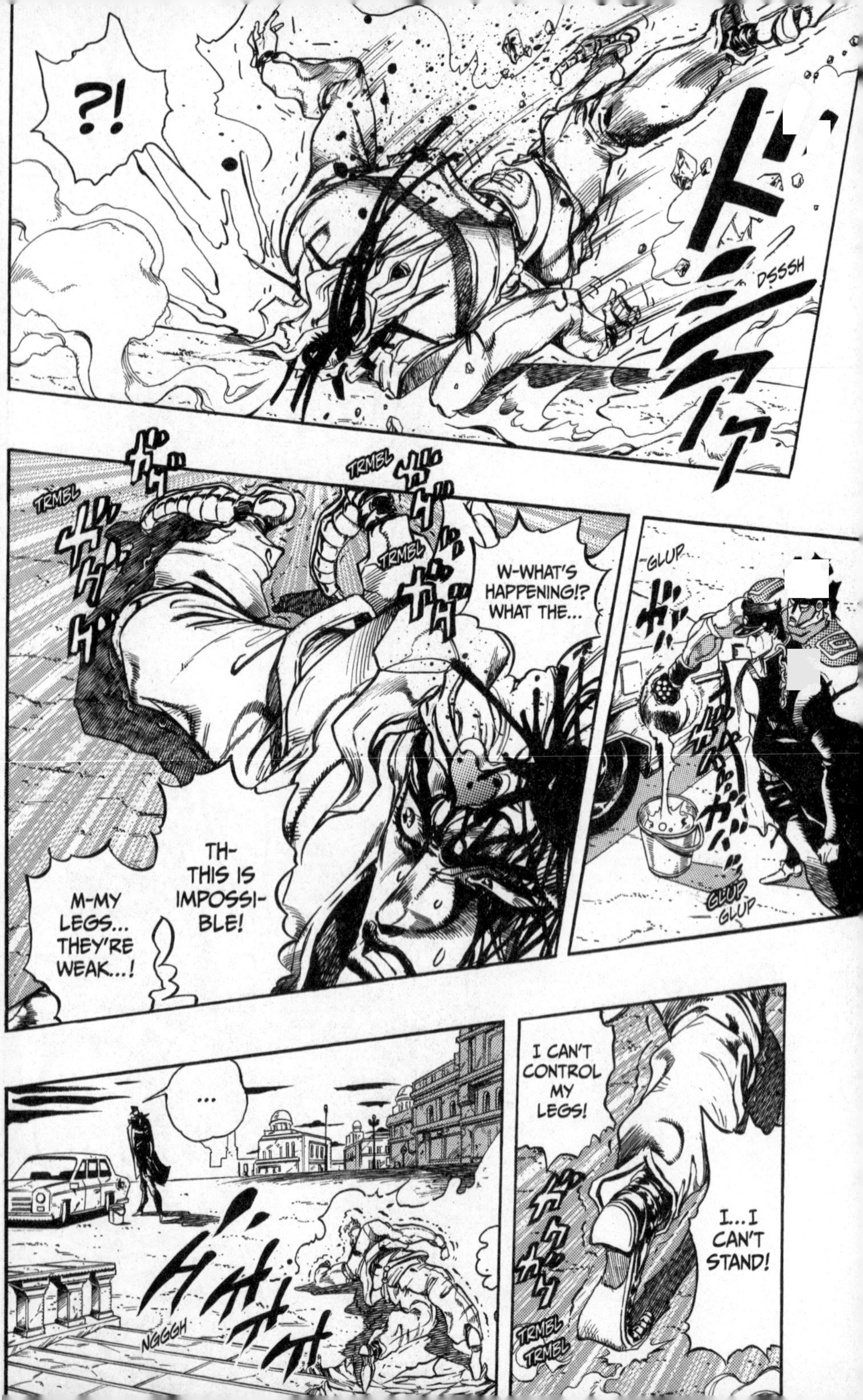
DSSSH
?!
GLUP
GLUP GLUP
TRMBL
TRMBL
W-WHAT'S HAPPENING!? WHAT THE...
TRMBL
TH- THIS IS IMPOSSIBLE!
M-MY LEGS... THEY'RE WEAK...!
I CAN'T CONTROL MY LEGS!
I...I CAN'T STAND!
TRMBL TRMBL
...
NGGGH

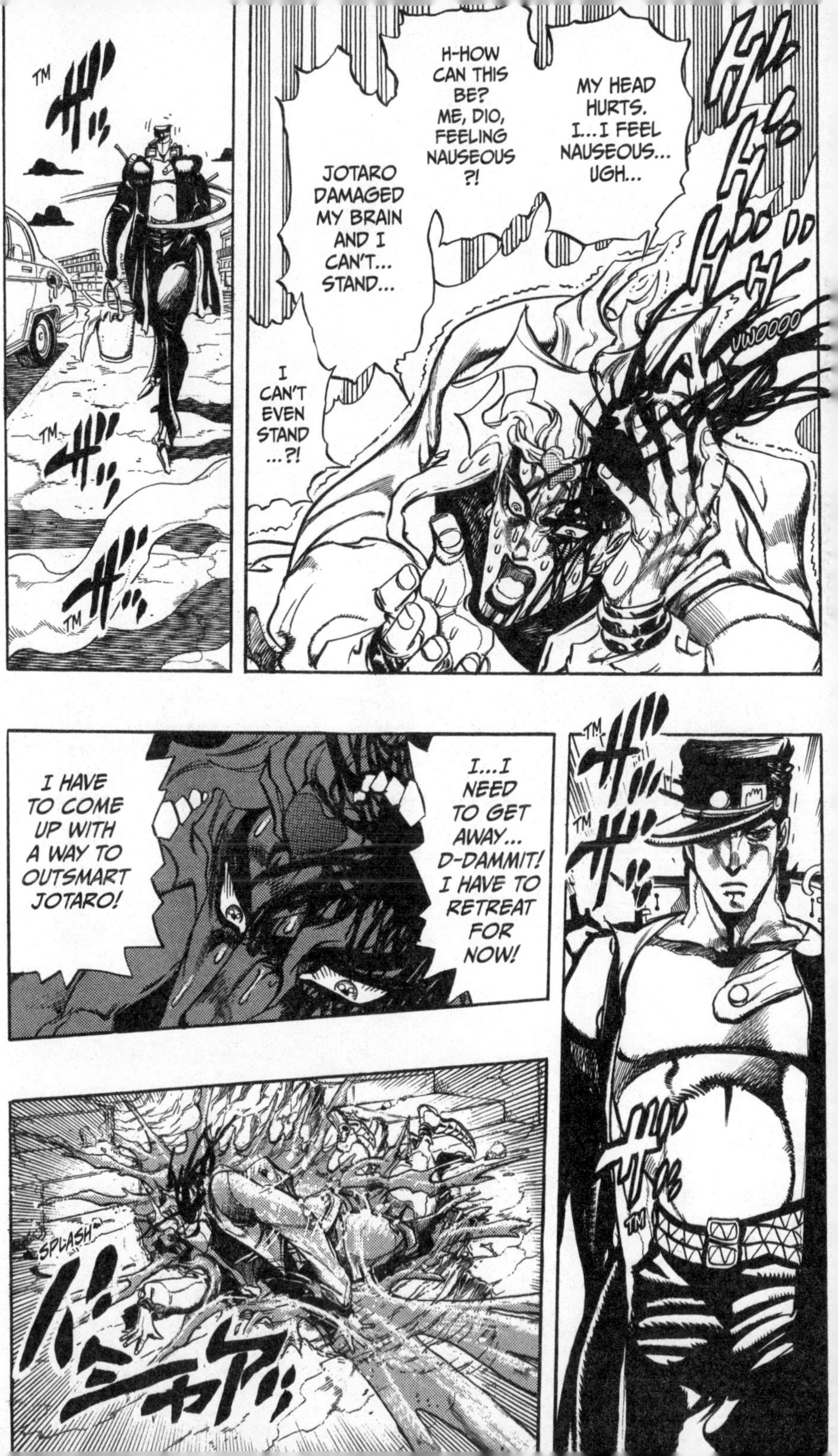

MY HEAD HURTS. I...I FEEL NAUSEOUS... UGH...
H-HOW CAN THIS BE? ME, DIO, FEELING NAUSEOUS?!
JOTARO DAMAGED MY BRAIN AND I CAN'T... STAND...
UWOOOO
I CAN'T EVEN STAND...?!
I...I NEED TO GET AWAY... D-DAMMIT! I HAVE TO RETREAT FOR NOW!
I HAVE TO COME UP WITH A WAY TO OUTSMART JOTARO!
SPLASH

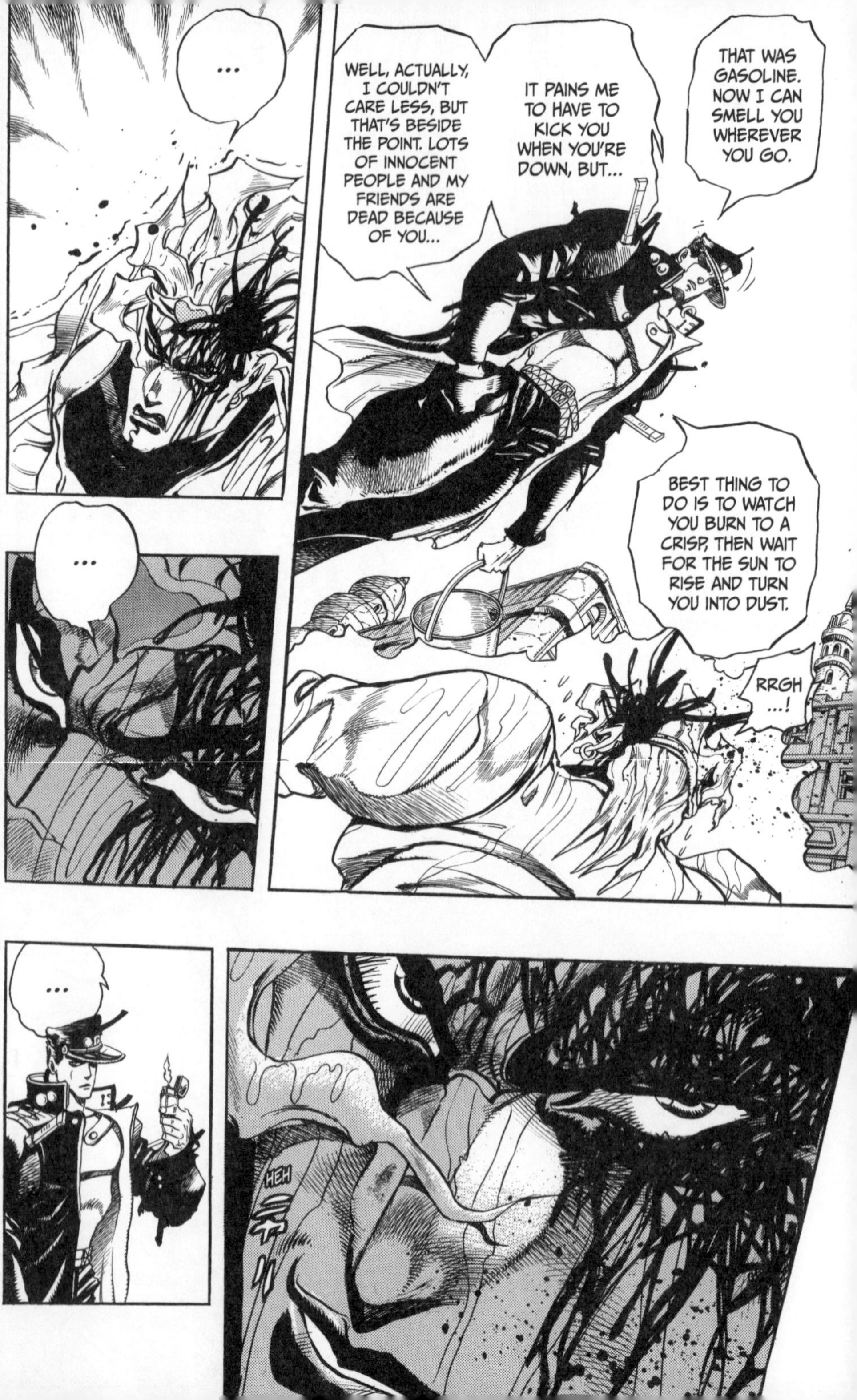
THAT WAS GASOLINE. NOW I CAN SMELL YOU WHEREVER YOU GO.
IT PAINS ME TO HAVE TO KICK YOU WHEN YOU'RE DOWN, BUT...
WELL, ACTUALLY, I COULDN'T CARE LESS, BUT THAT'S BESIDE THE POINT. LOTS OF INNOCENT PEOPLE AND MY FRIENDS ARE DEAD BECAUSE OF YOU...
BEST THING TO DO IS TO WATCH YOU BURN TO A CRISP, THEN WAIT FOR THE SUN TO RISE AND TURN YOU INTO DUST.
RRGH ...!
...
...
HEH
...

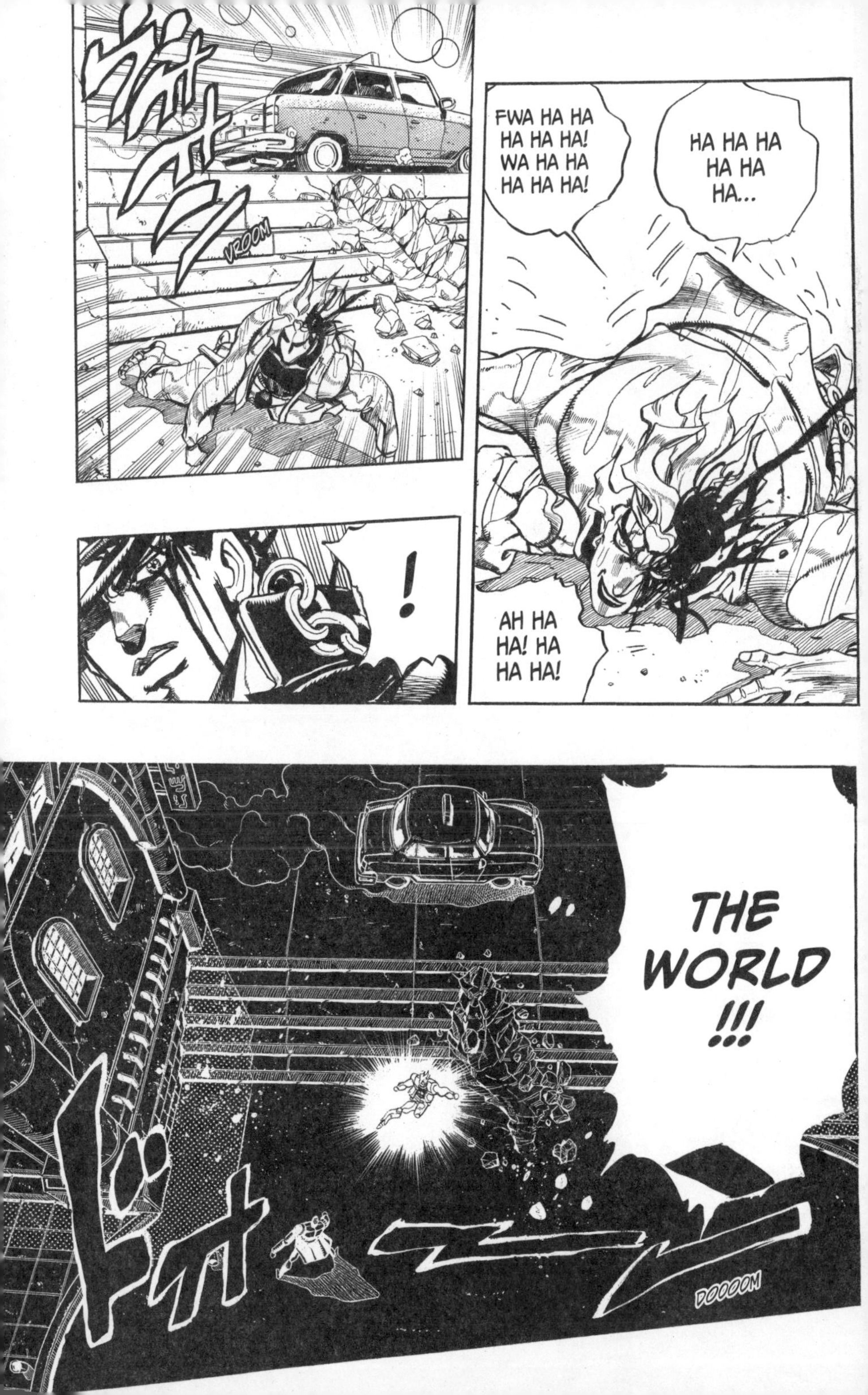
HA HA HA HA HA HA...
FWA HA HA HA HA HA! WA HA HA HA HA HA!
AH HA HA! HA HA HA!
VROOM
!
THE WORLD !!!
DOOOOM

SHF SHF

TWITCH

GRR...
RRRGH...

TWITCH

...

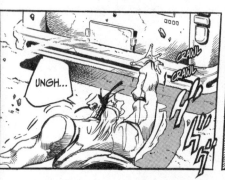

UNGH...

CRAWL
CRAWL

URG...

IF I CAN
JUST MAKE
IT...OVER
THERE...

CRAWL

GGH...

VROOM

AND NOW...
TIME WILL
START
AGAIN...

GGH...

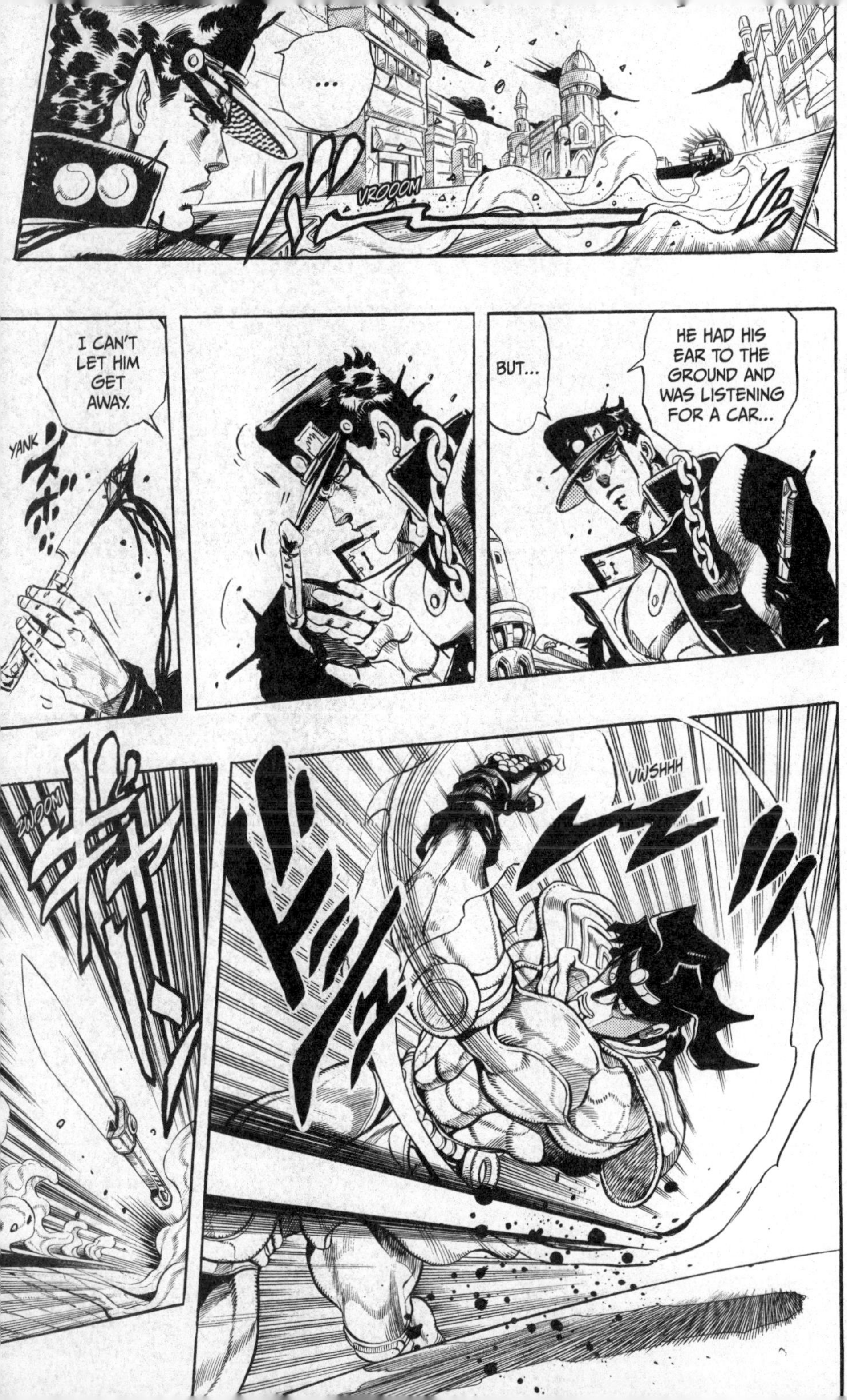
...
VROOOM
HE HAD HIS EAR TO THE GROUND AND WAS LISTENING FOR A CAR...
BUT...
I CAN'T LET HIM GET AWAY.
YANK
VWSHHH
ZWOOM

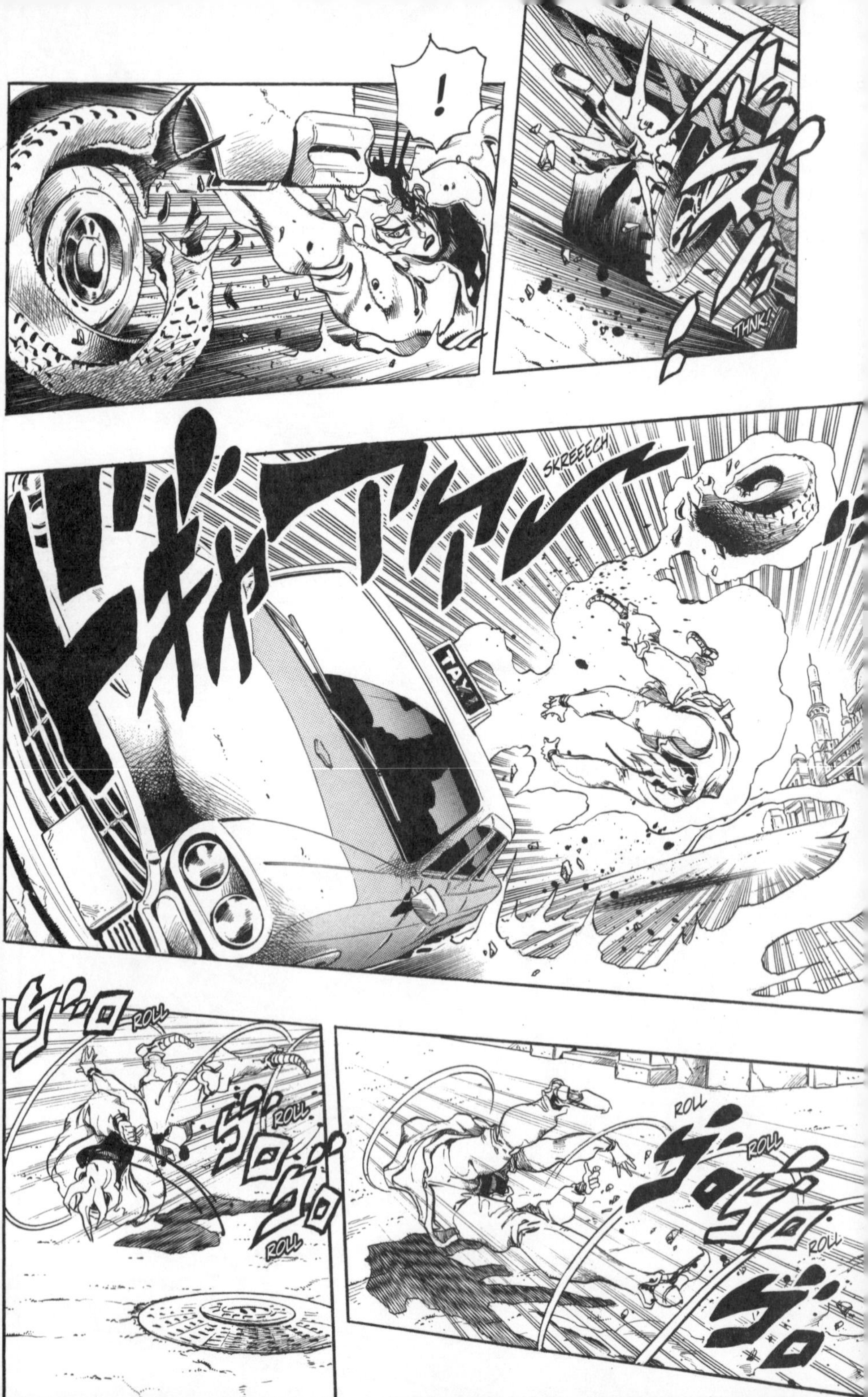

THNK!
!
SKREEECH
ROLL
ROLL
ROLL
ROLL
ROLL
ROLL

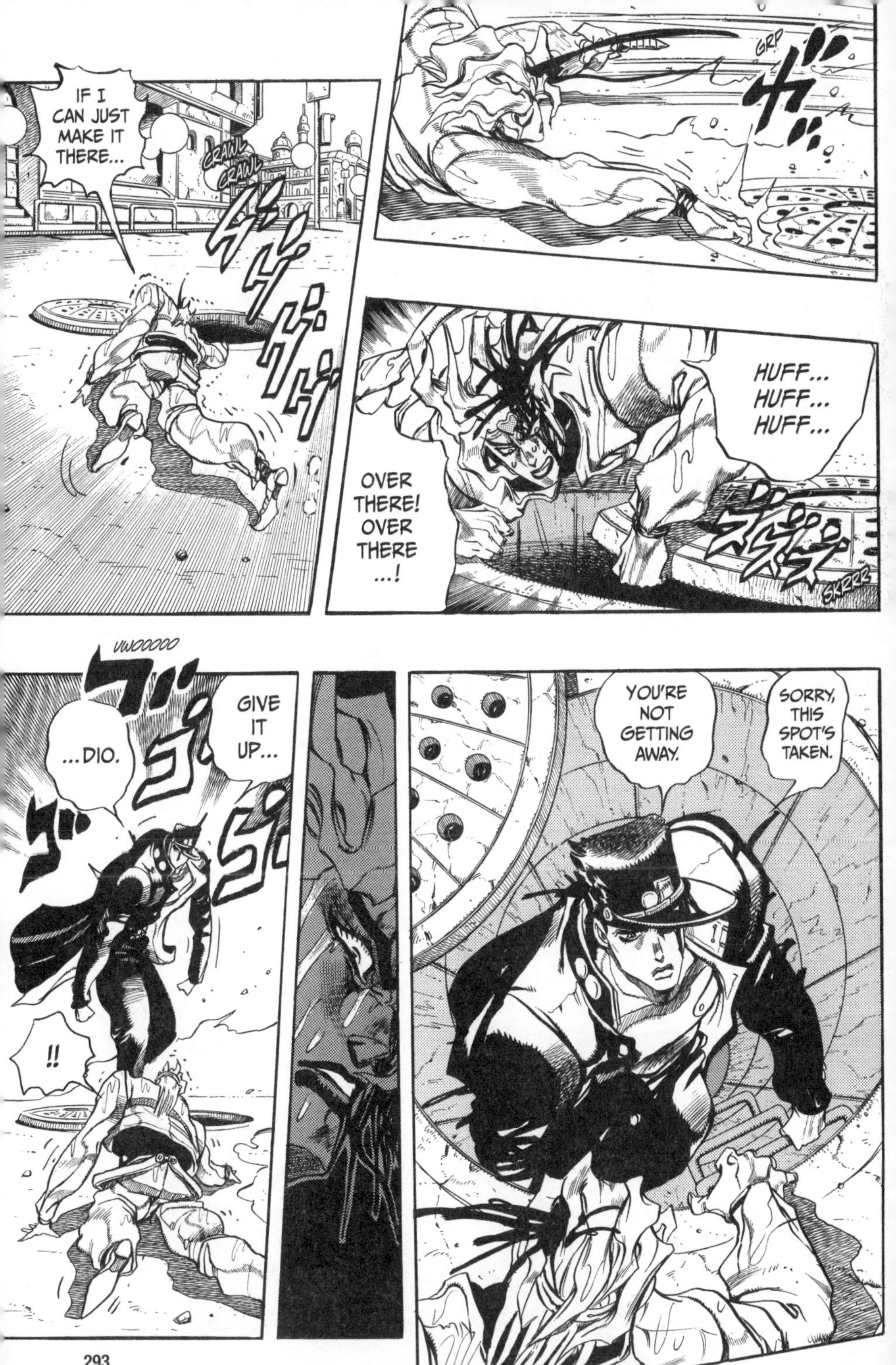
GRP
HUFF... HUFF... HUFF...
SKRRR
OVER THERE! OVER THERE ...!
IF I CAN JUST MAKE IT THERE...
CRAWL CRAWL
SORRY, THIS SPOT'S TAKEN.
YOU'RE NOT GETTING AWAY.
VWOOOOO
GIVE IT UP...
...DIO.
!!

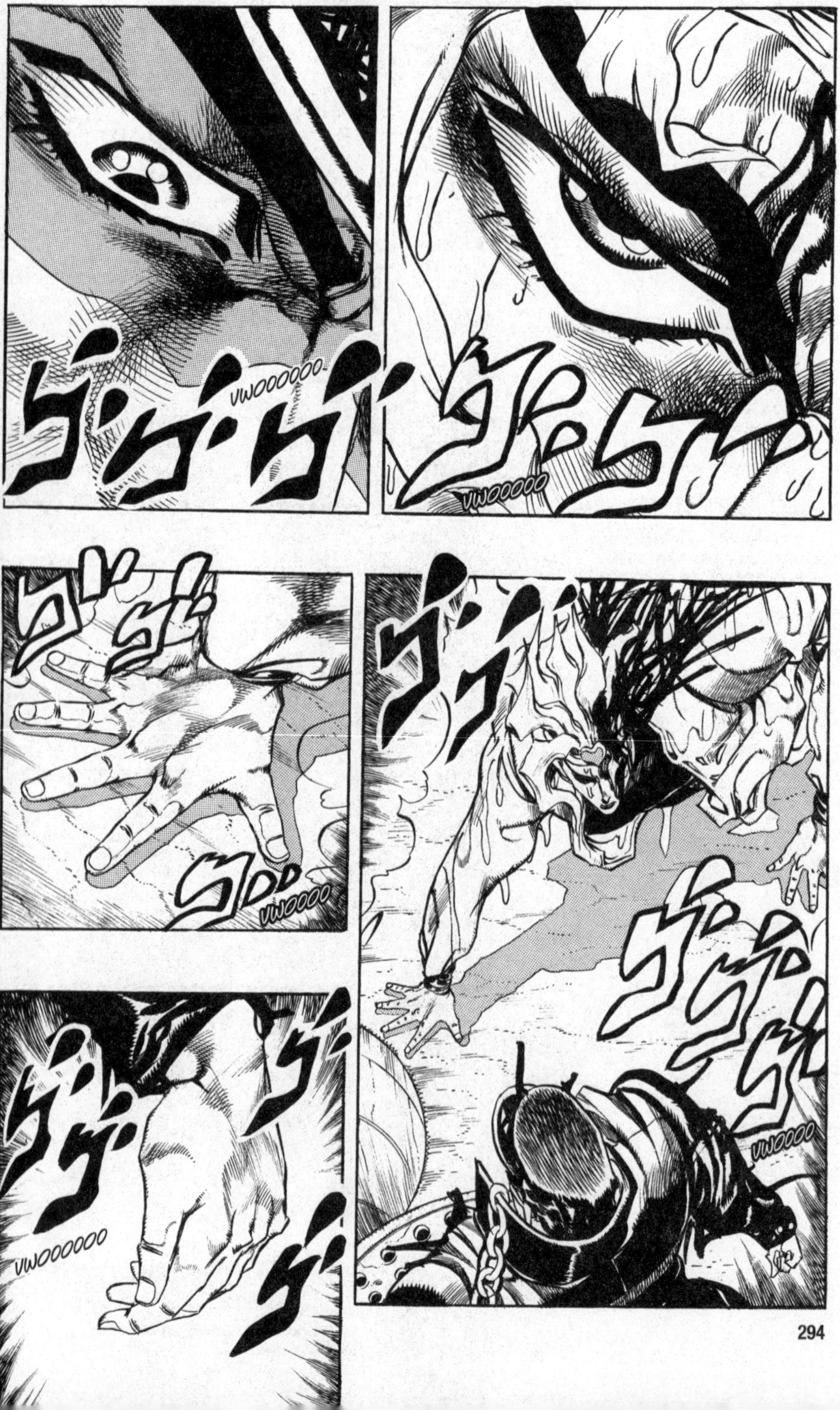
VWOOOOO
VWOOOOOO-
VWOOOO
VWOOOO
VWOOOOOO

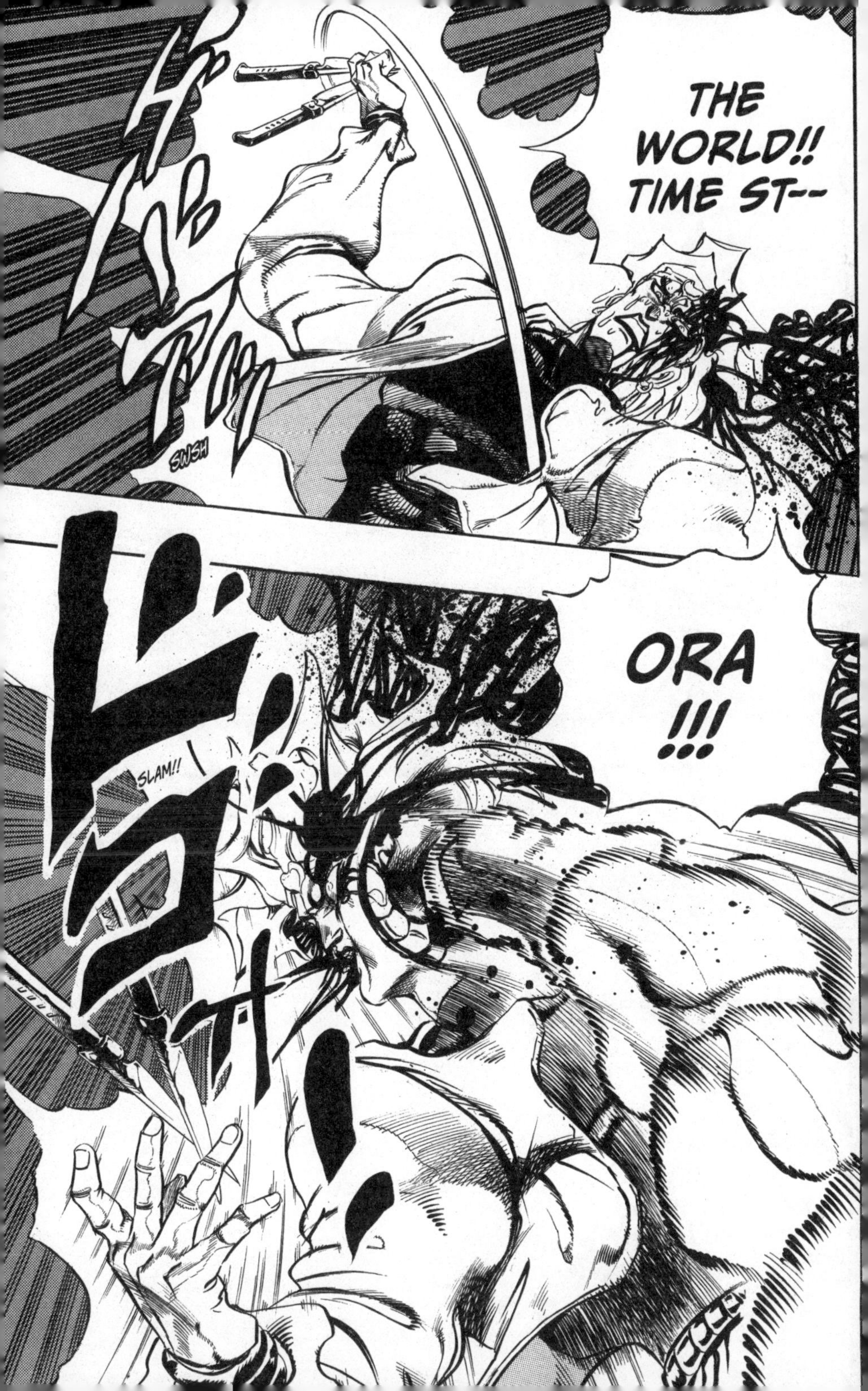
THE WORLD!! TIME ST--
SWSH
ORA !!!
SLAM!!

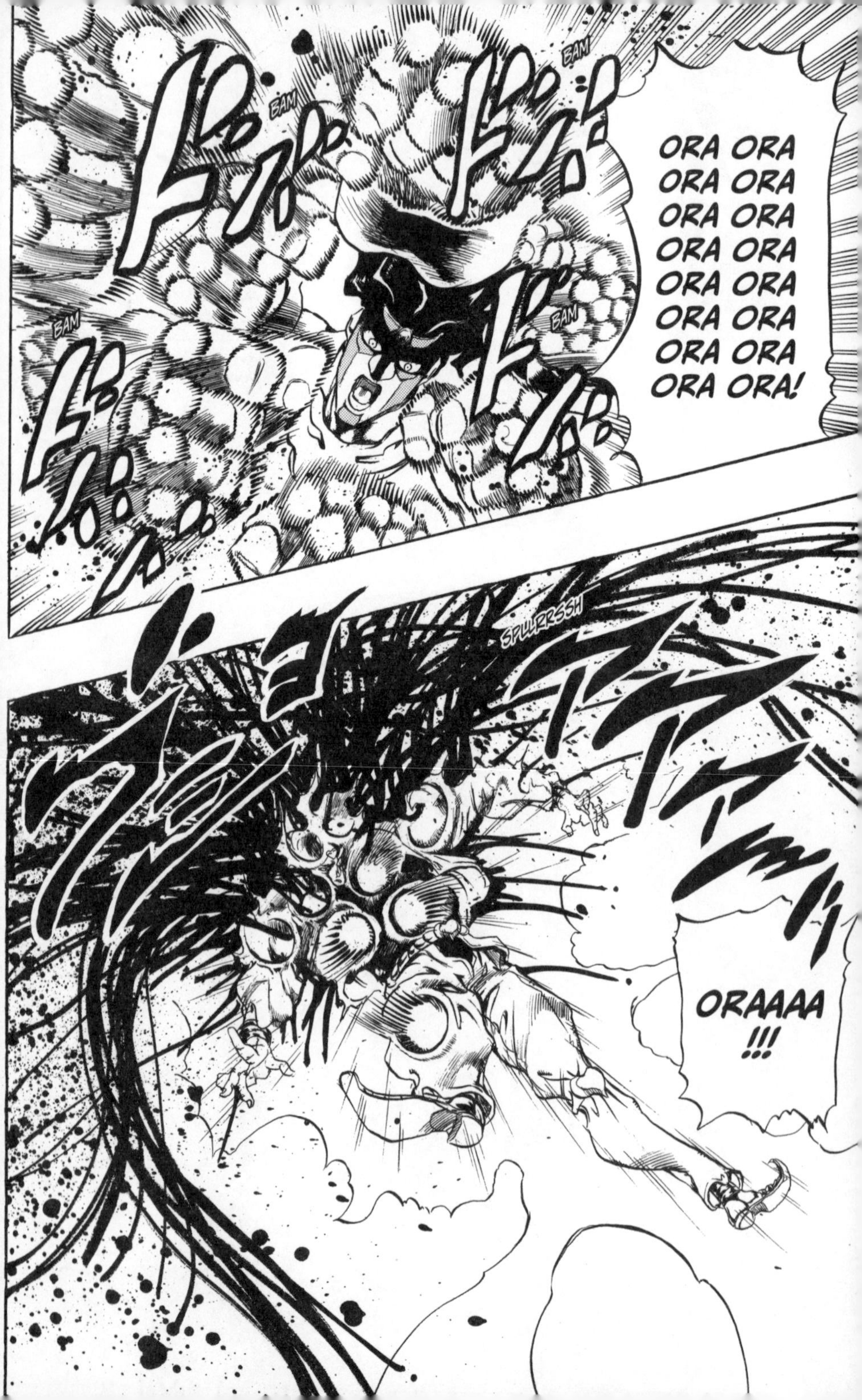
BAM
BAM
ORA ORA
ORA ORA
ORA ORA
ORA ORA
ORA ORA
ORA ORA
ORA ORA
ORA ORA!
BAM
BAM
SPLURRSSH
ORAAAA
!!!

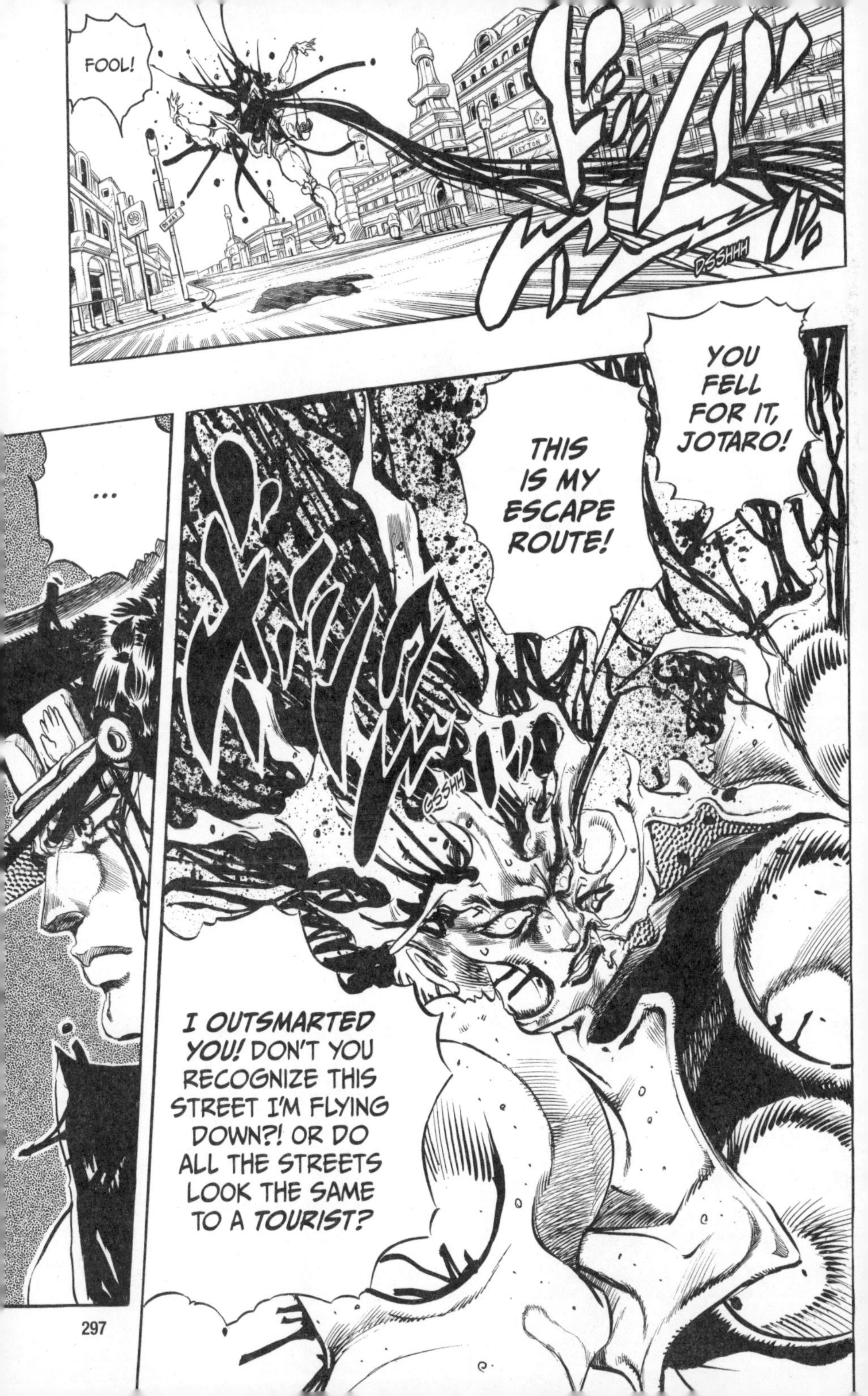
FOOL!
D-SSHHH
YOU FELL FOR IT, JOTARO!
THIS IS MY ESCAPE ROUTE!
GSSHH
I OUTSMARTED YOU! DON'T YOU RECOGNIZE THIS STREET I'M FLYING DOWN?! OR DO ALL THE STREETS LOOK THE SAME TO A TOURIST?
...

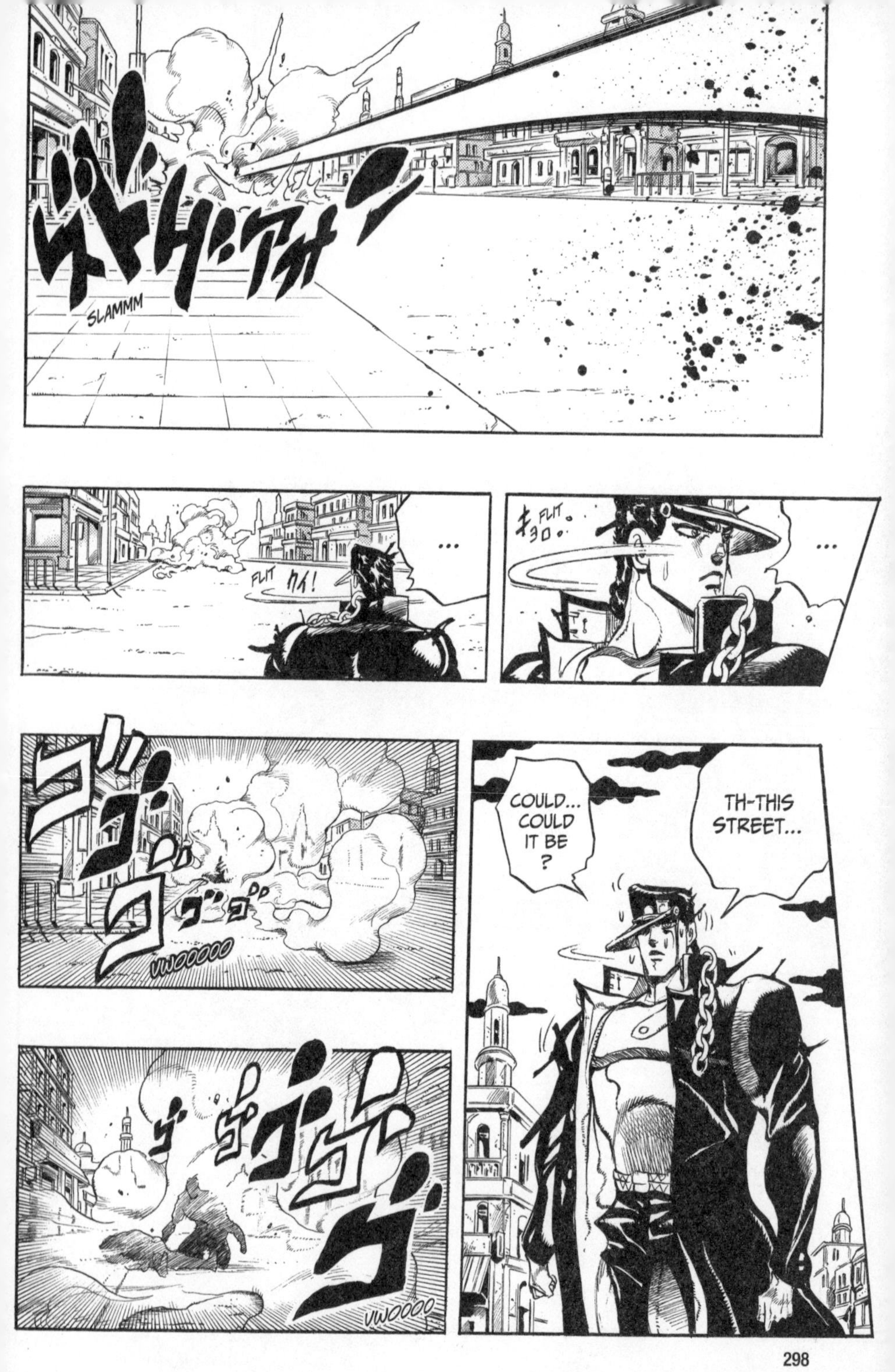
SLAMMM
FLIT
...
FLIT
...
TH-THIS STREET...
COULD... COULD IT BE?
VWOOOOO
VWOOOO

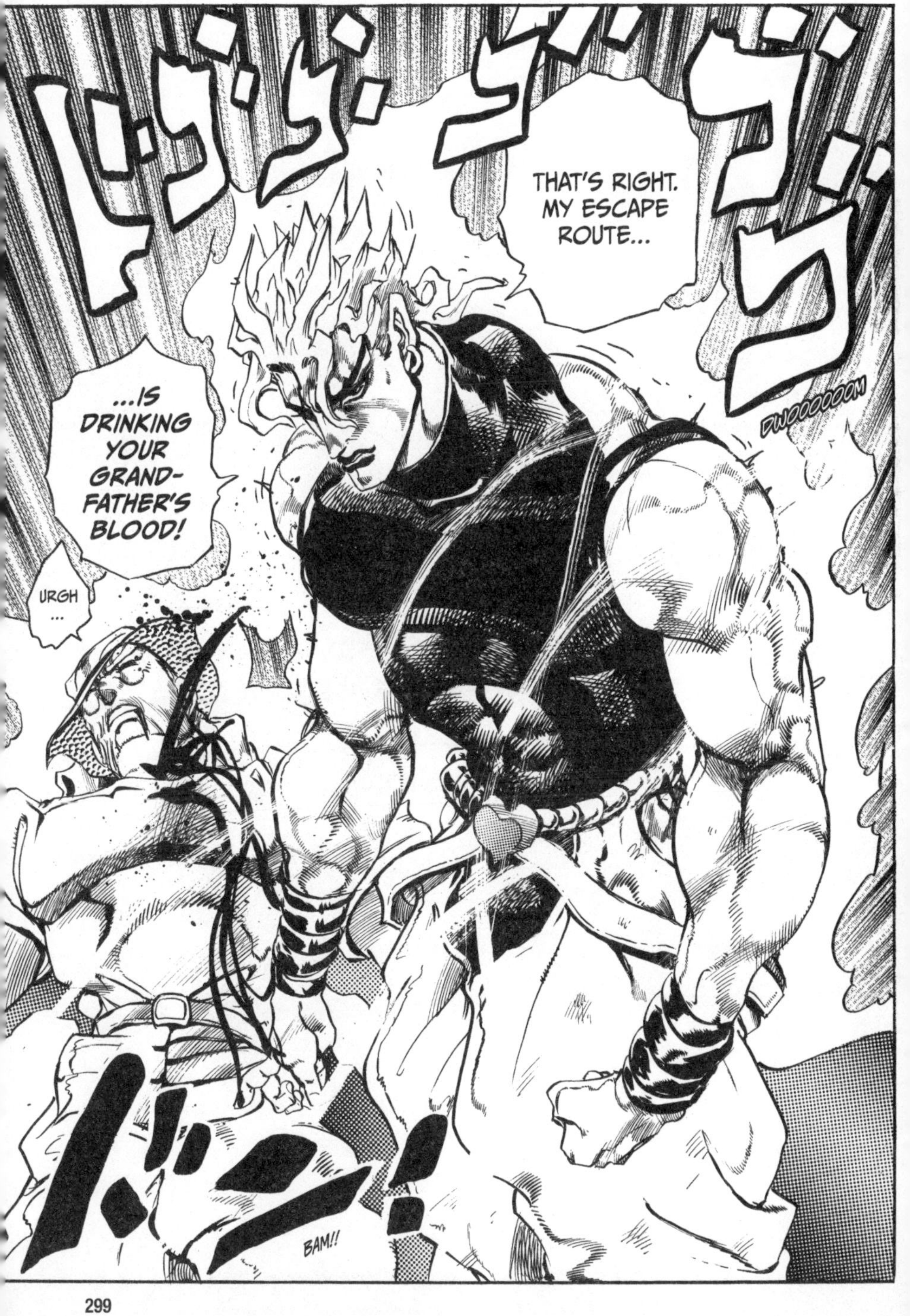
THAT'S RIGHT. MY ESCAPE ROUTE...
DWOOOOOOOM
...IS DRINKING YOUR GRAND-FATHER'S BLOOD!
URGH ...
BAM!!

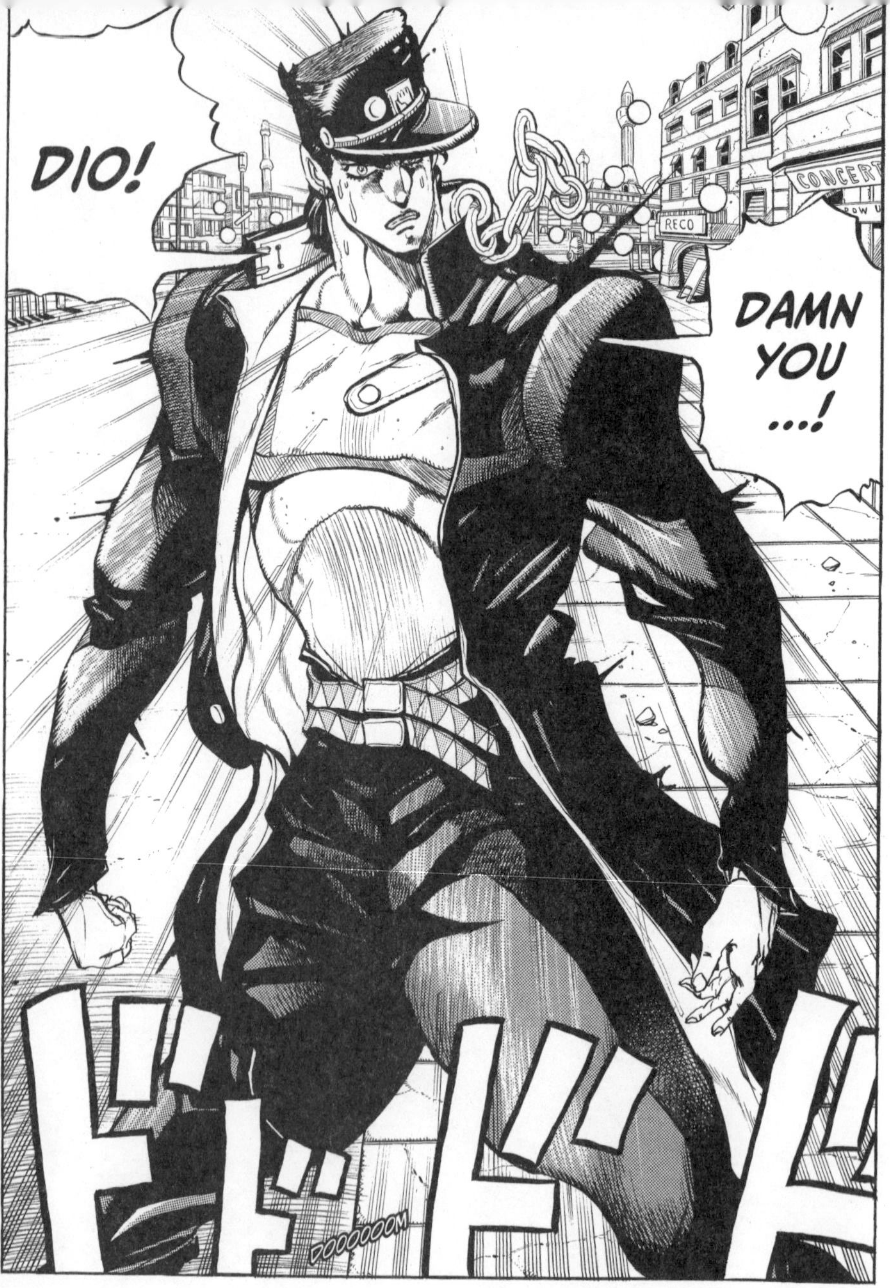
DIO!
DAMN YOU ...!
ドドドド
DOOOOOOM

CHAPTER 149: DIO's World PART 16

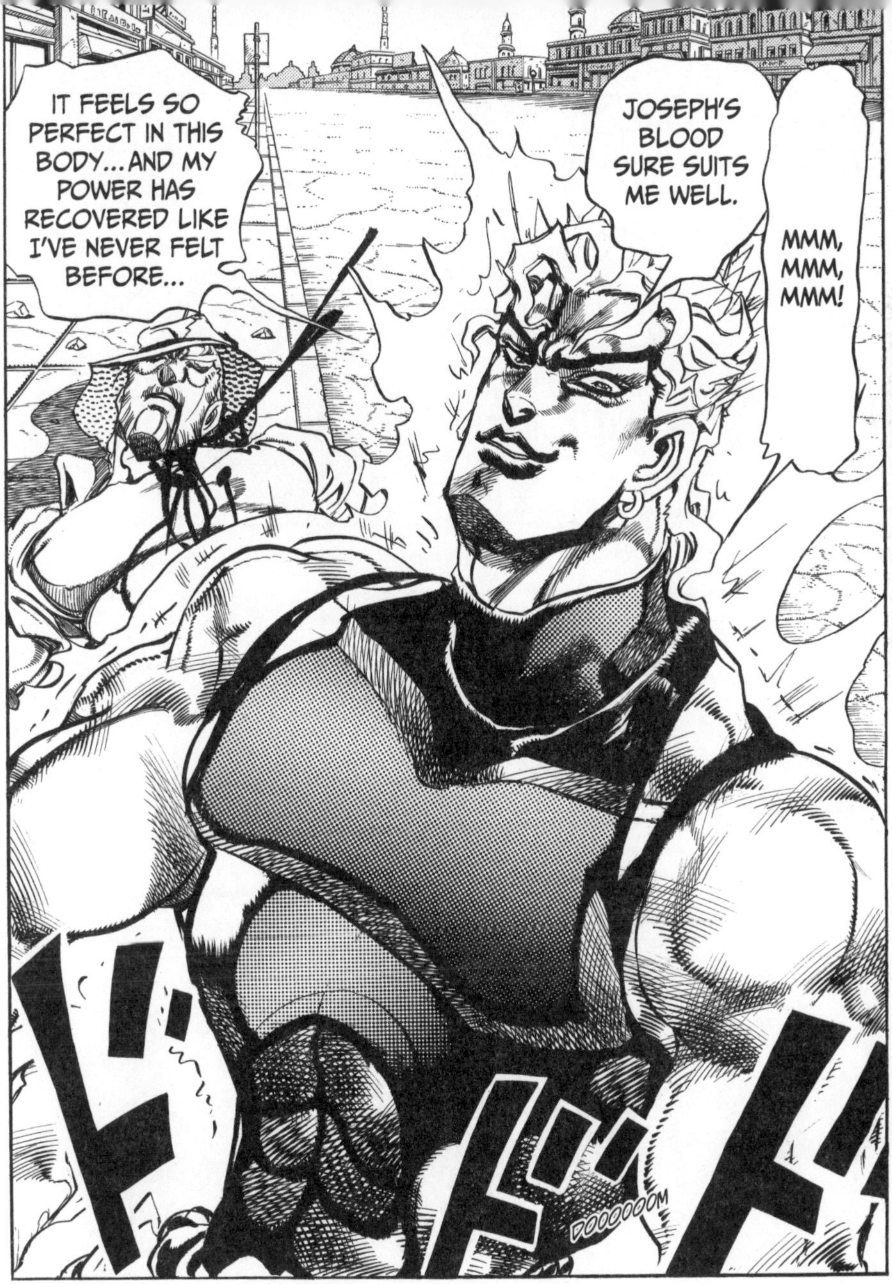
MMM, MMM, MMM!
JOSEPH'S BLOOD SURE SUITS ME WELL.
IT FEELS SO PERFECT IN THIS BODY...AND MY POWER HAS RECOVERED LIKE I'VE NEVER FELT BEFORE...
DOOOOOOM

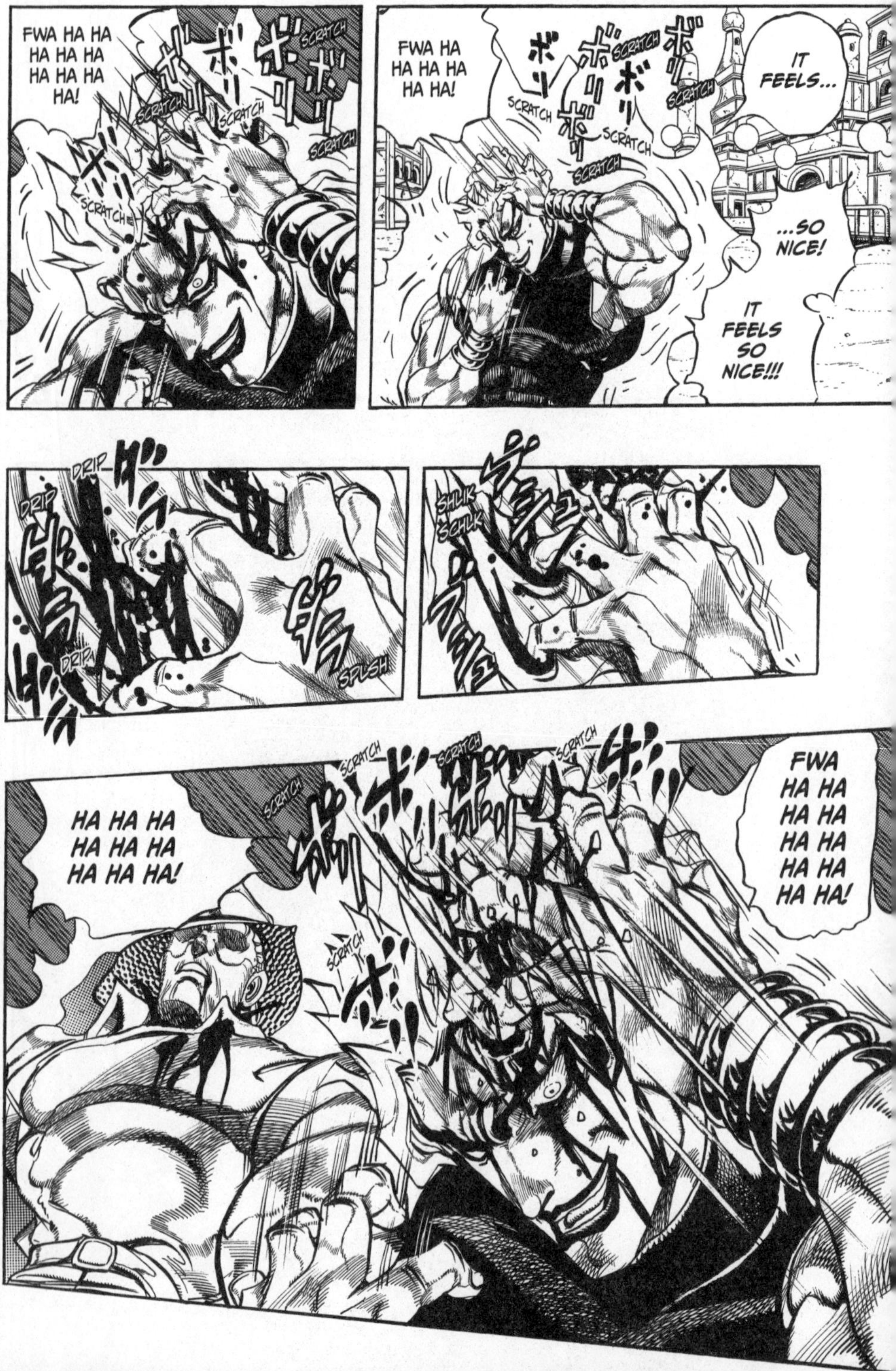
IT FEELS...
...SO NICE!
IT FEELS SO NICE!!!
SCRATCH
SCRATCH
SCRATCH
SCRATCH
SCRATCH
FWA HA HA HA HA HA HA HA!
SCRATCH
SCRATCH
SCRATCH
SCRATCH
FWA HA HA HA HA HA HA HA HA HA!
SHUK SHUK
DRIP
DRIP
DRIP
SPLSH
FWA HA HA HA HA HA HA HA HA HA HA HA!
SCRATCH
SCRATCH
SCRATCH
SCRATCH
SCRATCH
HA HA HA HA HA HA HA HA HA!

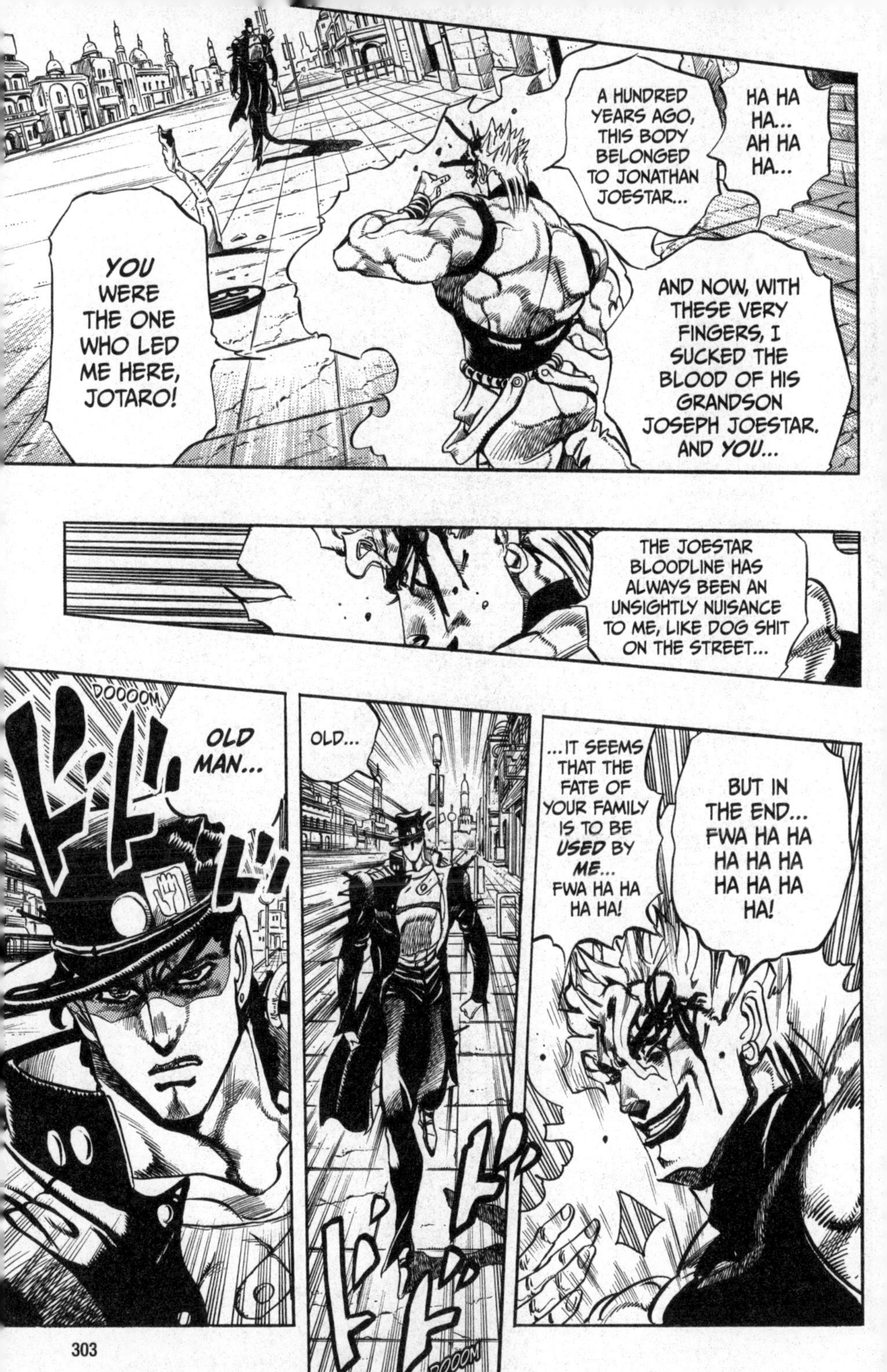
HA HA HA... AH HA HA...
A HUNDRED YEARS AGO, THIS BODY BELONGED TO JONATHAN JOESTAR...
AND NOW, WITH THESE VERY FINGERS, I SUCKED THE BLOOD OF HIS GRANDSON JOSEPH JOESTAR. AND *YOU*...
YOU WERE THE ONE WHO LED ME HERE, JOTARO!
THE JOESTAR BLOODLINE HAS ALWAYS BEEN AN UNSIGHTLY NUISANCE TO ME, LIKE DOG SHIT ON THE STREET...
...IT SEEMS THAT THE FATE OF YOUR FAMILY IS TO BE *USED* BY *ME*... FWA HA HA HA HA!
BUT IN THE END... FWA HA HA HA HA HA HA HA HA HA!
OLD...
DOOOM
DOOOOM
OLD MAN...

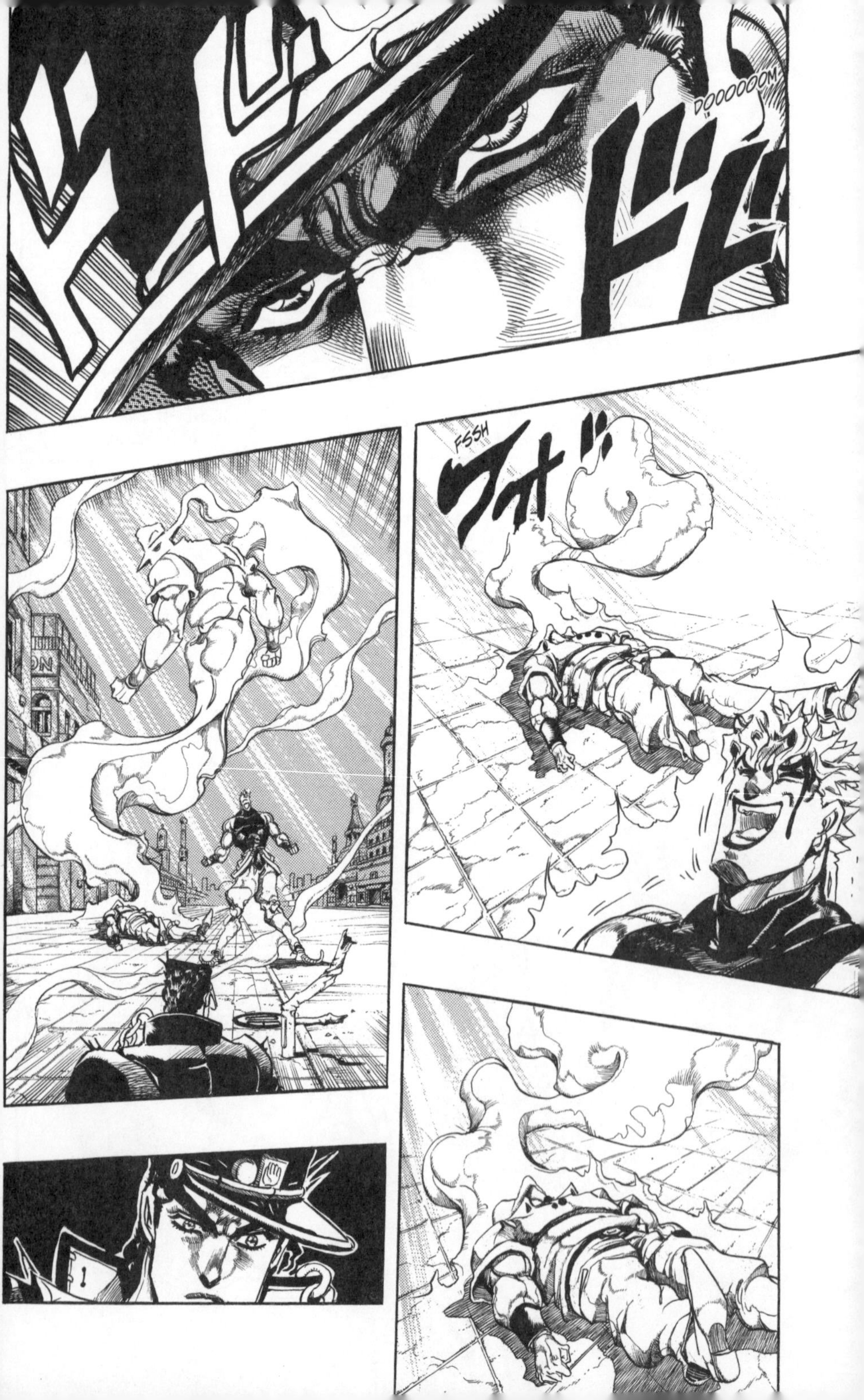
DOOOOOOM
FSSH

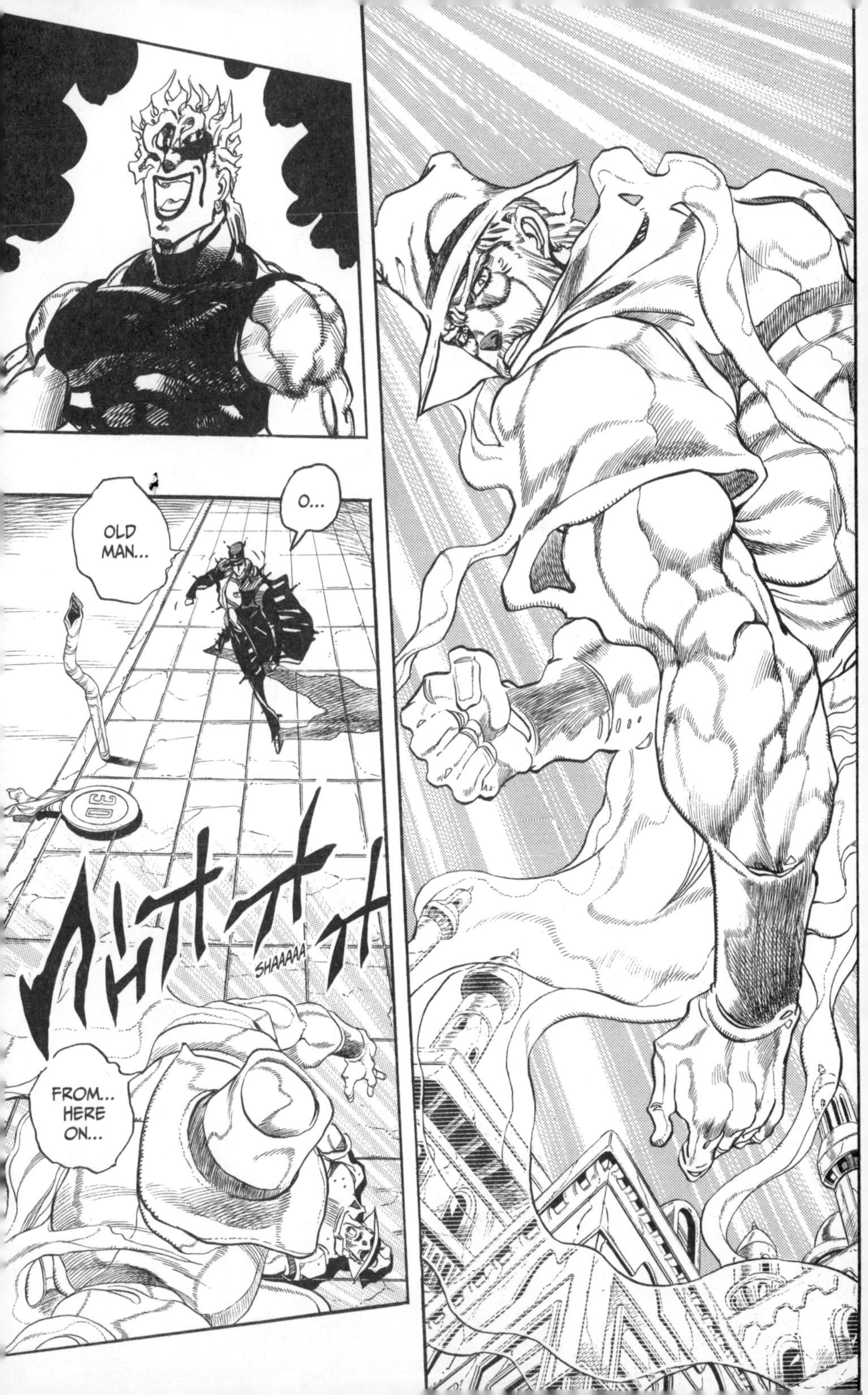
O...
OLD MAN...
SHAAAAA
FROM... HERE ON...

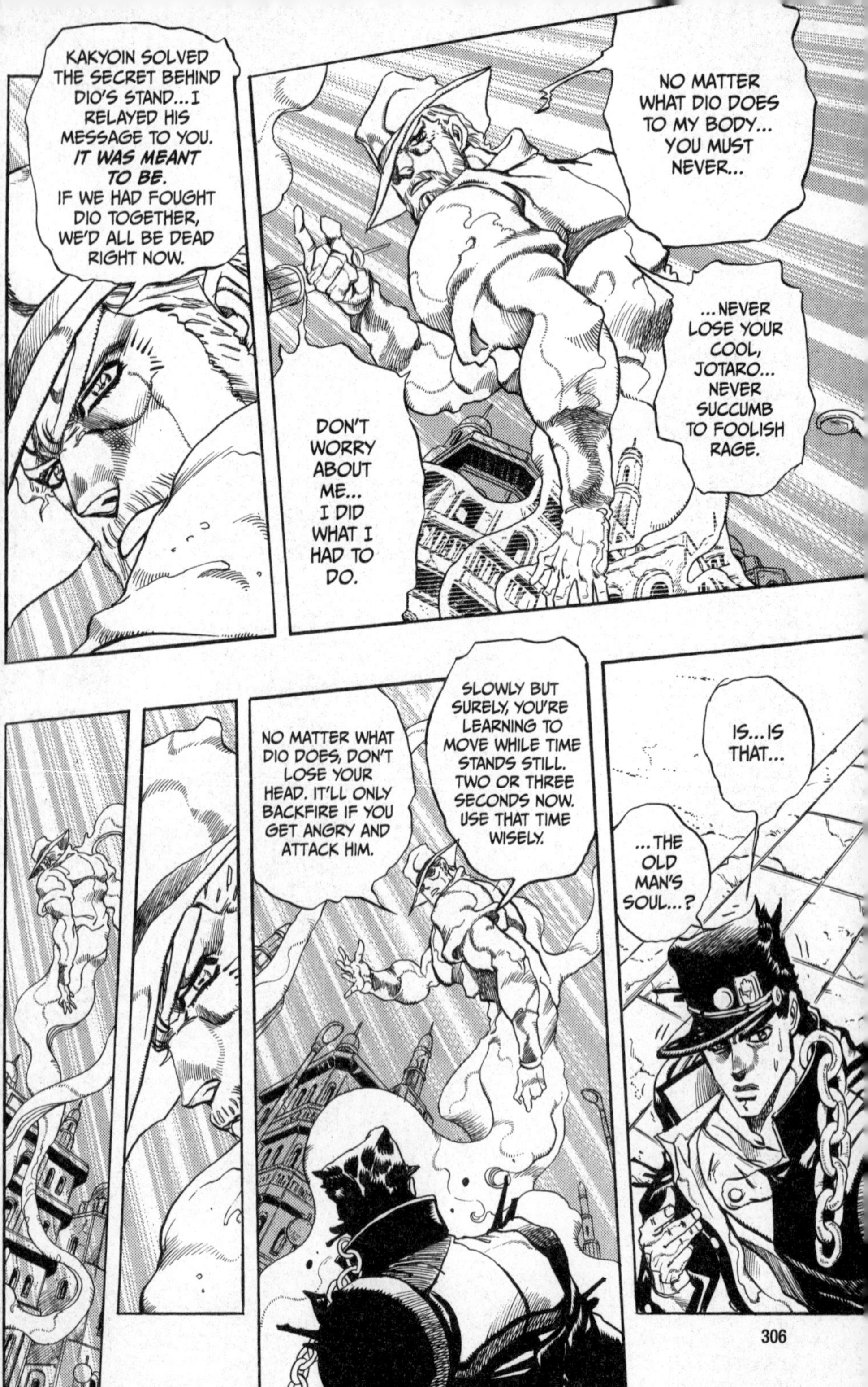

NO MATTER WHAT DIO DOES TO MY BODY... YOU MUST NEVER...
...NEVER LOSE YOUR COOL, JOTARO... NEVER SUCCUMB TO FOOLISH RAGE.
DON'T WORRY ABOUT ME... I DID WHAT I HAD TO DO.
KAKYOIN SOLVED THE SECRET BEHIND DIO'S STAND...I RELAYED HIS MESSAGE TO YOU. ***IT WAS MEANT TO BE.*** IF WE HAD FOUGHT DIO TOGETHER, WE'D ALL BE DEAD RIGHT NOW.
IS...IS THAT...
...THE OLD MAN'S SOUL...?
SLOWLY BUT SURELY, YOU'RE LEARNING TO MOVE WHILE TIME STANDS STILL. TWO OR THREE SECONDS NOW. USE THAT TIME WISELY.
NO MATTER WHAT DIO DOES, DON'T LOSE YOUR HEAD. IT'LL ONLY BACKFIRE IF YOU GET ANGRY AND ATTACK HIM.

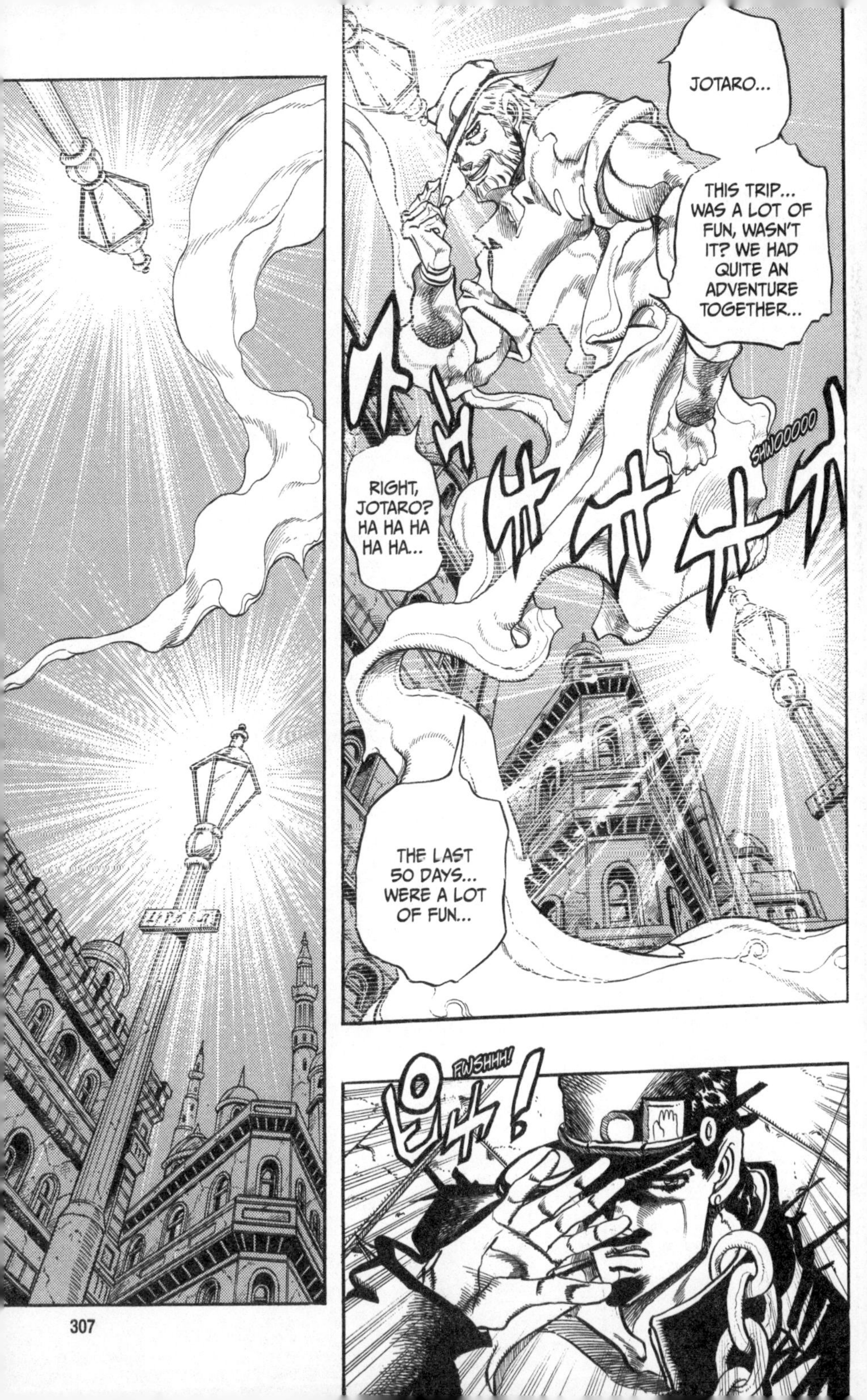
JOTARO...
THIS TRIP... WAS A LOT OF FUN, WASN'T IT? WE HAD QUITE AN ADVENTURE TOGETHER...
SHWOOOOO
RIGHT, JOTARO? HA HA HA HA HA...
THE LAST 50 DAYS... WERE A LOT OF FUN...
FWSHHH!

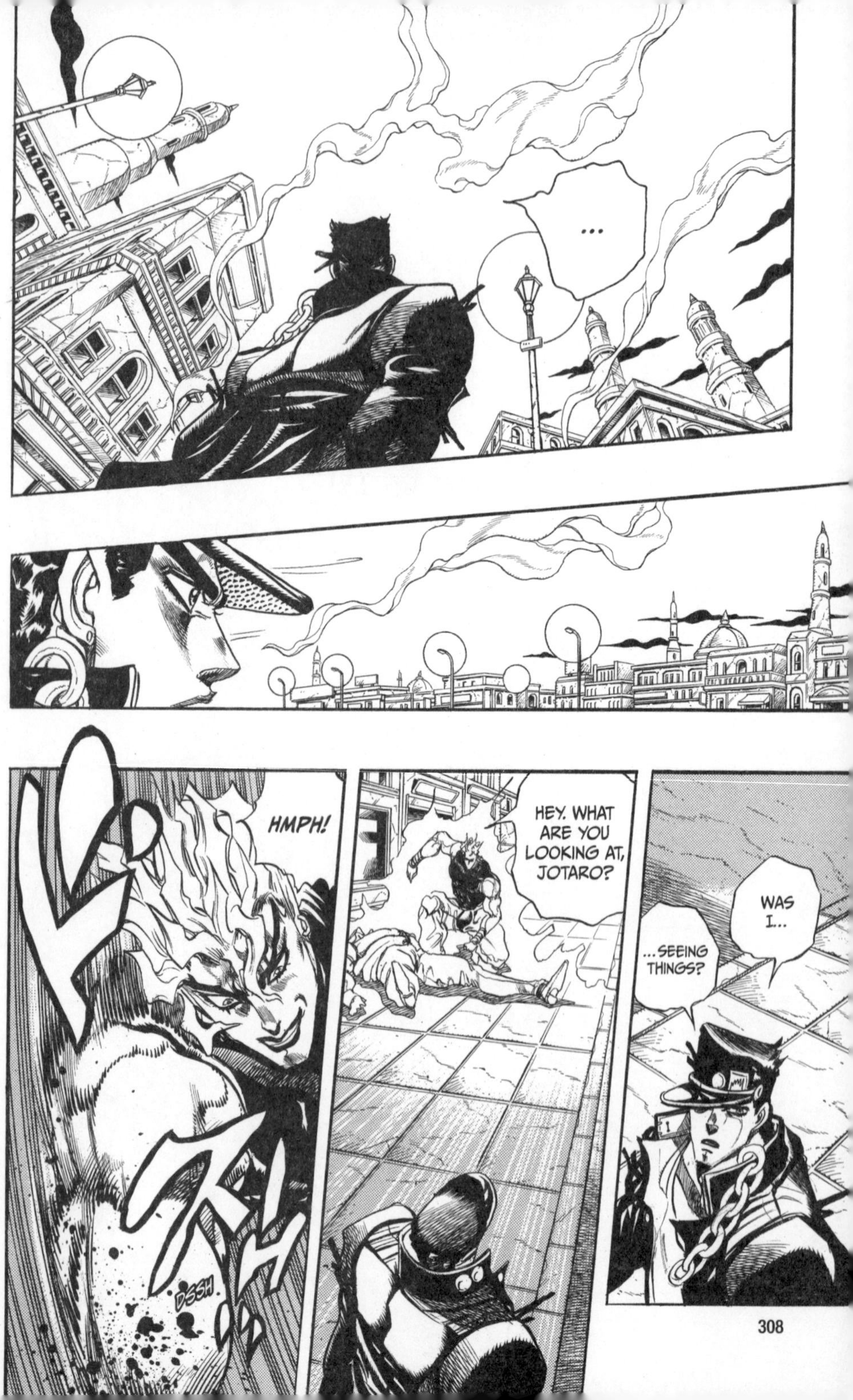
...
WAS I...
...SEEING THINGS?
HEY. WHAT ARE YOU LOOKING AT, JOTARO?
HMPH!
DSSH

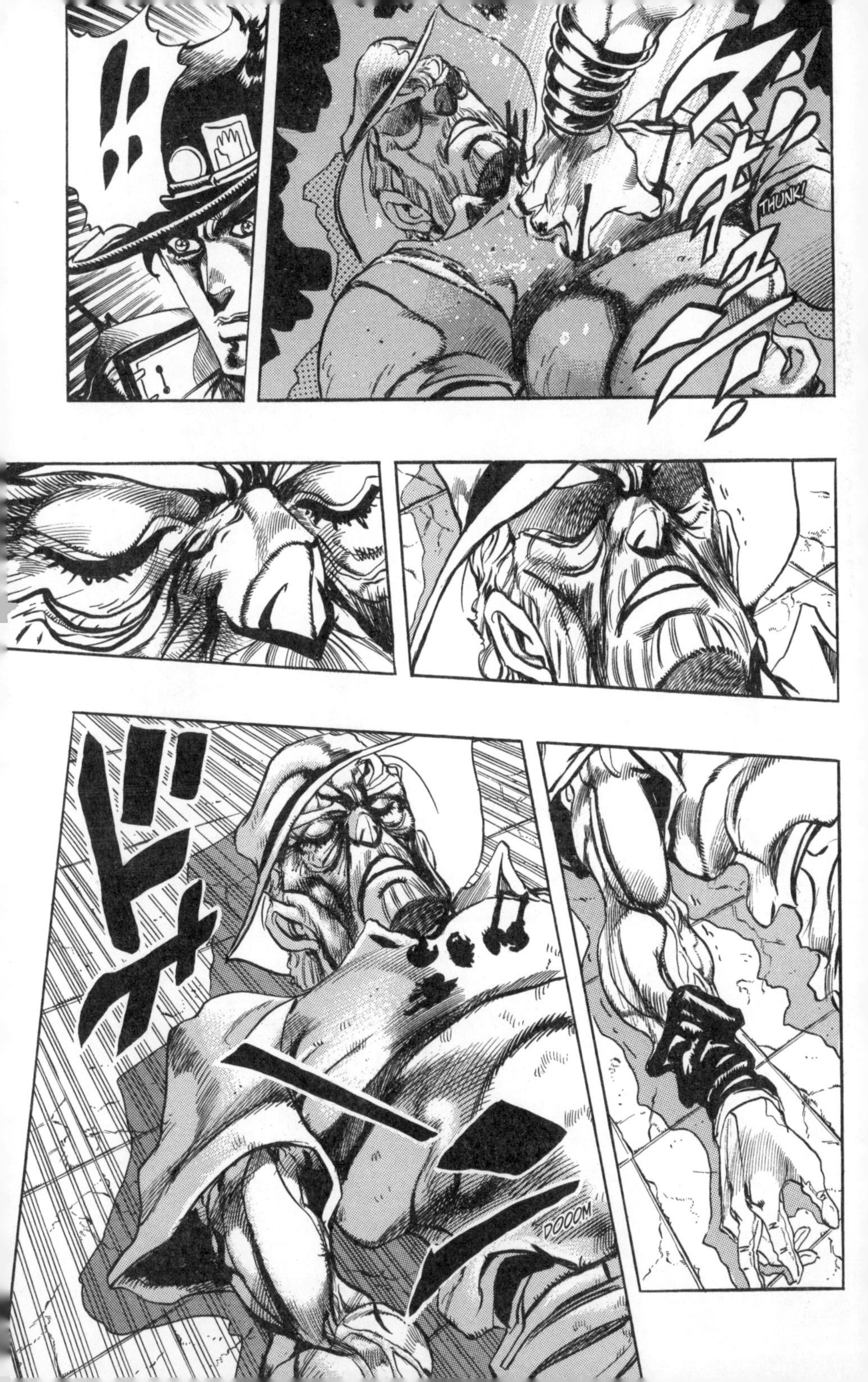
THUNK!
!!
DOOOM

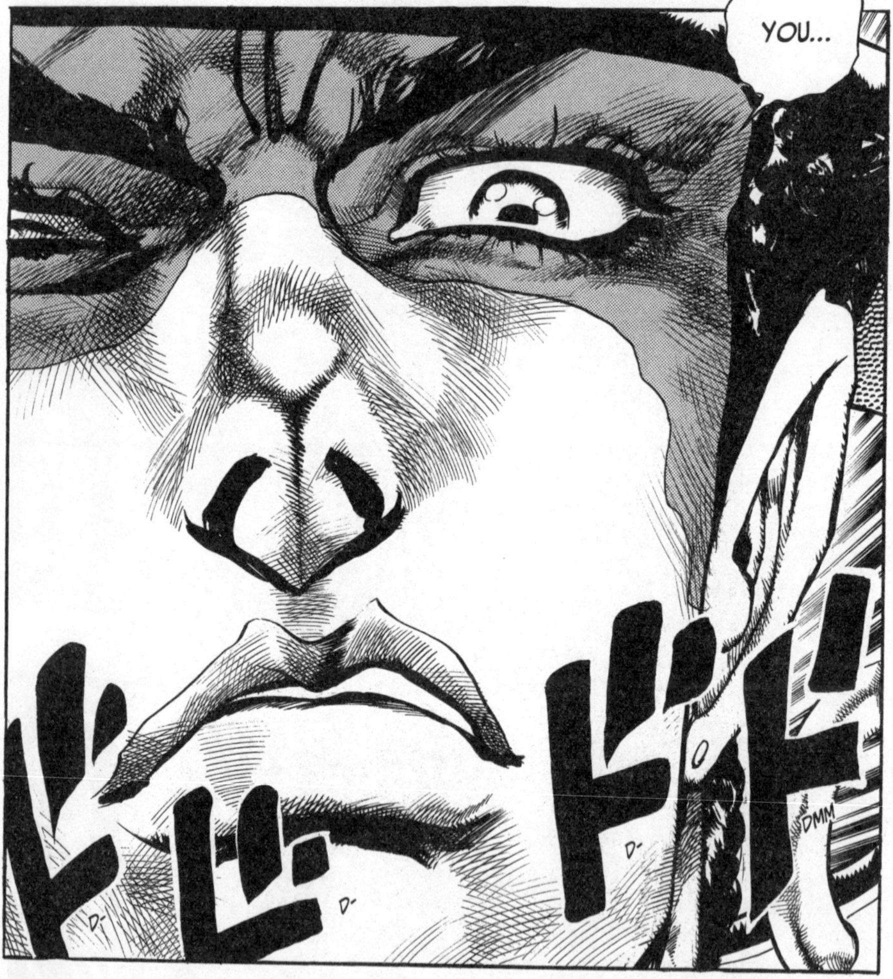
YOU...
D-
D-
D-
DMM
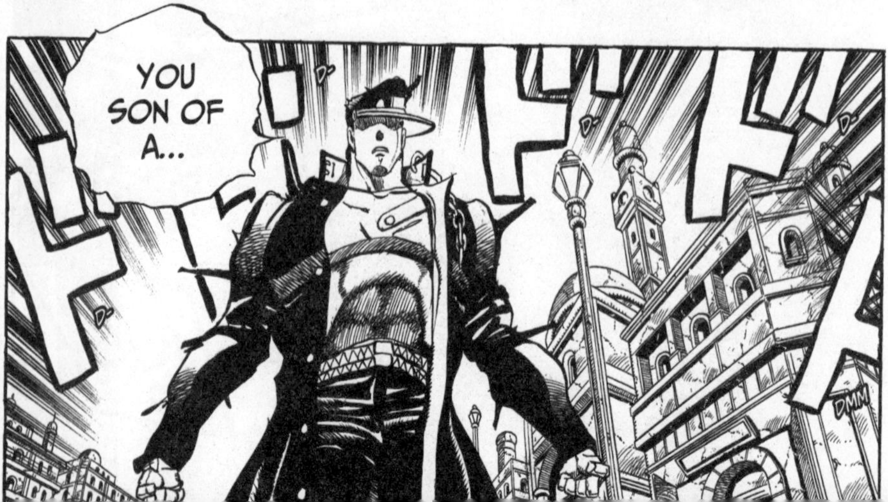
YOU SON OF A...
D-
D-
D-
D-
DMM

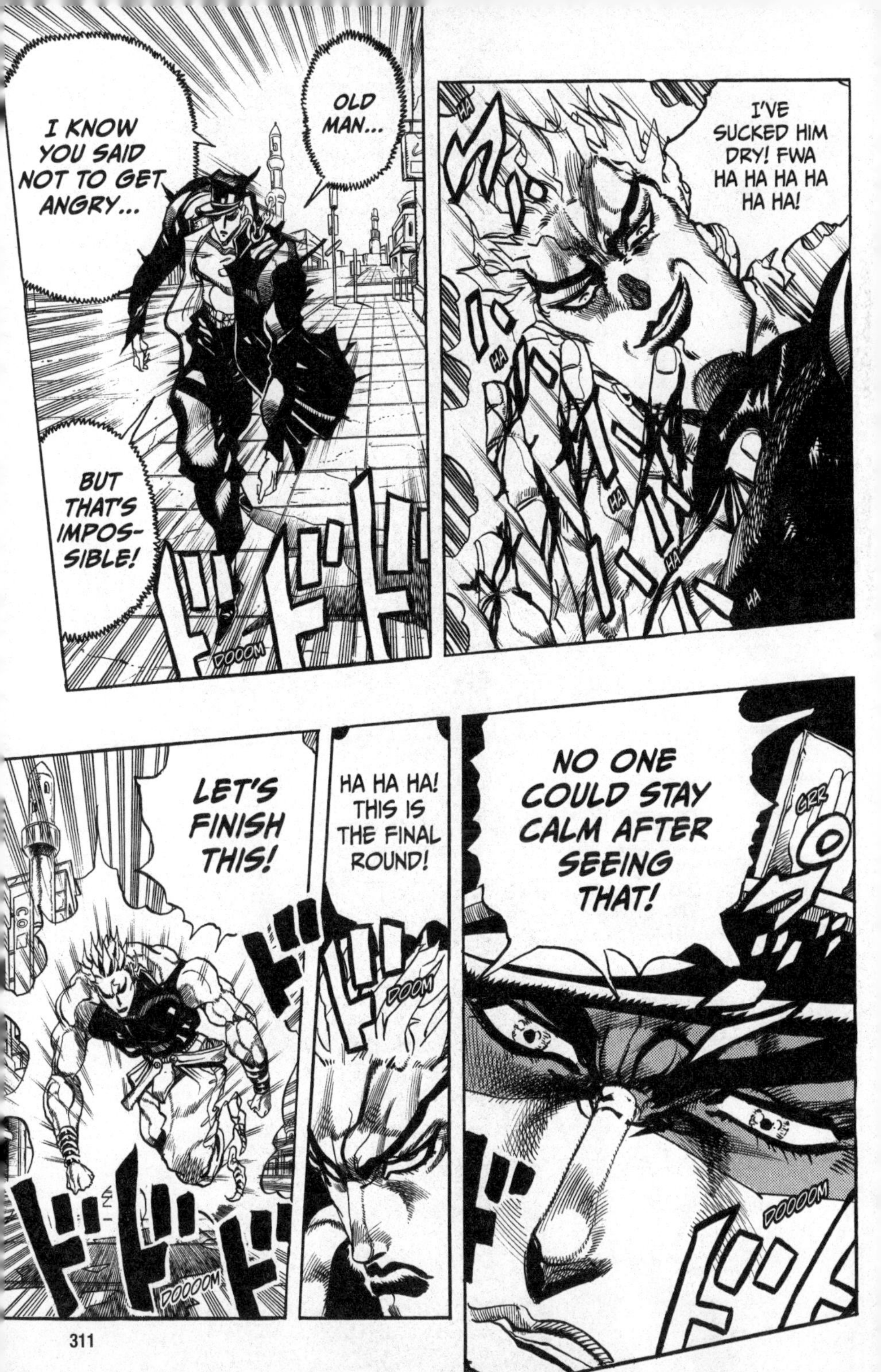
I'VE SUCKED HIM DRY! FWA HA HA HA HA HA HA!
HA
HA
HA
HA
HA
OLD MAN...
I KNOW YOU SAID NOT TO GET ANGRY...
BUT THAT'S IMPOSSIBLE!
DOOOM
NO ONE COULD STAY CALM AFTER SEEING THAT!
GRR
DOOOOM
HA HA HA! THIS IS THE FINAL ROUND!
DOOM
LET'S FINISH THIS!
DOOOOM

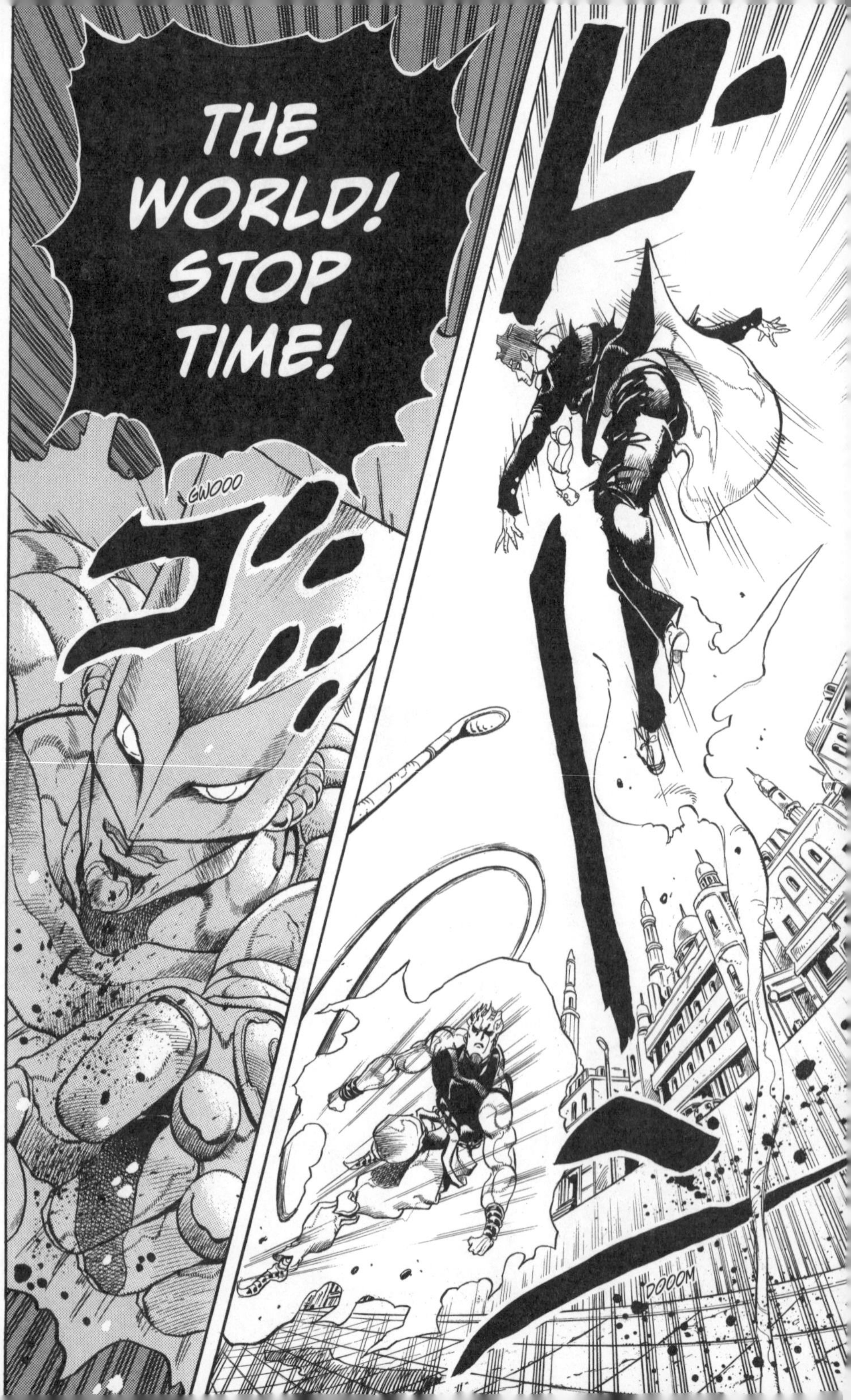
DOOOM
THE WORLD! STOP TIME!
GWOOO

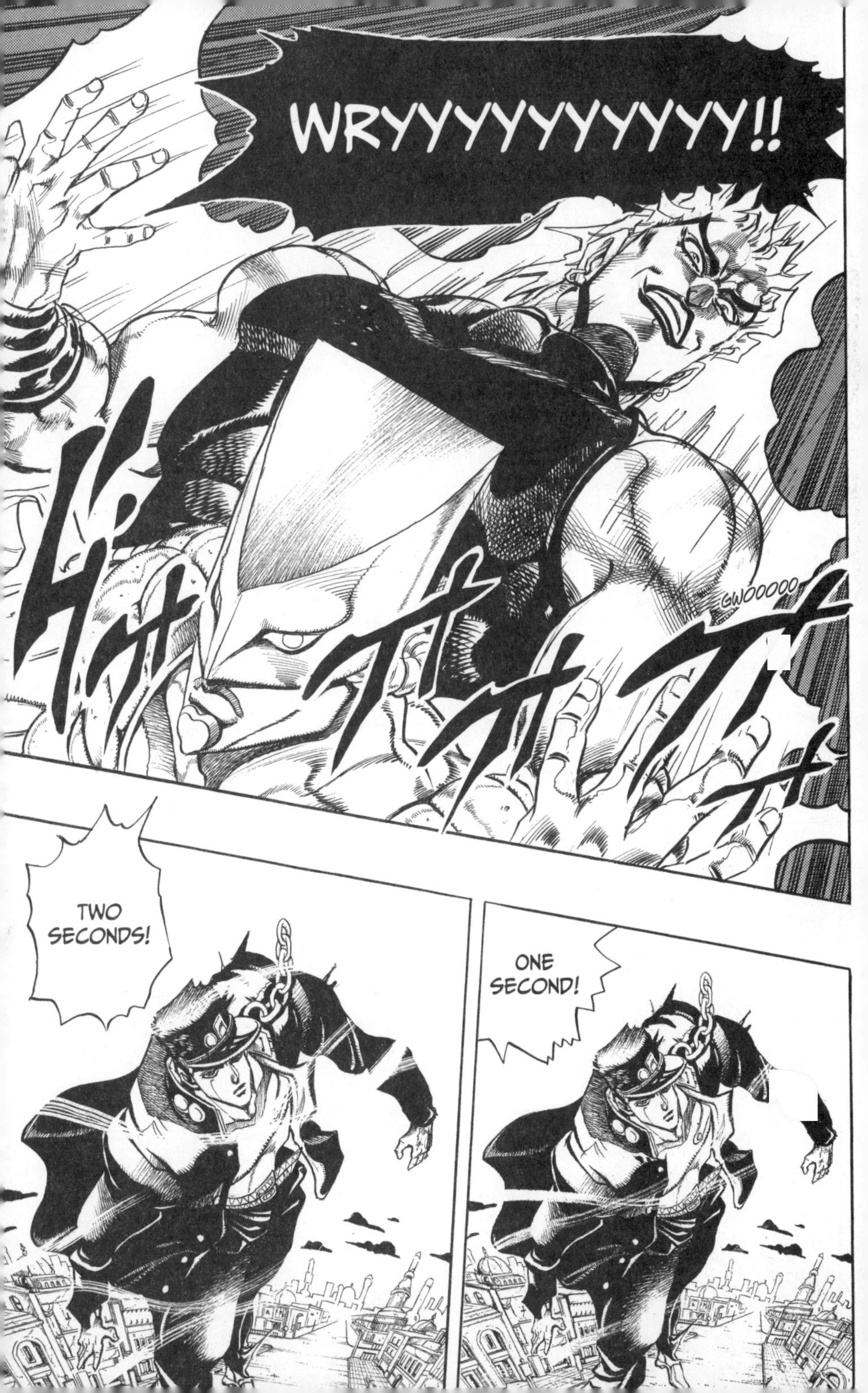
WRYYYYYYYYYYY!!
GWOOOOO
TWO SECONDS!
ONE SECOND!

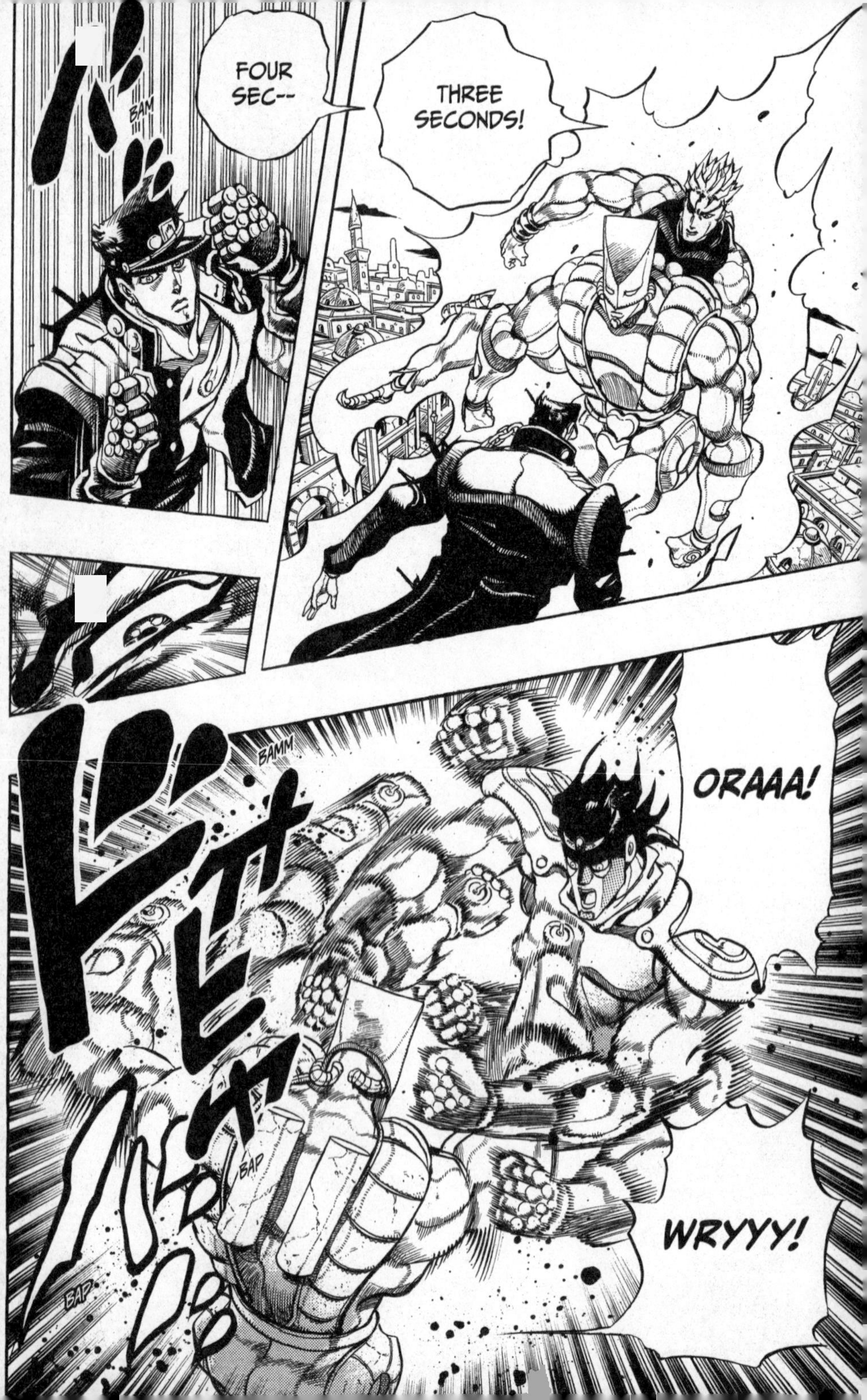
THREE SECONDS!
FOUR SEC--
BAM
ORAAA!
BAMM
WRYYY!
BAP
BAP

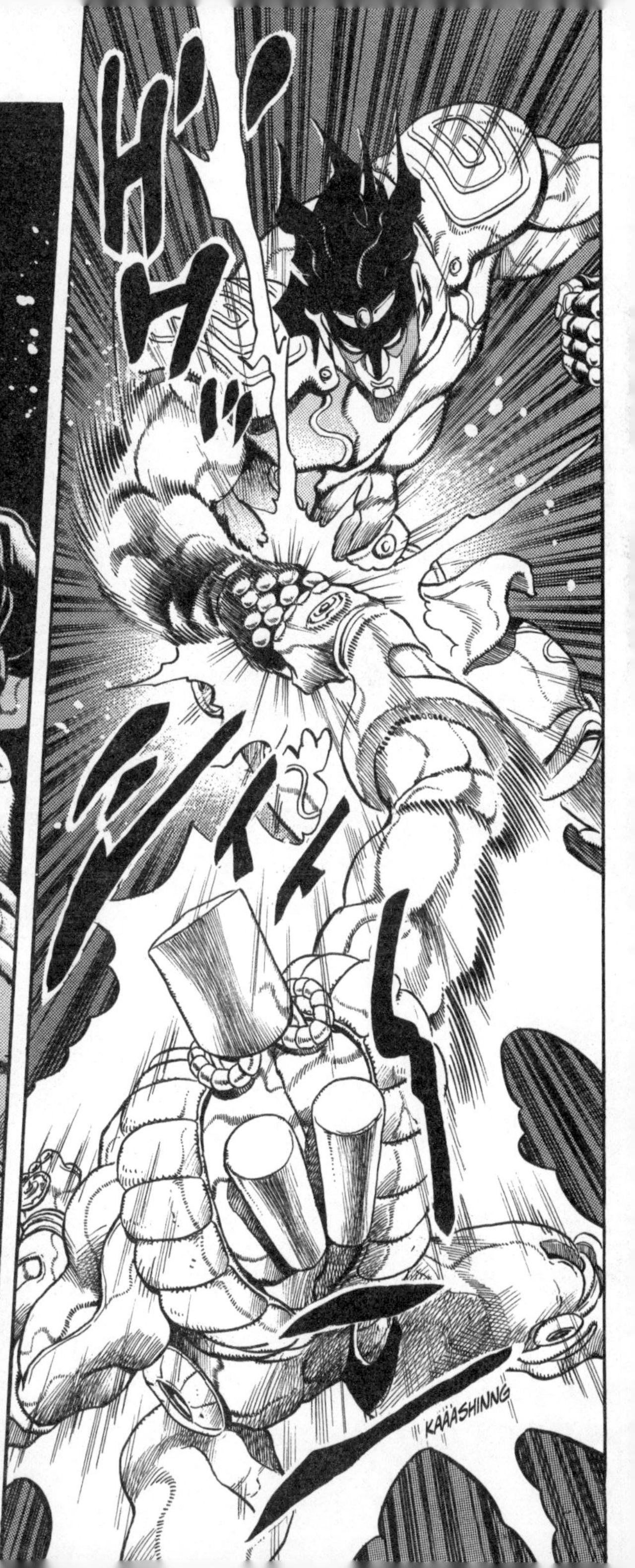
KAÄÄSHINNG
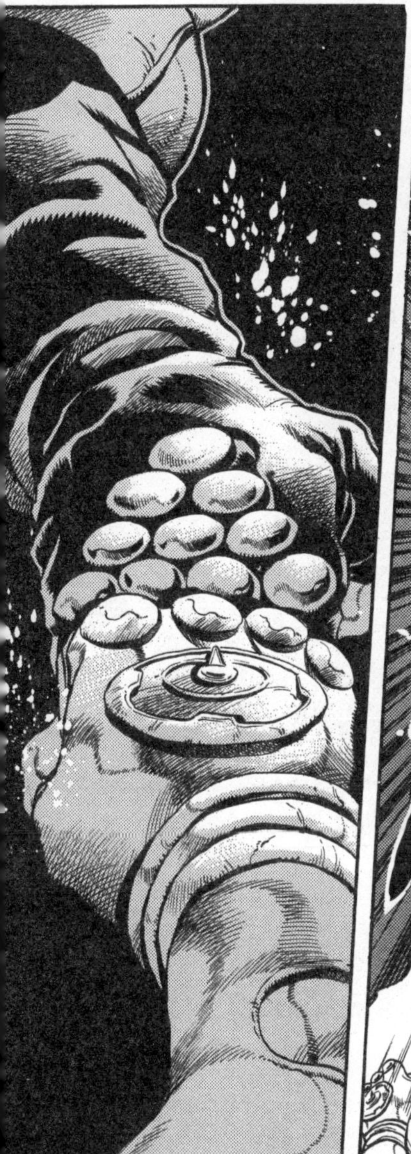

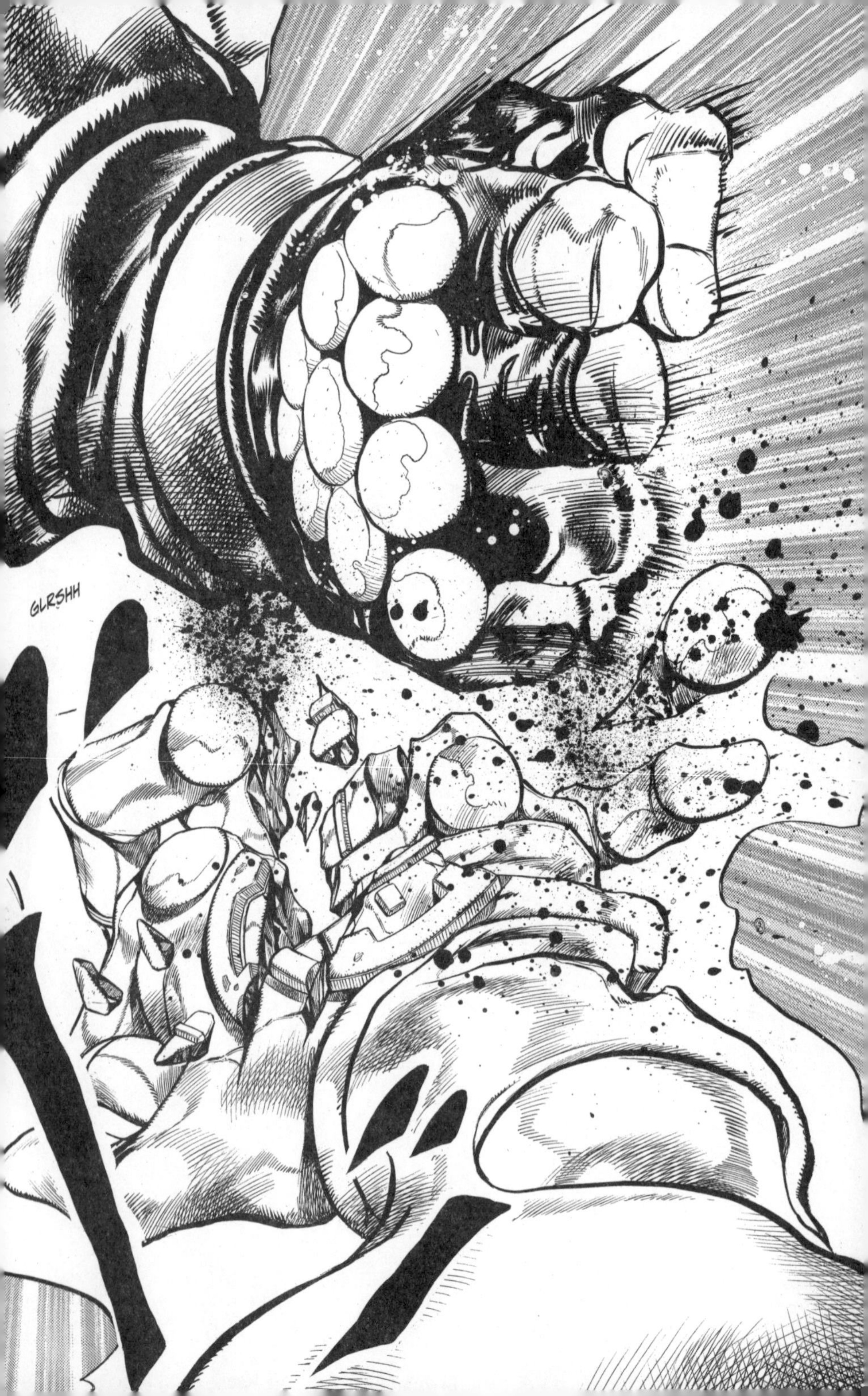
GLRSHH

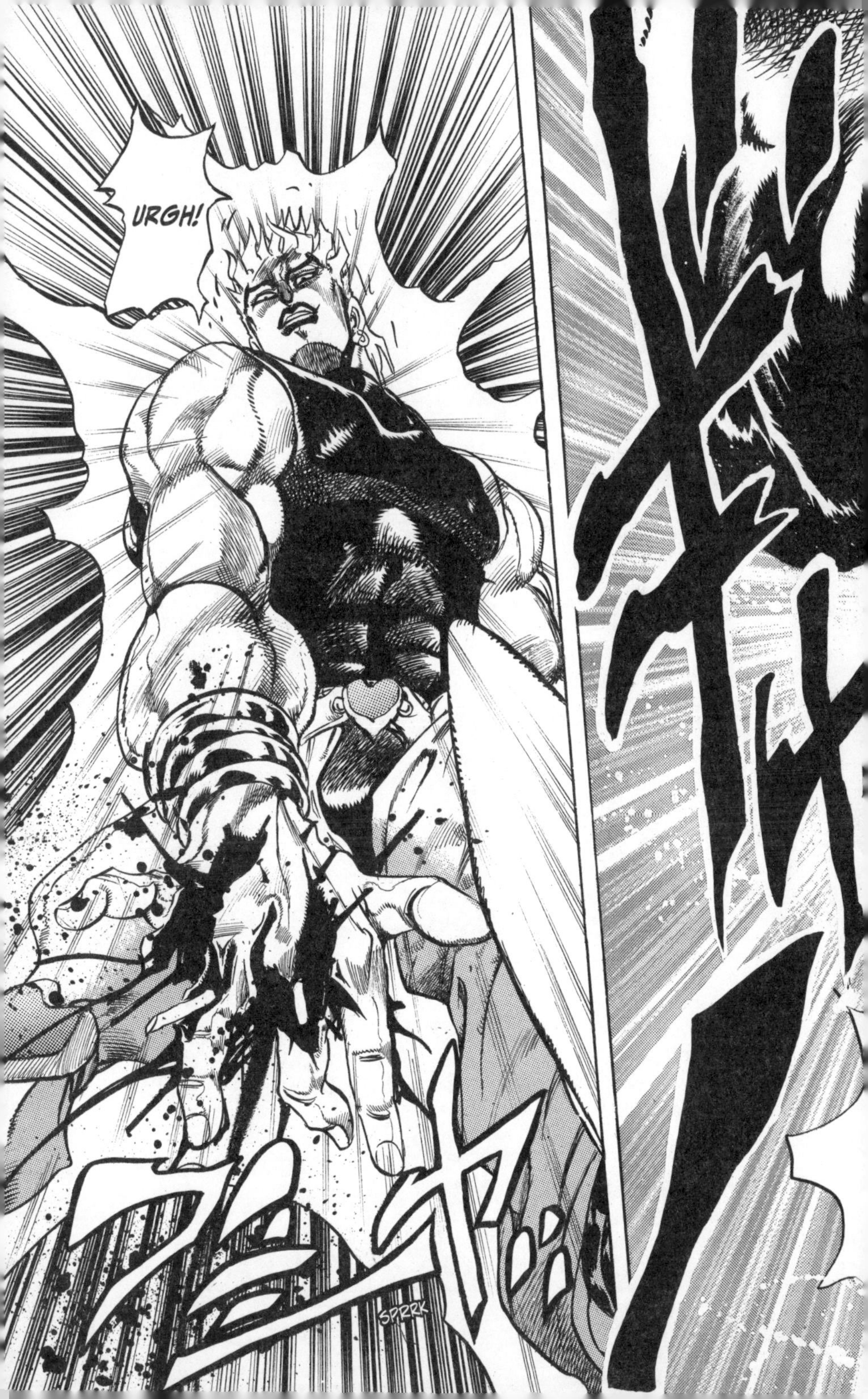
URGH!
SPRRK

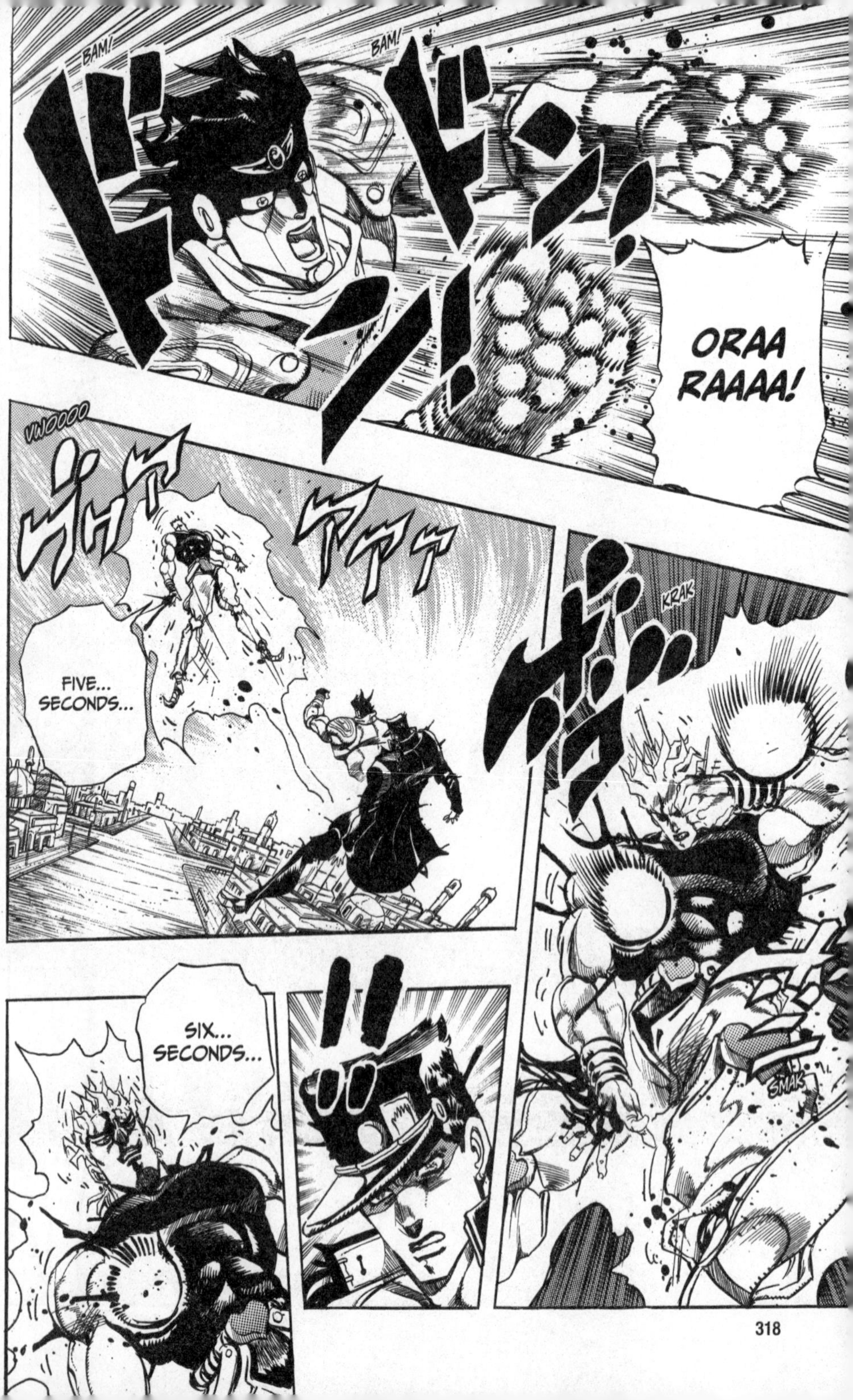
BAM!
BAM!
ORAA RAAAA!
KRAK
SMAK
VWOOOO
FIVE... SECONDS...
SIX... SECONDS...

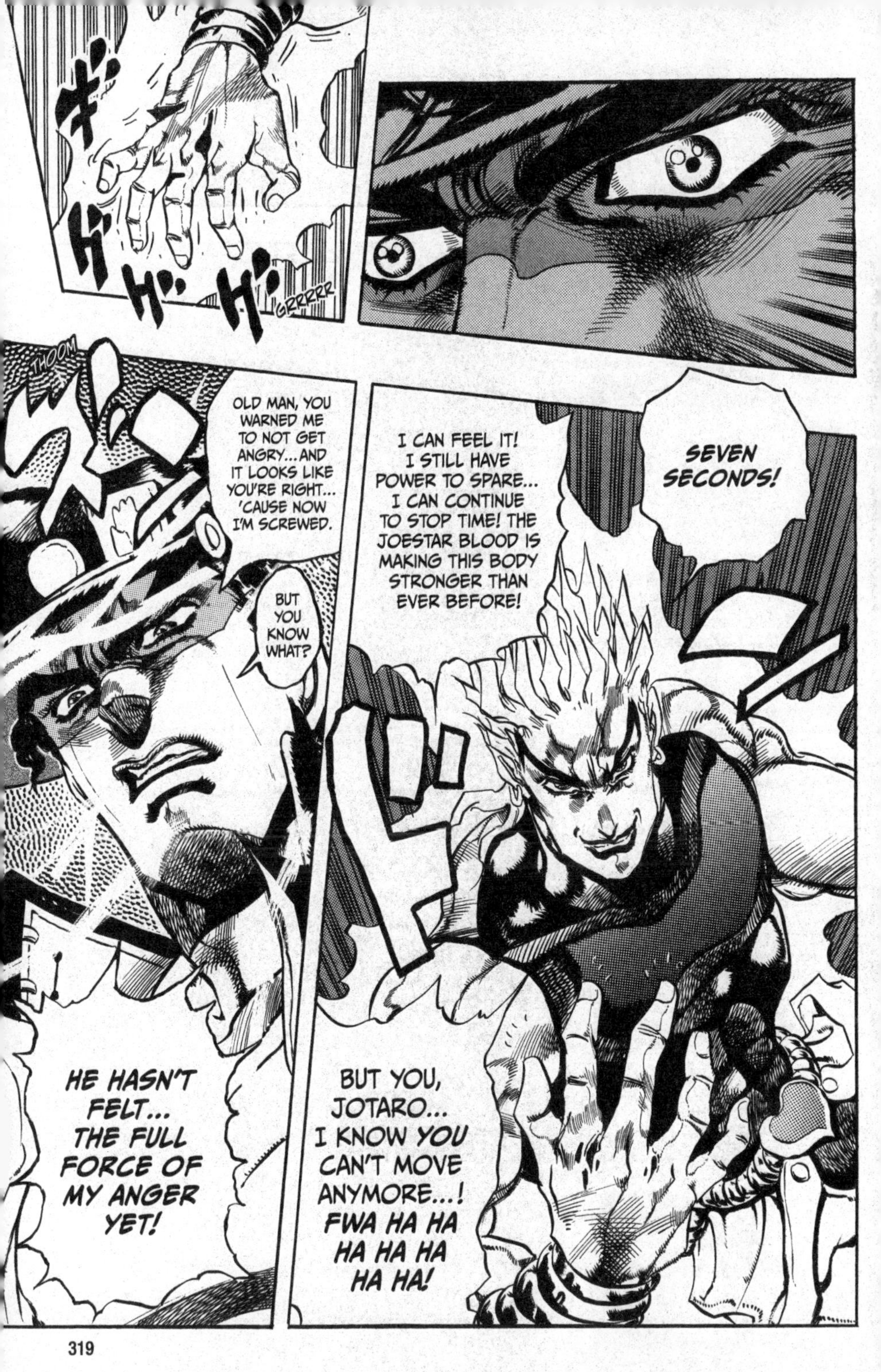
GRRRRR
SEVEN SECONDS!
I CAN FEEL IT! I STILL HAVE POWER TO SPARE... I CAN CONTINUE TO STOP TIME! THE JOESTAR BLOOD IS MAKING THIS BODY STRONGER THAN EVER BEFORE!
BUT YOU, JOTARO... I KNOW *YOU* CAN'T MOVE ANYMORE...! *FWA HA HA HA HA HA HA HA!*
THOOM
OLD MAN, YOU WARNED ME TO NOT GET ANGRY... AND IT LOOKS LIKE YOU'RE RIGHT... 'CAUSE NOW I'M SCREWED.
BUT YOU KNOW WHAT?
HE HASN'T FELT... THE FULL FORCE OF MY ANGER YET!

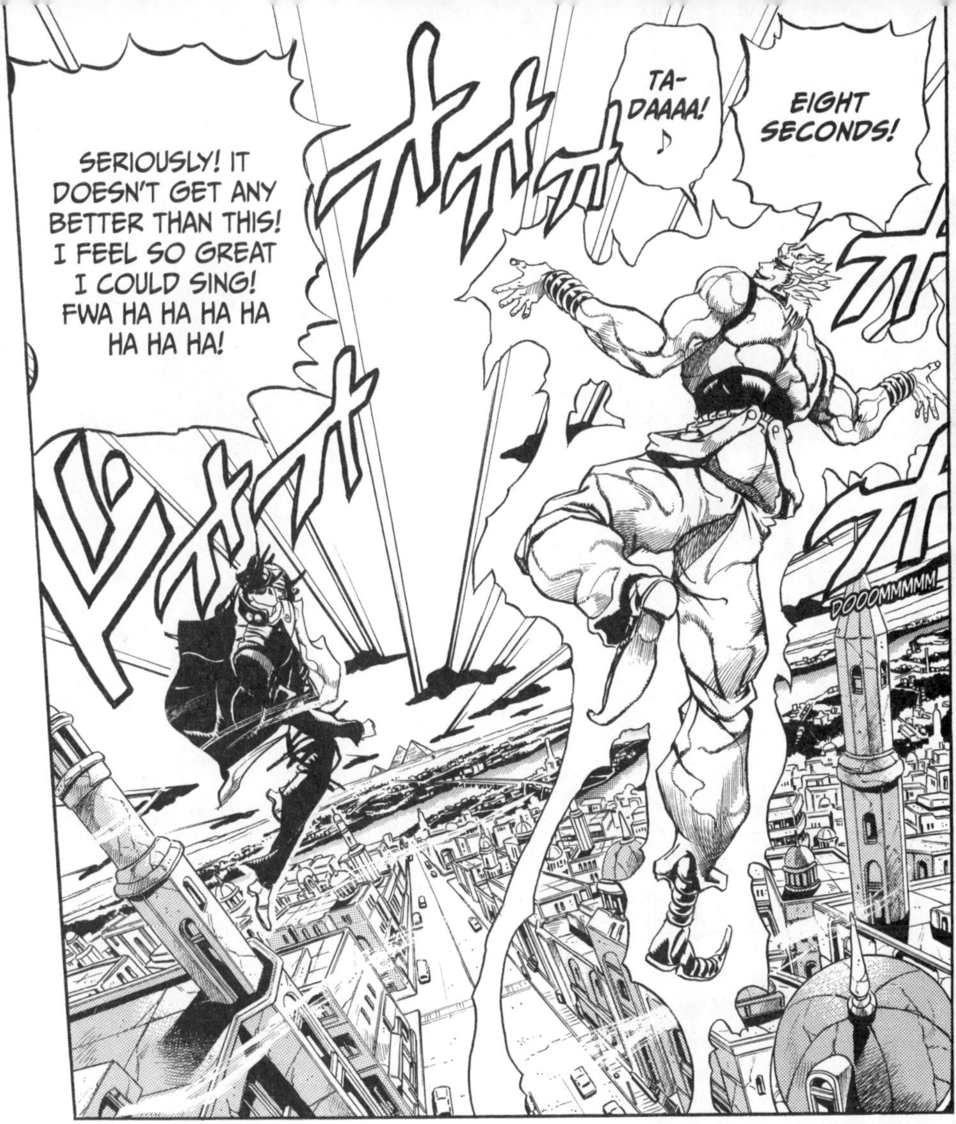
EIGHT SECONDS!
TA-DAAAA! ♪
SERIOUSLY! IT DOESN'T GET ANY BETTER THAN THIS! I FEEL SO GREAT I COULD SING! FWA HA HA HA HA HA HA HA!
DOOOMMMMM

CHAPTER 150: DIO's World PART 17

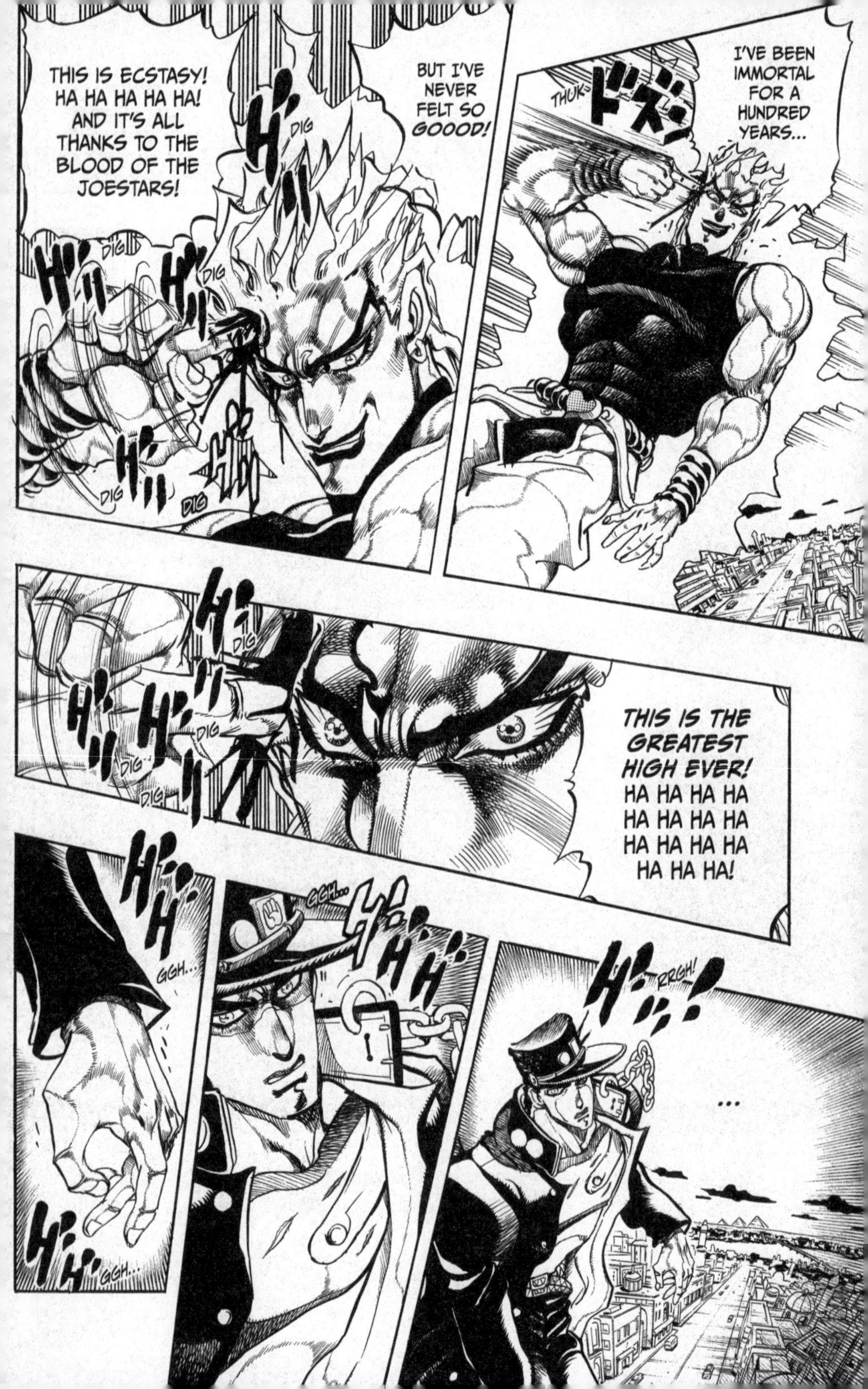
THUK
ドズッ
I'VE BEEN IMMORTAL FOR A HUNDRED YEARS...
BUT I'VE NEVER FELT SO GOOOD!
THIS IS ECSTASY! HA HA HA HA HA! AND IT'S ALL THANKS TO THE BLOOD OF THE JOESTARS!
DIG
DIG
DIG
DIG
DIG
THIS IS THE GREATEST HIGH EVER! HA HA HA HA HA HA HA HA HA HA HA HA HA HA HA!
DIG
DIG
DIG
DIG
RRGH!
...
GGH...
GGH...
GGH...

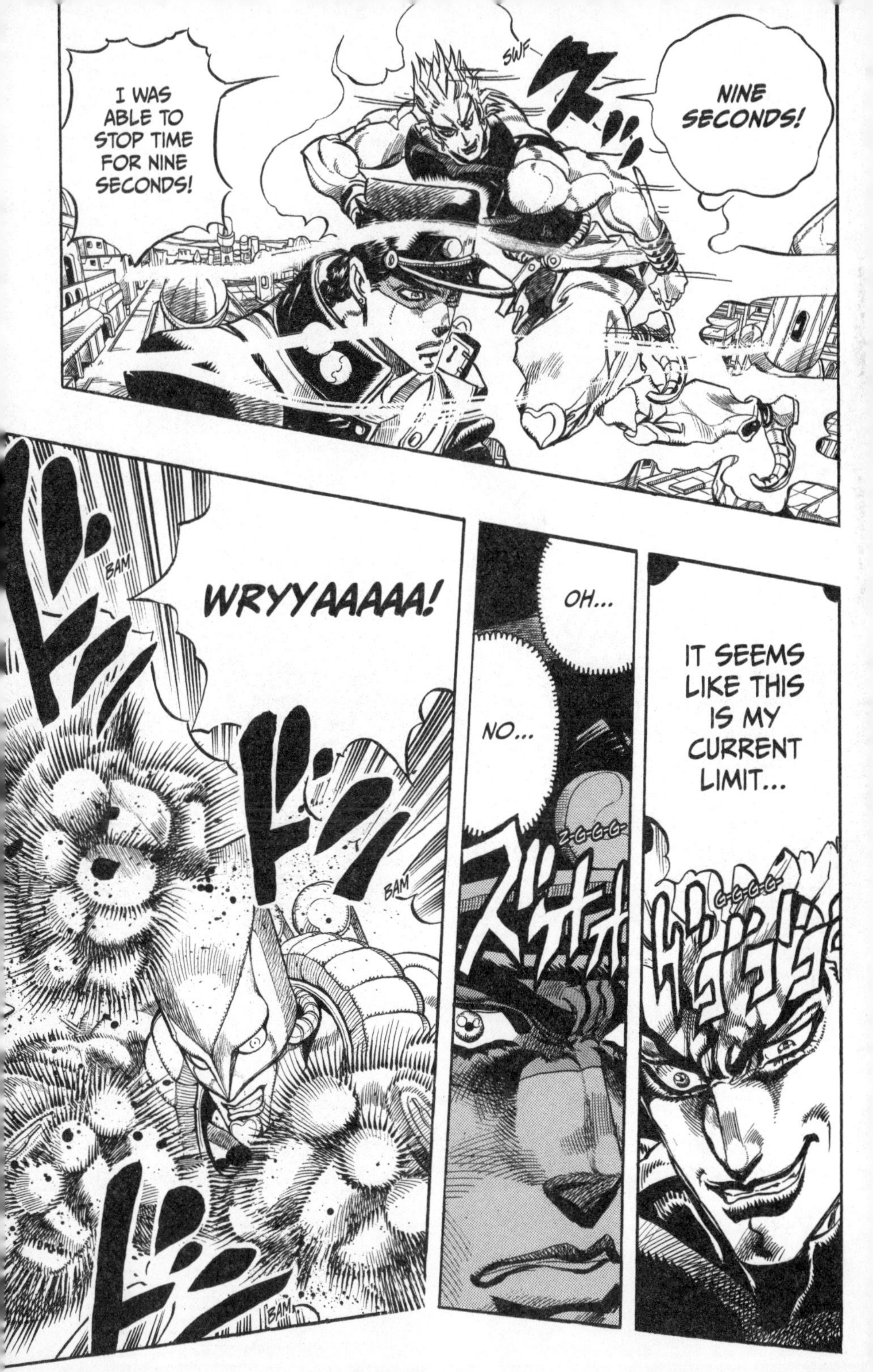
SWF
NINE SECONDS!
I WAS ABLE TO STOP TIME FOR NINE SECONDS!
IT SEEMS LIKE THIS IS MY CURRENT LIMIT...
G-G-G-G
OH...
NO...
Z-G-G-G
WRYYAAAAA!
BAM
BAM
BAM

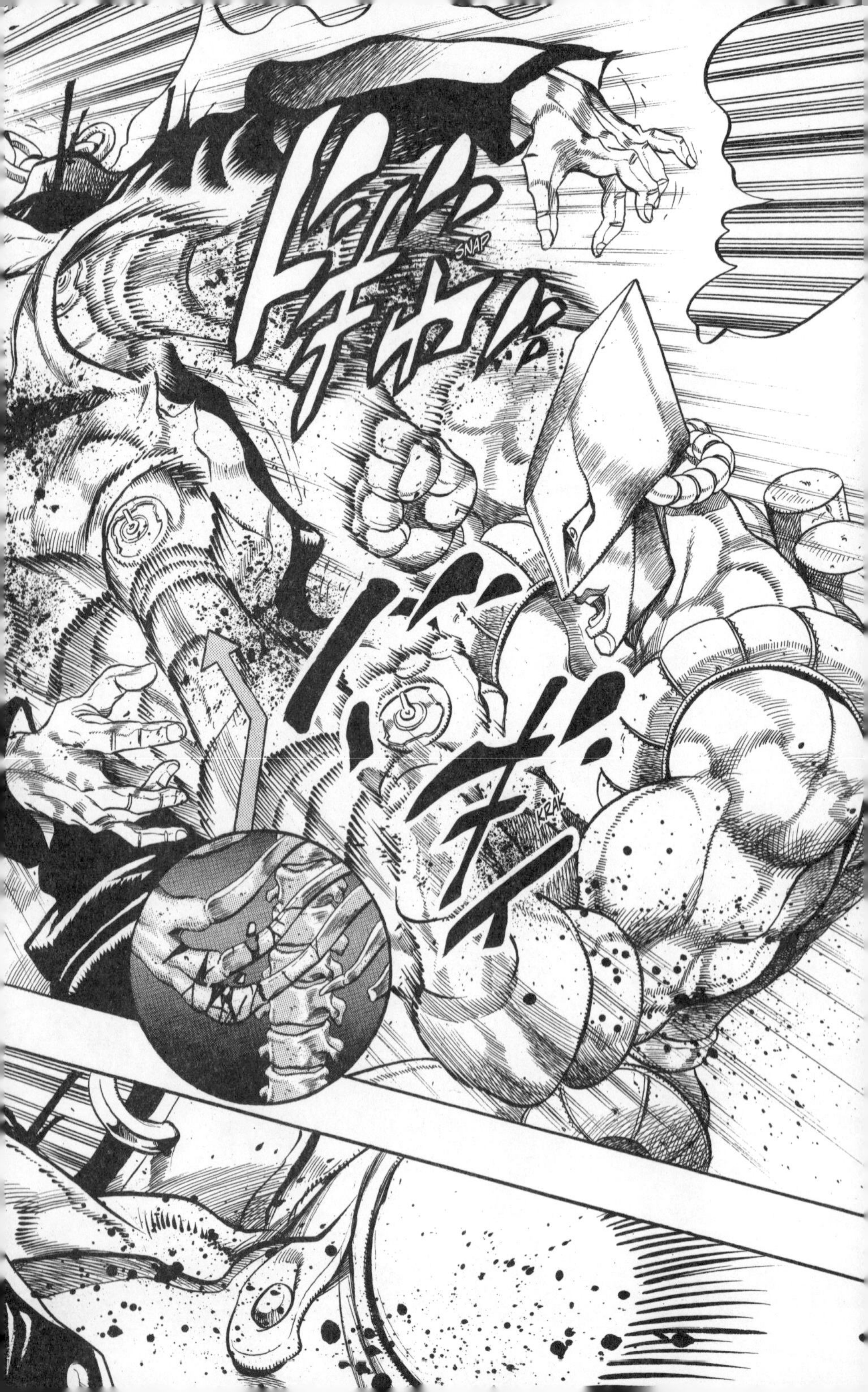
SNAP
KRAK

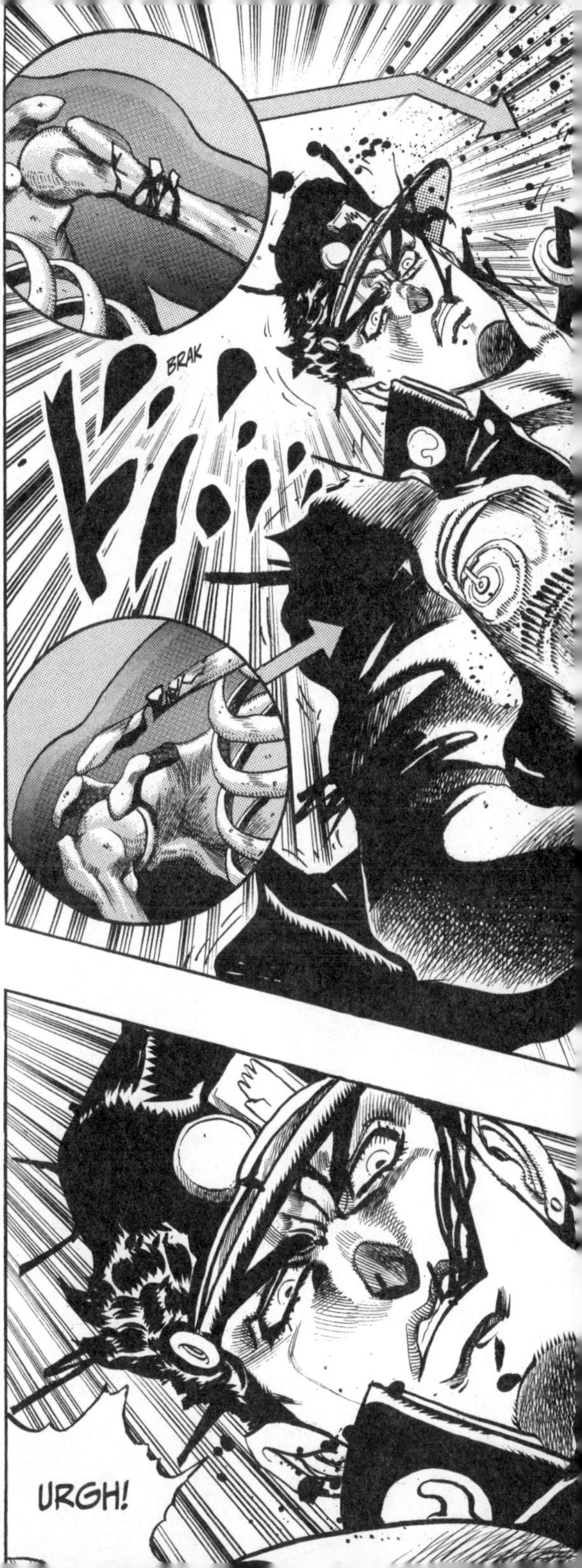
BRAK
URGH!

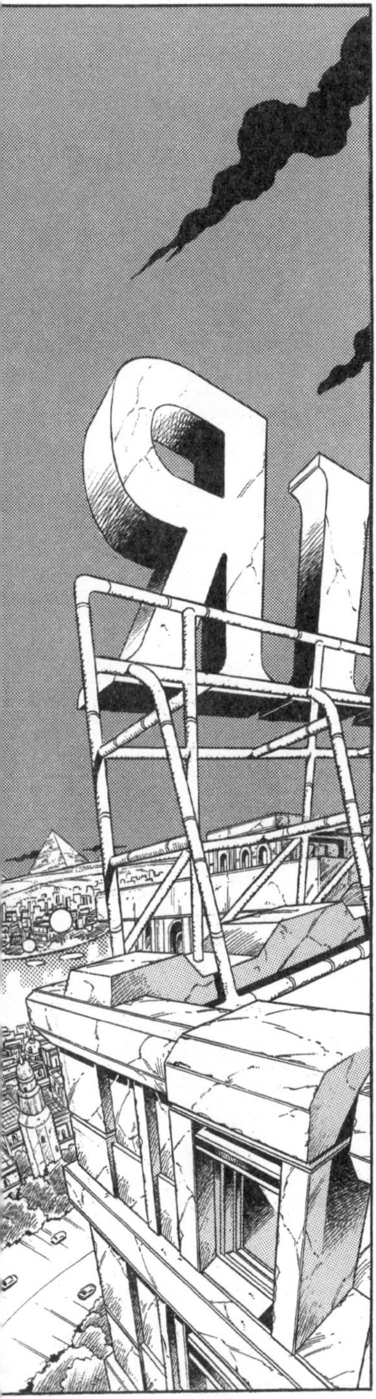

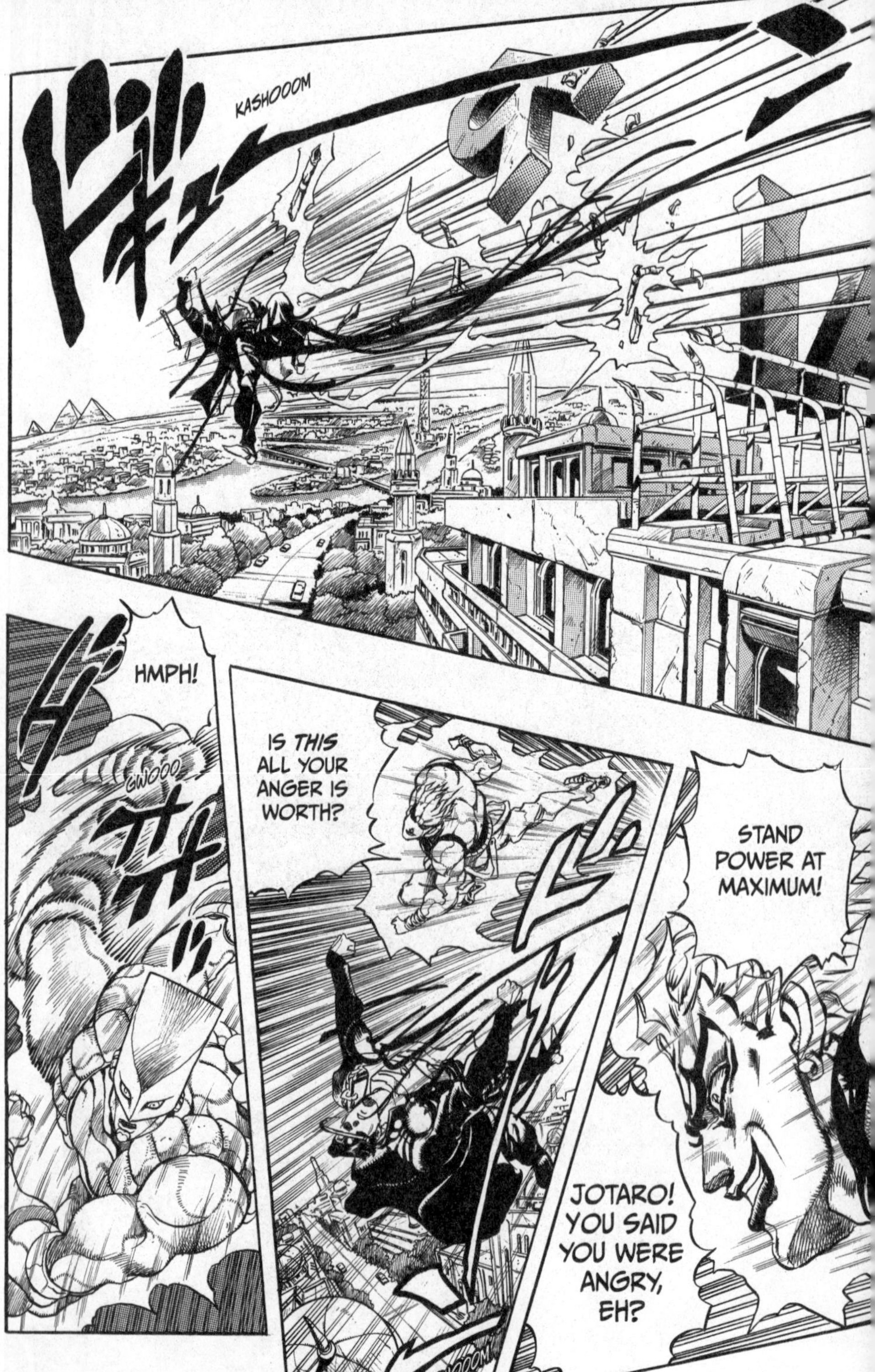
KASHOOOM
STAND POWER AT MAXIMUM!
JOTARO! YOU SAID YOU WERE ANGRY, EH?
IS THIS ALL YOUR ANGER IS WORTH?
VWOOOM
HMPH!
GWOOO

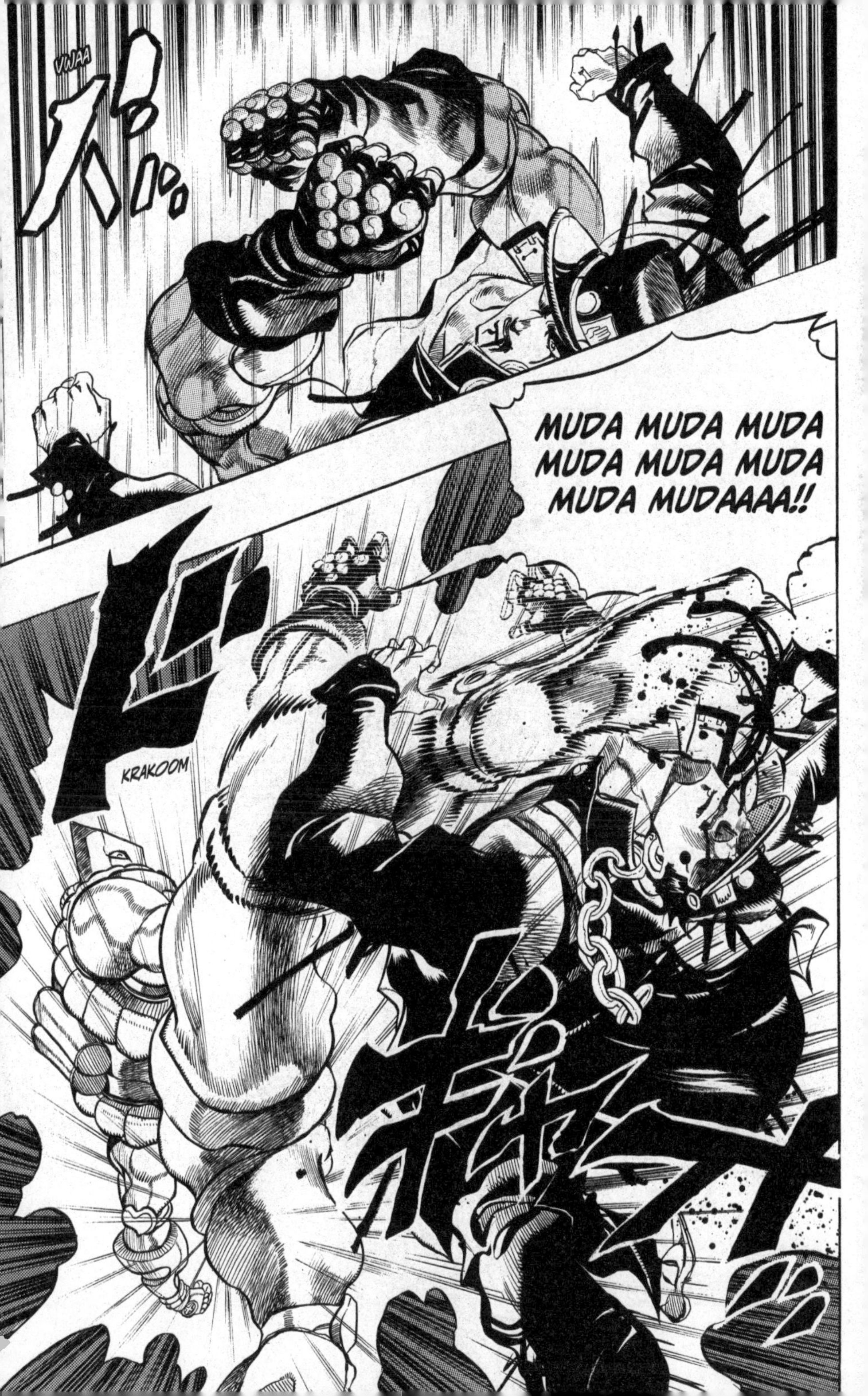
VWAA
MUDA MUDA MUDA
MUDA MUDA MUDA
MUDA MUDAAAA!!
KRAKOOM

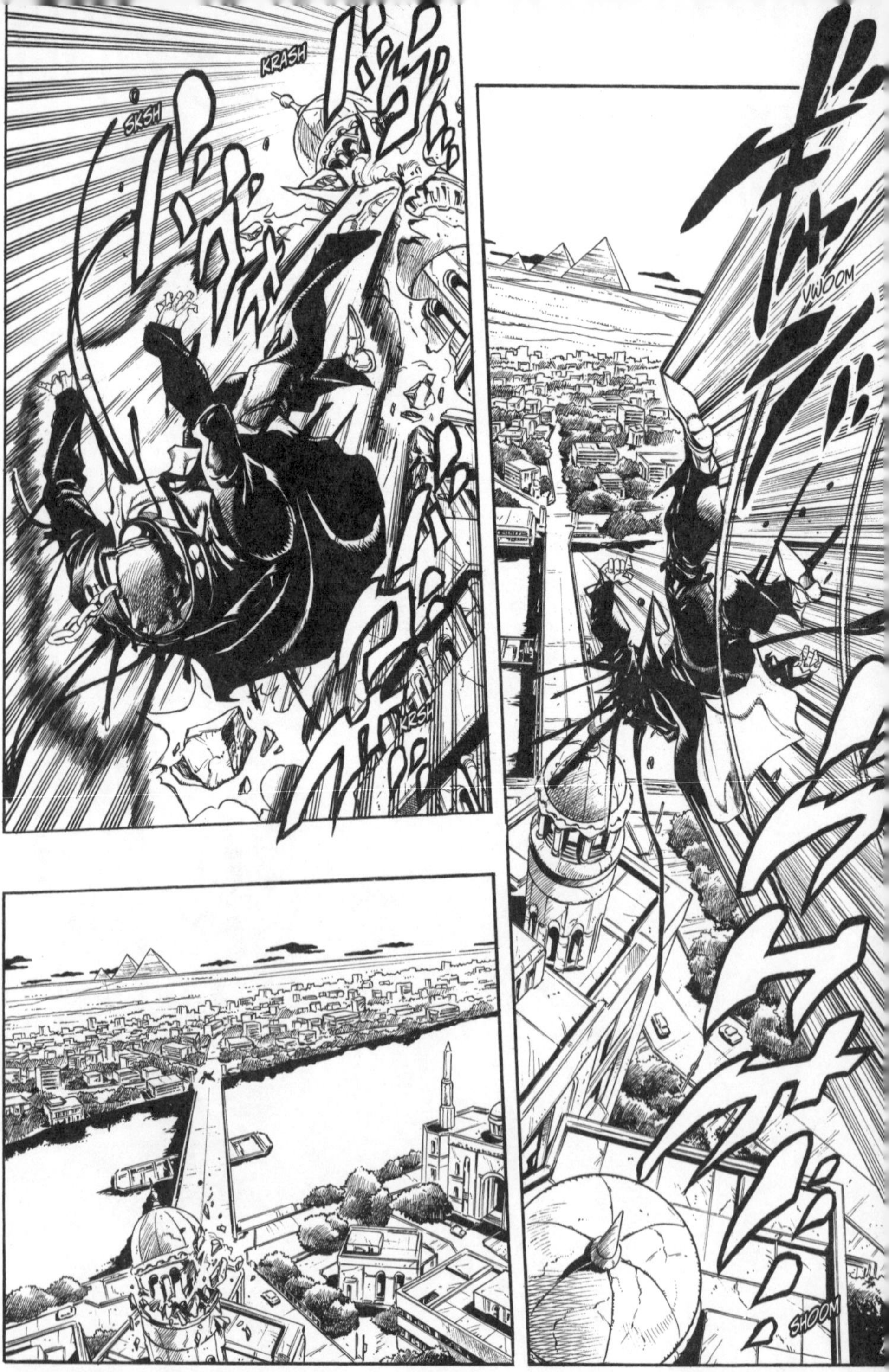
VWOOM
SHOOM
KRASH
SKSH
KRSH

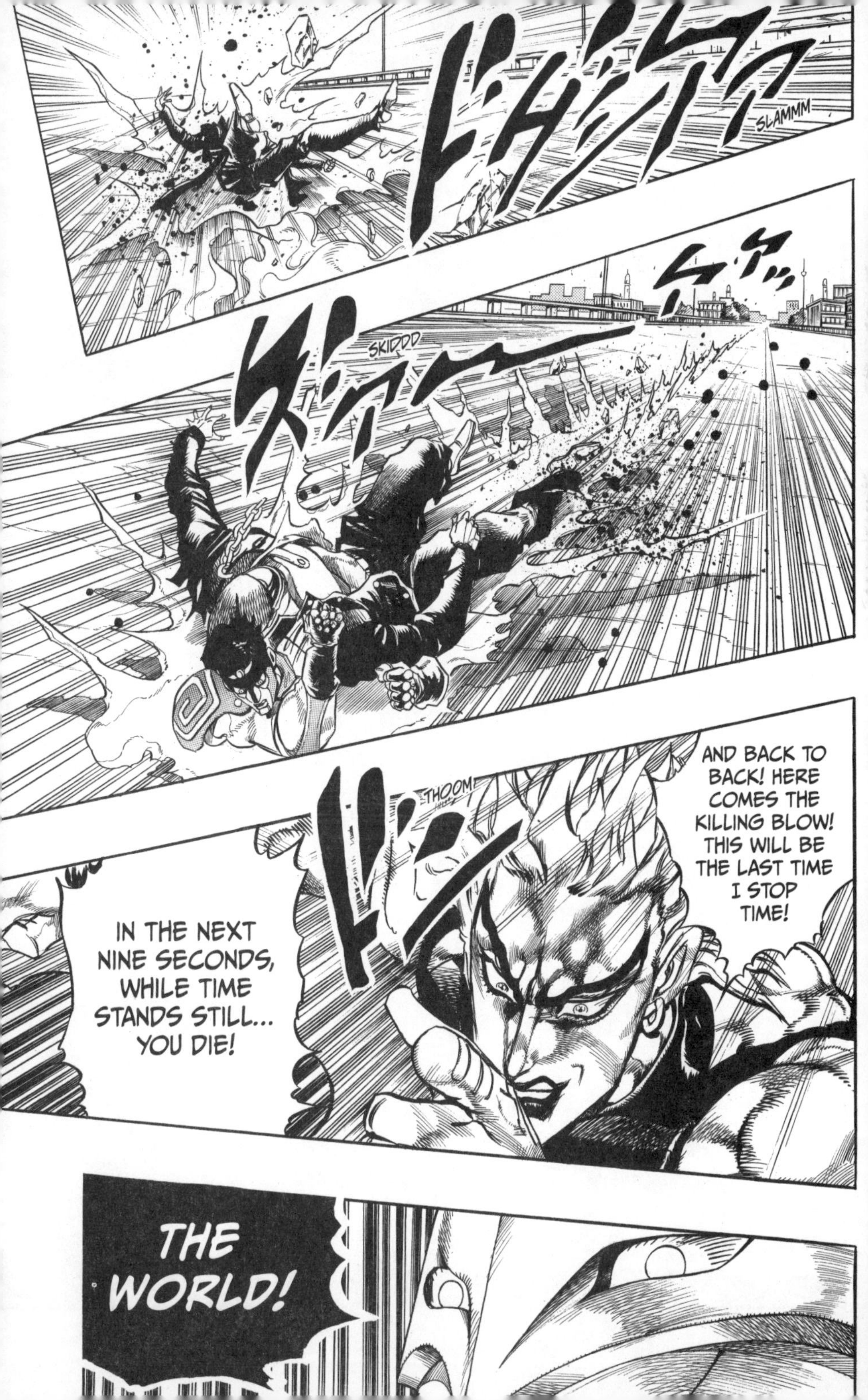

SLAMMM
SKIDDD
THOOM
AND BACK TO BACK! HERE COMES THE KILLING BLOW! THIS WILL BE THE LAST TIME I STOP TIME!
IN THE NEXT NINE SECONDS, WHILE TIME STANDS STILL... YOU DIE!
THE WORLD!

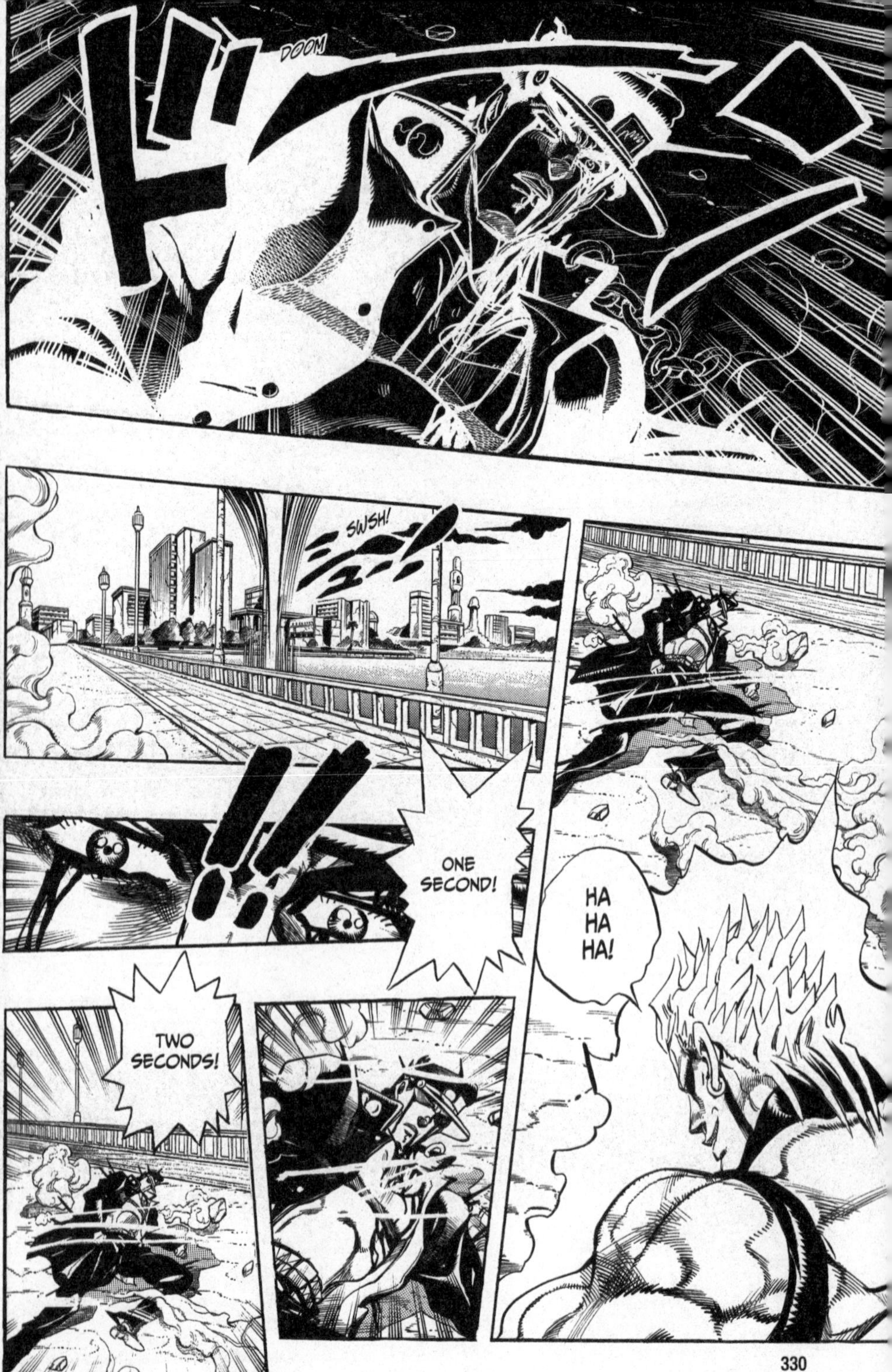
DOOM
HA
HA
HA!
SWSH!
ONE
SECOND!
TWO
SECONDS!

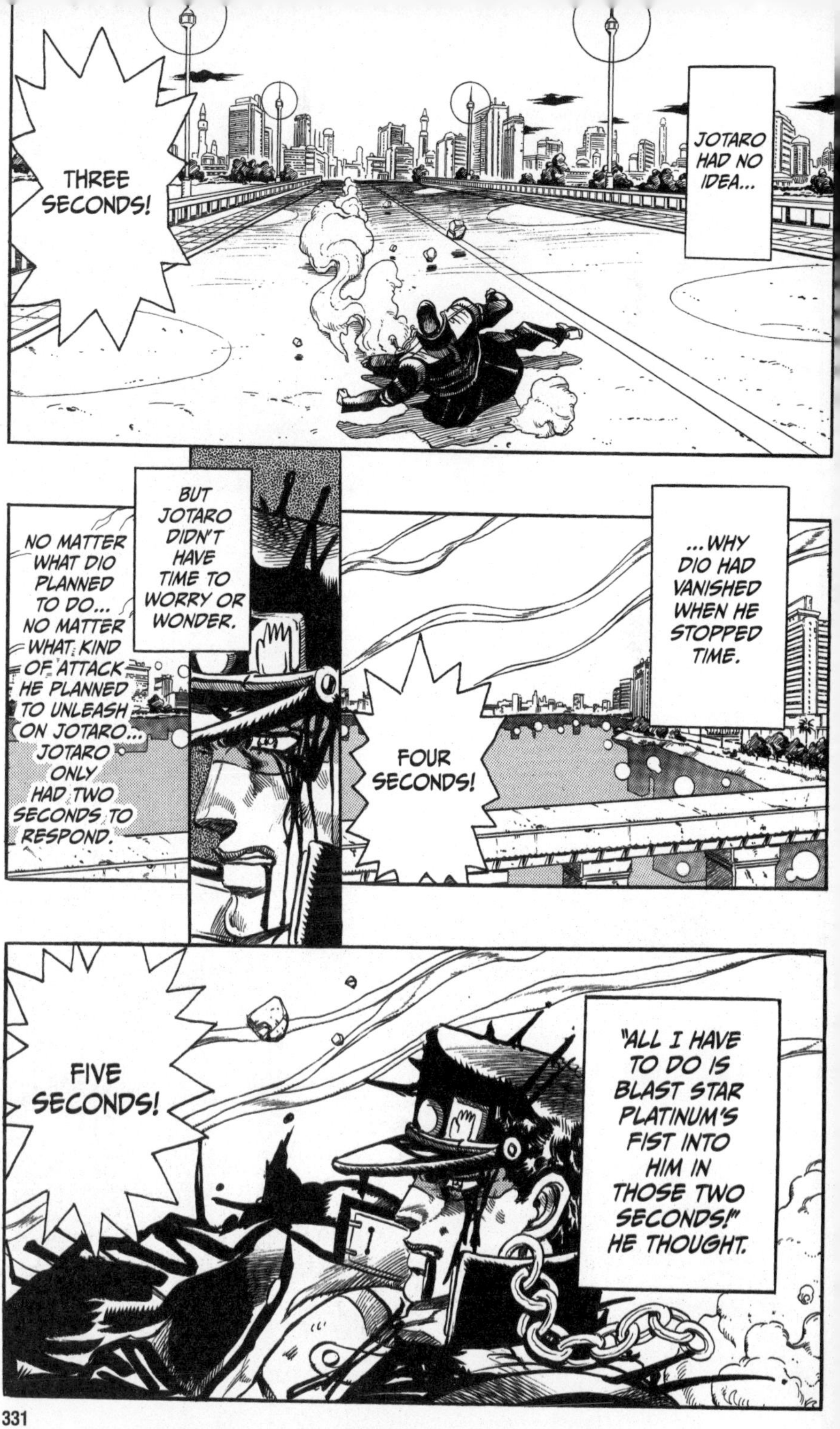
JOTARO HAD NO IDEA...
THREE SECONDS!
...WHY DIO HAD VANISHED WHEN HE STOPPED TIME.
FOUR SECONDS!
BUT JOTARO DIDN'T HAVE TIME TO WORRY OR WONDER.
NO MATTER WHAT DIO PLANNED TO DO... NO MATTER WHAT KIND OF ATTACK HE PLANNED TO UNLEASH ON JOTARO... JOTARO ONLY HAD TWO SECONDS TO RESPOND.
"ALL I HAVE TO DO IS BLAST STAR PLATINUM'S FIST INTO HIM IN THOSE TWO SECONDS!" HE THOUGHT.
FIVE SECONDS!

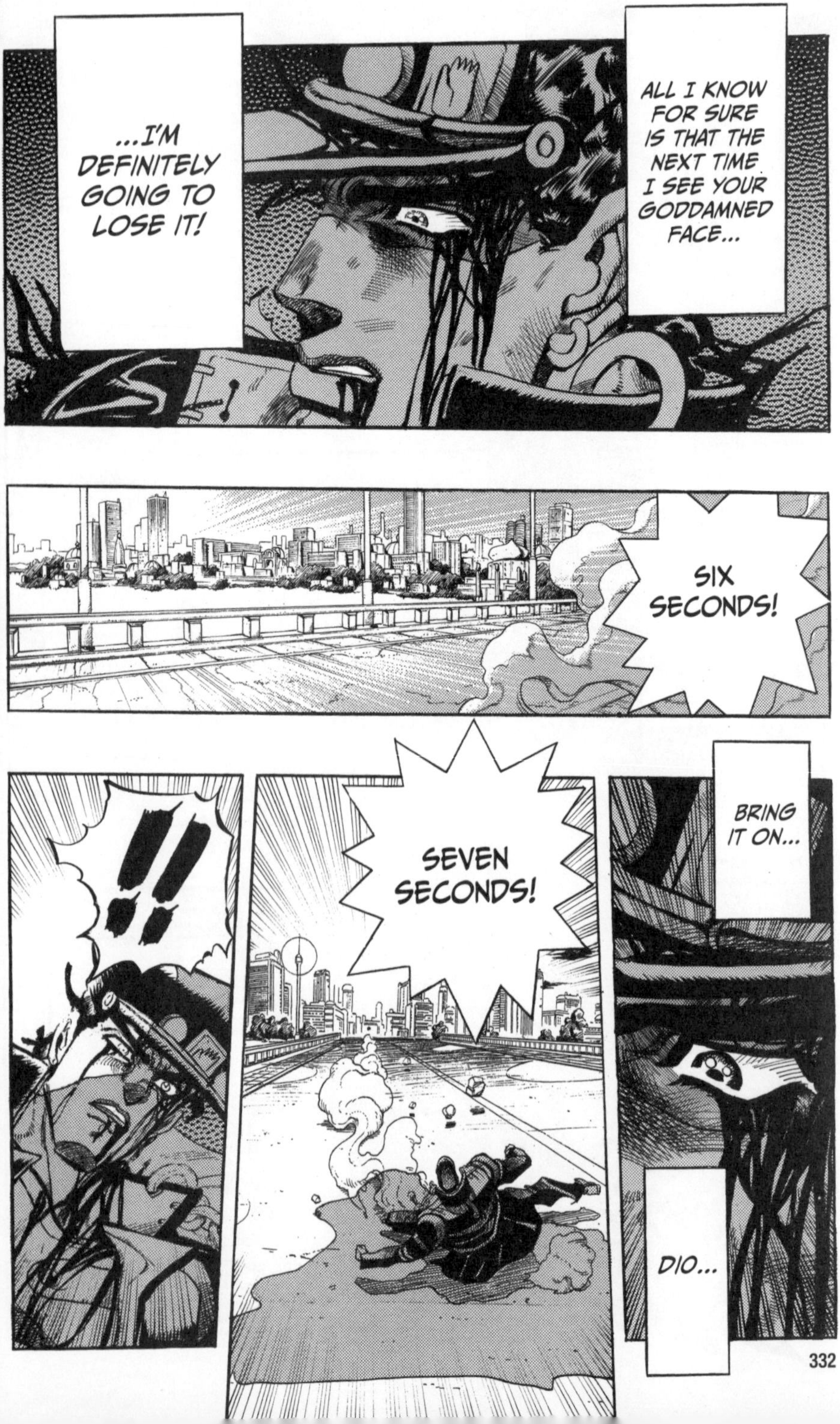
ALL I KNOW FOR SURE IS THAT THE NEXT TIME I SEE YOUR GODDAMNED FACE...
...I'M DEFINITELY GOING TO LOSE IT!
SIX SECONDS!
BRING IT ON...
DIO...
SEVEN SECONDS!
!!

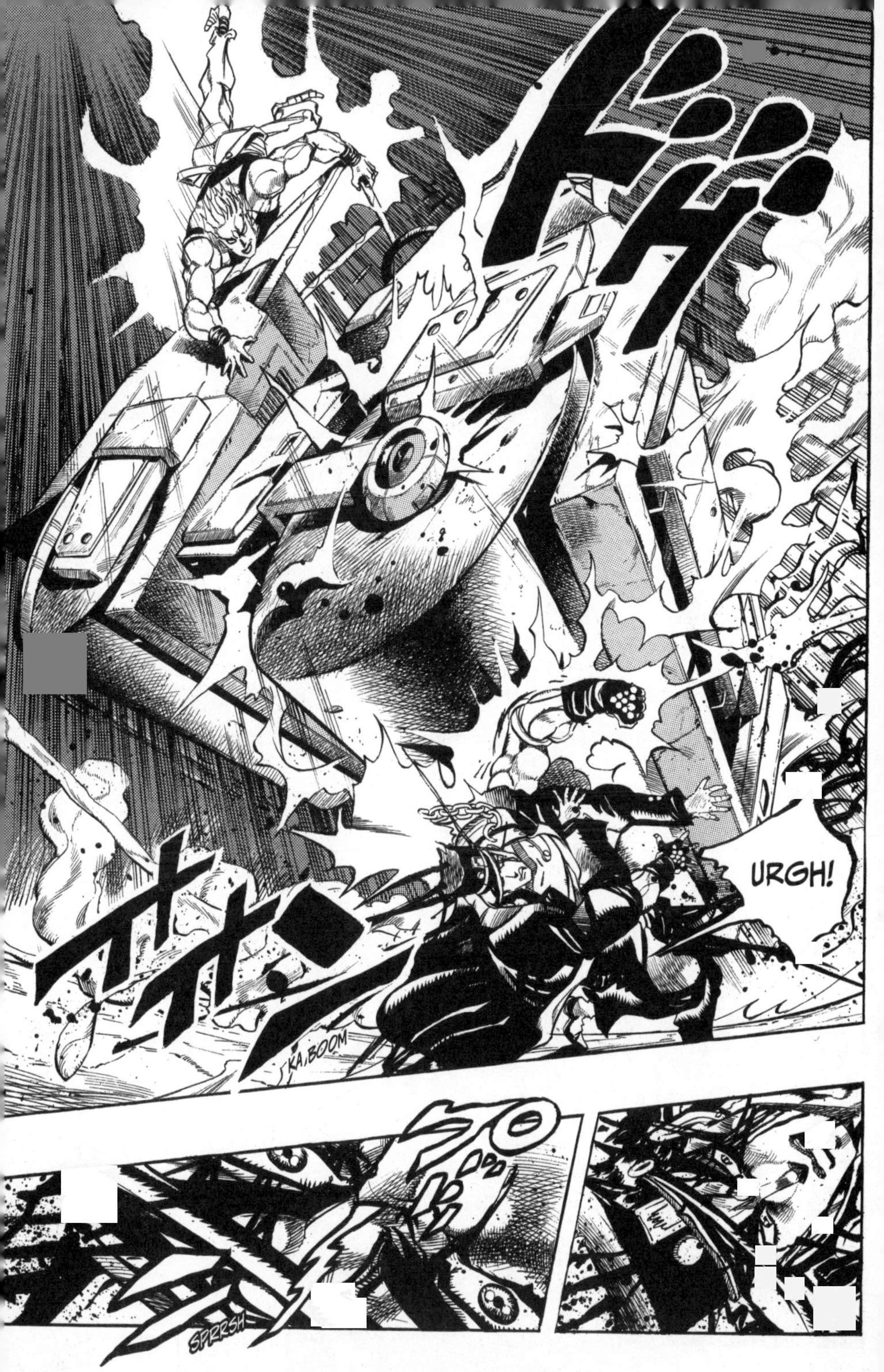
URGH!
KA-BOOM
SPRRSH

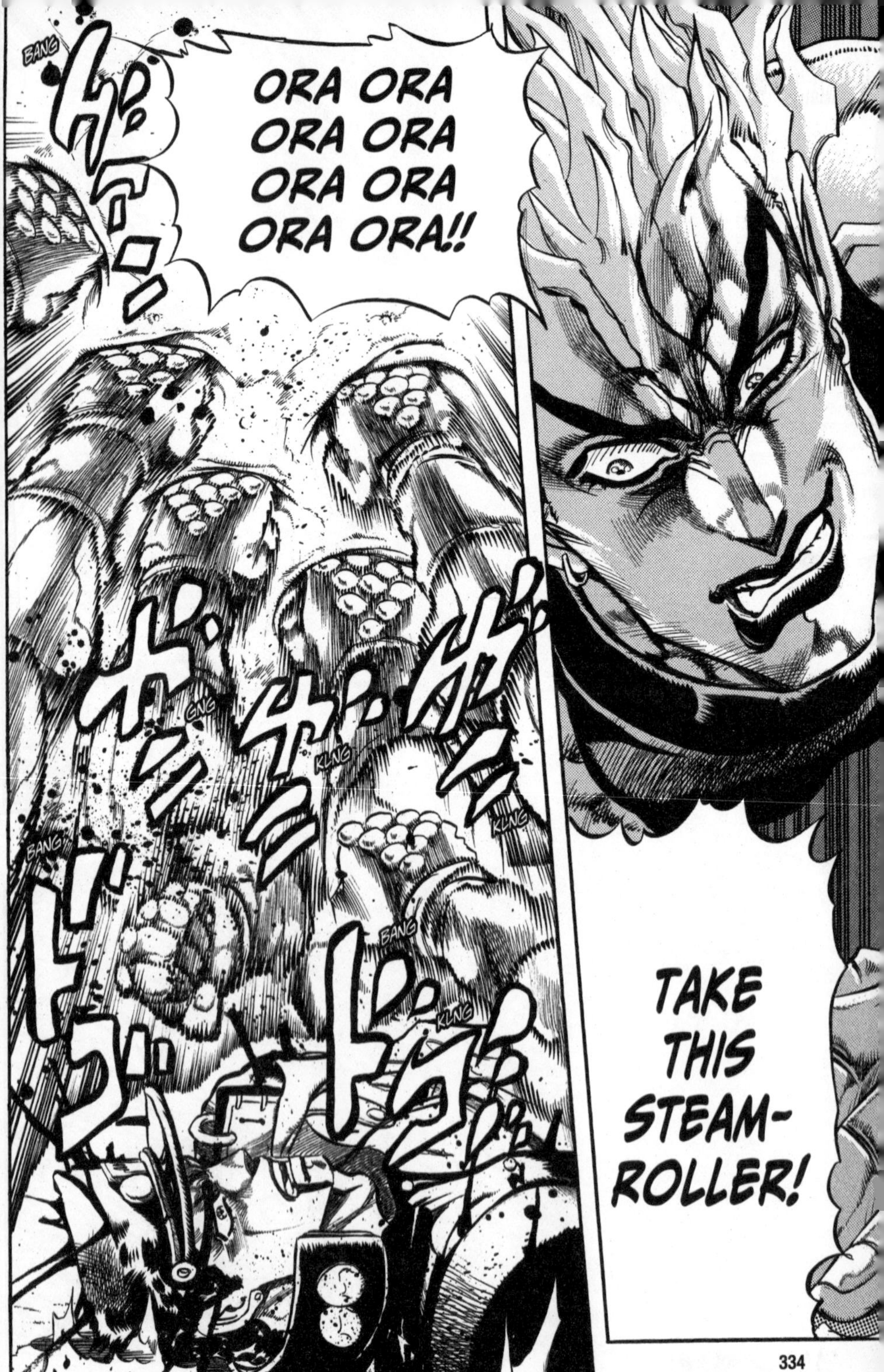
TAKE THIS STEAM-ROLLER!
ORA ORA ORA ORA ORA ORA ORA ORA!!
BANG
GNG
KLNG
KLNG
BANG
BANG
KLNG

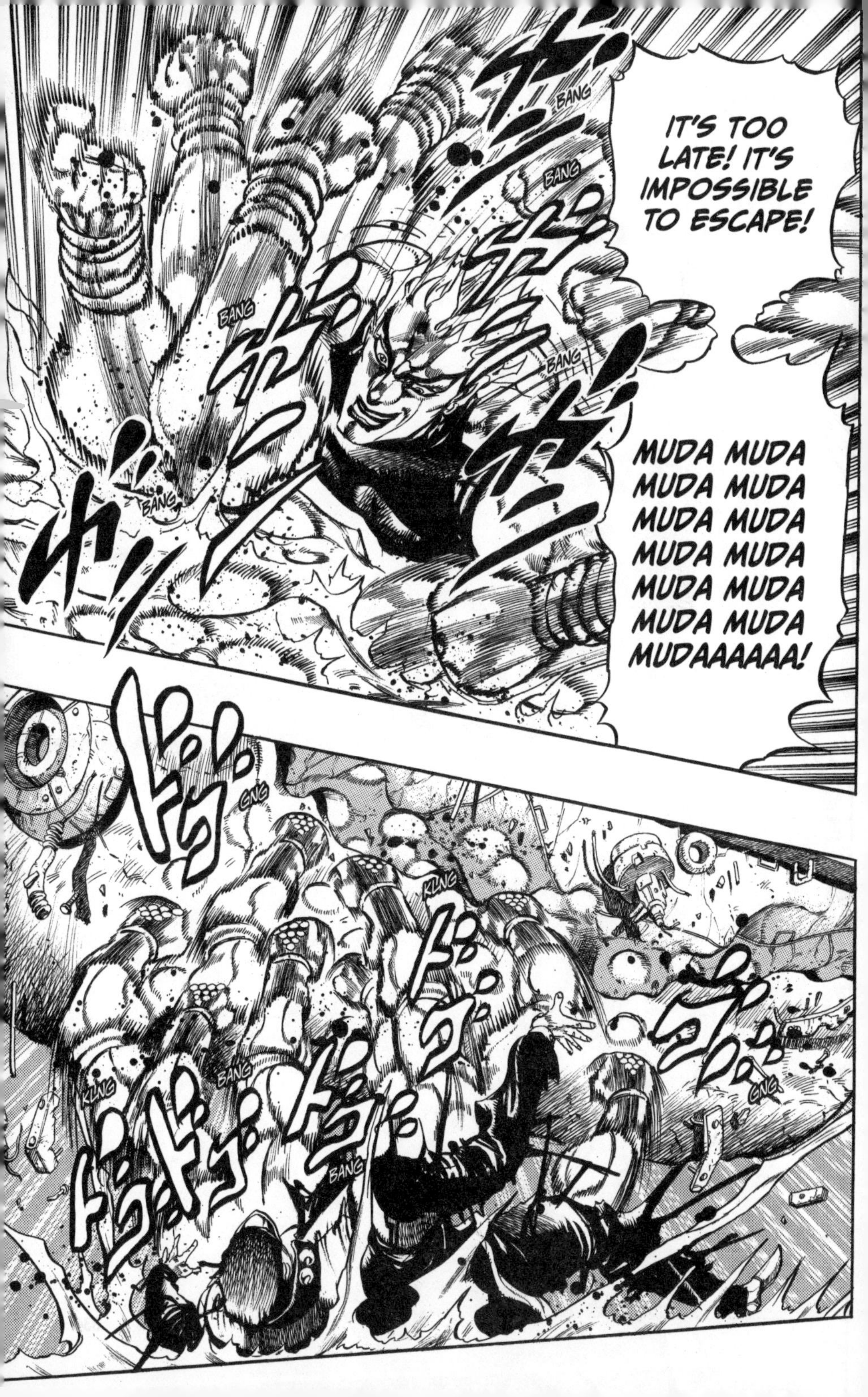
IT'S TOO LATE! IT'S IMPOSSIBLE TO ESCAPE!
MUDA MUDA MUDA MUDA MUDA MUDA MUDA MUDA MUDA MUDA MUDA MUDA MUDAAAAAA!
BANG
BANG
BANG
BANG
BANG
CNG
KLNG
BANG
BANG
KLNG
CNG

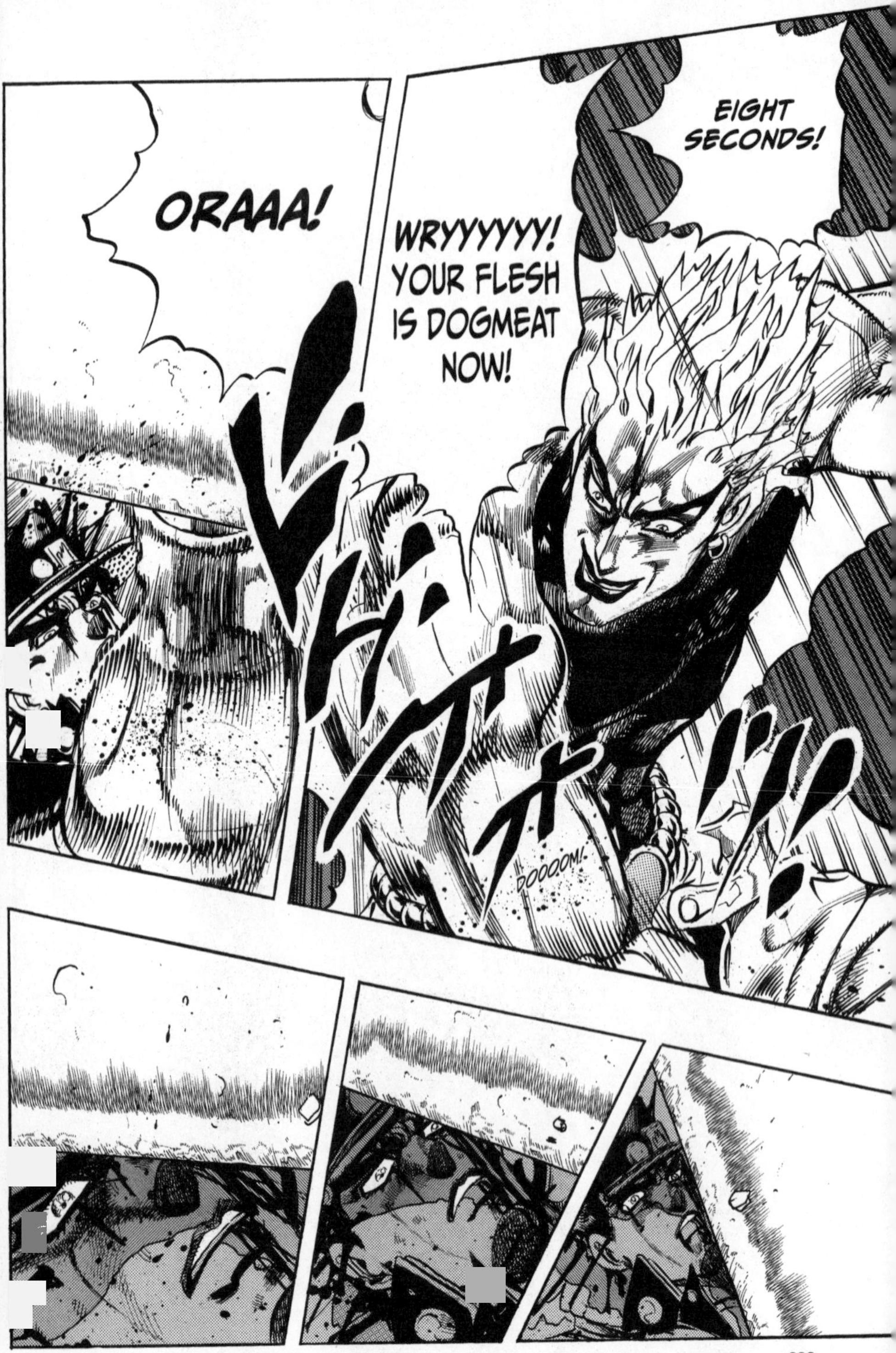
EIGHT SECONDS!
WRYYYYYY! YOUR FLESH IS DOGMEAT NOW!
DOOOOM!
ORAAA!

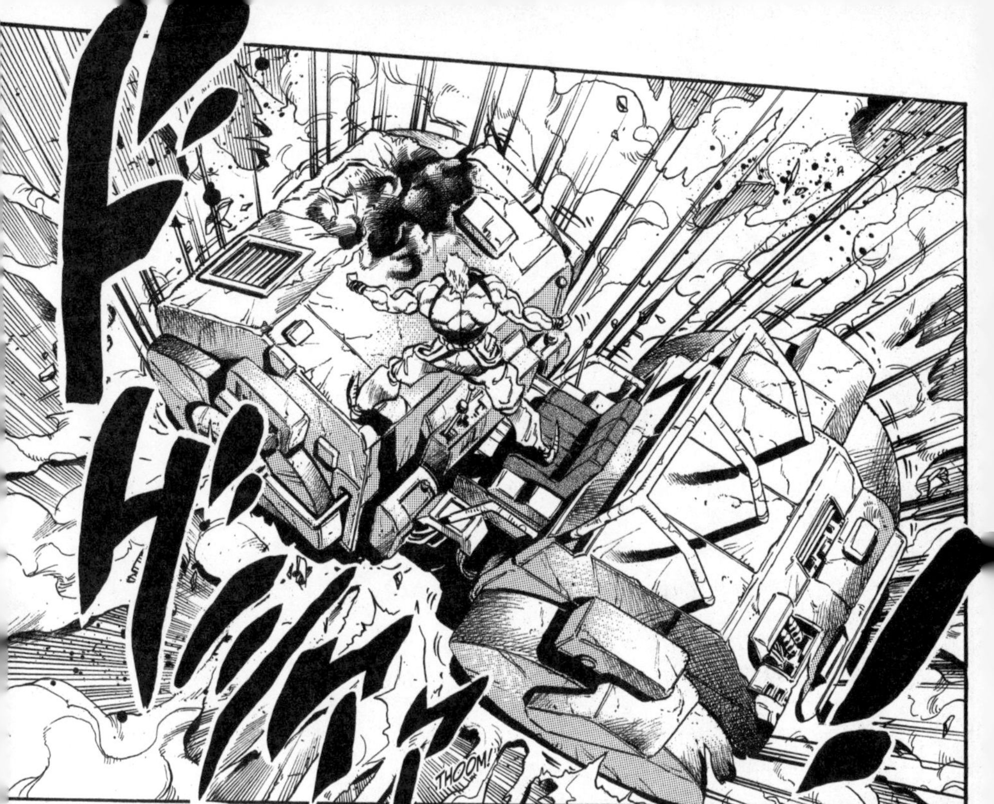
THOOM!
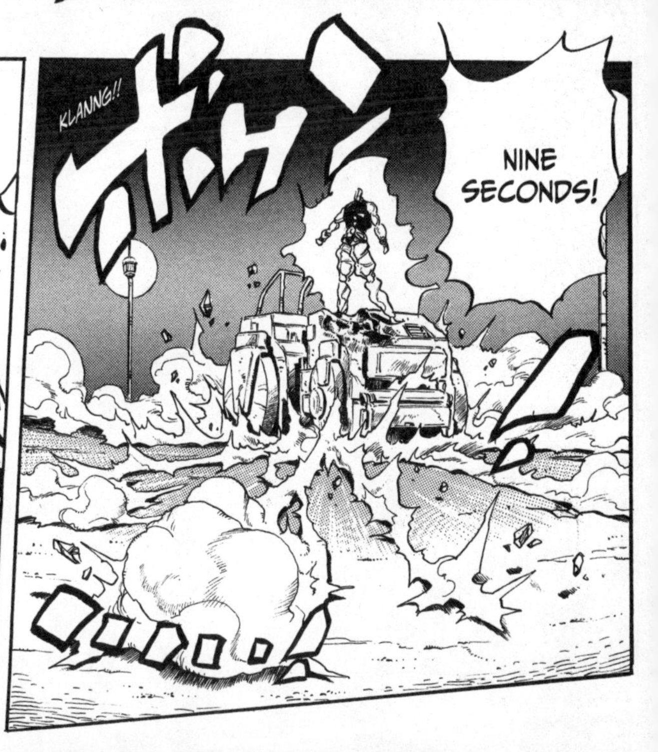
KLANNG!!
NINE SECONDS!
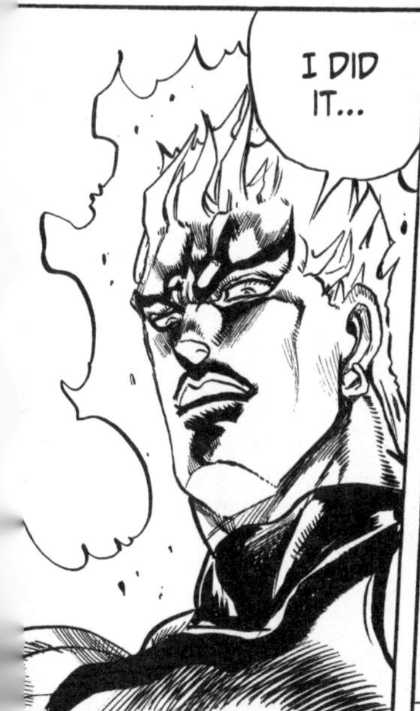
I DID IT...

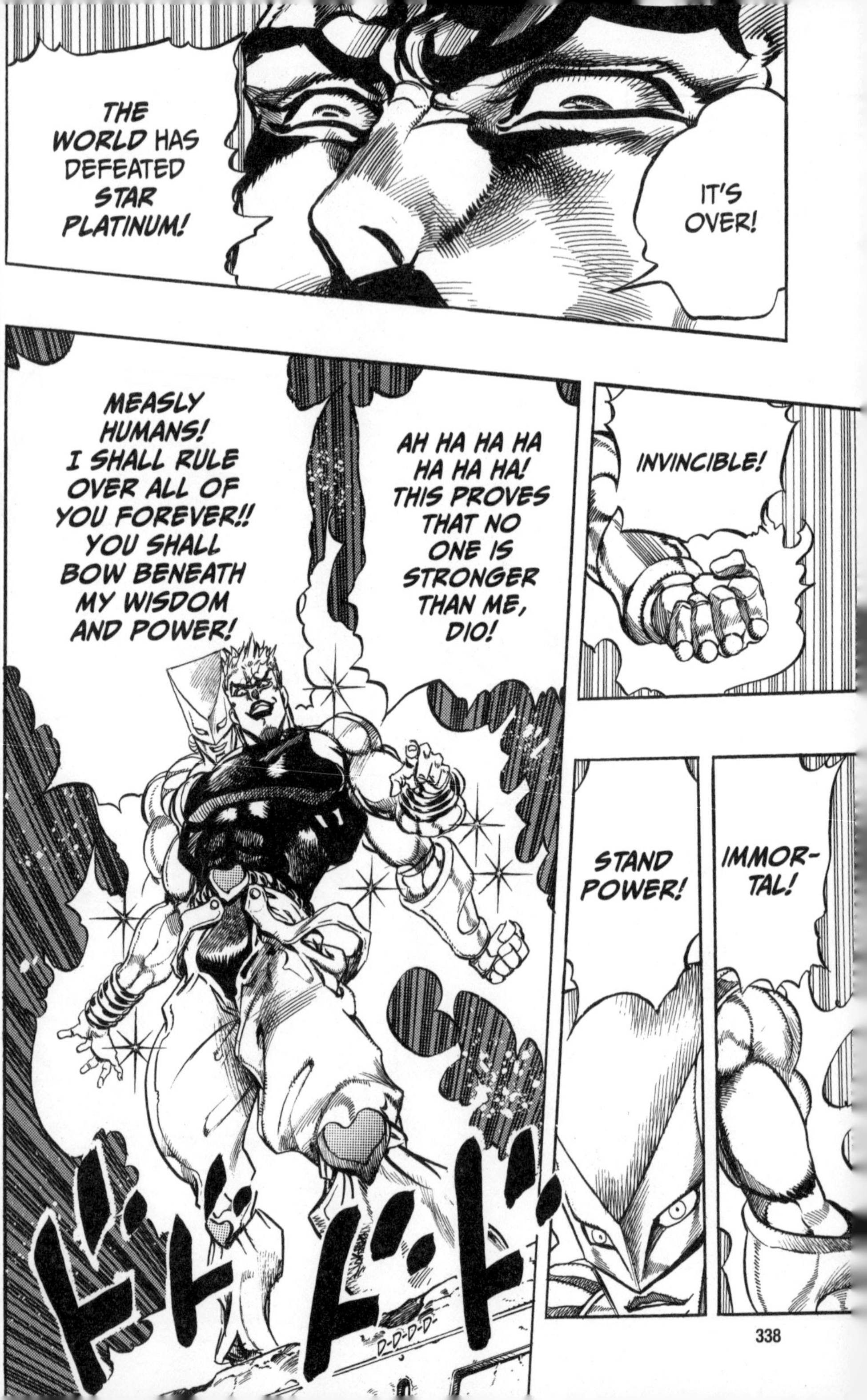
IT'S OVER!
THE WORLD HAS DEFEATED STAR PLATINUM!
INVINCIBLE!
IMMORTAL!
STAND POWER!
AH HA HA HA HA HA HA! THIS PROVES THAT NO ONE IS STRONGER THAN ME, DIO!
MEASLY HUMANS! I SHALL RULE OVER ALL OF YOU FOREVER!! YOU SHALL BOW BENEATH MY WISDOM AND POWER!
ドドドド
D-D-D-D-

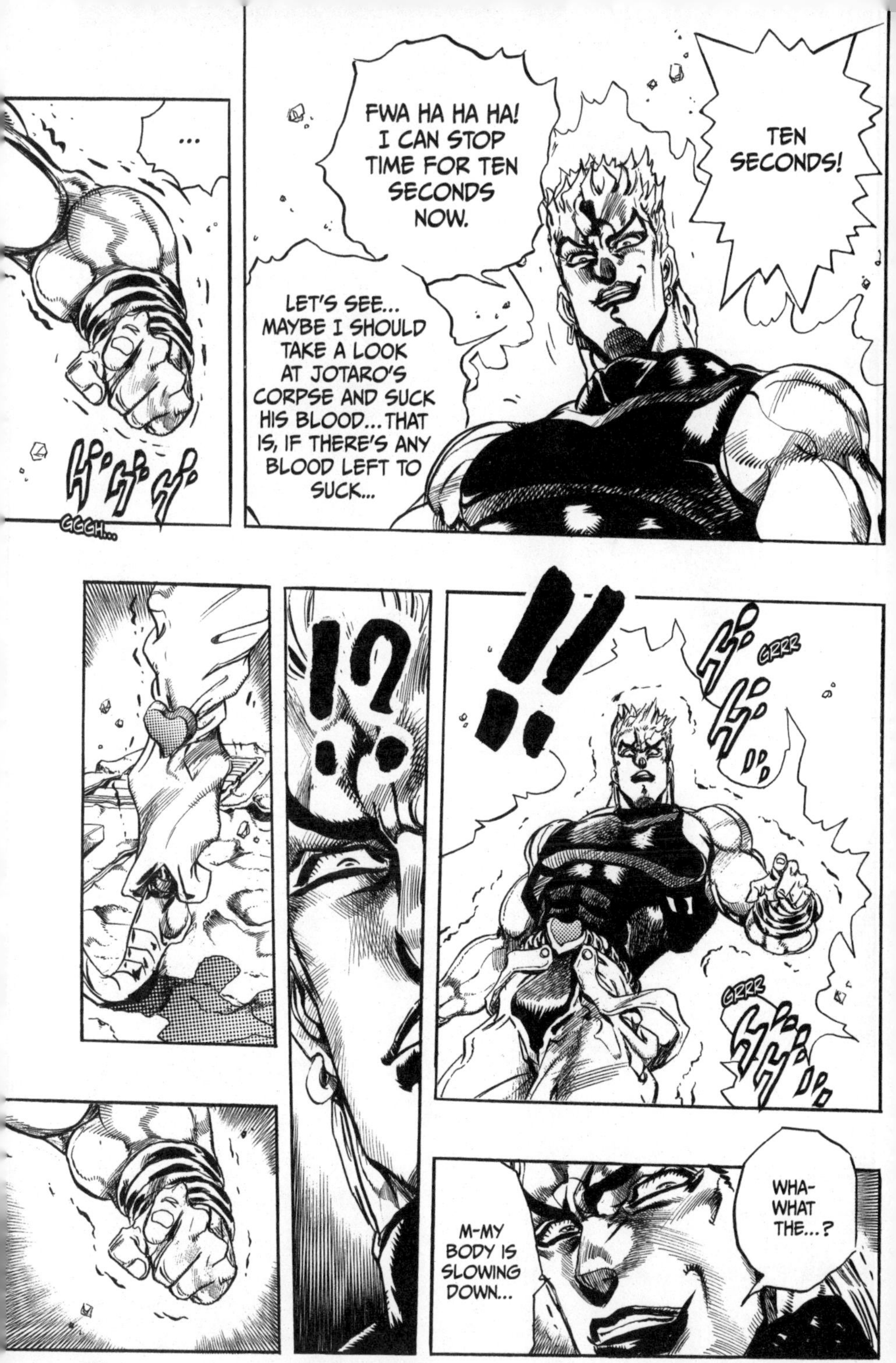
TEN SECONDS!
FWA HA HA HA! I CAN STOP TIME FOR TEN SECONDS NOW.
LET'S SEE... MAYBE I SHOULD TAKE A LOOK AT JOTARO'S CORPSE AND SUCK HIS BLOOD... THAT IS, IF THERE'S ANY BLOOD LEFT TO SUCK...
...
GGGH...
!!
GRRR
GRRR
!?
WHA- WHAT THE...?
M-MY BODY IS SLOWING DOWN...

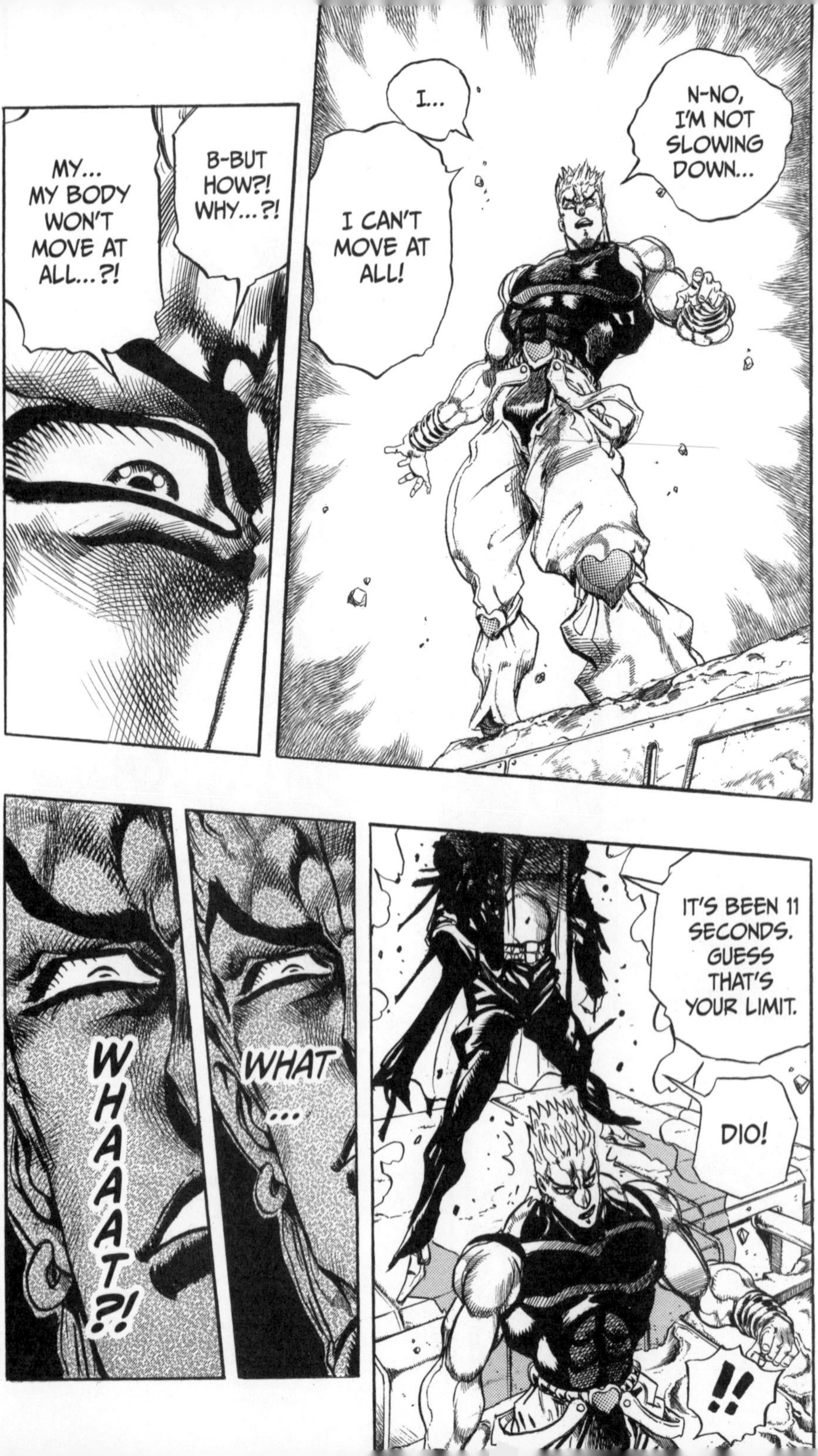
N-NO, I'M NOT SLOWING DOWN...
I...
I CAN'T MOVE AT ALL!
B-BUT HOW?! WHY...?!
MY... MY BODY WON'T MOVE AT ALL...?!
IT'S BEEN 11 SECONDS. GUESS THAT'S YOUR LIMIT.
DIO!
!!
WHAT...
WHAAAAT?!

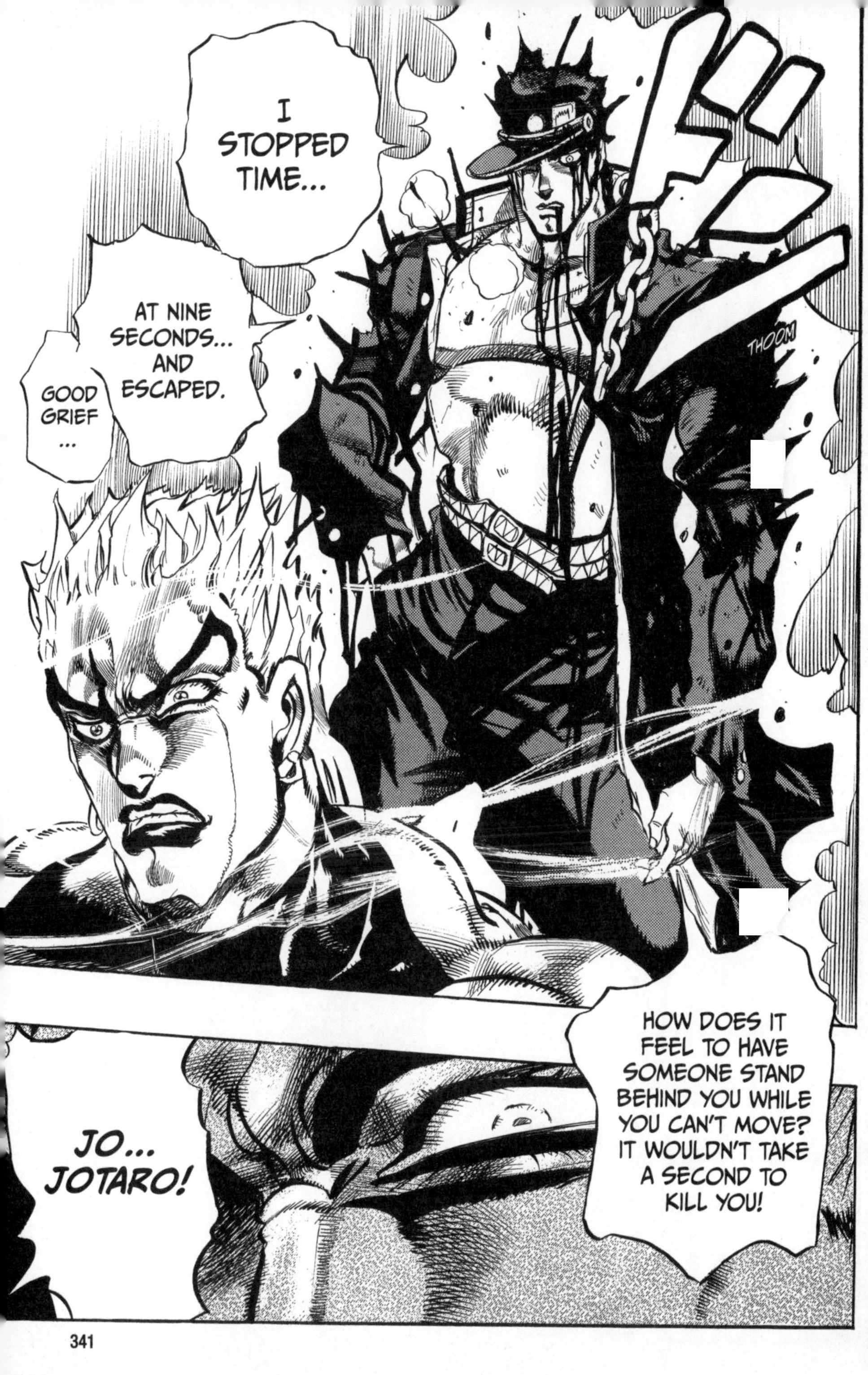
I STOPPED TIME...
AT NINE SECONDS... AND ESCAPED.
GOOD GRIEF...
THOOM
HOW DOES IT FEEL TO HAVE SOMEONE STAND BEHIND YOU WHILE YOU CAN'T MOVE? IT WOULDN'T TAKE A SECOND TO KILL YOU!
JO... JOTARO!

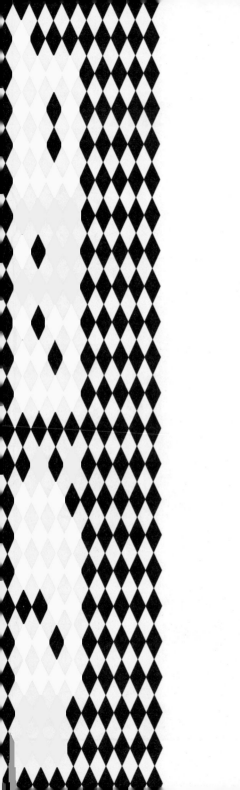

JoJo's
BIZARRE
ADVENTURE
1991

CHAPTER 151: DIO's World PART 18

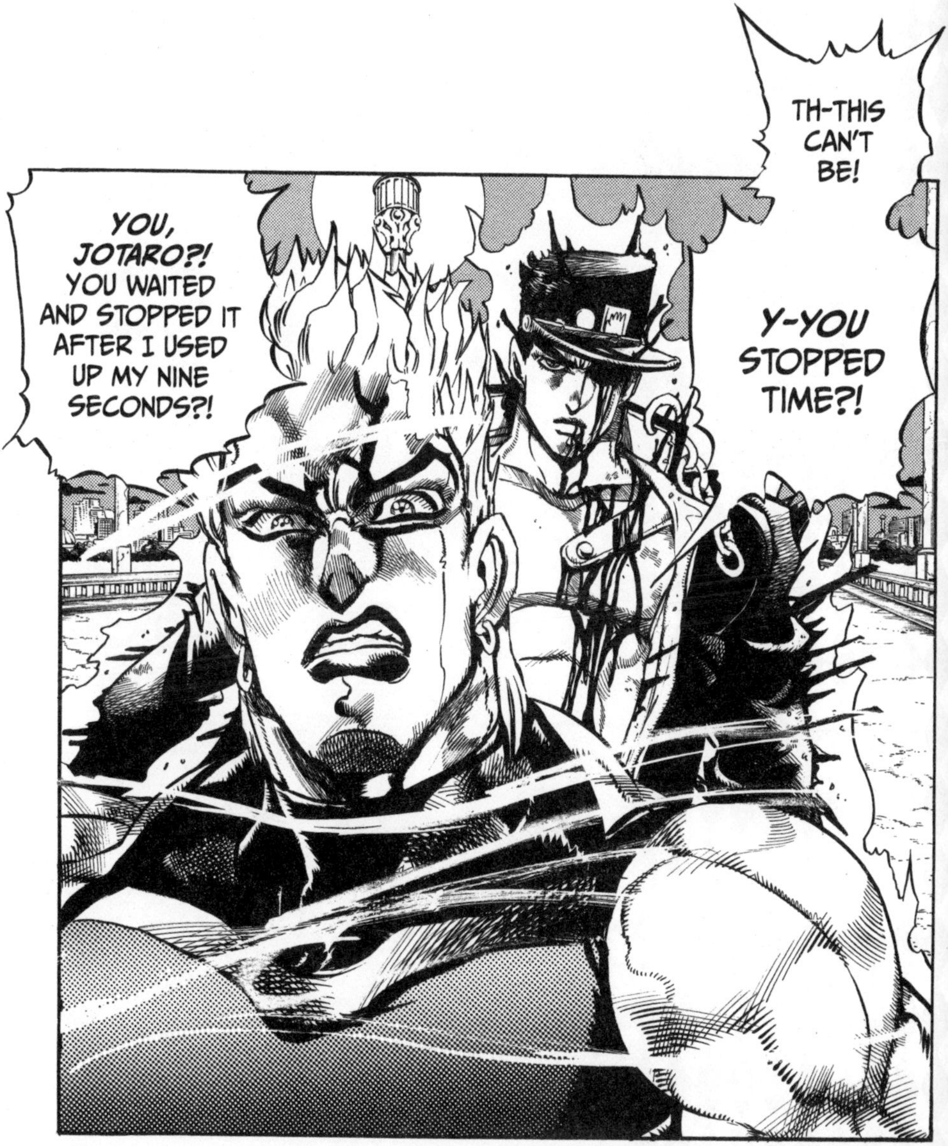
TH-THIS CAN'T BE!
Y-YOU STOPPED TIME?!
YOU, JOTARO?! YOU WAITED AND STOPPED IT AFTER I USED UP MY NINE SECONDS?!

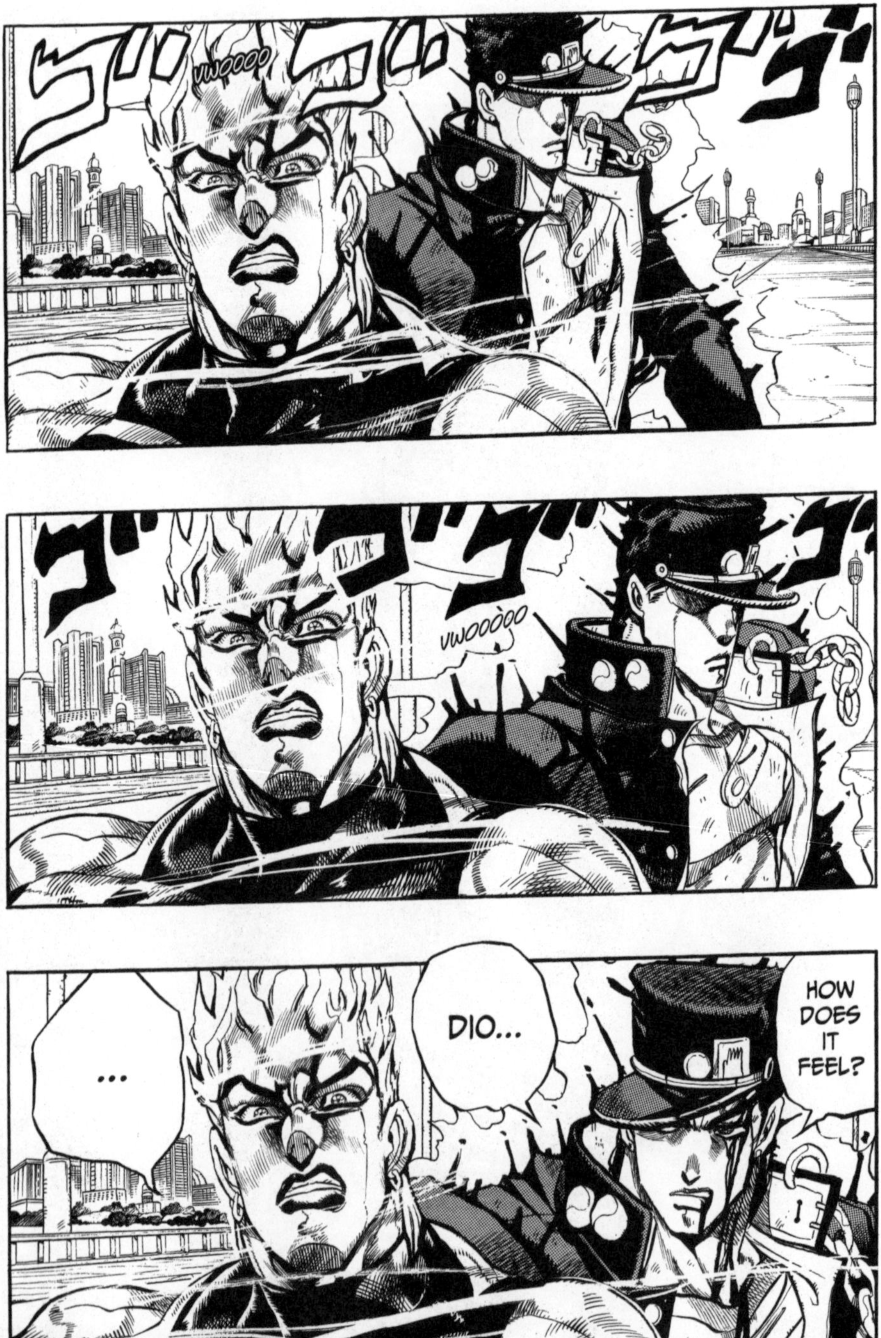
VWOOOO
VWOOOO
HOW DOES IT FEEL?
DIO...
...

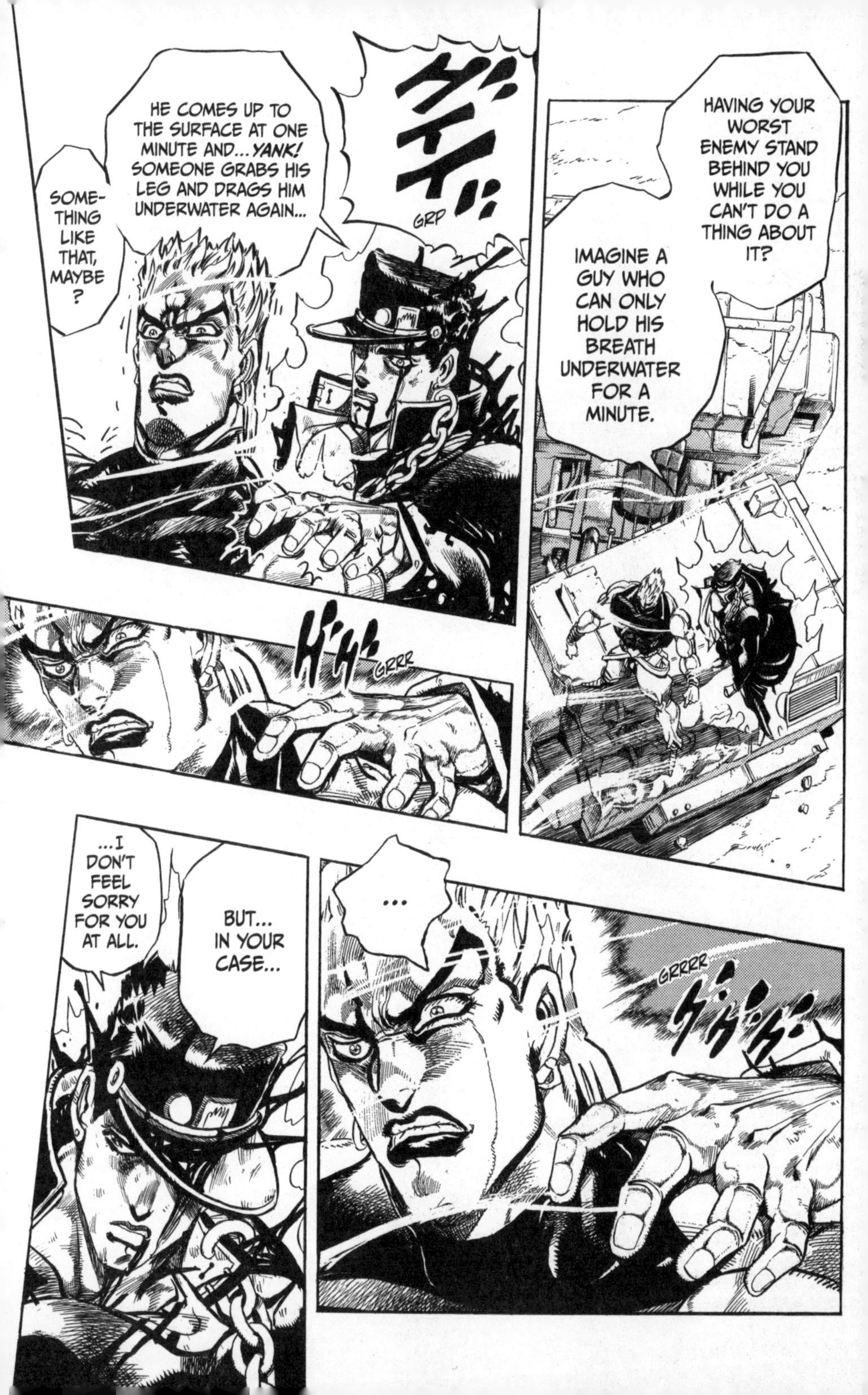
HAVING YOUR WORST ENEMY STAND BEHIND YOU WHILE YOU CAN'T DO A THING ABOUT IT?
IMAGINE A GUY WHO CAN ONLY HOLD HIS BREATH UNDERWATER FOR A MINUTE.
GRP
HE COMES UP TO THE SURFACE AT ONE MINUTE AND... YANK! SOMEONE GRABS HIS LEG AND DRAGS HIM UNDERWATER AGAIN...
SOMETHING LIKE THAT, MAYBE?
GRRR
...
GRRRR
BUT... IN YOUR CASE...
...I DON'T FEEL SORRY FOR YOU AT ALL.

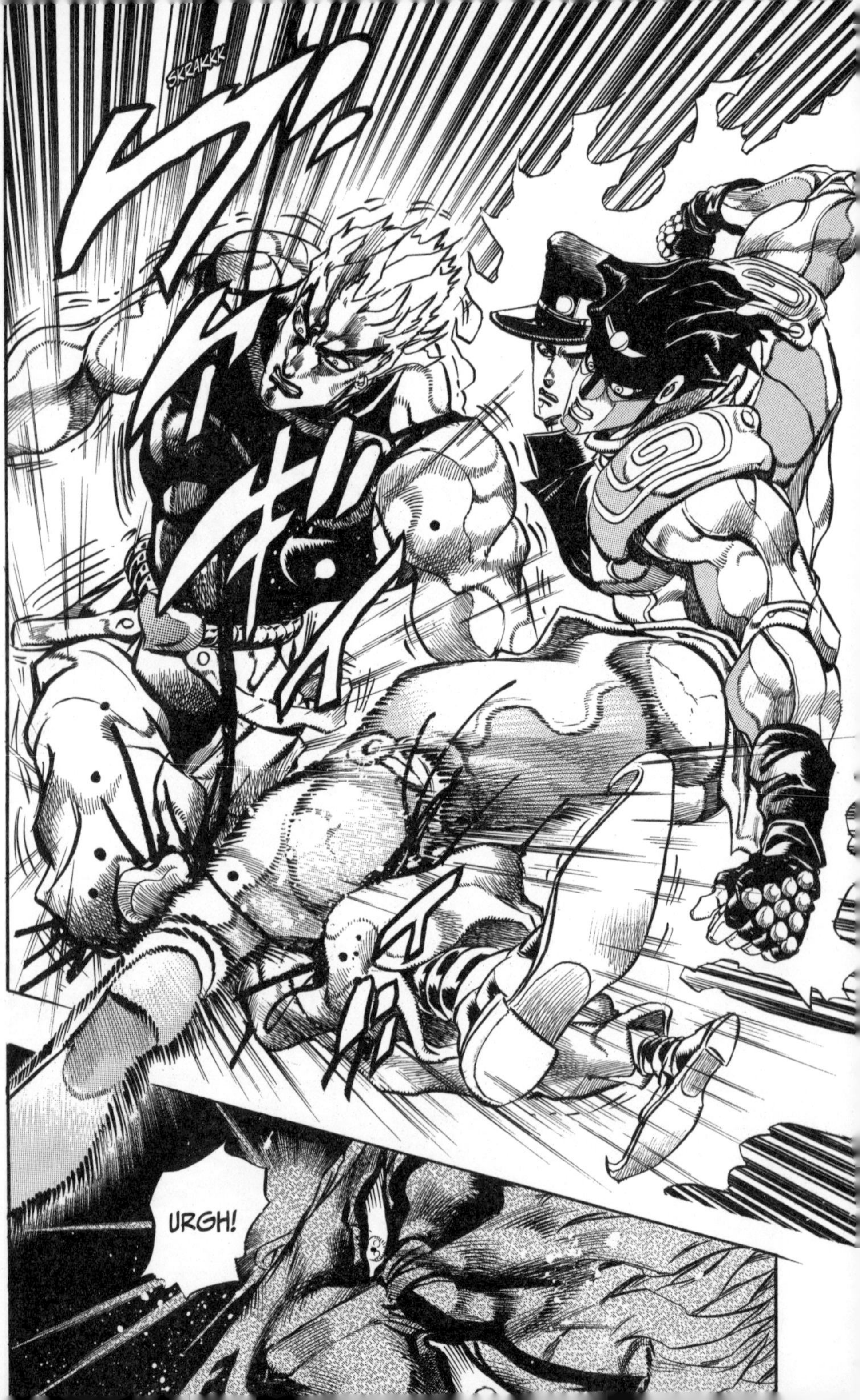
SKRAKKK
URGH!

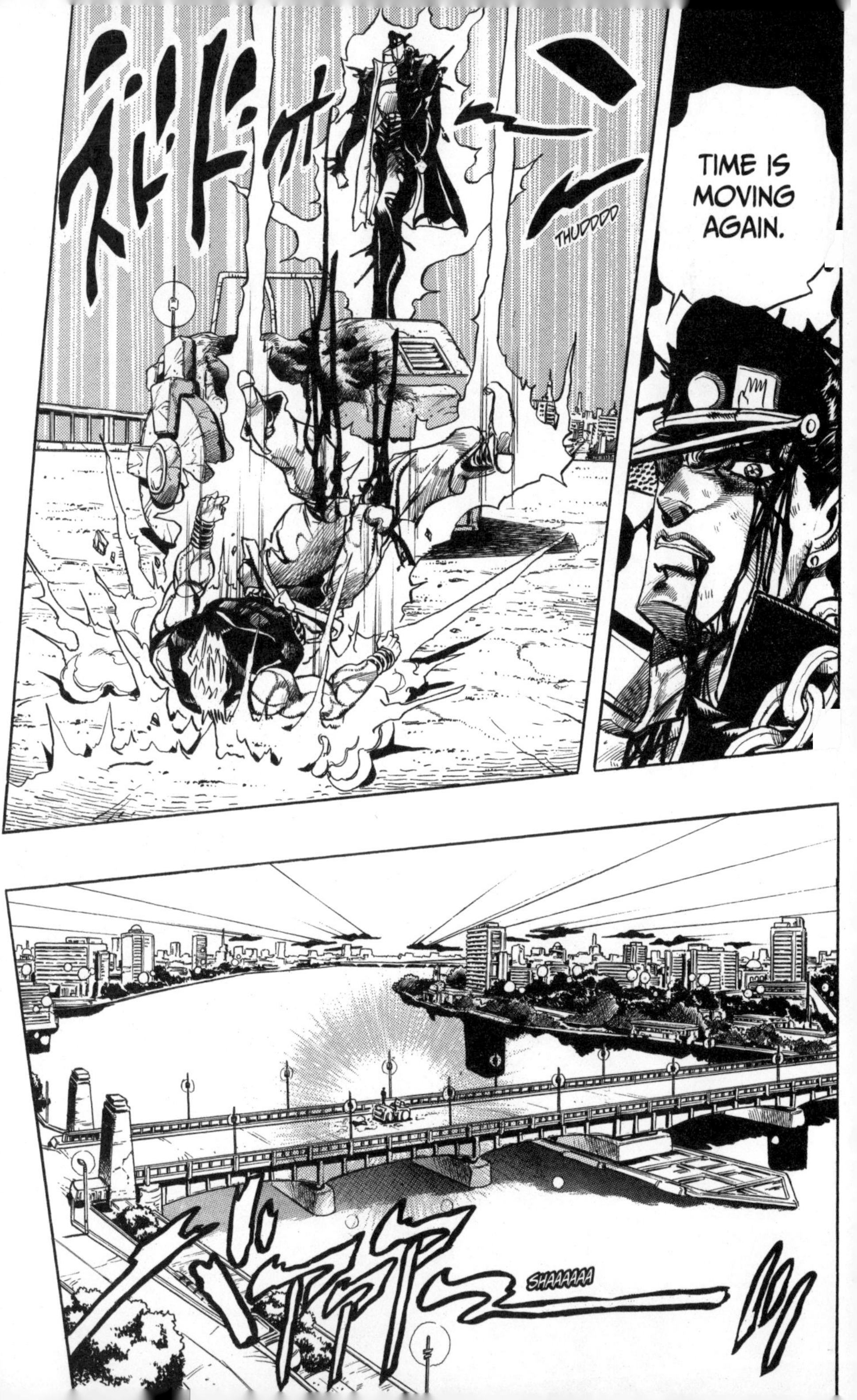
TIME IS MOVING AGAIN.
THUDDDD
SHAAAAAA

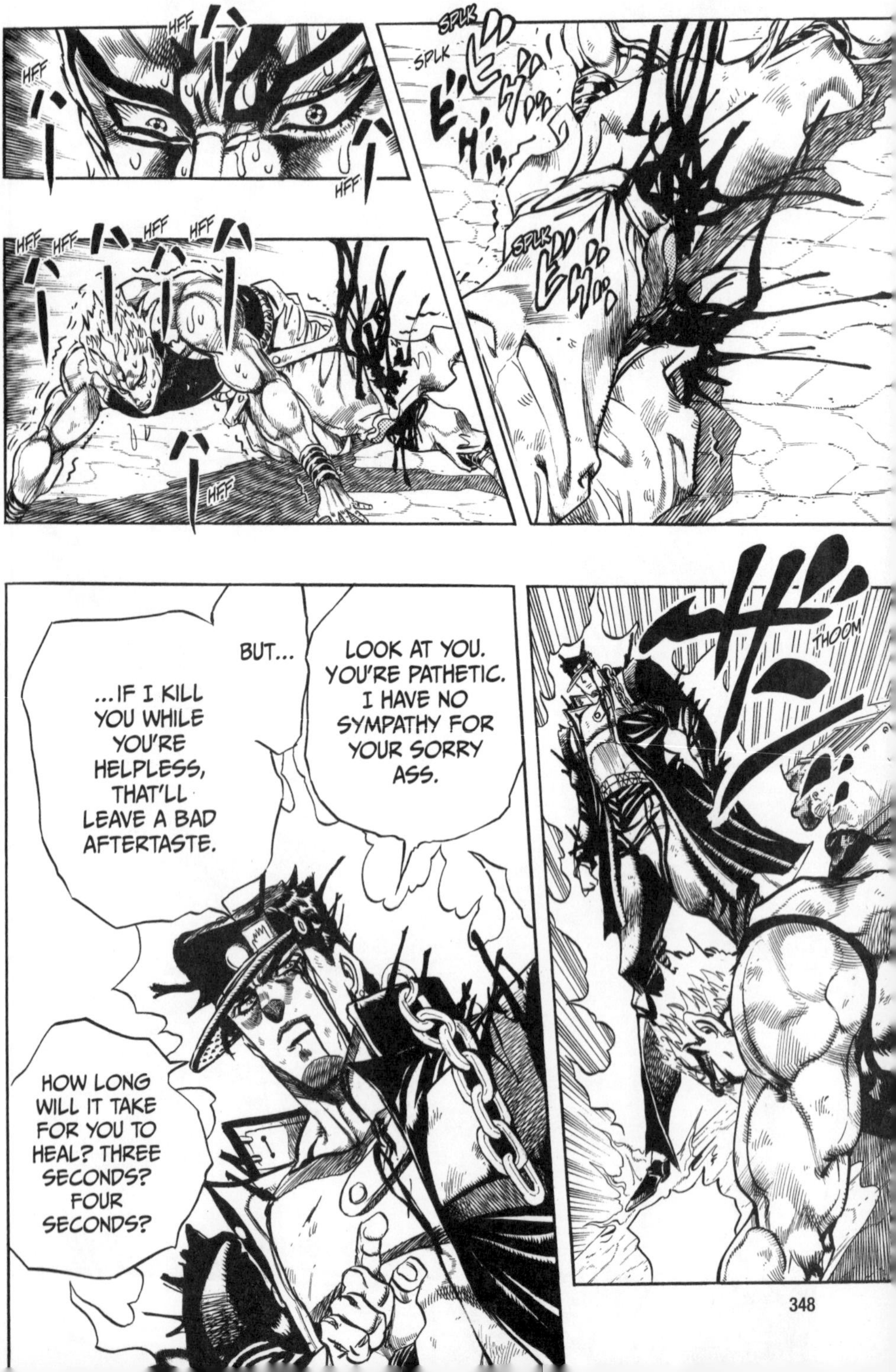
SPLK
SPLK
SPLK
HFF
HFF
HFF
HFF
HFF
HFF
HFF
HFF
THOOM
LOOK AT YOU. YOU'RE PATHETIC. I HAVE NO SYMPATHY FOR YOUR SORRY ASS.
BUT...
...IF I KILL YOU WHILE YOU'RE HELPLESS, THAT'LL LEAVE A BAD AFTERTASTE.
HOW LONG WILL IT TAKE FOR YOU TO HEAL? THREE SECONDS? FOUR SECONDS?

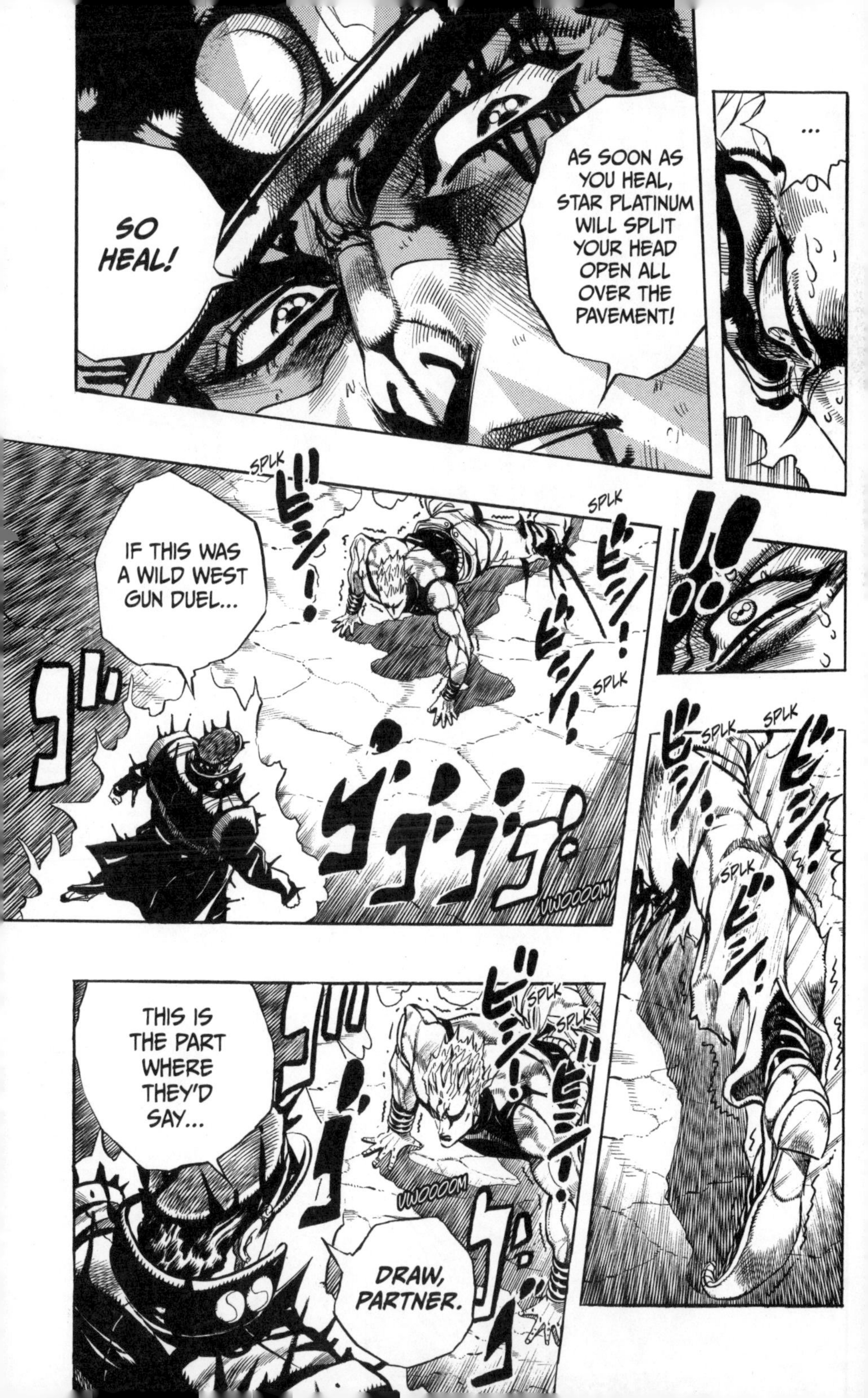

...
AS SOON AS YOU HEAL, STAR PLATINUM WILL SPLIT YOUR HEAD OPEN ALL OVER THE PAVEMENT!
SO HEAL!
SPLK
SPLK
SPLK
SPLK
IF THIS WAS A WILD WEST GUN DUEL...
VVOOOOM
SPLK
SPLK
SPLK
SPLK
SPLK
THIS IS THE PART WHERE THEY'D SAY...
VVOOOOM
DRAW, PARTNER.

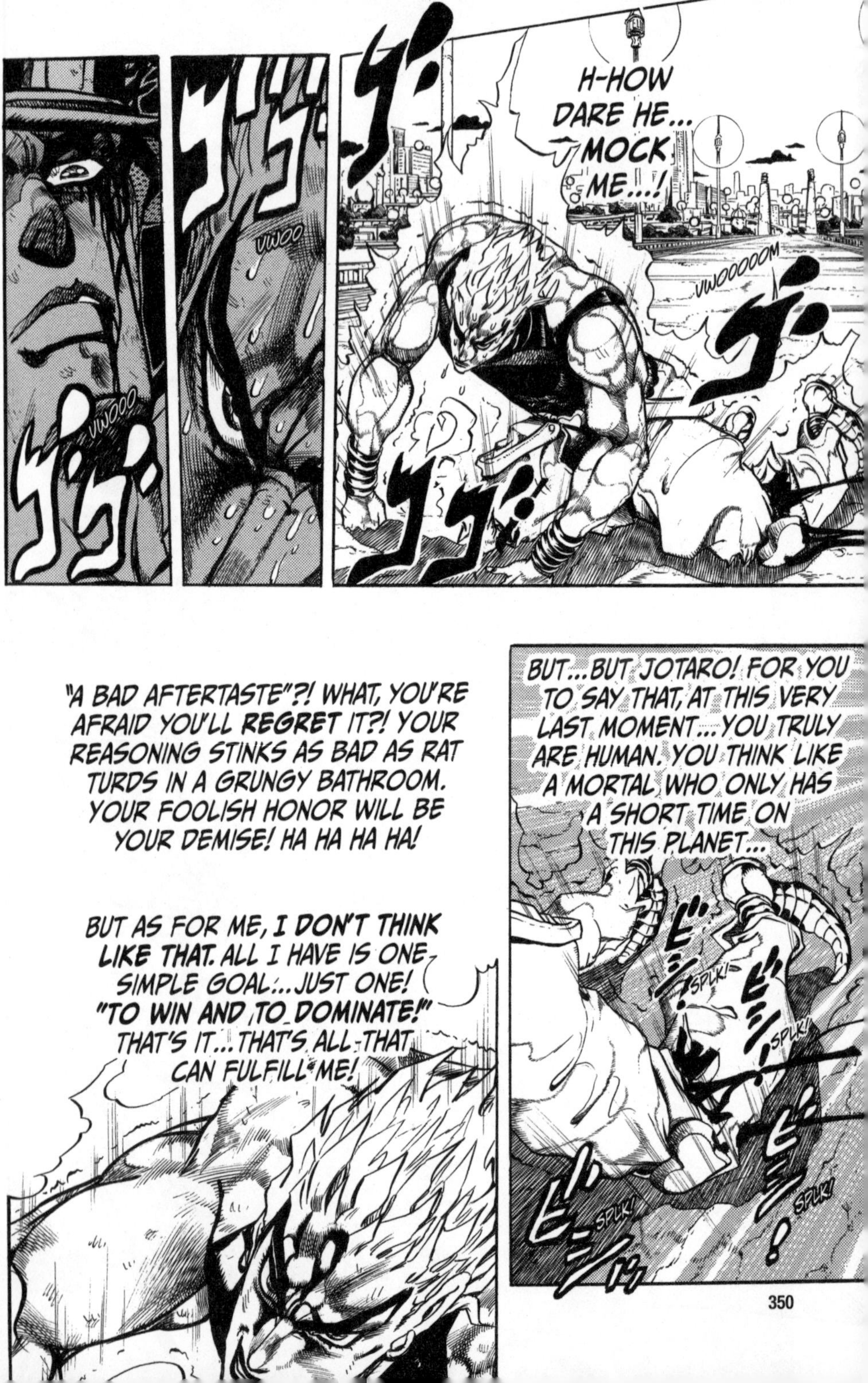
H-HOW DARE HE... MOCK ME...!
VWOOOOOM
VWOO
VWOOO
BUT...BUT JOTARO! FOR YOU TO SAY THAT, AT THIS VERY LAST MOMENT...YOU TRULY ARE HUMAN. YOU THINK LIKE A MORTAL WHO ONLY HAS A SHORT TIME ON THIS PLANET...
SPLK!
SPLK!
SPLK!
SPLK!
"A BAD AFTERTASTE"?! WHAT, YOU'RE AFRAID YOU'LL **REGRET** IT?! YOUR REASONING STINKS AS BAD AS RAT TURDS IN A GRUNGY BATHROOM. YOUR FOOLISH HONOR WILL BE YOUR DEMISE! HA HA HA HA!
BUT AS FOR ME, **I DON'T THINK LIKE THAT.** ALL I HAVE IS ONE SIMPLE GOAL...JUST ONE! **"TO WIN AND TO DOMINATE!"** THAT'S IT...THAT'S ALL THAT CAN FULFILL ME!

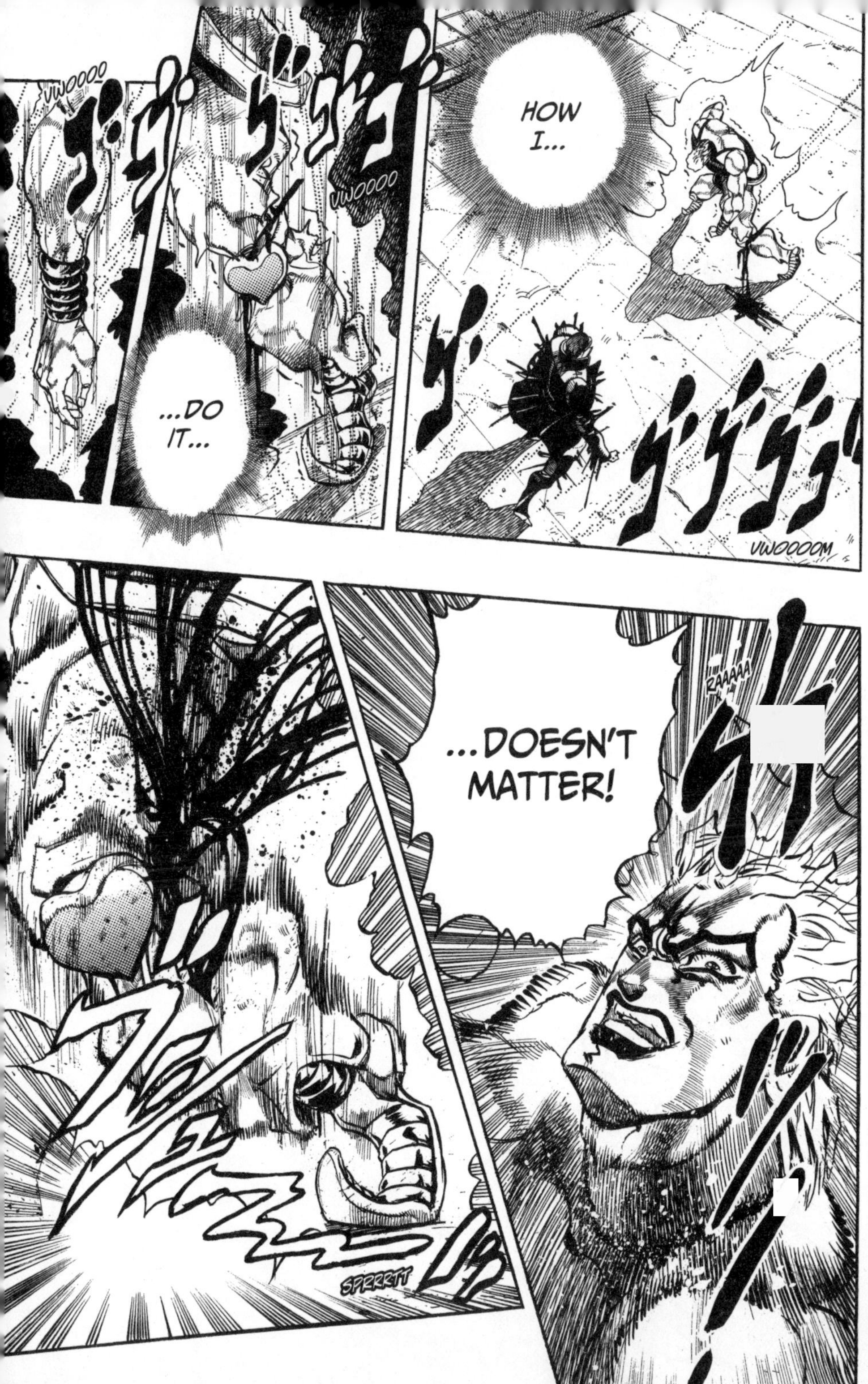
HOW I...
VWOOOOM
...DO IT...
VWOOOO
VWOOOO
...DOESN'T MATTER!
RAAAAA
SPRRRTT

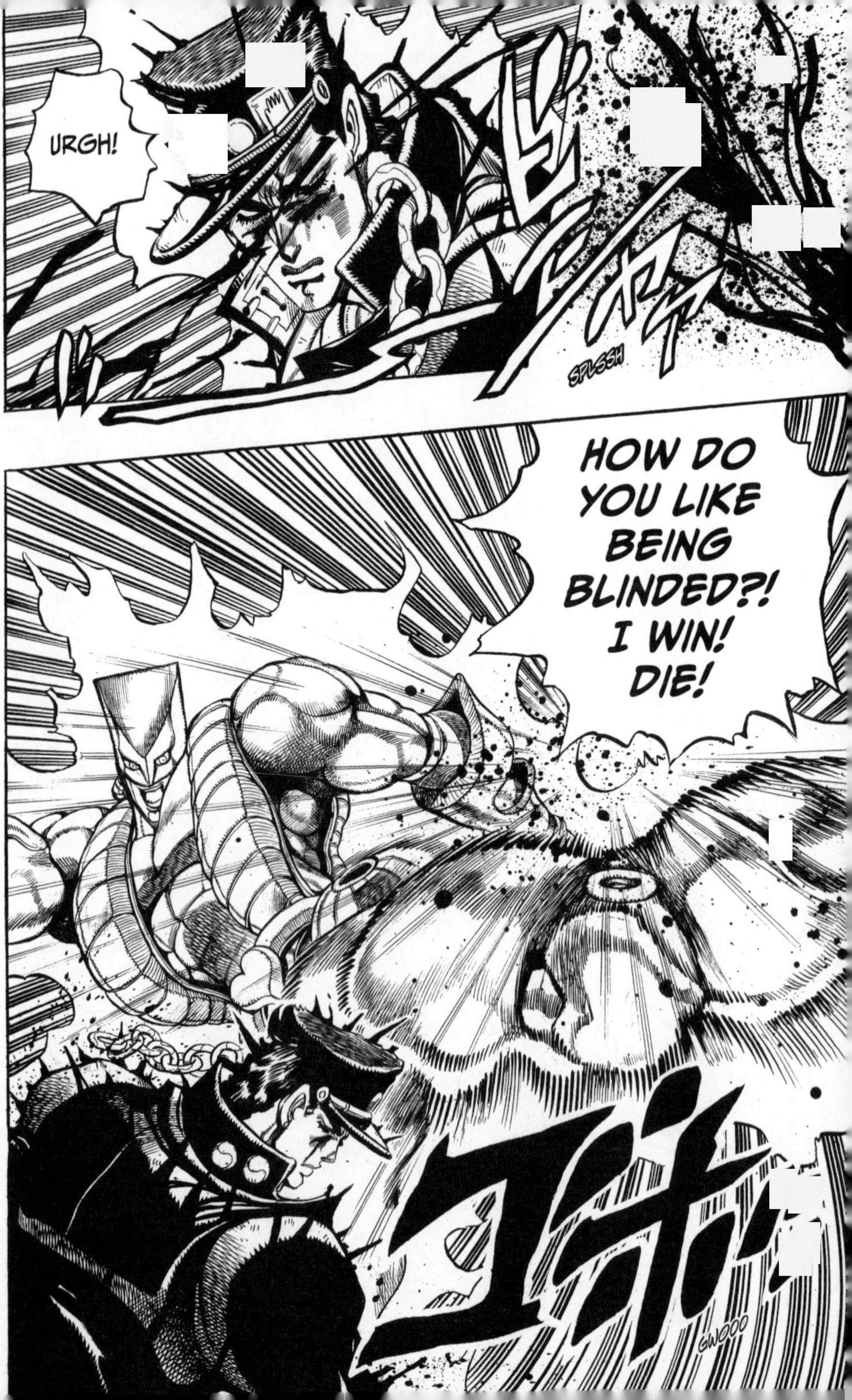
SPLSSH
URGH!
HOW DO YOU LIKE BEING BLINDED?! I WIN! DIE!
GWOOO

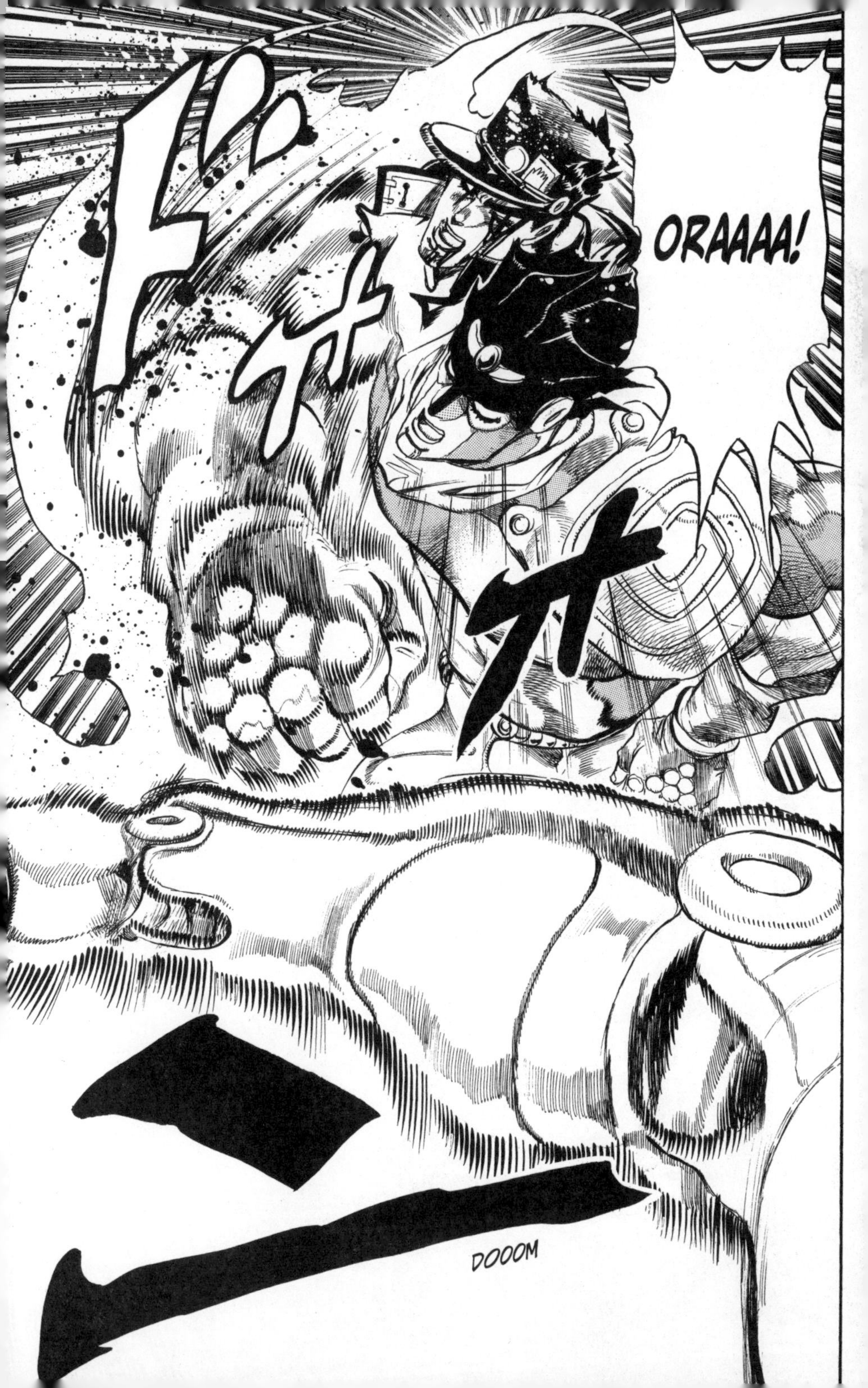
ORAAAA!
DOOOM

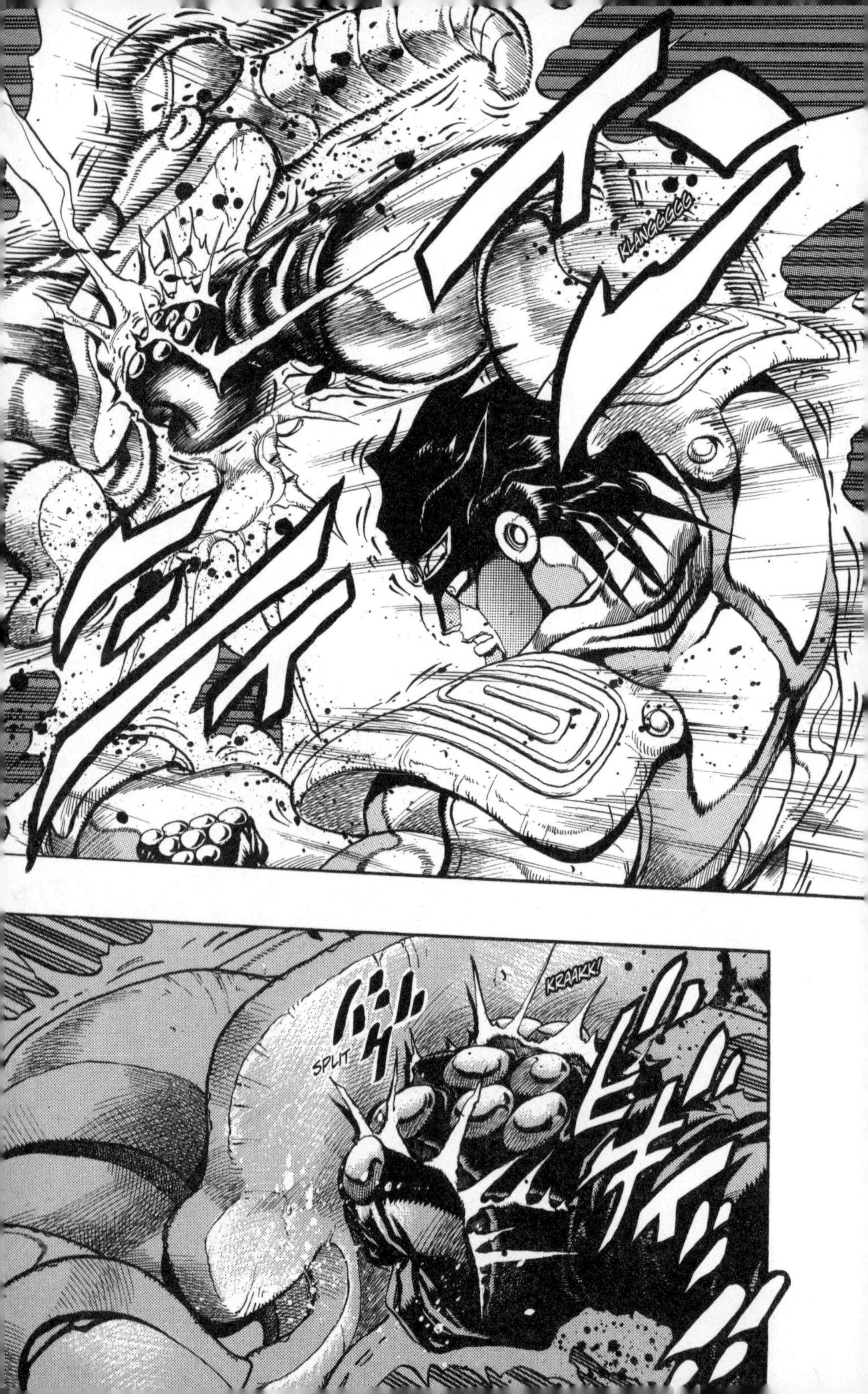
KLANGGGGG
KRAAKK!
SPLIT

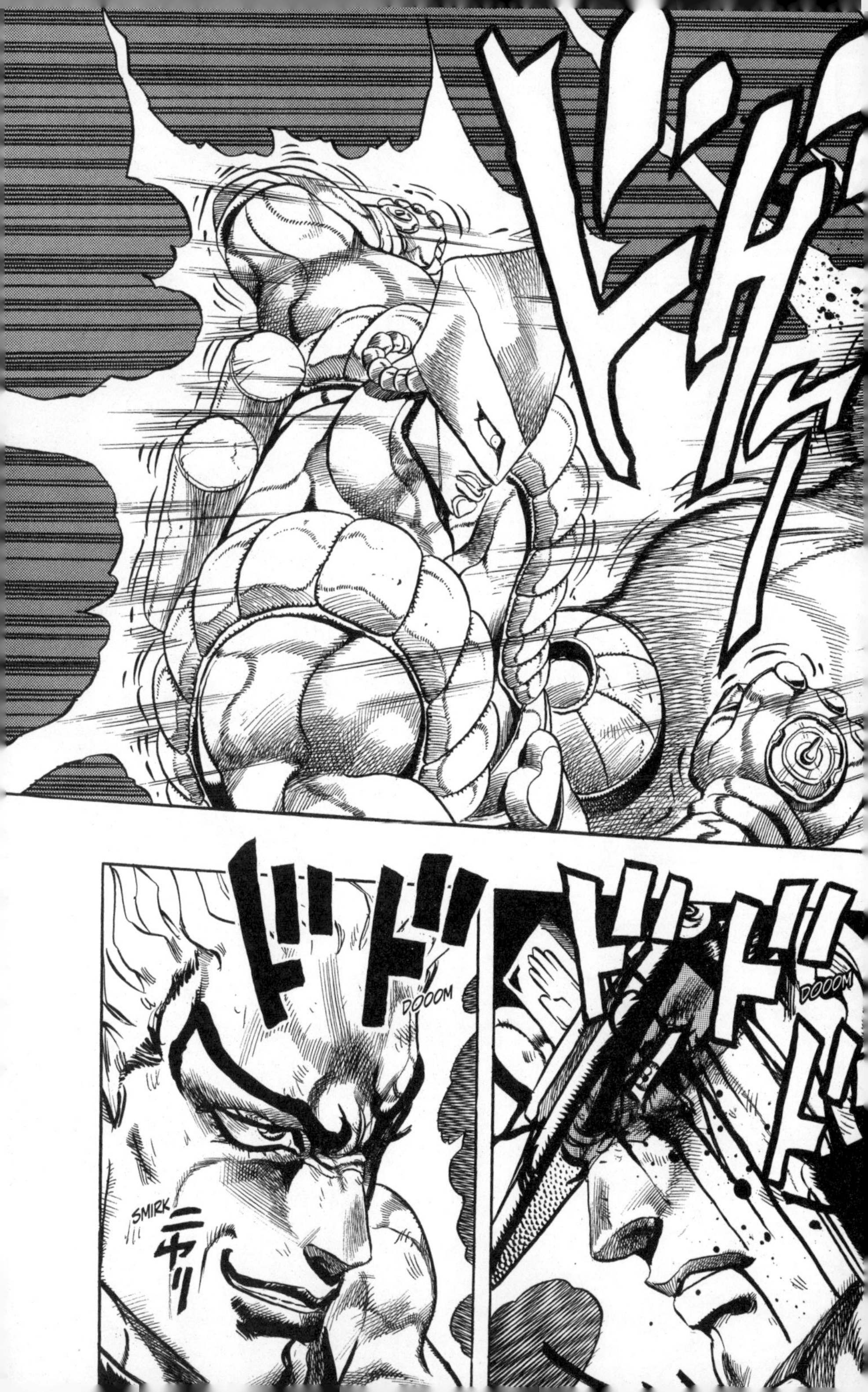
DOOOM
DOOOM
SMIRK
ニヤリ

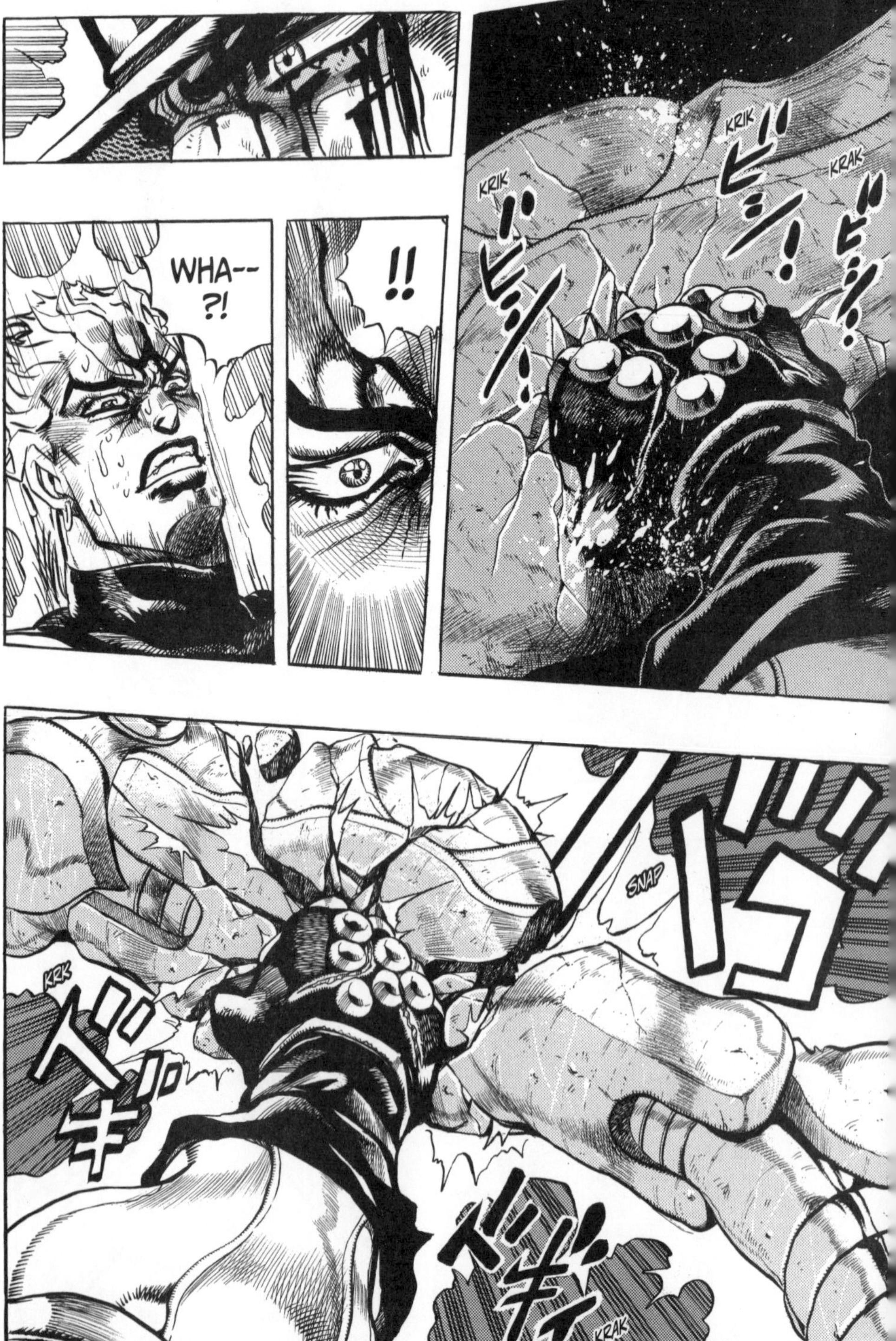
KRIK
KRAK
KRIK
!!
WHA--?!
SNAP
KRK
KRAK

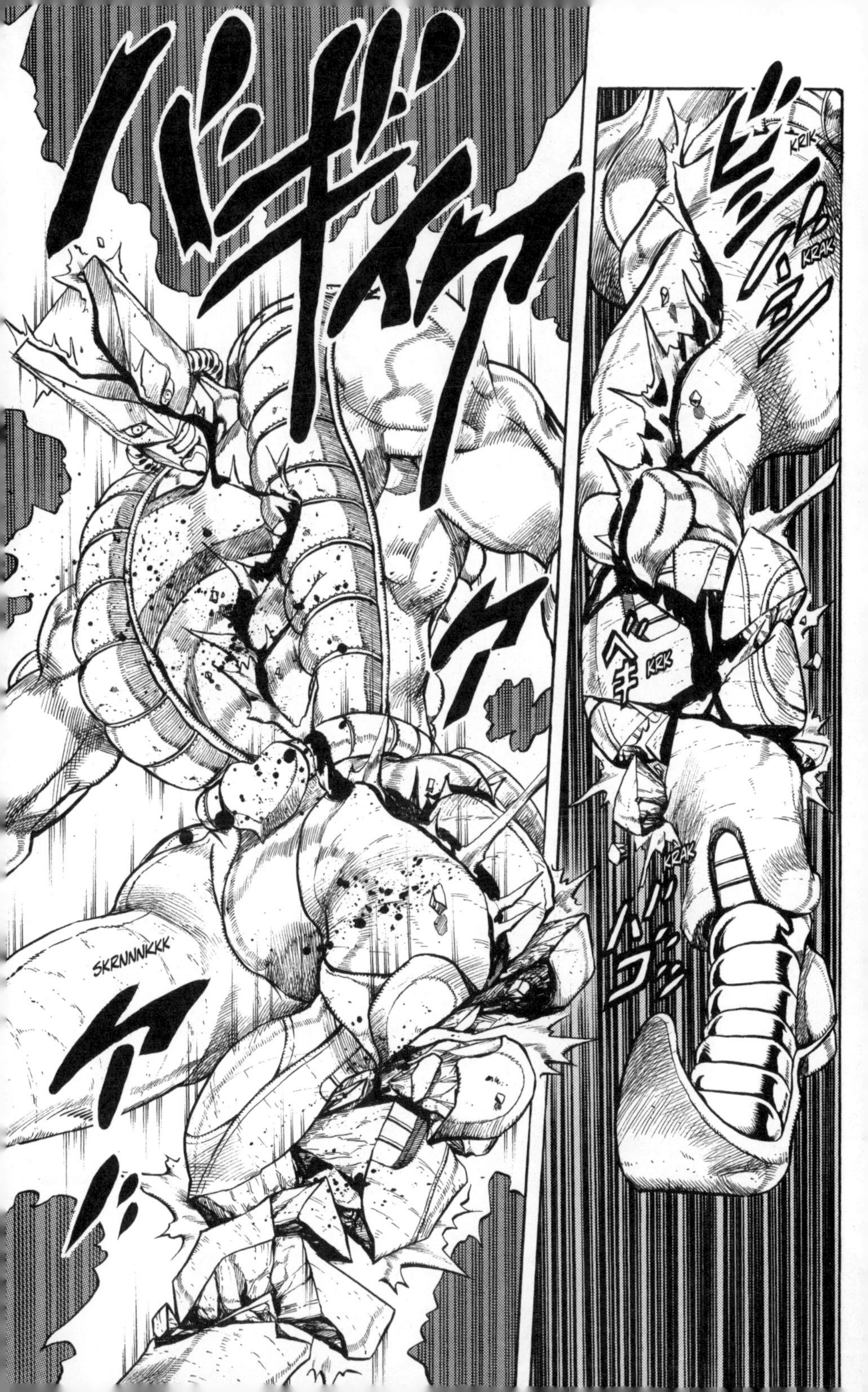
KRIK
KRAK
KRK
KRAK
SKRNNNKKK

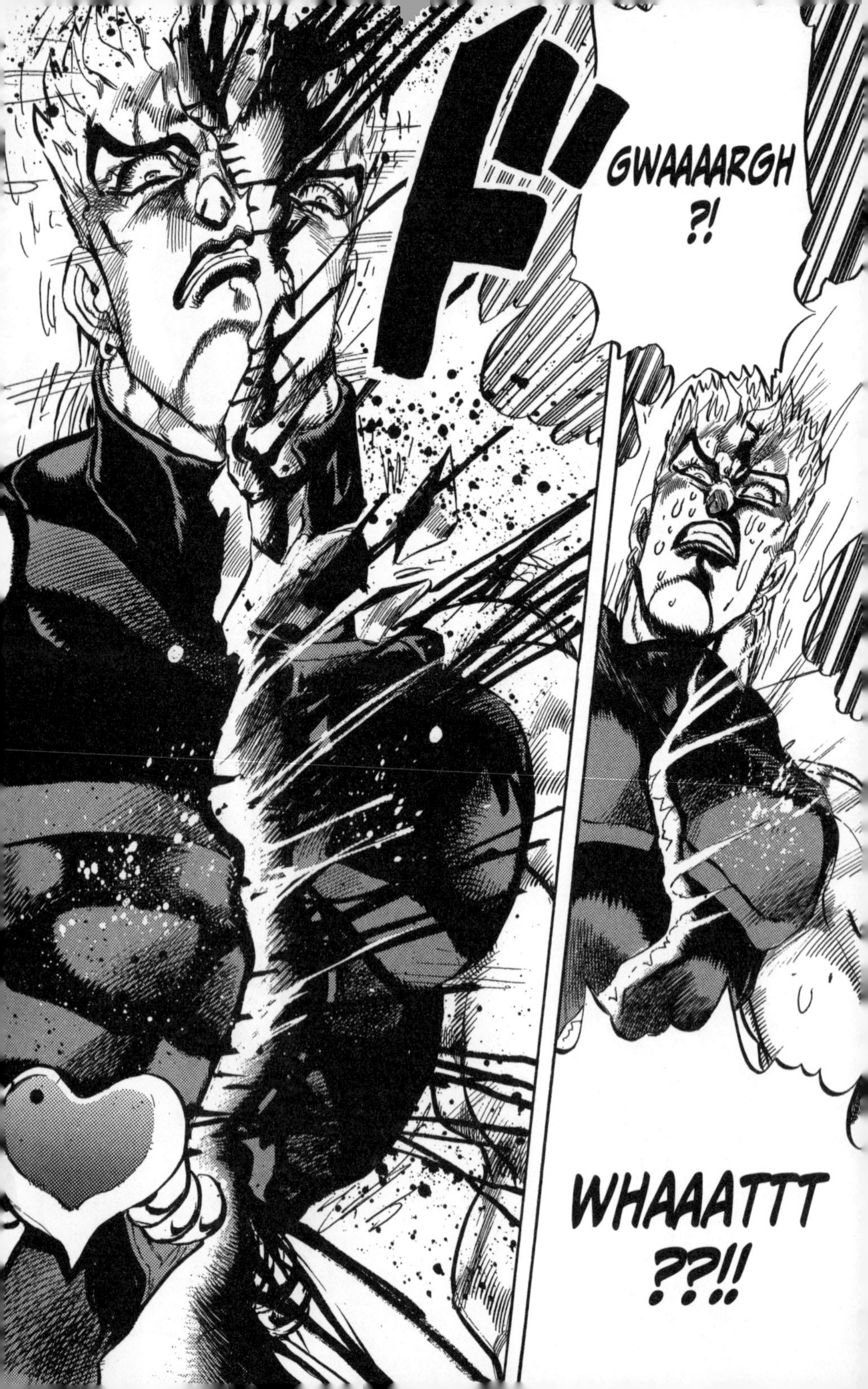
GWAAAARGH ?!
WHAAATTT ??!!

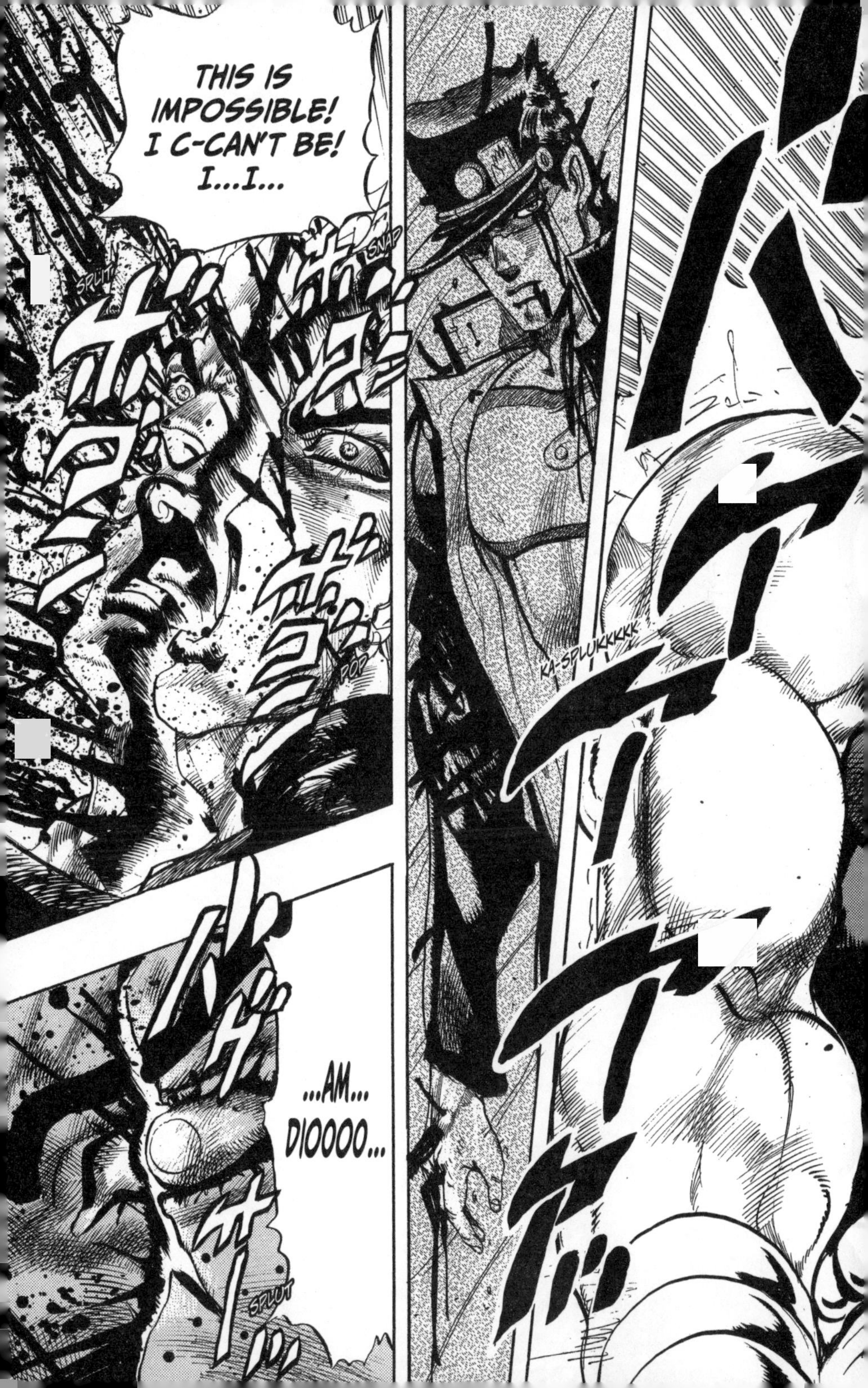
KA-SPLUKKKKK
THIS IS IMPOSSIBLE! I C-CAN'T BE! I...I...
SNAP
SPLUT
POP
...AM... DIOOOO...
SPLUT

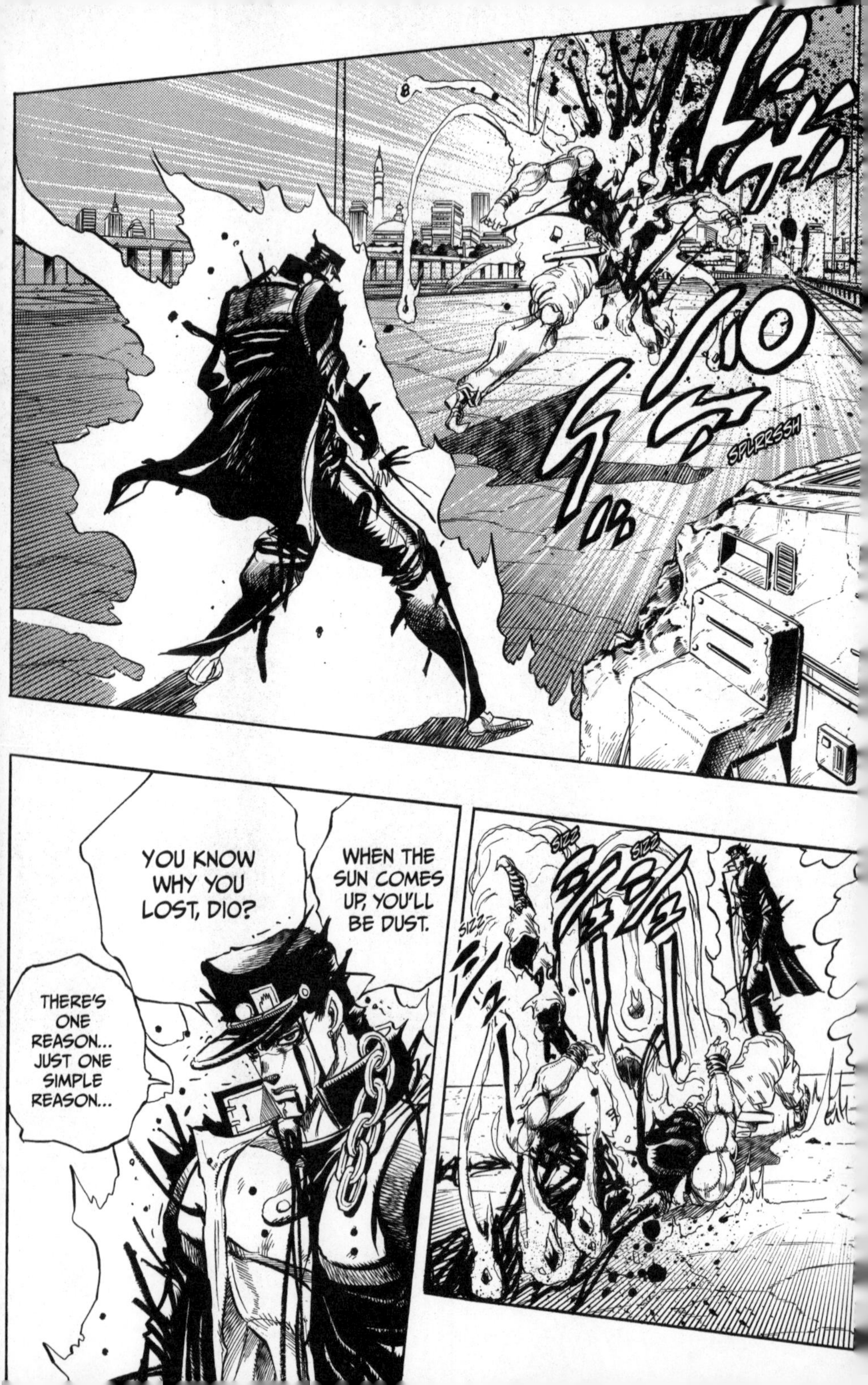
SPLRRSSH
SIZZ
SIZZ
SIZZ
WHEN THE SUN COMES UP, YOU'LL BE DUST.
YOU KNOW WHY YOU LOST, DIO?
THERE'S ONE REASON... JUST ONE SIMPLE REASON...

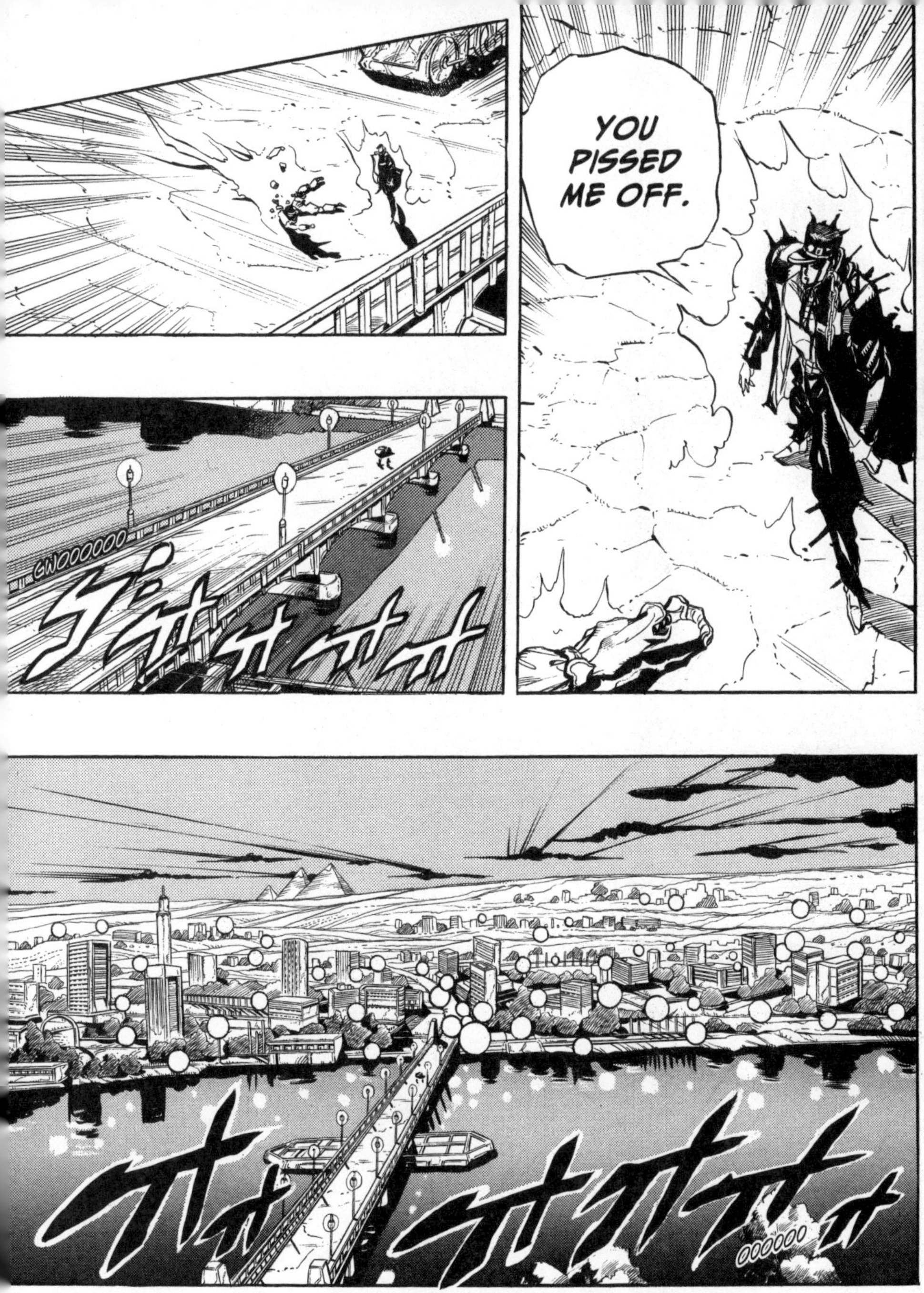
YOU PISSED ME OFF.
GWOOOOOO
OOOOOO

DIO · STAND: THE WORLD
- COMPLETELY ANNIHILATED... DEAD -

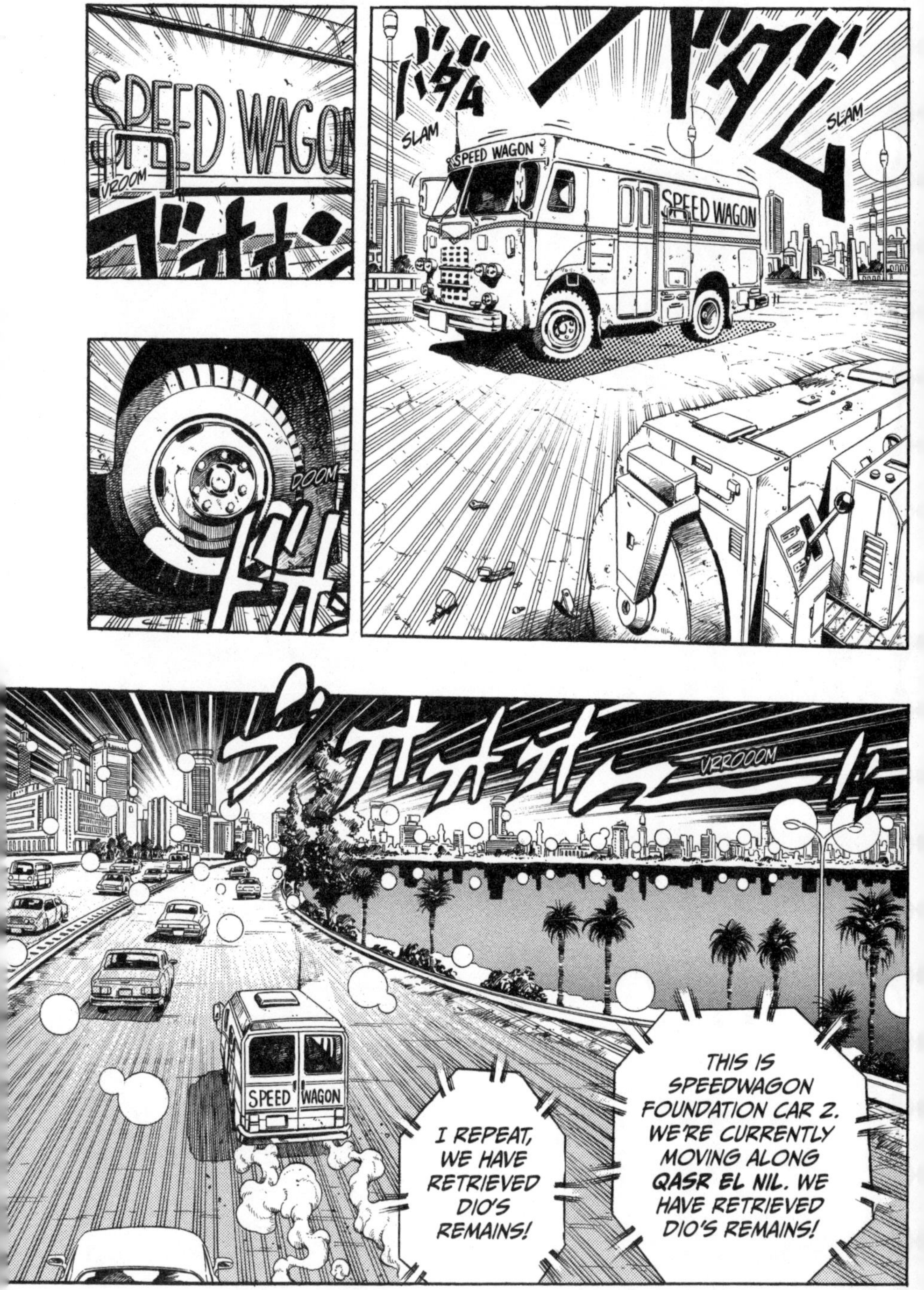
SLAM
SPEED WAGON
SPEED WAGON
SLAM
SPEED WAGON
VROOM
DOOM
VRROOOM
SPEED WAGON
THIS IS SPEEDWAGON FOUNDATION CAR 2. WE'RE CURRENTLY MOVING ALONG **QASR EL NIL**. WE HAVE RETRIEVED DIO'S REMAINS!
I REPEAT, WE HAVE RETRIEVED DIO'S REMAINS!

CHAPTER 152: The Faraway Journey, Farewell Friends

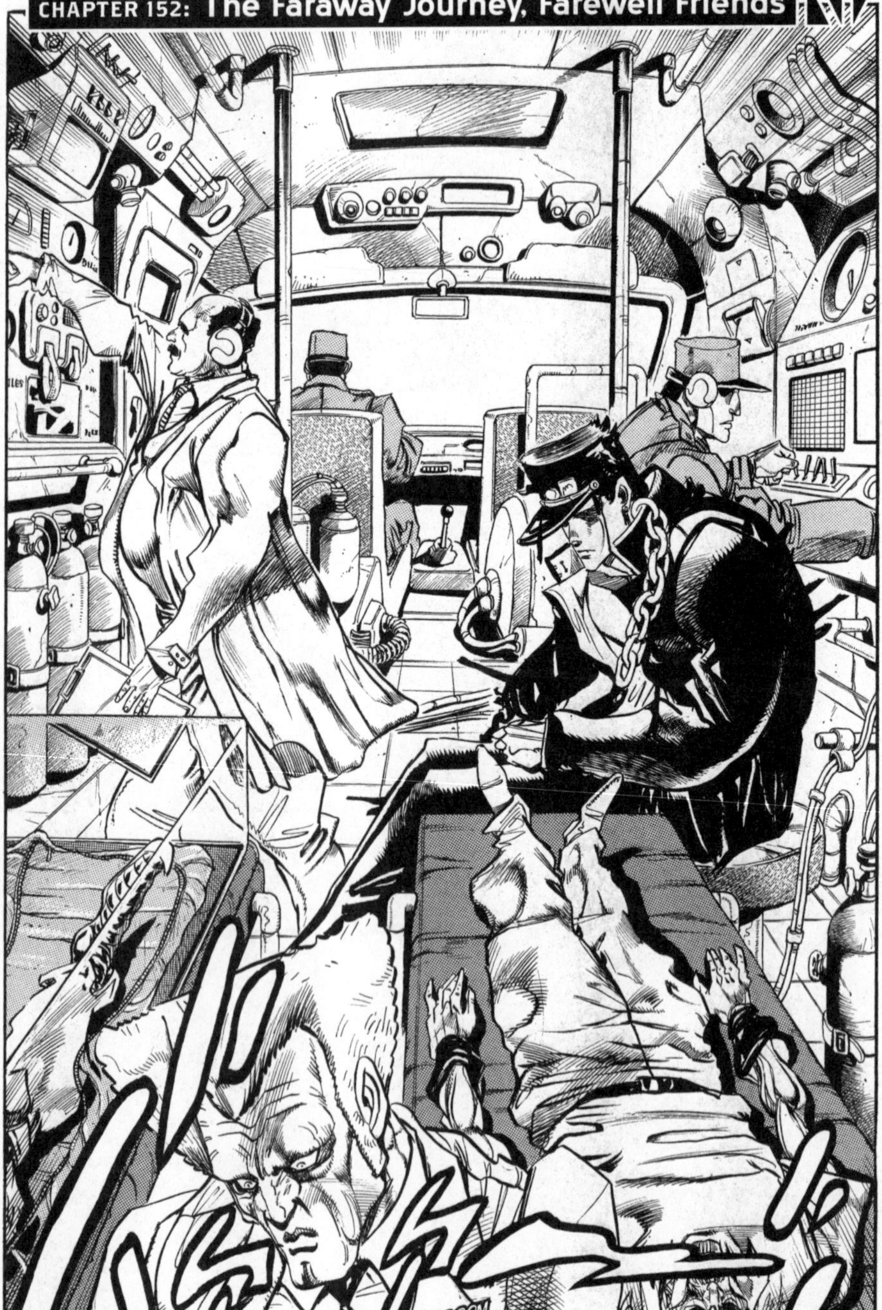
KABOOM

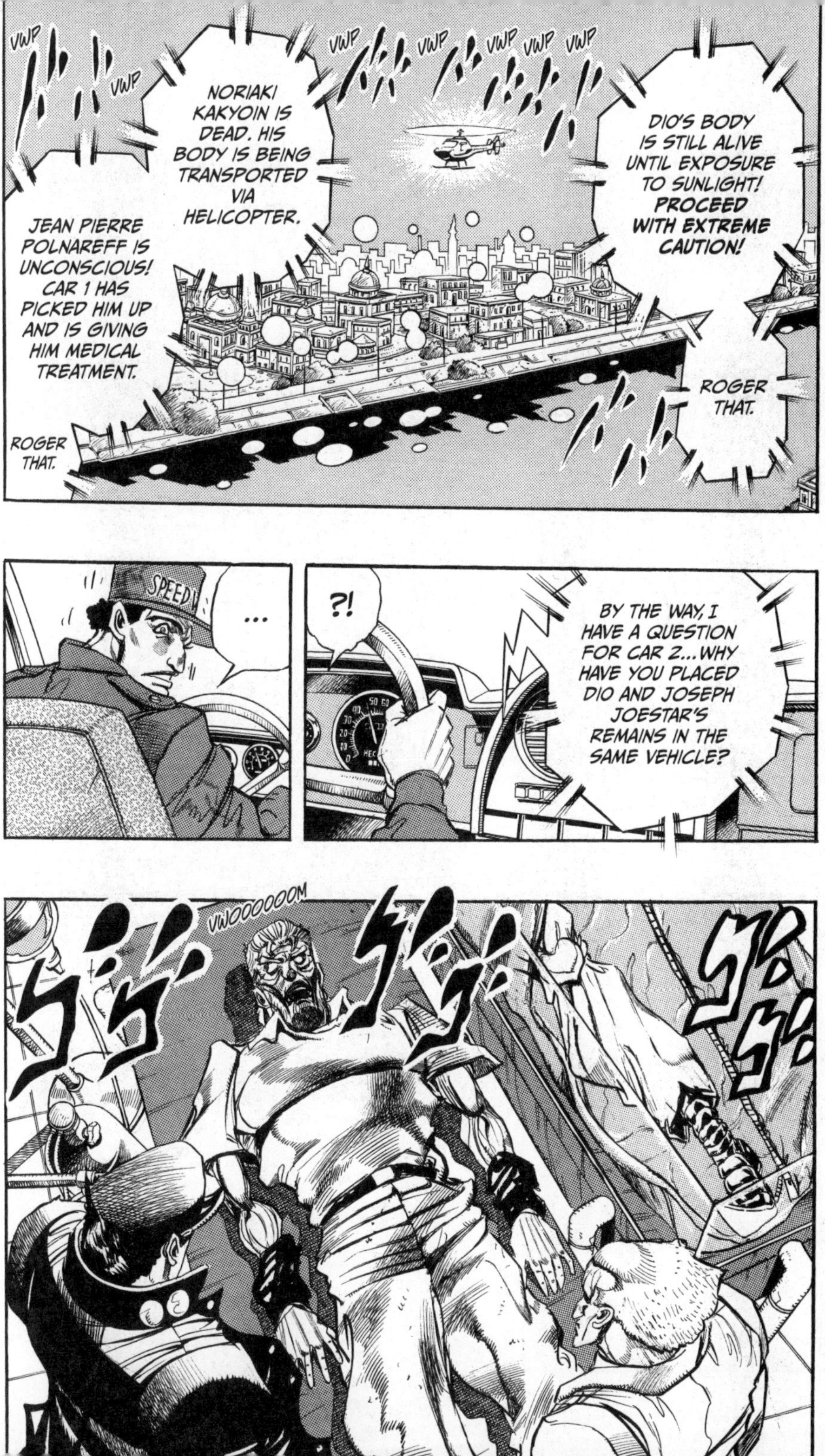
VWP
VWP
VWP
VWP
VWP
VWP
VWP
DIO'S BODY IS STILL ALIVE UNTIL EXPOSURE TO SUNLIGHT! **PROCEED WITH EXTREME CAUTION!**
ROGER THAT.
NORIAKI KAKYOIN IS DEAD. HIS BODY IS BEING TRANSPORTED VIA HELICOPTER.
JEAN PIERRE POLNAREFF IS UNCONSCIOUS! CAR 1 HAS PICKED HIM UP AND IS GIVING HIM MEDICAL TREATMENT.
ROGER THAT.
BY THE WAY, I HAVE A QUESTION FOR CAR 2...WHY HAVE YOU PLACED DIO AND JOSEPH JOESTAR'S REMAINS IN THE SAME VEHICLE?
?!
SPEED
...
VWOOOOOOM

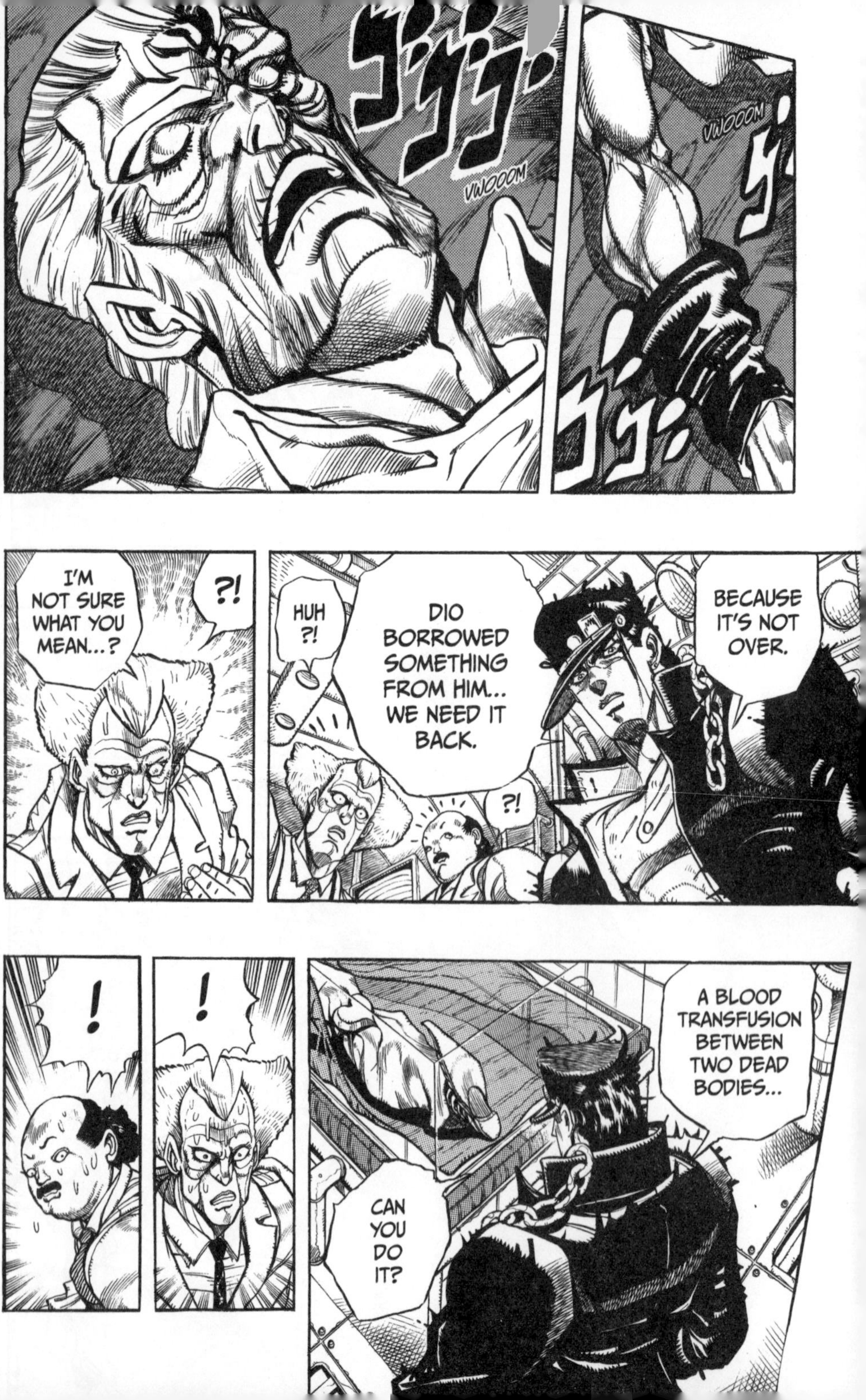
VWOOOM
VWOOOM
BECAUSE IT'S NOT OVER.
DIO BORROWED SOMETHING FROM HIM... WE NEED IT BACK.
HUH ?!
?!
?!
I'M NOT SURE WHAT YOU MEAN...?
A BLOOD TRANSFUSION BETWEEN TWO DEAD BODIES...
CAN YOU DO IT?
!
!

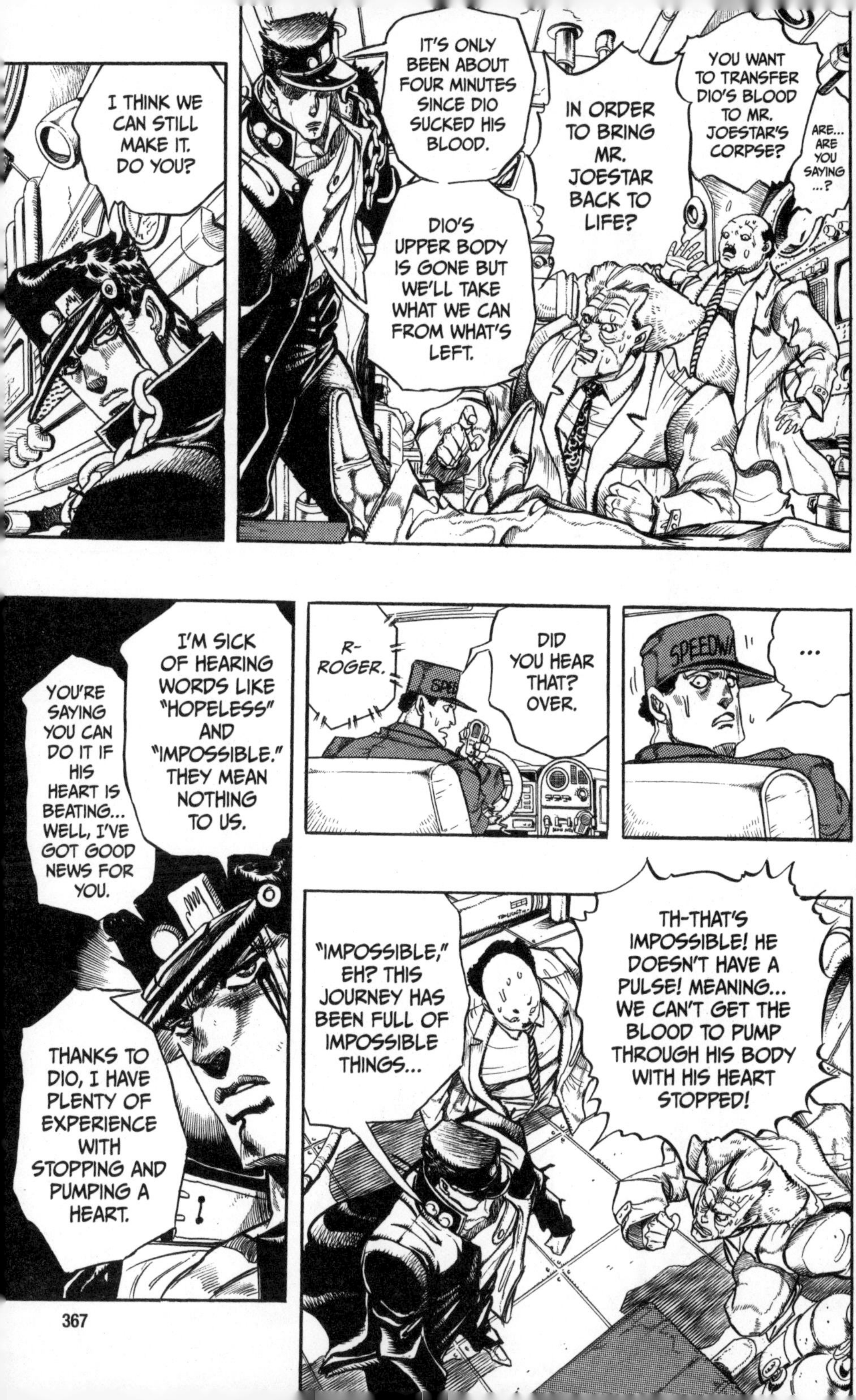
ARE... ARE YOU SAYING ...?
YOU WANT TO TRANSFER DIO'S BLOOD TO MR. JOESTAR'S CORPSE?
IN ORDER TO BRING MR. JOESTAR BACK TO LIFE?
IT'S ONLY BEEN ABOUT FOUR MINUTES SINCE DIO SUCKED HIS BLOOD.
DIO'S UPPER BODY IS GONE BUT WE'LL TAKE WHAT WE CAN FROM WHAT'S LEFT.
I THINK WE CAN STILL MAKE IT. DO YOU?
...
DID YOU HEAR THAT? OVER.
R-ROGER.
SPEEDWA
TH-THAT'S IMPOSSIBLE! HE DOESN'T HAVE A PULSE! MEANING... WE CAN'T GET THE BLOOD TO PUMP THROUGH HIS BODY WITH HIS HEART STOPPED!
"IMPOSSIBLE," EH? THIS JOURNEY HAS BEEN FULL OF IMPOSSIBLE THINGS...
I'M SICK OF HEARING WORDS LIKE "HOPELESS" AND "IMPOSSIBLE." THEY MEAN NOTHING TO US.
YOU'RE SAYING YOU CAN DO IT IF HIS HEART IS BEATING... WELL, I'VE GOT GOOD NEWS FOR YOU.
THANKS TO DIO, I HAVE PLENTY OF EXPERIENCE WITH STOPPING AND PUMPING A HEART.

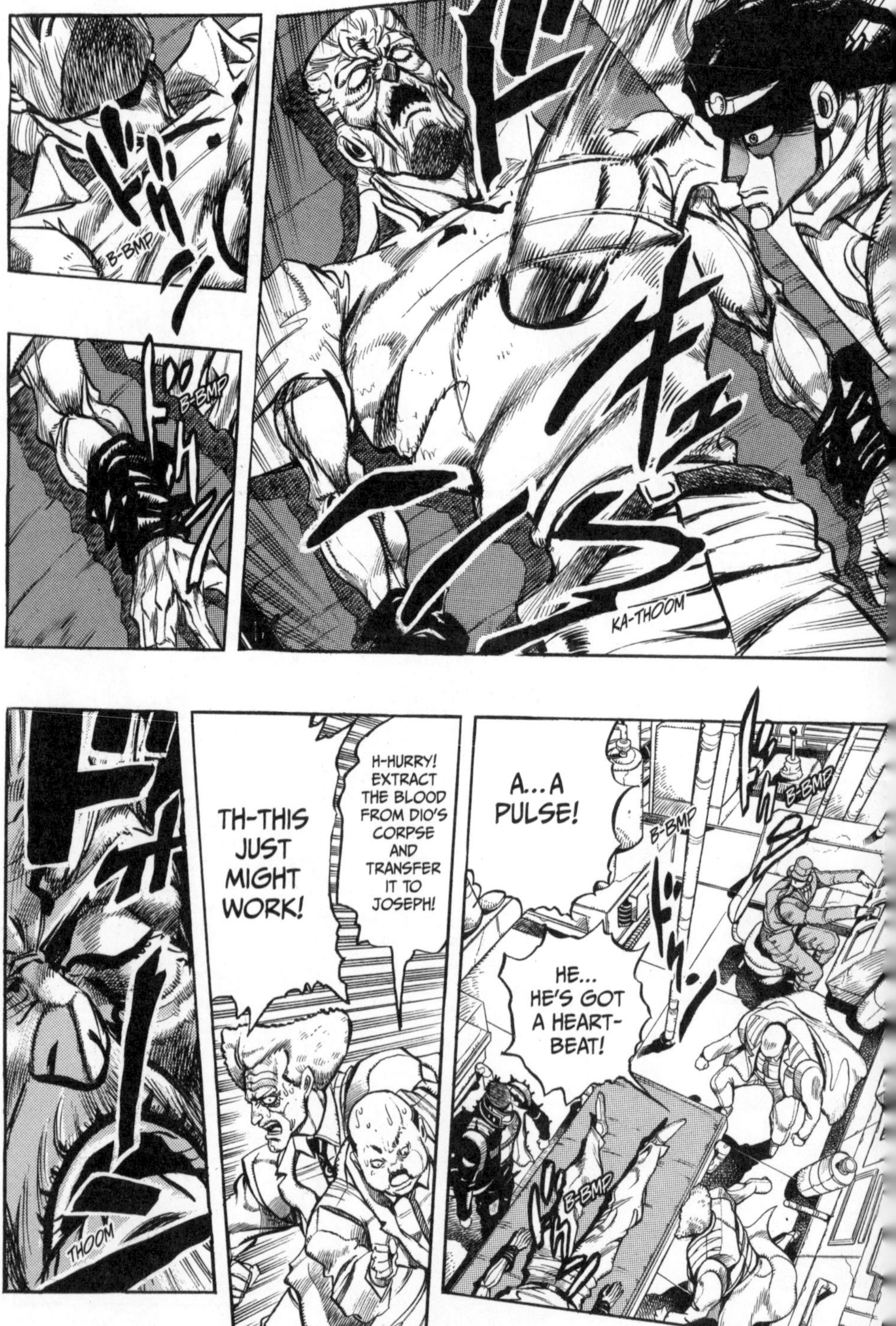
KA-THOOM
B-BMP
B-BMP
A...A PULSE!
B-BMP
B-BMP
HE... HE'S GOT A HEART-BEAT!
B-BMP
H-HURRY! EXTRACT THE BLOOD FROM DIO'S CORPSE AND TRANSFER IT TO JOSEPH!
TH-THIS JUST MIGHT WORK!
THOOM

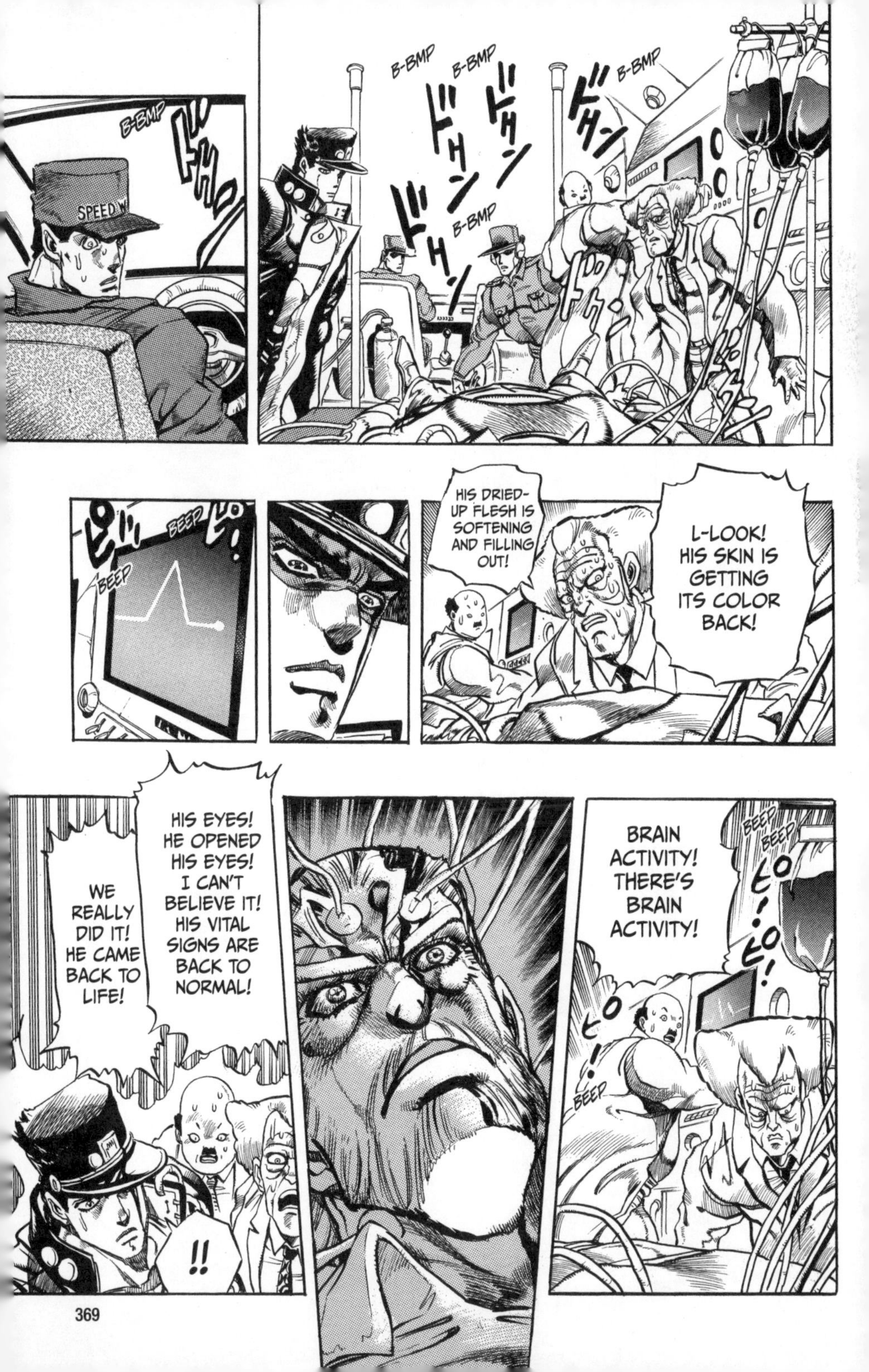
B-BMP
B-BMP
B-BMP
B-BMP
B-BMP
SPEED W
L-LOOK! HIS SKIN IS GETTING ITS COLOR BACK!
HIS DRIED-UP FLESH IS SOFTENING AND FILLING OUT!
BEEP
BEEP
BEEP
BEEP
BRAIN ACTIVITY! THERE'S BRAIN ACTIVITY!
BEEP
HIS EYES! HE OPENED HIS EYES! I CAN'T BELIEVE IT! HIS VITAL SIGNS ARE BACK TO NORMAL!
WE REALLY DID IT! HE CAME BACK TO LIFE!
!!

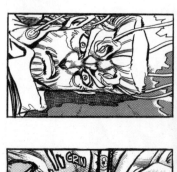

OLD MAN ?

GRIN

GLARE

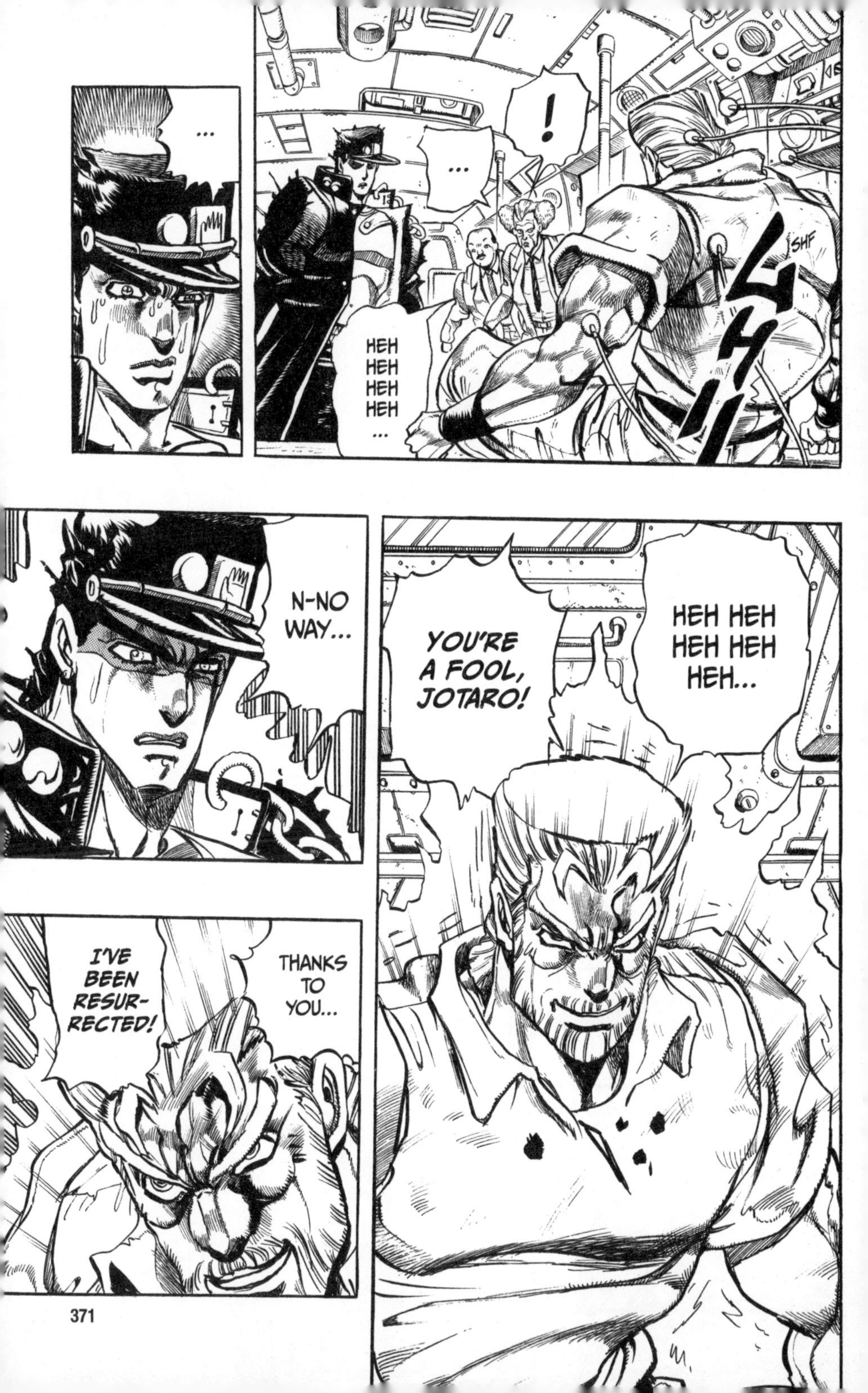
!
...
SHF
HEH HEH HEH HEH ...
...
HEH HEH HEH HEH HEH...
YOU'RE A FOOL, JOTARO!
N-NO WAY...
THANKS TO YOU...
I'VE BEEN RESUR-RECTED!

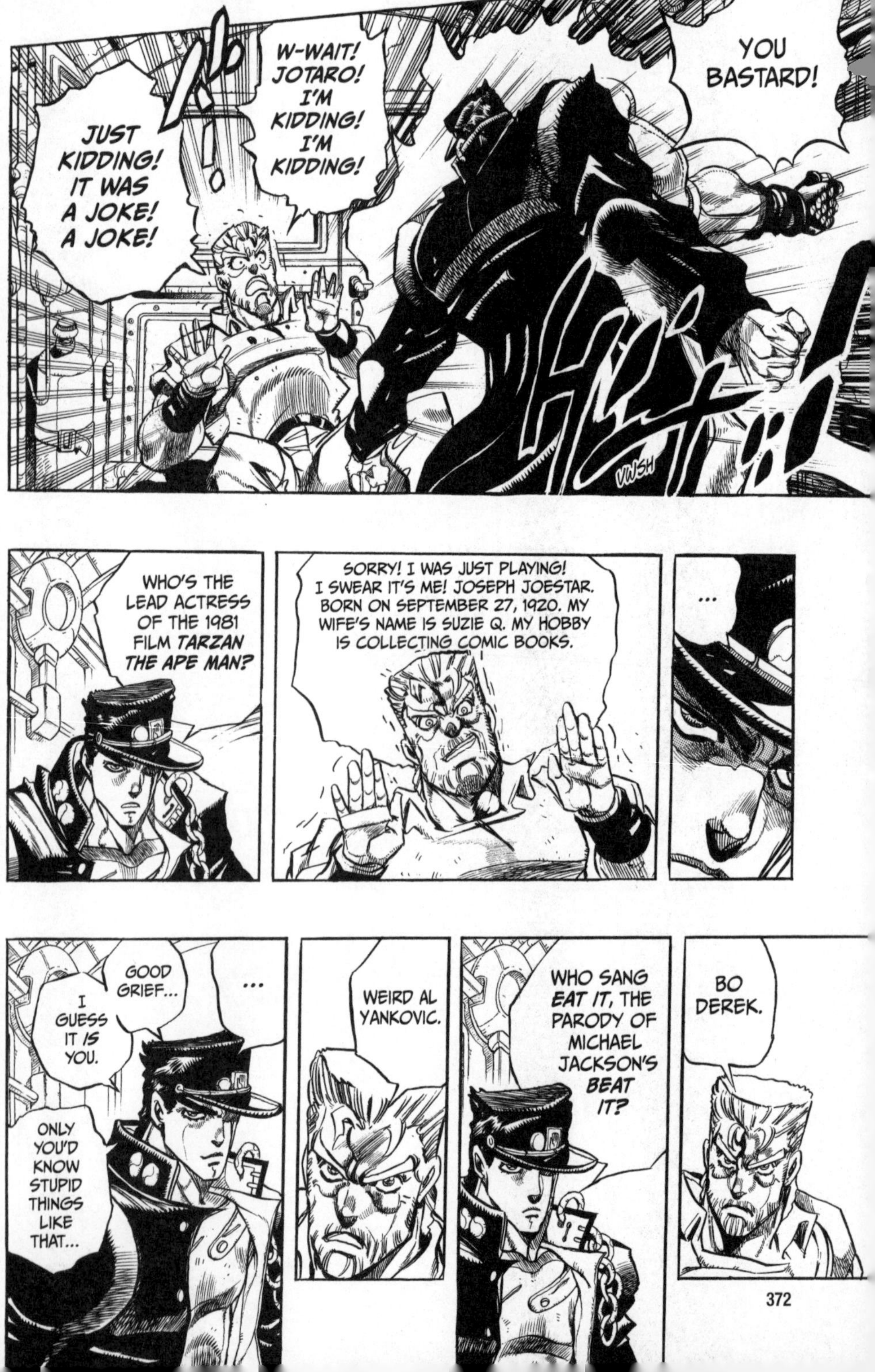

YOU BASTARD!
W-WAIT! JOTARO! I'M KIDDING! I'M KIDDING!
JUST KIDDING! IT WAS A JOKE! A JOKE!
VWSH
...
SORRY! I WAS JUST PLAYING! I SWEAR IT'S ME! JOSEPH JOESTAR. BORN ON SEPTEMBER 27, 1920. MY WIFE'S NAME IS SUZIE Q. MY HOBBY IS COLLECTING COMIC BOOKS.
WHO'S THE LEAD ACTRESS OF THE 1981 FILM *TARZAN THE APE MAN?*
BO DEREK.
WHO SANG *EAT IT*, THE PARODY OF MICHAEL JACKSON'S *BEAT IT?*
WEIRD AL YANKOVIC.
...
GOOD GRIEF...
I GUESS IT *IS* YOU.
ONLY YOU'D KNOW STUPID THINGS LIKE THAT...

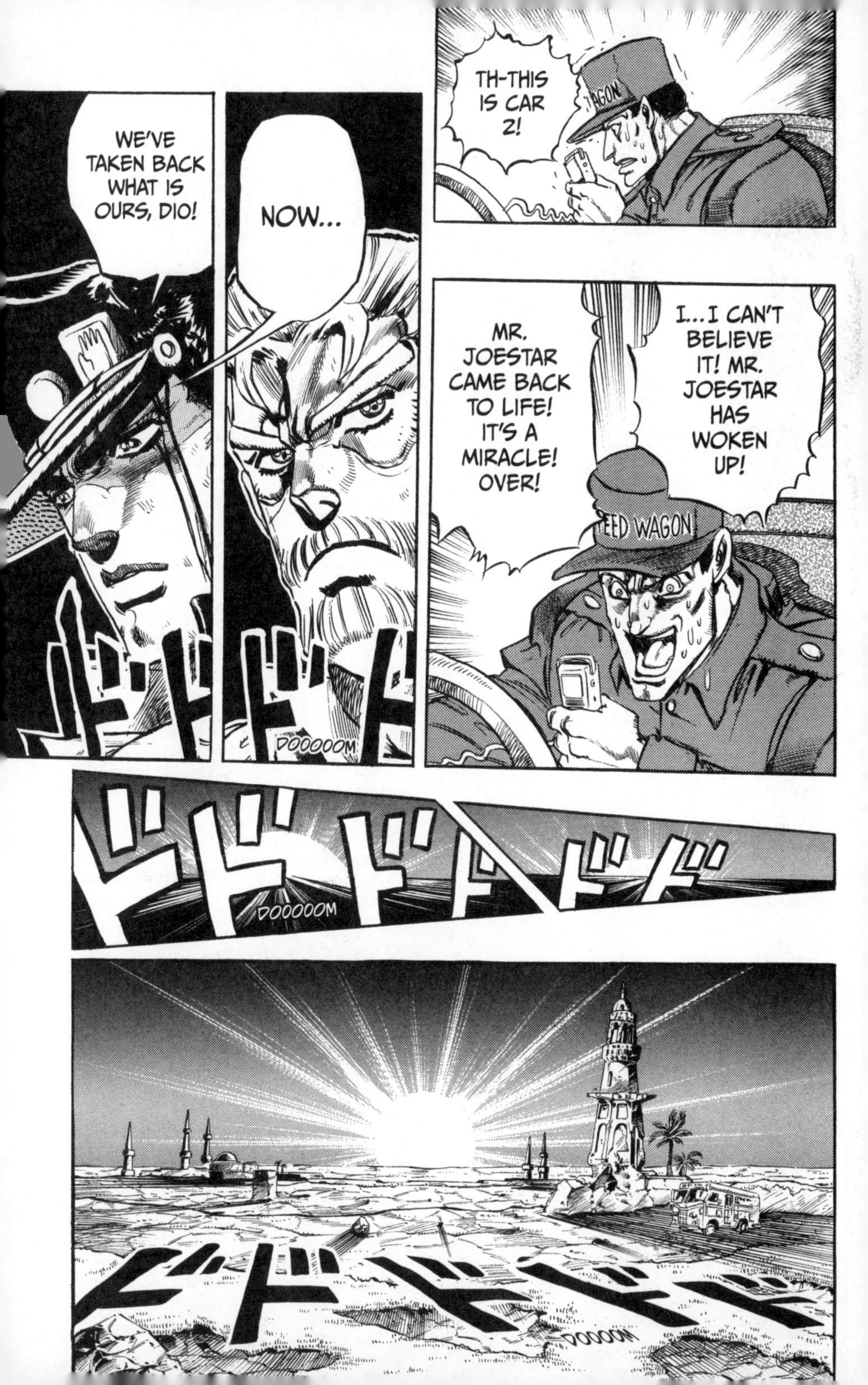
TH-THIS IS CAR 2!
I...I CAN'T BELIEVE IT! MR. JOESTAR HAS WOKEN UP!
MR. JOESTAR CAME BACK TO LIFE! IT'S A MIRACLE! OVER!
NOW...
DOOOOOM
WE'VE TAKEN BACK WHAT IS OURS, DIO!
DOOOOOM
DOOOON

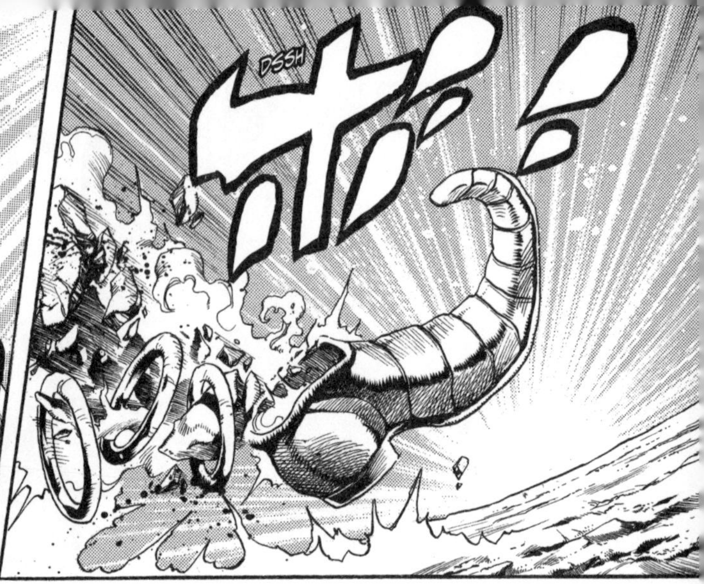
DSSH

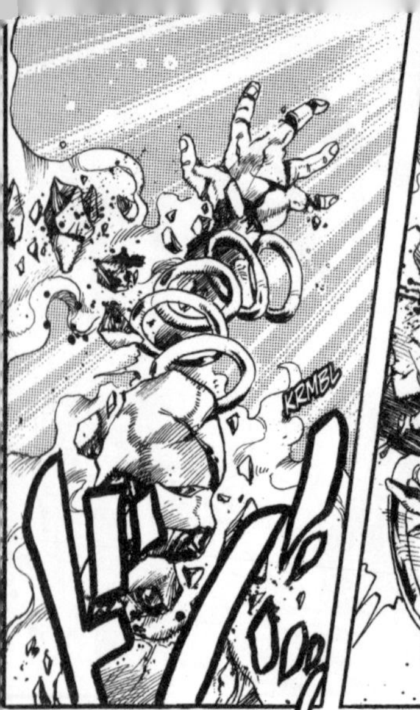
KRMBL

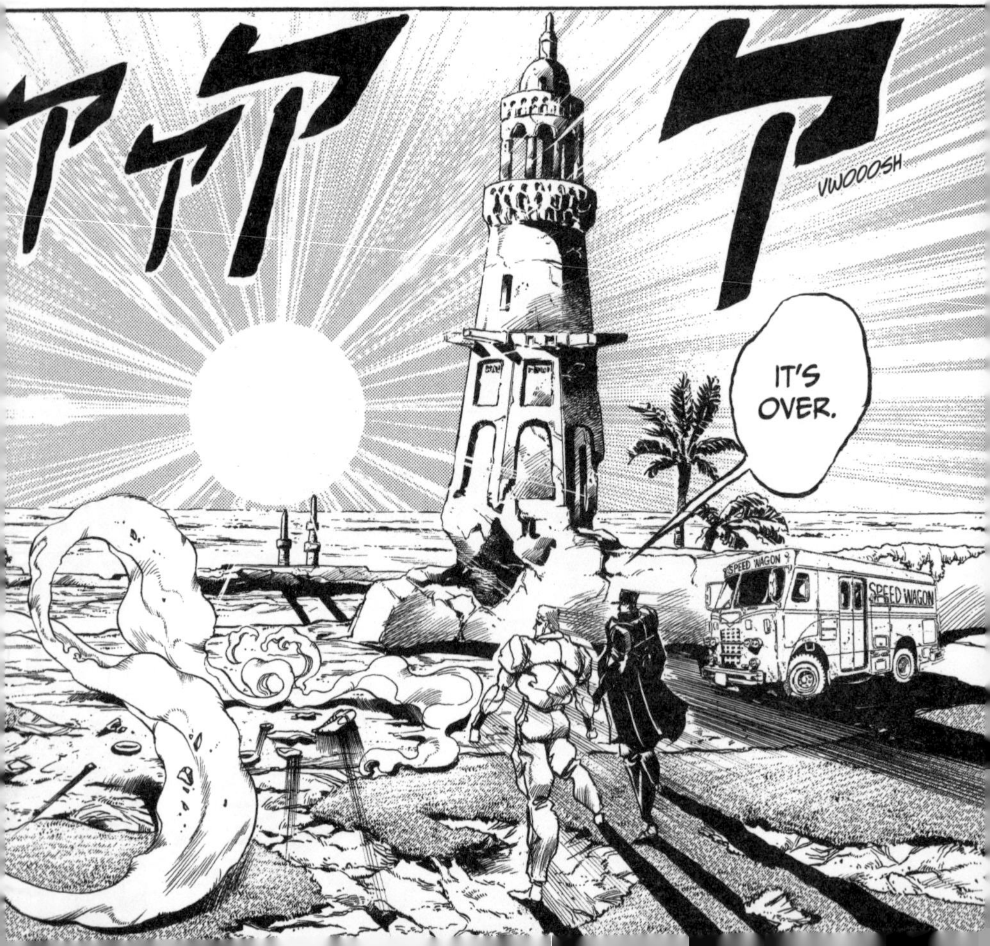
VWOOOSH
IT'S OVER.

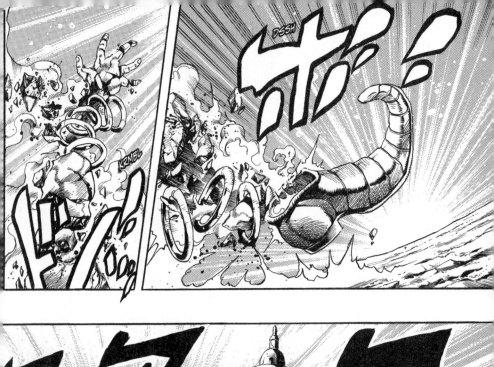

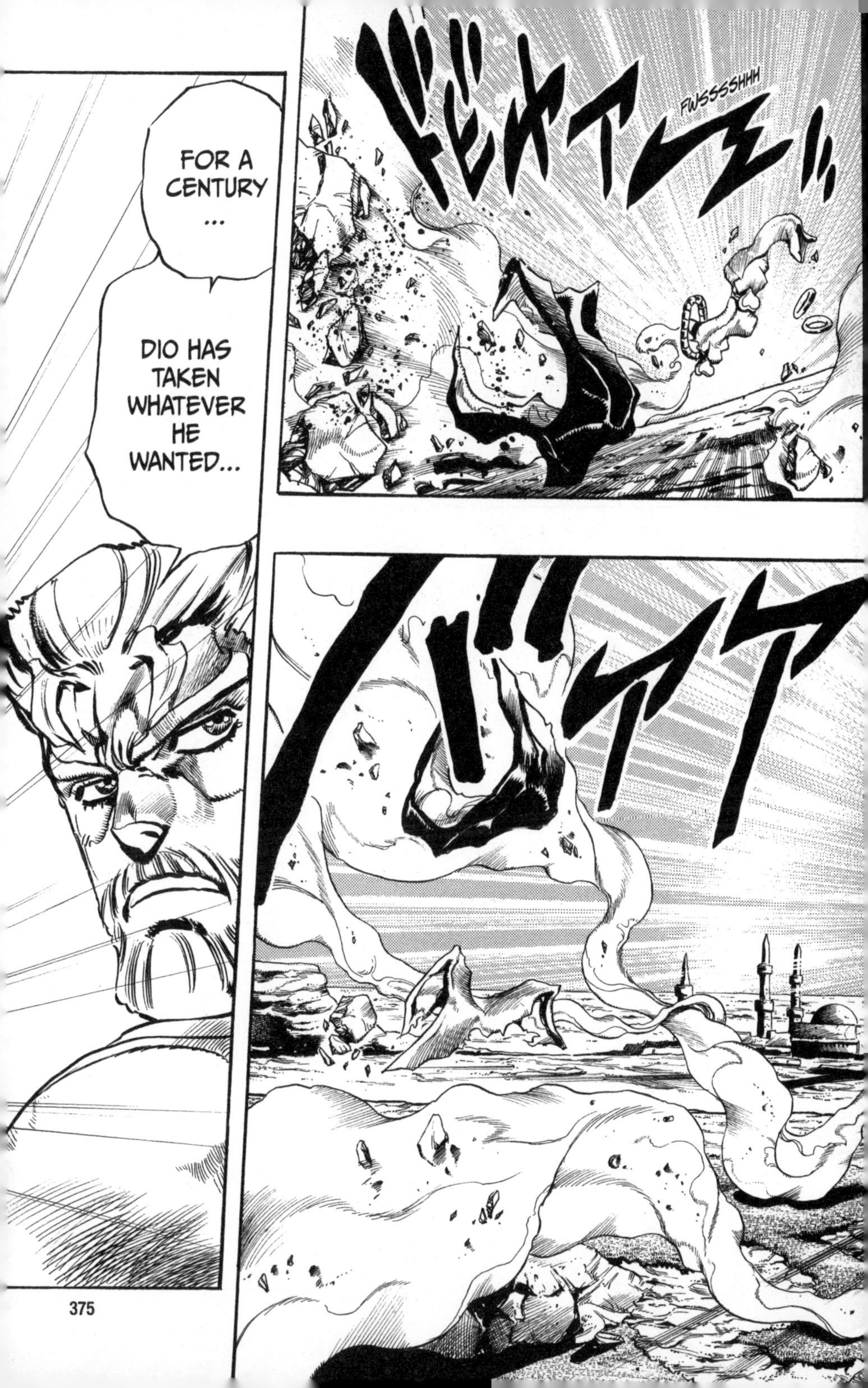
FWSSSSHHH
FOR A CENTURY ...
DIO HAS TAKEN WHATEVER HE WANTED...

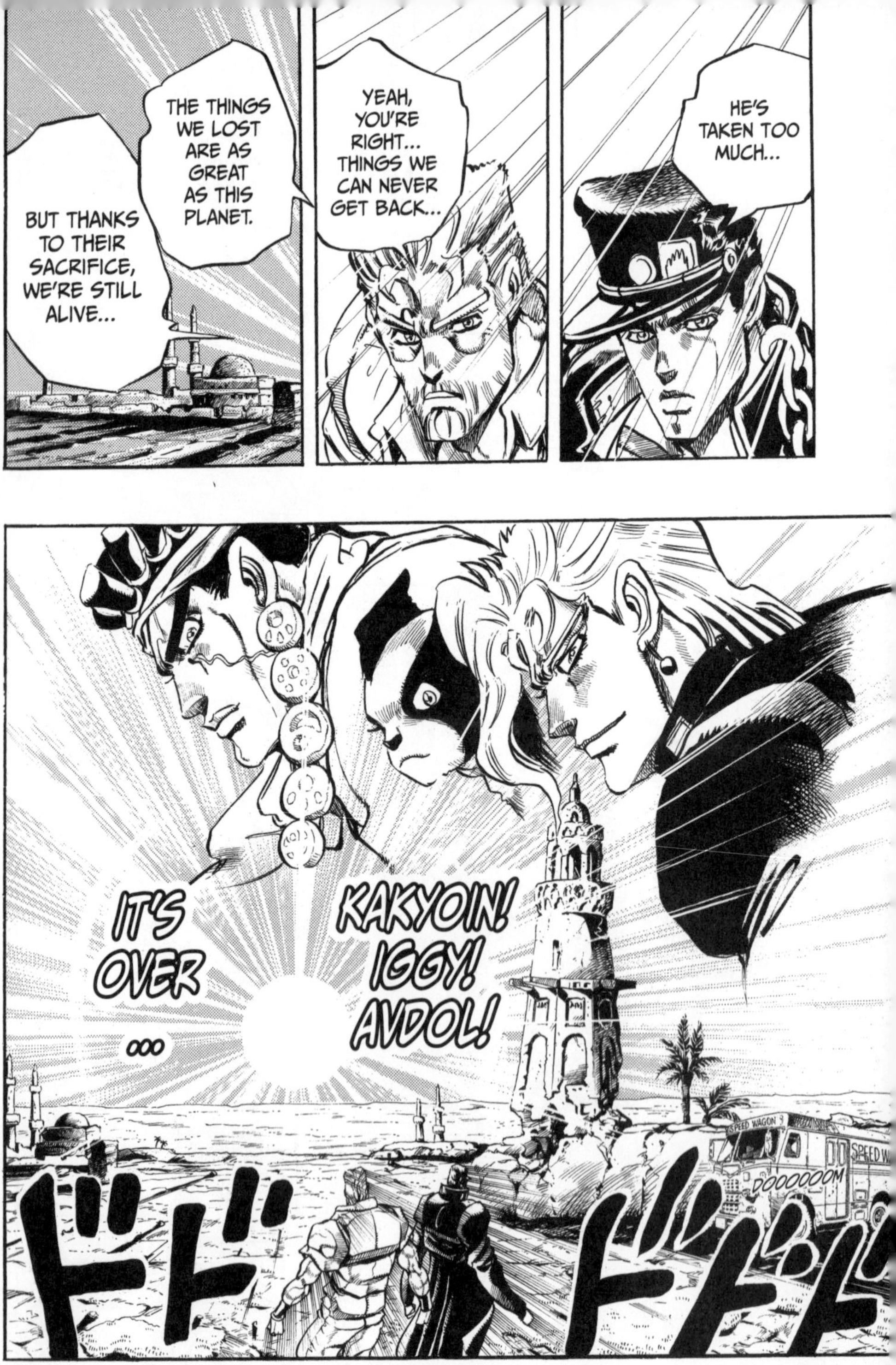
HE'S TAKEN TOO MUCH...
YEAH, YOU'RE RIGHT... THINGS WE CAN NEVER GET BACK...
THE THINGS WE LOST ARE AS GREAT AS THIS PLANET.
BUT THANKS TO THEIR SACRIFICE, WE'RE STILL ALIVE...
KAKYOIN! IGGY! AVDOL!
DOOOOOOM
IT'S OVER...

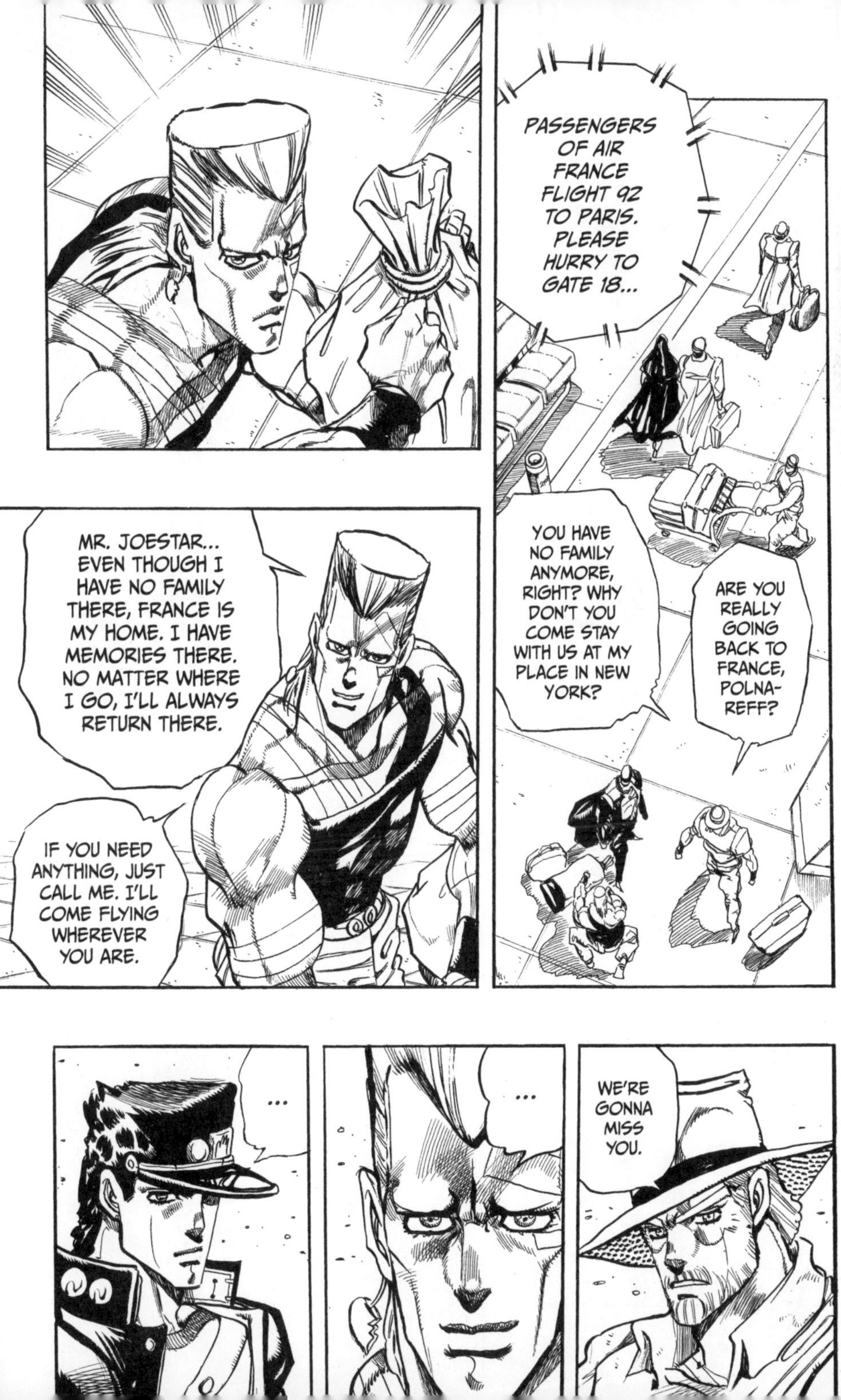
PASSENGERS OF AIR FRANCE FLIGHT 92 TO PARIS. PLEASE HURRY TO GATE 18...
ARE YOU REALLY GOING BACK TO FRANCE, POLNAREFF?
YOU HAVE NO FAMILY ANYMORE, RIGHT? WHY DON'T YOU COME STAY WITH US AT MY PLACE IN NEW YORK?
MR. JOESTAR... EVEN THOUGH I HAVE NO FAMILY THERE, FRANCE IS MY HOME. I HAVE MEMORIES THERE. NO MATTER WHERE I GO, I'LL ALWAYS RETURN THERE.
IF YOU NEED ANYTHING, JUST CALL ME. I'LL COME FLYING WHEREVER YOU ARE.
WE'RE GONNA MISS YOU.
...
...

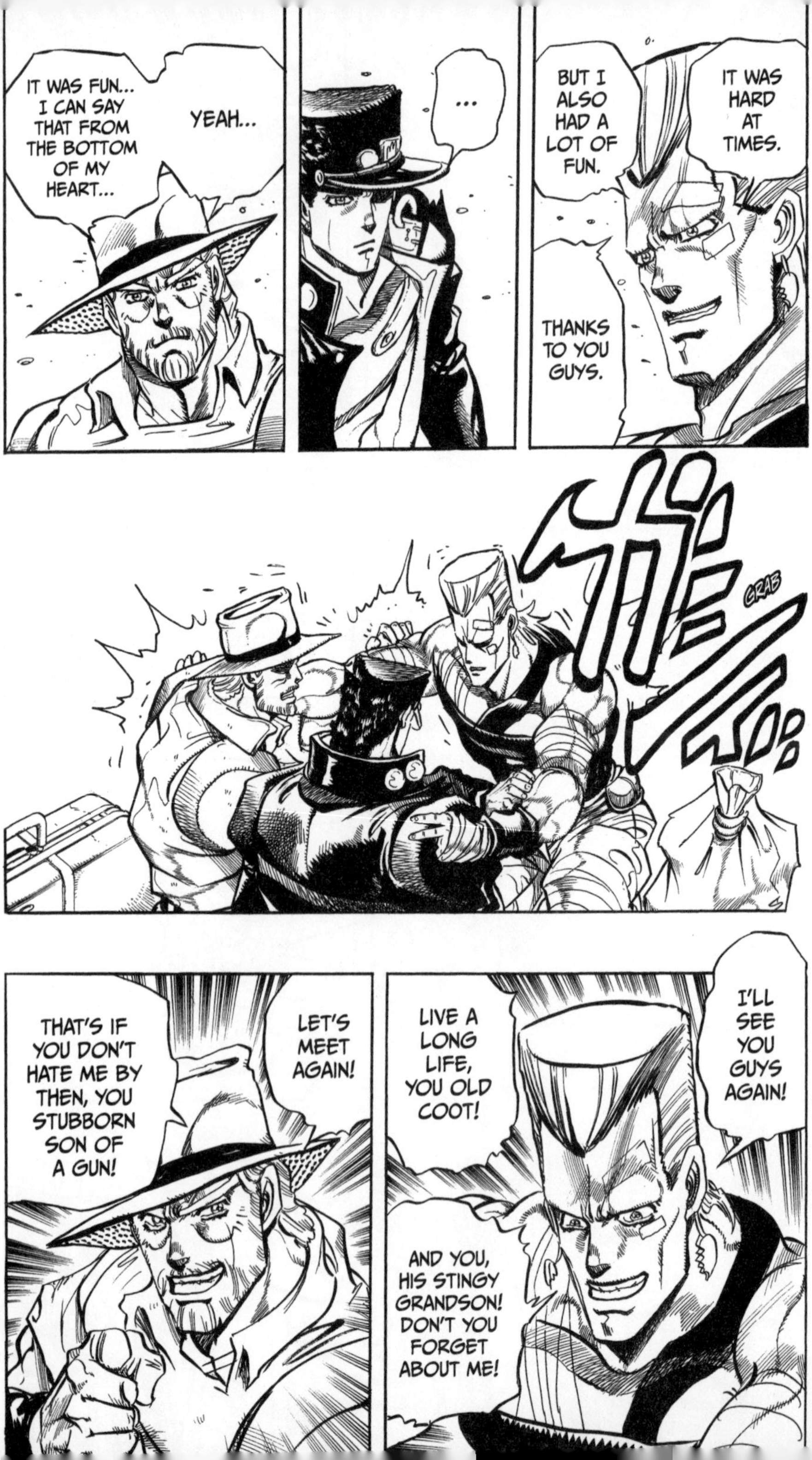
IT WAS HARD AT TIMES.
BUT I ALSO HAD A LOT OF FUN.
THANKS TO YOU GUYS.
...
YEAH...
IT WAS FUN... I CAN SAY THAT FROM THE BOTTOM OF MY HEART...
GRAB
I'LL SEE YOU GUYS AGAIN!
LIVE A LONG LIFE, YOU OLD COOT!
AND YOU, HIS STINGY GRANDSON! DON'T YOU FORGET ABOUT ME!
LET'S MEET AGAIN!
THAT'S IF YOU DON'T HATE ME BY THEN, YOU STUBBORN SON OF A GUN!

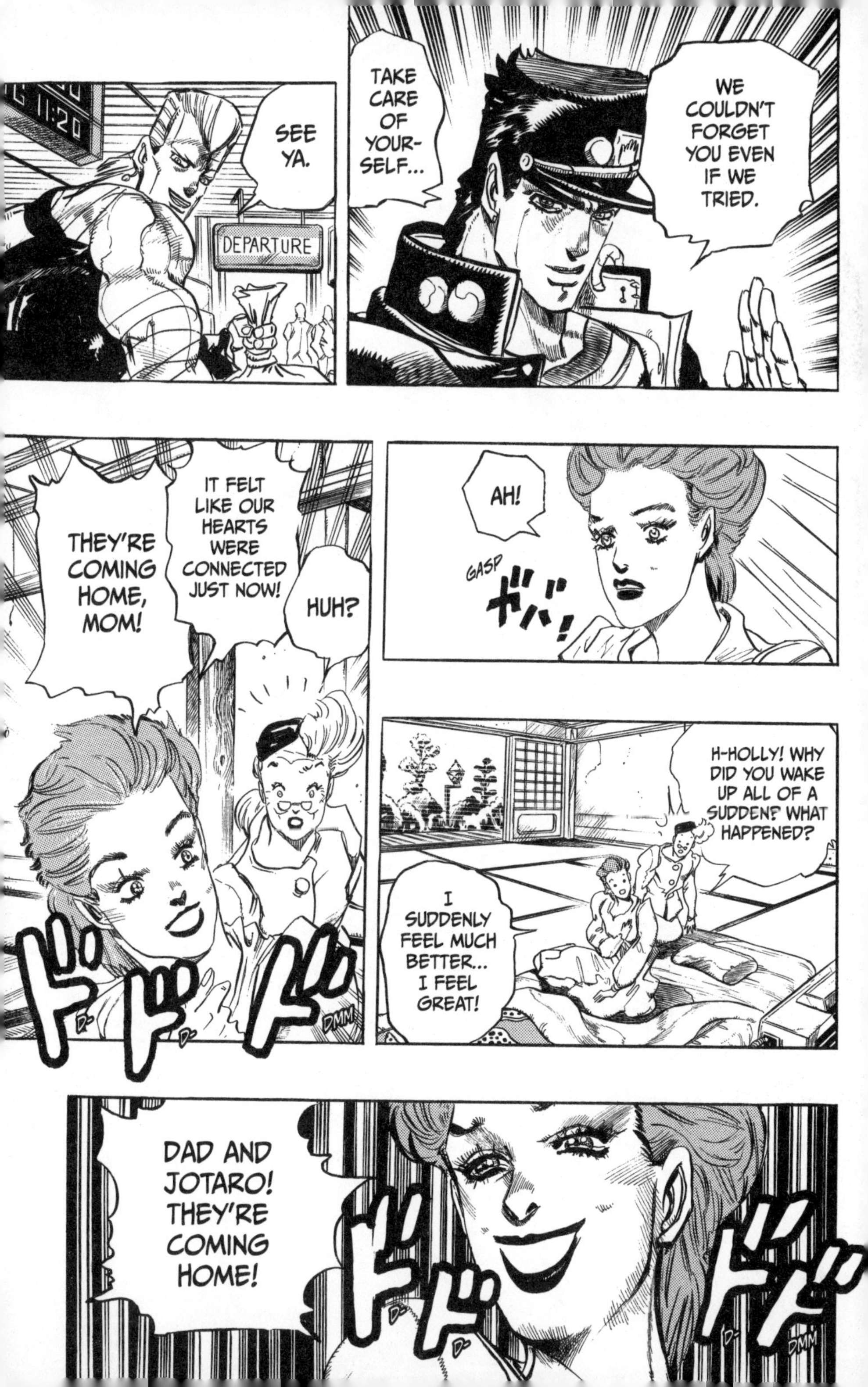
WE COULDN'T FORGET YOU EVEN IF WE TRIED.
TAKE CARE OF YOUR-SELF...
SEE YA.
11:20
DEPARTURE
AH!
GASP
ガバッ
H-HOLLY! WHY DID YOU WAKE UP ALL OF A SUDDEN? WHAT HAPPENED?
I SUDDENLY FEEL MUCH BETTER... I FEEL GREAT!
THEY'RE COMING HOME, MOM!
IT FELT LIKE OUR HEARTS WERE CONNECTED JUST NOW!
HUH?
ドドド
D- D- DMM
DAD AND JOTARO! THEY'RE COMING HOME!
ドドドド
D- D- D- DMM

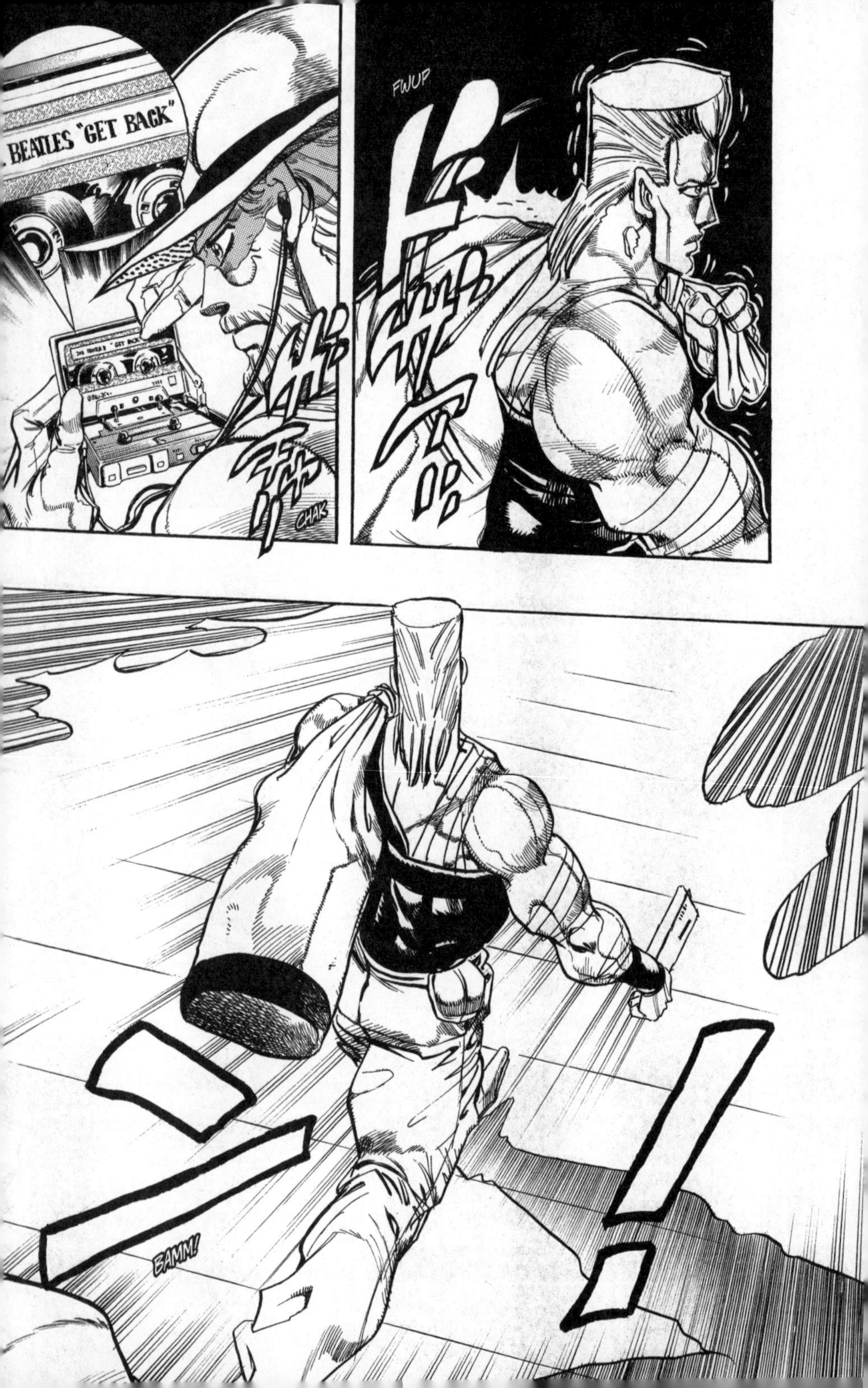
FWUP
BEATLES "GET BACK"
CHAK
BAMM!

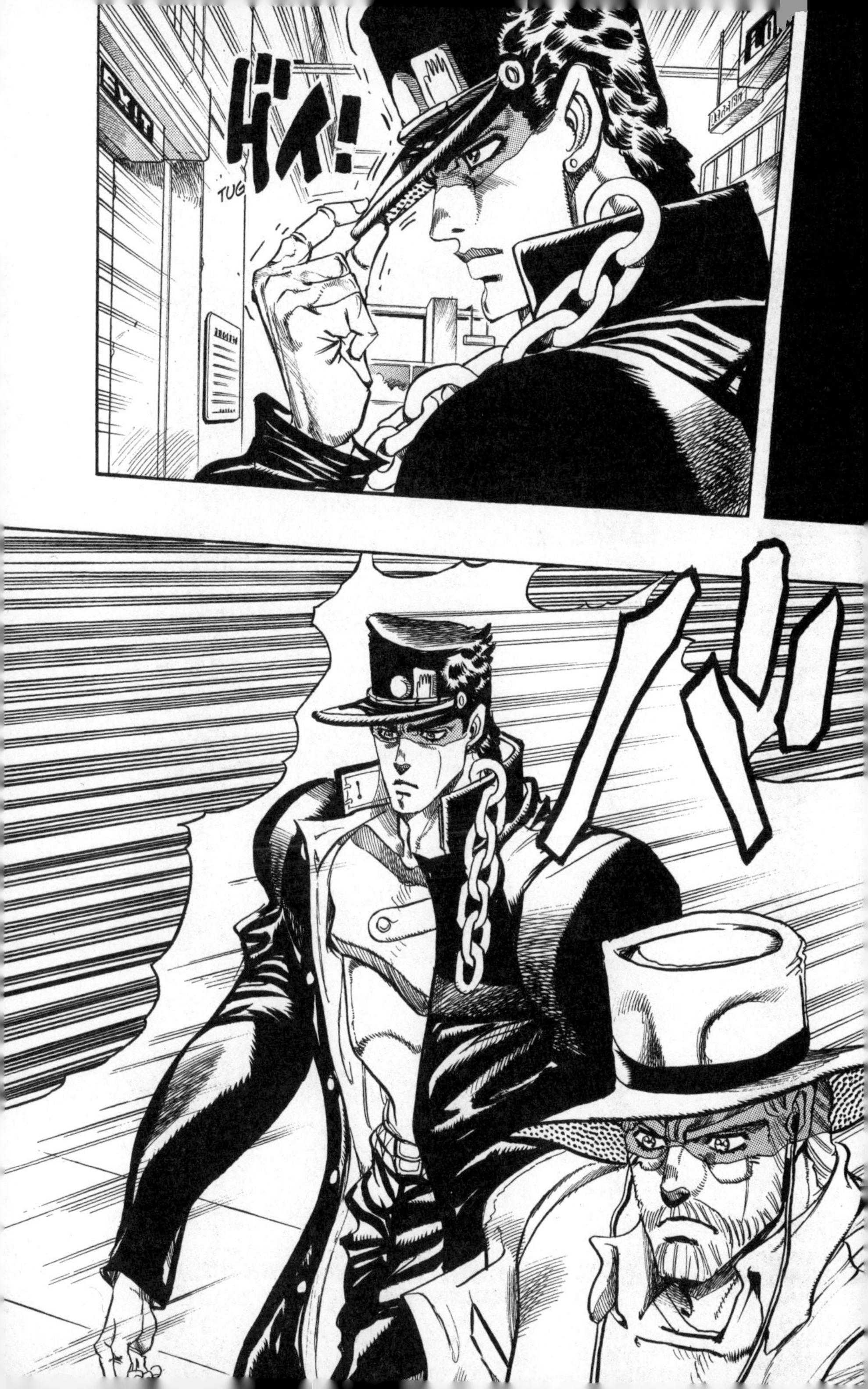
グイ!
TUG

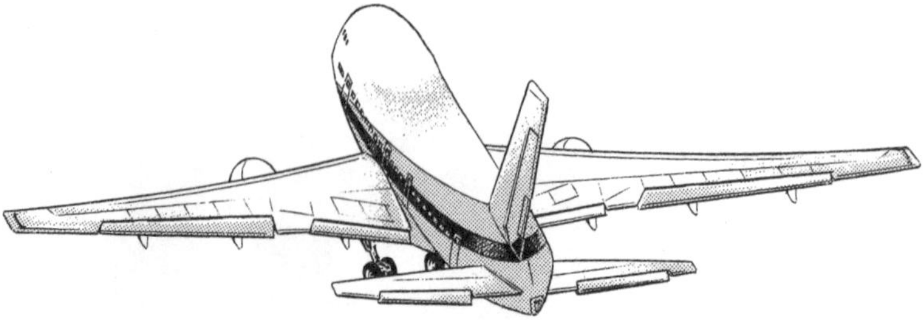

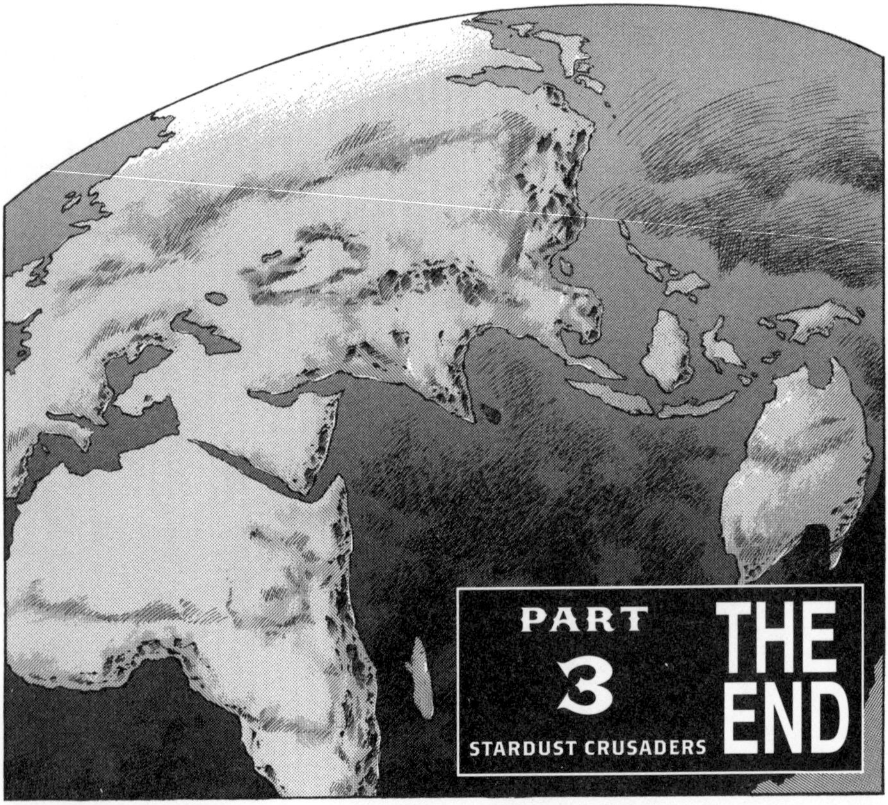
PART
3
STARDUST CRUSADERS
THE END

JOTARO AND FRIENDS' JOURNEY (After Arriving in Egypt)

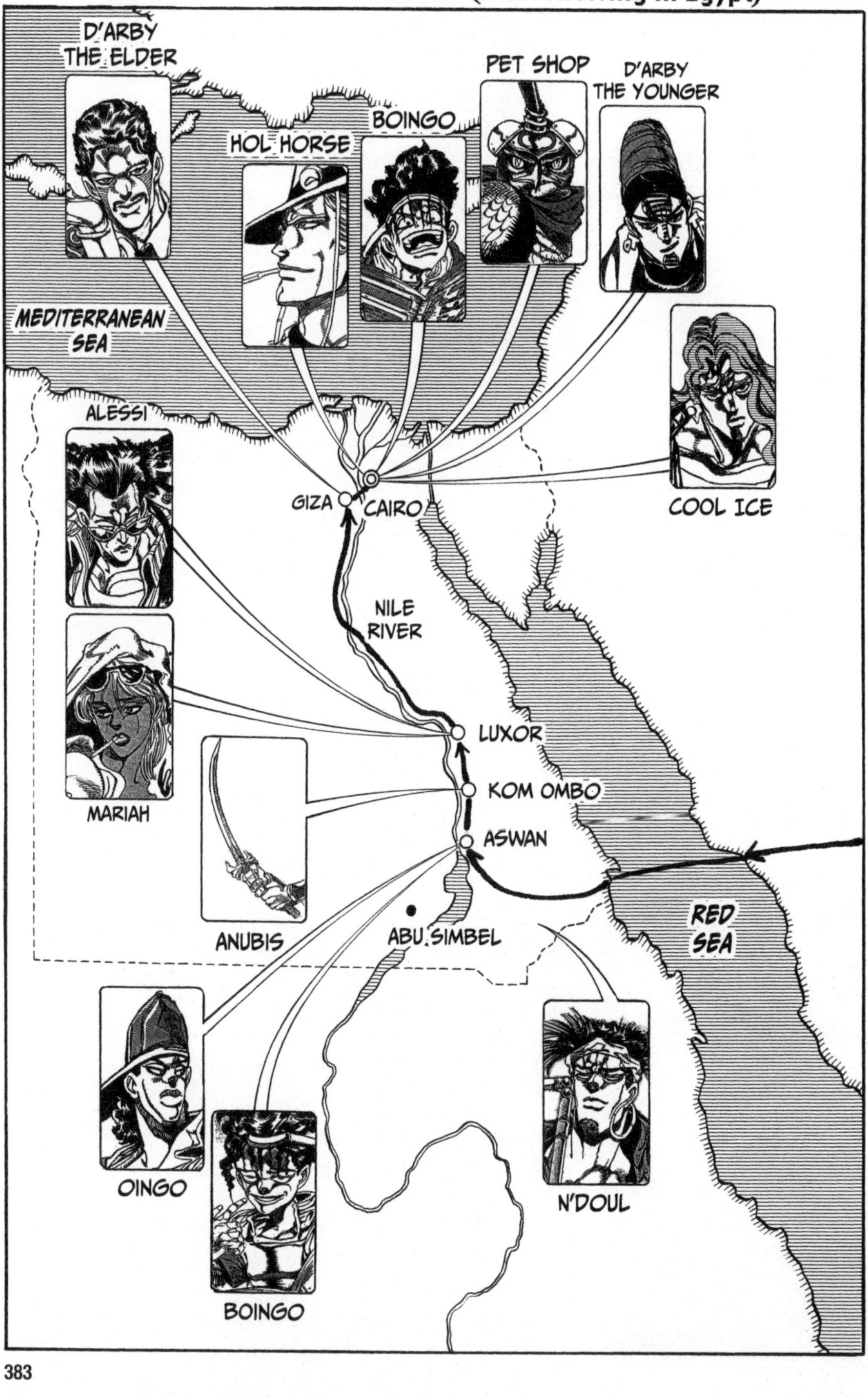
D'ARBY THE ELDER
HOL HORSE
BOINGO
PET SHOP
D'ARBY THE YOUNGER
MEDITERRANEAN SEA
ALESSI
GIZA
CAIRO
COOL ICE
NILE RIVER
LUXOR
KOM OMBO
ASWAN
MARIAH
ANUBIS
ABU SIMBEL
RED SEA
OINGO
BOINGO
N'DOUL

JOJO'S
BIZARRE ADVENTURE

10

END

To Be Continued

JoJo's BIZARRE ADVENTURE

10

Di

荒木飛呂彦が

語る

キャラクター

誕生秘話

Hirohiko Araki talks about character creation!

JoJo's BIZARRE ADVENTURE
PART 3
STARDUST CRUSADERS

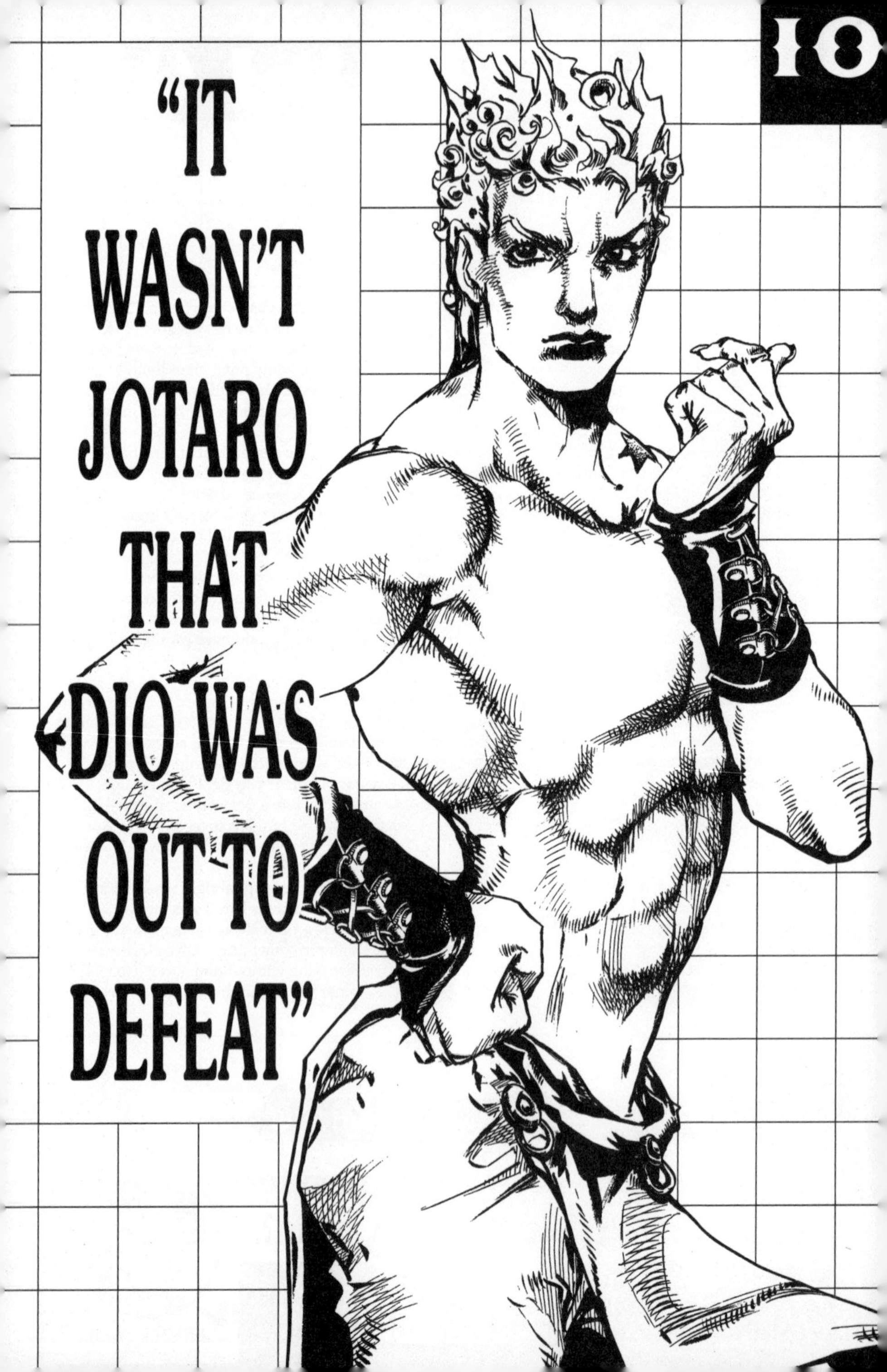
10
"IT WASN'T JOTARO THAT DIO WAS OUT TO DEFEAT"

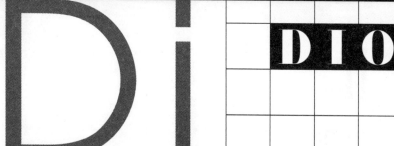

DIO

DIO—the archenemy of the Joestar family. Given that I was bringing back a character who had been at the bottom of the sea for a century, naturally he would have changed during the time he was down there—his malice ever growing. I wanted to make DIO feel like a final boss, and given that readers were really looking forward to his reintroduction, in order not to let them down, I not only put a lot of thought into his appearance, but his mind-set and thought process as well—in particular, how DIO would view his relationship to the Joestar family and the destiny they shared as an evolution from what it was in Part 1.

What is the destiny that DIO has to face? It's not to face off with Jotaro, the descendant of Jonathan. It's something invisible to the eye that lies behind their bloodline. It's what gives the Joestars their allies, the Hamon, Stands, and their uncanny luck…that's what I define as the Joestars' "destiny," and instead, what DIO is destined to do is to quash that and surpass it. As such, he doesn't view Jotaro himself as his archenemy—rather, DIO only views him as an obstacle to overcome in order to fulfill his destiny after his hundred-year slumber. In the end, DIO wasn't able to achieve his goal, but it's fun to imagine what things would have been like if he *had* been able to defeat Jotaro. I'm sure he would have beaten down anyone who he thought had the potential to challenge his position at the top of the food chain. Even after defeating Jotaro, perhaps someone else would inherit his will. After all, DIO had already experienced that once before. However, DIO is more of the reactionary type, so he probably would have continued to take root in Egypt and wait for his prey to come to him.

I had been working with DIO's character since Part 1, so I would often try and put myself in his shoes and imagine myself as a vampire. Those who put on the stone mask have to take the lives of others in order to keep on living. During the part where DIO is chasing after Joseph and Kakyoin, I wrote a scene where he takes a moment to marvel at the sight of cars. One would have to be an immortal vampire to experience something like that, so I actually found myself feeling a bit envious of him. If you slept long enough, for example, you could see a country instantly change from a monarchy into a democratic society—experiences that the average person could never have. As long as you had humans to feed on and you remained in good health, I think it would be pretty fun. Do vampires even get sick to begin with? (*laughs*)

Speaking of DIO, I'll never forget how my editor suddenly ended up in the hospital right when DIO and Jotaro were in the midst of their final battle. I remember panicking because Part 3 was rapidly approaching its end, and it's not like I could stop and wait for him! He would always give me really good, specific feedback on things like Stand designs. "This one is too similar to something you've already done, so try and differentiate their silhouettes a bit more." It was tough working without him. What's that? Did he give feedback on the design for DIO's The World? Hmm… I'm not sure about that one (*laughs wryly*).

The story behind the new illustration for JoJo Part 3 10!

Q. You already drew DIO naked for Part 1. Why did you do it again?

A. It makes him seem more like a Greek or Roman god.

Hirohiko Araki

In Parts 1 through 3, besides DIO, there are other examples of me drawing characters like this, such as the Pillar Men. However, I stopped doing it as much after I changed the setting to be a bit closer to home for Part 4 onward.

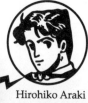

10

JOJO'S BIZARRE ADVENTURE

PART 3 STARDUST CRUSADERS

BY

HIROHIKO ARAKI

SHONEN JUMP EDITION
Translation ☆ Mayumi Kobayashi
Editor ☆ Jason Thompson

DELUXE HARDCOVER EDITION
Translation ☆ Evan Galloway
Touch-Up Art & Lettering ☆ Mark McMurray
Design ☆ Adam Grano
Editor ☆ David Brothers

First published in Japan in 1986 by SHUEISHA Inc., Tokyo.
English translation rights arranged by SHUEISHA Inc.

Original Japanese cover design by
MITSURU KOBAYASHI (GENI A LÒIDE)

Printed in the U.S.A.

Published by VIZ Media, LLC
P.O. Box 77010
San Francisco, CA 94107

10 9 8 7 6
First printing, February 2019
Sixth printing, February 2024

JO

ドドドド

JO